THE NEW STRATEGY OF STYLE

THE NEW STRATEGY OF STYLE

SECOND EDITION

- WINSTON WEATHERS
- OTIS WINCHESTER

Professors of Rhetoric and Writing
University of Tulsa

McGRAW-HILL BOOK COMPANY

New York   St. Louis   San Francisco   Auckland   Bogotá   Düsseldorf
Johannesburg   London   Madrid   Mexico   Montreal   New Delhi   Panama
Paris   São Paulo   Singapore   Sydney   Tokyo   Toronto

THE NEW
STRATEGY
OF STYLE

234567890DODO78321098

Library of Congress Cataloging in Publication Data

Weathers, Winston.
  The new strategy of style.

  First ed. published in 1967 under title: The
strategy of style.
  Includes index.
  1. English language—Rhetoric. I. Winchester, Otis, joint author. II. Title.
PE1408.W4443   1978   808'.042   77–20120
ISBN 0-07-068692-0

See Acknowledgments on pages 465–466. Copyrights included on this page by reference.

This book was set in Baskerville by National ShareGraphics, Inc.
The editors were Donald W. Burden and David Dunham;
the designer was Anne Canevari Green;
the production supervisor was Dominick Petrellese.
R. R. Donnelley & Sons Company was printer and binder.

CONTENTS

	List of Readings	vii
	Symbols Used in Marking Compositions	ix
	Preface	xiii
	An Introduction to Writing	xvii
1	Invention	1
2	Subject and Thesis	14
3	Classification and Order	29
4	Beginning and Ending	44
5	Expansion	61
6	Momentum	80
7	Emphasis	101
8	The Rhetorical Profile	126
9	Paragraphs	155
10	Paragraph Models	174
11	Sentences	213
12	Sentence Models	236
13	Words	290
14	Metaphors	310
15	Punctuation	326
16	The Popular Article	352
17	The Professional Article	376
18	The Personal Essay	402
19	The Formal Essay	419
20	The Critical Review	441
	A Note on Manuscripts and Publishing	458
	Acknowledgments	465
	Index	467

v

LIST
OF READINGS

John Updike, CENTRAL PARK 10
Kenneth Rexroth, THE ILIAD 24
E. M. Forster, MY WOOD 40
Yi-Fu Tuan, THE DESERT AND THE SEA 57
Mark Van Doren, THE CREATIVE HERITAGE 75
James Baldwin, ENCOUNTER ON THE SEINE:
    BLACK MEETS BROWN 94
Joan Didion, ON SELF-RESPECT 120
Dylan Thomas, A VISIT TO AMERICA 149
George Orwell, MARRAKECH 166
Norman Mailer, CITIES HIGHER THAN MOUNTAINS 208
John F. Baker, AN HONEST DAY'S WALK 230
Jane Howard, THE SEARCH FOR SOMETHING ELSE 286
Phyllis McGinley, SUBURBIA: OF THEE I SING 301
Christopher Morley, ON GOING TO BED 322
Richard M. Ketchum, J. P. MORGAN 347
Philip Kopper, LIFE IN STONE: A YOUNG MASTER'S
    ANTIQUE ART 366
Fred E. H. Schroeder, ENTER AHAB, THEN ALL:
    THEATRICAL ELEMENTS IN MELVILLE'S FICTION 391
Marya Mannes, A PLEA FOR FLIRTATION 413
J. H. Plumb, THE SORRY STATE OF HISTORY 433
Harold Taylor, ADMINISTRATION 101B 454

SYMBOLS USED IN MARKING COMPOSITIONS

BGL   The beginning of your composition is too long. Given the overall length of your composition, you are spending too much time "getting ready."

BGS   The beginning of your composition needs to be expanded, made longer. You have not written a long enough beginning to state clearly your subject/thesis or to establish your rhetorical profile.

BGX   The beginning of your composition is totally inadequate. It doesn't really lead into the body of your composition and seems simply "tacked on." Rewrite.

CL?   Your classification is not clear. There seems to be no clear reason why you have grouped your material the way you have.

CLB   Your classification system is too broad. You have too few categories and have put too many items into a single group. Increase the number of your categories.

CLX   Your classification system does not work. It is not appropriate to your subject/thesis.

DT   You need more details, illustrations, examples. At this point, your composition is too vague, general, abstract.

EDL   The ending of your composition needs to be shortened. You are taking too long to conclude. Your composition is beginning to "drag on."

EDS	The ending of your composition needs to be expanded, made longer. Your composition stops too abruptly.
EDX	Your composition's ending is totally inadequate. It doesn't seem related to the body of your composition. It seems simply "tacked on."
EL	Eliminate this material, this section of the composition.
EM	The material at this point needs greater emphasis.
EMX	Wrong emphasis given. You are emphasizing unimportant matters and neglecting to emphasize important ones.
EP	Your composition needs expansion at this point. Your material at this point is underdeveloped.
EPL	Your composition is overexpanded at this point. You need to cut back, trim.
GRX	A grammatical problem.
MOX	Faulty momentum. Your composition doesn't read easily at this point.
MTX	A metaphor problem. Either you have too many metaphors for your rhetorical profile or the metaphors presented are ludicrous, trite, difficult to picture.
NC	Meaning not clear.
OR?	Your reason for presenting your material in this order is not clear.
PC	Punctuation problem. Your punctuation either violates convention too radically, or just doesn't make sense. Confuses meaning.
PCRP	Punctuation not appropriate to this particular rhetorical profile. Consider all the punctuation possibilities at this point.
PG	You need to make a new paragraph at this point.
PGX	A paragraph problem. This paragraph is either poorly written or inadequately developed.
POL	Your composition needs a general polishing—you need to proofread it carefully and correct any typographical/ mechanical errors.

SYMBOLS USED IN MARKING COMPOSITIONS

PP   A more patterned paragraph might be helpful at this point in order to emphasize or call attention to what you are saying.

PPX   The patterned paragraph you have written is not appropriate at this point. It is too artificial within the rhetorical profile you are using and provides emphasis at the wrong point.

RP?   No particular rhetorical profile is identifiable, and your composition seems stylistically out of focus. For whom are you actually writing? What is the occasion for this piece of writing? How would you describe the overall rhetorical situation?

RPX   Your rhetorical profile is inappropriate. Reconsider the level and texture of your writing in consideration of your subject, your audience, the entire writing situation for this composition.

RPV   You need to bring some variation into the ways you are achieving your rhetorical profile. Don't rely upon just one or two writing devices to establish your level and texture.

S?   Just exactly what is the subject of your composition?

SNX   Something's wrong with this sentence. It is either poorly constructed or inappropriate to your general style.

SPX   Spelling error. Though words may sometimes be spelled in different ways, your spelling falls outside the range of acceptable spellings for this word.

SPRP You have spelled the word in a correct way, but this particular spelling is not the most appropriate for the rhetorical profile you are using.

SR?   Is this the best series to use? Can you alter the series in some way to make it more appropriate to your content?

SRX   This series is not well constructed and doesn't seem appropriate to your rhetorical profile.

STX   A stylistic shift does not work at this point. It creates emphasis at the wrong place and violates the general rhetorical profile unnecessarily.

STRX You have a structural problem with this composition. The beginning, middle, and end do not seem to be in appropriate proportion.

TH? Just exactly what is your thesis? It is not easy to determine what point you are trying to make in this composition.

THN Your thesis needs to be broadened somewhat. For this composition, it is too specialized.

THB Your thesis needs to be narrowed. For this composition, it is too broad and vast.

TR You need some sort of transition at this point in your composition.

TRX Faulty transition. You are using the wrong conjunction or transition word.

WX Wrong word. Look up this word in the dictionary.

WRP This is not the right word for this rhetorical profile. Either the word is too elaborate and exceptional, or it is too simplistic and ordinary.

GENERAL COMMENTS

Superior/sharable This work has satisfied the assignment in a superior way and it is work that can be shown to others without embarrassment.

Good This work fulfills the assignment in a satisfactory manner and does all the basic things a good composition should do. It has a clear and appropriate rhetorical profile, has good structure, and proceeds in an orderly and interesting way.

Adequate This work fulfills the assignment, and though it has some problems you need not revise the paper. Try to learn from the marks on your paper—and try to avoid the same problems in your next paper.

Revisable This composition needs revision. Study carefully the marks on it, confer with your instructor, and then redo the paper.

Not revisable This paper does not satisfy the assignment—but rather than revise it, you should simply attempt another composition on another subject.

PREFACE

Many students avoid writing because they have no "way of writing," no adequate prose style they can use when they wish—or need—to express themselves in writing. When forced to write, these students often fall back on jargon, cliché, and evasion to cover up their lack of craftsmanship.

Yet most serious students know that inarticulateness is a handicap, and they seriously wish to acquire a knowledge of the techniques of good composition.

Though one cannot learn all there is to know about good writing simply by reading a book, a student can be judiciously guided through many of the problems of writing and can be pointed in a direction that may lead to a meaningful and effective prose.

The New Strategy of Style begins, we believe, where some texts in composition end: our book aims for the development of a more provocative, stimulating—and flexible—kind of writing than has been fostered in recent years by advocates of communication-at-the-expense-of-artistry. The serious student can, we believe, pick up *The New Strategy of Style* and, with thought and practice (including the careful emulation of successful published pieces of writing), master the devices that spell the difference between boredom and interest, clumsiness and grace, aridity and vitality.

The premise of our book is that style is, more than anything else, the choosing between alternatives. We point out to the student that there is *more than one style,* that even though style is determined partly by the writer, partly by the occasion, partly by the audience, there is no one unchanging or ideal style that can be established, once and for all, for all writers and all occasions and all audiences.

We seek to guide students in making appropriate stylistic choices from all the possibilities available to them—first, by helping them identify and master the possibilities themselves and, second, by providing them with a rationale for making stylistic choices as they encounter diverse communication and rhetorical situations. We point out to students that the quality of words, the general structure and length of sentences, the structure and length of paragraphs, the incidence of metaphors and other rhetorical devices, and a host of minor determinants of style will all and always vary. In each of these areas a spectrum of possibilities presents itself—and this spectrum is, we believe, the great reality of style.

To help students achieve more completely a strategy of style, we have, in this *second edition* of our text, added five new chapters: one chapter dealing with invention and the process of discovering "something to say"; two chapters presenting sentence and paragraph models that the student can "imitate" (in what we call the copy-and-compose method) in order to develop a repertoire of ready-to-use sentence and paragraph patterns; and five chapters dealing with the basic and prevalent forms of prose writing—the essay, both formal and personal, the article, both professional and popular, and the critical review.

Each of the twenty chapters in the text introduces the student to a particular strategy of style or to a particular set of writing devices. After discussing the strategy or the devices, each chapter presents a brief checklist of questions to help the student review and bring into focus the chapter's major points. Then a complete composition is presented for detailed study—a composition reflecting the strategy or devices the chapter has discussed. Finally, a set of exercises is given, each designed to guide students toward mastering the material they have just read about.

The New Strategy of Style proceeds from a consideration of invention to a consideration of such basic composition matters as subject and thesis, order and classification, beginning and ending, expansion, momentum, emphasis. Then, in Chapter 8, the text deals with the crucial matter of the *rhetorical profile*—identifying nine general rhetorical areas in which most contemporary writing occurs, and presenting guidelines for adapting stylistic materials to particular writing situations, for selecting the devices and procedures most appropriate for a given subject, audience, occasion. Following the discussion of rhetorical profile, the text examines the key ingredients in establishing style—paragraphs, sentences, words, metaphors, and punctuation. And finally, the text analyzes and describes the essay, article, and review—the mastery of which forms prepares the student for writing many other contemporary prose forms.

(Obviously the sequence of this presentation can easily be varied by the teacher who wishes to do so. One possible alternative sequence would be this: Chapter 8, The Rhetorical Profile; Chapter 9, Paragraphs; Chapter 10, Paragraph Models; Chapter 11, Sentences; Chapter 12, Sentence Models; Chapter 13, Words, Chapter 14, Metaphors; Chapter 15, Punctuation; Chapter 1, Invention; Chapter 2, Subject and Thesis; Chapter 3, Classification and Order; Chapter 4, Beginning and Ending; Chapter 5, Expansion; Chapter 6, Momentum; Chapter 7, Emphasis; Chapter 16, The Popular Article; Chapter 17, The Professional Article; Chapter 18, The Personal Essay; Chapter 19, The Formal Essay; Chapter 20, The Critical Review. The text may also serve for either a one-semester course or a full-year course. In the full-year course, a reasonable procedure would be to deal with "the composition" the first semester (Chapters 1, 2, 3, 4, 5, 6, 7, 16, 17, 18, 19, and 20) and with "style" the second (Chapters 8, 9, 10, 11, 12, 13, 14, and 15). The text itself is, we believe, flexible—and the teacher may well find alternative sequences and divisions that are especially appropriate for a particular group of students.)

All in all, students who, through their study of *The New Strategy of Style,* adopt its philosophy of composition—a philosophy based upon stylistic decision making and the spectrum of possibilities—will, we believe, handle all their writing problems more effectively and more creatively. They will, with practice, be able to write with stylistic sensitivity, with a sense of appropriateness, with intelligent diversity.

As authors of *The New Strategy of Style* we wish to thank the University of Tulsa for supporting the writing and revision of this text and to thank teachers and friends at several universities, as well as students and former students, for their indirect assistance.

Winston Weathers
Otis Winchester

AN INTRODUCTION TO WRITING

To be a good writer, you must master as many of the principles and techniques of composition as you can. The more things you can do, the better off you will be. After all, good style is primarily a matter of wise choices from a wide range of possibilities. You need to develop a broad spectrum of stylistic achievements and then be able to move from one end of the spectrum to the other as occasion demands. By understanding that good writing is based, not upon a single, correct way of doing things, but upon your having at hand a variety of writing techniques, a set of options, you can achieve a truly creative approach to composition.

As you study the art of writing, you will, of course, hope to achieve a basic style of your own, a complex of writing practices that you can perform most easily and most meaningfully. You may, for instance, lean toward a simple style with short sentences, simple diction, a clear-cut exposition of ideas. Or you may lean toward a more elaborate style with long, complex sentences, a more learned vocabulary, a subtle and ingenious presentation of thought.

But having a style of your own does not mean that it should be inflexible or static. You must be able to vary wisely your basic manner of writing, adapting it to special circumstances; otherwise, you will be the victim of an unbending style that will actually make you lose a great many opportunities to write effectively. If you fail to diversify your writing skills, you may wind up like the pitcher who has only a fast ball—no knuckle ball or curve.

No exact formula can be given for matching a particular style to a particular circumstance, but you will learn from experience to make certain adjustments on certain occasions. You will learn to ask yourself a number of important questions: What am I writing about? Who will read what I have written? Why did I write it? And answering these questions, you will be able to make the decisions necessary for every writer.

In writing for children, for the uneducated, for those for whom English is a second language, you may obviously have to write in certain accommodating ways. In writing for one person, a group of persons, a million persons, you may have to make certain changes in your writing style. In proposing marriage, extending congratulations, criticizing and reprimanding, you will want to adopt the most appropriate writing manner possible.

If you are writing a paper to be read before the three thousand members attending the National Marketing Association, your style may be formal, expository, factual, straightforward. If you are writing a letter to your sweetheart back home, your style may be more personal, more lyrical, perhaps more evasive. If you are writing a hotheaded letter to the newspaper editor, your style may be angry, sarcastic, ironic, emphatic. But even in less clear-cut situations, stylistic adjustments will have to be made. Gradually, through experience, you will learn to make them.

The important thing to remember is this: Be prepared to do different things at different times. Though certain aspects remain constant in writing—the overall goals, the overall principles, certain established conventions of language—the greater part of the writing experience lies in the realm of the variable.

In the following chapters you will be presented with the strategies and tactics of good writing, with the various techniques that can lead you to clarity and effectiveness in your composition. But to make these techniques truly yours, you need to implement them with a serious and workable writing program—a program of study and performance that, faithfully followed, will make you a better writer.

First of all, *learn to read with an eye to style.* Read as widely as possible from the writer's point of view. Whenever you read a letter, story, essay, article, or book that pleases you, make a special effort to see exactly what the author has done with language. Try to discover some of the tricks and devices. Copy the passage out, word for word, just as it appears; then write a structurally similar version on quite a different topic and in words of your own. Don't be hesitant to use these stylistic forms.

As you become acquainted with the techniques of style, *practice them until they become automatic.* Though everyone, on occasion, must deliberate about what word to put down next, it would be difficult to write effectively if you had to deliberate all the time. It's like learning to drive: At first you have to think about shifting gears, putting on the brake, turning the steering wheel; with practice it becomes automatic. Only by writing will the strategies of good writing become relaxed and instinctive.

As you practice your writing techniques in order to achieve your own instinctive style, you will also want to develop *the important habit of revision and rewriting*. You will have gone a long way toward being a good writer when you realize that a great part of everyone's writing effort takes place in the revising and reshaping of the words originally written down. The following steps are followed by most good writers.

First, *jottings*: Jot down some preliminary notes for your article or essay. A list of main thoughts in about the order you expect to take them up is a good place to begin. You may have been putting down ideas over a period of time, just as they came to you. (No serious writer is ever without a note pad or some cards carried just for this purpose.) Sooner or later you must begin putting something down on paper, and you will write more fluently if these tentative efforts are jottings rather than a first draft or even an outline. If what you are writing is rather short and casual, such as a personal essay, and if you are reasonably familiar with your subject and a fairly confident writer, you may be able to make a first draft without further preliminaries. However, if you are writing something like a scholarly article or formal essay, you will probably need more of a synopsis or outline.

Second, *the outline*: Most writers find that their work goes more smoothly if they use some kind of outline, generally one of the following three. If your jottings are rather complete and orderly, they may already constitute a *preliminary* or *inventory* outline. But since it is easier to plan a short work in terms of topics scaled to paragraph size, you may find the *paragraph* outline even more useful. For a longer work on a difficult subject you may prefer the *noun-phrase* or *sentence* outline, one that is so detailed the writer needs only to flesh out the discussion and add transitions to have a first draft.

Remember this, however: You can overplan almost as easily as you can underplan. Jottings and outlines are useful because your materials can be more easily rephrased, juggled, or discarded at this stage than later. Do not let these prewriting gestures freeze your conceptions too soon; retain as much flexibility as possible not only in these early stages of writing but even through the final draft.

Third, *the rough draft*: In this first draft establish the general shape and accumulate most of the materials that will make up your work. Concentrate on the subject and thesis and overall unity, letting the finer points go until later. There is much to be said for writing as much as you can as rapidly as you can at this point, getting the materials down so you will have something to work with later, attaining a momentum that may lead you to write more knowledgeably and fluently than you supposed you could.

Fourth, *the controlled draft*: In this second draft you can begin trimming down, tightening up what you wrote earlier. Eliminate, expand, rearrange, rephrase. Especially consider proportion, emphasis, sentence and paragraph structure, and diction. Try to shape this draft toward the form the final work is to take.

Fifth, *the polished draft*: In this third draft clear up whatever problems remain. The general readability of your prose can often be greatly improved by a few final touches. And the accuracy of spelling, punctuation, and grammar needs to be checked.

Sixth, *the cold reading*: Put what you have written aside for at least 24 hours. Then give it a final critical reading. Remember that the reader has only these words; what they do not reveal of your thinking on this subject he or she will never know.

Seventh, *the finished manuscript*: All that remains now is to prepare a final copy of the article or essay—carefully proofreading to be sure it is absolutely neat and correct.

In summary, you are asked to read for style, to revise and rework your compositions through various drafts, and to master, one by one, by diligent practice, the particular strategies that are involved in good writing. If you do these things, you should find the writing experience increasingly pleasurable, and you should find your written compositions reaching your readers more immediately and effectively than ever before.

THE NEW
STRATEGY
OF STYLE

1.INVENTION

To develop the content of our writing—content that we can use when we begin to write for particular readers on particular occasions—we need to develop thoughtful, ongoing habits of *observing, experiencing, reading, imagining*. At times, these habits are of an informal, almost casual nature—permitting us to fill up our notebooks and journals with a variety of ideas and images. At other times, these habits are of a more formal, disciplined nature—providing us with organized research notes and data. In either case, we are developing the material that can become a part of our writing later on, providing it with substance and meaning.

To write well, you must have something to say—or you wouldn't get involved in this solitary, introspective, and sometimes painful business of putting words on paper. And whatever is on your mind will have to be *written by you,* for the ultimate source of your data is more or less personal. You have either observed and experienced and considered what you write about; or else you have read the account of what others have seen and done and thought and made it a part of your intellectual development. And although you inevitably draw upon the forms and techniques of other writers, the style in which you express yourself is uniquely your own. Planning for a piece of writing involves so much personal ingenuity that it is called *invention.*

Actually you must have a firm hold on the realities of your own life before you can expect to translate these realities into prose. Your ability to respond and ability to express are, in fact, related: you must see the world clearly and participate in it imaginatively before you can write about it; and you must possess an evocative language and literary vision of sorts before you can clearly comprehend this life of yours. So in preparing to write more expressively— in savoring what comes your way and searching out what does not, in retaining the significant, vital, and rewarding, and discarding the trivial, trite, and soporific—you are learning to live more richly.

OBSERVING

Invention begins with observation—seeing and smelling and hearing and tasting and touching, sensations that enable you to perceive the components of life and prose. Ordinarily you use these senses in specialized ways and for functional purposes. Driving to class, for example, you see the street ahead, you hear other cars passing, you feel the steering wheel vibrating in your hands—but observe little else. You rarely if ever use your senses simply for the purpose of observing. So you may think that observation comes naturally, but it doesn't. You know from experience that many times you look but do not see because of a psychological blindness.

You are blinded by the limitations of your vocabulary. You are often limited in your vision by not having the words, scientific or poetic, with which to conceptualize and describe what is in front of you. You may, for example, be accustomed to thinking of the clear sky as blue and only blue. But if you apply the word *green* to the sky, you see something you had not seen before—that sometimes the light glancing off summer foliage stains the sky a definite green, and that on many late afternoons the whole Western horizon is a broad band of vibrating green where the yellow of the setting sun blends with the blue of evening. Conceive it metaphorically—as "a sea of air," "a silk parasol," "a Wedgwood cup"—and your vision of the sky becomes immensely enlarged. In its way your perceptual vocabulary has more to say than your senses about what you observe.

Furthermore, your vision of the world is influenced by your motives: You are inclined to notice and value only those things that most affect you—the car, for example, because it takes you where you want to go and because it confers a certain status, a blue sky because it means a good day for tennis—and ignore those things which do not. Such a narrowness of vision excludes much of life and distorts the remainder. Some of this myopia is inescapably human. After all, it isn't possible to take in everything, and there are immediate practical demands made on your senses. But to some extent faulty vision deprives you of the best raw material for writing.

Of course, there are many different ways of seeing. When, for example, it suits your purpose to interpret what your senses tell you rather literally and objectively, when you are after a reasonably precise and comprehensive picture, you normally view the world and write about it from a "realistic" point of view. But when you choose to be highly subjective and selective in your responses, and to project the essence or effect of something, the result is a more "impressionistic" observation.

But however you choose to view your subject and whatever the nature of the subject is, *be observant.* For the great enemy of writers is vagueness, vagueness of impression and vagueness of expression, a vagueness that expects readers to be content with less rather than more, with generalizations rather than details, and with unexamined opinions rather than reasoned judgments. The cure for thin development, sketchy generalization, and excessive subjectivity is observation.

EXPERIENCING

The art of experiencing can be cultivated in much the same way as the art of observing. Writers inevitably draw upon their experience, not necessarily dramatic or adventurous, but experience from which they have wrung the greatest possible insight. More than others, writers know that having "an experience" depends less on the literal facts of their seeing and doing than upon the kind of awareness and imagination that they bring to it.

Despite the unsurpassed opportunity for experience these days, many seem dogged by ennui and downright boredom. And we are all inclined to be unappreciative of the familiar and commonplace. Many writers blame uneventful lives for their having nothing much to say. This contempt for the ordinary is based on pure illusion. What we suppose to be amazing and adventurous rarely is; and to go looking for it "out there somewhere" is seldom successful. The dullest and most insipid people are always boring us with tales about their wonderful experiences. And the cheapest and most tasteless aspects of our society are by-products of this naïve enthusiasm for titillating novelty. Moreover, the traditionally sensational experience is apt to be tiresome, despite its intensity, unless you avoid certain obvious traps. For one, so many clichés and false sentiments and bits of misinformation have come to be associated with these subjects that the experience itself is apt to be tarnished and the written account conventionally extravagant. And for another, the self-preoccupying circumstances of the events in which you played a starring role lead to such an excess of subjectivity that it is transformed either into something of interest only to you or into an unintended boast.

The commonplace ingredients of life are the most essential and real parts of our experience. The appeal of a subject often lies in its very commonness. Jane Austen sat in her parlor writing about what went on in ordinary middle-class parlors—and became for many the greatest of English novelists. Of course, if you have thwarted a mugging or sailed a catamaran to Hawaii, then by all means make the most of your unusual experience. But even if you have been a party to some extraordinary goings on, concentrate on those familiar details that link us all to life.

And never make the mistake of writing about exciting experiences in a dull way; it is far better to write about common experience in an uncommonly expressive way. Adventure is, after all, finally a matter of being exceptionally aware and articulate. The greatest contribution a writer can make to his readers is to recall them to a heightened awareness of their own experience, to make them sensitive to the transcendent realness in everyday and everyman.

Your participation in the broad activities and affairs of the world is largely a matter of choice. But neither the writer nor anyone who expects to derive the greatest meaning and satisfaction from life can afford to miss even apparently trivial fragments of experience, for to engage yourself even as a bystander is to become part of a much larger sweep of events. Experience—that totality of action that makes up an individual life, regardless of whether the encounters have been personal and direct or simply those of an onlooker—is finally the measure of your very existence.

Contemporary living offers unsurpassed opportunity for varied experience, if you take advantage of it. Your limited experience is often simply the result of having never given it a try, either because of a habit of remaining uncommitted, an unwillingness to work at developing the necessary skill, or a fear of risking failure. New experience is especially rich when you go into it with the awareness of a writer—expectant, resolved to find out all it has to offer, and intent on ultimately translating the events into a prose so vivid and animated that readers will be able to know vicariously much the same experience for themselves.

READING

Invention also involves *your ability to read,* for ingenuity is required there as well. In reading you are drawing on the observations and experiences of others—extending yourself well beyond the range of personal encounter. Whether for diversion, even as a kind of escape, or for cultural and professional reasons, reading makes a most remarkable contribution to the quality of your life. Through books you transcend the limitations imposed by time and space and all the other circumstances of your private existence. The alternatives to books and magazines and similar reading fare cannot begin to offer the quality or variety of data, the efficiency and convenience of such "packaging." The printed page remains one of the great technological achievements of history, perhaps the single *most* significant in terms of its cultural impact.

Also, from reading more than any other activity comes that perceptual vocabulary—the words, metaphors, symbols, allusions, and other verbal associations with which you grasp and shape life. For language and writing are not ways of expressing experience only, they are experience. At least any response more elaborate than vague feelings is likely to be essentially verbal, made of words. So your capacity for observation and experience, even of the simplest kind, is somewhat determined by the reading you have done by way of preparation.

Become a browser and buyer, a frequenter of bookstores and libraries. In bookstores don't become a victim of the "best-seller syndrome" or of the "what-everyone-else-is-reading complex"—not unless you can find time for your own sallies as well. To own your copy is one thing—to make it your own through a close reading, perhaps with underlinings and marginal notes, is quite another. Your shelves will invariably contain four kinds of books: writer's aids (like a dictionary, a thesaurus, *The New Strategy of Style*); reference books (possibly an encyclopedia, certainly titles dealing with your major interests: perhaps a travel guide to Spain or an auto racing annual); light reading (and other books which haven't made for themselves a special place in your esteem); and "touchstones," books so compelling and imitable that they remain on your shelves as models of effective writing. Such a collection of books and magazines "in reach," even if it numbers only a modest few paperbacks and old issues, is the best encouragement for a writer. Often a title from your personal library will get you started by suggesting a subject and even providing the data, and keep you going by serving as an example of smooth prose and of the finished product. But books from your own shelves are usually just a beginning.

Some leisurely moments spent exploring your way through the various rooms and stacks and reference materials of the library will make you feel more at home. But the quickest and most productive way of discovering what the library has to offer for your specific writing project is a fairly simple routine. A brief check of the standard reference works (encyclopedias, biographical dictionaries, almanacs, atlases), the periodical and newspaper indexes *(The Reader's Guide to Periodical Literature, The New York Times Index),* the special references (bibliographies and other reference works on specific fields of interest), and finally the card catalog will indicate what materials your library possesses. Most of your research effort will be spent sorting out the pertinent, authoritative, and recent from the irrelevant, opinionated, and outdated. From there to note taking to jottings is not a difficult process.

The most inventive aspect of research makes it seem like an extension of personal observation and experience. For even researched pieces are not facts-judgments-opinions gathered from here and there and strung together like beads on a string. To make proper use of your reading and research, you must make it your own. You were likely drawn to the books and articles in the first place because you were curious, interested, somewhat informed about the subject—or subjects, since it is often a combining process. For example, you have always been a dog lover; you recently made a visit to Spain, where in the Prado Museum you encountered a painting of Goya's that included a rather poignant portrait of a dog; a search of library sources on the dog in art and myth turns up, among other things, a book on the subject, Maria Leach's *God Had a Dog,* complete with its own bibliography; the standard art references, *The Encyclopedia of Painting* and *The Encyclopedia of Art,* contain other well-known paintings in which the presence of dogs is more than simply decorative; you recall Argos, Odysseus' old dog, from some assigned reading you did for a humanities course, and quite a different animal in Arthur Conan Doyle's "Hound of the Baskervilles"—and you mull over the various connections and implications until you come up with "an idea," the dual role of the dog in art and literature, where it is a symbol sometimes of loyalty and sometimes of terror, which you referred to in your paper as the "Argos" and "Cerberus" factors. Of course, the process of refining the subject to the point where it can be described by a thesis, identified by a title, and developed either in a short article or essay is still going on. But the line of thought is so much your own by this time that you seem always to be on familiar ground.

SPECULATING

The intellectual processes by which information is turned into insight are perhaps the most fascinating, surely the most illusive phase of invention. A certain amount of speculation was a part of your observing and experiencing, reading and researching. Whenever you paused to think about the various aspects of the subject, whenever you asked yourself "I wonder if . . . ," you were speculating. And the most interesting writing is often the product of subtle and ranging speculations. It is here that writers are apt to be too timid. The intellectual conversion of this assorted data of yours into something definite and meaningful is a procedure with infinite variations. But you will find that your imaginative leaps tend to be of three kinds: First, *you will frequently draw general conclusions from specific facts.* You may in rare instances be able to survey "all" the facts; but most of the time you will have to settle for "a sampling" of the facts; and occasionally you will prefer "a selection" of the facts. And the general conclusions you come up with are, as can be expected, sometimes quite probable and other times only possible. Except in obvious cases, such as those affecting human welfare (where accurate, representative, and pertinent facts are crucial, and where the line of argument leading to judgments and opinions must be absolutely clear), some of the most interesting generalizations can be wildly speculative. By trying first one possibility and then another, even if it means stretching a point here or ignoring a piece of contradictory evidence there, all kinds of conclusions might be drawn from the same collection of facts. For example, that creatures from outer space have changed from green monsters bent on the destruction of the earth in earlier science fiction to gentle and enlightened representatives of a superior race in more recent writing is not quite "true" according to the strictist rules of inductive logic (there are numerous exceptions and variations)—but doesn't such a conclusion make all kinds of revealing speculations possible? Doesn't it imply something about man's altered vision of himself and his society? This kind of selectivity leads immediately into the next pattern of invention on which writers rely.

Second, then, *you will variously separate and combine your facts to derive conclusions.* Actually a certain amount of analysis and synthesis always takes place. In order to grasp a subject, you examine its various parts; and to understand the function of individual components you reconstruct the whole. At one stage in your thinking you do this to see what you might discover about your material. Once again, whatever is under consideration can be separated into its parts or aspects or phases along any number of "natural" lines of division, depending on your purpose. And any subject can be organized in familiar and expected ways.

But nothing prevents you from coming up with imaginative or even outlandish alternatives; after all, the same parts can be assembled into a Volkswagen, a dune buggy, or a piece of junk sculpture. If, for example, you wanted to "make a statement" about American taste, you could do it quite interestingly in terms of "the chartreuse period, the pink lightning and charcoal black period, and the olive tone period." Such a treatment would arbitrarily divide the years 1945–1970 into three distinct periods, each characterized by the fashionable colors of the day, even though they would include such other expressions of the popular aesthetic as tail fins on cars and bell-bottom trousers. The separations and combinations you can make of any subject are virtually unlimited—and doesn't each reveal something different? Sooner or later you will find yourself stepping outside the immediate frame of reference, suggesting yet another process of invention.

And third, *you will make new connections and draw revealing analogies.* To perceive a relation between more or less comparable things or a similarity in some respect between things otherwise unlike can be an illuminating intellectual activity. There are the obvious connections, such as the relation between stress and fatigue in steel structures; and there are some not so obvious, like the link between the straight line and human culture. Actually there are some surprising parallels in so staid a field as economics, where the prices of gold and soybeans move together and where the ups and downs of the stock market seem to follow the rising and falling hemline of women's skirts. And what about the apparent connection between sunspots and oppressive weather and crimes of passion? What appears fanciful may turn out not to be at all.

But the writer is also interested in making connections, drawing analogies on purely intellectual grounds. That Hitler was the product of an unhappy home, or of the Treaty of Versailles, or of Wagnerian opera and Nietzschean philosophy, or even of the village bands and their patriotic music—these are possibilities worth contemplating. To treat the race car driver as a manifestation of St. George, out to slay the dragon of his own death fears, is moving from simple comparison in the direction of analogy.

Each of these processes by which you speculate upon the meaning of your materials is to a degree instinctive. At least these are the ways you have always thought about life. Sometimes you will have to be more accurate and orderly than you usually are in order to avoid illogical and fallacious conclusions. At other times, however, when new light needs to be shed on an old subject, or when novel and innovative ideas are demanded, or simply when you wish to write interestingly, your speculations will take a more audacious turn.

As you carry out these activities of invention, you write words on paper, of course, for at some point invention—which has to do mainly with getting a firm hold on your ideas—shades into writing. After all, you can hardly know what to think until you begin to put it down. So: You write down your observations, your reading notes, your imaginative ideas. You keep a commonplace book or a journal. You take notes on file cards and keep them in a box, or folder. You jot things down, write notes to yourself, record the present moment for future use. You involve yourself in what might be called prewriting—the prewriting of invention, the developing and discovering of material—and you create for yourself a rich storehouse from which to draw as you begin to focus upon particular writing assignments and particular writing needs: as you begin to choose subjects, develop theses, illustrate and expand topics, and otherwise engage in writing a composition for others to read.

SUMMARY CHECKLIST

As you consider the prospect of writing, ask yourself these questions:

1. Have I made it a rule to be alive to what goes on around me and to participate?
2. Am I a browser and buyer, a frequenter of bookstores and libraries?
3. Do I make it a habit to speculate freely upon the fruits of my observing and experiencing, reading and researching?
4. Am I committed to the process of invention by which readable and interesting prose is created?
5. Have I made it a habit to jot down my notes each day— notes to which I can refer when I take on the task of writing a composition?

THE WHOLE COMPOSITION

A complete perceptual experience is composed of many separate sensory observations, selected and arranged to create a more extended picture of something. John Updike's "On the First Day of Spring" is a collection of notes relating to a single afternoon. Written in the form of a list, as if he were trying to teach himself to be a better observer, it represents a sort of compositional missing link showing the evolutionary step in writing between preliminary thoughts and the finished essay. Instead of telling the reader *about* the scene or giving his *general impressions* of it, Updike presents him with the raw materials, the various sights and sounds most acutely suggestive of that first day of spring in Central Park.

Central Park

John Updike

On the afternoon of the first day of spring, when the gutters were still heaped high with Monday's snow but the sky itself was swept clean, we put on our galoshes and walked up the sunny side of Fifth Avenue to Central Park. There we saw:

Great black rocks emerging from the melting drifts, their craggy skins glistening like the backs of resurrected brontosaurs.

A pigeon on the half-frozen pond strutting to the edge of the ice and looking a duck in the face.

A policeman getting his shoe wet testing the ice.

Three elderly relatives trying to coax a little boy to accompany his father on a sled ride down a short but steep slope. After much balking, the boy did, and, sure enough, the sled tipped over and the father got his collar full of snow. Everybody laughed except Youngster, who sniffled.

Four boys in black leather jackets throwing snowballs at each other. (The snow was deliciously soggy, and packed hard with one squeeze.)

Seven men without hats.

Twelve snowmen, none of them intact.

Two men listening to the radio in a car parked outside the Zoo; Mel Allen was broadcasting the Yanks-Cardinals game from St. Petersburg.

A tahr (*Hemitragus jemlaicus,* as the Zoo's identifying sign termed him) pleasantly squinting in the sunlight.

An aoudad absently pawing the mud and chewing.

A yak with its back turned.

Empty cages labelled "Coati," "Orang-outang," "Ocelot."

A father saying to his little boy, who was annoyed almost to tears by the inactivity of the seals, "Father [Father Seal, we assumed] is very tired; he worked hard all day."

Most of the cafeteria's out-of-doors tables occupied.

A pretty girl in black pants falling on them at the Wollman Memorial Rink.

"BILL & DORIS" carved on a tree. "MEG & FUDGE" written in the snow.

Two old men playing, and six supervising, a checkers game.

The Michael Friedsam Foundation Merry-Go-Round, nearly empty of children but brimful of calliope music.

A man on a bench near the carrousel reading, through sunglasses, a book on economics.

Crews of shinglers repairing the roof of the Tavern-on-the-Green.

A woman dropping a camera she was trying to load, the film unrolling in the slush and exposing itself.

A little colored boy in aviator goggles rubbing his ears and saying, "He really hurt me." "No, he didn't," his nursemaid told him.

The green head of Giuseppe Mazzini staring across the white softball field, unblinking, though the sun was in its eyes.

Water murmuring down walks and rocks and steps. A grown man trying to block one rivulet with snow.

Damp chartreuse patches of grass under trees and on unshaded slopes.

Things like brown sticks nosing through a plot of cleared soil.

A tire track in a piece of mud far removed from where any automobiles could be.

Footprints around a "KEEP OFF" sign.

Two pigeons feeding each other.

Two showgirls, whose faces had not yet thawed the frost of their makeup, threading indignantly through the slush.

A plump old man saying "Chick, chick" and feeding peanuts to squirrels.

Many solitary men throwing snowballs at tree trunks.

Many birds calling to each other about how little the Ramble has changed.

One red mitten lying neglected under a poplar tree.

An airplane, very bright and distant, slowly moving through the branches of a sycamore.

Exercises

1. Write a brief diary of an afternoon on the order of John Updike's "On the First Day of Spring"—perhaps in the same listlike pattern and elliptical style.

2. Examine the simplest, most commonplace object in sight and make an exhaustive list of its attributes. Or recall the dullest, most routine chore in your day and list its procedures. Exclude all other thoughts. Keep coming back to the task until the size of the list astonishes you.

3. Force yourself to see the world as you never saw it before. Imagine that the connections between your sensory organs and brain were crossed; describe the feel of a color, the sound of an odor. Or suppose you suddenly became almost painfully hypersensitive to a particular physical sensation; describe, for example, the nausea, dizziness, and insecurity caused by the slightest motion. Or suppose you could from a point quite outside observe yourself casually and dispas-

sionately as an animated object moving through a land-scape; describe this utter stranger as he wakes up in the morning, shows off, has his tonsils removed.

4. Begin a writer's journal in which you record some of the details and incidents and thoughts of your days for possible future reference—but mainly as a stimulus for your own alertness and imagination.

5. Begin a writer's notebook in which you collect brief passages from your reading that hold special appeal, particularly for their style.

6. To illustrate the relation between literature and life in your own experience, recall ways in which a story or drama or other form of verbal art has shaped your style of living. Jot down the title of a novel, short story, poem, play, television or movie scenario that you found especially compelling. Next, cite lines or relate events or describe characters or report other of its features that for some reason linger most vividly in your memory. Assuming that you are conscious of this impressionable influence, how might the work have shaped your style of thinking or acting? Even if its effect was no more profound than prompting you to buy a turtleneck sweater or to resolve to look up your own ancestral roots, write a paragraph or so in which you relate the effect of a work upon your way of acting and talking and dressing, upon your attitudes and ideals and values.

7. Writers often keep journals as a means of learning the art of observing. The act of putting your perceptions into prose makes a connection between the word and the thing that strengthens your hold on both. Evidently begun as explorations in the art of observing, the "inscapes" from the journals of Gerard Manley Hopkins, many of them one-sentence records of fleeting perceptions, are virtual prose haiku illustrating the connection between words and sense experience—"Moonlight hanging or dropping on treetops like blue cobweb," "Winds housing in trees."

As an exercise in both observing and writing, for the arts complement one another, write half a dozen or such *inscapes* of your own. Some of you will have better luck composing them on the spot or shortly afterward; others will be able to revive a sensory experience long after it was observed. The important point is to concentrate as much of the perceptual encounter as possible into a few well-chosen, evocative words. Emphasize the scene or object itself rather than your feelings about it. (If you have supplied your readers with sufficient detail, they will experience the emotion without its being mentioned.) And be specific, concrete, and selective, stretching your vocabulary and your perceptual reach at the same time.

Of a fountain you could write, "Wind dried the emerald moss to a chalky turquoise"; of a stop at the corner joint, "My beer mug left an olympic flag of rings on the bar"; of an errand to the administration building, "The marble halls shimmered like congealed water."

2. SUBJECT AND THESIS

When we begin to think about writing a specific composition, we ask two crucial questions: *What am I writing about? What point am I trying to make?* Obviously, we need a *subject*. And obviously, we need a *thesis*—something as specific and meaningful as possible to say about the subject. On some occasions and for certain readers, we are given a subject and thesis and are asked to write a composition using them. For other readers on other occasions, we must determine a subject and thesis of our own. In either case, we tailor the subject and thesis to the writing situation: to the audience, to the occasion, to the literary form in which we are writing.

Every composition, large or small, has a specific subject and thesis. Even so thrilling a message as "Keep off the grass" has a subject, "grass," and a thesis, "keep off." Sometimes you are given the subject and thesis—as when you are asked to write a laudatory report on the achievements of the corporation for distribution to the shareholders, or when you are writing a note of condolence to a bereaved family, or when you are asked to write the official statement setting forth government or institutional policy. At other times, you select the subject and thesis on your own—as when you simply want to write a letter to a friend back home, or when you are asked to read a paper "on anything you like" at the next club meeting, or when you are assigned a research paper on "some topic that interests you." Sometimes the writing situation—the reader, the occasion, the form—practically dictates what the subject and thesis will be. But at other times, the writing situation is an open one—and it is up to you to select a subject and thesis that will be appropriate and meaningful.

Your major task—whether your subject and thesis be given or freely chosen—will be to choose and state in words a specific topic and a specific idea about that topic. The task seems simple enough, but many writers find themselves in trouble because they cannot choose from their subject matter a specific item that they can adequately handle; they do not distinguish between their subject and thesis; they do not state the thesis clearly and understandably, for themselves or for their readers.

THE SUBJECT

Your first problem is simply this: What specific subject am I writing about on this occasion? You must decide whether you're writing about apples, cider making, or Vermont. Without a specific subject your communication becomes a hodgepodge of statements that may do for idle conversation—"What are you two talking about?" "Oh, nothing in particular. Just this and that"—but will not do at all for serious communication.

Your main problem in selecting a subject is in narrowing it down to workable size. All too frequently writers burden themslves with subjects that are too big and broad. Admittedly, a too specialized or personal subject may mean very little to your reader. Yet most often you err in the other direction; too frequently, you will decide to talk about apple pies in general when you would be better off talking about the Dutch apple pies that mother used to bake. Your first task in choosing a subject is to pick one limited enough in scope so that, within the bounds of your composition, you can do the subject justice. Is there a formula for this decision? No. But experience and common sense will tell you when you have the proper-size subject to handle. Isn't it obvious that in a fifty-word memo you can't do the subject of suspension bridges justice? You may do justice to the color of the suspension bridge over Jones River, but you can't deal with bridges in general, anywhere, anytime. When you state your subject, you commit yourself to a reasonable discussion of it; if your subject is too broad for the time and space available within your composition, you can't expect to succeed in your writing.

Here are some possible subjects, with an evaluation of them in consideration of the sort of writing in which they are to appear:

Composition	Subject	Evaluation
A 15-word telegram	The virtues of the two-party political system as opposed to a multiparty political system	Subject too extensive for the form.
A 60,000-word book	My favorite fishing spot	Subject too limited for the form.
A 60,000-word book	Literature	Subject too extensive for the form. Certainly a book can be written on "literature" if the subject is limited in some way.
A 60,000-word book	Twentieth-century Canadian literature	More likely. Subject suitable for book-length consideration.
A 4,000-word essay	Edgar Allan Poe	Subject too extensive for an essay. Subject would be difficult to handle even in book form; in an essay it would be impossible.
A 4,000-word essay	Sea images in the writing of Edgar Allan Poe	More possible. This seems to be a subject one could adequately discuss in an essay.
A 15-word telegram	Rejection of an invitation to dinner	Probably would work.
A 2,000-word essay	My favorite fishing spot	Would work.

THE THESIS

A serious composition must have, however, more than a well-chosen subject. You may announce that you are going to talk about Charlie Chaplin's film *City Lights,* but your reader is going to ask you why. The reason you give is your thesis. If you say you are going to discuss the proposition, "Chaplin's *City Lights,* more than any other cinematic exercise, captures the spirit and dilemma of the twentieth-century alienated man," you have the basis for real discussion. The thesis may be extravagant, but at least it is something to prove or demonstrate or explain. You not only have a subject, but you have something to say about the subject.

A good thesis either should tell readers something of significance that they did not know before or that they did not previously accept or agree with, or should tell them something they knew or agreed with before, providing also an explanation or proof or analysis that was not available or acceptable before. If your subject is apples, and your thesis is "Apples are red," you're off to a bad start simply because you have not told your readers anything significant that they did not already know. If, however, you have a thesis that "aardvarks are dangerous when removed from their natural habitat," you may conceivably have a reasonable thesis for an essay, simply because you are telling your readers something, possibly significant, that they did not know. If you write on the thesis "Alan Thompson was the first mayor of Centerville," you may be telling readers something they did not know, but they may not consider it worth knowing. If, however, you tell readers that "Abraham Lincoln was a great President because he was able to maintain the right balance between his spiritual predilections and his political know-how," you may be telling readers something they know but in addition may be giving them a new explantion of it. Obviously the selection of a good thesis depends a great deal upon the knowledge you have of your readers.

Sometimes a thesis is acceptable even though it introduces neither novelty nor explanation. You sometimes will write a thesis that does not tell the reader anything new and does not offer any new explanation or proofs, if you accompany this "do nothing" thesis with another thesis that proposes a universal truth. You may write an essay on the thesis "It is no longer possible to bake or get Dutch apple pies like those mother used to bake" (a thesis that does not tell readers anything significant that they didn't already know) if you accompany that thesis with one that says, "Time passes, and what was typical of past generations is not typical of a new generation. The old days are gone." This "truth of mutability" is the universal observation that validates the otherwise insipid or insignificant thesis.

Here are some theses with evaluations of their significance:

A two-party political system is more effective in a populous society than a multiparty system would be. (This could be a workable thesis; certainly it has importance or significance. The danger would lie in the fact that the reader may already "know" this thesis; you may not be telling him anything he hasn't already agreed to. In such a case it might be wise to modify the thesis to include proofs or arguments that are new to the reader.)

My favorite camping spot is in Minnesota. (This thesis certainly has little significance. Why would anyone want to read a discussion of it?)

Poe's sea images represent his symbolic concern with the positive, life-giving experiences that other parts of his work seem to deny. (This is a usable thesis, since it presents something that is probably new to the reader, and, in the literary world at least, has a certain significance.)

Fishing is the best single activity a man can engage in in order to "settle his soul." (The thesis may have some value, since anything that helps our souls may be considered significant. Yet is it new? Hasn't the reader probably encountered this thesis before?)

The portrayal of violence on television should be greatly curtailed, as the result either of voluntary network action or of regulatory action by the federal government. (This thesis would have significance for many readers, and though it is not a new idea, it might be developed into a worthwhile discussion if the details used to support it prove novel and sensible.)

The National Gallery in Washington, D.C., contains the most representative collection of great European paintings to be found in the Western Hemisphere. (For a specialized audience, this thesis might be significant in that it is "debatable." Essentially a thesis of evaluation, it calls for a great deal of definition and a detailed demonstration of how the National Gallery collection satisfies the criterion of "most representative"; in other words, it is a thesis that seems likely to generate a substantial composition.)

Napoleon's dramatic career can be better understood if we realize that he was at heart a frustrated author. (Significant enough, in educated circles, and new enough to make it a usable thesis.)

Theses ultimately have to be evaluated in terms of "occasion" and "audience"—and what is significant and novel in one instance may not be in another. Simple theses of definition and identification— "The newly discovered virus is a lethal member of the mumps family"—may be highly significant and novel propositions to be proved and demonstrated—even though the thesis is a simple equation of "this is that." Complex theses of evaluation and analysis— "Beethoven's string quartets demonstrate both his musical skill and his philosophical insight"—may be equally desirable given other kinds of writing situations.

PLACEMENT

After you have decided upon your subject and thesis, your next decision is one of placement. Subject and thesis exist in words, and the verbalization of the subject and thesis must occur in your essay. Obviously, no set formula for this verbalization can be given; subject and thesis may occur in declarative statements, in question-and-answer patterns, even in the subtleties of metaphors and symbols. And obviously, too, the verbalization can occur at just about any point in your composition; since every part of your composition is supposedly devoted to the subject-thesis, it is reasonable that an expression of the subject-thesis would be pertinent at any place within the writing. But you must take care, if you do nothing else, to present the subject and the thesis as clearly as possible at certain vital locations.

You will usually state the subject in one of three places: (1) in the first sentence of the composition, (2) in the last sentence of the first paragraph of the composition, (3) in the first sentence of the first paragraph following any sort of preliminary material that is not an essential part of the composition proper.

Which place you choose depends upon what sort of beginning you are using for your essay. The normal beginning calls for the subject in the first sentence; the delayed beginning calls for the subject in the last sentence of an introductory paragraph or in the first sentence of the text proper. Unless you have a reason to do otherwise, always mention your subject in the first sentence of your composition. Unless you desire to intrigue your reader with some preliminary material, you will have no reason to delay stating your subject.

As for placing your *thesis,* you have a more elaborate decision to make. You may place it at any of the following positions:

At the Climax
In some compositions, your thesis can be the climax of the essay, and in these cases your thesis will occur at the very end of the middle part of the essay, since most essays have their climax at that location.

In the Conclusion
In those essays in which the thesis is not the climax but is a conclusion to be drawn from the middle part, or is to be a restatement of an earlier presentation of the thesis, the thesis will occur in the conclusion of the essay.

At the Climax and in the Conclusion Both
In certain cases the thesis may be presented figuratively or illustratively in the climax and then overtly or literally in the conclusion; or in some cases, just to the contrary: a literal, concise statement of the thesis occurs at the climax, followed by a figurative restatement in the conclusion.

At the Beginning
Even though the thesis is presented toward the end of the composition, you may also wish to present it, as writers do most of the time, at the beginning of the essay. Certainly if you are writing a business or technical report you may well wish to communicate your thesis as soon as possible, even though you will, of course, state it again at the end of the writing. Only if you are writing a personal, more leisurely essay, will you wish—for effect—to limit the revelation of your thesis to the last portion of the composition. At the beginning of the composition, the thesis may be stated:

> In the first sentence of the first paragraph.

> In the last sentence of the first paragraph, at the conclusion of an inductive paragraph.

> In either of the above positions, but with the entire "first paragraph" following one or more paragraphs of prelude material not actually a part of the composition proper.

Exceptional Cases
In rare and exceptional cases, the thesis may be stated in the beginning of the essay and not toward the end. This occurs, however, only in pieces of writing like newspaper stories or technical reports, which follow the journalistic "who-what-when-where-why" plan in revealing and presenting information.

In exceptional cases you may avoid stating the thesis at all. You may use an *implied thesis*. You will leave it up to your reader to decide what the thesis is. This, of course, is a very tricky business. You must remember, first of all, that though you do not state the thesis within the composition, it still must be a statable thesis that you have articulated to yourself. And, second, you will use the implied thesis in only the most sophisticated of situations. The implied thesis is limited almost exclusively to fiction or fictionlike writing, that is, highly poetic or lyrical essays that are chiefly concerned with creating aura and impression rather than communicating ideas.

CONSISTENCY OF CONTENT

In your verbalization and placement of subject and thesis you are contributing to the overall goal of unity. A good composition needs a consistency of subject matter, a consistency of content. You must stick to the subject and thesis as you write.

To achieve the desired unity and consistency, *keep in mind, first of all, that the subject is not stated once and once only.* Everything you say in a composition should be related to your subject, and therefore your subject should be mentionable at any given point in your writing, and you should not let it go unmentioned for any great length of time.

Make frequent reference to the subject throughout your composition, especially in the topic sentences of your paragraphs. Even in those topic sentences in which you do not verbalize the subject, you should be able to insert a mention of the subject and still have the topic sentence make sense. Rule: Mention your subject at least once a page, either straightforwardly or obliquely; if the composition doesn't make sense with so frequent a mentioning of the subject, you have probably wandered afield.

Second, *make sure every paragraph in your writing relates directly or indirectly to your thesis.*

Third, *do not digress from your subject and thesis except for rhetorical purposes.*

You can test the consistency of content in your essays in several ways. First, write down your thesis. Then make a list of all your topic sentences and either confirm the relationship of each topic sentence to the thesis or show that the topic sentences are connected with each other in a logic that leads to the thesis. This unity of content can be demonstrated, on a miniature scale, in a single paragraph:

When a man falls in love, he may reveal his condition by several symptomatic behaviors. Sleeplessness may fall upon him. Nervousness may plague him. Fancifulness may afflict him. He may giggle at the wrong moment, choke up at inappropriate times. He may forget his umbrella on rainy days, clutch it to him on fair days. He may speak frequently of the beauties of the world. He may purchase large supplies of roses, candies, perfumes, and assorted doodads.

To confirm the unity of this paragraph you can check each sentence against the topic sentence. Though you would not write or leave the paragraph in the following condition, you can see in this paraphrase how unity is built into the paragraph:

When a man falls in love, his condition may be revealed to him and to others in several ways. Sleeplessness may fall upon him. [*And sleeplessness will reveal to him and to others that he is in love.*] Nervousness may plague him. [*And this nervousness reveals to the man and to others that he is in love.*] Etc.

Here is a paragraph that begins on the same note as the one above and quickly loses its way:

When a man falls in love, he may reveal his condition by several symptomatic behaviors. Sleeplessness may fall upon him. Nervousness may plague him. Nervousness can also be caused by drinking too much coffee or by staying up too late at night to study. Fancifulness may afflict him. He may, indeed, giggle at the wrong time, choke up at the inappropriate time. Inappropriateness, in fact, causes a lot of trouble for a lot of people. He may forget his umbrella on rainy days, clutch it to him on fair days. He may speak frequently of the beauties of the world. He may purchase large supplies of roses, candies, perfumes, and assorted doodads. All of which goes to prove that love can cost you a lot of money.

Such a paragraph fails because the sentences do not relate back to a central idea nor do they proceed in a rational way to the revelation of a topic sentence.

Here are two "outlines" in which the placement of subject and thesis is indicated:

Napoleon—Frustrated Author
Napoleon Bonaparte always wanted to write a successful novel (subject). When he was a young man, Napoleon actually tried his hand at writing fiction (subject). He wrote . . . (subject). And he also wrote . . . (subject). But all his writings were mediocre . . . (subject). When the opportunity to enter politics came along, he took it—partly perhaps because he knew he would never be a success as a writer. (Thesis.)

Napoleon Bonaparte entered politics because he had failed as a writer (subject and thesis).

Napoleon had always wanted to write a successful novel. When he was a young man, he tried his hand at fiction. He wrote. . . . And he also wrote. . . . But all his writings were mediocre. . . . (Thesis restated.)

Your decisions concerning a specific subject and thesis are not, of course, the only decisions you have to make in writing. Writing involves a long chain of decisions that finally penetrate the area of minute details. But the decisions you make about the subject and thesis are among the most important. Until these decisions are made, many others cannot be made. If you choose your subject and your thesis wisely, you will avoid a great many problems that would otherwise show up later on in your writing.

SUMMARY CHECKLIST

As you prepare to write a given composition, ask yourself these questions:

1. Have I limited my subject to a specific subject that I can handle adequately within the space and time limitations before me?
2. Have I a definite point I wish to make about the specific subjects? Do I have a clear, expressible thesis?

After you have written your composition, ask yourself these questions:

1. Even though it may be stated frequently elsewhere, is my subject stated clearly at some reasonable point in the beginning of my composition?
2. Even though it may be stated frequently elsewhere, is my thesis at least stated clearly and understandably toward the end of my composition?

THE WHOLE COMPOSITION

In the following essay, you will find both the subject and thesis presented in the first paragraph. The subject is "the first work of Western European literature" and the thesis is that the *Iliad* "has remained incomparably the greatest" literary work in the Western literary tradition. Throughout the essay, in every paragraph, reference is made to the subject (note that Rexroth uses "the *Iliad*," "Homer," and "first work of Western European literature" interchangeably as subject words) even though each paragraph is devoted to some separate and special topic of its own. In the last two paragraphs the thesis is twice restated: ". . . in the *Iliad*, he constructed a dramatic architecture of a cogency never to be surpassed"; ". . . the *Iliad* is the paramount classic of that art."

The Iliad
Kenneth Rexroth

The best-qualified critics have always agreed that the first work of Western European literature has remained incomparably the greatest. In itself this is a revelation of the nature of the human mind and of the role of works of art. This is a popular judgment as well as a critical one. Today, over 2,500 years old, Homer competes successfully with current best-sellers, detective stories, and the most sensational and topical nonfiction.

Modern Americans may be the heirs of Western civilization, but all the elements of that civilization have changed drastically since Homer's day. The office worker who reads Homer on the subway bears little superficial resemblance either to Homer's characters or to his audience. Why should two long poems about the life of barbaric Greece have so great an appeal?

It was the fashion in the nineteenth century to deny the existence of Homer and to break up the *Odyssey* and *Iliad* into collections of folk ballads. Nothing disproves those theories more than this public reception. The *Iliad* and the *Odyssey* have been read by such a vast diversity of men because, as unitary works of art, they deal with universal experience with unsurpassed depth, breadth, and intensity. Each poem shows the powerful insight and organization that comes from the artistic craft of a complete person.

Men have argued about the *Iliad* for so long and raised so many side issues that it is easy for a critic to forget that it is formally a tragedy, saturated with a tragic sense of life and constructed with the inevitability of the tragedies of Orestes or Macbeth. It is a double tragedy—of Achilles and the Greeks, and of Hector and the Trojans, each reinforcing the other. To modern taste, the heroes are not Greeks, who are portrayed as quarreling members of a warrior band, but the Trojans, men of family united in the community of the city-state.

Homer, like most later writers of epic—Teutonic, Irish, or Icelandic—portrays heroic valor as fundamentally destructive, not just of social order but of humane community. The Greeks are doomed by their characteristic virtues. Achilles sulks in his tent. Agamemmon has stolen his girl. The Greek camp is beset with a disorder that wastes all good things. Underlying disorder is violence.

Violence is not approved of in itself by the Greeks, but all the values they most admire—the nobility, pride and power, glamour and strength of barbaric chieftains—flourish only in the context of violence and must be fed by it continuously. Failure of these values provokes shame, the opposite of the assumption of responsibility, and shame provokes disaster.

On the other side of the wall the Trojans go their orderly and dignified ways. None of them approves of the crime of Paris but he is a member of the family of the King of Troy and the citizens of Troy are members one of another. So they assume his guilt in an act of collective responsibility. When the Greeks arrived before the walls of Troy, the Trojans could have thrown Paris and Helen out of the city. The invaders would have gone their way. When the *Iliad* opens, the Greeks have been fighting for ten years and are worn out with the moral attrition of war, while the Trojans have grown ever closer together in the consciousness of doom. "Our lot is best, to fight for our country," says Hector, and Homer implies a contrast with the Greeks who are fighting for themselves, each for his own valor and pride.

Greeks and Trojans are not the only protagonists of this tragedy. There is another community—the gods of Olympus. In the vast literature of Homeric criticism, I have never read a mention of what kind of community this was, of where in Homer's day he could have found an earthly parallel to such a group of people. The court of Zeus is precisely a court like those to be found in the great empires of ancient Near East in Egypt, Babylon, or Persia. After Homer, for a few hundred years, Greek society strove to rise above the tyrant and the court of the tyrant. The Greeks of the classical period looked on the rulers of Persia or Egypt and their provincial imitators in the Greek world as at once frivolous and dangerous, because, in Greek opinion, they were motivated not by the moral concensus of a responsible community but by the whims of what today we would call a collection of celebrities.

Homer contrasts the societies of the Greeks, the Trojans, and the Olympian gods as the three forms of political association that prevailed in the Heroic Age (a time that in fact, 400 years before, must have seemed almost as remote to him as his age does to us), namely the barbaric war band, the ancient, pre-Greek City-state, and the imperial court. He also contrasts men and gods as two disparate orders of being. The gods may behave like painted and perfumed courtiers of the Persian King of Kings, but they function also as conceptual forms of the forces of nature and of the forces that operate within the human personality on nonhuman levels. In this role, too, the tragedy of the *Iliad* reveals them as frivolous, dangerous, and unpredictable.

True, Homer speaks worshipfully at times of the gods, and especially of Zeus, but in terms of standardized flattery, empty of moral content. For Homer, utterly unlike the Jew or Moslem or Christian, the supernatural is devoid of value altogether. Value arises only in the relations of men. He contrasts two different systems of relationships, the epic chivalry of the Heroic Age war band of the Greeks, and the Trojan community of mutual respect and responsibility. The conflicts and resolutions and tragedies that beset the interactions of these human beings are all the good and evil there is in the *Iliad.* The gods contribute only chance, fate, doom, as amoral as so many roulette wheels.

Homer has been read for almost 3,000 years, and is read today by millions, because he portrayed men in the nightbound world of insensate circumstance as being each man to his fellow the only light there is, and all men to each other as the source of the only principle of order. This, says Homer, is the human condition. Out of it in the *Iliad* he constructed a dramatic architecture of a cogency never to be surpassed.

Each time I put down the *Iliad,* after reading it again in some new translation, or after reading once more the somber splendor of Greek, I am convinced, as one is convinced by the experiences of a lifetime that somehow, in a way beyond the visions of artistry, I have been face to face with the meaning of existence. Other works of literature give this insight, but not so powerfully, so uncontaminated by evasion or subterfuge. If the art of poetry is a symbolic criticism of value, the *Iliad* is the paramount classic of that art. Its purity, simplicity, definition, and impact reveal life and expose it to irrevocable judgment, with finality, at the beginning of European literature.

Exercises

1. Convert the following list of broad, general subject areas into more limited, specific subjects that might be used in compositions of 2,000 words.

   Nuclear Arms Race

   Energy Resources

   Atlantic Fishing Rights

   Neckties

   Office Equipment

   Women Poets

Jazz

Chicago

Skiing

Urban Transportation

2. Modify a subject in various ways to make it suitable for a 15-word telegram, a 50-word memo, a 1,000-word essay, a 4,000-word essay, a 60,000-word book.

3. Without stopping to consider whether you are actually ready to write or not, list a dozen or so subjects which hold a special interest for you and about which you have some passing knowledge or expertise. Draw the subjects from as great a variety of personal sources as possible—classes, work, hobbies, reading, current affairs, conversation with friends, etc. Now arrange or number the subjects on your list according to their relative "human interest." In a paragraph or so consider what the subjects holding the greatest interest for your readers have in common.

4. Write an effectively limited and phrased thesis for each of the following subjects: books, national psychology, professors, poetry, dormitory (barrack) living, poor students and rich students, faraway places.

5. For a single subject write half a dozen possible theses. Check each to make sure it satisfies the basic requirements of a good thesis.

6. You have at some time or other been forced to look at experience from a new angle because of a rare or unexpected occurrence: a childhood illness, the first stirrings of romance, a youthful criminal adventure, perhaps nothing more definite than a day so beautiful it left you shaken. Make a list of three such subjects, devising a thesis for each that would enable you to avoid the pitfalls in such writing—the tendency to be imprecise and effusive, to fall back on generalized cliché and sentiment. (For example, that you suffer excruciating headaches does not make very compelling reading; even your vivid description of a day in misery is not likely to evoke much response; but a thesis in which you allude to the exquisite pleasure of feeling nothing after having endured pain as the greatest sensual delight is the kind of insight around which you could compose an interesting brief essay.) Pick the most likely and try it out on the class, either as simply a subject and thesis briefly described or as an essay of from one to three paragraphs.

7. Make three quick essay outlines (in the manner of the illustrations on pages 22–23) indicating, in each outline, the most effective placement of the thesis. You may wish to develop some of the thesis statements written for the preceding exercises.

3.CLASSIFI-CATION AND ORDER

When we have decided what it is we want to say, and when we have accumulated—through the processes of invention—a body of material to support our subject and thesis, we turn to the task of classifying and ordering. We want now to organize our ideas and data into sensible, relevant groups and to arrange the groups into sensible, relevant sequences. We ask ourselves these questions: *Which of my ideas and data go together? Can I simplify my material into a small number of homogeneous groups? In what order should I present these groups in my composition? Which point in my argument or demonstration should I present first, which second?* Our thoughtful answers to these questions help us write a well-structured composition, with some sort of logical—and meaningful—pattern to it.

Seldom is experience of any kind presented to the writer in a form that can be transformed directly into prose. The raw materials for writing are usually more or less jumbled, and to express whatever thoughts come to mind at ramdom is not to write clearly and effectively.

Writers must first *classify* their materials, grouping them in some reasonable way, deciding what to include and in what proportions. They must then *order* their material, considering the sequence in which the elements of their compositions should occur. In other words, they must make sure they have some definite reason for presenting a particular selection of ideas. And they must make sure they have some definite reason for presenting one idea first, another second, another third.

CLASSIFICATION

Having developed a body of material by the processes of invention, you need to classify the material—by (1) eliminating unnecessary material that does not pertain to the specific subject-thesis you have established and (2) gathering your material into a small number of groups, each group being in some way relevant to the subject-thesis.

Suppose, for instance, that you are preparing to write a composition on the major economic capitals of the world—the cities that seem to dominate world trade and world finance. You have already done a great deal of research and have established your thesis: *Economic capitals cannot be correlated with national or area populations.* You need now to organize the eighteen capitals on your list into groups for discussion. Even if each capital receives some individual attention in your composition, you still need to base your composition on a smaller number of items—in this case, groups of capitals.

Your basic list of economically important cities might go something like this: New York, London, Amsterdam, Paris, Buenos Aires, Rio de Janeiro, Cairo, Rome, Istanbul, Moscow, Peking, Hong Kong, Sidney, Tokyo, San Francisco, Mexico City, Chicago, Houston. Now how do you organize them? A reasonable way would be to group them according to country: the United States, England, Holland, France, Brazil, Argentina, Egypt, Italy, Turkey, Russia, China, Australia, Japan, Mexico. But where do you put Hong Kong? And besides that, you still have too many groups.

You will probably prefer to divide the world up into homogeneous population areas, each area as large as possible. Something like this: the United States, Latin America, Western Europe, Russia, Middle East, China, Far East (excepting China), and Australia. Under these eight headings you can now place your eighteen capitals:

United States: New York, San Francisco, Chicago, Houston

Western Europe: London, Amsterdam, Paris, Rome

Latin America: Buenos Aires, Rio de Janeiro, Mexico City

Middle East: Cairo, Istanbul

Russia: Moscow

China: Peking

Far East: Hong Kong, Tokyo

Australia: Sidney

With this classification, you can probably discuss your thesis with some ease. Certainly you have organized your material to show that the United States, with a population of around 200 million, has four times the number of economic capitals as does China with a population around 800 million. Your classification is pertinent to what you have to say. Also, your eight groups give you a workable number of items to arrange.

What you are trying to obtain, obviously, is a quantity of information, details, and ideas, classified into a few meaningful groups. As you organize your material, you will do well to try for a particular number of groups. Most often you will write a better composition if you have no fewer than three and no more than nine basic parts or groups with which to deal. You may, of course, on occasion have only two parts, in a very short balanced essay, but in general, even in a balanced essay, four, six, or eight parts will do better, for with that number you can achieve your balance and at the same time give your composition substance.

If you have more than nine parts, you begin to face the problem of having a tedious series of topics, a tedious series that should in fact be reduced to three or four larger topics. Most readers simply will not stay with you if you take them through a series of more than nine units. Psychologists tell us that reader retention deteriorates as the number increases.

This ideal quantity is a rule of thumb writers rarely disregard. Indeed, most prose is ordered around five, six, or seven topics. Readers find this a convincing and adequate number whether the work is a book or a short essay. Length, complexity, form, and naturally the subject-thesis have some bearing on what constitutes the ideal number of parts for a work, but the average remains remarkably constant. And there is, in modern prose, a clear tendency to prefer fewer parts.

ORDER

Once you have gathered your material into no more than nine groups (or at least into a reasonably small number of groups), you are ready to *order* your material. You will have to order your material *within each class* and will have to *order the classifications within the essay as a whole.* If you are still writing on the subject "The Economic Capitals of the World" and have classified your material—the eighteen separate cities—into (1) the United States, (2) Western Europe, (3) Latin America, (4) the Middle East, (5) Russia, (6) China, (7) the Far East, and (8) Australia, you now must order the particular cities within each area and you must decide in what order you will present the groups as a whole. Just as you must order the sentences within a paragraph and must order the paragraphs within each part of an essay, you must order the large sections themselves into some reasonable sequence.

In the case of the economic capitals you have several possibilities for order. You could order the groups alphabetically:

Australia

China

Far East

Latin America

Middle East

Russia

United States

Western Europe

but the alphabetical order really has little significance, just as a numerical order would have little significance if you were arbitrarily to assign each group a number. You want to order on the basis of subject-thesis, obviously, and you want to find not only a reasonable basis for order, but as significant a basis as possible. If your thesis in this case indicates no preference for one group over another, then you can well order the groups on the basis of geography. You can start with the United States and simply circle the globe. Yet this ordering would present some problems; after the United States would you go south to Latin America or east to Western Europe? If, however, your thesis has something to do with an evaluative relationship among the groups, you may use an emphatic kind of order—order on the basis of population, on the basis of economic importance, on the basis of historical significance. You may, using some such emphatic order, come up with a list like this:

China

Russia

Western Europe

United States

Latin America

Far East

Middle East

Australia

with the list preceeding from the most to the least populous.

Another possible order would be on the basis of the number of cities within each group: United States, Western Europe (which group first?), Latin America, Middle East (which group first?), Russia, China, Australia (which group first?). Still another sequence would be based on economic importance: United States, Western Europe, Russia, Far East, Latin America, China, Middle East, Australia.

Regardless of which order you finally decide upon, you have the additional task of ordering the cities within each group. For instance, in your discussion of the United States, in what order would you discuss the cities?

The primary rule of order is to *use some reasonable and significant order that supports your thesis.* Though there may be a great variety of ordering possibilities, certain kinds of order are more generally used than others, and these popular forms of order should be given your first consideration: *spatial* order, *chronological* order, *cause-and-effect* order, and *emphatic* order.

Spatial Order

The ordering of details or parts according to physical or spatial considerations is common when the writer is dealing with something that has area or geographical location. In spatial order, you can take up the details in sequence, moving from east to west, top to bottom, center to periphery, left to right, large to small. You may use spatial order if the major parts of your composition deal with such things as the furniture in your room, a tour of the Louvre, a trip across the country, a walk across the campus, the arrangement of your garden. The details in a description of a blackjack tree could effectively be presented in this manner: the leathery leaves, the close-branched crown, the dead lower limbs, the short trunk, the exposed upper roots.

If you are very careful, you can "skip around" in geographical order. You may, for instance, wish to compare Maine with California, Minnesota with Texas, Oregon with Florida. Or in a discussion of the countryside of Britain you might refer to the rolling hills and green meadows of the South of England and the Midlands, Salisbury Plain, the Devon moors, the level fields and watery horizons of the East, the lakes in the North, and the Scottish Highlands. You are still operating within an acceptable spatial order, though, if in your skipping around you don't get lost and if there is a reasonableness to what you are doing—and if your reader is familiar with the spatial concept or physical entity you are referring to. Remember, too, that no particular direction dominates spatial order. You can move from left to right, or right to left; north to south, east to west, or whichever way you wish.

Some examples of spatial order are these:

Old Smith Hall, the main building on the campus: the great stone steps; the bleak, ivy-covered facade; the ancient steeple room with the four stained-glass windows; the thin, needlelike spire.

A study of Michelangelo's *Moses:* the sweep of marble hair; the furrowed brow; the piercing eyes; the famous hands; the strong angle of the body; the firmly planted feet.

The provinces and territories of Canada: the maritime provinces—Newfoundland, Nova Scotia, New Brunswick, Prince Edward Island; the larger provinces—Quebec, Ontario, Manitoba, Saskatchewan, Alberta, British Columbia; the territories—Northwest Territory, Yukon.

The Chicago Symphony: the violins; the flutes, oboes, bassoons, trumpets, horns; the violas, cellos, bass viols; timpani.

One note of caution: Spatial order may not necessarily be the best kind of order in dealing with spatial things. If you are dealing with the thesis that "The National Gallery contains the most representative collection of European paintings in the Western Hemisphere," it may be a great mistake to proceed through the National Gallery's collection spatially—room by room, gallery by gallery. Or if you are dealing with "The development of democratic practices in the American colonies," you many not necessarily discuss those practices colony by colony in spatial or geographical order.

Chronological Order

The ordering of details or parts according to chronology or age considerations is common when the writer is dealing with something that exists in time, has definite stages of development, has a significant history. In chronological order, you can take up the details in sequence moving from past to present, old to new, early to late. You may use chronological order if the major parts of your essay deal with such things as the events at a party, the growth of the carrots in your vegetable garden, the course of the American Revolution, a typical evening's television programming.

Remember that time can be progressive or regressive, and therefore your chronological order can move either from early to late or from late to early. Progressive order is by far the more common: Browning is born in 1812, is privately educated at home, publishes his first poems in 1833, travels on the Continent, publishes *Bells and Pomegranates* in 1841–1846. Reversing the order of details may be useful if your main purpose is to explain the last event in terms of what came before. You may, for example, discuss the gradual perfecting of Browning's dramatic monologue by beginning with "Andrea del Sarto" in the 1855 volume and working backward through his earlier efforts to the plays.

Other variations of chronological order are these: (1) An *in medias res* beginning, looking first at exciting or important details out of their chronological order, then backing up and proceeding in a regular progressive time sequence. You could begin with Browning's emergence as a major poet in the 1860s, then revert to a progressive time sequence and discuss the man's life from his birth in 1812 to his death in 1889. Ordinarily the *in medias res* passage is little more than an allusion, the second time around receiving a more detailed treatment. Sometimes, however, the opening material is dwelt on at such length that what you have is a variation of the regressive approach. (2) Use of the *flashback,* interrupting the regular progressive time sequence to pick up some antecedent material that has bearing on what is going on at the moment. In the course of interpreting Browing's religious views you might find it necessary to discuss the early influence of his mother's conventional and highly emotional religious attitudes. The flashback is a device for economy since with it the writer can skip over a less important phase, later dealing with the relevant details as necessary. (3) Use of the *foreshadowing technique,* interrupting the regular progressive time sequence to pick up some advance material in order to demonstrate the significance of the material at hand. The importance of Browning's buying a faded, watermarked volume in a Florentine book stall in 1860 is heightened if you tell your reader, by glancing ahead, that it will suggest the plot for *The Ring and The Book.* Foreshadowing can be a quick reference or a passage of some length.

Some examples of chronological order are these:

The Beethoven Symphonies: No. 1 (1799); No. 2 (1802); No. 3, *Er-*

oica (1803); No. 4 (1806); No. 5 (1805–1807); No. 6, the *Pastoral Symphony* (1808); No. 7 (1812); No. 8 (1812); No. 9, the *Choral Symphony* (1817–1823).

Presidential Assassinations: Kennedy, McKinley, Garfield, Lincoln.

The University's Architecture: Old Smith Hall (1873), the Fine Arts Lyceum (1885), the Johnson Memorial Library (1910), the Chemistry Building (1927), Radio and Television Center (1949), Data Processing Center (1960).

The University's Architecture: The recently completed, magnificently appointed buildings of the postwar era—Radio and Television Center (1949), Data Processing Center (1960). These great buildings are the culmination of an architectural development dating back to Old Smith Hall (1873) and becoming more evident in all the major buildings since that time: the Fine Arts Lyceum (1885), the Johnson Memorial Library (1910), the Chemistry Building (1927).

One note of caution: In selecting chronological order, be sure that it is actually the most appropriate one to use. Especially in dealing with theses in the areas of history and literature, you may be tempted to use chronological order when some other order would be preferable. For instance, if you are writing about "Tudor Monarchs of England," you may be tempted to proceed chronologically without giving due thought to other possibilities; on second thought, you may decide that in developing your thesis, "Characteristics of both liberal and conservative social policies appeared during the Tudor era," a chronological order would not be the most satisfactory. Or chronological order may not serve you particularly well if you are writing on the thesis that "Emma Bovary and Anna Karenina provided models of attempted liberation for nineteenth-century feminists." In comparing Emma and Anna, you may not wish at all to deal with the early novel first, the later novel second, and you certainly may not wish to proceed through each novel in a chronological way. In dealing with either history or literature, you may find that chronological order comes first to mind but in actuality it leads you too often to tedious plot summaries and historical sequences that do not serve the particular thesis with which you are working.

Cause-and-Effect Order

The ordering of details or parts according to cause-and-effect considerations is common when the writer is dealing with something which is a complex of simultaneous but interrelated operations or events. In cause-and-effect order, you can take up the details in sequence moving from first cause to final effect, from fundamental event to final events. You may use cause-and-effect order if the major parts of your essay deal with such things as the operation of a grandfather's clock, the firing of a Cape Kennedy rocket, the nature of a violin's harmonics, the burning of a light bulb.

For variation *you can reverse the cause-and-effect order and have an effect-and-cause order.* Using the normal cause-to-effect sequence, you are likely to create a climactic effect, but if you reverse the procedure and give the effect first, cause second, you create an anticlimactic effect. Your choice will depend a great deal on the kind of essay you are writing: In a technical report you may wish to give the effect first, the cause later; in a mystery story, you may wish to give all the causes first, the effect—or solution—only last.

Some examples of cause-and-effect order:

The Nature of Dante's Greatness: His residing in Florence caused his exposure to the infant Renaissance and to the great faith of the Church inherited from the Middle Ages. This combination of influences, joined with Dante's own aesthetic capacity, enabled him to illuminate the old order with a new vision.

Private Responses to Natural Symbols: The Rainbow. With Wordsworth, many men are stimulated by the rainbow. A certain awesome joy arises in them, a joy that actually, on inspection, is created not only by the rainbow itself, but by the complex nature of its occurrence: Hot and cold air meet in the skies to make a storm; the storm washes the sky clean with rain but leaves the sky filled with a vast number of minute liquid mirrors; the mirrors reflect the western sun; a rainbow explodes upon the horizon; joy rises in the heart and mind.

Emphatic Order

The ordering of details or parts according to their rank or importance is common when the writer is dealing with something that has degrees of value or significance. In emphatic order, you can take up the details in sequence, moving from most valuable to least valuable, most important to least important, most beautiful to least beautiful, most mysterious to least mysterious. You may use emphatic order if the major parts of your composition deal with such things as the jewels in a rare collection, the Beethoven symphonies, the loves in your life, the subjects you are taking this semester in college.

Variation can be achieved by choosing either a climactic or an anticlimactic presentation: moving from least important to most important is climactic; moving from most important to least important is anticlimactic. This consideration must be kept in mind when you are deciding whether or not your subject-thesis calls for a climactic or anticlimactic presentation to a particular audience on a particular occasion. If you decide you want a climactic essay and you are using emphatic order, you must be sure that you move from least important to most important; otherwise, your order will contradict your intended climax.

Some examples of emphatic order:

Best-sellers in American Fiction: *Gone with the Wind, Anthony Adverse, To Kill a Mockingbird, Herzog, The Caine Mutiny.*

The Skyscrapers of New York: Singer, Woolworth, Chase Manhattan, Chrysler, Empire State, World Trade Center.

Major American Cities: Detroit, Houston, Philadelphia, Los Angeles, Chicago, New York.

Major Cultural-Ideological Movements in America: puritanism, protestant fundamentalism, Catholicism, deism, humanism.

Using these basic kinds of order, you will be able to arrange effectively and coherently any groups of material with which you may have to work. You will frequently have a choice among orders. You will, of course, pick the order that is not only inherently reasonable, as far as your material is concerned, but that is most appropriate to your thesis. If you are working with the American Revolution, you may have organized your material in terms of the various battle sites—Lexington, Bunker Hill, Yorktown. You may order these groups chronologically or spatially or emphatically. Any of these three orders would work. You will choose the one that works best.

As you develop your sense of classification and order, you will find yourself greatly strengthened as a writer. As you more and more think in these terms, you will find that many of your writing problems are solved even before you begin writing. Certainly more and more of your writing problems will be solved in the early drafts of your composition.

SUMMARY CHECKLIST

To help you discipline yourself in classification and order, use this checklist of do's and don't's as you do your prewriting work of jotting down ideas and constructing an outline. Use this checklist again after your first draft, asking yourself if you have done what the checklist advises.

1. Have I provided myself a body of information, knowledge, data, details that is pertinent to the subject about which I am writing?

2. Have I organized this body of material into no more than nine major parts or groups?

3. Have I organized the material within each part into as many subordinate parts as necessary? Again, no major part should contain more than nine subordinate parts.

4. Have I ordered, first of all, the major parts? Decide in what sequence you are going to present the major parts.

5. Have I ordered, next, the subordinate parts within each major part? Decide in what sequence you are going to present the subordinate parts within each major part.

6. Have I ordered the paragraphs within each subordinate part, if there are subordinate parts? If there are no subordinate parts, simply order the paragraphs within the major parts.

7. Have I used the most suitable form of order in each part of my essay? The order that you use in arranging the major parts need not be the same order you use in arranging the subordinate sections within any one major part. Likewise, there need be no consistency of ordering methods from paragraph to paragraph, from one subordinate section to another.

THE WHOLE COMPOSITION

Having a good many thoughts about owning a piece of property, E. M. Forster classifies his reactions to ownership into four major groups: His wood makes him feel (1) enormously stout, (2) endlessly avaricious, (3) pseudocreative, and (4) intensely selfish. Notice how clearly Forster—having established the question, "What is the effect of property upon the character?"—labels his classifications: "In the first place, . . ." "In the second place, . . ." etc. Forster orders these reactions into an emphatic and climactic list.

Notice that Forster spends more time with each succeeding group to indicate increasing emphasis; and, with the final group, he makes a radical break in parallelism to indicate climax.

Forster's summary in the last sentence ties the essay into a neat package, a perfectly prepared and structured piece of writing.

My Wood

E. M. Forster

A few years ago I wrote a book which dealt in part with the difficulties of the English in India. Feeling that they would have had no difficulties in India themselves, the Americans read the book freely. The more they read it the better it made them feel, and a cheque to the author was the result. I bought a wood with the cheque. It is not a large wood—it contains scarcely any trees, and it is intersected, blast it, by a public footpath. Still, it is the first property that I have owned, so it is right that other people should participate in my shame and should ask themselves, in accents that will vary in horror, this very important question: What is the effect of property upon the character? Don't let's touch economics; the effect of private ownership upon the community as a whole is another question—a more important question, perhaps, but another one. Let's keep to psychology. If you own things, what's their effect on you? What's the effect on me of my wood?

In the first place, it makes me feel heavy. Property does have this effect. Property produces men of weight, and it was a man of weight who failed to get into the Kingdom of Heaven. He was not wicked, that unfortunate millionaire in the parable, he was only stout; he stuck out in front, not to mention behind, and as he wedged himself this way and that in the crystalline entrance and bruised his well-fed flanks, he saw beneath him a comparatively slim camel passing through the eye of a needle and being woven into the robe of God. The Gospels all through couple stoutness and slowness. They point out what is perfectly obvious, yet seldom realized: that if you have a lot of things you cannot move about a lot, that furniture requires dusting, dusters require servants, servants require insurance stamps, and the whole tangle of them makes you think twice before you accept an invitation to dinner or go for a bathe in the Jordan. Sometimes the Gospels proceed further and say with Tolstoy that property is sinful; they approach the difficult ground of asceticism here, where I cannot follow them. But as to the immediate effects of property on people, they just show straight-forward logic. It produces men of weight. Men of weight cannot, by definition, move like the lightning from the East unto the West, and the ascent of a fourteen-stone bishop into a pulpit is thus the exact antithesis of the coming of the Son of Man. My wood makes me feel heavy.

In the second place, it makes me feel it ought to be larger.

The other day I heard a twig snap in it. I was annoyed at first, for I thought that someone was blackberrying, and depreciating the value of the undergrowth. On coming nearer, I saw it was not a man who had trodden on the twig and snapped, but a bird, and I felt pleased. My bird. The bird was not equally pleased. Ignoring the relation between us, it took fright as soon as it saw the shape of my face, and flew straight over the boundary hedge into a field, the property of Mrs. Henessy, where it sat down with a loud squawk. It had become Mrs. Henessy's bird. Something seemed grossly amiss here, something that would not have occurred had the wood been larger. I could not afford to buy Mrs. Henessy out, I dared not murder her, and limitations of this sort beset me on every side. Ahab did not want that vineyard—he only needed it to round off his property, preparatory to plotting a new curve—and all the land around my wood has become necessary to me in order to round off my wood. A boundary protects. But—poor little thing—the boundary ought in its turn to be protected. Noises on the edge of it. Children throw stones. A little more, and then a little more, until we reach the sea. Happy Canute! Happier Alexander! And after all, why should even the world be the limit of possession? A rocket containing a Union Jack, will, it is hoped, be shortly fired at the moon. Mars. Sirius. Beyond which . . . But these immensities ended by saddening me. I could not suppose that my wood was the destined nucleus of universal dominion—it is so very small and contains no mineral wealth beyond the blackberries. Nor was I comforted when Mrs. Henessy's bird took alarm for the second time and flew clean away from us all, under the belief that it belonged to itself.

In the third place, property makes its owner feel that he ought to do something to it. Yet he isn't sure what. A restlessness comes over him, a vague sense that he has a personality to express—the same sense which, without any vagueness, leads the artist to an act of creation. Sometimes I think I will cut down such trees as remain in the wood, at other times I want to fill up the gaps between them with new trees. Both impulses are pretentious and empty. They are not honest movements towards money-making or beauty. They spring from a foolish desire to express myself and from an inability to enjoy what I have got. Creation, property, enjoyment form a sinister trinity in the human mind. Creation and enjoyment are both very, very good, yet they are often unattainable without a material basis, and at such moments property pushes itself in as a substitute, saying, "Accept me instead—I'm good enough for all three." It is not enough. It is, as Shakespeare said of lust, "The expense of spirit in a waste of shame": it is "Before, a joy proposed; behind, a dream." Yet we don't know how to shun it. It is forced on us by our economic system as the alternative to starvation. It is also forced on us by an internal defect in the soul, by the feeling that in property may lie the germs of self-development and of exquisite or heroic deeds. Our life on earth is, and ought to be, material and carnal. But we have not yet learned to manage our materialism and carnality properly; they are still entangled with the desire for ownership, where (in the words of Dante) "Possession is one with loss."

And this brings us to our fourth and final point: the blackberries.

Blackberries are not plentiful in this meagre grove, but they are easily seen from the public footpath which traverses it, and all too easily gathered. Foxgloves, too—people will pull up the foxgloves, and ladies of an educational tendency even grub for toadstools to show them on the Monday in class. Other ladies, less educated, roll down the bracken in the arms of their gentlemen friends. There is paper, there are tins. Pray, does my wood belong to me or doesn't it? And, if it does, should I not own it best by allowing no one else to walk there? There is a wood near Lyme Regis, also cursed by a public footpath, where the owner has not hesitated on this point. He had built high stone walls each side of the path, and has spanned it by bridges, so that the public circulate like termites while he gorges on the blackberries unseen. He really does own his wood, this able chap. Dives in Hell did pretty well, but the gulf dividing him from Lazarus could be traversed by vision, and nothing traverses it here. And perhaps I shall come to this in time. I shall wall in and fence out until I really taste the sweets of property. Enormously stout, endlessly avaricious, pseudo-creative, intensely selfish, I shall weave upon my forehead the quadruple crown of possession until those nasty Bolshies come and take it off again and thrust me aside into the outer darkness.

Exercises

1. List in exhaustive detail the contents of the room in which you are now seated—discussing its structure, decoration, and furnishings—and organize what you have on the basis of one scheme, then another—for example, function, composition, configuration. What can you now say about the room that was indefinite and inexpressible before? Notice how each organization permits quite different sets of conclusions.

2. Use your observation in a three- to five-paragraph descriptive essay. Call it "The Academic Pad" or something of the kind. Think of it as a model study in organization and order.

3. If you were to write an essay dealing with the religious beliefs of the Presidents of the United States, into how many groups would you divide the Presidents and in what order would you present the groups for discussion? Write out in full your classification, indicating not only the order of the groups but also the order in which you would present the individual Presidents within each group.

4. Classify a body of material constituting a subject according to one system, then another, then still another—coming up with an extensive and varied set of possibilities. With a lit-

tle imagination virtually any information can be classified many different ways, from the most explicit and utilitarian to the most fanciful and suggestive. (While you usually classify your materials according to the requirements of your purpose or thesis, you may sometimes try out one or another system in the early stages of your planning just to see what it might reveal about your subject.)

5. Human beings, with unfortunate results when it becomes the basis for a prejudicial view, are frequently classified according to the familiar divisions suggested by sex, race, religion, nationality, and so on. These somewhat tired categories often seem to overlook the uniqueness of individuality that other fresh and imaginative classifications might assert. List some possibilities (like the notion that everyone is either a Platonist or an Aristotelian).

6. Many classifications and their consequent orderings are based on standard ways of perceiving experience. For example, we are accustomed to dealing with the concepts of size (large, small), location (top, north), value (best, most), etc., not realizing that even our concept of color is based on an arbitrary division of the spectrum and as such is an imposed classification. Consider this for a moment, then see if you can come up with a system of classification for some material which seems not to rely on one of the standard bases.

7. Check the three outlines you wrote earlier (Chapter 2, exercise 7) against the advice given here about classification, ideal quantity, and order. Modify the outlines if necessary until they demonstrate sound practice.

4. BEGINNING AND ENDING

After we have organized the body of our composition, we give thought to what words we shall actually use to start our composition and what words we shall actually use to bring our composition to a close. Though we often write the beginning and ending of our composition after the middle portion of the composition is completed, we should never think of the beginning and ending as unimportant sentences and paragraphs that can simply be "stuck on." We need, rather, to acquaint ourselves with the various kinds of beginnings and endings that are standard fare in good writing, select the particular kinds that would seem to work best in the particular writing situation confronting us, write out several versions, and revise both beginning and ending until they are smoothly integrated into the composition as a whole.

Every successful piece of writing has a beginning and an end. Yet a world of difference lies between a blunt starting-stopping and an effective beginning-conclusion. You will realize better the difference between the two as you begin to understand the function and pattern of your composition's opening and closing sections.

BEGINNINGS

The major observation about a composition's beginning is that it exists primarily to prepare or condition the reader for the main body of the writing. The beginning is primarily a place where the stage is set or the reader is intrigued; where the reader is quickly acclimated to the general feeling, perspective, and approach of your composition; where you hope you lure the reader to read on.

To orient your reader, you try to make as many of the necessary commitments as you can for the entire composition. That is, you will establish the voice you are using in this particular work. The tone, the stylistic manner, the attitude of your composition will be established in the first few sentences.

As you start work on your beginning, you must decide whether to write a direct beginning or delayed beginning. In the direct beginning, as the name implies, you roll up your sleeves and go right to work. In the delayed beginning, you take a running leap at the beginning from some removed point.

The Direct Beginning

If you choose to write the direct beginning—the normal choice for the standard composition, certainly for anything that professes utility or economy—you will want to do the following things: (1) state the subject in the first sentence of the first paragraph; (2) devote the first paragraph primarily to an identification or definition of the subject, or a synopsis or foreshadowing of the material to be covered in detail in the middle; (3) if you are writing the most prevalent kind of composition, in which the thesis is stated in the beginning as well as toward the end, state the thesis in the first sentence of the first paragraph, or state it in the last sentence of the beginning.

An example of the direct beginning would be the following paragraph:

George Washington has recently been denigrated by certain historians of noted scholarship who feel that the actual historical first President has been getting lost in a maze of sentimental idealization and pathological hero worship. Not denying Washington his inevitable place in the history books, a place he won by serving his nation at the most critical time in its history, these historians are actually attacking the great father figure

that Washington has become, a father figure of classical proportions—honest, brave, and true. They are attacking the image of perfect citizen and perfect leader.

In the preceding paragraph, the first sentence contains
a statement of the subject "George Washington" and the
thesis "George Washington has recently been denigrated by certain
historians. . . ." The beginning as a whole is an elaboration upon
the subject-thesis statement and at the same time a synopsis, in miniature, of the material to be covered in the middle of the composition. The same beginning could have been written, of course, so that
the subject alone appeared in the first sentence, and the thesis did
not appear until the last part of the paragraph—a simple variation
of this most prevalent form of the beginning.

George Washington is more than an historical figure; he is a mythic
hero. Serving his nation at the most critical time in its history,
Washington inevitably took his place in the history books. But he
soon went beyond the history books to become a father figure of
classical proportions—honest, brave, and true. He became the symbol of the perfect citizen and perfect leader. And it is this *apotheosis
of Washington* that *has led to some of the recent denigration of the first President* on the part of those who appreciate historical facts but not historical fancies.

The subject is italicized in the first sentence; the thesis is italicized
in the last sentence.

The Delayed Beginning
Both the above paragraphs are direct beginnings. But you can write
a delayed beginning, in which the announcement of the subject or
subject-thesis is delayed until some other matter is taken care of—
such as an attention-getting device, an anecdote, a generalization
that will serve as background for your particular subject-thesis, a
vivid description, a suspenseful or dramatic incident, an ironic or
paradoxical observation.

Look, for instance, at the following paragraphs:

George Washington has recently been denigrated by certain historians of noted scholarship who feel that the actual historical President
has been getting lost in a maze of sentimental idealization and
pathological hero worship. Not denying Washington his inevitable
place in the history books, a place he won by serving his nation at

the most critical time in its history, these historians are actually attacking the great father figure that Washington has become, a father figure of classical proportions—honest, brave, and true. They are attacking the image of perfect citizen and perfect leader.

This denigration of Washington is, however, but one of *the twentieth-century attacks upon popular heroes.* Other attacks have been leveled at Abraham Lincoln, Theodore Roosevelt, and Woodrow Wilson. In fact, nearly any public figure on his way to becoming a part of popular lore is in danger of being whittled down to size by those scholarly historians who see in too much popular mythology something of a national menace. Some historians feel that *a national mythology can be a dangerous instrument in the hands of the overly chauvinistic who would manipulate it, not for the national good, but for mass exploitation.*

Of these two paragraphs, the first is merely a prologue, a delaying example. The true beginning does not occur until the second paragraph: the subject stated in the first sentence of the second paragraph, the thesis stated in the last sentence of the paragraph.

You may rightfully ask, of course: How do I know that the first paragraph is now not a part of the true beginning, when just one example back, it was the true beginning? The answer is this: The first paragraph in the example immediately above has now only a topic sentence developed into a normal paragraph and does not contain the thesis of the whole composition, for in relationship to the paragraph that follows, the first paragraph does not make the commitment for the whole essay. If the first paragraph remains the subject-thesis paragraph, then the second paragraph in the example becomes an unfortunate digression at an unfortunate place in the composition's structure. Far more likely is it that the second paragraph is the true beginning, making the author's commitments for the entire essay.

Another kind of delayed beginning is the simple inductive paragraph in which both the subject and thesis are unstated until the last sentence. For example:

After a bitter and frustrating war, a nervous peace settled over the American colonies. After a confused and sometimes labyrinthine struggle during that peace, a new government was formed. It was time, in 1788, for the new American people to seek the best leadership possible for their government. They looked down into Virginia and called to office the man who exemplified leadership itself. In 1789, *George Washington* took office as the first President and *became the prototype of all successful Presidents.*

Opening Sentences

Whatever form of beginning you are using, you should take into consideration the value and effect of various possible opening sentences. Though obviously you can open with any kind of sentence you choose, there are a few standard openings: (1) The short, simple sentence, the direct opening. (Murder was Capone's business.) (2) The loose, multiclaused sentence, a rather high-flown opening. (Murder was a business that Capone had developed into the dimensions of a big American corporation.) (3) The sentence beginning with a short modifying word, phrase, or clause, a rather standard, general opening. (Cold and calculating, Capone made murder his business.) (4) The sentence beginning with a long phrase or clause, a smooth-flowing and serious, even at times dramatic, opening. (Having made murder his business, Capone developed a strong, affluent empire in the underworld.) Some well-known examples of such opening sentences are these:

New York is a city of things unnoticed.—Gay Talese, New York

It used to be easy to hate Hollywood. For me it was no trouble at all. But that was years ago.—Orson Welles, Twilight in the Smog

Young men and women beginning to write are generally given the plausible but utterly impracticable advice to write what they have to write as shortly as possible, as clearly as possible, and without other thought in their minds except to say exactly what is in them.—Virginia Woolf, The Patron and the Crocus

Seven thousand Romaine Street is in that part of Los Angeles familiar to admirers of Raymond Chandler and Dashiell Hammett: the underside of Hollywood, south of Sunset Boulevard, a middle-class slum of "model studios" and warehouses and two-family bungalows.—Joan Didion, The Howard Hughes Underground

In an age gone stale through the complex of bureaucratic interdependencies, with its tedious labyrinth of technical specializations, each contingent upon the next, and all aimed to converge into a single totality of meaning, it is a refreshing moment indeed when one comes across an area of human endeavor absolutely sufficient unto itself, pure and free, no strings attached—the cherished and almost forgotten l'art pour l'art.—Terry Southern, Twirling at Ole Miss

No doubt the opening sentence is one of the most important single sentences you will write in any given composition. You should therefore try to make it appropriate to the general manner of the essay and as readable and uninvolved as possible.

Also give consideration on special occasions to opening sentences based on *a quotation from another author,*

In his Journal for July 10–12, 1841, Thoreau wrote: "A slight sound at evening lifts me up by the ears, and makes life seem inexpressibly serene and grand. It may be in Uranus, or it may be in the shutter." The book into which he later managed to pack both Uranus and the shutter was published in 1854. . . . —E. B. White, A Slight Sound at Evening

Fine writing, according to Mr. Addison, consists of sentiments which are natural, without being obvious. There cannot be a juster and more concise definition of fine writing.—David Hume, Of Simplicity and Refinement in Writing

a question,

How many people have read Belchamber today? Of the few who have read it, how many, besides myself, have carried out scraps of its wisdom and wit, its tact and its bitterness, for the last thirty years?—E. M. Forster, Howard Overing Sturgis

Why should any words be called obscene? Don't they all describe natural human functions?—Barbara Lawrence, Four-Letter Words Can Hurt You

Anybody here remember the fashion forecast of 1960?—Veronica Geng, The Blue Jeans Craze

a proverb or aphorism,

"Finders keepers, losers weepers," runs the ancient taunt by which boys justify their acquisitive instincts.—Carlos Baker, The Function of the Critics

"A village without an ikon: a head without an eye," says a proverb more comminatory than most, for the psychic life of these small Aegean communities is the healthiest where it can be focused upon some such arbiter of fate.—Lawrence Durrell, The Saint of Soroni

a one-word or virtual sentence, that is, a noun, verb, or adjective,

Thursday, 28 November. Nantucket light. In cold, sunny afternoon the bright red lightship bobbing to starboard is the first sign that our ten-day pre-school voyage is coming to an end; we are as happy as the discoverers of Virginia in 1584.—Cyril Connolly, Blueprint for a Silver Age: Notes on a Vist to America

Battersea Rise! What a thrill the name gives me in the publisher's list! Is it just a fancy title, or can it really be the house which once belonged to my family?—E. M. Forster, Battersea Rise

Ten o'clock Sunday morning in the hills of North Carolina.—Tom Wolfe, The Last American Hero Is Junior Johnson. Yes!

a piece of dialogue,

"But, sir, I don't think I really deserve it, it was mostly bull, really." This disclaimer from a student whose examination we have awarded a straight "A" is wonderously depressing.—William G. Perry, Jr., Examanship and the Liberal Arts: A Study in Educational Epistemology

The professor looked into the faces of the freshmen in Philosophy I. "How many of you," he asked, *"believe in the existence of God?"—Michael Novak,* God in the Colleges

"I wish poets could be clearer," shouted my wife angrily from the next room. Here is a universal longing.—E. B. White, Poetry

These are irregular openings that have a certain attention-getting quality. You should be able and willing to use them to vary your own writing practices, and to help you create appropriate beginnings. You will not use them as often as you will the regular sentence openings, but you should have them in your repertoire. They are especially valuable in the creation of delayed beginnings.

As you give your attention to your composition's beginning, keep in mind that, regardless of the kind of opening, *you are not compelled to write a long beginning.* Since the length of the beginning is strictly a matter of proportion—anywhere from one-third to one-ninth the length of your essay proper—the beginning does not even have to be one paragraph long, if the composition it is serving does not call for that substantial a beginning. A one- or two-sentence beginning may be quite adequate for some short compositions. If you do write a one- or two-sentence beginning, you may go ahead and incorporate the beginning into a paragraph that serves also as the first paragraph of the middle, or you may set off the beginning as a miniature paragraph of its own.

In general, you should write as short a beginning as is proportionally fitting. Do only what has to be done in the beginning. Your chief task in any writing is in the middle of the composition, in the essay proper. Also you will do well to avoid the startling or pretentious beginning. Some writers, perhaps taking the cue from advertising, think a reader must always be tricked into an essay. Most serious readers resent this attitude. The gimmick of surprise, overassertive, or argumentative beginnings is almost always bad because it gives the wrong impression. Readers expect the first sentences to set the tone of the essay and are confused when they don't. An off-key beginning marks you as an unsophisticated writer and suggests that you really have little to say. The tone itself should be intriguing enough to hold your reader.

You should, however, recognize the validity of the delayed beginning in special cases—in writing essays of a more personal or lyrical quality, in writing humor perhaps, or in dealing with ideas that do need some legitimate preparation if the reader is to "stay with you" into the composition. Even in the case of legitimate delayed beginnings, however, you still will want to accept the responsibility for stylistic commitment in your opening sentences.

A number of things should usually be avoided in beginnings. *Do not employ the obvious, labeled opening save in the case of certain scientific or technical reports.* "In this paper I plan to discuss . . ." has the virtue of clarity, but little else to recommend it. And rarely make reference, in your beginning, to the title of your composition.

Also avoid the overworked dictionary-definition beginning: "*Webster's* defines 'uxoricide' as the 'murder of a wife by her husband.' " And above all, sidestep the time-consuming opening that publicizes the subject's popularity: "The subject of solar energy has been much in the news lately and many articles and books have been written on the matter. Of interest to many people for several decades, solar energy is now being discussed by an increasing number of responsible people. . . ." (If justifying of subject and thesis seems absolutely necessary, it should be done as subordinately as possible and not in so prominent a position as a beginning.)

Although what you do in your opening paragraph is important, don't worry about the beginning too much until at least a rough draft of the composition is completed. Some writers grow so concerned over the beginning that they never get beyond it. A certain psychological block occurs. If you have any trouble whatsoever in moving from the beginning of your composition into the middle proper, drop the beginning immediately. Do not linger over it. If you have a chronic problem with getting beyond the beginning, you should develop the habit of postponing your writing of the beginning altogether. Simply make a few notes, then get on with the essay. You can always come back later and write the beginning.

Here are some well-known beginnings that demonstrate various approaches the writer can take in getting his essay under way:

I do not claim that I can tell a story as it ought to be told. I only claim to know how a story ought to be told, for I have been almost daily in the company of the most expert story-tellers for many years.

There are several kinds of stories, but only one difficult kind—the humorous. I will talk mainly about that one. The humorous story is American, the comic story is English, the witty story is French. The humorous story depends for its effect upon the manner of the telling; the comic story and the witty story upon the matter.—Mark Twain, How to Tell a Story

A Poor Relation—is the most irrelevant thing in nature,—a piece of impertinent

correspondency,—an odious approximation,—a haunting conscience,—a preposterous shadow, lengthening in a noontide of your prosperity,—an unwelcome remembrancer,—a perpetually recurring mortification,—a drain on your purse,—a more intolerable dun upon your pride,—a drawback upon success,—a rebuke to your rising,—a stain in your blood,—a blot on your scutcheon,—a rent in your garment,—a death's head at your banquet,—Agathocles' pot,—a Mordecai in your gate,—a Lazarus at your door,—a lion in your path,—a frog in your chamber,—a fly in your ointment,—a mote in your eye,—a triumph to your enemy, an apology to your friends,—the one thing not needful,—the hail in harvest,—the ounce of sour in a pound of sweet.—Charles Lamb, Poor Relations

In the feeding and safeguarding of their progeny insects and spiders exhibit some interesting analogies to reasoning and some crass examples of blind instinct. The case I propose to describe here is that of the tarantula spiders and their archenemy, the digger wasps of the genus Pepsis. It is a classic example of what looks like intelligence pitted against instinct—a strange situation in which the victim, though fully able to defend itself, submits unwittingly to its destruction.—Alexander Petrunkevitch, The Spider and the Wasp

I do not believe in Belief. But this is an age of faith, and there are so many militant creeds that, in self-defense, one has to formulate a creed of one's own. Tolerance, good temper and sympathy are no longer enough in a world which is rent by religious and racial persecution, in a world where ignorance rules, and science, who ought to have ruled, plays the subservient pimp. Tolerance, good temper and sympathy—they are what matter really, and if the human race is not to collapse they must come to the front before long. But for the moment they are not enough, their action is no stronger than a flower, battered beneath a military jack-boot. They want stiffening, even if the process coarsens them. Faith, to my mind, is a stiffening process, a sort of mental starch, which ought to be applied as sparingly as possible. I dislike the stuff. I do not believe in it, for its own sake. Herein I probably differ from most people, who believe in Belief, and are only sore they cannot swallow even more than they do. My law-givers are Erasmus and Montaigne, not Moses and St. Paul. My temple stands not upon Mount Moriah but in that Elysian Field where even the immoral are admitted. My motto is: "Lord, I disbelieve—help thou my unbelief."

I have, however, to live in an Age of Faith—the sort of epoch I used to hear praised when I was a boy. It is extremely unpleasant really. It is bloody in every sense of the word. And I have to keep my end up in it. Where do I start?—E. M. Forster, What I Believe

ENDINGS

Though a good ending cannot salvage a poor composition, certainly a bad ending can spoil an otherwise good piece of writing. The ending deserves as much attention as does any other part of your composition.

The ending, even more than the beginning, is a product of the essay proper. Yet you nearly always have a choice as to the kind of ending you write. A basic kind of ending is the one that, in effect, *summarizes the entire composition,* or at least makes a quick review, ties up in a neat bundle the essence of the composition. Another kind of basic ending is the one that is a *conclusion reached* as the result of information given in the central part of the composition, a kind of final total, a sum of the various statements made in the essay proper.

Suppose you write an essay that works this way: Thesis: The Santa Fe Trail was the most important of the trading routes that pierced the Western frontier. Essay proper: The Chisholm Trail, the Sedalia Trail, the Oregon Trail, the Mormon Trail, the Santa Fe Trail. The ending of this composition may simply be a resume of the middle part. Ending: All these trails played an important part in the opening of the West, but whereas the others were more specialized and limited in their handling of traffic, the Santa Fe Trail became a major Western thoroughfare.

Or suppose you write an essay roughly outlinable in this way: Thesis: The fatal weakness of Russian communism lies in its inability to adjust to a changing world. Essay proper: (1) Communism preaches a form of absolutism. (2) Absolutism inhibits science and the arts. (3) An inhibited culture cannot adjust to political and cultural upheavals outside itself. The ending of this composition may be an outgrowth of the arguments in the middle. Ending: Therefore, Russian communism will be destroyed simply by the passage of time and the advances made by other countries.

You should note that in both kinds of endings—summary and conclusion—something new should be presented, not something new that suddenly changes the entire complexion of your essay, but some new illumination. In the conclusion ending, the conclusion being reached is in itself new material and will do the job. But in the summary ending, you must guard against a simple repetitive list of what you have been talking about. Even if you are reviewing your basic topics, you should throw them into a new light of some sort. If in the example given above of a summary ending, the body of your composition had been devoted to explaining how limited each of the trails was, in the summary you might point out briefly how valuable each trail was even though the Santa Fe Trail was the most important of them all. Also, it is wise, in the summary ending especially, not to present the thesis word for word as it was presented in the beginning; a slight variation simply in phrasing gives a better tone to your ending.

Both kinds of endings may be written in one of two basic forms: a regular or direct ending, and a prolonged ending. *The direct ending, summary or conclusion, has as its essential characteristic the statement of the composition's thesis. The prolonged ending has, in addition to a statement of the composition's thesis, one of the following: statement of a greater truth that the thesis illustrates, or some illustrative material or anecdote.*

Here are two examples of endings. The first demonstrates the summary conclusion, in which very briefly the reader is reminded of the general substance of the composition, and the thesis is reiterated (no doubt the thesis was also presented in the beginning of this particular composition). The second example demonstrates the conclusion ending, with the thesis presented as evolving from the middle of the composition (this could be the first overt expression of the thesis in this composition). The ending of the second example goes on to present a concluding idea that could well be the basis for another composition.

The seventh major effort the successful executive must make is to keep abreast of the times. Many executives find themselves isolated on some lonely island of out-dated knowledge, out-dated concepts, and out-dated attitudes. They are consequently unable to maintain vigorous leadership of a corporation that must play its role not in the past but in the ever-changing present. Successful executives, therefore, must read as extensively as possible, observe the vagaries not only of the business world but of the social and political world as well, acquaint themselves with the issues of their day—issues in science, religion, and art, as well as economics. They must not become locked in the tidy closet of their executive functions, or they will find the office crumbling around them, their executive functions isolated phenomena in a world that once was, but is no longer. [This paragraph is the last paragraph in the essay proper.]

None of these seven efforts is easy, of course. Rare are the people who find themselves with a decent liberal education, with a working technical education, with a well-organized and disciplined mind, with the vitally necessary communications tools of the day, with genuine psychological insight into their own behavior and the behavior of their colleagues, their employees, and their customers, with the necessary stamina and energy to survive under corporation pressures, and with the time and inclination to maintain their awareness of the vast, wonderful world in which they live. Rare indeed are such people. Yet the successful executive must be just such a rare person. *The successful executive is one who will work hard to become the exceptionally qualified person who will make the seven necessary efforts that are an essential part of the corporation leader's everyday life.* [This is a direct summary ending—a review is given of the middle material and nothing follows the thesis.]

Napoleon finally came to consider literature merely a tool in a vast propaganda campaign. As the affairs of empire became more involved, widespread, and burdensome, Napoleon saw little value in a literature that did no more than entertain and provoke and stimulate. What good were the old romantic novels? The lyric poems? The charming eclogues? Napoleon urged upon France an attitude that resulted in a dearth of serious literature. The age became one of functional writings: memoirs, letters, pamphlets, bulletins, military and political documents. Napoleon's own writings and the writings that he encouraged were increasingly utilitarian. [This is the last paragraph in the middle part of the essay.]

In other words, *Napoleon's own sense of utility, his own sense of political and military destiny kept him from becoming the author who, as a young man, he had wanted to be.* He was frustrated by the demands of the times, by the demands of his own role in history. The young man who wanted to write romantic novels had to give way to the mature man who used literature as a political and military weapon. Even though all his life he kept up a peripheral interest in great literature—reading the classics, reading the masters of European literature—he discouraged its own composition in France, and he suppressed his own creative tendencies. Though his literary talents were no doubt meager, Napoleon might have become a mediocre novelist of an early nineteenth-century vintage, an imaginative, slightly flamboyant writer of adventures, creating empires on paper rather than on the real map of Europe. *Napoleon is the suppressed author, frustrated by other calls within him, by other and greater opportunities presented to him.* [If the essay ended here, it would have a direct conclusion ending.]

Perhaps the enigmatic Napoleon can be rewardingly understood this way as the frustrated author who, denying himself the literary life, went on to fulfill his sense of the dramatic and romantic in the wars he fought, in the nations he made, in the triumphs he achieved. Perhaps Napoleon, in part at least, can be seen as the author who, frustrated in the medium of words, merely shifted to another medium, the medium of military and political action, *and wrote his novel, his epic poem, and ultimately his tragedy in the very real affairs of his time.* [But the essay went on with a prolonged conclusion ending.]

You will find that, regardless of the kind of ending you write, you do well to write as quick and emphatic an ending as possible. Try to avoid a tedious collection of afterthoughts or a laborious review of what has already been said. Also, you should remember to write an ending of a length proportionate with the beginning—though the ending can be slightly shorter than the beginning without violating their proportionate relationship, and the ending may be—in an especially short composition—no more than the last sentence or two of the composition's final paragraph.

You will write a stronger ending, of course, if you don't tell your reader things he can deduce for himself. Restating your thesis is one thing, but drawing an obvious moral or explaining a self-evident implication is quite another. Even though you may, on occasion, present in the ending those subtle generalizations that your reader may not realize by himself, you should not hammer home a platitude or spell out for a reader a truth he has already formulated on the basis of the information you have given him.

And one last warning: Don't rush to label your conclusion. Such phrases as "Thus we can see" and "In conclusion" are not usually advisable save in certain scientific and technical reports.

Here are some well-known endings that demonstrate various ways to "get out" of an essay:

Thus truth, frankness, courage, love, humility, and all the virtues range themselves on the side of prudence, or the art of securing a present well-being. I do not know if all matter will be found to be of one element, as oxygen or hydrogen, at last, but the world of manners and actions is wrought of one stuff, and begin where we will, we are pretty sure in a short space, to be mumbling our ten commandments.—Ralph Waldo Emerson, Prudence

I have not here been considering the literary use of language, but merely language as an instrument for expressing and not for concealing or preventing thought. Stuart Chase and others have come near to claiming that all abstract words are meaningless, and have used this as a pretext for advocating a kind of political quietism. Since you don't know what Fascism is, how can you struggle against Fascism? One need not swallow such absurdities as this, but one ought to recognize that the present political chaos is connected with the decay of language, and that one can probably bring about some improvement by starting at the verbal end. If you simplify your English, you are freed from the worst follies of orthodoxy. You cannot speak any of the necessary dialects, and when you make a stupid remark its stupidity will be obvious, even to yourself. Political language—and with variations this is true of all political parties, from Conservatives to Anarchists—is designed to make lies sound truthful and murder respectable, and to give an appearance of solidity to pure wind. One cannot change this all in a moment, but one can a least change one's own habits, and from time to time one can even, if one jeers loudly enough, send some worn-out and useless phrase—some jackboot, Achilles' heel, hotbed, melting pot, acid test, veritable inferno, or other lump of verbal refuse—into the dustbin where it belongs.—George Orwell, Politics and the English Language

Yet who reads to bring about an end, however desirable? Are there not some pursuits that we practice because they are good in themselves, and some pleasures that are final? And is not this among them? I have sometimes dreamt, at least, that when the Day of Judgment dawns and the great conquerors and lawyers and statesmen come to receive their rewards—their crowns, their laurels, their names carved indelibly upon imperishable marble—the Almighty will turn to Peter and will say, not without a certain envy when He sees us coming with our books under our arms, "Look, these need no reward. We have nothing to give them here. They have loved reading."—*Virginia Woolf,* How Should One Read a Book?

SUMMARY CHECKLIST

A good place to stop and make sure that your composition has a reasonable and controlled structure is at the completion of your first draft. If the first draft reveals structural haziness or uncertainty—no need to go further. You cannot cover up bad structure or the absence of structure.

As you look over your first draft ask yourself these questions:

1. Does this composition have a recognizable beginning, middle, and end?
2. Are the beginning, middle, and end in an acceptable proportion to each other?
3. Does the beginning clearly identify the subject of the composition?
4. Does the ending clearly state the thesis of the essay?

THE WHOLE COMPOSITION

The following essay gives good demonstration of a delayed beginning. The first paragraph is essentially anecdotal and joins with the second paragraph to make up the total beginning. By the end of the second paragraph, the author has made his general stylistic commitments, has announced his thesis, and has stated his subject, though the statement of subject is somewhat oblique until the opening sentence of the third paragraph. Paragraphs 3 to 7 constitute the essay proper—the large middle part of the composition that contains the bulk of classified and ordered material. The last paragraph serves as the ending and is legitimately shorter than the delayed beginning. Note that the ending is primarily one of summary, restating the thesis in a somewhat lyrical manner.

The Desert and the Sea

Yi-Fu Tuan

In popular astronomy much has been written on the possibility of life on planets other than earth in the solar system. The judicious conclusion is usually negative; to judge by terrestrial criteria, life is either not possible or can occur only in very lowly form on our sister planets. In a short story I have read not long ago, Arthur C. Clarke has amusingly turned the table on this perhaps rather complacent view of earthlings. He made a Martian astronomer speculate on the possibility of terrestrial life. The Martian's conclusion, couched in language that parodies our own unlovely blend of impartiality and chauvinism when we consider such matters, is—no. Life is not possible on earth—at least not intelligent life. His chief reason is that the earth's atmosphere contains too much of the dangerously reactive oxygen. Another is that, unlike Mars *"almost three quarters of the planet earth is covered with liquid."* (Underlining Martian's).

I like the story. It has the merit of reviving a geographical fact which familiarity has consigned to oblivion. The story jars, however slightly, our good-natured anthropocentrism which we reinforce each time we repeat the confident tale of man's mastery over nature, of the progressive changes he has wrought on the face of the earth. In our complacency we forget too easily that much of it is in fact (as yet) little affected. It is little affected because it is quite unsuited to human use and habitation. We are land animals but, as the Martian astronomer correctly surmises, three-fourths of the earth's surface is water. We need fertile soils in moist climates for our livelihood but almost a quarter of the earth's land area suffers from drought so severe that human habitation in large numbers is nearly impossible.

The desert and the sea are among the great open spaces of the earth which discourage human encroachment. The impact of the population "explosion" in the last fifty years, for instance, fell on lands that respond more or less readily to human endeavor—on compliant soils that already support many people. On the other hand, the "explosion" (to press the metaphor) has barely singed the desert, much less the sea. The ease with which this simple fact can elude us was brought home to me one day by a trivial incident. A map of world population by Dr. Alfred Soderlund of Sweden arrived. I had looked forward to it for I have been lecturing on population pressure to my geography class and needed a large wall map to dramatize the theme of a crowded earth. The expectation was foolish; for when the map was unfurled before the class we were confronted by what seemed at first sight just a blank outline of continents and oceans. The population pattern does appear on it of course, but finely as dots rather than as colored layers—a gross form of generalization popular with school atlases. The Soderlund map shows us where people are more accurately than the population maps we usually see. It reveals the smallness of the inhabited portion of the earth compared with the great extent of open space.

There is a grain of comfort to be drawn from the discouraging fact of the earth's intractability over so much of its surface. When we need food for the proliferation of our species, the prospect of desert and sea does indeed give us cause for dismay. But when we hunger for a reality and beauty not of our own making, the very intransigent permanence of so much unplowable surface argues for our gratitude. And it cannot be denied that we do occasionally feel this hunger. In the United States it is confessed in the demand for the preservation of wilderness. We desire wildernesses not only because we need fresh air, a change of scene, or a pleasant background for the family picnic. We desire them also because (to confirm our sanity) we need to believe in the existence of an independent world—one that does not immediately reflect our images. Too much of nature, by yielding to man's itch and power to transform, does just that. We look, and see only ourselves in the shape of our handiwork. Prairies are touched up and become corn fields; mud-flats, rice paddies; swamps, gardens; and the fundamental design of matter itself has, upon close scrutiny, dissolved into a mere tracery of our powerful instruments.

The desert, however, has grit. It repels the human imprint. It resists our attempt to transform it into a vast suburbia for human propagation. It corrals human effort into isolated spots and ribbons surrounded by sterility and a forbidding stillness. The stillness of the desert, as Aldous Huxley says, is so massive that it can absorb even jet planes. "The screaming crash mounts to its intolerable climax and fades again, mounts as another of the monsters rips through the air, and once more diminishes and is gone. But even at the height of the outrage the mind can still remain aware of that which surrounds it, that which preceded and will outlast it."

The sea also resists. It says no to us. "I thought of those great, pure and beautiful things which say no to us," Morten meditated in a story by Isak Dinesen. "For why should they say yes to us, and tolerate our insipid caresses? Those who say yes, we get them under us, and we ruin them and leave them, and find when we have left them that they have made us sick. The earth says yes to our schemes and our work, but the sea says no; and we, we love the sea ever."

The desert and the sea cover the major portion of the earth's surface. They discourage human familiarity. We ask for bread and they give us stone. We need fresh water and they give us salt. But it is said that man has other needs than bread. The desert and the sea . remind us of this fact by vaunting an impersonal beauty which cannot be eaten and yet sustains. . . . At any rate the sheer size of so much recalcitrant earth conduces us to relax a little in the acceptance that the earth is not all plasticine suppliant to the touch of our fingers.

Exercises

1. Write beginnings and endings for three abbreviated compositions (merely outline the middle section). Exemplify the

direct and delayed beginning, and the summary and conclusion ending. Briefly explain your choices.

2. Choose an article or essay that you find especially effective. Identify the exact nature of the beginning and ending.

3. Convert the following opening sentences into *(a)* question beginnings, *(b)* quotation beginnings, *(c)* dialogue beginnings:

Long-range plans for protecting the American economy must include a reduction in income taxes.

Robert Frost should have been given a Nobel prize.

English is a suitable language for both poetry and science.

4. While there is no "standard" beginning and ending to compare with the fairy tale's "Once upon a time. . . . And they lived happily ever after," see if you can't come up with three examples of something equivalent for the article and essay.

5. Consider the very popular *in medias res* (Latin, "into the midst of things") beginning of fiction, epic, and drama. Which examples in the chapter (or text) seem to borrow something from such beginnings? Find an article or essay that seems to plunge the reader into the subject first and then explain later.

6. Look at the current issue of one of the national magazines that publishes nonfiction—e.g., *Atlantic, Harper's, The New York Times Magazine, The New Yorker, The American Scholar, Saturday Review.* Copy out the beginnings and endings of at least two or three pieces. Analyze each beginning and ending—what kind is it? how does it relate to the entire composition? how effective is it?

7. Start a collection of especially effective beginnings and endings that you encounter in your reading. Use these beginnings and endings as models—writing, in your exercise book, similar beginnings and endings on various subjects for various hypothetical compositions.

8. Consider again the three outlines you wrote earlier (Chapter 3, exercise 7). Does your preliminary thinking check with the advice given here about structure? Modify the outlines until they do and write out the beginnings and endings.

5.EXPANSION

One of the secrets of good writing is to present just the right amount of information and to discuss a subject just long enough—neither to be too succinct nor to be too garrulous. Often, after we've written the first draft of a composition, we find that material can be eliminated—because it is redundant or irrelevant. But equally often we find that material needs to be *added*—if our readers are fully to understand what we're trying to say. We should always read over our early drafts and ask ourselves: *Do I tell enough? Have I skipped over some major point in my argument? Would a few more examples and details bring my ideas into better focus?* Identifying any areas of thinness and sparsity in our composition, we can use the devices of controlled expansion to provide the "fullness of expression" that promotes clarity and comprehension.

Many times communication fails because our messages are too succinct. Though succinctness and economy are traditional virtues in writing, they can become vices as well. One of the great secrets of effective writing is that of controlled expansion—a secret that needs to be brought out in the open in an age sorely addicted to memos, telegrams, notes, and other abbreviated messages.

Economical writing is always valued, of course. If you can speak your piece in one word rather than in ten, so much the better. But brevity has its limitations. Sometimes, more words save more time. When you think of economy, you must not only take into consideration word count or reading time, but must consider the time necessary for reader understanding and comprehension. If a reader has to spend too much time figuring out what you are saying or guessing at your emphasis or puzzling over your attitude and position, then you have been uneconomical—no matter how few words you may have used.

CONTROLLED EXPANSION

You need to develop a sense of expansion in order to develop your basic ideas to their maximum usefulness in the prewriting stage of your thinking; give adequate "flesh" to your ideas as you organize them into a writing structure; and elaborate certain areas of your communication when, after having finished the basic composition, you discover that certain areas need increased emphasis—perhaps for the sake of proper proportion or balance—or increased clarity that at times can come only through a more detailed presentation of an idea.

You will want to be aware, of course, of the difference between a genuinely controlled elaboration and a false kind of word growth that actually defeats the purpose of serious composition. This false kind of word growth is something of a hop-skip-and-jump game, a running from idea to idea, without any overall control. If, for instance, you start with the idea that "Books are the mark of an educated person," and then let your mind simply go, you may come up with an expansion that reads like this:

Books are the mark of an educated person.

An educated person is a happy person.

Happy people live longer.

A long life is certainly to be desired.

People probably live longer in the United States than in many other countries.

In many countries, malnutrition causes a high mortality rate.

This sort of uncontrolled "expansion" may be acceptable in a college bull session, at the bridge table, or in your daydreams. It may even beneficially serve you when you need to fish around for ideas. (In fact, we all need at times simply to let our minds go and see what shows up; we may discover ideas we have not anticipated.) But this sort of uncontrolled expansion is simply a preliminary, prewriting game. It must give way to a more genuine, controlled, and useful kind of expansion when you are in the process of composition and communication.

METHODS OF EXPANSION

Several recognizable and acceptable techniques of controlled expansion are available to the writer; you should master these techniques so that when occasion demands you can whip out the most appropriate technique and fill in a picture that you otherwise might have to leave blank and void. The two basic forms of expansion that you will use over and over again are the horizontal method and the vertical method. You will use both of these methods equally.

In the *horizontal method,* you expand by going on to another idea that has some logical attachment to its predecessor. You expand by going on to a new but related idea. You can expand upon the idea that "books are the mark of an educated person" by next writing, "and educated people are the keepers of the nation." Next: "As keepers of the nation, educated people have a great influence on the lives of all people, educated or not. Books that are the mark of the educated people thus become an influence in the lives of those who may not even be aware that certain books exist." This is an example of expansion by growth, development, addition.

Some of the words and phrases we use to lead our thoughts in a horizontal direction are these: *and, on the other hand, next, therefore, thus, consequently, with the result that, which leads to.* Such words and phrases serve as signposts of horizontal expansion and they help us develop our theses and ideas in a sequential way. We may, for instance, begin with an idea, "The growing world food crisis necessitates the identification of new food resources," and expand it horizontally this way:

1. The growing world food crisis necessitates identification of new food resources.

2. On the other hand, it necessitates the reduction in world food needs.

3. Consequently, the solution to the crisis must involve both increased research in the area of food production and increased concern with, and control of, population growth.

4. This realization of a "double task" leads to the issue of serious government intervention in both the business-economic sector and in the private sociobehavior sector.

5. We may, therefore, face a crisis of "government intervention" at the very same time we face the crisis of food itself.

6. And the result may be that our solution to the food crisis will be delayed because the solution is rooted in something more important to many human beings than hunger itself: the issue of democracy and political freedom.

Obviously, there is a danger in the horizontal method. It may too easily become that kind of hop-skip-and-jump method of uncontrolled word growth. The add-on method, properly used, however, is controlled by some overall idea: in the case of an essay or total composition, by the subject-thesis; in a paragraph by the topic. This controlling idea guides the expansion carefully toward predetermined ends.

The *vertical method* of expansion is a method of analysis, detail, and illustration. If you were to expand upon the statement "Books are the mark of an educated person" by the vertical method, you could come out with something like this: "As depositories of knowledge, books are prized by educated people. As instruments of stimulation, books are cherished by educated people. As vehicles of beauty, books are treasured by educated people." In this example, you have not "added on" to the idea, but you have enlarged the idea by "going into it," by analyzing it into parts.

Some of the words and phrases we use to lead our thoughts in a vertical direction are these: *for example, in particular, on closer examination, to repeat, which is not, the parts of which are, in comparison, in contrast, the causes of which are.*

Whenever you come to a place in your writing where you need to expand, you must decide which sort of expansion to use. In some instances, you need to add on more ideas, or you need to break into your writing and put in some necessary ideas to make a sequence of ideas more understandable; in both cases, you will be using the horizontal method of expansion. In other instances, you need to pause in a sequence of ideas and expand by going "in depth" or vertically into a particular idea, by enlarging an idea to the point that it can be clearly seen, understood, and made effective.

In the composition as a whole, one method of expansion or the other will usually dominate, simply because of the nature of the thesis. If your thesis happens to be "Music is the purest of the arts," the thesis itself will call for a vertical method of expansion. If, however, your thesis happens to be "The causes of the present-day energy crisis are rooted in a complex of political, social, and economic factors," you could possibly be led to the horizontal method, especially if you trace out a chronological development of the present-day energy crisis. In either case, however, the total essay will finally be an almost equal combination of both methods. The thesis itself may be expanded by one method or the other, but the total fabric of the composition will involve both methods.

Let us see how this might work: Thesis: "If automobile pollution continues unabated, we can expect an increase in a good many social and physical diseases in our large metropolitan areas." This thesis may develop as follows.

1. If automobile pollution continues unabated, we can expect an increase in a good many social and physical diseases in our large metropolitan areas.

2. (Vertical expansion) Automobile pollution—in current large doses—definitely contributes to the high incidence of cancer, heart disease, bronchial ailments, and to the high incidence of social dissatisfactions and to the general deterioration of our "quality of life" with the blighting of our parks, our lawns, etc.

3. (Horizontal expansion) And if our large metropolitan areas become increasingly "diseased," the entire fabric of American culture and economy will be threatened.

4. (Horizontal expansion) Surely it behooves the American public to protect its "health" on all fronts by insisting on regulations and ordinances curtailing the use of the automobile in modern society.

5. (Vertical expansion) Regulations and ordinances may come from municipal governments, but more likely they will have to come from state and federal governments.

6. (Vertical expansion) Such regulations and ordinances will have to restrict the licensing of drivers, regulate the kinds of fuel to be used, prescribe the actual construction of automobile engines, control the operation of automobiles in city areas, and the like.

7. (Horizontal expansion) Those who resist such regulations and ordinances on the part of governments will actually be resisting the maintenance of good health in American society.

8. (Horizontal expansion) Surely even the most laissez-faire Americans will—when they think about the consequences—agree to cooperate in bringing about the necessary government-controlled abatement of automobile pollution.

Let us look at yet another thesis to be expanded: Thesis: "The causes of present-day political conservatism are rooted in postwar disillusionment." The demonstration of this thesis may be seen in the following elaboration:

Following World War II, many young people were disillusioned to find themselves involved not in peace, but in a lingering "cold" conflict.

As a result, they sought an escape from the problems of a cold war by creating a kind of isolated world, removed from world issues at large.

This neoisolationism developed not only into a rejection of world problems, but into an extreme emphasis upon a detached nationalism. Advocating nationalism at the expense of internationalism, these people began to interpret nationalism as a matter of preservation and conservation, rather than as a matter of new frontiers and new procedures.

This elaboration of the thesis involves the setting forth of sequential ideas, ideas added onto one another, moving from point A to point D. The horizontal method becomes, then, the dominant method of expansion. Note, however, that subsequent expansion may be of the vertical kind. You may need, in your further expansion, either to fill in with detailed sequential steps, between these four big steps—a further horizontal expansion. Or you may need to go in depth concerning each one of these four stages of conservatism's evolution.

Given the four sequential steps, resulting from elaboration of the thesis, ask yourself the following questions: Do I need to expand by adding a fifth step or a step prior to the first? Do I need to expand by adding interior steps between the first and the second, the second and the third, the third and the fourth? Do I need to expand by going into detail about any one of the steps in particular?

You will have to expand, of course, if you are going to have anything more than a thesis, with four steps simply listed beneath it. The quickest, most satisfactory composition will probably develop simply by expanding vertically each of the steps. For instance, the first step, "Following World War II, many young people were disillusioned to find themselves involved not in peace, but in a lingering 'cold' conflict," will probably be expanded by exploring the statement (the vertical method) rather than by trying to create a sequence of ideas out of it.

Following World War II, many young people were disillusioned to find themselves involved not in peace, but in a lingering "cold" conflict. They found their lives suddenly entangled in such diverse problems as that of the bomb; newly emerging, inexperienced nations; the population explosion. They found themselves confronted with great ideological issues, great momentous struggles between East and West. They found themselves burdened with the enigma of their own military victory turning into a moral responsibility for the welfare of much of the world. Everywhere they turned, young Americans found problems and obligations rather than serenity and halcyon days.

You will perhaps come up with a final essay having the following plan of expansion:

Introductory paragraph, stating subject and thesis. Subject elaborated vertically in this paragraph.

Paragraph devoted to step 1: Expansion vertically. Particular elaboration by description and examples.

Paragraph devoted to step 2: Expansion vertically. Description and contrast—contrasting isolated world with the informed world.

Paragraph devoted to step 3: Expansion vertically. Structure, illustration.

Paragraph devoted to step 4: Expansion vertically. Description and contrast.

Final paragraph, restating the thesis in new terms. Summary of the development—horizontal expansion.

You will use the horizontal method of expansion most frequently in (1) the elaboration of those theses that especially call for chronological, cause-and-effect, or such development, wherein the development lets go one idea as it proceeds to the outgrowth of that idea; (2) summarizing paragraphs dealing with sequential events; (3) transitional paragraphs dealing with sequential events; and (4) any narrative passage recounting a sequence of actions.

You will use the vertical method of expansion most frequently in (1) the elaboration of those theses that especially call for an analytical, descriptive, or parts-of-the-whole development; (2) regular paragraphs that do not move from idea to idea within themselves but devote themselves to the elaboration of a single topic.

Here are some individual paragraphs that illustrate the difference between horizontal and vertical expansion.

I saw a fox some sixty rods off, making across the hills on my left. As the snow lay five inches deep, he made but slow progress, but it was no impediment to me. I yielded to the instinct of the chase. But he slipped into the wood, and I gracefully yielded him the palm.

    This inadequately developed paragraph would be improved by horizontal expansion, the addition of narrative details about the chase.

Suddenly, looking down the river, I saw a fox some sixty rods off, making across to the hills on my left. As the snow lay five inches deep, he made but slow progress, but it was no impediment to me. So, yielding to the instinct of the chase, I tossed my head aloft and bounded away, snuffing the air like a fox-hound, and spurning the world and the Humane Society at each bound. It seemed the woods rang with the hunter's horn, and Diana and all the satyrs joined in the chase and cheered me on. Olympian and Elean youths were waving palms on the hills. In the meanwhile I gained rapidly on the fox; but he showed a remarkable presence of mind, for, instead of keeping up the face of the hill, which was steep and unwooded in that part, he kept along the slope in the direction of the forest, though he lost ground by it. Notwithstanding his fright, he took no step which was not beautiful. The course on his part was a series of most graceful curves. It was a sort of leopard canter, I should say, as if he were nowise impeded by the snow, but was husbanding his strength all the while. When he doubled I wheeled and cut him off, bounding with fresh vigor, and Antaeus-like, recovering my strength each time I touched the snow. Having got near enough for a fair view, just as he was slipping into the wood, I gracefully yielded him the palm. He ran as though there were not a bone in his back, occasionally dropping his muzzle to the snow for a rod or two, and then tossing his head aloft when satisfied of his course. When he came to a declivity he put his forefeet together and slid down it like a cat. He trod so softly that you could not have heard it from any nearness, and yet with such expression that it would not have been quite inaudible at any distance. So, hoping this experience would prove a useful lesson to him, I returned to the village by the highway of the river.—Henry David Thoreau, Journals

    The following paragraph is also inadequately developed:

Visited my nighthawk on her nest. Could hardly believe my eyes when I stood within seven feet and beheld her sitting on her eggs. It was enough to fill one with awe. Another step, and the bird fluttered down the hill close to the ground, with a wobbling motion, as if touching the ground now with the tip of one wing, now with the other, so ten rods to the water, which it skimmed close over a few rods, then rose and soared in the air above me.

    Since the narrative framework of this paragraph is rather more complete than in the previous example of an inadequately developed paragraph, it would be improved by *vertical* expansion, a descriptive and reflective comment on the nighthawk.

Visited my nighthawk on her nest. Could hardly believe my eyes when I stood within seven feet and beheld her sitting on her eggs, her head to me. She looked so Saturnian, so one with the earth, so sphinx-like a relic of the reign of Saturn which Jupiter did not destroy, a riddle that might well cause a man to go dash his head against a stone. It was not an actual living creature, far less a winged creature of the air, but a figure in stone or bronze, a fanciful production of art, like the gryphon or phoenix. In fact, with its breast toward me, and owing to its color or size no bill perceptible, it looked like the end [of] a brand, such as are common in a clearing, its breast mottled or alternately waved with dark brown and gray, its flat, grayish, weather-beaten crown, its eyes nearly closed, purposely, lest those bright beads should betray it, with the stony cunning of the sphinx. A fanciful work in bronze to ornament a mantel. It was enough to fill one with awe. The sight of this creature sitting on its eggs impressed me with the venerableness of the globe. There was nothing novel about it. All the while, this seemingly sleeping bronze sphinx, as motionless as the earth, was watching me with intense anxiety through those narrow slits in its eyelids. Another step, and it fluttered down the hill close to the ground, with a wobbling motion, as if touching the ground now with the tip of one wing, now with the other, so ten rods to the water, which [it] skimmed close over a few rods, then rose and soared in the air above me. Wonderful creature, which sits motionless on its eggs on the barest, most exposed hills, through pelting storms of rain or hail, as if it were a rock or a part of the earth itself, the outside of the globe, with its eyes shut and its wings folded, and, after the two days' storm, when you think it has become a fit symbol of the rheumatism, it suddenly rises into the air a bird, one of the most aerial, supple, and graceful of creatures, without stiffness in its wings or joints! It was a fit prelude to meeting Prometheus bound to his rock on Caucasus.—Henry David Thoreau, Journals

While you may elaborate horizontally by giving simply a preceding or following event or idea, you may elaborate vertically by using any one of a vast number of methods. In fact, your greatest writing effort—as far as expansion is concerned—will be in using the vertical method, and it is the vertical method that requires your greater study.

In mastering the vertical method, you must first give consideration to the following matters:

Generalities require particulars, abstractions require concretes, opinions require evidence. Each makes the other meaningful. A generality is a broad statement, applicable to many cases; it is like a summary, or a conclusion, or an outline regardless where stated. A specific detail, the stuff of an expanded statement, is a statement about a particular case. Ordinarily numerous specific details are required to explain or support a generality.

Notice in the following paragraph how the general idea enables the reader to make sense of the details, and how the details make the generalization believable and interesting:

At the beginning of World War I the American Air Force was, strangely, an anachronism. Pilots wore spurs and jodhpurs and flew missions formerly assigned the cavalry. They were commanded by cavalry officers who typically made their inspections on horseback and insisted that every hangar be equipped with hitching posts. A commission looking into the military uses of the airplane shortly before the war began concluded that as a weapon its usefulness would be limited to stampeding the horses of the enemy cavalry. For a time it looked as if the airplane was as obsolete as the horse in war.

(Admittedly a specific statement can sometimes be substituted for a general one: Such a general statement as "At the beginning of World War I the American Air Force was, strangely, an anachronism" can be translated into specific terms and do just as good a job. "At the beginning of World War I American pilots wore spurs and jodhpurs and flew missions formerly assigned the cavalry." But more often both the generalization and the details are necessary and useful.)

Equate the quantity of specific detail to the generalization and to the situation. You see the necessity of details, but you can't list all the details reflected in any generalization. How many is enough? The answer requires an illustration:

Old linoleum smells hung in the dead air. Flies flung themselves against the window panes. Dark brown paint peeled from the table-top, revealing patterns of indeterminate color beneath. The waitress made some ritualistic motions in the middle of it with a sodden rag, then banged down three pieces of bent silverware and a glass of tepid water. She covered both with a greasy blotched menu and stood there impatiently picking her teeth. I mumbled something about not being ready to order. Really I was nauseated.

The paragraph could have been longer. There were other smells, sounds, and sights. The writer could have mentioned "the odor of stale beer," "the sick roach wriggling on its back in the corner," "the moisture-stained wallpaper," but each of these is from a class of descriptive details already represented in "the linoleum smells," the "flies," the "paint peeled from the tabletop." And the same could be said for all the details in the paragraph. So the first rule about quantity is: *Select each detail to represent a whole class of details.*

The second rule governing quantity is more intangible: *The more mature and interested your reader, the more details you should provide.* For example, a piece of closely reasoned, formal prose for a critical reader will inevitably contain more detail than lighter informal prose written to entertain. An unsupported generalization might not trouble the second reader while it wouldn't satisfy the first. But in either situation details are essential.

Both of the following paragraphs are successful. But the first and most detailed of the two appears in a rather sizable, scholarly book directed to the more specialized reader.

The foregoing discussion provides the elements for a definition of what is ordinarily understood to be "a novel," namely, that it is a long, fictitious, prose narrative. The word "long" is necessarily relative. As a pragmatic distinction, a "short story" can be heard or read at a single sitting, whereas a "novel" extends through an indefinite number of sessions. This original difference came to be reinforced by later influences: a short story is usually one of several items in a magazine, which satisfies its customers by providing as much diversity as possible, whereas a novel has to be long enough to make a volume by itself, of sufficient bulk to justify its cost. Through these external pressures, two clearly unlike techniques were developed: the short story has a single action, with unity of mood and strict limitation of characters; the novel is expected to have a slower tempo, a wider range of character and scene, and a more complex action. In practice, the maximum length of a short story is perhaps 10,000 words; the minimum length of a novel, perhaps 70,000. Various authors have experimented with works in the intervening area, and some of these have proved to be excellent achievements; but they are so few in proportion to the other two types, and their media of publication are so restricted, that not even a satisfactory name for such stories has been accepted. The term "novelette" has acquired a contemptuous connotation, and "long short story" is absurd.—Lionel Stevenson, The English Novel

And the second and less detailed paragraph is from a brief, introductory book for the general reader.

The novel may be defined then as the form of written prose narrative of considerable length involving the reader in an imagined real world which is new because it has been created by the author. The converse of this statement is part of the definition: any form of literature which is oral, poetry, description, exposition, drama, short, fact, fantasy, fable, or formula is not *a novel.—Katherine Lever,* The Novel and the Reader

Your presentation of details in the horizontal method of expansion will usually involve one of the following categories of details.

1. Causes. Describe a situation rather briefly and then devote most of your composition to showing what caused it. Effect to cause.

Idea: The noble California condor is in serious danger of extinction. Direction of expansion: Kill-happy hunters, coyote exterminators using poisoned meat, and the encroachment of civilization on the nesting grounds in the form of roads and recreation facilities are the principal causes of this situation.

2. Consequences. Discuss the causes first and proceed from these to a consideration of the results. Cause to effect.

Idea: Night drivers should not smoke.

Direction of expansion: The glowing cigarette tip and irritants in the smoke limit night vision and increase the chance of accidents.

Your presentation of details in the vertical methods of expansion will usually involve one of the following categories. Though the list is not definitive, it does represent the major kinds of details you will use in vertical expansion.

1. Description. Marshal details to create a mental image of something—an object, scene, event, person, emotion.

Idea: The sycamore is an impressive tree.

Direction of expansion: The sycamore often grows to be 80 or 90 feet in height and is the largest hardwood tree in North America; its white-barked limbs are gnarled and widespread; and it is a dramatic sight against the blue summer sky or in the gray winter woods.

2. Structure, parts, makeup. Use details to indicate the qualities of something, to tell what it's made of and how it's put together. This method is similar to description but more technical, less suggestive.

Idea: Wood and fabric are still used extensively in light plane construction.

Direction of expansion: The main spar and ribs in the wing are of wood; the engine wall, instrument panel, and other fuselage parts are generally plywood; most light planes are either all fabric-covered or have fabric-covered control surfaces—rudder, elevators, ailerons.

3. Examples. Cite representative specific cases to make a general statement clear and meaningful. Examples can precede or follow the statement.

Idea: Henry Vaughan's later, religious poetry is strikingly superior to his earlier, secular verse.

Direction of expansion: "To Amoret Gone from Him," the best of his earlier verse, is a conventional lover's complaint; his earlier secular poems have none of the inspiration of "The Retreate" or the mighty lines of "The World."

4. Illustration. As in giving examples cite representative cases, but here depend on the reader to infer the general idea.

Idea: Milers train for their event by running long distances over grueling courses.

Direction of expansion: Landy ran long distances over beach sand; Snell ran over a hilly cross-country course; O'Hara ran 140 miles a week, much of it along railroad right of way.

5. Restatement. Repeat the idea, each time in slightly different form.

Idea: The cow pond reflected the moonlight.

Direction of expansion: The mirrored image of a full moon glowed cooly; shimmering reflections rode every ripple; the dappled light glanced toward the willows at the far end and splashed back again; three mud hens swam in bull's-eyes of light.

6. Denials and negations. Tell what your subject is not in order to illustrate what it is.

Idea: Snails make ideal pets for children.

Direction of expansion: Snails are not vicious. Snails do not eat a great deal. Snails are not expensive. Snails are not noisy.

7. Comparisons. Point out how things are alike by describing one then the other or by describing two things part by part.

Idea: The lynx and bobcat are, except for superficial differences, the same animal.

Direction of expansion: Both are handsome, bobbed-tail cats with soft, spotted fur; both grow to about 3 feet and weigh up to 25 pounds; both hunt by night and live mainly on a diet of rabbits, ground squirrels, mice, snakes, and birds.

8. Contrasts. Point out how things are unlike by describing one then the other or by describing two things part by part.

Idea: The wings of birds that soar above water are differently shaped from those of birds that soar above land.

Direction of expansion: The wings of ocean-soaring birds are long and narrow, while those of land-soaring birds are comparatively short and broad. The primary feathers on sea birds are short and close together leaving a sharp trailing edge, while those of land birds are large and spaced leaving a serrated wing tip.

Your task as a writer is to employ both the horizontal and vertical methods of expansion in order that you may adequately develop your composition, in order that you may give body to the initial outline of thoughts you have. Your task is also to master, in particular, the use of details in the vertical method, since it calls for a very definite technical skill.

SUMMARY CHECKLIST

1. Have I actually written a full composition, or have I simply written a synopsis of a composition?

2. In the series of ideas that I present in my composition, have I started or stopped too soon? One of the mistakes you may make in horizontal expansion is dealing with too limited a slice of events or ideas. You may present only ideas 3, 4, 5, and 6, when you need to present ideas 1, 2, 7, and 8 as well.

3. In the series of ideas that I present in my composition, have I skipped over certain necessary events or ideas within the sequence? You may have your boundaries well established, but you may need to give more of the inner steps. You may present ideas 1, 3, 5, and 7, and have overlooked the necessary ideas 2, 4, and 6.

4. In my vertical expansion of ideas, have I erred in the direction of too much generalization? You may need to be more concrete and precise in your expansion.

5. In my vertical expansion of ideas, have I erred in the direction of irrelevancy? You may have sufficient quantity in your expansion, but your details may contribute little to your reader's understanding of your idea.

THE WHOLE COMPOSITION

Mark Van Doren develops his thesis both horizontally and vertically in the following essay. Starting with the idea that "Men are imitators, not creators," he proceeds horizontally through a set of subsequent ideas: Artists, like all men, are imitators, not creators; to be good imitators, artists must be good observers, good noticers; to check on their ability to observe, good artists must compare their work with that of other artists; the young person who wants to become a good artist must adapt a similar program of imitation and learning.

At the same time, Van Doren expands upon each of these basic ideas in a vertical manner. Notice in the second paragraph, for instance, how he makes the idea of man's imitative nature more convincing by stating the idea in a variety of ways. Notice in the third paragraph how vertical expansion is achieved by using Shakespeare as an example.

The essay finally turns out to be, of course, the product of both forms of expansion—vertical and horizontal methods woven together, criss-crossing back and forth to create the full-bodied composition.

The Creative Heritage

Mark Van Doren

Before the creative spirit can be communicated to the young, or to those of any age who do not have it yet, it must be defined with all possible care, lest it be misunderstood at the very outset. Misunderstanding in this case can be serious; indeed, it can be fatal to the spirit in question. And the commonest form of misunderstanding consists of supposing that man ever does create anything—that is to say, causes it to come into existence, brings it into being, or originates it. Man simply does not have that power, though sometimes he seems to think so. His genius and his glory lie in an altogether different direction: he is an imitator, not a creator.

To call him an imitator may seem to belittle him, but it might be well to consider whether any other creature can do even that. No other creature can. All creatures, including man, find themselves in a world they did not make and could not have made. And man alone is capable of comprehending what this means. He alone can see the world as something outside of himself which he can reflect in that unique mirror, his mind. It is a unique mirror in that it is more than quicksilver and glass. It studies, it penetrates, it sees parts of things in relation to one another; in the scientist it combines and recombines those parts so that something entirely new may seem to result. But it is not entirely new, any more than the so-called creations of the artist are entirely new—made up, so to speak, out of things that had no previous existence. The scientist and the artist are alike in that they begin with existence, and go on from there to imitations or reconstructions of it, which by their brilliance can blind us to the fact that nothing after all has been brought into being. All that has happened is that being itself has become clearer and more beautiful to us than it was before. This is a superb achievement, and it does not belittle man to claim that he is capable of it. Rather do we then perceive his ultimate, his incomparable distinction.

The greatest artists are the most lifelike: the best imitators of life. Their works, we say, are so much like life that they might be life themselves. But they are not life; they are like life, and it gives us happiness to realize that this is so. If Shakespeare is the best of poets, the reason surely is that he misses less than other poets do of the world he renders. We say he leaves nothing out; he sees everything in its full form and at its right value, and, finally, he causes what he sees, and what he makes us see, to glow with its own natural color. But he does not make us see what was never there. We had seen it too, over and over. The difference now is that we love it more, and behold it with a deeper intelligence. There is nothing new in Shakespeare except this beauty in everything, which he has helped us see more completely than we had considered possible. No man could have done more for other men.

Was Shakespeare, then, "original"? What would it mean to call him so? He has never in fact been paid the compliment, if compliment it is. Nor can he be imagined as ever desiring that it should be paid him. He would rather have been praised as true—true to the life he found himself living with others. He would rather have heard it said of him that he noticed this life in all of its particulars. He was the greatest of noticers. And the child or the youth who has ambitions to be an artist should be asked if *he* is a noticer. What we call creation is nothing but noticing—and then, of course, reflecting and rendering what has been noticed. But first of all, noticed. The artist has good eyes and ears, and uses them as most of us do not. He uses them to observe and relish what is *there,* outside himself or in; for he notices too how his own mind works, and lets none of its operations elude him. Yet his own mind, being the human mind, is like all other minds, just as the world outside of it is the same world for us all. We did not make our minds any more than we made the world they have the gift to mirror. The most original artist knows this the most humbly, and is the most likely to wish that we would judge his works by their truth, comparing it to what we already know.

He is also the most willing that we should compare his account of life with the accounts of other artists. To the extent that he competes with them, he expects to be measured by a standard common to all artists, and this standard is the truth, the whole truth, and nothing but the truth. If originality means trying something that no one ever tried before and no one will ever try again, then comparison ceases to be possible. The good artist prefers to be measured for results that can be stated. He is not, of course, concerned in any of his works with the whole truth at once. Particular truth is his practical aim. And toward this end he has selected a form which he will make as perfect as he can. The best art comes out of many attempts by many artists to write the same poem, paint the same picture, compose the same symphony or song. As soon as this is done perfectly—by Shakespeare, by Congreve, by Mozart, by Rembrandt—the effort moves into another field. But it was concerted effort on the part of many persons who accepted the same rules. The artist who triumphed was original only in the intensity and the fullness with which he realized the possibilities of the form. The form was before him, as his success will live after him.

A young person who wants to practice a given art should be convinced that it is indeed an art. It is a way of imitating life, and there are demands which it makes upon anyone who woos it. The chief of these demands are knowledge and love, not only of life itself, but of the means men take to reflect it. The artist loves his art, too, and in his apprentice days learns to love the masters who preceded him in its practice. The artist imitates other artists, and surpasses them if he can. But he begins by trying what they tried, and the better the artists he imitates, the faster he will improve—as Keats did, once he discovered Shakespeare, Milton, and Spenser. Left to himself, Keats might never have been impressive. He might have gone on merely trying to express himself. The proper business of the artist is not to express himself; it is to express the world, and the dimensions of the world are most clearly seen in the works of great artists. We can make them clearer still, but that will be hard work. The good artist will not hesitate to undertake it.

Nor will he feel that he loses anything by learning. He will understand that the more he knows about life, and about the art he is compelled to practice, the better he will be. Compelled is not too strong a word for the desire that moves him. The good artist is born as well as made: born with the desire to do what we find him doing. But he *must* be made. So he delights to learn. Granted that he might never have written a poem if he had never read one, or painted a picture if he had never seen one—granted this, he now proceeds as if he were free, as in fact he is, to be first in the field if he can. He will never be free to be first, however, unless he understands that he is also last—the last to try what has been tried by a long line of artists before him. He goes to school to his art, and likes it.

Imitation and learning. We learn about life, and we learn to imitate it. To communicate the importance of these essentials is the best way to inspire a beginning artist. For one thing, it may relieve him of certain terrors, lest creation be the mysterious, the magic process it is all too frequently represented to him as being. The only mysterious matter is that some of us have the desire to be artists and some do not. But given the desire, the next thing to understand is that knowledge plays an indispensable role in the formation of the poet, the painter, the sculptor, the musician. It has been said that the more a lawyer knows about everything, the better a lawyer he will be. And so of doctors, and divines, and statesmen. And precisely the same thing is true of artists. They do not start from scratch; they start by scratching—by peering, by digging, by diving and coming up again. Their art was there before them, just as life was, which they will now set out to render. Nor will they lose by being in a given case just one kind of artist instead of another. Nobody ever felt sorry for Shakespeare because he was nothing but a poet, for Rembrandt because he was nothing but a painter, for Bach because he was nothing but a musician. Each had his own way—but it was the way of others too—of learning all there was for him to learn. Or for him to make us learn. For it is well to remember how much we learn from artists. What we learn is not absolutely new, but we learn it in the most delightful of senses. We recognize it. Which means that we know it again, and better; more deeply, more clearly, more humbly with respect to its power and beauty.

It was said a long time ago that there is nothing new under the sun. It could also have been said—and doubtless it was—that there is nothing newer than this morning's sunrise, or the infant born today. Life, which never changes, is always starting over. And so is any art. The newest poet may be the best. But we shall not say this of him if there is no basis for comparison with others. The basis is his knowledge of the thing he imitates and of the art by which that is to be done. Inspiration is largely emulation of the artists we adore. But first of all, there must be some artists we adore. We must know and love them before we can surpass them. And so with life. We must know and love it before we can imitate its grandeurs.

Exercises

1. Jot down three possible ideas. Then write additional thoughts to illustrate how you would expand each idea horizontally, vertically. (You will frequently find one more natural than the other, but usually both are possible.)

2. Write down a half-dozen generalities—like "Communication failure is the world's tragedy" or "Few novels make good movies." (They can even be clichés.) Then transform each into meaningful statements by writing four or five accompanying details or by substituting a specific statement for the general statement.

3. Point out the method of expansion used in each paragraph of an essay or article that you find especially effective. Which method is used most frequently? Is the essay as a whole developed in the horizontal or vertical fashion?

4. Indicate the method you would use in expanding the following generalizations into paragraphs:

Destroy the American automobile and you destroy America.

The Greek deities exemplify natural phenomena.

Teaching machines can never replace professors.

5. The most interesting expansions of an idea almost always require details of one kind or another. But many subjects cannot be researched in the usual sense. For example, people who are good cooks often bear the faint scars of old

burns on their forearms, seem more conscious of scents and odors than others, and sometimes in restaurants murmur to themselves such things as "This could do with a pinch of oregano." Expand on this list of remembered observations regarding "the good cook." Now come up with another topic of the kind and expand upon it with a similar list.

6. If you were to write a brief essay in which you concluded that the "real" motives behind human actions were "You've got to do something" and "One thing leads to another," how might it be expanded and with what kind of material? Compose such an essay in from one to three paragraphs. Or, if you have been describing the hectic life of your circle (or someone else's) and conclude with the line "If things get too bad we can always have a party," what does this suggest about the foregoing detail and the method of expansion? Write a brief essay, perhaps in dialogue, to go with this line.

7. Consider once again the outlines you wrote earlier (Chapter 4, exercise 8). Are you using a method of expansion appropriate to the thesis? Indicate how you plan to expand each paragraph in the middle section; you may need to enlarge the outlines somewhat in order to make this clear.

6.MOMENTUM

After our composition has achieved its basic shape, we want to be sure our readers will be able to move easily through the words that we have written. Not only must we present our readers with adequately developed and reasonably arranged material, but we must *guide* our readers through the composition—from sentence to sentence, paragraph to paragraph; from one point to another, from this idea to that. By using the devices of *momentum* and the devices of *transition,* we can effect a continuity that provides a "smooth ride" for our readers from the beginning of our composition to the end. By helping them see the connections and relationships between and among the parts of our composition, we enable our readers to concentrate—as we would wish—upon what we have to say.

Reading some prose is, unfortunately, like trying to sleep on a milk train—all jerks and jolts. The end of every paragraph is a whistle stop, and every period a clackety-clack where the rails join.

This is a milk-train paragraph:

Gertrude Stein said of the postwar American writers, "You are all a lost generation." Most were born around 1900 and were thoroughly steeped in the genteel traditions of a tottering age. World War I left many spiritually defeated. They streamed to Paris with their baggage of despair and cynical hedonism to write about the lost years.

The sentences are abrupt and disjointed; it isn't enough that they are related and orderly—though no manner of tinkering would help if they weren't.

Now read this swifter version:

Gertrude Stein said of the postwar American writers, "You are all a lost generation." And they were. Most of them were born around 1900 and were thoroughly steeped in the genteel traditions of a tottering age. Many fought in World War I and were spiritually defeated by it. And when it was over, some streamed to Paris with their baggage of despair and cynical hedonism to write about the lost years.

Add a short transitional sentence ("And they were."), a transitional clause ("And when it was over"), a pronoun reference ("them"); revise the last three sentences, making them parallel (adding "some" to carry out the pattern begun by "most" and "many"); and the paragraph has momentum. In reading it, you move easily from one thought to the next without stopping to ponder the relationship.

If you work from an outline, which makes no provision for the devices of momentum, and write at a somewhat tedious pace, word by word, sentence by painful sentence, gaps will inevitably appear in your train of thought. (Rereading your own prose will not always disclose these gaps since you may unconsciously supply the missing details and connections.) And you will be surprised to find that what was perfectly clear and swift for you is slow going for your reader. As you write, think in terms of whole paragraphs and larger patterns. Put your composition aside for a few days; then read it as if it were written by someone else; this will often expose the remaining seams.

You may even wish to read your composition aloud—perhaps into a tape recorder if one is available—so that you can actually hear the momentum, or lack of it, in your writing. If you read your work aloud and find yourself stumbling and stalling through your sentences at particularly awkward spots, you will want to do the necessary rewriting that will give your composition its wanted smoothness and flow.

THE DEVICES OF MOMENTUM

As you work to give your prose a motion that makes readers want to read on and remember, keep in mind that good style is always a matter of knowing and using a full spectrum of possibilities. To achieve momentum, you should give consideration to each of the following devices:

Before all else, you must make sure that a *strand of an idea* runs through the paragraph and the composition. You must create a sense of inevitability in the way the thoughts in a particular paragraph or composition occur. You did, of course, give attention to the order of ideas in the planning stage, but problems are apt to linger.

In this paragraph "the plight of the desert" is expressed in every sentence, and the train of thought—"Kalahari . . . late in the year . . . grass . . . trees . . . leaf . . . sand . . . [sand] . . . [sand]" —carries naturally from sentence to sentence.

We were still deep in the Kalahari, moving slowly through a difficult tract of country into which the rains as yet had been unable to break. Since it was already late in the year, the plight of the desert was frightening. Almost all the grass was gone and only the broken-off stubble of another season left here and there, so thin, bleached and translucent that its shadow was little more than a darker form of the sunlight. The trees, most of them leafless, stood exposed against the penetrating light like bone in an X-ray plate. The little leaf there was looked burnt out and ready to crumble to ash on touch. Under such poor cover the deep sand was more conspicuous than ever, saffron at dawn and dusk, and sulphur in between. There was no shade anywhere solid enough to cool its burning surface. What there was seemed scribbled on it by the pointed thorns like script on some Dead Sea Scroll.—Laurens van der Post, The Heart of the Hunter

In some cases, where the logical connections are not as obvious as they are in conventional expository paragraphs, it is still possible to relate the separate sentences through the *use of recurring images associated with the idea or with the repeated indirect references to the idea.*

This paragraph employs, in the prevailing insect metaphor, similar images and symbols to fuse the separate sentences:

Mankind in the mass has often been compared, cynically or otherwise, to insects. To the historian proper the image of an ant-heap is almost inevitable. When he looks back into the past, he sees no great men or famous names, but myriads of

minute and nameless human insects, hurrying this way and that, making wars and laws, building and destroying cities and civilizations. The swarm ebbs and flows over the earth and through the centuries, the groups converging and coalescing or breaking up and scattering. The story of this ant-heap, of its impersonal groups and communities and of their ebb and flow upon the earth, is history.—Leonard Sidney Woolf, After the Deluge

Through *repetition and pronoun references* you can easily clarify the relation of thoughts to each other and to the larger idea. Yet writers are often warned against repetition. This is bad advice. Seldom are repeated words the real cause of monotony. Furthermore, this is one of the most natural ways to maintain the momentum of your prose, especially when you can't depend on the logical progression of sentences to carry your reader along.

A sense of momentum is achieved in this paragraph through the use of repetition; "education" is mentioned at least once in every sentence:

Well, what I mean by Education is learning the rules of this mighty game. In other words, education is the instruction of the intellect in the laws of Nature, under which name I include not merely things and their forces, but men and their ways; and the fashioning of the affections and of the will into an earnest and loving desire to move in harmony with those laws. For me, education means neither more nor less than this. Anything which professes to call itself education must be tried by this standard, and if it fails to stand the test, I will not call it education, whatever may be the force of authority, or of numbers, upon the other side.—Thomas Henry Huxley, Lay Sermons

In the following paragraph, minor variations—"contemporary music . . . listener . . . eclectic listener . . . contemporary music . . . musical taste . . . broad-minded listener . . . chamber music"—enable the writer to carry the thought from sentence to sentence without risking monotony:

Contemporary music is unusually rich in that it provides the listener with a great variety of aesthetic experiences. An eclectic listener can find in contemporary music a full spectrum of forms, styles, and presentations. From highly calculated, traditionally constructed symphonies to provocative jazz improvisations, contemporary music serves every possible musical taste, and the broad-minded listener who wants hootenanny on Monday, chamber music on Tuesday, dance tunes on Wednesday need only reach out and help himself to the particular arrangement of fare he desires.

Repetition from paragraph to paragraph is equally effective:

Napoleon launched his *Egyptian Campaign* with high hopes. . . .

But France did not have the resources to support a drawn-out *campaign* in *Egypt.*

And the British fleet complicated supplying an army in *Egypt* by. . . .

Had the French public known the full story of Napoleon's defeat in the *Egyptian Campaign* they would have. . . .

A warning, however: Repetition must never become too obvious or mechanical. In the following passage, repetition makes the paragraph coherent, but the prose style is indeed plodding:

A. E. Housman was born in Shropshire. A county on the Welsh border, Shropshire is largely agricultural. Plowing, mowing, harvesting, and other agricultural activities figure importantly in Housman's poetry. His poetry is characterized by. . . .

The writer makes too much of a point getting from one thought to the next and uses repetition too exclusively. He should have written something like this:

A. E. Housman was born in Shropshire, an agricultural county on the Welsh border. His poetry abounds with allusions to plowing, mowing, and harvesting, and with. . . .

The best alternative to simple repetition is, of course, *the reference pronoun.* You can't always use a pronoun in place of a noun; sometimes it's difficult, sometimes impossible. But when you can use a pronoun in one sentence to refer to a noun in the preceding, you have achieved the effect of a repeated word without risking either the monotony of repetition or the confusion of a different, even though synonymous, word.

In the following paragraph momentum is achieved partly through pronoun reference:

This is a snail shell, round, full and glossy as a horse chestnut. Comfortable and compact, it sits curled up like a cat in the hollow of my hand. Milky and opaque, it has the pinkish bloom of the sky on a summer evening, ripening to rain. On its smooth symmetrical face is pencilled with precision a perfect spiral, winding inward to the pinpoint center of the shell, the tiny dark core of the apex, the pupil of the eye. It stares at me, this mysterious single eye—and I stare back.—Anne Morrow Lindbergh, Gift from the Sea

(A final warning: be sure the antecedent of your pronoun is unmistakably clear. In the following sentence "he" could refer to either man: "Jackson told Lee that he was late coming up." Rewritten, the sentence is clear: "Jackson admitted to Lee that he was late coming up.")

Synonyms and antonyms can be an aid to momentum if you are sure the reader will be quick to make the association. A synonym might answer when you hesitate to repeat a word or use a pronoun. Variety is sometimes desirable if it can be achieved without confusing your readers or impressing them with your misdirected inventiveness. Alluding to the same object as a "device," an "instrument," a "mechanism" would be risky; since the words are indefinite to begin with and mean not quite the same thing in any case, some confusion is certain to occur. While there is undoubtedly a synonymic momentum in "football game . . . intersectional tilt . . . gridiron battle . . . pigskin rivalry," none but an inept writer would even distantly approximate it in serious writing. However, the momentum achieved through a play on synonyms in this series of paragraph beginnings is clear and at the same time useful since each new term carries with it implications not present in simply "General Gordon":

Charles George Gordon first came to the attention of. . . .

"Chinese Gordon," as the public thereafter knew him, became the most. . . .

When the Egyptian garrisons were hard pressed in the Sudan, *Victoria's General* was sent. . . .

The *martyr to England's imperialistic ambitions.* . . .

And notice how the momentum of this paragraph is subtly sustained by the use of synonyms—"great downs . . . colossal contours . . . landscape . . . lifting of the whole land":

With my stick and my knife, my chalks and my brown paper, I went out on the great downs. I crawled across those colossal contours that express the best quality of England, because they are at the same time soft and strong. The smoothness of them has the same meaning of great cart-horses, or the smoothness of the beech-trees; it declares in the teeth of our timid and cruel theories that the mighty are merciful. As my eyes swept the landscape, the landscape was as kindly as any of its cottages, but for power it was like an earthquake. The villages in the immense valley were safe, one could see, for centuries; yet the lifting of the whole land was like the lifting of one enormous wave to wash them all away.—G. K. Chesterton, A Piece of Chalk

Readers associate antonyms quite as easily. If anything, words that stand in clear opposition to one another are safer to use than synonyms, for we are quick to see many dichotomous relationships (as in *past* and *present, Heaven* and *Hell, first* and *last*) and ready to move from a discussion of one to the other. Some antonyms (like *happiness* and *sorrow*) are real in that the words describe opposite things; but some (like *comedy* and *tragedy*) are artificial; the words are more contrasting than oppositional.

The somewhat antonymous relation of *straight* and *curved* is one of the devices connecting the sentences in the following paragraph:

Strange that we should think in straight lines, when there are none, and talk of straight courses, when every course, sooner or later, is seen to be making the sweep round, swooping upon the centre. When space is curved, and the cosmos is sphere within sphere, and the way from any one point to any other point is round the bend of the inevitable, that turns as tips of the broad wings of the hawk turns upwards, leaning upon the air like the invisible half of the ellipse. If I have a way to go, it will be round the swoop of a bend impinging centripetal towards the centre. The straight course is hacked out in wounds, against the will of the world.—D. H. Lawrence, Mornings in Mexico

The obvious connection between *question and answer* is frequently used to achieve momentum. The one is, without the other, an unfinished statement. In order to complete it, the reader looks to what follows.

The momentum in dialogue is often supplied by a question-and-answer scheme:

Stop!
What?
That!
Darn it, what was I doing?
Using your thumb as a pusher, that's what.

And even in ordinary prose, questions and answers contribute effectively to momentum:

What place is this, to which the squalid street conducts us? A kind of square of leprous houses, some of which are attainable only by crazy wooden stairs without. What lies beyond this tottering flight of steps, that creak beneath our tread?—a miserable room, lighted by one dim candle, and destitute of all comfort, save that which may be hidden in a wretched bed. Beside it, sits a man: his elbows on his knees: his forehead hidden in his hands. "What ails that man?" asks the foremost officer. "Fever," he sullenly replies, without looking up. Conceive the fancies of a fevered brain, in such a place as this!—Charles Dickens, New York

A *pro-con* series of statements operates much like questions and answers, especially if the subject is clearly controversial. There are, of course, many variations, but ordinarily suggestions for a proposal are balanced by the evidence against, or the advantages of one are contrasted with the disadvantages in another. In any case, you often expect a statement in support to be answered by one in opposition and this clearly contributes to momentum.

The momentum of this passage is sustained partly by the pro-con relation of its thoughts:

Petrol has acted like magic on the place. Miraculous stuff, petrol! But the king-fishers do not like it. Nor does the lane wander any more. It has been disci-plined, and we know how good is discipline. The lane is broad, it is direct. It has no dust, and lost its smell of herbs. The old walnut trees do not lean over broken pales there. There are no trees. The lane has become a straight road with a surface like polished ebony. It is, in fact, a highway for motorcars. It becomes dangerous, every Sunday morning, with an endless flying procession of engines on their way to the coast; the chain reverses towards evening. We do not hear the corncrake anymore, when coolness and silence fall at eventide; we hear klaxons. We have no peppermint fields; we have filling stations.—H. M. Tom-linson, A Lost Wood

Notice how few words are needed to suggest the pro-con shape of an argument:

Most people believe that. . . .

But they overlook. . . .

Notice how the. . . .

And how the. . . .

In view of this it seems incredible that people persist in. . . .

Of course, some attribute this to. . . .

But. . . .

And. . . .

Therefore. . . .

Although *parallelism* can be used on any level, it is especially ef-fective for achieving momentum within the paragraph. Casting your sentences in a similar syntactical mold establishes a rhythm that en-ables your readers to move swiftly from one sentence to the next. They accustom themselves to a sentence pattern and expect you to stick with it as long as the thoughts are parallel.

Consider the parallelism in this paragraph:

The coffee-house was a most important political institution. No Parliament had sat for years. The municipal council of the City had ceased to speak the sense of the citizens. Public meetings, harangues, resolutions, and the rest of the modern machinery of agitation had not yet come into fashion. Nothing resembling the modern newspaper existed. In such circumstances the coffee-houses were the chief organs through which the public opinions of the metropolis vented itself.— Thomas Macaulay, The History of England from the Accession of James the Second

TRANSITIONS

Transitional words and phrases indicating the relationship between the new sentence, paragraph, or division and the one before are probably the most versatile kind of transition. You can add the words—usually at or near the beginning—without rephrasing the sentence or paragraph. And you can depend on your reader's seeing the logical relationship the words indicate.

You will, of course, vary the weight of a transition according to what you expect of it. To link a paragraph with a paragraph, a single word may do. Even to link several paragraphs with several other paragraphs may require only a word. But the larger the sections and the more obviously separate they are, the stronger the transitional device—sometimes a full sentence, or even a full paragraph. (Just as in a long book, an entire chapter may be needed to make a transition from one big section to another.)

And you will use relatively fewer or more transitional devices depending on the circumstances. When the thoughts expressed are relatively simple and their connections clear enough in context, you may use only a few transitional gestures. However, when the continuity of ideas is weaker or when you wish to emphasize their relation, you will use more. In any case, make a conscious effort to use transitions liberally, to use such a variety that your reader is not made overly aware of their presence, and to use transitions any time their presence is essential. Because of the absence of a single word, the following sentences seem to stand back and glare at each other:

Intercollegiate football has its place. If I were in charge of a college athletic program, I would shift the emphasis to track and field, a sport that invites wider participation and involves fewer of the risks.

But restores the logical relation of the sentences by pointing out the contrast between them:

Intercollegiate football has its place. But if I were in charge of a college athletic program, I would shift the emphasis to track and field, a sport that invites wider participation and involves fewer of the risks.

Notice, likewise, the importance of transitional words in this paragraph:

The city is everywhere dominant, so much so that many have come to regard urbanization as synonymous with civilization, and the synthetic environment as the natural one. Yet a love of the country persists. And those who dismiss it as romantic escapism are ignorant of the numerous articulate and reasoned defenses of this nearly lost culture. Of course some of the agrarianism is a result of disillusionment with city life. But there remains a strong faith in rural life as the noblest and best way. Thus, if the city is to be a wholly satisfying design for living, some provision must be made among all the concrete and steel for something of the earth, the trees, and the sky.

Yet . . . and . . . of course . . . but . . . thus—a great many transitional words for so short a paragraph, especially since they take the first position in each but the first sentence, yet most are clearly essential to its momentum.

You will get more mileage out of *connectives and conjunctions* if you do these two things: (1) Develop a large vocabulary of such words; don't always use *and, or, but,* and *however.* (2) And use them with precision; don't use *also* when you mean *yet,* or *thus* when you mean *furthermore.*

This list, although far from exhaustive, suggests the variety and significance of transitional words.

To introduce an addition or comparison: and, also, again, next, in addition, besides, finally, last, furthermore, moreover, likewise, similarly.

To introduce a contrast, qualification, or concession: but, however, yet, still, in spite of, in contrast, on the contrary, on the other hand, nevertheless, at the same time, though, although, of course, after all.

To introduce a summary or conclusion: then, thus, therefore, consequently, hence, to summarize, to sum up, in short, in brief, in conclusion, to conclude, as a result.

To suggest passage of time: immediately, soon, while, until, presently, shortly, thereafter, afterward, in the meantime, meanwhile, lately, since.

To introduce an example or point out particular aspects: for example, for instance, thus, to illustrate, in particular.

Numbers and words with similar functions are one of your most useful transitional devices. A *first* suggests a *second*, and a *to begin with* implies a *finally*. But be careful. What seems to you an effectively developed enumeration may seem to your reader an instance of compulsive list making. Use these transitional words only when you have an authentic series of steps or parts and only when you want to make certain the reader knows it.

Notice the effect of *first, second,* and *third* in this paragraph:

There be three degrees of this hiding and veiling of a man's self. The first: closeness, reservation, and secrecy, when a man leaveth himself without observation or without hold to be taken what he is. The second: dissimulation, in the negative, when a man lets fall signs and arguments that he is not that he is. And the third: simulation, in the affirmative, when a man industriously and expressly feigns and pretends to be that he is not.—Francis Bacon, Of Simulation and Dissimulation

However, in the following paragraph, *first, second, third* would have been too formal:

"Throwing" a calf is easy once you learn to use his efforts rather than your own. First, get in close to the calf's left side. Next, reach over the calf grabbing his flank (the fleshy web just forward of the rear leg) with your right hand and his ear with your left. Then, squeeze the ear, and as the calf jumps pull up on the flank. If your coordination has been good and if you've been quick he will be flat on his side, ready to hog-tie. Throwing a calf is not only easy, it's a misnomer.

Transitions are best when unobtrusive. Numbers have a habit of being obtrusive when they take the first position in every topic sentence. The following example illustrates how to use them inconspicuously:

. . . the three aspects of poetry. . . .
Poetry is characterized, *first,* by its emotional content. . . .
Rhythmic form, the *second* attribute of poetry, is. . . .
And, *third,* the pleasurable effect of poetry. . . .

The *transitional sentence* usually mentions what has been discussed and what will be discussed in the same breath. In doing this it frequently uses one or more of the transitional devices already referred to. Almost always it is the first sentence in the first paragraph of the new division; often it doubles as the topic sentence.

This example is all these things:

Though technically a defeat, Thermopylae was a moral victory and the key to Greek success in the Persian Wars. . . .

The author has been reviewing the Battle of Thermopylae; he is next going to show that it was the turning point in the long war with Persia; he uses a transitional word *though;* and the statement is undoubtedly intended to serve as a topic sentence.

Notice the transitional sentences joining the following paragraphs:

In any case national life itself must frequently exasperate him, because it is the medium in which he is expressing himself, and every craftsman or artist is repelled by the resistance of his medium to his will. All men should have a drop or two of treason in their veins, if the nations are not to go soft like so many sleepy bears.

Yet to be a traitor is most miserable. *All the men I saw in the prisoner's dock were sad as they stood their trials, not only because they were going to be punished. They would have been sad even if they had never been brought to justice.—Rebecca West,* The Meaning of Treason

Like other legends deeply rooted in folklore, the Atlantis story may have in it an element of truth. In the shadowy beginnings of human life on earth, primitive men here and there must have had knowledge of the sinking of an island or a peninsula, perhaps not with the dramatic suddenness attributed to Atlantis, but well within the time one man could observe. The witness of such a happening would have described it to their neighbors and children, and so the legend of a sinking continent might have been born.

Such a lost land lies today beneath the waters of the North Sea. *Only a few scores of thousands of years ago, the Dogger Bank was dry land, but now the fishermen drag their nets over this famed fishing ground, catching cod and hake and flounders among its drowned tree trunks.—Rachel L. Carson,* The Sea around Us

The transitional paragraph joins one major divison of a paper to another in situations where shorter transitional elements would be inadequate. It says three things: "This is what I've been talking about; this is what I'm going to talk about; and this is how the two relate." Here is an example:

These are problems Australia must overcome if she is to support more than a modest population at the present high standards of living. And none of them appears overwhelming for already the barren continent is changing. The Australians, a vigorous and resourceful people, are using a number of modern techniques to make their country more prosperous and habitable.

You can emphasize any one of the three functions of the transitional paragraph. It may be primarily a summary of what has already been said:

Before we turn to the solutions modern techniques offer, let us review the problems Australia must overcome if she is to support more than a modest population at the present high standards of living. We have demonstrated that sheer physical size is no advantage when the central four-fifths of the continent is a land of scant rainfall, low fertility, and high temperature. It is largely because of this that the population remains concentrated along the eastern and southern seaboard where, out of touch with the problems imposed by this trilogy of natural handicaps, they contribute little to their solution. Australian planners are trying to break this vicious circle in several ways.

And it can be used principally to introduce the next topic:

These are handicaps Australia must overcome if she is to support more than a modest population at the present high standards of living. Now let us look at some of the things the inventive and vigorous Australians are doing to solve their problems. I will concentrate on the deep wells, irrigation schemes, and chemical fertilizer plants since these, it seems to me, hold the answer to the most immediate problems. Air service, which also deserves special notice, is revolutionizing freight and passenger transportation and bringing people into closer touch with inland areas. The numerous comforts and conveniences that make life in the bush more bearable, like air conditioning and regular postal service, will be briefly discussed since, insignificant as they seem, these are things that will attract settlers to rural areas.

or a set of illustrations:

This discussion of changing Australia becomes much more meaningful when translated into more familiar terms. Imagine yourself a sheep rancher in South Australia, a businessman in Melbourne, a New Australian miner in Kalgourlie as I describe the effect modern techniques for overcoming the natural handicaps of the Australian continent will have on their lives.

And the transitional paragraph can briefly allude to what has been said and what will be said, but dwell at greater length on the relation between the two:

We have discussed the major natural problems Australia must overcome if she is to support more than a modest population at the present high standards of living. Now let us look at some of the solutions offered by modern techniques. No one imagines that the handicaps of scant rainfall, low fertility, and high temperature will be wholly overcome; yet deep wells, irrigation schemes, and chemical fertilizers offer some promise. The enormous problem of distance has already made Australia one of the most air-minded nations in the world. And the difficult living conditions of the bush are being improved by such comforts and conveniences as air conditioning and regular postal service. These are the challenges that inspire vigor in a people, when they are provided with the means for the solution of their problems.

Transitional paragraphs are usually short because they do not advance the thought. A paragraph of one sentence will often be enough to clarify the organization of the essay and to direct your reader from one part to another:

Now let us turn from the natural problems faced by the Australians to the solutions offered by modern techniques.

Certainly you should not feel compelled to write a sizable paragraph, for it seldom contains a topic sentence and rarely develops a central idea in the same way as does a conventional paragraph.

As you practice the devices of momentum, including the full range of transitional devices, you will find them more frequently appearing in your writing without your conscious manipulation of them. Though at first you may need to plant them artificially as guideposts, you will find, after a while, that momentum has become part and parcel of the way you write, even on first drafts. Until that day comes, however, you should check your writing carefully, especially on the second and third drafts, to see that a reasonable momentum is maintained.

SUMMARY CHECKLIST
Ask yourself these questions:

1. Is the movement of thought in the composition uniformly smooth-flowing? Do any lapses, any abrupt turns remain?
2. Specifically: Is there a strand of an idea running through the composition? Are the sentences so fused that the paragraphs create a single impression? Are the paragraphs and larger sections so joined that the reader, aware always of

the shape of the whole composition, moves easily from one to the next?

3. Do I use the devices of momentum and transitions liberally? Always where their presence is required?

4. At the same time, do I use the most appropriate methods for achieving momentum? Do I use transitional words and phrases in their most exact sense? And do I use such a variety of the devices of momentum and transitions that the reader is not made overconscious of their existence?

THE WHOLE COMPOSITION

James Baldwin uses at one level or another literally all the familiar devices of momentum and transitions—yet no more than any articulate writer. To point them all out would be tedious, but notice how the insistent repetition of "American Negro in Paris," "Negro," "American Negro" constantly reminds the reader that the essay is about the American Negro in Paris and the alienation of the American Negro generally. And notice how smoothly Baldwin moves from one paragraph to the next: "Negro entertainer" in the second paragraph picks up the idea of the first; "face from home" in paragraph 3 is a synonymic reference to "traditional kinfolk" in the last sentence of paragraph 2; "poverty" in one paragraph is an indirect reference to "choose between cigarettes and cheese at lunch" in the preceding; "thus . . . on the other hand . . . yet" are standby transitional words; and paragraphs 7 and 10 are almost wholly transitional.

Notice the devices of momentum in the complex series of parallels in paragraph 12 and the devices in such a sentence as this: "His white countrymen, by and large, fail to justify his fears, *partly* because the social climate does not encourage an outward display of racial bigotry, *partly* out of their anxiousness of being ambassadors, and *finally*, I should think, because they are themselves relieved at being no longer forced to think in terms of color."

Because of the quantity and variety and precision of his transitional methods, the momentum of Baldwin's essay is irresistible— and yet natural.

Encounter on the Seine: Black Meets Brown

James Baldwin

In Paris nowadays it is rather more difficult for an American Negro to become a really successful entertainer than it is rumored to have been some thirty years ago. For one thing, champagne has ceased to be drunk out of slippers, and the frivolously colored thousand-franc note is neither as elastic nor as freely spent as it was in the 1920's.

The musicians and singers who are here now must work very hard indeed to acquire the polish and style which will land them in the big time. Bearing witness to this eternally tantalizing possibility, performers whose eminence is unchallenged, like Duke Ellington or Louis Armstrong, occasionally pass through. Some of their ambitious followers are in or near the big time already; others are gaining reputations which have yet to be tested in the States. Gordon Heath, who will be remembered for his performances as the embattled soldier in Broadway's *Deep Are the Roots* some seasons back, sings ballads nightly in his own night club on the Rue L'Abbaye; and everyone who comes to Paris these days sooner or later discovers Chez Inez, a night club in the Latin Quarter run by a singer named Inez Cavanaugh, which specializes in fried chicken and jazz. It is at Chez Inez that many an unknown first performs in public, going on thereafter, if not always to greater triumphs, at least to other night clubs, and possibly landing a contract to tour the Riviera during the spring and summer.

In general, only the Negro entertainers are able to maintain a useful and unquestioning comradeship with other Negroes. Their nonperforming, colored countrymen are, nearly to a man, incomparably more isolated, and it must be conceded that this isolation is deliberate. It is estimated that there are five hundred American Negroes living in this city, the vast majority of them veterans studying on the G.I. Bill. They are studying everything from the Sorbonne's standard *Cours de Civilisation Française* to abnormal psychology, brain surgery, music, fine arts, and literature. Their isolation from each other is not difficult to understand if one bears in mind the axiom, unquestioned by American landlords, that Negroes are happy only when they are kept together. Those driven to break this pattern by leaving the U.S. ghettos not merely have effected a social and physical leave-taking but also have been precipitated into cruel psychological warfare. It is altogether inevitable that past humiliations should become associated not only with one's traditional oppressors but also with one's traditional kinfolk.

Thus the sight of a face from home is not invariably a source of joy, but can also quite easily become a source of embarrassment or rage. The American Negro in Paris is forced at last to exercise an undemocratic discrimination rarely practiced by Americans, that of judging his people, duck by duck, and distinguishing them one from another. Through this deliberate isolation, through lack of numbers, and above all through his own overwhelming need to be, as it were, forgotten, the American Negro in Paris is very nearly the invisible man.

The wariness with which he regards his colored kin is a natural extension of the wariness with which he regards all of his countrymen. At the beginning, certainly, he cherishes rather exaggerated hope of the French. His white countrymen, by and large, fail to justify his fears, partly because the social climate does not encourage an outward display of racial bigotry, partly out of their awareness of being ambassadors, and finally, I should think, because they are themselves relieved at being no longer forced to think in terms of color. There remains, nevertheless, in the encounter of white Americans and Negro Americans the high potential of an awkward or an ugly situation.

The white American regards his darker brother through the distorting screen created by a lifetime of conditioning. He is accustomed to regard him either as a needy and deserving martyr or as the soul of rhythm, but he is more than a little intimidated to find this stranger so many miles from home. At first he tends instinctively, whatever his intelligence may belatedly clamor, to take it as a reflection on his personal honor and good-will; and at the same time, with the winning generosity, at once good-natured and uneasy, which characterizes Americans, he would like to establish communication, and sympathy, with his compatriot. "And how do *you* feel about it?" he would like to ask, "it" being anything—the Russians, Betty Grable, the Place de la Concorde. The trouble here is that any "it," so tentatively offered, may suddenly become loaded and vibrant with tension, creating in the air between the two thus met an intolerable atmosphere of danger.

The Negro, on the other hand, via the same conditioning which constricts the outward gesture of the whites, has learned to anticipate: as the mouth opens he divines what the tongue will utter. He has had time, too, long before he came to Paris, to reflect on the absolute and personally expensive futility of taking any one of his countrymen to task for his status in America, or of hoping to convey to them any of his experience. The American Negro and white do not, therefore, discuss the past, except in considerately guarded snatches. Both are quite willing, and indeed quite wise, to remark instead the considerably overrated impressiveness of the Eiffel Tower.

The Eiffel Tower has naturally long since ceased to divert the French, who consider that all Negroes arrive from America, trumpet-laden and twinkle-toed, bearing scars so unutterably painful that all of the glories of the French Republic may not suffice to heal them. This indignant generosity poses problems of its own, which, language and custom being what they are, are not so easily averted.

The European tends to avoid the really monumental confusion which might result from an attempt to apprehend the relationship of the forty-eight states to one another, clinging instead to such information as is afforded by radio, press, and film, to anecdotes considered to be illustrative of American life, and to the myth that we have ourselves perpetuated. The result, in conversation, is rather like seeing one's back yard reproduced with extreme fidelity, but in such a perspective that it becomes a place which one has never seen or visited, which never has existed, and which never can exist. The Negro is forced to say "Yes" to many a difficult question, and yet to deny the conclusion to which his answers seem to point. His past, he now realizes, has not been simply a series of ropes and bonfires and humiliations, but something vastly more complex, which, as he thinks painfully, "It was much worse than that," was also, he irrationally feels, something much better. As it is useless to excoriate his countrymen, it is galling now to be pitied as a victim, to accept this ready sympathy which is limited only by its failure to accept him as an American. He finds himself involved, in another language, in the same old battle: the battle for his own identity. To accept the reality of his being an American becomes a matter involving his integrity and his greatest hopes, for only by accepting this reality can he hope to make articulate to himself or to others the uniqueness of his experience, and to set free the spirit so long anonymous and caged.

The ambivalence of his status is thrown into relief by his encounters with the Negro students from France's colonies who live in Paris. The French African comes from a region and a way of life which—at least from the American point of view—is exceedingly primitive, and where exploitation takes more naked forms. In Paris, the African Negro's status, conspicuous and subtly inconvenient, is that of a colonial; and he leads here the intangibly precarious life of someone abruptly and recently uprooted. His bitterness is unlike that of his American kinsman in that it is not so treacherously likely to be turned against himself. He has, not so very many miles away, a homeland to which his relationship, no less than his responsibility, is overwhelmingly clear: His country must be given—or it must seize—its freedom. This bitter ambition is shared by his fellow colonials, with whom he has a common language, and whom he has no wish whatever to avoid; without whose sustenance, indeed, he would be almost altogether lost in Paris. They live in groups together, in the same neighborhoods, in student hotels and under conditions which cannot fail to impress the American as almost unendurable.

Yet what the American is seeing is not simply the poverty of the student but the enormous gap between the European and American standards of living. *All* of the students in the Latin Quarter live in ageless, sinister-looking hotels; they are all forced continually to choose between cigarettes and cheese at lunch.

It is true that the poverty and anger which the American Negro sees must be related to Europe and not to America. Yet, as he wishes for a moment that he were home again, where at least the terrain is familiar, there begins to race within him, like the despised beat of the tom-tom, echoes of a past which he has not yet been able to utilize, intimations of a responsibility which he has not yet been able to face. He begins to conjecture how much he has gained and lost during his long sojourn in the American republic. The African before him has endured privation, injustice, medieval cruelty; but the African has not yet endured the utter alienation of himself from his people and his past. His mother did not sing "Sometimes I Feel Like a Motherless Child," and he has not, all his life long, ached for acceptance in a culture which pronounced straight hair and white skin the only acceptable beauty.

They face each other, the Negro and the African, over a gulf of three hundred years—an alienation too vast to be conquered in an evening's good-will, too heavy and too double-edged ever to be trapped in speech. This alienation causes the Negro to recognize that he is a hybrid. Not a physical hybrid merely: in every aspect of his living he betrays the memory of the auction block and the impact of the happy ending. In white Americans he finds reflected—repeated, as it were, in a higher key—his tensions, his terrors, his tenderness. Dimly and for the first time, there begins to fall into perspective the nature of the roles they have played in the lives and history of each other. Now he is bone of their bone, flesh of their flesh; they have loved and hated and obsessed and feared each other and his blood is in their soil. Therefore he cannot deny them, nor can they ever be divorced.

The American Negro cannot explain to the African what surely seems in himself to be a want of manliness, of racial pride, a maudlin ability to forgive. It is difficult to make clear that he is not seeking to forfeit his birthright as a black man, but that, on the contrary, it is precisely this birthright which he is struggling to recognize and make articulate. Perhaps it now occurs to him that in his need to establish himself in relation to his past he is most American, that this depthless alienation from oneself and one's people is, in sum, the American experience.

Yet one day he will face his home again; nor can he realistically expect to find overwhelming changes. In America, it is true, the appearance is perpetually changing, each generation greeting with short-lived exultation yet more dazzling additions to our renowned facade. But the ghetto, anxiety, bitterness, and guilt continue to breed their indescribable complex of tensions. What time will bring Americans is at last their own identity. It is on this dangerous voyage and in the same boat that the American Negro will make peace with himself and with the voiceless many thousands gone before him.

Exercises

1. Write a dozen possible topic sentences, each employing a different transitional device.
2. Jot down three statements. Then incorporate in each a transitional word, first one and then another, from the different classes on page 89. Describe how the meaning of the sentence shifts with each new version.
3. Circle all the devices of momentum in one of your compositions (either written for this purpose or for an earlier exercise) and connect with lines those which act in concert. In addition to illustrating the pervasiveness of transitions and other devices, does this graphic view disclose any lapses in the momentum of your essay?
4. Transitional words suggest momentum so forcefully that they can make even nonsense seem to be getting somewhere. Write a paragraph on the order of "While tum-de-dum is both snip and snap, and biff is neither boom nor bang, rumpty-tumpty is, of course, rumpty-tumpty, . . ." in which you employ a great many transitional words and perhaps, other devices of momentum. (Such verbal play is good practice for writers. After all, Dylan Thomas attributed some of his skill to his experience as a sound man with BBC, where he mimicked animal noises!)
5. Identify the major device used in each of the following paragraphs to achieve momentum. Rewrite one of the paragraphs using yet another method.

Gilbert White's *Natural History of Selborne* is undoubtedly one of the most tranquil books in the language. A country parson's record of the animals and plants, geography and weather of his native parish, it was not in the beginning intended for publication. When he was forty-seven, White began sending his observations to an interested friend, and twenty-one years later, in 1788, discovered he had a book. It was an immediate success and was widely admired at a time when a great many people were writing about nature. Although there is enough science in it to justify White's designation as the first great English field naturalist, this is not what makes *The Natural History of Selborne* immortal. Rather, it is the spirit of contented homeliness.

When I was a little boy, I was permitted to take violin lessons.

Permitted I say? Forced, rather. I was forced to take violin lessons and I hated them. Every Saturday morning at ten o'clock I would trudge the seven blocks to the violin teacher's studio and suffer through an agonizing forty minutes of saw, count, saw, count, saw. And worse than that, every afternoon after school, I was confined to quarters for a ghastly hour for the express purpose of sawing and counting on my own. My Saturday mornings were ruined. My afternoons were spoiled. My youth was transfigured into an off-beat and out-of-tune nightmare from which I thought I might not possibly wake.

6. Point out the methods of momentum used in a short article or essay that you find especially swift and smooth.
7. Consider once more the outlines you wrote earlier (Chapter 5, exercise 7); enlarge each paragraph heading until it is a complete sentence, making sure each contains a transitional device.

7.EMPHASIS

Whenever we decide that some word, sentence, or paragraph in our composition is saying something especially important, we must indicate that significance to our readers. One of our obligations as writers is to *direct* our readers' attention— pointing out those parts of our composition that we want our readers especially to notice. We do this "pointing out" by using the devices of emphasis— we repeat a word or an idea, we increase the length of a sentence or a paragraph, we place a word or sentence or paragraph in a prominent position, or we make a noticeable shift in style.

Are all ideas of equal importance in a composition? No. Must the really important ideas in your composition receive special attention? Yes.

Sometimes a particular sentence or paragraph needs to stand out because it is making a major point in your composition or is setting forth one of your major ideas. You can, of course, openly label those parts of your composition you wish to emphasize: "Especially important is the idea that . . .," or "You will want to give special consideration to the fact that . . .," or "The following information is the most essential part of my argument." Just as often, however, you will want to bypass such labeling, or complement it, by using other devices of emphasis—for the sake of variety if nothing else.

THE WORD

To emphasize a word, you may do four things: repeat the word; place the word in an attention-getting position; contrast the quality of the word with that of surrounding words; or, in rare cases, set off the word typographically in some manner.

Word Repetition

An easy form of word emphasis is simply word repetition. Though simple repetition is to be used judiciously and cautiously, it can become an effective instrument. Consider, for instance, Franklin D. Roosevelt's famous "again and again and again." Repeating a word for emphasis is simply an established human way of calling attention to words.

In the following sentences, you will note that the word being emphasized cannot be overlooked. Though the device of word repetition is so obvious you would not want to use it very often, nevertheless it is a good one to keep in mind when in some moment of crisis or desperation you do want to hammer home a certain word within a sentence.

I love everything that's old: old friends, old times, old manners, old books, old wine; and, I believe, Dorothy, you'll own I have been pretty fond of an old wife.—Oliver Goldsmith, She Stoops to Conquer

The van of the Caucasians, and the rear of the Mongolians, must intermix. They must talk together, and trade together, and marry together.—Thomas Hart Benton, The Superior Race

Madame du Châtelet was certainly a most remarkable creature—tiresome, but not too tiresome, and therefore an ideal mate for a very tiresome man.—E. M. Forster, How They Weighed Fire

Perhaps the main guiding principle of modern architecture is economy: economy

of material, economy of means, economy of expression.—Lewis Mumford, The Culture of Cities

Now read these same sentences without the device of repetition and note that the words which were important in the first instance are now no more significant than any of the other words about them.

I love everything that's old: friends, times, manners, books, wine; and, I believe, Dorothy, you'll own I have been pretty fond of you.

The van of the Caucasians, and the rear of the Mongolians, must intermix. They must talk and trade and marry together.

Madame du Châtelet was certainly a most remarkable creature—tiresome, but not too much so, and therefore an ideal mate for a very tedious man.

Perhaps the main guiding principle of modern architecture is economy of material, means, expression.

Word Position

Placing a word in an attention-getting position is a more useful and desirable method of emphasis. The attention-getting positions in a sentence are, of course, those held by the first word and the last word. When you have something very important to tell, don't you naturally tell it at the very beginning of your conversation or save it for the very end of your conversation as a big surprise? The first word in a sentence (not counting the articles *the, a,* and *an)* is emphasized simply because it is the first word that the reader encounters; the last word in a sentence is emphasized simply because it is the last one the reader sees drop over the horizon in farewell. Whether you have even thought about it or not, you yourself respond more to the first and last words in a sentence—unless some other word has been given some special, more powerful emphasis to make up for its having neither first nor last position.

In the following sentences, what words stand out for you?

Novels are more popular than novellas.

Soames broke the news to Victoria, Albert, and Palmerston.

After the war was over, a peace treaty was signed.

For most of us, the words "novels . . . novellas," "Soames . . . Palmerston," "after . . . signed" have a slight emphatic edge over their fellow words.

Likewise, in these sentences, the importance of opening and closing position is quite obvious:

Of these public and private scenes, and of the first years of my own life, I must be indebted not to memory, but to information.—Edward Gibbon, Autobiography

The proper force of words lies not in the words themselves, but in their application.—William Hazlitt, On Familiar Style

Ugly and drab furnishings cannot be justified economically.—Robert Sommer, Hard Architecture

Now consider what happens to a word when it is put in a different place in a sentence. What happens to the emphasis in Gibbon's sentence if we move things around?

Of the first years of my own life, and of these public and private scenes, I must be indebted to information but not to memory.

Or to Hazlitt's emphasis?

The proper force of words lies in their application, not in the words themselves.

Or to Robert Sommer's?

Furnishings that are ugly and drab cannot be economically justified.

Ask yourself in which of the following sentences the word *however* stands out the most.

However, I shall not do as you have asked.
I, however, shall not do as you have asked.
I shall, however, not do as you have asked.
I shall not, however, do as you have asked.
I shall not do as you have asked, however.

For most people, the first and fifth sentences give the greatest emphasis to *however*—(a fact that leads to a well-established rule of style: never begin or end a sentence with a conjunctive adverb unless you consciously, deliberately want to call the reader's attention to it). *However* is buried and deemphasized in the second, third, and fourth sentences.

Other things can happen in a sentence, of course, to overcome the power of the first-last positions and give a greater emphasis to a word occurring elsewhere. But when everything else is equal, the first-last words will carry an inherent emphasis, not because of what they are, but because of where they are. Whether you intend it or not, you give emphasis to certain words simply by placing them where you do—and sometimes the emphasis can have important consequences. In the following sentences, what words are naturally emphasized and what might be the implications?

Arnold Brown and Bill Woodstock have invented an important new electronic counting device.

Bill Woodstock and Arnold Brown have invented an important new electronic counting device.

An electronic counting device, both new and important, has been invented by Arnold Brown and Bill Woodstock.

In the first sentence, Bill Woodstock may feel that Arnold Brown is receiving a fraction more recognition than he deserves, and Arnold Brown may feel likewise about Bill Woodstock in sentence 2. In the third sentence, Bill Woodstock has the edge over Arnold Brown, for Woodstock is in a "tail end" position—not a deemphasizing place—and Arnold Brown is beginning to be buried inside the sentence. Reading sentence 3 rapidly, wouldn't you remember Bill Woodstock more readily than Arnold Brown, since "Bill Woodstock" is the last name you encounter? Observe, also, in sentence 3 that the words *new* and *important* have lost some of the emphasis they would have had in such a sentence as this:

A new, important electronic device has been invented by Arnold Brown and Bill Woodstock.

Position is, obviously, a powerful tool in word emphasis. Merely by moving a word in a sentence you can put it in the light or in the shade.

Stylistic Shift

Another strong method of word emphasis is the sudden shifting to a new level of diction. Since emphasis is primarily a matter of calling attention to a situation and since a good way to get attention, on any occasion, is to do something different from what has been going on or different from what the neighbors are doing, a shift in word diction is an effective way of making a particular word stand out in a sentence. Here is an example:

He put the little bird in the aviary and wouldn't let it out.

In this sentence, the word *aviary* differs in its dictional level from all the other words in the sentence—it has three syllables, is of Latin origin, is not as commonly used as the other words. The emphasis would not fall on *aviary*, however, if all the words in the sentence were of *aviary's* level. Consider this:

He stationed the petite oriole in the aviary and adamantly refused to permit its exit.

Now *aviary* has lost its emphasis—for it no longer stands out; it is of the same general vocabulary level that prevails throughout the sentence. When you come to *aviary*, no shift in diction occurs.

In the following sentences you should have no difficulty in recognizing the word being emphasized by dictional shift.

The young man with the fine blond hair left the rail and returned almost at once with a victorious air and a pair of binoculars.—Walter Van Tilburg Clark, Why Don't You Look Where You're Going?

They cannot understand the middle-class diffidence of the young men who wear collars and ties and finger-rings.—D. H. Lawrence, Twilight in Italy

The second type is the smug professor—the one with a kind of feline complacency and an imperturbable confidence that he is most clever and most knowing. He has proved to himself that he is a pretty smart fellow.—George C. Williams, Some of My Best Friends Are Professors

The increasing crowd stares with beatific placidity.—Arnold Bennett, The Author's Craft

The scene was made even more sententious by the fact that it was Sunday.— Anatole Boyard, Sunday Dinner in Brooklyn

Typographical Emphasis

Typographical emphasis is, no doubt, the least effective and reliable method. Italicizing a word, capitalizing the word, setting the word off in quotation marks—these are all easily done and they do call attention to a word.

When man developed the idea of private property, woman's destiny was "sealed." At this time women were cut off from the more adventurous activities of war, forays, explorations, to stay home to protect *and* maintain *what men had achieved by their far-reaching pursuits.—Elizabeth Hardwick,* The Subjection of Women

We're all intellectuals about something.—*Randall Jarrell,* The Intellectual in America

Man is, properly speaking, based upon Hope, he has no other possession but

Hope; this world of his is emphatically the Place of Hope.—Thomas Carlyle,
Sartor Resartus

*Indeed, our "savage" ancestors are still very near us, and not merely in our ca-
pacity for savagery.—Herbert Joseph Muller,* The Uses of the Past

Yet their obviousness and their frequent overuse work against them.
Judicious use of typographical devices of emphasis can, indeed, contribute to a good style, but the careless and constant use of them
jades the reader to the point that he is unable to respond. In the following paragraph you see the failure to achieve emphasis, simply
because the typographical devices are too frequent and too varied.
Restlessness and laughter result; not the emphasis desired.

We set sail one *dark* and *lonely* night over the "inky" sea that was in-
distinguishable from the "inky" sky. We sailed what seemed FOR-
EVER before I gained any sense of direction. I had to put my *entire
trust* in the "mysterious" captain. I must admit I was frightened and
anxious!!

This inadequate paragraph not only uses a weak technique of
emphasis, but uses it too abundantly. If every other word is emphasized, then no word stands out. Emphasis, after all, is a matter of
discrimination.

THE SENTENCE

To emphasize a particular sentence in the midst of many sentences,
you will usually do one of four things: convert your sentence—if it is
a simple one—into the independent clause of a complex sentence;
make the sentence you wish to emphasize longer than those around
it; place the sentence you wish to emphasize at the beginning or end
of the paragraph in which it occurs; write the sentence to be emphasized in a slightly different style.

Making a Simple Sentence into the Independent Clause of a Complex Sentence

This is perhaps the most frequent form of sentence emphasis. You
can achieve emphasis by converting a simple sentence into an independent clause; the independent clause will contrast with an accompanying subordinate element. In the sentences,

After he finished work last night, he went to the movie.

When the spiritual energy is directed on something outward, then it is thought.—Ralph Waldo Emerson, Intellect

Plausible as the theory sounds, great risks are attached to it.—Virginia Woolf, The Patron and the Crocus

the second clause is emphasized simply because of its grammatical construction. Likewise in the sentences,

He took the trip abroad because he wanted to do so.

They published hundreds of books which are never noticed at all.—Henry James, Criticisms

I would like to go back to school so that I can become economically independent, support myself, and, if need be, support those dependent upon me.—Judy Syfers, Why I Want a Wife

the first clause is emphasized by its independence.

By combining a sentence with its neighboring sentences, you can make the sentence to be emphasized an independent clause, and make the other sentences, not to be emphasized, dependent clauses. This is done quite easily.

Twenty new novels have been published this week.
Most critics think Bruce Robinson's novel is the best.
Bruce Robinson wrote last year's best seller, *Roses in the Rain.*

Assuming that you wish to emphasize the second sentence, you can do so by making the second sentence an independent clause within a complex sentence:

Most critics think that Bruce Robinson, who wrote last year's best seller *Roses in the Rain,* has written the best of the twenty new novels published this week.

Here are some similar problems:

After she arrived, I took a day's vacation from work. I drove her up to Lake Tohee and showed her the famous view from the island.

If the second sentence is to receive greater emphasis than the first, you can combine the two sentences into one complex one:

Having taken a day's vacation from work after she arrived, I drove her up to Lake Tohee and showed her the famous view from the island.

Or consider the possibility of emphasizing one of the following sentences,

I have just quoted from Mr. Coleridge's poems.
I repeated those lines once before while walking on a road.
The road commanded a delicious prospect.
How glad I was to walk along that road!

by combining them into one sentence—as Hazlitt did—to emphasize the sentence dealing with walking rather than those dealing with poetry:

How proud, how glad I was to walk along the high road that commanded the delicious prospect, repeating the lines which I have just quoted from Mr. Coleridge's poems!—William Hazlitt, On Going a Journey

The following paragraph has no emphasized sentences, for no sentence stands out from the rest.

I worked until five o'clock last Saturday. At five thirty, I ate my evening meal in the corner restaurant. At six, I went to the double-feature movie. At ten o'clock I left the movie and had some pie and coffee. By eleven o'clock, I was fast asleep in my bed.

If you wish any one of the events in the paragraph to stand out, you can see to it that an independent clause is created to contrast with a dependent clause. As the paragraph stands now, every event is equally important. But if you rewrite it, you can begin to point out to your reader that some of the events are more important than others:

After working until five o'clock last Saturday, I ate my evening meal in the corner restaurant. And after attending the double-feature movie from six until ten, I had some pie and coffee in the restaurant again before I managed to hit the sack in my own apartment around eleven.

Obviously the main idea in this pedestrian set of statements is that the narrator ate in the restaurant. All other ideas have been subordinated so that the independent clauses dealing with the restaurant begin to stand out.

Length of Sentence

Another obvious way to emphasize a particular sentence, of course, is simply by making it noticeably longer or noticeably shorter than other sentences around it. If most of the sentences in a paragraph run an average of ten to fifteen words, a sentence of some twenty-five words will be unusual and will be emphasized—and so will a sentence two or three words in length. Here are some examples:

Mary, with her money, bought a single lovely doll with golden hair. Jane, with her money, bought a dozen different toys, all trinkets actually, that would be broken in a week's time, but which were to her, at the moment, a vast quantity of glorious treasure.

By giving the second sentence greater length it rises in importance above the first sentence.

But you can also emphasize the second sentence by greatly reducing it in length:

Mary, with her money, bought a single, lovely golden-haired doll all dressed up in a pink taffeta evening gown. Jane bought a dozen trinkets.

In the following paragraph, the fourth sentence has been emphasized by its length.

Eugene O'Neill must be recognized as America's greatest playwright. The remarkable plays that he wrote in the twenties and thirties actually founded American theater. His experiments in form and technique paved the way for all the significant theatrical achievements in this century. His tragic vision, a vision that prevails from the early sea plays to the late historical plays and personal confessions, added a depth of meaning to the American theater, a grand sense of tragic darkness that will forever balance out any shallowness or superficiality that may occur in American drama. Though O'Neill may someday fall out of fashion, he can never be really dethroned.

The sentence that stands out in the next paragraph is the long last one:

In Western civilization there are two lines of teachers from whom all modern teaching stems: the Greek philosophers and the Hebrew prophets. Outside the Jewish community the influence of the Greeks is far wider, stronger, and more varied—with the exception of the teaching of Jesus himself. In this book we are not concerned with what is taught, but with how teaching is done; yet in con-

tent, also, our schools and our universities are much more Greek than Hebrew. The Greek teachers claimed to be following the movement of Reason. The Hebrew prophets knew they were uttering the voice of God. We admire both, but we are apt to think that while a group of men who are in touch with God can change the world by a rare and miraculous intervention, it needs the steady work of reason to keep the place going and to train the young.—*Gilbert Highet,* The Art of Teaching

But in the following sentence groups, sentences have been emphasized by making them noticeably shorter than their neighbors:

I thought ten thousand swords must have leaped from their scabbards to avenge even a look that threatened her with insult. But the age of chivalry is gone. That of sophisters, economists, and calculators, has succeeded; and the glory of Europe is extinguished forever.—*Edmund Burke,* Reflections on the Revolution in France

I believe all scholars lie like this. An ancient friend of mine, a clergyman, tells me that in Hesiod he finds a peculiar grace that he doesn't find elsewhere. He's a liar. That's all. Another man, in politics and in the legislature, tells me that every night before going to bed he reads over a page or two of Thucydides to keep his mind fresh.—*Stephen Leacock,* Homer and Humbug

It was once a land of giants, black-bearded men, who came up from the coastal fisheries and sometimes took a small boy in their boat to see the odd harvest of their nets. It was full of dark pools and distant heights, of birds and animals, of hopes and panics and surprises. It is not at all like that now.—*Ivor Brown,* A Sentimental Journey

Position of Sentence

Sentences, like words, can also be emphasized by position. They can be placed first or last in a paragraph and receive special consideration thereby. If everything else is equal and no counteracting emphatic device is used in another sentence, the first and last sentences of a paragraph are the most important.

The great tragic artists of the world are four, and three of them are Greek. It is in tragedy that the pre-eminence of the Greeks can be seen most clearly. Except for Shakespeare, the great three, Aeschylus, Sophocles, Euripides, stand alone. Tragedy is an achievement peculiarly Greek. They were the first to perceive it and they lifted it to its supreme heights. Nor is it a matter that directly touches only the great artists who wrote tragedies; it concerns the entire people as well, who felt the appeal of the tragic to such a degree that they would gather thirty thousand strong to see a performance. In tragedy the Greek genius penetrated farthest and it is the revelation of what was most profound in them.—*Edith Hamilton,* The Greek Way

In such a paragraph, only position gives emphasis to particular sentences. When all the sentences in a paragraph are primarily alike and no one sentence is given any special attention, the first and last sentences automatically receive most notice. This situation can give rise to a control of reader attention simply by your stating first and last what you want your reader to notice and by *not* mentioning first or last those things you wish to be read with as little attention as possible. Consider for instance this paragraph from a student's letter to the folks back home:

I'm finding college an extremely rewarding experience. I like most of my teachers all right, even though some of the courses are rather dull. And I'm making better grades after flunking my first two exams in history. What with all the parties and coke dates, I've had a little trouble finding time to study. But I'm definitely holding my own grade-wise now and I'm finding it can really be fun to dig in and get the message in my classes. I'm on a good schedule now and it's paying off.

Wisely, the student put first and last the positive statements and buried the less fortunate news he had to reveal. If he had ignored the prime importance of first and last position, he might have written a paragraph like this:

I flunked my first two exams in history, but don't worry. Some of my courses are dull, but I'm making better grades now. I like most of my teachers all right and I'm finding college an extremely rewarding experience. I'm finding it can really be fun to dig in and get the message in my classes. I'm on a good schedule now and it's paying off and I'm definitely holding my own grade-wise. I have had a little trouble finding time to study, though, what with all the parties and coke dates.

And note that in the following paragraph those sentences mentioning President Taylor and his daughter occur first and last; sentences mentioning Major Seaton, Speaker Winthrop, the ambassadors, the wife of the Russian minister, two Louisiana beauties are all presented inside the paragraph, in less emphatic position.

On the night of March 4, President Zachary Taylor entered the enormous ballroom of the Washington Armory, decorated with flags and insignia. Leaning on the arms of Major Seaton and Speaker Winthrop, the President accepted the cheers and waving handkerchiefs with delight spread across his face. Behind him, escorted by two ambassadors, walked the young and handsome wife of the Russian minister, Madame Bodisco, "enveloped in a cloud of crimson satin and

*glistening with diamonds." After her, stepped two Louisiana beauties, a blonde
and a brunette, then "Miss Betty," the President's twenty-two-year-old daughter
who, because of her mother's "disinclination," was to act as White House hostess during her father's term. The President's daughter was dressed in white, a
simple flower in her hair. Again and again the crowd cheered her as she
walked toward the center of the ballroom.—Grace Steele Woodward,* The
Man Who Conquered Pain

Stylistic Shift

Finally, with sentences, as with words, emphasis can be achieved by
shifting to a different kind of sentence. Although there is scarcely a
limit to the kinds of stylistic shift that can take place, some of the
more common are these: from loose sentences to a periodic sentence,
or from periodic sentences to loose; from statements to question, or
questions to statement; from nonmetaphorical sentences to a metaphorical style, or from metaphors to nonmetaphors; from simple sentences to a complex one, or complex sentences to a simple one; from
sentences lacking balance or parallelism to a sentence with balance
or parallelism.

Here are examples of various kinds of change that can take
place:

*It doesn't do, this retracing of a boyhood's steps. One knew, of course, that look-
ing backward is like looking through an opera-glass reversed. But the distortion
is worse than one imagined. One shouldn't have gone. The return has been a
cowardly assault upon romance, a butchering of innocent memories. Far better
have left the old house to be, in mind's eyes, grandiose, mysterious, abounding in
dark possibilities.—Ivor Brown,* A Sentimental Journey

(The fifth sentence rises to emphasis with the balanced metaphors;
the emphasis is maintained in the next sentence with the three parallel adjectives.)

*I often wondered what the author of Notices to Mariners looks like. I have tried
to represent him to myself as a monk, a man who has renounced the vanities of
the world, and for preference belonging to the Order of Trappists who are bid-
den to remember death—memento mori—and nothing else. A sobering
thought! Just suppose the author of Notices to Mariners acquiring convivial
habits and sitting down to write a Notice in that happy frame of mind when
nothing matters much and one letter of the alphabet is as good as another.—Joseph Conrad,* Outside Literature

(The sentence "A sobering thought!" achieves an emphasis it would
not otherwise have simply because it stands in sharp contrast to the
sentences preceding and following it.)

A slave may have a soul, and possess it in patience, but not an automaton. Made homogeneous by machinery, we have but one name now; we are the nation. And when our governing machines multiplying and expanding, claiming greater space for their wheels, flatten and unify still more the ancient, varied, and familiar things which we did not know were good till they had gone, we feel as though our identity will soon be traceless.—H. M. Tomlinson, A Lost Wood

(The third sentence shifts radically both in length and in structure—it is highly periodic in contrast with the two fairly loose sentences that precede it.)

The Greek notion of felicity, on the other hand, is perfectly conveyed in these words of a great French moralist: "C'est le bonheur des hommes,"—when? when they abhor that which is evil?—no; when they exercise themselves in the law of the Lord day and night?—no; when they die daily?—no; when they walk about the New Jerusalem with palms in their hands?—no; but when they think aright, when their thought hits: "quand ils pensent juste."—Matthew Arnold, Culture and Anarchy

(Here, the last sentence—presented as a clause in a compound sentence—is emphasized because of the shift to the declarative after a series of questions.)

Clearly there is something quite unusual about the voice of a first-class opera singer. Quite apart from the music, the intrinsic quality of such a voice can have a forceful impact on the listener. Moreover, a well-trained singer produces sounds that can be heard distinctly in a large opera house even over a high level of sound from the orchestra, and can do so week after week, year after year. If a second-rate singer or a completely untrained one tried to be heard over an orchestra, the result would be a scream and the singer's voice would soon fail. Is it only training that makes the difference? Or is the instrument that produces an excellent singer's voice itself different from other people's?—Johan Sundberg, The Acoustics of the Singing Voice

(In these sentences, questions become emphatic following declarative sentences.)

The whole thing was so familiar, the first feeling of oppression and heat and a general air around camp of not wanting to go very far away. In midafternoon (it was all the same) a curious darkening of the sky, and a lull in everything had made life tick; and then the way the boats suddenly swung the other way at their moorings with the coming of a breeze, out of the new quarter, and the premonitory rumble. Then the kettle drum, then the snare, then the bass drum and cymbals, then crackling light against the dark, and the gods grinning and lick-

ing their chops in the hills. Afterward the calm, the rain steadily rustling in the calm lake. . . .—E. B. White, Once More to the Lake

(In this paragraph, the sentence describing the storm is emphasized by the shift to metaphor.)

I can think of no one objection that will possibly be raised against this proposal, unless it should be urged that the number of people will be thereby much lessened in the kingdom. This I freely own, and it was indeed one principal design in offering it to the world. I desire the reader will observe, that I calculate my remedy for this one individual kingdom of Ireland and for no other that ever was, is, or I think ever can be upon earth. Therefore let no man talk to me of other expedients: of taxing our absentees at 5s. a pound: of using neither clothes or household furniture except what is of our own growth and manufacture: of utterly rejecting the materials and instruments that promote foreign luxury: of curing the expensiveness of pride, vanity, idleness, and gaming in our women: of introducing a vein of parsimony, prudence, and temperance: of learning to love our country, in the want of which we differ even from Laplanders and the inhabitants of Topinamboo: of quitting our animosities and factions. . . .—Jonathan Swift, A Modest Proposal

(Here is a great and classic example of shifting to increasing parallelism to emphasize an idea.)

THE PARAGRAPH

With paragraphs you can employ the same basic devices of emphasis that you use with words and sentences—*the devices of position, length, and stylistic shift.* To make one paragraph stand out above the other paragraphs around it, you can make sure the paragraph to be emphasized occurs first.

Position of Paragraph

A. In the face of an extended drought, lasting for some four months, the farmers of western Oklahoma felt compelled to support any rainmaking scheme that was presented to them. Though often their better judgment told them they were being foolish, they nevertheless crossed their fingers and hoped that somehow the normal meteorological laws might be suspended just for a little while, and that in some mysterious way rain might be made to fall.

B. First they tried the quack rainmakers. A veritable parade of idiots with vast complicated pseudoscientific instruments filed through western Oklahoma, all with confident promises that within twenty-four hours and with $2,000 cash they would make the clouds gather, the skies rumble, and the rain descend.

C. Second, the farmers tried prayer and fasting. Almost daily meetings were held in church, in revival tents, in the seclusion of pious homes, with increasingly thin and wan workers of the soil imploring God to soak the prairie good, to flood the creeks, to overlook their sins and meannesses just this once.

D. Third, they tried a whole week of imported Hopi Indian dances. Bedecked in colorful regalia, a dozen hardy old redskins picked up some easy cash by stomping around every afternoon from two until four, waving chicken feathers at the sun, hinting constantly that the gods would show great favor "in just the next few days."

E. Not until September, after all the crops were burned to a crisp, did the farmers give up on the rainmaking schemes and put their last and final trust in the inevitable laws of nature. When it was too late for hope, the farmers returned to reason. They simply waited, waited for the rain that had to come someday, the rain that would come in its own way, that they could not beguile by threats or pleas, proddings or entertainment.

In these five paragraphs a certain emphasis is achieved simply by location. Paragraphs *A* and *E*, first and last, have more attention-getting qualities to them than do paragraphs *B, C,* and *D*. The three middle paragraphs, however, form a composition unit of their own in which paragraphs *B* and *D* have more emphasis than does paragraph *C*.

Because of the emphatic position of paragraphs *A* and *E*, a reader is led to give his chief attention to the general situation, to the final triumph of reason, and is led to give less attention to the criticism of specific rainmaking schemes. Furthermore, the reader is led to give more attention to the first and third rainmaking schemes than to the second, a judicious decision on the part of a writer who may be aware of the religious sensibilities of his audience. The writer has, in effect, deemphasized his criticism of prayer and fasting by calling attention to other paragraphs.

Length of Paragraph

Another basic method to be used in emphasizing the paragraph is that of a difference in length. Let us suppose that in this five-paragraph composition you have decided that you want special attention given to paragraph *D*. Of the three rainmaking schemes criticized, you decide you want your reader to keep particularly in mind the effort of the Hopi Indians. You will have to rewrite the Hopi Indian paragraph so that it is longer than paragraphs *B* and *C*.

Third, they tried a whole week of imported Hopi Indian dances. Bedecked in colorful regalia—yellow head bands, green loin cloths, white moccasins—a dozen hardy old redskins picked up some easy cash by stomping around every afternoon from two until four, waving dyed chicken feathers at the sun, hinting constantly—by means of deep somber grunts—that the gods would show great favor "in just the next few days." The Indians even danced twice on Saturday, threw in a hot drummer, jazzed up the whole performance with a combo of gourd rattlers. But ne'er a drop did fall.

This paragraph now assumes an importance it did not previously have. You could even make the paragraph longer and thereby increase its emphasis—yet you must remember that each emphatic device has its limits—it must not violate the general harmony of a piece of writing. To make this one paragraph longer than all the rest of the composition would be ludicrous and totally ineffective.

Stylistic Shift

Finally, paragraphs can be emphasized by some change in writing style. By giving a paragraph a special stylistic flavor that its fellow paragraphs do not have, you call attention to it. Although numerous stylistic shifts can be made in paragraphs, the most frequently used are these: from random sentences to a definite pattern of sentences; from a nonmetaphorical style to a metaphorical style; from a standard diction to a more formal diction or a more colloquial diction.

The following paragraph groups give examples of various shifts from a prevailing paragraph style to a different or exceptional one:

A. If we arbitrarily divide novels into two classes—the succinct and the expansive—we may make the general observation that serious novels are moving away from the vast nineteenth-century panoramic style to a modern miniature manner. Not that the long novel has disappeared. Indeed great, rich novels are still written. But by and large a greater percentage of serious, worthwhile novels are on the brief, terse, intense side—more, indeed, than ever before. Since World War II, scarcely a single, long, in-depth novel has been a critical or popular success, while some of the most highly praised and most rapidly purchased novels have been thin little pieces of carefully controlled literature.

Perhaps, really, it is a question of time. Perhaps the shorter novel is increasingly popular because people have less time to spend in reading. Yet that explanation does not quite seem adequate when we consider the vast amounts of time that are now given to leisure pursuits in the Western world or when we consider the vast amounts of time people spend simply in the waste of television watching.

Even though our hurriedness may account in part for the short novel's popularity, some other issue must also be involved. I think the success of the short novel must be attributed to some more subtle psychological reality. I think it has something to do with a search for simplicity.

After all we are a hurried, harried, busy people on the move, busy solving new and complicated social problems, busy waging cold wars and hot little battles all over the world, struggling as always for a new and better materialism.

Here, the second paragraph represents a stylistic shift into a paragraph of sentence pattern. Whereas no patterning of the sentences occurs in the first paragraph, in the second paragraph a definite pattern, based upon sentence length, occurs—short to long to short.

B. Through even an inexpensive, two-inch reflecting telescope one can begin to see some of the treasures of the skies that would otherwise be invisible. With magnification of eighty to ninety times, the moon becomes an exciting new landscape of planes and curves, Saturn becomes the unbelievable spinning top of the heavens, and Jupiter becomes a vast world accompanied by her own set of moons. Though the small telescope may not penetrate very deeply into mysteries of the heavens, it does pull back the veil far enough to convince most viewers that they live in an unbelievably exciting universe, a universe that must not be accepted at face value, must not be accepted just for what it seems to the naked eye. The small telescope, properly used, may change one's mind about a lot of important things—things like religion and philosophy and beauty and truth and reality.

Thus a telescope, though small, is the magic wand that transforms. With it in our hands, we seem to change the very profile of the reality in front of us. And it is the magic key that opens. With it in our hands, we can open sealed dark doors and step into new rooms of mystery and splendor. And it is a Promethean torch that illuminates. With it in our hands, we kindle light in the dark corners of the universe and even in some of the dark corners of our own thinking. With it, for instance, Galileo kindled a fire against the dark shadows of his age, threw open a door into a bigger, more startling cosmos, transformed human vision so that people could see what they did not even know existed. And finally, a telescope is a veritable mirror that reflects, not only heavens into our eyes, but reveals to us our own image, our own greater image, the image of an increasingly enlightened mankind, for by seeking out the dimensions of our cosmic home, we more truly discover who we are.

(In the above case, the second paragraph represents a stylistic shift into a more intense metaphorical style.)

C. In October, the University announced its plans for a newly organized honors program to get under way at the beginning of the next academic year. The new program is essentially an accelerated version of the present honors system and is designed to serve the University's superior students more effectively. No freshman student may participate in the program, but any sophomore, with an A or A-minus average, may apply for admission. No more than fifty students will be admitted to the honors class in any one year, in order that the tutorial and seminar approach may be more frequently employed.

If the new honors program succeeds, the University will greatly benefit. If the new honors program fails, the University will have learned a profitable lesson. The question being asked is simply this: Do superior students deserve a more expensive education? Do they deserve a more difficult education? The University has decided to let the superior student answer the question, if he will. By giving the superior student a more flexible schedule, a more advantageous relationship with his instructors, a more challenging subject matter, a higher standard to meet, the University hopes the superior student will flourish as never before.

(The second paragraph in this pair is emphasized by a stylistic shift to a more formally constructed paragraph, with a greater use of balance and parallelism.)

SUMMARY CHECKLIST
Because emphasis is an important part of your writing technique, you should examine your composition and ask these questions.

1. Have I called adequate attention to the key ideas and statements in my composition? Will my reader know, without question, what points in my composition I consider truly important?
2. Have I, in particular, highlighted—using the devices of emphasis—those areas in my composition that should, if my composition is structurally sound, be of major significance?
3. Have I highlighted, emphasized the climax of my composition, that part of the composition that occurs at the end of the middle section? Have I emphasized my thesis? Have I emphasized those conclusions I have reached by logical argument?

4. Have I used my devices of emphasis liberally enough and with enough variation so that my composition is not simply a flat, barren plain of monotonous prose but has increasing peaks of interest and stylistic excitement?

THE WHOLE COMPOSITION

The following essay is not notably emphatic; that it contains not a single exclamation point is characteristic of its low-keyed appeal to sensibleness. And yet, despite the numerous allusions and anecdotes, you never lose sight of either the main point or its line of development. The subject, "self-respect," is alluded to in a sentence that is emphasized by its comparative brevity and by its prominent position as the final sentence of the first paragraph. And the repetition of "self-respect" throughout the essay keeps it before the reader.

You will recognize at once Joan Didion's use of such simple devices as italics (*"could not possibly respect themselves,"* for example), paired dashes (which set off and thereby emphasize "—the willingness to accept responsibility for one's own life—"), and the colon (in such lines as "To have that sense of one's intrinsic worth which constitutes self-respect is potentially to have everything: the ability to discriminate, to love and to remain indifferent").

The author frequently shifts to a noticeably shorter sentence (like "It does not at all") or to a longer one to achieve emphasis. In her hand the long periodic sentences and the frequent use of balance and parallelism are inevitably dramatic touches. And so are the metaphors, allusions, and anecdotes upon which the essay relies for much of its substance. (While emphasis is largely a matter of contrast, the energy and interest of Joan Didion's writing sustains a high level of intensity throughout.) After giving "On Self-Respect" a careful reading, can you explain how these devices of emphasis work and identify still others?

On Self-Respect

Joan Didion

Once, in a Dry Season, I wrote in large letters across two pages of a notebook that innocence ends when one is stripped of the delusion that one likes oneself. Although now, some years later, I marvel that a mind on the outs with itself should have nonetheless made painstaking record of its every tremor, I recall with embarrassing clarity the flavor of those particular ashes. It was a matter of misplaced self-respect.

I had not been elected to Phi Beta Kappa. This failure could scarcely have been more predictable or less ambiguous (I simply did not have the grades), but I was unnerved by it; I had somehow thought myself a kind of academic Raskolnikov, curiously exempt from the cause-effect relationships which hampered others. Although even the humorless nineteen-year-old that I was must have recognized that the situation lacked real tragic stature, the day that I did not make Phi Beta Kappa nonetheless marked the end of something, and innocence may well be the word for it. I lost the conviction that lights would always turn green for me, the pleasant certainty that those rather passive virtues which had won me approval as a child automatically guaranteed me not only Phi Beta Kappa keys but happiness, honor, and the love of a good man; lost a certain touching faith in the totem power of good manners, clean hair, and proven competence on the Stanford-Binet scale. To such doubtful amulets had my self-respect been pinned, and I faced myself that day with the nonplused apprehension of someone who has come across a vampire and has no crucifix at hand.

Although to be driven back upon oneself is an uneasy affair at best, rather like trying to cross a border with borrowed credentials, it seems to me now the one condition necessary to the beginnings of real self-respect. Most of our platitudes notwithstanding, self-deception remains the most difficult deception. The tricks that work on others count for nothing in that very well-lit back alley where one keeps assignations with oneself: no winning smiles will do here, no prettily drawn lists of good intentions. One shuffles flashily but in vain through one's marked cards—the kindness done for the wrong reason, the apparent triumph which involved no real effort, the seemingly heroic act into which one had been shamed. The dismal fact is that self-respect has nothing to do with the approval of others—who are, after all, deceived easily enough; has nothing to do with reputation, which, as Rhett Butler told Scarlett O'Hara, is something people with courage can do without.

To do without self-respect, on the other hand, is to be an unwilling audience of one to an interminable documentary that details one's failings, both real and imagined, with fresh footage spliced in for every screening. *There's the glass you broke in anger, there's the hurt on X's face; watch now, this next scene, the night Y came back from Houston, see how you muff this one.* To live without self-respect is to lie awake some night, beyond the reach of warm milk, phenobarbital, and the sleeping hand on the coverlet, counting up the sins of commission and omission, the trusts betrayed, the promises subtly broken, the gifts irrevocably wasted through sloth or cowardice or carelessness. However long we postpone it, we eventually lie down alone in that notoriously uncomfortable bed, the one we make ourselves. Whether or not we sleep in it depends, of course, on whether or not we respect ourselves.

To protest that some fairly improbable people, some people

who *could not possibly respect themselves,* seem to sleep easily enough is to miss the point entirely, as surely as those people miss it who think that self-respect has necessarily to do with not having safety pins in one's underwear. There is a common superstition that "self-respect" is a kind of charm against snakes, something that keeps those who have it locked in some unblighted Eden, out of strange beds, ambivalent conversations, and trouble in general. It does not at all. It has nothing to do with the face of things, but concerns instead a separate peace, a private reconciliation. Although the careless, suicidal Julian English in *Appointment in Samarra* and the careless, incurably dishonest Jordan Baker in *The Great Gatsby* seem equally improbable candidates for self-respect, Jordan Baker had it, Julian English did not. With that genius for accommodation more often seen in women than in men, Jordan took her own measure, made her own peace, avoided threats to that peace: "I hate careless people," she told Nick Carraway. "It takes two to make an accident."

Like Jordan Baker, people with self-respect have the courage of their mistakes. They know the price of things. If they choose to commit adultery, they do not then go running, in an access of bad conscience, to receive absolution from the wronged parties; nor do they complain unduly of the unfairness, the undeserved embarrassment, of being named co-respondent. In brief, people with self-respect exhibit a certain toughness, a kind of moral nerve; they display what was once called *character,* a quality which, although approved in the abstract, sometimes loses ground to other, more instantly negotiable virtues. The measure of its slipping prestige is that one tends to think of it only in connection with homely children and United States senators who have been defeated, preferably in the primary, for reelection. Nonetheless, character— the willingness to accept responsibility for one's own life—is the source from which self-respect springs.

Self-respect is something that our grandparents, whether or not they had it, knew all about. They had instilled in them, young, a certain discipline, the sense that one lives by doing things one does not particularly want to do, by putting fears and doubts to one side, by weighing immediate comforts against the possibility of larger, even intangible, comforts. It seemed to the nineteenth century admirable, but not remarkable, that Chinese Gordon put on a clean white suit and held Khartoum against the Mahdi; it did not seem unjust that the way to free land in California involved death and difficulty and dirt. In a diary kept during the winter of 1846, an emigrating twelve-year-old named Narcissa Cornwall noted coolly: "Father was busy reading and did not notice that the house was being filled with strange Indians until Mother spoke about it." Even lacking any clue as to what Mother said, one can scarcely fail to be impressed by the entire incident: the father reading, the Indians filing in, the mother choosing the words that would not alarm, the child duly recording the event and noting further that those particular Indians were not, "fortunately for us," hostile. Indians were simply part of the *donnée*.

In one guise or another, Indians always are. Again, it is a question of recognizing that anything worth having has its price. People who respect themselves are willing to accept the risk that the Indians will be hostile, that the venture will go bankrupt, that the liaison may not turn out to be one in which *every day is a holiday because you're married to me*. They are willing to invest something of themselves; they may not play at all, but when they do play, they know the odds.

That kind of self-respect is a discipline, a habit of mind that can never be faked but can be developed, trained, coaxed forth. It was once suggested to me that, as an antidote to crying, I put my head in a paper bag. As it happens, there is a sound physiological reason, something to do with oxygen, for doing exactly that, but the psychological effect alone is incalculable: it is difficult in the extreme to continue fancying oneself Cathy in *Wuthering Heights* with one's head in a Food Fair bag. There is a similar case for all the small disciplines, unimportant in themselves; imagine maintaining any kind of swoon, commiserative or carnal, in a cold shower.

But those small disciplines are valuable only insofar as they represent larger ones. To say that Waterloo was won on the playing fields of Eton is not to say that Napoleon might have been saved by a crash program in cricket; to give formal dinners in the rain forest would be pointless did not the candlelight flickering on the liana call forth deeper, stronger disciplines, values instilled long before. It is a kind of ritual, helping us to remember who and what we are. In order to remember it, one must have known it.

To have that sense of one's intrinsic worth which constitutes self-respect is potentially to have everything: the ability to discriminate, to love and to remain indifferent. To lack it is to be locked within oneself, paradoxically incapable of either love or indifference. If we do not respect ourselves, we are on the one hand forced to despise those who have so few resources as to consort with us, so little perception as to remain blind to our fatal weaknesses. On the other, we are peculiarly in thrall to everyone we see, curiously determined to live out—since our self-image is untenable—their false notions of us. We flatter ourselves by thinking this compulsion to please others an attractive trait: a gist for imaginative empathy, evidence of our willingness to give. *Of course* I will play Francesca to your Paolo, Helen Keller to anyone's Annie Sullivan:

no expectation is too misplaced, no role too ludicrous. At the mercy of those we cannot but hold in contempt, we play roles doomed to failure before they are begun, each defeat generating fresh despair at the urgency of divining and meeting the next demand made upon us.

It is the phenomenon sometimes called "alienation from self." In its advanced stages, we no longer answer the telephone, because someone might want something; that we could say *no* without drowning in self-reproach is an idea alien to this game. Every encounter demands too much, tears the nerves, drains the will, and the specter of something as small as an unanswered letter arouses such disproportionate guilt that answering it becomes out of the question. To assign unanswered letters their proper weight, to free us from the expectations of others, to give us back to ourselves— there lies the great, the singular power of self-respect. Without it, one eventually discovers the final turn of the screw: one runs away to find oneself, and finds no one at home.

Exercises

1. Write versions of the same sentence to exemplify each of the four methods of emphasizing words.

2. Write four paragraphs, each emphasizing the same sentence in a different way, to exemplify the four methods of emphasizing sentences.

3. Evaluate the emphasis achieved in the following paragraph. Which words seem emphasized? Which sentences? Does any one sentence seem more emphatic than the others to you?

Wiseman extends our understanding of our common life the way novelists used to—a way largely abandoned by the modern novel and left to the journalists but not often picked up by them. What he's doing is so simple and so basic that it's like a rediscovery of what we knew, or should know. We often want more information about the people and their predicaments than he gives, but this is perhaps less a criticism of Wiseman's method than it is a testimonial to his success in making us care about his subjects. With fictional movies using so little of our shared experiences, and with the bit TV news "specials" increasingly using that idiot "McLuhanite" fragmentation technique that scrambles all experience—as if the deliberate purpose were to make us indifferent to the life around us—it's a good sign when a movie sends us out wanting to know more and feeling that there is more to know. Wiseman is probably the most sophisticated intelli-

gence to enter the documentary field in recent years.—Pauline Kael,
High School and Other Forms of Madness

4. Identify the methods used to emphasize individual sentences in the following paragraphs. Then rewrite each of the paragraphs using yet other methods of emphasis.

Voltaire's *Candide* is probably the most enduring satire ever to be written upon the human experience in general. Though primarily an attack upon Leibniz's optimism, *Candide* manages to touch, scathingly, upon all our human foibles. So accurate is *Candide* in describing human error and stupidity that generation after generation recognizes itself within its pages. Other great satires have been written, of course, but *Candide* is without question the most widely read and the most widely understood.

I like to go to the park just to watch all the people having a good time. Most people seem to enjoy themselves thoroughly whenever they get out in the open. In the sunshine, among the trees and flowers, how impossible to be gloomy or depressed.

The airliner circled Le Bourget for a long thirty minutes, unable to descend because of low ceiling. At ten thirty, however, the fog lifted and ground control gave the go-ahead for an immediate landing. At exactly ten thirty, the big jet-engined bird swooped down from the skies, gently touched earth, shook its great wings, and settled to rest.

The candle had burned itself out. The room had fallen into utter darkness. If ever a ghost were going to appear, now was the time for it.

5. Identify the methods used to emphasize paragraphs and sentences in a short article or essay of your choosing; point out the methods used to emphasize words in one of the paragraphs.

6. Can you think of still other means for achieving emphasis, unconventional and impractical perhaps, but possible—like colored inks, appropriately scented paper, pop-up figures on the order of those in children's books? Discuss some possibilities. Possibly try out your favorite. Writing is not always confined to even lines of text on white paper. And with the newer printing equipment you are going to see increasingly more of such experiment—usually for empahsis.

7. Consider the outlines you wrote earlier (Chapter 6, exercise 7): What paragraphs do you wish to emphasize? What methods will you employ?

8. THE RHETORICAL PROFILE

In all our writing efforts, we try to adjust our style, so far as possible, to the needs of the moment. Obviously, we write for different people at different times, write about different subjects and theses on different occasions. And we try to take the "differences" into consideration as we establish the style for a particular composition. A good writer is a flexible writer: as we give thought to particular rhetorical situations we do what we can with both the *level* and the *texture* of our style to give our composition just the right profile, just the right stylistic quality that will make the composition both accessible and meaningful to its intended readers.

Your writing has a rhetorical profile whether you try to attain it or not. If it is an effective profile, it will be appropriate to your subject, harmonious within itself, and consistently maintained throughout your piece of writing.

Rhetorical profile is established primarily by the quality of diction, the general structure and length of sentences, the structure and length of paragraphs, and the quantity of metaphor and other poetic devices. What you do in these four areas creates the general style of your prose.

Even within the limits of journalistic prose, different rhetorical profiles can be created by changing your way of writing:

On May 2, Tim Hagerty announced his candidacy for the United States Senate. Mr. Hagerty is a life-time resident of Brownsville, Ohio, and he has served seven terms as mayor of that city. He is owner of the Brownsville Hardware Store and is a prominent figure in the Methodist Layman's League. He is married and has five children and two grandchildren. Mr. Hagerty's campaign headquarters will be located in the First National Bank Building, with Mrs. Oliver Smith acting as campaign manager.

Tim Hagerty plunged into politics like a daredevil swimmer attacking the Atlantic Ocean. Trumpeting the news of his candidacy for the United States Senate, Hagerty quickly swung open, early May 3, the doors at his campaign headquarters in the First National Bank Building and put Mrs. Oliver Smith in charge of all the inevitable shenanigans and maneuverings that make a political campaign what it is. Hagerty is no greenhorn in politics, of course. A Brownsvillian all his life, Hagerty ran city hall for over a decade as "his honor the mayor." Nor is Hagerty lacking in the characteristics a good politician needs: he's married, he's the proud father of five, the prouder grandfather of two, he's a successful businessman, and he's managed to keep a finger or two in such upstanding organizations as the Methodist Layman's League.

Timothy Hagerty, a life-time resident of Brownsville, Ohio, and seven times that city's mayor, announced on May 2 his candidacy for the United States Senate. Owner of the Brownsville Hardware Store, a prominent Methodist layman, father of five and grandfather of two, Mr. Hagerty has established campaign headquarters in the First National Bank Building, with Mrs. Oliver Smith in charge.

These paragraphs, though saying just about the same thing, differ distinctly in their manner. The first is ordinary, straightforward, flat. The second is breezy, slangy, excited. The third is restrained, distant, formal.

Actually, there are two basic ways of identifying any given rhetorical profile: you can identify the *level* and you can identify the *texture*. There are three standard and traditional levels—formal, informal, and colloquial. And there are three general categories of texture—elaborate, common, and restrained. The categories in either case are, of course, arbitrary, for a profile occurs more on a spectrum than in clearly delineated groups.

In the paragraph examples concerning Mr. Hagerty's candidacy, you would probably identify the first as informal in level, restrained in texture; the second as colloquial in level, elaborate in texture; the third as formal in level, common in texture.

LEVEL

Though no precise formula can be given as to when you should use a particular level of style, you can keep this general principle in mind: The more educated your audience and the more serious your subject matter, the more inclined you should be to increase the formality of your composition.

Speaking to a highly intelligent audience on a very serious subject, you would speak on the formal level; you certainly would not speak colloquially. Speaking to an uneducated audience, however, even if on a serious subject, you might possibly speak on the colloquial or informal level. Again, experience will be your teacher.

Your first task is to be able to write on various levels so that you can make the adjustment to audience and subject that finally seems best to you.

The Formal Level

You can achieve a formal level of writing if, first of all, you establish a formal diction. Without necessarily seeking to use "big words" exclusively, you certainly can include less familiar words *(magnitude, raze, sporadic)* and words outside everyday usage ("Relatively unorthodox events seemed to occur every time the professor announced an examination," "The committee authorized our firm to raze the building in as expeditious a way as possible"). You can also use words more Greco-Latin than Anglo-Saxon in etymology *(veritable, community, vital, hydraulic, angel, citizen, patriotic, dental, urban, luxurious)* and words frequently more polysyllabic than monosyllabic *(polychromous, antiquarian, orientation;* "The professors frequently commented on their different experiences"). At the same time you will want to avoid contractions, slang, or regional idioms, and you will want to avoid using the impersonal *you.* Here is a paragraph written with formal diction:

This attitude of mind is not peculiar to historians. In every field of intellectual activity, men of science are reconstructing the cosmos in terms of the evolutionary hypothesis. We are most of us quite proud of having reduced the universe to unstable equilibrium, and yet there is one thing that seems to be exempt from the operation of this law of change and adaptation which incessantly transforms everything else—truth itself: everything is unstable except the idea of instability. It is true, the Pragmatists are asking whether, if everything is subject to the law change, truth be not subject to the law of change, and reality as well—the very facts themselves. But whatever scientists may think of this notion, historians have not yet been disturbed by it. For them, certainly, truth is a fixed quality: the historical reality, the "fact," is a thing purely objective, that does not change; a thing, therefore, that can be established is this idea, that it has been formulated in a law of history.—Carl L. Becker, Detachment and the Writing of History

In addition to using a formal diction, you can also achieve formality in your writing if you write more substantial sentences than usual; use abundantly the full range of grammatical types—compound, complex, compound-complex; and frequently use periodic sentences—that is, sentences of some length that delay stating the subject and predicate to the very end. ("After the show, unable to get a cab and realizing the hotel was only seven blocks away, he decided to walk.") Usually you should write longer and more involved paragraphs.

These are not all the things you can do to be formal, but they are clues, in general, to the formal manner.

Here are two paragraphs that give a taste of the formal. In these paragraphs you will recognize some of the things done and some of the things not done in order to maintain the desired level.

The atmosphere of education in which he lived was colonial, revolutionary, almost Cromwellian, as though he were steeped, from his greatest grandmother's birth, in the odor of political crime. Resistance to something was the law of New England nature; the boy looked out on the world with the instinct of resistance; for numberless generations his predecessors had viewed the world chiefly as a thing to be reformed, filled with evil forces to be abolished, and they saw no reason to suppose that they had wholly succeeded in the abolition; the duty was unchanged. That duty implied not only resistance to evil, but hatred of it. Boys naturally look on all force as an enemy, and generally find it so, but the New Englander, whether boy or man, in his long struggle, with a stingy or hostile universe, had learned also to love the pleasure of hating; his joys were few.—Henry Adams, The Education of Henry Adams

Philosophiren, *says Novalis, is* dephlegmatisiren, viviciciren. *The service of philosophy, or speculative culture, towards the human spirit, is to rouse, to startle it to a life of constant and eager observation. Every moment some form grows perfect in hand or face; some tone on the hills or the sea is choicer than the rest; some mood or passion or insight or intellectual excitement is irresistibly real and attractive to us—for that moment only. Not the fruit of experience, but experience itself, is the end. A counted number of pulses only is given to us of a variegated, dramatic life. How many we see in them all that is to be seen in them by the finest senses: How shall we pass most swiftly from point to point, and be present always at the focus where the greatest number of vital forces unite in their purest energy?*—*Walter Pater,* The Renaissance

The Informal Level

To achieve an informal level of style, you can do the following: You can use a medium-quality diction—that is, some contractions *(can't, isn't, we're);* some popular idioms *(out and around, get in touch with, figure out)* but less real slang and an avoidance of the more radical neologisms; a more equal mixture of Greco-Latin and Anglo-Saxon words than you maintained on the formal level *(city, walk, cattle, beef);* a more equal mixture of monosyllabic and polysyllabic words *(fright, despair, inconvenience, joy, intrepid, kind;* "The boy advertised his talents in the school paper"); and words from a more ordinary vocabulary *(advertise, consideration, sidewalk, business)* with a mixture of the familiar and less-than-familiar words ("Reverence for life is a doctrine that many religious persons profess"). You may, if you wish, make judicious use of the impersonal *you.* Here is a paragraph that makes use of informal diction:

I've often thought that we should all try to support at least one philanthropic organization in our community. I know we all have plenty of demands made upon our pocketbook, but nevertheless, we should all try to do something worthwhile—and not just individually. I can't afford to build a hospital all by myself, but by giving to the Community Hospital Society, I can contribute to better medical services in our town. By channeling our money into responsible organizations, we can do together many of the fine things we couldn't do by ourselves.

As for sentences on the informal level, write those that are more definitely simple—though you can still use, of course, a fair share of complex and compound sentences. You can use both loose and periodic sentences, but will tend toward the loose. You can write sentences that average out at about a dozen words in length. ("No one could say why he had come. Uninvited, he showed up at the party just as though he were an honored guest. But what were we to do? He obviously was unwilling to leave, and we, obviously, were unprepared to evict him.") Your paragraphs can be of ordinary length—say seven to ten sentences.

The following paragraphs demonstrate the informal level of writing:

In the course of a day's walk, you see, there is much variance in the mood. From the exhilaration of the start, to the happy phlegm of the arrival, the change is certainly great. As the day goes on, the traveller moves from the one extreme towards the other. He becomes more and more incorporated with the material landscape, and the open-air drunkenness grows upon him with great strides, until he posts along the road, and sees everything about him, as in a cheerful dream. The first is certainly brighter, but the second stage is more peaceful. A man does not make so many articles towards the end, nor does he laugh aloud; but the purely animal pleasures, the sense of physical well-being, the delight of every inhalation, of every time the muscles tighten down the thigh, console him for the absence of the others, and bring him to his destination still content.—Robert Louis Stevenson, Walking Tours

There is, in fact, considerable mobility between vocations. I, for one, started out as a scientist and wound up, for various reasons—not wholly voluntary—working at a desk instead of a laboratory bench. Several promising engineers and administrators have left us for the ministry or for teaching. We have a few who have reversed the procedure.

So, if we can concede that people in the main have decent, honorable, and reasonable standards of taste and behavior, I think we can say that those in the business world average out at about the same level as any other. Any disfigurement which society may suffer will come from man himself, not from the particular vocation to which he devotes his time.—Crawford H. Greenewalt, The Culture of the Businessman

The Colloquial Level

As for the colloquial level, you can use a low or popular level of diction—that is, ordinary and simple words in general use, words that individually are of great familiarity *(hope, friendship, advertisements, night, day, airplane, car, children, music);* a good many slang phrases and popular idioms *(moonlighting, jet set, man, A-okay, get away with it, dig in).* But note: Popular street expressions have a way of becoming respectable; words that were colloquial diction last year may suddenly be informal diction this year; you have to pay attention to language if you want to be up to date, to recognize an idiom. On the colloquial level, you can also use, without restraint, the impersonal *you.* Here is a paragraph written with colloquial diction:

Man, what a time we had! You can't say we were scared, but when Charlie said he heard a bobcat out in the bushes, we sure decided to get out of there. I'm a city boy and not a bit equipped to deal with the wild animal forces of the natural world. I admit I was one of the first to hightail it out of the tent, into the car, and back to town.

You can have the woods. I'll take the good old steel and concrete of the metropolis.

You can, on the colloquial level, also maintain a rather steady flow of short, simple sentences—or long, loose sentences of a rambling quality, and created simply by compounding a great number of simple sentences. ("I told him I wouldn't go. I don't like night fishing. I'd rather watch TV than sit out on some dirty river bank and wait for a catfish to take a nibble at my line and then to find out it got away anyhow.") Your paragraphs will generally be short and simple.

These paragraphs are written on the colloquial level—the second two more so than the first:

Every year since I've lived in Arkansas, I've had the urge to pick cotton. Everyone I know picked cotton in his or her youth, and speaks with nostalgia of the good times and the fun. "You never picked cotton?" is asked in a "You poor thing. What kind of childhood did you have?" voice. My miserable, deprived childhood barely even hinted that cotton grew anywhere except in the medicine chest.—Dorothy Otis Wyre, Cotton Picker

Madrid is a mighty pretty place. You will see the time soon when there will be a tremendous Tourist travel to Spain. But you sure want to get ready to change your hours. Shows start in the Theaters at night at a quarter of eleven, and then nobody comes in till the second act, about 12 o'clock. Dinner is never before 9:30 or 10 o'clock at night.

The most miserable and lonesome half day I ever spent in my life was one morning in Madrid. I got up at 8:30 and went out on the street. Well, from then to noon I had Madrid entirely to myself. They commenced piling out for Coffee about eleven. That don't mean the working people don't work; they do. You will see them going to it at night in the fields and in the city up to and after nine o'clock.—Will Rogers, Letters of a Self-made Diplomat to His President

In creating these various rhetorical levels, you can make special use of the difference that exists between *contracted* and *uncontracted words* and the difference between the *third person singular pronoun* and the *second person impersonal* you. In these differences, you can find a helpful device in distinguishing between the rhetorical levels.

Contractions

You will certainly want to keep a full measure of contractions in your dictional equipment. Save on the formal level, contractions are always acceptable and they offer you some definite stylistic advantages. Contractions can help establish the colloquial or informal level of your composition, and they also offer a valuable contrast to noncontracted expressions: by having on hand both *do not go* and *don't go,* you can more easily establish a norm from which to deviate for variation or emphasis; "Do not go near the water," for instance, may be forcefully emphatic in a context in which contractions abound, or "Don't go near the water" may be forcefully intimate, even emotional, in a context in which contractions do not appear. Contractions, in other words, provide alternatives, help give you a greater choice in diction—and choice is always good.

You can use contractions, also, to help preserve the rhythm of your sentences. Many times *let's, can't,* or *won't* will simply permit a sentence to flow more easily than would *let us, cannot, will not.*

Note, however, that too many contractions and their cluttering apostrophes—"Let's build a fence so those who can't read won't go near the water"—may run counter to your purpose by slowing your reader to an unconversational pace.

Here are three paragraphs showing how level can vary simply as a result of using or not using contractions:

Some of our members simply will not volunteer to take part in the food bazaar we have planned for next Saturday afternoon. They claim they have done all they intend to do for the organization— that they have already been worked to the limit of their energies. What do you think we should do? Should we or should we not demand their resignation?

Some of our members simply will not volunteer to take part in the food bazaar we've planned for next Saturday afternoon. They claim they've done all they intend to do for the organization—that they've already been worked to the limit of their energies. What do you think we should do? Should we or should we not demand their resignation? [Note the emphasis now given to those phrases left uncontracted.]

Some of our members simply won't volunteer to take part in the food bazaar we've planned for next Saturday afternoon. They claim they've done all they intend to do for the organization—that they've already been worked to the limit of their energies. What do you think we should do? Should we or shouldn't we demand their resignation?

The Impersonal *You*

You can use the impersonal *you* to indicate colloquial or informal levels of diction and to establish something of a pseudo-personal, even confidential, tone in your writing. Whereas you would say in formal writing, "If one wants to develop an effective prose style, one should begin by reading widely and critically," you are certainly entitled, in less formal composition, to shift to the second person, "If you want to develop an effective prose style, you should begin by reading widely and critically."

There are some dangers, however: *You must not confuse the impersonal* you *with the personal* you; on those rare occasions when your composition is directed to and refers to a specific, named audience, you may run into the awkward situation of saying in one sentence, "Those of you gathered here tonight," and in another sentence, "You are never sure, in this world, about the loyalty of your friends," leaving the reader uncertain as to the meaning of the second *you.*

And *you should not shift back and forth in the same composition between the third person and the impersonal* you. The effect of such a passage as this—"One can never find in youth any real happiness. You may look all you want, but you always have to accept a substitute for happiness. One finds happiness only in maturity, because in maturity you are at last ready fully to appreciate and respond to the experiences of life"—is not variety but confusion.

Here are two paragraphs demonstrating the acute change in level as a result of shifting from the third person singular to the impersonal *you.*

When a person comes to the end of his college days, he often feels compelled to take a backward look over the four most important years in his life. He begins to examine all his courses in a new light, to weigh them by new standards of measurement. He begins to evaluate professors with a new and sympathetic eye, to overlook what once was dull and onerous, to concentrate upon what now seems to be wisdom and insight. And as he walks away from classrooms and laboratories and libraries of his college, the new graduate begins to treasure what once he scorned.

When you come to the end of your college days, you often feel compelled to take a backward look over the four most important years in your life. You begin to examine all your courses in a new light, to weigh them by a new standard of measurement. You begin to evaluate professors with a new and sympathetic eye, to overlook what once was dull and onerous, to concentrate upon what now seems to be wisdom and insight. And as you walk away from classrooms and laboratories and libraries of your college, you begin to treasure what once you scorned.

TEXTURE

Just as certain subjects and audiences call for compositions to be written at certain levels, they also call for compositions to be written with certain textures—certain degrees of richness and intricacy. In general, you can *increase* the elaborateness and intricacy of your composition's texture as the simplicity and clarity of your subject matter increases. Vice versa, you can *decrease* the richness and complexity of your composition's texture as you deal with subject matter of a more complex and difficult nature.

Your control of texture will come primarily with your control of diction, and in writing effectively, you must be prepared to increase—or decrease—the general vividness and intensity of your vocabulary as the occasion demands. You will, in general, always be moving toward a more elaborate diction if you do the following things:

Make your nouns more specific. You can achieve increasing vividness and intensity by moving from *person* to *man* to *author, novelist, W. Somerset Maugham*. A general word (like *person*) applies to many, while a specific word *(W. Somerset Maugham)* applies to only one.

Make your nouns more concrete. You can achieve increased vividness by moving from *beauty* to *clouds* to *thunderhead*. An abstract word *(beauty)* refers to the quality of physical things, while a concrete word *(thunderhead)* refers to the physical thing itself and the sights, sounds, smells, and other sensations associated with it.

(Note: You can, of course, use both specific and general nouns, both abstract and concrete nouns in your writing; if you limited yourself to using only specific and concrete words, you would write only in a matter-of-fact way about physical realities; if you limited yourself to only indefinite and abstract nouns, you would write only in a nebulous, vague way about ideas, concepts, and qualities. But to achieve an elaborate texture, you move in a direction of the definite, specific, concrete noun; to simplify texture you move toward the broad, general, abstract noun.)

Here are two paragraphs, the first of low dictional texture, the second of increased intensity as the result of moving the nouns to the more vigorous end of the noun spectrum:

The country store was an interesting place to visit. In the very heart of the city, it had the air of a small-town grocery store combined with a feed and hardware supply house. There were flower seeds and milk churns, coal buckets and saddle blankets, all mixed together. Walking down the crowded aisles, you felt you had gone back to the past—to the time of pot-belly stoves and kerosene lamps and giant pickle jars. You could smell the grain, you could touch the harnesses, you could even sit down in the old wooden chair. When you finally left the store and were once more in the activity of the city, you felt as you sometimes do when you come out of an old movie into the bright light of reality.

Charlie's Country Store was an interesting *emporium*. In the very heart of Minneapolis, Charlie's had the *charm* of a small-town *grocery* combined with a feed and hardware supply house. There were flower seeds and milk churns, coal buckets and saddle blankets, all mixed together. Walking down its crowded *passageways,* you felt you had gone back to *nineteenth-century America*—to the *lost years* of pot-belly stoves and kerosene lamps and giant pickle *crocks*. You could smell the *cornmeal,* you could touch the harnesses, you could even sit down in the old wooden *rocker.* When you finally left this anachronism and were once more in the *bustle* of the city, you felt as you sometimes do when you come out of an old *cinema* into the bright *glare* of reality.

Make your adjectives more specific. You can achieve increasing vividness by moving from "red" to "crimson," from "a few" to "seven," from "an ugly pine" to "a lifeless, sterile pine" to "a lightning-struck, sparsely needled pine." The more specific your adjective the more definitely in focus does your statement become.

Present your adjectives in varied form. By moving from the simple, ordinary adjective-in-front-of-the noun presentation of your modifiers, you achieve a richer and therefore more elaborate diction. Remember you have all of these possibilities for adjective placement: "the sweet candy" (adjective-noun); "the sweet and sticky candy" (adjective, adjective, noun); "the sweet, sticky candy" (adjective, adjective, noun); "the sweet candy and the sticky" (adjective, noun, adjective); "the candy, sweet and sticky" (noun, adjective, adjective).

Note: By showing the definite qualities of nouns, adjectives make *them* more specific and concrete—"watery horizon," "taciturn chap," "the girl, aloof and confident." Adjectives are used not only to tell what kind, but to tell how many ("several days") and which one ("first snowfall"). They can be used to modify either nouns ("A lone, sparsely needled, wind-contorted pine dominated the ridge") or pronouns ("He was inscrutable"). They may be single words ("He practices high living and plain thinking"), phrases ("The clouds in the west are cumulonimbus"), or clauses ("The man who passed is evidently a native").

Beware, however, of being trapped by the ease with which you can use adjectives. Don't overuse adjectives by attaching them to every noun in a piece of description.

An ancient Roman fountain with its sparkling jets, gleaming rocks, and undulating sheen was the chief attraction of the unfrequented square. (Rather write: "A Roman fountain with its sparkling jets, gleaming rocks, and undulating sheen monopolized the square.")

And don't overuse them by piling them on the nouns:

An old, gnarled, apple tree, covered with pink blossoms, grew near the front stoop of the grey, weather-beaten Pennsylvania Dutch farmhouse. (Decide what you want to emphasize and concentrate on that: "An old, gnarled apple tree, covered with pink blossoms, grew near the farmhouse stoop.")

Avoid the series of nouns used as adjectives:

He is a Yale graduate-school English professor. (It would be less awkward and confusing to write either, "He is an English professor in Yale's graduate school," or "He is a product of Yale's graduate school and an English professor.")

Do not use an adjective at all when the noun alone would do the job:

His petulant behavior was very irritating to me. ("His petulance irritated me" suffices.)

And don't use those tired inexact adjectives, like *beautiful* and *good*, or those adjectives that stick like leeches to certain nouns, as *shrewd move, bitter attack, important factor.*

Here are two paragraphs, the second of more elaborate dictional texture because of a greater concern with the adjectives:

Charlie's Country Store was an interesting emporium. In the very heart of Minneapolis, Charlie's had the charm of a small-town grocery combined with a feed and hardware supply house. There were flower seeds and milk churns, coal buckets and saddle blankets, all mixed together. Walking down its crowded passageways, you felt you had gone back to nineteenth-century America—to the lost years of pot-belly stoves and kerosene lamps and giant pickle crocks. You could smell the cornmeal, you could touch the harnesses, you could even sit down in the old wooden rocker. When you finally left this anachronism—and were once more in the bustle of the city—you felt as you sometimes do when you come out of an old cinema into the bright glare of reality.

Charlie's Country Store was a *spell-binding* emporium. In the very heart of Minneapolis, Charlie's had the *dubious* charm of a small-town grocery combined with a feed and hardware supply house. There were *zinnia* seeds and milk churns, *shiny* coal buckets and *garish* saddle blankets, all mixed together. Walking down its *quaint* passage-ways—*narrow, poorly lighted, but nevertheless immaculate*—you felt you had gone back to nineteenth-century America—to the lost years, the *faintly remembered* days of *squat* pot-belly stoves and *sturdy* kerosene lamps and *rotund, ceramic* crocks—meant for pickles or pastries. You could smell the cornmeal, you could touch the *leather* harnesses, you could even sit down in the *stern* wooden rocker. And when you finally left this anachronism—and were once more in the bustle of the city—you felt as you sometimes do when you come out of an old cinema into the *blinding* glare of a *rocket-age* reality.

Make your verbs more specific. You can achieve increasing vividness and intensity by moving from *went* to *walked* to *strolled* (or any one of the other possibilities: *ambled, crawled, crept, hurried, hustled, paced, ran, rushed, sauntered, shuffled, slouched, staggered, stumbled, tiptoed, tripped, trotted, weaved*), or moving from *look* to *peer*, from *sit* to *slouch*.

Make your verbs more active. You can achieve increasing intensity by moving from forms of the verb *to be* to more active, though ordinary verbs; to those highly volatile verbs that indicate some definite action: "He is a fast driver," to "He speeds down the highways," to "He jets down the turnpike." You can readily see the increasing elaborateness in these sets of verbs: *is, am, are, was, have been—come, sit run, go, say, laugh—spit, careened, jabbed, pounded, slouched, collapsed.*

(*Note:* You will use all verbs, of course, from the forms of the verb *to be*—undoubtedly the weakest of verbs as far as stylistic intensity is concerned, and therefore never to be used more than 50 percent of the time!—through a whole wide world of ordinary verbs, to the treasure house of intense, truly active, dynamic verbs. But to achieve textual elaboration, you will always move up the spectrum in the direction of specific, action verbs; to simplify texture you will move toward the weak, being verbs.)

Here are three paragraphs, indicating the increasingly elaborate texture that can be achieved simply by altering the verbs:

Charlie's Country Store was an interesting emporium. In the very heart of Minneapolis, Charlie's had the charm of a small-town grocery combined with a feed and hardware supply house. There were flower seeds and milk churns, coal buckets and saddle blankets, all mixed together. Walking down its crowded passageways, you felt you had gone back to nineteenth-century America—to the lost years of pot-belly stoves and kerosene lamps and giant pickle crocks. You could smell the cornmeal, you could touch the harnesses, you could even sit down in the old wooden rocker. When you finally left this anachronism and were once more in the bustle of the city, you felt as you sometimes do when you come out of an old cinema into the bright glare of reality.

Charlie's Country Store *remained, always,* an interesting emporium. In the very heart of Minneapolis, Charlie's *possessed* the charm of a small-town grocery combined with a feed and hardware supply house. You *found* flower seeds and milk churns, coal buckets and saddle blankets, all mixed together. Walking down its crowded passageways, you felt you had returned to nineteenth-century America—to the lost years of pot-belly stoves and kerosene lamps and giant pickle crocks. You could smell the cornmeal, you could touch the harnesses, you could *settle down* in an old wooden rocker. When you finally left this anachronism and *stepped* once more into the bustle of the city, you felt as you sometimes do when you step out of an old cinema into the bright glare of reality.

Charlie's Country Store always *remained* an interesting emporium. In the very heart of Minneapolis, Charlie's *boasted* the charm of a small-town grocery combined with a feed and hardware supply house. You *discovered* flower seeds and milk churns, coal buckets and saddle blankets, all mixed together. *Sauntering* down its crowded passageways, you felt you *had wandered* back to nineteenth-century America—to the lost years of pot-belly stoves and kerosene lamps and giant pickle crocks. You could smell the cornmeal, you could *fondle* the harnesses, you could *snuggle into* the old wooden rocker. When you finally left this anachronism and *plunged* once more into the bustle of the city, you felt as you sometimes do when you step from an old cinema into the bright glare of reality.

Make judicious use of adverbs to lift the dictional texture indirectly. Adverbs can make verbs more specific by telling how ("tread lightly"), when ("playing tonight"), where ("swam there"), and how much ("less useful"). They can be used to modify not only verbs ("He writes well"), but adjectives ("She is an extremely handsome woman"), and other adverbs ("He writes rather badly").

Infrequently adverbs are also used to modify verbals ("By studying diligently he graduated with honors"; "The bride, smiling happily, clung to her husband's arm"; "Rover has learned to wait faithfully").

Adverbs may be single words ("The government he defied angrily"), phrases ("He yodeled with gusto"), or clauses ("The man flew because he loved the lonely heights").

An adverbial style, in which the qualities of things are combined with their actions, can be forcefully vivid and immediate. The verb in this sentence is rather flat: "The gunboat *Virginia* moved down the James." Changing the verb to something more specific, like "steamed," would be an improvement in the direction of elaboration, but with adverbs the sentence can be just as elaborate: "The gunboat *Virginia* moved slowly and cumbrously down the James."

Effective as they are in increasing texture, adverbs are risky. Many of the jaded verbs in your prose were seduced by a lone adverb. While "he walked slowly" is more descriptive than simply "he walked," it is not as descriptive as "he ambled." Before you permit an adverb to go with a verb, be sure the verb needs an escort. Most will not. Even more than adjectives, adverbs must be watched. Since most adverbs end in *ly,* it is usually easy to tell when they are being overworked in a sentence. The monotonous repetition of such sounds in "World War I crept quietly and relentlessly upon a morally unprepared Europe" warns that you have more than enough adverbs. "World War I crept quietly and relentlessly upon an unprepared Europe" is an improvement.

And especially avoid those tiresome intensifying adverbs—like *very, so,* and *really*—as well as those weakening adverbs which seem invariably to tag along with certain words—*fully recognize, seriously consider,* and *totally concerned.*

Make your whole dictional style more verbal-adverbial than adjectival. Whenever you can translate the adjectival expression—"the tall tree"—into a verbal one—"the tree towered"—your diction will be intensified. You can always make your diction more vivid and interesting by moving from neutrality, to adjectives, to adjectives supplanted by equally effective verbs and verbals: "The clouds were gathering overhead," "the dark clouds gathered overhead," "the clouds darkened overhead," or "the clouds gradually darkened overhead."

Here are three paragraphs in which an increasing textual elaboration is achieved by moving from a neutral style, to an adjectival style, to a verbal-adverbial style:

From the gardens of Chaillot, one can see the Eiffel Tower of Paris rising up through the trees. The tower is taller than any other structure in Paris, but because it is not an enclosed structure, it does not seem to hurt the Parisian skyline as perhaps it would if it were a solid block of masonry or steel. Rather, because it is open, it is almost like a lacework seen through the Chaillot greenery, and the tower gives to Paris that aura of lightness and loveliness that keeps one from thinking about the strength and sturdiness underneath.

From the *luxuriant* gardens of Chaillot, one can see the *incredible* Eiffel Tower of Paris rising up through the trees. The tower is taller than any other structure in Paris, but because it is not an enclosed structure, *opaque and ponderous,* it does not seem to hurt the gentle Parisian skyline as perhaps it would if it were a solid block of masonry or steel. Rather, because it is splendidly open, it is almost like a castle of *earth-colored* lace, seen through the Chaillot greenery, and the tower, *now aged and mellowed,* gives to Paris that *famous* aura of lightness and loveliness that keeps one from thinking about the *complex* strength and sturdiness underneath.

From the gardens of Chaillot, one can see the Eiffel Tower *sweeping incredibly* up through the trees. The tower *overshadows* any other structure in Paris, but because it is not an enclosed structure, it *fails to smudge* the Parisian skyline as perhaps it might if it *struggled skyward* as a solid block of masonry or steel. Rather, because it *climbs so openly* into the heavens, it *resembles* lacework seen through the Chaillot greenery, and the tower gives Paris that aura of lightness and loveliness that *prevents* one's pondering the strength and sturdiness underneath.

With all these dictional possibilities in mind, you can manage to establish fairly easily any one of the three standard textures that you may need on a particular writing occasion.

Elaborate Texture

To achieve an elaborate or intricate texture you can, first of all, employ a vivid diction. (You can use more active and vigorous verbs than usual—*dashed, wrangled, shiver, stream, protrude;* you can use very few forms of the verb *to be;* you can use a language generally more picturesque and sensory in quality—"a bevy of matrons," "a nauseating sunset," "regiments of cannas," "TV tremors"; you can use more varied and specific descriptive and modifying terms—"the grotesque music, dissonant and formless, spilled over the imprisoned audience.")

You can write sentences more balanced, definite, and parallel ("Having nowhere to go, nowhere to remain, I wandered aimlessly through the city's dark and empty streets"); you can make judicious use of the rhetorical question; and you can employ a great abundance of metaphors and poetic devices. And you can give attention to sound (alliteration, assonance) and rhythm.

Here are some paragraphs written with intricate or elaborate texture. Note, however, that the *level* of the writing differs in each case.

This is the difference between those two luminaries in literature, the well-accomplished scholar, and the divinely inspired enthusiast; the first *is, as the bright morning star; the* second, *as the rising sun. The writer who neglects these two rules above will never stand alone; he makes one of a group, and thinks in wretched unanimity with the throng: Incumbered with the notions of others, and impoverished by their abundance, he conceives not the least embryo of new thought; opens not the least vista thro' the gloom of ordinary writers, into the bright walks of rare imagination, and singular design; while the true genius is crossing all public roads into fresh untrodden ground; he, up to the knees in antiquity, is treading the sacred footsteps of great examples, with the blind veneration of a bigot saluting the papal toe; comfortably hoping full absolution for the sins of his own understanding, from the powerful charm of touching his idol's infallibility.—Edward Young,* Conjectures on Original Composition *[Formal level]*

This timeless Grecian Etna, in her lower-heaven loveliness, so lovely, so lovely, what a torturer! Not many men can really stand her, without losing their souls. She is like Circe. Unless a man is very strong, she takes his soul away from him and leaves him not a beast, but an elemental creature, intelligent and soulless. Intelligent, almost inspired, and soulless, like the Etna Sicilians. Intelligent daimons, and humanly, according to us, the most stupid people on earth. Ach, horror! How many men, how many races, has Etna put to flight? It was she who broke the quick of the Greek soul. And after the Greeks, she gave the Romans, the Normans, the Arabs, the Spaniards, the French, the Italians, even the English, she gave them all their inspired hour and broke their souls.—D. H. Lawrence, Sea and Sardinia *[Informal level]*

Challenged by "the new American leisure," we are a nation grimly rededicated. Horizontal, crammed with Miltown, we will relax or bust. Our emblem, in fact our uniform, is a politer pajama.

It just caught on, like rabbits in Australia or t.b. among the Eskimos. You can't blame Mr. Truman for the sport shirt. Nor is the dervish at fault who designs it; nor the woman who buys it; nor, certainly, the reclining American who wears it. . . . When he puts it on, he is not of sound mind. Lately mangled and extruded by the subway, railway, or parkway, he is weary, desperate, prone to grab at straws—in a word suggestible. He sheds his working get up and is reborn in another ritual garment, of spinnaker cut this time, and radio-active hue. He feels fine, now: comfortable, attractive, emancipated, off his feet.—Crary Moore, The Big Stop *[Informal to colloquial level]*

Common Texture

You can create common texture by using a more ordinary diction. (You can use a fair share of forms of the verb *to be;* both action and general words; nouns both general and specific. You can use a moderate amount of descriptive and modifying language with less adjectival variation than for elaborate texture.) You can write sentences with parallelism and balance—and without. You can use a scattering of metaphors.

Here are two paragraphs with common texture:

For the first day or two I felt stunned, overwhelmed. I could only apprehend my felicity; I was too confused to taste it sincerely. I wandered about, thinking I was happy, and knowing that I was not. I was in the condition of a prisoner in the Old Bastile, suddenly let loose after a forty years' confinement. I could scarce trust myself with myself. It was like passing out of Time into Eternity— for it is a sort of Eternity for a man to have his Time all to himself. It seemed to be that I had more time on my hands than I could ever manage. From a poor man, poor in Time, I was suddenly lifted up into a vast revenue; I could see no end of my possessions; I wanted some steward, or judicious bailiff, to manage my estates in Time for me.—Charles Lamb, The Superannuated Man *[Informal level]*

In Brownsville tenements the kitchen is always the largest room and the center of the household. As a child I felt that we lived in a kitchen to which four other rooms were annexed. My mother, a "home" dressmaker, had her workshop in the kitchen. She told me once that she had begun dressmaking in Poland at thirteen; as far back as I can remember, she was always making dresses for the local women. She had an innate sense of design, a quick eye for all the subtleties in the latest fashions, even when she despised them, and great boldness. For three or four dollars she would study the fashion magazines with a customer, go with the customer to the remnants store on Belmont Avenue to pick out the material, argue the owner down—all remnants stores, for some reason, were supposed to be shady, as if the owners dealt in stolen goods—and then for days would patiently fit and baste and sew and fit again.—Alfred Kazin, A Walker in the City *[Informal level]*

Restrained Texture

And, finally, to create a restrained texture, you can use relatively passive diction. (You can use few action verbs, a quantity of *being* verbs, a rather general vocabulary all around; you can use simple adjective modification—a single adjective in front of a noun, *the blue sky, the swirling clouds, the miserable child,* with no adjectival variation into double adjectives before the noun, or predicate adjectives, or adjectival prepositional phrases.) You can use few or no metaphors. You can avoid definite sound patterns or rhythms. And you can write ordinary sentences, without either balanced or parallel phrasing.

The following paragraphs are written with a restrained texture:

In its initial character, the gangster film is simply one example of the movies' constant tendency to create fixed dramatic patterns that can be repeated indefinitely with a reasonable expectation of profit. One gangster film follows another as one musical or one Western follows another. But this rigidity is not necessarily opposed to the requirements of art. There have been very successful types of art in the past which developed such specific and detailed conventions as almost to make individual examples of the type interchangeable. This is true, for example, of Elizabethan revenge tragedy and Restoration comedy.—Robert Warshow, The Gangster as Tragic Hero *[Informal level]*

What has been thus far said applies to Poetry in general; but especially to those parts of composition where the Poet speaks through the mouths of his characters; and upon this point it appears to authorize the conclusion that there are few persons of good sense, who would not allow that the dramatic parts of composition are defective, in proportion as they deviate from the real language of nature, and are colored by a diction of the Poet's own, either peculiar to him as an individual Poet or belonging simply to Poets in general; to a body of men who, from the circumstances of their compositions being in metre, it is expected will enjoy a particular language.—William Wordsworth, Preface to Lyrical Ballads *[Formal level]*

The combination of level and texture makes up the general rhetorical profile of a composition. Obviously, you have nine general profiles to use: formal, elaborate; formal, common; formal, restrained; informal, elaborate; informal, common; informal, restrained; colloquial, elaborate; colloquial, common; colloquial, restrained.

RHETORICAL PROFILE SELECTION

You should try to choose the profile that is most appropriate on any particular writing occasion. Each time you write, you should determine the general rhetorical situation—and hence the appropriate rhetorical profile—by asking yourself these questions: (1) For whom am I writing? (2) What am I trying to say to the reader? (3) What is the occasion for this particular communication? (4) What role do I play on this particular occasion in relation to my reader? Your answers to these questions will help to bring the rhetorical situation into focus—and will help you, in turn, determine the profile that you can most effectively use in the composition that you are preparing.

You may, for instance, determine that you are writing (1) for a teen-age audience, (2) about the need for better nursing care for the elderly, (3) at a high school conference on "Looking Ahead to Your Future in American Society," (4) which you are addressing as a representative of a particular religious denomination. Or you may determine that you are writing (1) as a college history major, (2) for a group of retired business people, (3) about the need to preserve historical buildings in American cities, (4) at a time when cities are tending to raze old downtown buildings in order to create modern pedestrian malls and the like.

Rhetorical situations vary a great deal, of course: Are you writing for young people or old people, educated people or uneducated people, city dwellers or country dwellers? Are you writing about a difficult complex subject or a well-known ordinary subject, about the deadly serious or the trivial, about a beloved American hero or about some unknown citizen? Are you writing on a highly public occasion or on a private occasion, writing an address to be read at a national conference or writing a message to be read at a friend's birthday party? Ar you writing as a teacher or as a student, as friend or foe, as "one of the group" or as an "outside authority figure"?

Most of the time, you may well write on the informal level with a common texture; this is the most prevalent rhetorical profile in writing and it will serve you well on most occasions. And you may well avoid, 90 percent of the time, those extreme profiles—elaborate formality or restrained colloquialism—simply because the one can become extremely high-flown, pompous, syrupy, or stiff, while the other can easily become dull, banal, lethargic, and boring.

Yet rhetorical situations do vary—and each time you write, you need to describe the rhetorical situation to yourself as clearly as possible and thus select the most fitting profile for the composition at hand. The judicious choice of profile must, ultimately, be the result of your observation of human beings, your own good taste, your awareness of how people respond to different writing manners. Only experience and practice will guide you to accurate decisions.

RHETORICAL CONSISTENCY

The choice of rhetorical profile, once made, becomes the prevailing manner of your piece of writing. One of the chief characteristics of a good piece of writing is its unity and consistency—that is, the same profile on the seventh page as on the third page. If you fail to achieve unity, your reader will become lost in a maze of seemingly unrelated rhetorical profiles, will be caught in a meaningless "up and down" of writing behavior. His constant readjustment to your diverse writing techniques will get in the way of his appreciation of your content and your ideas.

Unity of rhetorical profile does not mean, of course, that every last word must be colloquial level, common texture simply because the prevailing profile is so defined. But it does mean that colloquial level, common texture—once chosen—should remain your basic choice. Likewise, it does not mean that every last sentence will be formal, elaborate texture even if the prevailing profile happens to be so—but it does mean that your sentences *in general* should be of a formal and elaborate quality. Rhetorical unity does not mean that every paragraph will be the same length or be organized in the same way, but it does mean that your paragraphs will have a general rhetorical likeness about them.

Here are some paragraphs demonstrating both unity and disunity in the rhetorical profile:

Even a casual glance at a major book publisher's catalog nowadays informs one of the cultural revolution taking place in modern America. Aware that Americans are truly becoming "culture consumers," leading book publishers are reaching out into such formerly unprofitable areas as the literary classics, the anthropology monographs, and the political critiques. The publishers are turning out an increasingly wide range of tomes on every conceivable subject of interest to the serious-minded reader.

One can, also, simply make an examination of any bookstore or book-selling newsstand. Martin Buber, John Milton, and Margaret Mead are famous nowadays in every stall, on every shelf. Greek philosophy and natural history studies are no longer overwhelmed by the historical romance or the detective novel. Culture is becoming popular, and book publishers are busily making their contribution to this phenomenon of our times.

(Those two paragraphs maintain a fairly consistent profile—high informal level, of a common texture.)

Lady Fitzsimmons represents, without question, that quality of perfect gentility that once flourished but is now fast disappearing in both British and American social life. Lady Fitzsimmons exudes graciousness and warmth, has a real knack for making folks feel at home, and practices a genuine humility without stooping to weakness, officiousness, or stupidity. She's the most—anyway you look at it. Look at her recent behavior when attacked in the tabloids: not a word in reply, not a gesture in defiance, simply a quiet and serene waiting for the storm to pass. Lady Fitzsimmons may be an anachronism, but she is to be cherished nevertheless. She may be the last survivor of an age no longer possible, but as long as she is with us we ought to learn just as much as we can from her about living a really nice life and getting along with people.

(That paragraph has a totally mixed-up profile, wandering—for no purpose—from formality to colloquialism, from elaborate to restrained texture.)

Regardless of the profile you choose for any given composition, you should be committed to it after the first few paragraphs of your writing. The first few paragraphs of a composition tell the reader what kind of writing is going to prevail throughout. The reader is oriented to a writing manner; the profile is established. You must make sure, obviously, that the commitment given in the opening pages of your work matches the profile that actually maintains in the essay as a whole. You will have committed yourself, and you should not violate the promises you have made.

You cannot wait until a composition is half over to establish your rhetorical profile; as a writer you cannot fumble around with the profile, hoping to discover some prevailing writing manner along the way or hoping that a prevailing profile will somehow mysteriously evolve out of your composition. Even if you have no particular rhetorical profile in mind when you begin writing, after a few paragraphs—certainly with the completion of *the beginning*—you have no choice left. Whatever you have done in the beginning, you must do throughout the composition.

VARIATION

You will wish, of course, even as you maintain rhetorical unity, to avoid the sin of monotony. You will want—within the confines of your essay's profile—to achieve some sort of variety. If you fail to achieve variety, your reader may well fall asleep and never finish traveling the clean-swept road you have spread out for him. Though variety may seem to contradict the idea of unity, the two goals, unity and variety, are actually complementary. Variation within a prevailing profile does not mean total destruction of that profile. Unity can still prevail even though you throw in a few judicious curves along the road. There is a difference obviously between a calculated variation and a truly disrupting detour.

Within any one of the nine general categories of rhetorical profiles there is room for variation; one always has a choice of words, choice of sentence structures and lengths, paragraph structures and lengths, kinds of metaphors, degrees of metaphor, and the like. Though you may employ a highly sensory diction in order to establish an elaborate texture, you can keep in mind that human beings have five different senses. Not all your images need to be visual, or aural, or tactile. Though you may decide that simple short sentences will help you to establish the colloquial level you have in mind, you nevertheless can write a moderately long loose sentence once in a while; fifteen short simple sentences in a row would so blind your reader he wouldn't recognize one rhetorical profile from another.

Proper variation hangs on the prevailing, chosen manner of writing, but makes slight, easy gestures away from it, always returning very quickly, and never really violating the basic profile.

SUMMARY CHECKLIST

By the time you have completed the second draft of your composition, you should be able to identify the prevailing rhetorical profile of your essay and you should be able to check it out for unity, appropriateness, and variation.

Ask yourself these questions:

1. What is the rhetorical situation in which this composition will have to exist? Have I determined with some clarity (*a*) the kind of reader for whom I'm writing, (*b*) what it is I want to say, (*c*) why I am writing this composition at this particular time, (*d*) who I am in this particular situation?
2. What is the prevailing rhetorical profile of this composition?
3. Is the profile of this composition appropriate to the situation?
4. Is this profile affirmed by the time the beginning section of the composition has been read?
5. Is the profile—to which I committed myself in the beginning—maintained throughout the composition?
6. Do I maintain ample variation, variation that relieves monotony but does not violate unity?

THE WHOLE COMPOSITION

By using vigorous diction, rich metaphors, a wide variety of sentence forms, Dylan Thomas creates in this essay an elaborately textured piece of writing on the informal level. The opening sentence indicates the profile—with sharp vocabulary ("glazed," "heady supper"); metaphor and alliteration ("streams and sings"); and a carefully constructed circular journey from the opening phrase, "Across the United States of America," to the concluding phrase, "on the United States of America."

Such expressions as "on this and that," "on, say, ceramics," and "there they go" occur throughout the essay as constant reminder of level. Such expressions as "fat poets with slim volumes," "washing sherry," and "flush of ignorance and fluency" occur throughout as constant reminder of texture.

Certainly the use of dialogue, parenthetical expressions, mock nomenclature, rhetorical questions, paragraphs of sharply contrasting length—all these establish and maintain an exceptionally clear profile. You will recognize a good many more rhetorical devices contributing to texture as you read the composition.

A Visit to America

Dylan Thomas

Across the United States of America, from New York to California and back, glazed again, for many months of the year there streams and sings for its heady supper a dazed and prejudiced procession of European lecturers, scholars, sociologists, economists, writers, authorities on this and that and even, in theory, on the United States of America. And, breathlessly between addresses and receptions, in planes and trains and boiling hotel bedroom ovens, many of these attempt to keep journals and diaries. At first, confused and shocked by shameless profusion and almost shamed by generosity, unaccustomed to such importance as they are assumed, by their hosts, to possess, and up against the barrier of common language, they write in their note-books like demons, generalizing away, on character and culture and the American political scene. But, towards the middle of their middle-aged whisk through middle-western clubs and universities, the fury of the writing flags; their spirits are lowered by the spirit with which they are everywhere strongly greeted and which, in ever-increasing doses, they themselves lower; and they begin to mistrust themselves, and their reputations—for they have found, too often, that an audience will receive a lantern-lecture on, say, ceramics, with the same uninhibited enthusiasm that it accorded the very week before to a paper on the Modern Turkish Novel. And, in their diaries, more and more do such entries appear as "No way of escape!" or "Buffalo!" or "I am beaten," until at last they cannot write a word. And twittering all over, old before their time, with eyes like rissoles in the sand, they are helped up the gangway of the homebound liner by kind bosom friends (of all kinds and bosoms) who boister them on the back, pick them up again, thrust bottles, sonnets, cigars, addresses into their pockets, have a farewell party in their cabin, pick them up again, and, snickering and yelping, are gone: to wait at the dockside for another boat from Europe and another batch of fresh, green lecturers.

There they go, every spring, from New York to Los Angeles: exhibitionists, polemicists, histrionic publicists, theological rhetoricians, historical hoddy-doddies, balletomanes, ulterior decorators, in love with steaks, men after millionaires' widows, men with elephantiasis of the reputation (huge trunks and teeny minds), authorities on gas, bishops, best sellers, editors looking for dollars, existentialists, serious physicists with nuclear missions, men from B.B.C. who speak as though they had the Elgin Marbles in their mouths, potboiling philosophers, professional Irishmen (very lepri-corny), and I am afraid, fat poets with slim volumes. And see,

too, in that linguaceous stream, the tall monocled men, smelling of
saddle soap and club arm-chairs, their breath a nice blending of
whisky and fox's blood, with big protruding upper-class tusks and
county moustaches, presumably invented in England and sent
abroad to advertise *Punch,* who lecture to women's clubs on such
unlikely subjects as "The History of Etching in the Shetland
Islands." And the brassy-bossy men-women, with corrugated-iron
perms, and hippo hides, who come, self-announced, as "ordinary
British housewives," to talk to rich minked chunks of American
matronhood about the iniquity of the Health Services, the criminal
sloth of the miners, the visible tail and horns of Mr. Aneurin Bevan,
and the fear of everyone in England to go out alone at night
because of the organized legions of cosh boys against whom the
police are powerless owing to the refusal of those in power to equip
them with revolvers and to flog to ribbons every adolescent offender
on any charge at all. And there shiver and teeter also, meek and
driven, those British authors unfortunate enough to have written,
after years of unadventurous forgotten work, one bad novel which
became enormously popular on both sides of the Atlantic. At home,
when success first hit them, they were mildly delighted; a couple of
literary luncheons went sugar-tipsy to their heads, like the washing
sherry served before those luncheons; and perhaps, as the lovely
money rolled lushly in, they began to dream in their moony writers'
way, of being able to retire to the country, keep wasps (or was it
bees?), and never write another lousy word. But in come the literary
agent's triggermen and the publisher's armed narks: "You must go
to the States and make a Personal Appearance. Your novel is killing
them over there, and we're not surprised either. You must go round
the States lecturing to women." And the inoffensive writers, who've
never dared lecture anyone, let alone women—they are frightened
of women, they do not understand women, they write about women
as creatures that never existed, and the women lap it up—these
sensitive plants cry out. "But what shall we lecture about?"

"The English Novel."

"I don't read novels."

"Great Women in Fiction."

"I don't like fiction or women."

But off they're wafted, first class, in the plush bowels of the
Queen Victoria with a list of engagements long as a New York
menu or a half-hour with a book by Charles Morgan, and soon they
are losing their little cold-as-goldfish paw in the great general
glutinous handshake of a clutch of enveloping hostesses. I think, by
the way, that it was Ernest Raymond, the author of *Tell England,*
who once made a journey round the American women's clubs, being
housed and entertained at each small town he stopped at by the

richest and largest and furriest lady available. On one occasion he stopped at some little station, and was met, as usual, by an enormous motor-car full of a large hornrimmed business man, looking exactly like a large hornrimmed business man on the films—and his roly-poly pearly wife. Mr. Raymond sat with her in the back of the car, and off they went, the husband driving. At once, she began to say how utterly delighted she and her husband and the committee were to have him at their Women's Literary and Social Guild, and to compliment him on his books. "I don't think I've ever, in all my life, enjoyed a book so much as *Sorrel and Son*," she said. "What you don't know about human nature! I think Sorrel is one of the most beautiful characters ever portrayed."

Ernest Raymond let her talk on, while he stared, embarrassed, in front of him. All he could see were the three double chins that her husband wore at the back of his neck. On and on she gushed in praise of *Sorrel and Son* until he could stand it no longer. "I quite agree with you," he said. "A beautiful book indeed. But I'm afraid that I didn't write *Sorrel and Son*. It was written by an old friend of mine, Mr. Warwick Deeping."

And the large hornrimmed double-chinned husband at the wheel said without turning: "Caught again, Emily."

See the garrulous others, also, gabbing and garlanded from one nest of culture-vultures to another: people selling the English way of life and condemning the American way as they swig and guzzle through it; people resurrecting the theories of surrealism for the benefit of remote parochial female audiences who did not know it was dead, not having ever known it had been alive; people talking about Etruscan pots and pans to a bunch of dead pans and wealthy pots in Boston. And there, too, in the sticky thick of lecturers moving across the continent black with clubs, go the foreign poets, catarrhal troubadours, lyrical one-night-standers, dollar-mad nightingales, remittance-bards from at home, myself among them booming with the worst.

Did we pass one another, en route, all unknowing, I wonder, one of us, spry-eyed, with clean, white lectures and a soul he could call his own, going buoyantly west to his remunerative doom in the great State University factories, another returning dog-eared as his clutch of poems and his carefully typed impromptu asides? I ache for us both. There one goes, unsullied as yet, in his Pullman pride, toying, oh boy, with a blunderbuss bourbon, being smoked by a large cigar, riding out to the wide open spaces of the faces of his waiting audience. He carries, besides his literary baggage, a new, dynamic razor, just on the market, bought in New York, which operates at the flick of a thumb, but cuts the thumb to the bone; a tin of new shaving-lather which is worked with the other, unbleeding, thumb and covers not only the face but the whole bath-room and, instantly freezing, makes an arctic, icicled cave from which it takes two sneering bellboys to extract him; and, of course, a nylon shirt. This, he dearly believed from the advertisements, he could himself wash in his hotel, hang to dry overnight, and put on, without ironing, in the morning. (In my case, no ironing was needed, for, as someone cruelly pointed out in print, I looked, anyway, like an unmade bed.)

He is vigorously welcomed at the station by an earnest crewcut platoon of giant collegiates, all chasing the butterfly culture with net, note-book, poison-bottle, pin and label, each with at least thirty-six terribly white teeth, and is nursed away, as heavily gently as though he were an imbecile rich aunt with a short prospect of life, into a motor-car in which, for a mere fifty miles or so travelled at poet-breaking speed, he assures them of the correctness of their assumption that he is half-witted by stammering inconsequential answers in an over-British accent to the genial questions about what international conference Stephen Spender might be attending at the moment or the reactions of British poets to the work of a famous American whose name he did not know or catch. He is then taken to a small party of only a few hundred people all of whom hold the belief that what a visiting lecturer needs before he trips on to the platform is just enough martinis so that he can trip off the platform as well. And, clutching his explosive glass, he is soon contemptuously dismissing, in a flush of ignorance and fluency, the poetry of those androgynous literary ladies with three names who produce a kind of verbal ectoplasm to order as a waiter dishes up spaghetti—only to find that the fiercest of these, a wealthy huntress of small, seedy lions (such as himself), who stalks the middle-western bush with ears and rifle cocked, is his hostess for the evening. Of the lecture he remembers little but the applause and maybe two questions: "Is it true that the young English intellectuals are really psychological?" or, "I always carry Kierkegaard in my pocket. What do you carry?"

Late at night, in his room, he fills a page of his journal with a confused, but scathing account of his first engagement; summarizes American advanced education in a paragraph that will be meaningless to-morrow, and falls to sleep where he is immediately chased through long, dark thickets by a Mrs. Mabel Frankincense Mehaffey, with a tray of martinis and lyrics.

And there goes the other happy poet bedraggedly back to New York which struck him all of a sheepish never-sleeping heap at first but which seems to him now, after the ulcerous rigours of a lecturer's spring, a haven cosy as toast, cool as an icebox, and safe as skyscrapers.

Exercises

1. Write paragraphs to exemplify each of these rhetorical profiles—the formal, restrained; informal, common; colloquial, elaborate.

2. Write three versions of the same paragraph to illustrate the fine distinctions between monotonously unvaried (as much as you can in so short a passage), interestingly varied, and inconsistent rhetorical profile.

3. Identify the rhetorical profile used in each of the following paragraphs. What variations in level and texture do you find in each paragraph? Rewrite two of the paragraphs so that a new rhetorical profile is established.

Seldom does one encounter greatness in the tawdry, hurried lives of the twentieth century. Not that greatness is necessarily the product of leisure or aristocracy, but certainly the evidence supports the notion that somehow the busy, ordinary marketplace is not likely to be the scene of great events and deeds performed by great men. One asks, Why should this be so? But no easy answer presents itself.

The alienated man of the twentieth century is a bundle of disturbing emotions. Fear. Anxiety. Anger. And these emotions, uncorralled by a disciplining society, lead everyman to what Dostoevsky called, as long ago as 1880, "malignant individualism." That sick and sterile individualism that feeds on its own alienation, rejecting any salutary contact with the world. The alienated everyman of the twentieth century, rejecting community, fosters those forces within himself that make his return to community also impossible.

My Uncle Sibelius was a rich man. He had made a great deal of money in South America. He had dabbled in gold, in silver, in tin—and with lucky fingers. By the time he was forty, he had amassed enough money to let him return to the United States, build a mansion, spend his days in idle pastimes. He lived what seemed to be the perfect life.

4. Point out the various techniques used to achieve the rhetorical profile in a short article or essay that you have found especially readable.

5. Jokes, witty stories, and humorous passages often exploit the comic possibility in surprisingly inappropriate rhetorical profiles—as when a couple of hobos eat a scavanged

meal from rusty tin cans, discussing it in the language of the elegant dining room. Comic writing *is* difficult, but try your hand at a passage which employs either an inappropriate rhetorical profile or an incongruous mixture of levels and textures for humorous effect.

6. Consider the outlines you wrote earlier (Chapter 7, exercise 7). What should be the prevailing rhetorical profiles? Do the beginnings make this commitment? Are the outlines and endings consistent? If not, modify the essays until they reflect good practice.

9. PARAGRAPHS

Most writers concentrate early in the writing process on their paragraphs. A basic unit of composition, the paragraph is an orderly series of sentences developing a single, unified idea. It is seldom shorter than fifty words, but may run to as many as four or five hundred words. The essential characteristic of the good paragraph is *effective structure*—with all the sentences in the paragraph obviously related to one another in content and obviously arranged, sequentially, one sentence after another, in some reasonable way.

You can bring sentences together into useful paragraph units by paying close attention to established methods of paragraph construction. As you construct paragraphs, you will be dealing with such questions as: Does *this particular* paragraph need a topic sentence—and if it does, where should the topic sentence be located? How should *this* paragraph begin? How should *this* paragraph end? How long should *this* paragraph be? The following suggestions can help guide you into some basic paragraph-writing practices that will help you write the most appropriate paragraphs in any given rhetorical situation.

Construct most of your paragraphs around a topic sentence. Every paragraph deals with one topic. Sometimes this means only that the paragraph contains several loosely related, somewhat coordinate ideas. But usually it means the paragraph consists of closely related sentences elaborating upon a single topic stated in some emphatic place. Since the topic sentence is very likely a major idea in the essay, writing a paragraph is largely a matter of elaborating upon the topic sentence until it has been satisfactorily supported or explained. Occasionally, of course, the topic sentence little more than names the subject of the paragraph; but ordinarily it makes a statement about the subject which the additional sentences serve to complement. In any case, you must learn to write manageable topic sentences. The self-evident topic sentence dooms the paragraph to superfluity:

The dome of St. Peter's is 390 feet high and 137 feet in diameter.

The sweepingly general topic sentence dooms the paragraph to superficiality:

There are more than four hundred churches in Rome, seven of which are major monuments.

(Of course amazing things are possible. Writers have in single paragraphs dealt with immensities and minutiae.) Learn to fulfill in subsequent sentences what you promise in the topic sentence:

To the ancient Greeks the ocean was an endless stream that flowed forever around the border of the world, ceaselessly turning upon itself like a wheel, the end of earth, the beginning of heaven. *This ocean was boundless; it was infinite. If a person were to venture far out upon it—were such a course thinkable—he would pass through gathering darkness and obscuring fog and would come at last to a dreadful and chaotic blending of sea and sky, a place where whirlpools and yawning abysses waited to draw the traveler down into a dark world from which there was no return.—Rachel Carson,* The Sea around Us

(Any sentence that didn't contribute to a somewhat impressionistic description of the mysterious ocean from the ancients' point of view would have been out of place.)

A good topic sentence names the subject and, indirectly, sets the limits of the paragraph; suggests the kind of details the paragraph will contain and implies something of their order; and makes a quick transitional reference to the preceding paragraph.

Place the topic sentence where it will best serve the paragraph. You have several alternatives. Sometimes you will prefer one to the other simply for the sake of variety. But ordinarily you will have other reasons for your choice.

You may state your topic in the *first sentence.* The deductive, generalization-followed-by-details approach is the most common and undoubtedly the best in a routine, expository paragraph.

In relation to their Southern background, the cultural history of Negroes in the North reads like the legend of some tragic people out of mythology, a people which aspired to escape from its own unhappy homeland to the apparent peace of a distant mountain; but which, in migrating, made some fatal error of judgment and fell into a great chasm of mazelike passages that promise ever to lead to the mountain but end ever against a wall. *Not that a Negro is worse off in the North than in the South, but in the North he surrenders and does not replace certain important supports to his personality. He leaves a relatively static social order in which, having experienced its brutality for hundreds of years—indeed, having been formed within it—he has developed those techniques of survival to which Faulkner refers as "endurance," and an ease of movement within explosive situations which makes Hemingway's definition of courage, "grace under pressure," appear mere swagger. He surrenders the protection of his peasant cynicism—his refusal to hope for the fulfillment of hopeless hopes—and his sense of being "at home in the world" gained from confronting and accepting (for day-to-day living, at least) the obscene absurdity of his predicament. Further, he leaves a still authoritative religion which gives his life a semblance of metaphysical wholeness; a family structure which is relatively stable; and a body of folklore—tested in life-and-death terms against his daily experience with nature and the Southern white man—that serves him as a guide to action.—Ralph Ellison,* Harlem Is Nowhere.

Meanwhile the Georgians had rediscovered the direct speech of Wordsworth; but they relied uncritically upon the spirit of his pastoral lyrics. *They echoed his assurances of natural beauty, and extended his confidence in the benign power of the country scene. They avoided the uglier impli-*

cations of rural life, the losing struggles with the soil, poverty and hunger, the spiritual barrenness, and the economic failures. Theirs was a poetry of happy dawns, song-filled dusks, peace-breathing nights.—Louis Untermeyer, Modern British Poetry

You may state your topic in the *last sentence.* The inductive, details-followed-by-generalization approach is useful in persuasive writing, where it's sometimes wise to support an opinion before expressing it, and in narration and description, where suspense is always a good thing.

A painter told me that nobody could draw a tree without in some sort becoming a tree; or draw a child by studying the outlines of its form merely—but by watching for a time his motions and plays, the painter enters into his nature and can then draw him at will in every attitude. So Roos "entered into the inmost nature of a sheep." I knew a draughtsman employed in a public survey who found that he could not sketch the rocks until their geological structure was first explained to him. In a certain state of thought is the common origin of very diverse works. It is the spirit and not the fact that is identical. By a deeper apprehension, and not primarily by a painful acquisition of many manual skills, the artist attains the power of awakening other souls to a given activity.—*Ralph Waldo Emerson,* History

There are naïve people all over the world—some of them scientists—who believe that all problems, sooner or later, will be solved by Science. The word Science itself has become a vague unreasonable noise, with a very ill-defined meaning and a powerful emotional charge; it is now applied to all sorts of unsuitable subjects and used as a cover for careless and incomplete thinking in dozens of fields. But even taking Science at the most sensible of its definitions, we must acknowledge that it is as imperfect as all other activities of the human mind.—*Gilbert Highet,* Man's Unconquerable Mind

The church stands high on the summit of this granite rock, and on its west front is the platform; the eye plunges down, two hundred and thirty-five feet, to the wide sands or the wider ocean, as the tides recede or advance, under an infinite sky, over a restless sea, which even we tourists can understand and feel without books or guides; but when we turn from the western view, and look at the church door, thirty or forty yards from the parapet where we stand, one needs to be eight centuries old to know what this mass of encrusted architecture meant to its builders, and even then one must still learn to feel it. The man who wanders into the twelfth century is lost, unless he can grow prematurely young.—*Henry Adams,* Mont-Saint-Michel and Chartres

Or you may, on some rare occasion, wish to state the topic somewhere within the paragraph.

The Olympic Hermes is a perfectly beautiful human being, no more, no less. Every detail of his body was shaped from a consummate knowledge of actual bodies. Nothing is added to mark his deity, no aureole around his head, no mystic staff, no hint that here is he who guides the soul to death. The significance of that statue to the Greek artist, the mark of the divinity, was its beauty, only that. *His art had taken form within him as he walked the streets, watched the games, noted perpetually the people he lived among. To him what he saw in those human beings was enough for all his art; he had never an impulse to fashion something different, something truer than his truth of nature. In his eyes the Word had become flesh; he made his image of the eternal what men could be. The Winged Victory is later Greek; the temple of the Acropolis was built to the Wingless Victory.—Edith Hamilton,* The Greek Way

Largo *has come to imply breadth and dignity;* grave, *pathos and heaviness;* adagio, *a tender or elegiac quality. Owing to the fact that musical practice changed considerably from the eighteenth century to the nineteenth,* some of these terms carry with them a certain ambiguity. *To the earlier period* andante *meant a "going" pace—that is, a fair degree of movement. To the nineteenth century it implied a slowish gait. Both meanings came to be accepted, which caused some confusion. Beethoven was not sure whether andantino was to be understood as being a bit slower or faster than andante. The above terms may be modified by adverbs such as* molto *(very),* meno *(less),* poco *(a little), and* non troppo *(not too much).—Joseph Machlis,* The Enjoyment of Music: An Introduction to Perceptive Listening, *rev. ed.*

Nevertheless, I am the last person to question the importance of genuine literary education, or to suppose that intellectual culture can be complete without it. An exclusively scientific training will bring about a mental twist as surely as an exclusively literary training. *The value of the cargo does not compensate for a ship's being out of trim; and I should be very sorry to think that the Scientific College would turn out none but lopsided men.—T. H. Huxley,* Science and Culture, and Other Essays

Or you may wish to state the topic in the first sentence, and again in the last; or you may state the topic more than once anywhere within the paragraph. In longer, more difficult paragraphs this is especially good practice. And it's almost routine when you want to emphasize strongly an idea, such as the main point of the whole essay.

Language, of course, is our prime instrument of conceptual expression. *The things we can say are in effect the things we can think. Words are the terms of our thinking as well as the terms in which we present our thoughts, because they present the objects of thought to the thinker himself. Before language communicates ideas, it gives them form, makes them clear, and in fact makes them what they are. Whatever has a name is an object for thought. Without words, sense experience is only a flow of impressions, as subjective as our feelings; words make it objective, and carve it up into* things and facts *that we can note, remember, and think about.* Language gives outward experience its form and makes it definite and clear.—*Susanne K. Langer,* Philosophical Sketches

In default of a recognized term, I have called the perfection or virtue of the intellect by the name of philosophy, philosophical knowledge, enlargement of mind, or illumination; terms which are not uncommonly given to it by writers of this day; but, whatever name we bestow on it, it is, I believe, as a matter of history, the business of a University to make this intellectual culture its direct scope, or to employ itself in the education of the intellect,—*just as the work of a Hospital lies in healing the sick or wounded, of a Riding or Fencing School, or of a Gymnasium, in exercising the limbs, of an Almshouse, in aiding and solacing the old, of an Orphanage, in protecting innocence, of a Penitentiary, in restoring the guilty. I say, a University, taken in its bare idea, and before we view it as an instrument of the Church, has this mission; it contemplates neither moral impression nor mechanical production; it professes to exercise the mind neither in art nor in duty; its function is intellectual culture; here it may leave its scholars, and it has done its work when it has done as much as this.* It educates the intellect to reason well in all matters, to reach out towards truth, and to grasp it.—*John Henry Newman,* The Idea of a University

But you may choose not to state the topic at all. In narrative and descriptive writing the topic is usually obvious enough. And occasionally, as in a summary or transition, you will write an expository paragraph that contains several loosely related ideas but doesn't develop any particular one of them.

I went up hurriedly, in pyjamas and oil-skins. Day had not come, but it was not night; night was lifted slightly in the east on a wedge of rose, though the wind was still bleak out of darkness. We were somewhere near the Berlengas. What was this? My friend the chief officer pointed astern without a word. We were passing a ghost ship, under all canvas. The barque was so close that I could see the length of her deck. She was silent, and more pale than the twilight. She was tall, and tinctured faintly with rose. Had we steamed back into another age? Was the past so near? I could see two men on her poop, but they were not looking at us. Only my friend, and the bridge of our liner, were material. My friend spoke, "I thought you would like to see her; it may be the last time. Isn't she a beauty?"—H. M. Tomlinson, A Lost Wood

None of them knew the color of the sky. Their eyes glanced lower, and were fastened upon the waves that swept toward them. These waves were of the hue of slate, save for the tops, which were of foaming white, and all of the men knew the colors of the sea. The horizon narrowed and widened, and dipped and rose, and at all times its edge was jagged with waves that seemed thrust up in points like rocks.—Stephen Crane, The Open Boat

If there was no more to be said than this, it would still be worth saying. To some extent the air would be cleared and we would know where we stand. Those to whom a man is, first of all, a mere figuring machine, would be clearly separated from those to whom consciousness is the essential condition of all those activities which define the human being. But there is more to be said, and there are conclusions to be drawn.—Joseph Wood Krutch, The Measure of Man

We have now pointed out one great class of rocks, which, however they may vary in mineral composition, colour, grain, or other characters, external and internal, may nevertheless be grouped together as having a common origin. They have all been formed under water, in the same manner as modern accumulations of sand, mud, shingle, banks of shells, reefs of coral, and the like, and are all characterized by stratification or fossils, or by both.—Charles Lyell, Elements of Geology

The more experience you have with writing paragraphs, the less you'll have to depend on explicitly stated topic sentences—but the more you'll respect them.

Conclude most of your paragraphs with a terminal sentence.. If the topic sentence doesn't take the end position or isn't repeated there in one form or another, you must do something to bring the paragraph to a close. Otherwise the paragraph will end on the crest of a thought or trail off into silence. Any sentence that concludes one paragraph and looks forward to the next will answer; it need not be particularly obvious; the quick, quiet conclusion is usually best. The terminal sentence may be definitely the last in a series of points or illustrations, or it may be a new angle or an afterthought. But more often the terminal sentence doesn't further elaborate the idea of the paragraph; instead it briefly reiterates or summarizes the main thought and so implies that it is done. Whatever form it takes, the terminal sentence frequently employs two devices of conclusion—*final transitions (then, finally, so)* and *high pointing*, an increase in rhetorical texture. Both devices are particularly essential in paragraphs occurring at the climax and in the ending of a composition.

Here are some typical terminal sentences:

. . . And so for Hegel the tree of wisdom bore bitter fruit.

. . . Thus the pendulum of reaction dooms even the greatest literary work to its hour of darkness.

. . . By the end of the century even the most zealous optimists knew that a day of reckoning was near.

. . . When at last he achieved his goal, he declared openly and forthrightly, that all had been in vain—his world seemed empty now, his life a tremendous vacuum, his heart the proverbial and unfortunate hollow shell.

And here are some paragraphs containing effective terminal sentences:

The characteristic motive of English poetry is love of nature, especially of nature as seen in the English rural landscape. From the "Cuckoo Song" of our language in its beginnings to the perfect loveliness of Tennyson's best verse, this note is ever sounding. It is persistent even amid the triumph of the drama. Take away from Shakespeare all his bits of natural description, all his casual allusions to the life and aspects of the country, and what a loss were there! The reign of the iambic couplet confined, but could not suppress, this native music; Pope notwithstanding, there came the "Ode to Evening" and that "Elegy" which, unsurpassed for beauty of thought and nobility of utterance in all the treasury of our lyrics, remains perhaps the most essentially English poem ever written.—George Gissing, The Private Papers of Henry Ryecroft

Yet one good look at the street would revive her. I see her now, perched against the windowsill, with her face against the glass, her eyes almost asleep in enjoyment, just as she starts up with the guilty cry—"What foolishness is this in me!"—and goes to the stove to prepare supper for us: a moment, only a moment, watching the evening crowd of women gathering at the grocery for fresh bread and milk. But between my mother's pent-up face at the window and the winter sun dying the fabrics—"Alfred, see how beautiful"—she has drawn for me one single line of sentience.—Alfred Kazin, A Walker in the City

And that is all they do remark. That is all they have witnessed. They will not, and could not, give intelligible and interesting particulars of the affair (unless it were as to the breed of the dog or the number of the bus-service). They have watched a dog run over. They analyse neither their sensations nor the phenomenon. They have witnessed it whole, as a bad writer uses a cliché. They have observed—that is to say, they have really seen—nothing.—Arnold Bennett, The Author's Craft

Sport, then, in this mechanized society, is no longer a mere game empty of any reward other than the playing: it is a profitable business: millions are invested in arenas, equipment, and players, and the maintenance of sport becomes as important as the maintenance of any other form of profit-making mechanism. And the technique of mass sport infects other activities: scientific expeditions and geographic explorations are conducted in the manner of a speed stunt or a prize-fight—and for the same reason. Business or recreation or mass spectacle, sport is always a means: even when it is reduced to athletic and military exercises held with great pomp within the sports arenas, the aim is to gather a record-breaking crowd of performers and spectators, and thus testify to the success or importance of the movement that is represented. Thus sport, which began originally, perhaps, as a spontaneous reaction against the machine, has become one of the mass duties of the machine age. It is a part of that universal regimentation of life—for the sake of private profits or nationalistic exploit—from which its excitement provides a temporary and only a superficial release. Sport has turned out, in short, to be one of the least effective reactions against the machine. There is only one other reaction less effective in its final result: the most ambitious as well as the most disastrous. I mean war.—Lewis Mumford, Sport and the "Bitch-Goddess"

Write a full-length paragraph. The trend toward shorter paragraphs is for many writers a trap. And if you begin writing before you're ready, if you don't know how to expand your ideas, if you write in pen or double-spaced type, you may fall into it. There is a great deal of difference between an underdeveloped paragraph:

The grasshoppers consumed the crops and covered the ground with their bodies. But the destruction and inconvenience went unnoticed because of the surprise, the revulsion—and the terror.

and a short paragraph:

A cloud of grasshoppers rolled across the landscape and rattled against the farm buildings and bent down the crops. Fields of ripe wheat and tall corn moved as if stirred by some ghostly breeze. Behind the main flood of consuming hoppers, bare fallen stems and stalks rippled still. Tree leaves went, then grass. Clothes left on lines went next, then paper signs. Walks and highways were greased with the crackly bodies of hoppers. But the destruction and inconvenience went unnoticed because of the surprise, the revulsion—and the terror.

So write a full-length paragraph; plan for five or six sentences, one or two hundred words, not more than two or three paragraph indentations on a typewritten (double-spaced) page. Sometimes you'll need to strike out irrelevant or superfluous details; but more often you'll need to expand paragraphs or combine shorter paragraphs.

Of course this doesn't mean all your paragraphs should be metronomically regular. Even though paragraphs vary much less in length than sentences, you will write shorter paragraphs when the material is sharply divided, or treated rather cursorily, or hurried and excited; or when you wish to introduce a series of paragraphs, to make a transition, to emphasize a thought.

If the wealth resulting from prosperous industry is to be spent upon the gratification of unworthy desires, if the increasing perfection of manufacturing processes is to be accompanied by an increasing debasement of those who carry them on, I do not see the good of industry and prosperity.—T. H. Huxley, Science and Culture

Yet amidst the disintegration were sprouting, invisible to contemporaries, the green shoots of the Renaissance to come. In human affairs as in nature, decay is compost for new growth.—Barbara Tuchman, History as Mirror

Meanwhile Armstrong was transporting the television camera away from the Lem to a position where it could cover most of their activities. Once properly installed, he revolved it through a full panorama of their view in order that audiences on earth might have a clue to what he saw. But in fact the transmission was too rudimentary to give any sense of what was about them, that desert sea of rocks, rubble, small boulders, and crater lips.—Norman Mailer, Of a Fire on the Moon

And you will sometimes write longer paragraphs when the material is more unified, or is considered in some detail, or is leisurely:

The charts of the world which have been drawn up by modern science have thrown into a narrow space the expression of a vast amount of knowledge, but I have never yet seen any one pictorial enough to enable the spectator to imagine the kind of contrast in physical character which exists between Northern and Southern countries. We know the differences in detail, but we have not that broad glance and grasp which would enable us to feel them in their fulness. We know that gentians grow on the Alps, and olives on the Apennines; but we do not enough conceive for ourselves that variegated mosaic of the world's surface which a bird sees in its migration, that difference between the district of the gentian and of the olive which the stork and the swallow see far off, as they lean upon the sirocco wind. Let us, for a moment, try to raise ourselves even above the level of their flight, and imagine the Mediterranean lying beneath us like an irregular lake, and all its ancient promontories sleeping in the sun: here and there an angry spot of thunder, a grey stain of storm, moving upon the burning field; and here and there a fixed wreath of white volcano smoke, surrounded by its circle of ashes; but for the most part a great peacefulness of light, Syria and Greece, Italy and Spain, laid like pieces of a golden pavement into the sea-blue, chased, as we stoop nearer to them, with bossy beaten work of mountain chains, and glowing softly with terraced gardens, and flowers heavy with frankincense, mixed among masses of laurel, and orange, and plumy palm, that abate with their grey-green shadows the burning of the marble rocks, and of the ledges of porphyry sloping under lucent sand. Then let us pass farther toward the north, until we see the orient colours change gradually into a vast belt of rainy green, where the pastures of Switzerland, and poplar valleys of France, and dark forests of the Danube and Carpathians stretch from the mouths of the Loire to those of the Volga, seen through clefts in grey swirls of rain-cloud and

flaky veils of the mist of the brooks, spreading low along the pasture lands: and then, farther north still, to see the earth heave into mighty masses of leaden rock and heathy moor, bordering with a broad waste of gloomy purple that belt of field and wood, and splintering into irregular and grisly islands amidst the northern seas, beaten by storm, and chilled by ice-drift, and tormented by furious pulses of contending tide, until the roots of the last forests fail from among the hill ravines, and the hunger of the north wind bites their peaks into barrenness; and, at last, the wall of ice, durable like iron, sets, deathlike, its white teeth against us out of the polar twilight. And, having once traversed in thought this gradation of the zoned iris of the earth in all its material vastness, let us go down nearer to it, and watch the parallel change in the belt of animal life: the multitudes of swift and brilliant creatures that glance in the air and sea, or tread the sands of the southern zone; striped zebras and spotted leopards, glistening serpents, and birds arrayed in purple and scarlet. Let us contrast their delicacy and brilliancy of colour, and swiftness of motion, with the frost-cramped strength, and shaggy covering, and dusky plumage of the northern tribes; contrast the Arabian horse with the Shetland, the tiger and leopard with the wolf and bear, the antelope with the elk, the bird of paradise with the osprey: and then, submissively acknowledging the great laws by which the earth and all that it bears are ruled throughout their being, let us not condemn, but rejoice in the expression by man of his own rest in the statutes of the lands that gave him birth. Let us watch him with reverence as he sets side by side the burning gems, and smooths with soft sculpture the jasper pillars, that are to reflect a ceaseless sunshine, and rise into a cloudless sky: but not with less reverence let us stand by him, when, with rough strength and hurried stroke, he smites an uncouth animation out of the rocks which he has torn from among the moss of the moorland, and heaves into the darkened air the pile of iron buttress and rugged wall, instinct with work of an imagination as wild and wayward as the northern sea; creations of ungainly shape and rigid limb, but full of wolfish life; fierce as the winds that beat, and changeful as the clouds that shade them.—John Ruskin,
The Stones of Venice

In general, look to your subject; if your view of it has been complete and orderly, your paragraphing will be also.

SUMMARY CHECKLIST
Ask yourself these questions:

1. Are the major ideas in my composition projected in terms of paragraphs?
2. Are most paragraphs constructed around a topic sentence? Is the topic sentence truly descriptive of the paragraph' content? And is the topic sentence always placed wh⸍ will best serve the paragraph?
3. Do the sentences in each paragraph proceed in s

derly fashion—chronologically or geographically or the like?

4. Are most paragraphs concluded with a terminal sentence?
5. Do I—except in special situations—write fully developed paragraphs of five or six sentences, one or two hundred words?

THE WHOLE COMPOSITION

You will immediately notice the variety of paragraphs in George Orwell's essay. Several (notably the first paragraph) are of one sentence, some of ten and eleven sentences.

There is also a varied placement of topic sentences: The second paragraph contains no clear topic sentence. The third contains a topic sentence *within* the paragraph. In the fifth paragraph, the topic sentence is first; in the eleventh, it is last; in the seventeenth paragraph, the topic is stated in the first sentence and again in the last.

But topic sentence or no, each paragraph deals with a separate thought, parts of the larger subject. And, more important, the length and form of each is adequate to the thought: for example, "I was feeding one of the gazelles in the public garden" needs no further comment; "But what is strange about these people is their invisibility" requires considerable explanation. Furthermore, the casualness of the essay's overall organization places greater emphasis on the individual paragraphs.

Marrakech

George Orwell

As the corpse went past the flies left the restaurant table in a cloud and rushed after it, but they came back a few minutes later.

The little crowd of mourners—all men and boys, no women— threaded their way across the market-place between the piles of pomegranates and the taxis and the camels, wailing a short chant over and over again. What really appeals to the flies is that the corpses here are never put into coffins, they are merely wrapped in a piece of rag and carried on a wooden bier on the shoulders of four friends. When the friends get to the burying-ground they hack an oblong hole a foot or two deep, dump the body in it and fling over it a little of the dried-up, lumpy earth, which is like broken brick. No gravestone, no name, no identifying mark of any kind. The burying-ground is merely a huge waste of hummocky earth, like a derelict building-lot. After a month or two no one can even be certain where his own relatives are buried.

When you walk through a town like this—two hundred thousand inhabitants, of whom at least twenty thousand own literally nothing except the rags they stand up in—when you see how the people live, and still more how easily they die, it is always difficult to believe that you are walking among human beings. All colonial empires are in reality founded upon that fact. The people have brown faces—besides, there are so many of them! Are they really the same flesh as yourself? Do they even have names? Or are they merely a kind of undifferentiated brown stuff, about as individual as bees or coral insects? They rise out of the earth, they sweat and starve for a few years, and then they sink back into the nameless mounds of the graveyard and nobody notices that they are gone. And even the graves themselves soon fade back into the soil. Sometimes, out for a walk, as you break your way through the prickly pear, you notice that it is rather bumpy underfoot, and only a certain regularity in the bumps tells you that you are walking over skeletons.

I was feeding one of the gazelles in the public gardens.

Gazelles are almost the only animals that look good to eat when they are still alive, in fact, one can hardly look at their hindquarters without thinking of mint sauce. The gazelle I was feeding seemed to know that this thought was in my mind, for though it took the piece of bread I was holding out it obviously did not like me. It nibbled rapidly at the bread, then lowered its head and tried to butt me, then took another nibble and then butted again. Probably its idea was that if it could drive me away the bread would somehow remain hanging in mid-air.

An Arab navvy working on the path nearby lowered his heavy hoe and sidled slowly towards us. He looked from the gazelle to the bread and from the bread to the gazelle, with a sort of quiet amazement, as though he had never seen anything quite like this before. Finally he said shyly in French:

"*I* could eat some of that bread."

I tore off a piece and he stowed it gratefully in some secret place under his rags. This man is an employee of the Municipality.

When you go through the Jewish quarters you gather some idea of what the medieval ghettoes were probably like. Under their Moorish rulers the Jews were only allowed to own land in certain restricted areas, and after centuries of this kind of treatment they have ceased to bother about overcrowding. Many of the streets are a good deal less than six feet wide, the houses are completely windowless, and sore-eyed children cluster everywhere in unbelievable numbers, like clouds of flies. Down the centre of the street there is generally running a little river of urine.

In the bazaar huge families of Jews, all dressed in the long black robe and little black skull-cap, are working in dark fly-infested booths that look like caves. A carpenter sits crosslegged at a prehistoric lathe, turning chair-legs at lightning speed. He works the lathe with a bow in his right hand and guides the chisel with his left foot, and thanks to a lifetime of sitting in this position his left leg is warped out of shape. At his side his grandson, aged six, is already starting on the simpler parts of the job.

I was just passing the coppersmiths' booths when somebody noticed that I was lighting a cigarette. Instantly, from the dark holes all round, there was a frenzied rush of Jews, many of them old grandfathers with flowing grey beards, all clamouring for a cigarette. Even a blind man somewhere at the back of one of the booths heard a rumour of cigarettes and came crawling out, groping in the air with his hand. In about a minute I had used up the whole packet. None of these people, I suppose, works less than twelve hours a day, and every one of them looks on a ciagarette as a more or less impossible luxury.

As the Jews live in self-contained communities they follow the same trades as the Arabs, except for agriculture. Fruit-sellers, potters, silversmiths, blacksmiths, butchers, leatherworkers, tailors, water-carriers, beggars, porters—whichever way you look you see nothing but Jews. As a matter of fact there are thirteen thousand of them, all living in the space of a few acres. A good job Hitler wasn't here. Perhaps he was on his way, however. You hear the usual dark rumours about the Jews, not only from the Arabs but from the poorer Europeans.

"Yes, mon vieux, they took my job away from me and gave it to a Jew. The Jews! They're the real rulers of this country, you know. They've got all the money. They control the banks, finance—everything."

"But," I said, "isn't it a fact that the average Jew is a labourer working for about a penny an hour?"

"Ah, that's only for show! They're all moneylenders really. They're cunning, the Jews."

In just the same way, a couple of hundred years ago, poor old women used to be burned for witchcraft when they could not even work enough magic to get themselves a square meal.

All people who work with their hands are partly invisible, and the more important the work they do, the less visible they are. Still, a white skin is always fairly conspicuous. In northern Europe, when you see a labourer ploughing a field, you probably give him a second glance. In a hot country, anywhere south of Gibraltar or east of Suez, the chances are that you don't even see him. I have noticed this again and again. In a tropical landscape one's eye takes in everything except the human beings. It takes in the dried-up soil, the prickly pear, the palm tree and the distant mountain, but it always misses the peasant hoeing at his patch. He is the same colour as the earth, and a great deal less interesting to look at.

It is only because of this that the starved countries of Asia and Africa are accepted as tourist resorts. No one would think of running cheap trips to the Distressed Areas. But where the human beings have brown skins their poverty is simply not noticed. What does Morocco mean to a Frenchman? An orange-grove or a job in Government service. Or to an Englishman? Camels, castles, palm trees, Foreign Legionnaires, brass trays, and bandits. One could probably live there for years without noticing that for nine-tenths of the people the reality of life is an endless, back-breaking struggle to wring a little food out of an eroded soil.

Most of Morocco is so desolate that no wild animal bigger than a hare can live on it. Huge areas which were once covered with forest have turned into a treeless waste where the soil is exactly like broken-up brick. Nevertheless a good deal of it is cultivated, with frightful labour. Everything is done by hand. Long lines of women, bent double like inverted capital L's, work their way slowly across the fields, tearing up the prickly weeds with their hands, and the peasant gathering lucerne for fodder pulls it up stalk by stalk instead of reaping it, thus saving an inch or two on each stalk. The plough is a wretched wooden thing, so frail that one can easily carry it on one's shoulder, and fitted underneath with a rough iron spike which stirs the soil to a depth of about four inches. This is as much as the strength of the animals is equal to. It is usual to plough with a cow and a donkey yoked together. Two donkeys would not be quite strong enough, but on the other hand two cows would cost a little more to feed. The peasants possess no harrows, they merely plough the soil several times over in different directions, finally leaving it in rough furrows, after which the whole field has to be shaped with hoes into small oblong patches to conserve water. Except for a day or two after the rare rainstorms there is never enough water. Along the edges of the fields channels are hacked out to a depth of thirty or forty feet to get at the tiny trickles which run through the subsoil.

Every afternoon a file of very old women passes down the road outside my house, each carrying a load of firewood. All of them are mummified with age and the sun, and all of them are tiny. It seems to be generally the case in primitive communities that the women, when they get beyond a certain age, shrink to the size of children. One day a poor old creature who could not have been more than four feet tall crept past me under a vast load of wood. I stopped her and put a five-sou piece (a little more than a farthing) into her hand. She answered with a shrill wail, almost a scream, which was partly gratitude but mainly surprise. I suppose that from her point of view, by taking any notice of her, I seemed almost to be violating a law of nature. She accepted her status as an old woman, that is to say as a beast of burden. When a family is travelling it is quite usual to see a father and a grown-up son riding ahead on donkeys, and an old woman following on foot, carrying the baggage.

But what is strange about these people is their invisibility. For several weeks, always at about the same time of day, the file of old women had hobbled past the house with their firewood, and though they had registered themselves on my eyeballs I cannot truly say that I had seen them. Firewood was passing—that was how I saw it. It was only that one day I happened to be walking behind them, and the curious up-and-down motion of a load of wood drew my attention to the human being beneath it. Then for the first time I noticed the poor old earth-coloured bodies, bodies reduced to bones and leathery skin, bent double under the crushing weight. Yet I suppose I had not been five minutes on Moroccan soil before I noticed the overloading of the donkeys and was infuriated by it. There is no question that the donkeys are damnably treated. The Moroccan donkey is hardly bigger than a St. Bernard dog, it carries a load which in the British Army would be considered too much for a fifteen-hands mule, and very often its pack-saddle is not taken off its back for weeks together. But what is peculiarly pitiful is that it is the most willing creature on earth, it follows its master like a dog and does not need either bridle or halter. After a dozen years of devoted work it suddenly drops dead, whereupon its master tips it into the ditch and the village dogs have torn its guts out before it is cold.

This kind of thing makes one's blood boil, whereas—on the whole—the plight of the human beings does not. I am not commenting, merely pointing to a fact. People with brown skins are next door to invisible. Anyone can be sorry for the donkey with its galled back, but it is generally owing to some kind of accident if one even notices the old woman under her load of sticks.

As the storks flew northward the Negroes were marching southward—a long, dusty column, infantry, screw-gun batteries, and then more infantry, four or five thousand men in all, winding up the road with a clumping of boots and a clatter of iron wheels.

They were Senegalese, the blackest Negroes in Africa, so black that sometimes it is difficult to see whereabouts on their necks the hari begins. Their splendid bodies were hidden in reach-me-down khaki uniforms, their feet squashed into boots that looked like blocks of wood, and every tin hat seemed to be a couple of sizes too small. It was very hot and the men had marched a long way. They slumped under the weight of their packs and the curiously sensitive black faces were glistening with sweat.

As they went past a tall, very young Negro turned and caught my eye. But the look he gave me was not in the least the kind of look you might expect. Not hostile, not contemptuous, not sullen, not even inquisitive. It was the shy, wide-eyed Negro look, which actually is a look of profound respect. I saw how it was. This wretched boy, who is a French citizen and has therefore been dragged from the forest to scrub floors and catch syphilis in garrison towns, actually has feelings of reverence before a white skin. He has been taught that the white race are his masters, and he still believes it.

But there is one thought which every white man (and in this connection it doesn't matter twopence if he calls himself a socialist) thinks when he sees a black army marching past. "How much longer can we go on kidding these people? How long before they turn their guns in the other direction?"

It was curious, really. Every white man there had this thought stowed somewhere or other in his mind. I had it, so had the other onlookers, so had the officers on their sweating chargers and the white N.C.O.'s marching in the ranks. It was a kind of secret which we all knew and were too clever to tell; only the Negros didn't know it. And really it was like watching a flock of cattle to see the long column, a mile or two miles of armed men, flowing peacefully up the road, while the great white birds drifted over them in the opposite direction, glittering like scraps of paper.

Exercises

1. Jot down several ideas for a composition. Write out some of the topic sentences that might be developed from each idea. Then develop each topic sentence into a complete paragraph of some five or six sentences.
2. Write a topic-sentence-first expository paragraph, a topic-sentence-last persuasive paragraph, a topic-sentence-first-and-last climactic paragraph, and a no-topic-sentence narrative paragraph.
3. Where are the topic sentences in the following paragraphs? Rewrite the paragraphs to change the position of the topic sentences.

The eighteenth century was a crucial period for Shakespeare's reputation. On point of being recognized as the greatest of English writers, the playwright had not yet attained the untouchable position Romantic critics were to assign him—those who praised his natural genius also had to apologize for his ignorance of the rules. And the popular theater and the world of scholarship, both claiming him, worked at cross purposes—while the critics searched for authoritative texts, the actors and producers were busy editing the plays until it was difficult to tell what was truly Shakespeare and what was Nahum Tate, Thomas Otway, Colley Cibber, David Garrick, or one of the other "improvers." Still, the discussion kept alive the whole question of his quality.

I have a recurring vision of white birds rolled in a round cup of green northern sky and thrown down the long reach of the sea. Each wears a numbered aluminum band, an amulet. And though I cannot see beyond the horizon, I know thereby the fate of each. Some fall in the sea, some in the desert, some in the grassy plains, some in the icy waters. For I am a student of the arctic tern, a diminutive white bird that wheels around the world on tireless, tapered wings.

4. Identify the topic sentence in each paragraph of a short article or essay that appeals to you.

5. Whole essays are sometimes expressed in a single paragraph. Taking the following examples—all by Logan Pearsall Smith—as your model, compose such a micro- or mini-essay.

At the Window
But then I drew up the curtain and looked out of the window. Yes, there it still was, the old External World, still apparently quite unaware of its own non-existence. I felt helpless, small-boyish before it: I couldn't pooh-pooh it away.

My Map
The "Known World" I called the map, which I amused myself making for the children's schoolroom. It included France, England, Italy, Greece, and all the odd shores of the Mediterranean; but the rest I marked "Unknown"; sketching into the East the doubtful realms of Ninus and Seriramis; changing back Germany into the Hercynian Forest; and drawing pictures of the supposed inhabitants of these unexploited regions, Dog-Apes, Satyrs, Paiderasts and Bearded Women, Cimerians involved in darkness, Amazons, and Headless Men. And all around the Map I coiled the coils, and curled the curling waves of the great Sea Oceanus, with the bursting cheeks of the four Winds blowing from the four hinges of the World.

Paradise Regained
The fields and old farm, the little river, the village church among elms, the formal gates of the park with the roofs of the Great House beyond, all made, in the evening air, a dream-like picture. I was strangely happy: and

how familiar was every detail of the scene before me! There was the trout-stream I had fished in, there were the meadows I had galloped over;—through how many countless, quiet English years had I not lived here, and loved and hunted, courting innumerable vicars' daughters from cover to cover of all the countless, mild, old-fashioned novels of English country life I have dreamed away my own life in reading?

6. Complete the unwritten paragraph of the three compositions you have been preparing (Chapter 8, exercise 6), shifting the position of or even suppressing the topic sentences where necessary.

10. PARAGRAPH MODELS

Writing is a skill, and like playing a violin or throwing a Frisbee, it may be learned by observing how others do it—then by trying to imitate, carefully and thoughtfully, the way it was done. In writing, we can consciously imitate the paragraphs of master stylists and make established paragraph forms a part of our basic repertoire. First, we should read a model paragraph, understand what is being said, and try to grasp the sense of structure and style that prevail in the model. Next, in our own handwriting, we should make an exact copy—down to every comma, dash, and period. Then we should choose a subject of our own, one distinct and different from that of the model, and write our own paragraph—saying what we want to say—but imitating, as much as possible, the manner and style, structure and syntax, formality and texture of the original.

In the following models, the more common paragraph forms are presented first and the more stylistic ones second—all labeled and described. As you study and imitate the models, concentrate upon the structure of each paragraph and consider the potential use of each one in achieving various rhetorical profiles. Obviously, as you develop your skill in composing the various kinds of paragraphs, you will be able to write with increasing flexibility and appropriateness.

BASIC PARAGRAPH FORMS

1 THE TOPIC-SENTENCE-FIRST PARAGRAPH

The characteristic motive of English poetry is love of nature, especially of nature as seen in the English rural landscape. From the "Cuckoo Song" of our language in its beginnings to the perfect loveliness of Tennyson's best verse, this note is ever sounding. It is persistent even amid the triumph of the drama. Take away from Shakespeare all his bits of natural description, all his casual allusions to the life and aspects of the contry, and what a loss were there! The reign of the iambic couplet confined, but could not suppress, this native music; Pope notwithstanding, there came the "Ode to Evening" and that "Elegy" which, unsurpassed for beauty of thought and nobility of utterance in all the treasury of our lyrics, remains perhaps the most essentially English poem ever written.—George Gissing, The Private Papers of Henry Ryecroft

In this paragraph by George Gissing, the first sentence, the topic sentence, names the subject and makes a general assertion about it: "The characteristic motive of English poetry is love of nature, especially of nature as seen in the English rural landscape." Following are four sentences which explain and support the generalization by naming several English literary works—"Cuckoo Song," "Ode to Evening," and "Elegy [Written in a Country Churchyard]"—and writers—"Tennyson," "Shakespeare"—in which this "characteristic motive" is apparent. The topic sentence is in effect restated in each of the subsequent sentences: "this note is ever sounding," "It is persistent . . .," "his bits of natural description . . . casual allusions to the life and aspects of the country," "this native music." To further emphasize the truth of his assertion, Gissing declares that this *nature* element persists *even* in drama and despite the iambic couplet and Pope's influence. The terminal sentence expresses the thought that one of the most pastoral lyrics is also "perhaps the most essentially English poem ever written," echoing the "characteristic motive of English poetry" of the topic sentence. The topic sentence is reasonably terse and straightforward, as most effective topic sentences are; the subsequent sentences are with a single exception more complex and suggestive; and the paragraph is rounded out by a magnificently long and elaborate terminal sentence, effectively climaxing Gissing's whole statement.

This topic-sentence-first paragraph is not part of a long and detailed treatment of the subject but rather a kind of allusion: a concise and, as far as it goes, complete appreciation of the love of nature revealed in English poetry.

. *Copy* Gissing's paragraph; then *compose* a similar topic-sentence-first paragraph. Express a general assertion in the first sentence, explain and support it in several subsequent sentences, echo the general assertion from time to time, and certainly refer to it once again in the terminal sentence.

2 | THE TITLE-SENTENCE-FIRST PARAGRAPH

First, then, a few general remarks about the Sun. It is the nearest of the stars— a hot self-luminous globe. Though only a star of moderate size, the Sun is enormously greater than the Earth and the other planets. It contains about 1,000 times as much material as Jupiter, the largest planet, and over 300,000 times as much as the Earth. Its gravitational attraction controls the motions of the planets, and its rays supply the energy that maintains nearly every form of activity on the surface of the Earth. There are some exceptions to this general rule: for instance, the upheaval of mountain ranges and the outbursts of volcanoes.—Fred Hoyle, The Nature of the Universe

The title sentence names the subject but does not go on to make any assertion about it as a conventional topic sentence would. In narrative and descriptive writing, especially in fiction where regular use of a standard topic sentence is apt to seem overly formal, you may simply wish to identify the subject without saying anything specific about it. Even in expository writing, introductory, transitional, and summary paragraphs are frequently begun with a title sentence rather than a topic sentence. And if a complement in the first sentence is to be the topic of the paragraph, you may wish to invert the sentence, as Charles Doughty did when he wrote "Pleasant, as the fiery heat of the desert daylight is done, is our homely evening fire" at the head of a paragraph in which he listed a number of other things which were also pleasant. Or you may, as is often done, phrase the title sentence as a question. While a title sentence may be placed anywhere in the paragraph, it rarely appears in any but first place.

In the exemplary title-sentence-first paragraph, Fred Hoyle tells the reader that he is going to make "a few general remarks about the Sun," declining at this time to make any particular point about the subject. Even though this sentence does not occur in the first paragraph, it is nevertheless an introduction, background for what is to come later. The paragraph is unified by the reference pronouns, "it" and "its" that refer always to "the Sun," and by the sentences that are parallel in structure, especially the second, fourth, and fifth. Since this paragraph of quite short, uncomplicated sentences was written simply to express a variety of basic facts about the sun, a title sentence was sufficient. Such a paragraph does not call for a standard terminal sentence, there being nothing to reiterate or summarize. The title-sentence-first paragraph is by nature unemphatic; it is not intended as a prevailing paragraph pattern but only as an occasional alternative.

Copy Hoyle's paragraph; then *compose* a similar title-sentence-first paragraph. Make sure that the context supports such an exceptional pattern; compensate for the inherent problems—chief among them an apparent lack of any definite purpose—by keeping the paragraph short and simple, and by maintaining its unity and momentum through pronoun reference, parallel structure of some of the sentences, and other means.

3 THE TOPIC-SENTENCE-LAST PARAGRAPH

There are naive people all over the world—some of them scientists—who believe that all problems, sooner or later, will be solved by Science. The word Science itself has become a vague unreasonable noise, with a very ill-defined meaning and a powerful emotional charge; it is now applied to all sorts of unsuitable subjects and used as a cover for careless and incomplete thinking in dozens of fields. But even taking Science at the most sensible of its definitions, we must acknowledge that it is as imperfect as all other activities of the human mind.—Gilbert Highet, Man's Unconquerable Mind

The inductive, details-followed-by-generalization pattern is useful in persuasive writing, where you are often wise in giving reasons before expressing your opinions; in expository writing, where your conclusion might not be understood without some preliminary explanation; and in narration and description, where a certain amount of suspense is always desirable. When a topic sentence replaces the terminal sentence, it assumes some of the functions of the terminal sentence and is likely to be something of a summary or conclusion. Since the main statement of the paragraph is expressed at the climax, the topic-sentence-last paragraph is a somewhat emphatic pattern.

Gilbert Highet's is a persuasive paragraph, relying rather more upon emotional appeals and sheer verbal force than reasoned arguments. Still, if the reader accepts the implications and assertions expressed in the earlier sentences of the paragraph, then the final sentence—the topic sentence since it is clearly the main point of the paragraph—is in the broad sense an inductively derived conclusion. At any rate, coming where it does at the end of an unusually short and charged paragraph, the topic sentence is not likely to be overlooked.

Copy the Highet sentence; then *compose* a similar topic-sentence-last paragraph in which the earlier sentences explain and support the major assertion at the end of the paragraph.

4 THE INTERNAL-TOPIC-SENTENCE PARAGRAPH

The Olympic Hermes is a perfectly beautiful human being, no more, no less. Every detail of his body was shaped from a consummate knowledge of actual bodies. Nothing is added to mark his deity, no aureole around his head, no mystic staff, no hint that here is he who guides the soul to death. The significance of that statue to the Greek artist, the mark of the divinity, was its beauty, only that. His art had taken form within him as he walked the streets, watched the games, noted perpetually the people he lived among. To him what he saw in those human beings was enough for all his art; he had never an impulse to fashion something different, something truer than this truth of nature. In his eyes the Word had become flesh; he made his image of the eternal what men could be. The Winged Victory is later Greek; the temple on the Acropolis was built to the Wingless Victory.—Edith Hamilton, The Greek Way

When you feel that preliminary explanation and support is needed for your topic sentence and you also wish to elaborate upon the main thought after it has been expressed, you may choose to place the topic sentence somewhere within the paragraph. Such a deductive-inductive paragraph would seem to combine the best of both the topic-sentence-first and -last alternatives, and to some extent it does. At the same time, however, it so obscures and deemphasizes the main thought of the paragraph by placing it in the middle that the internal-topic-sentence paragraph is seldom written. Still, at times this will be the most natural kind of paragraph to write, and you must simply do what you can to compensate for any inherent drawbacks.

In the Edith Hamilton paragraph the topic sentence, "The significance of that statue to the Greek artist, the mark of the divinity, was its beauty, only that," is preceded by three sentences. Each of the sentences makes some essential preliminary observation—"The Olympic Hermes is a perfectly beautiful human being . . . shaped from a consummate knowledge of actual bodies . . . nothing is added to mark his deity." And the topic sentence is followed by another three sentences, excluding the terminal sentence, all emphasizing the preoccupation of the Greek artist with "man" and "what man could be." In the first clause the terminal sentence expresses something of a new thought—that the "Winged Victory," a notable exception to the artist's normal preoccupation, "is later Greek"—but in the final clause it implies that the best Greek art was inspired by the actual appearance of things. You do not have to read very far in the paragraph to realize that even the first sentence, although not a topic sentence, encompasses much of the meaning of the paragraph. Thus, Edith Hamilton compensates for the unemphatic position of the topic sentence by alluding to it in the first sentence and in the last and, indeed, at other points in the paragraph.

Copy the Hamilton paragraph; then *compose* a similar internal-topic-sentence paragraph. Be sure the topic sentence is more effective for having both a kind of prologue and epilogue, and emphasize the topic sentence through some means other than position which is, by the nature of this pattern, lost to you.

5 THE REITERATED-TOPIC-SENTENCE PARAGRAPH

Language, of course, is our prime instrument of conceptual expression. The things we can say are in effect the things we can think. Words are the terms of our thinking as well as the terms in which we present our thoughts, because they present the objects of thought to the thinker himself. Before language communicates ideas, it gives them form, makes them clear, and in fact makes them what they are. Whatever has a name is an object for thought. Without words, sense experience is only a flow of impressions, as subjective as our feelings; words make it objective, and carve it up into things and facts that we can note, remember, and think about. Language gives outward experience its form and makes it definite and clear.—Susan K. Langer, Philosophical Sketches

Paragraphs in which the topic is stated in the first sentence and again in the last or more than once anywhere in the paragraph are fairly common. To be sure, in many paragraphs you will allude from time to time to the topic in some way even though you do not actually restate the topic sentence. However, in longer, more difficult paragraphs it often is wise to repeat, in essence, the topic sentence. When you wish to emphasize an idea rather forcibly, you will certainly consider writing the reiterated-topic-sentence paragraph.

In the model paragraph, Susan Langer makes a general assertion in the first sentence, explains it in the middle sentences, and restates the generalization in the final sentence. Both statements of the topic, "Language, of course, is our prime instrument of conceptual expression" and "Language gives outward experience its form and makes it definite and clear," are eminently clear and succinct. Indeed, the entire paragraph is an example of first-class formal expository prose and a fine illustration of the inverse relation between the comparative difficulty of a thought and the simplicity of its expression. Obviously, this is a key paragraph, for the author's concern at this point is not so much with moving on in the essay as with making doubly sure that this particular idea is understood absolutely; hence, the middle sentences in the paragraph are devoted to a discussion of the topic rather than to a presentation of details.

Copy the Langer paragraph; then *compose* a similar reiterated-topic-sentence paragraph. Since your readers, having learned something from the discussion coming before, will be better informed the second time they encounter the topic, you can state it as a more explicit and categorical generalization.

6 THE DUAL-TOPIC-SENTENCE PARAGRAPH

The great and simple appeal of fiction is that it enables us to share imaginatively in the fortunes of these created beings without paying the price in time or defeat for their triumphs and frustrations. One moves with them in lands where one has never been, experiences loves one has never known. And this entrance into lives wider and more various than our own in turn enables us more nicely to appreciate and more intensely to live the lives we do know. It is impossible to say how much novelists teach us to look at our fellow beings, at "their tragic divining of life upon their ways." The novelist is, in one sense, your true philosopher. For any marshaling of people into a story implies a conception of fate and a philosophy of nature. The least obviously philosophical of novelists, in the choice he makes of events, in the construction he makes of circumstances, indicates and implies what the world, his world, is like. Where novelists, like some of those in our own day, Hardy and Anatole France and Thomas Mann, are philosophers, they are so in a more rich and living sense than the philosophers of the academy. They imply themselves or express through their characters a total appraisal of existence. They document their estimates with the whole panorama of human experience. They not only judge but create a world. It is difficult to find in current philosophy a universe more complete and comprehensive than that of a novelist whose mind has ranged over eternity and whose eyes and imagination have traveled widely in time.—Irwin Edman, Arts and the Man: A Short Introduction to Aesthetics

Most paragraphs develop a single, rather unified idea; but some few, among them dual-topic-sentence paragraphs, do not. The train of thought in such a paragraph moves in a systematic way from the consideration of one idea to the consideration of a closely related second idea. In no sense does the paragraph begin here, lose its direction, and wind up over there. Rather, the writer chooses to fuse thoughts that, like clauses in a compound sentence, are so much a product of the same deliberation that it seems only natural to keep them together. Such a paragraph is written around two separate but related topic sentences, one stated at or near the beginning and the second at or near the end.

Irwin Edman's dual-topic-sentence paragraph begins with one generalization, "The great and simple appeal of fiction is that it enables us to share imaginatively in the fortunes of these created beings without paying the price in time or defeat for their triumphs and frustrations," and concludes with a second, "It is difficult to find in current philosophy a universe more complete and comprehensive than that of a novelist whose mind has ranged over eternity and whose eyes and imagination have traveled widely in time." Each is stated in the most reasonable and emphatic place. But coming as it does at the end, the final topic sentence in Edman's paragraph, and in most dual-topic-sentence paragraphs, is the more important and emphasized. The first couple of sentences develop the first idea, the final several the second. The discussion moves in a clear way from one idea to the next, making the turn in these two sentences, "It is impossible to say how much novelists teach us to look at our fellow beings, at 'their tragic divining of life upon their ways.' The novelist is, in one sense, your true philosopher." (Incidentally, when the source of a short quotation is not relevant, you can insert the quotation into your own prose, and use quotation marks to identify it as borrowed; you do not need to name the author.)

Copy the Edman paragraph; then *compose* a similar dual-topic-sentence paragraph in which a second principal idea emerges logically and inevitably from the first.

7 THE IMPLIED-TOPIC-SENTENCE PARAGRAPH

The fields and old farm, the little river, the village church among elms, the formal gates of the park with the roofs of the Great House beyond, all made, in the evening air, a dream-like picture. I was strangely happy; and how familiar was every detail of the scene before me! There was a trout-stream I had fished in, there were the meadows I had galloped over;—through how many countless, quiet English years had I not lived here, and loved and hunted, courting innumerable vicars' daughters from cover to cover of all the countless, mild, old-fashioned novels of English country life which I have dreamed away my own life in reading?—Logan Pearsall Smith, All Trivia

You will write a great many paragraphs in which the topic is, for one reason or another, not stated at all in so many words. In narrative and descriptive writing the topic of a paragraph is often obvious enough. And summary and transitional paragraphs that contain a number of related ideas but do not develop any particular one of them are sometimes not written around a topic sentence. Such implied-topic-sentence paragraphs expect more of the reader than conventional paragraphs. The reader must, in effect, put together a topic sentence from the details in the paragraph or do without what is, in expository prose at least, something of a necessity. Such paragraphs demand more of the writer as well, for it is just as easy for the writer to lose the way. To compensate for the apparent lack of any definite point, special attention must be given to selecting and arranging details and to connecting sentences in a way that gives an extraordinary sense of momentum in the paragraph.

The model implied-topic-sentence paragraph by one of the finest stylists in English, Logan Pearsall Smith, is a descriptive-expository paragraph without a conventional topic sentence. The final sentence is almost one; at least in a surprising way it locks all the previously expressed details into place. It is, however, as complicated and ranging a sentence as any of the three in the paragraph and is even phrased as a question. But you would not expect a short personal reverie to employ the familiar patterns of informative prose. This is, by the way, a good illustration of the possibilities of the paragraph, for the essay, *Paradise Regained*, consists of only this one paragraph.

Copy the Logan Pearsall Smith paragraph; then *compose* a similar, short implied-topic-sentence paragraph. Conclude it with a sentence that does not express the topic matter-of-factly but contains what the reader needs to know to organize the paragraph in some meaningful way.

8 THE SINGLE-SENTENCE PARAGRAPH

If the wealth resulting from prosperous industry is to be spent upon the gratification of unworthy desires, if the increasing perfection of manufacturing processes is to be accompanied by an increasing debasement of those who carry them on, I do not see the good of industry and prosperity.—T. H. Huxley, Science and Culture

The usual full-length paragraph consists of five or six sentences, one or two hundred words. Exceptions are the single-sentence paragraph, the abbreviated paragraph, and the extended paragraph.

Now and then you will write a paragraph of only one sentence.

When introducing a series of paragraphs, or making a transition from one part of an essay to another, or quickly summarizing the discussion up to the point, or emphasizing an important point—say the thesis of your essay—by simple isolation, the single-sentence paragraph might well serve. While this is an exceptional paragraph pattern, there will be times when a sentence alone will suffice, when additional explanation and support will be superfluous.

T. H. Huxley chose to express a major idea from his essay as a single-sentence paragraph. The sentence stands as an effective paragraph partly because it is clearly and forcefully stated and partly because it summarizes by repeating, most emphatically, an assertion that is basic to the essay and one about which the author has already said a good deal. The paragraph has, you will note, periodicity, parallelism, and repetition—of "prosperous industry" as "industry and prosperity."

Copy the Huxley paragraph; then *compose* a similar single-sentence paragraph—one which, while it may serve as an introduction, transition, or summary—is mainly a device for emphasis. Take special pains with the design of the sentence, for no ordinary statement deserves the prominence of being a single-sentence paragraph.

9 THE ABBREVIATED PARAGRAPH

Philosophy commonly distinguishes between what we may conveniently call "Experience" and "Nature." In the first of these categories is included the whole realm of human perception; in the second the whole realm of phenomena which occur outside of man; and philosophy is concerned with the traffic which goes on between them.—Joseph Wood Krutch, Experience and Art

An abbreviated paragraph is simply an exceptionally short one. You will write short paragraphs when the materials of your essay are sharply divided or cursorily treated or hurried and excited or for the same reasons you may have written single-sentence paragraphs, that is, for introductions, transitions, or summaries. There is a world of difference between an abbreviated paragraph and an underdeveloped one. If you try to write without thinking through and researching your subject or if you do not know how to expand your ideas, you are probably writing underdeveloped paragraphs—a bad habit even the trend toward shorter paragraphs will not hide. In the long run giving too many details is less destructive to effective writing than giving too few. The abbreviated paragraph is short because its objectives have been carefully limited, not because it has been arbitrarily abridged. Furthermore, the abbreviated paragraph should be written only occasionally and then only where a shorter paragraph clearly serves the purpose better than one of more usual length.

Joseph Wood Krutch's model abbreviated paragraph is a kind of internal introduction devoted expressly to defining certain important terms and laying out the subject of inquiry. Krutch wants to make sure the reader understands that "Experience," "Nature," and "Philosophy" are key words having particular meanings. For the sake of clarity and emphasis and because he preferred not to enlarge upon the subject at this point, Krutch chose to write an abbreviated paragraph of only two sentences—the first setting forth the terms "Philosophy," "Experience," and "Nature," and the second defining each of these key words in relation to the others.

Copy the Krutch paragraph; then *compose* a similar abbreviated paragraph of no more than two or three average-length sentences.

10 | THE EXTENDED PARAGRAPH

I was witness to events of a less peaceful character. One day when I went out to my wood-pile, or rather my pile of stumps, I observed two large ants, the one red, the other much larger, nearly half an inch long, and black, fiercely contending with with one another. Having once got hold they never let go, but struggled and wrestled and rolled on the chips incessantly. Looking farther, I was surprised to find that the chips were covered with such combatants, that it was not a duellum, *but a* bellum, *a war between two races of ants, the red always pitted against the black, and frequently two red ones to one black. The legions of these Myrmidons covered all the hills and vales in my wood-yard, and the ground was already strewn with the dead and dying, both red and black. It was the only battle which I have ever witnessed, the only battlefield I ever trod while the battle was raging; internecine war; the red republicans on the one hand, and the black imperialists on the other. On every side they were engaged in deadly combat, yet without any noise that I could hear, and human soldiers never fought so resolutely. I watched a couple that were fast locked in each other's embraces, in a little sunny valley amid the chips, now at noon-day prepared to fight till the sun went down, or life went out. The smaller red champion had fastened himself like a vice to his adversary's front, and through all the tumblings on that field never for an instant ceased to gnaw at one of his feelers near the root, having already caused the other to go by the board; while the stronger black one dashed him from side to side, and, as I saw on looking nearer, had already divested him of several of his members. They fought with more pertinacity than bulldogs. Neither manifested the least disposition to retreat. It was evident that their battle-cry was Conquer or die. In the meanwhile there came along a single red ant on the hill-side of this valley, evidently full of excitement, who either had despatched his foe, or had not yet taken part in the battle; probably the latter, for he had lost none of his limbs; whose mother had charged him to return with his shield or upon it. Or perchance he was some Achilles, who had nourished his wrath apart, and had now come to avenge or rescue his Patroclus. He saw this unequal combat from afar—for the blacks were nearly twice the size of the red—he drew near with rapid pace till he stood on his guard within half an inch of the combatants; then, watching his opportunity, he sprang upon the black warrior, and commenced his operations near the root of his right fore-leg, leaving the foe to select among his own members; and so there were three united for life, as if a new kind of attraction had been invented which put all other locks and cements to shame. I should not have wondered by this time to find that they had their respective musical bands stationed on some eminent chip, and playing their national airs the while, to excite the slow and cheer the dying combatants. I was myself excited somewhat even as if they had been men. The more you think of it, the less the difference. And certainly there is not the fight recorded in Concord history, at least, if in the history of America, that will bear a moment's comparison with this, whether for the numbers engaged in it, or for the patriotism and heroism displayed. For numbers and for carnage it was an Austerlitz or Dresden. Concord Fight! Two killed on the patriots' side, and Luther Blanchard wounded! Why here every ant was a Buttrick,—"Fire! for God's sake fire!"—and thousands shared the fate of Davis and Hosmer. There was not one hireling there. I have no doubt that it was a principle they fought for, as much as our ancestors, and not to avoid a three-penny tax on their tea; and the results of this battle will be as important and memorable to those whom it concerns as those of the battle of Bunker Hill, at least.—Henry David Thoreau,* Walden

An extended paragraph is, of couse, an exceptionally long one. When the materials of your essay fall naturally into larger blocks, when the subject lends itself to greater detail and depth, and when the mood is leisurely and absorbed, you will tend to write longer paragraphs. Closely reasoned, formal prose for the critical reader, because it contains more detail, is conceived in terms of longer paragraphs. Even here, however, when writers wish to be absolutely clear, they will shift to paragraphs of average or even shorter length. An unusually long paragraph even in a scholarly work is a special paragraph pattern written to serve a specific purpose. For example, the extended paragraph in a passage of otherwise normal-length paragraphs is a device of emphasis.

Henry David Thoreau chose to write an extended paragraph because he wanted to project the episode of the ants as something complete and coherent, a kind of essay within an essay. He could have broken the passage into four or five paragraphs of average length; but since the subject, which was neither obscure nor difficult, lent itself to the extended paragraph, Thoreau saw every reason to regard the paragraph as a flexible convention capable of infinite variation and elaboration. Long paragraphs are apt to become dull affairs; however, this one is not. Conflict, the basic ingredient of a fictional plot, is present in the narrative and so is suspense; there is in Thoreau's description an abundance of solid perceptible detail;

the expository reflections are quick and pertinent. Thoreau has, in short, compensated brilliantly for any tediousness that may result from an abundance of words.

Copy the Thoreau paragraph; then *compose* a similar extended paragraph. Overcome any inclination to dullness by being especially lively and vivid.

11 THE PARAGRAPH OF NARRATIVE DETAILS

Once, thinking it might be my maternal duty to catch an inside glimpse of the houses to which my son has entrée, I committed the error of calling for him at a residence whose marble exterior and wrought-iron garage door should have forewarned me of the elaborate juvenile goings-on in there. A butler answered the bell. Butlers have an over-refining effect on me and in their presence I hear myself using the broad "a" on words like "hat." I murmured my son's name and the fact that I had come to fetch him. After I had made it plain that I was my child's mother and not his governess, the butler reluctantly led me up a carved stone stairway, opened a period door, and thrust me into a completely dark room. I was greeted by the whoops and catcalls of fifteen small boys and it was some moments before I realized that a moving picture was being shown and that I was standing between the screen and the projection machine. There was nothing to do but drop to a crouching position. My eyes were by now getting focussed— the way they do in the Blue Grotto—and in the dusk I could distinguish, over on a couch across the room, a pair of adults whom I presumed to be the parents of the child host. Fearing to cut off any more breathless moments of "Our Gang," I approached their presence in a crouching shuffle that must have seemed like a definite throwback to the Neanderthal Man. This startled them a good deal, but what startled them much more was my announcement that I was the mother of such-and-such a boy. Even in the gloom I could see their shocked astonishment. It was all very well for the nursemaids, waiting below, to crash the gate, but for a parent! They did manage, though, to utter a few polite phrases and we all three simulated an animated interest in the film, which was blessedly nearing its custard-pie finale. The lights flashed on and the party was pronounced over. My son and I thanked our hosts and departed, I sheepishly, he triumphantly with a considerable quantity of loot in the way of candy, favors, and, I later found out, a few of the birthday gifts of the unsuspecting host.—Cornelia Otis Skinner, It's a Wise Parent

When you are confronted by a topic of paragraph size in which chronology or age considerations are a major factor, a story or a historical occurrence or some kind of process, you will likely discover yourself writing a paragraph of narrative details. In such a paragraph you will probably take up the details in sequence moving from earlier to later, older to newer, past to present, or possibly even from the past to the future. Time, however, is something that can be managed in a variety of ways. You could order the details within a paragraph regressively almost as well as progressively, moving from later to earlier, newer to older, or present to past. Or you might, even in the framework of a single paragraph, be able to accommodate an *in medias res* beginning, a flashback, or foreshadowing. But taking the art of storytelling, specifically at the paragraph level, the problem is one of selecting and arranging the details in such a way as to provide for a good deal of motivated action, anticipation or surprise, character development, natural and lively dialogue, and casually introduced description.

The model passage is a conventional paragraph of narrative details, moving from "I committed the error of calling for him," through a sequence of related acts, to "my son and I thanked our hosts and departed." The paragraph is also a classic example of the most instinctive form of verbal art, storytelling. Notice in Cornelia Otis Skinner's anecdote how the basic narrative is expanded and somewhat delayed by a variety of allusions and asides. In the first three sentences the only strictly narrative details are probably "I committed the error of calling for him" and "a butler answered the door." The descriptive "marble exterior and wrought-iron garage door" and the reflective "butlers have an over-refining effect on me and in their presence I hear myself using the broad 'a' on words like 'hat' " are nevertheless essential if the passage is to be effective or, indeed, to have any point at all. Here, as in most instances, the story line—the narrative thread—is not really as significant as the related observations and commentary. The best raconteurs are not necessarily people with a good story but are people who know how to use the narrative to best advantage—not only for expressing events in some chronological way but as a compelling framework for other kinds of expository details.

Copy the Skinner paragraph; then *compose* a similar paragraph of narrative details, making it an equally complete and, if possible, entertaining anecdote. The humor in this passage is more obvious than subtle, but it is successful because it is neither exaggerated nor familiar. Everyone has felt ridiculous at being thrust into a novel and awkward situation, and certainly you would react so under the circumstances Cornelia Otis Skinner describes.

12 THE PARAGRAPH OF DESCRIPTIVE DETAILS

A marvellous stillness pervaded the world, and the stars, together with the serenity of their rays, seemed to shed upon the earth the assurance of everlasting security. The young moon recurved, and shining low in the west, was like a slender shaving thrown up from a bar of gold, and the Arabian Sea, smooth and cool to the eye like a sheet of ice, extended its perfect level to the perfect circle of a dark horizon. The propeller turned without a check, as though its beat had been part of the scheme of a safe universe; and on each side of the Patna *two deep folds of water, permanent and sombre on the unwrinkled shimmer, enclosed within their straight and diverging ridges a few white swirls of foam bursting in a low hiss, a few wavelets, a few ripples, a few undulations that, left behind, agitated the surface of the sea for an instant after the passage of the ship, subsided splashing gently, calmed down at last into the circular stillness of water and sky with the black speck of the moving hull remaining everlastingly in its centre.—Joseph Conrad,* Lord Jim

When you are dealing with a paragraph topic in which physical or spatial considerations are most prominent, as when you are writing about an object or scene, you will undoubtedly compose a paragraph of descriptive details. In such a paragraph you take up the details in sequence, moving from top to bottom, left to right, center to periphery, large to small, east to west, and so on. Unlike narration, in which there is a natural progression of details, description has no real standard; you have greater freedom in ordering paragraph details to fit the circumstances. If the reader is familiar with the subject, you can "skip around" as long as you have good reasons and do not lose your reader.

The problem of selection is sometimes greater in descriptive writing than in narrative, where it is easier to separate the relevant from the irrelevant. In description the object or scene is before you, imaginatively if not actually, and the parts and materials and shapes and colors and textures are so varied and so complex that you have difficulty deciding what details are essential to convey the picture. Generalized observations are not as a rule especially effective; overall impressions and essences can best be suggested by more detailed impressions. Choose those details which describe features of the subject pertinent to the discussion. Select each detail to represent a whole class of details. Whenever you can, express descriptive detail in terms of motion. And avoid those clichés which seem especially prevalent in descriptive writing.

Joseph Conrad's is a remarkably effective paragraph of descriptive details. Even more than the night passage of a ship through the Arabian Sea, he is describing an atmosphere of "marvellous stillness." Every detail, every image, every reflective observation is selected and expressed accordingly. Everything about the passage suggests serenity and permanence, even the frequently alliterated sounds of the words—the mellifluous *m*'s and *l*'s, the *s*'s and *r*'s—and the long rhythms. The paragraph begins as an unearthly vision, focuses for a moment on the *Patna*, slides away on the waves trailing behind, and ends on the same detached note upon which it opened.

The language is the most striking feature of the paragraph; every word is so explicitly descriptive and so evocative of the scene Conrad wished to describe.

Copy the Conrad paragraph; then *compose* a similar paragraph of descriptive details. The secret of writing lyrical prose—and, indeed, of writing poetry—is learning to present a quantity of specific descriptive detail. So even though atmospheric and scenic effects are basic objectives of the paragraph, begin with the clearest possible view of your subject and describe it in the most exact language. Imaginative descriptive writing is not so different from the most literal, scientific kind as you might suppose; indeed, the methods and problems of both are quite similar.

13 THE PARAGRAPH OF EXAMPLES AND ILLUSTRATIONS

The worship of the oak tree or of the oak god appears to have been shared by all the branches of the Aryan stock in Europe. Both Greeks and Italians associated the tree with their highest god, Zeus or Jupiter, the divinity of the sky, the rain, and the thunder. Perhaps the oldest and certainly one of the most famous sanctuaries in Greece was that of Dodona, where Zeus was revered in the oracular oak. The thunderstorms which are said to rage at Dodona more frequently than anywhere else in Europe, would render the spot a fitting home for the god whose voice was heard alike in the rustling of the oak leaves and in the crash of thunder. Perhaps the bronze gongs which kept up a humming in the wind round the sanctuary were meant to mimick the thunder that might so often be heard rolling and rumbling in the coombs of the stern and barren mountains which shut in the gloomy valley. In Boeotia, as we have seen, the sacred marriage of Zeus and Hera, the oak god and the oak goddess, appears to have been celebrated with much pomp by a religious federation of states. And on Mount Lycaeus in Arcadia the character of Zeus as a god both of the oak and of the rain comes out clearly in the rain charm practised by the priest of Zeus, who dipped an oak branch in a sacred spring. In his latter capacity Zeus was the god to whom the Greeks regularly prayed for rain. Nothing could be more natural; for often, though not always, he had his seat on the mountains where the clouds gather and the oaks grow. On the Acropolis at Athens there was an image of Earth praying to Zeus for rain. And in time of drought the Athenians themselves prayed, "Rain, rain, O dear Zeus, on the cornland of the Athenians and on the plains."—James George Frazer, The Golden Bough

You can make a general statement clearer and more meaningful by citing concrete and specific cases. This is, to be sure, the *raison d'être* of the great majority of paragraphs, most consisting of a general statement supported and explained by details. The examples and illustrations may be intended to prove the general statement or simply to make it more vivid. The examples may come before or after the general statement. And the paragraph may consist of a great number of such details; several examples, each stated in a sentence or two; or a single, extended example. At any rate, the richness such detail provides is essential to effective writing, and fluent writers are those who have learned to expand their basic ideas with the most apt and lively detail.

The paragraph of examples and illustrations by James George Frazer is in the tradition of popular scholarship. Frazer uses examples to prove the general truth of the assertion that "the worship of the oak tree or of the oak god appears to have been shared by all the branches of the Aryan stock in Europe." At the same time, the specific examples are almost equally important, as much the point of the essay as the basic idea. Finally, the examples are so sensitively set forth and so ranging that Frazer's classic on mythology is a rich work quite apart from its historical facts and learned hypotheses.

Copy the Frazer paragraph; then *compose* a similar paragraph of examples and illustrations in which you cite specific, representative cases to make a general statement more valid, pertinent, and, above all, more vivid.

14 | THE PARAGRAPH OF COMPARISONS OR ANALOGIES

Yet if one looks closely one sees that there is no essential difference between a beggar's livelihood and that of numberless respectable people. Beggars do not work, it is said; but then, what is work? A navvy works by swinging a pick. An accountant works by adding up figures. A beggar works by standing out of doors in all weathers and getting varicose veins, chronic bronchitis, etc. It is a trade like any other; quite useless, of course—but, then, many reputable trades are quite useless. And as a social type a beggar compares well with scores of others. He is honest compared with the sellers of most patent medicines, high-minded compared with a Sunday newspaper proprietor, amiable compared with a hire-purchase tout—in short, a parasite, but a fairly harmless parasite. He seldom extracts more than a bare living from the community, and, what should justify him according to our ethical ideas, he pays for it over and over in suffering. I do not think there is anything about a beggar that sets him in a different class from other people, or gives most modern men the right to despise him.—George Orwell, Down and Out in Paris and London

In a paragraph of comparisons or analogies you illuminate the subject by demonstrating its similarity to something else. If the ideas or things are from the same plane of experience, whether the reader immediately recognizes this or is surprised to discover the resemblances, it is a case of simple comparison; but if the ideas or things are from quite different planes of experience, you have an analogy, a metaphorical comparison. Sometimes in such a paragraph you compare only to clarify some aspect of the main topic; while at other times, the object of the paragraph is the fact that these ideas or things are in a real way similar, and the comparison itself is most important. In a paragraph of comparisons or analogies you can point out how two or more items are alike by describing first one and then the other or by describing each of them part by part. Whatever form the paragraph takes, you select details according to how pertinent they are to the comparison.

The George Orwell quotation is a paragraph of comparisons. He makes this clear in the first sentence when he writes, "there is no *essential* difference between a beggar's livelihood and that of number-less respectable people." He then proceeds to compare a beggar's work favorably with that of navvys, accountants, sellers of patent medicines, Sunday newspaper proprietors, and hire-purchase touts. And he concludes with what is the immediate reason for the comparison, "I do not think there is anything about a beggar that sets him in a different class from other people, or gives most modern men the right to despise him." Orwell is, of course, less concerned with the status of beggars than with exposing the social hypocrisy that condemns some men to inhuman labor and others to exceedingly dull work, extols some respectable tradesmen while despising others no less useless and parasitical. (Incidentally, notice the transitional touches in "Yet . . .," emphasized words set apart in roman, and Orwell's use of the dash.)

Copy the Orwell paragraph; then *compose* a similar paragraph of comparisons. If you would prefer to write a paragraph of analogies, find an effective well-written example upon which to pattern your own.

15 | THE PARAGRAPH OF CONTRASTS

At first sight those Great Twin Brethren of the Victorian era, Tennyson and Browning, are wildly unlike. What greater contrast could there be than between a tall black-cloaked, black-bearded, black-blooded recluse in the Isle of Wight, and a sociable frisking little gentleman, who drew from Tennyson the growl that Browning would certainly "die in a white tie," and from a lady who had met him at dinner the question—"Who was that too exuberant financier?"; between a poet whose style was as meticulously polished as he was himself shaggy and unkempt, and a poet who might wear evening-dress himself, but often left his hastily scribbled poems as fuzzy and prickly and tangled as a furze-bush; between the writer of Tithonus, *with an immeasurable sadness underlying his talk about "the larger hope," and the writer of* Rabbi Ben Ezra, *who looked on the world and, behold, it was very good, with an even better one to follow? They are as different as the lady in the Japanese story, who kept butterflies, from her neighbour, the lady who preferred creeping things and caterpillars. The contrast had already struck contemporaries. FitzGerald found in Tennyson unforgettable things, in Browning only "Cockney sublime, Cockney energy": Carlyle wrote, "Alfred knows how to jingle, Browning does not," and again of Browning, "I wish he had taken to prose. Browning has far more ideas than Tennyson, but is not so truthful. Tennyson means what he says, poor fellow. Browning has a meaning in his twisted sentences, but he does not really go into anything or believe much about it. He accepts conventional values."—F. L. Lucas,* Ten Victorian Poets

A paragraph can as easily be based upon a contrast as upon a comparison, or it can involve both contrast and comparison. In the paragraph of contrasts, you illuminate a subject by pointing out the ways in which it is unlike something else. Sometimes the contrast itself is the object of the paragraph; sometimes one or the other or even both subjects are vivified by the contrast. As with comparisons you can contrast ideas or things by first discussing one and then turning to the other or by shifting from one to the other and then back again, taking up the differences part by part. In any case, you expand the paragraph with details that are relevant to the contrast.

In the first sentence of the model paragraph of contrasts, F. L. Lucas presents the subjects, "Tennyson and Browning," noting that they are "wildly unlike." With the words "what greater contrast could there be," he introduces a quick review of superficial differences in physical appearance, social grace, and poetic method. With the observation that "the contrast had already struck contemporaries," he moves on to FitzGerald's and Carlyle's assessment of more basic dissimilarities between the poets. It would be difficult to present a more vivid sketch of two personalities in so brief a paragraph than F. L. Lucas has done here, principally because the contrast serves to emphasize strongly the distinctive qualities of each.

Copy Lucas's paragraph; then *compose* a similar paragraph contrasting two objects, two ideas, two experiences, two persons, two places, or what have you. After establishing your basic contrast, give a vivid series describing the side of the contrast that is most pleasant and appealing. Then conclude your paragraph by restating the contrast.

16 THE PARAGRAPH OF CAUSES AND CONSEQUENCES

The angle of the earth causes the rays of the sun to fall more directly on the equatorial than on the polar regions. As a result, the air at the equator is warmed more rapidly than elsewhere and, according to the well-known behavior of the warm air, rises; this expanding warm air flows poleward aloft, resulting in an increased weight of air over the poles. Hence the equatorial low pressure areas and the polar highs. The earth, of course, is constantly rotating on its axis from west to east and this sets up deflections and eddies in the returning air near the surface. The general result is a secondary low pressure area at about 60° (the subpolar low), and a secondary high pressure at about 30° (the horse latitudes), with prevailing east winds in the polar regions and near the equator (the polar easterlies and the trades), and prevailing west winds in the middle latitudes (the westerlies).—Marston Bates, Where Winter Never Comes: A Study of Man and Nature in the Tropics

The details in a paragraph are often the causes of an event or situation or the consequences of one. Such a paragraph of causes and consequences usually emphasizes one or the other: Either it is a quick statement of a cause and a more detailed discussion of the consequences; or else it is a brief account of a consequence and a more exhaustive treatment of the causes. Sometimes causes and consequences are the same, as a series of events, each the result of some previous condition and each giving rise to another.

Marston Bates's is clearly a paragraph of causes and consequences. The prime cause of this particular series of meteorological consequences is stated in the first sentence, "The angle of the earth causes the rays of the sun to fall more directly on the equatorial than on the polar regions." The sentences following describe events that are both consequences of this situation and at the same time operate as causes in a complex sequence of events clarified by Bates's methodical use of transitional terms: "as a result," "resulting," "hence," "and this sets up," and "the general result." In this moderately brief and carefully explicit paragraph, the author has expressed an amazing quantity of information about weather (notice even the parenthetical detail), and more important than that, he has demonstrated the complex causal relation of the phenomena. In this case the pattern inherent in the subject is reflected rather clearly in the pattern of the paragraph.

Copy the Bates paragraph; then *compose* a similar paragraph of causes and consequences. Simplify what is actually a collection of almost simultaneous events by showing how each one is in a sense the result of an earlier event and the cause of a later one. Remind the reader of the causal relations by a generous use of the most exact transitional expressions.

17 THE PARAGRAPH OF RESTATEMENTS

One of the greatest dangers of living in large towns is that we have too many neighbors and human fellowship is too cheap. We are apt to become wearied of humanity; a solitary green tree sometimes seems dearer to us than an odd thousand of our fellow citizens. Unless we are hardened, the millions of eyes begin to madden us; and forever pushed and jostled by crowds we begin to take more kindly to Malthus, and are even willing to think better of Herod and other wholesale depopulators. We begin to hate the sight of men who would appear as gods to us if we met them in Turkestan or Patagonia. When we have become thoroughly crowd-sick, we feel that the continued presence of these thousands of other men and women will soon crush, stamp, or press our unique, miraculous individuality into some vile pattern of the streets; we feel that the spirit will perish for want of room to expand in: and we gasp for an air untainted by crowded humanity.—J. B. Priestley, A Road to Oneself

In order to be clear if not emphatic you can spend an entire paragraph enlarging upon a general statement not by going into detail about it or by going on to another related idea, but by in effect repeating the original thought. Each of the subsequent sentences in J. B. Priestley's paragraph, even though differently phrased and somewhat extended by the addition of new detail, is basically a restatement of the first. Priestley has simply said "One of the greatest dangers of living in large towns is that we have too many neighbors and human fellowship is too cheap" in a variety of ways. When you encounter a thought over which you wish to linger or about which you want to be absolutely clear and emphatic, consider writing a paragraph of restatements.

Copy the Priestley paragraph; then *compose* a similar paragraph of restatements in which every sentence is a variation on a theme. To do so without seeming to spin your wheels demands a lively, vivid, and provocative style.

18 THE PARAGRAPH OF DENIALS AND NEGATIONS

How does war look when pinned out in the biologist's collection? In the first place, he is able to say with assurance that war is not a general law of life, but an exceedingly rare biological phenomenon. War is not the same thing as conflict or bloodshed. It means something quite definite: an organized physical conflict between groups of one and the same species. Individual disputes between members of the same species are not war, even if they involve bloodshed and death. Two stags fighting over a harem of hinds, or a man murdering another man, or a dozen dogs fighting over a bone, are not engaged in war. Competition between two different species, even if it involves physical conflict, is not war.

When the brown rat was accidentally brought to Europe and proceeded to oust the black rat from most of its haunts, that was not war between two species of rat; nor is it war in any but a purely metaphorical sense when we speak of making war on the malaria mosquito or the boll-weevil. Still less is it war when one species preys upon another, even when the preying is done by an organized group. A pack of wolves attacking a flock of sheep or deer, or a peregrine killing a duck is not war. Much of nature, as Tennyson correctly said, is "red in tooth and claw"; but this only means what it says, that there is a great deal of killing in the animal world, not that war is the rule of life.—Julian Huxley, On Living in a Revolution

You can sometimes most effectively explain a topic by telling what it is not as a means of indicating precisely what it is. Usually, such a paragraph of denials and negations is accompanied by a more conventional and positive explanation, but in order to clear away any misconceptions it is often essential to eliminate the popular alternatives—especially in dealing with subjects about which a good deal of prejudice, misinformation, and ignorance have accumulated.

Julian Huxley, in the model paragraph, poses a question in the first sentence and answers it in the second, a negatively phrased topic sentence, "In the first place, he is able to say with assurance that war is not a general law of life, but an exceedingly rare biological phenomenon." Then in a series of "is not" statements supported by numerous examples, Huxley explains and supports the paragraph's basic assertion by alluding to several forms of biological competition and dispute and predatory killing which, though physical conflict is involved, are not war and are not suggestive "that war is the rule of life," as he concludes in the final reiteration of the topic sentence. Clearly, a repetition of denials and negations is almost always emphatic, so much so that such a paragraph is written chiefly for that reason.

Copy the Julian Huxley paragraph; then *compose* a similar paragraph of denials and negations, with an opening rhetorical question, a negatively phrased topic sentence, a series of "is not" sentences supported by examples, and a closing reiterated topic sentence.

SPECIAL STYLISTIC PARAGRAPH FORMS

Any one of the basic paragraphs you have just studied can be given additional characteristics of structure and form that will make it special and noticeable.

Admittedly, you will write basic paragraphs most of the time, and you will choose one basic paragraph or another depending on what you have to say. The logic of your arguments and the rationale for your illustrations will determine the kind of basic paragraph you write. Your decision to write a topic-sentence-first paragraph or a topic-sentence-last paragraph will depend primarily upon content and the general direction of your thinking in any particular composition.

You will always be faced, however, with certain stylistic considerations: the need for variation, the need to indicate emphasis, and the need to establish a much more elaborate and extraordinary style in certain compositions. To satisfy these needs, you may wish to give some of your basic paragraphs a more stylistic posture, a more precise architecture, or some particular turn in arrangement in length. In general, a stylistic paragraph will result when you pay careful attention to sentence forms, sentence lengths, and sentence repetitions, and when you give a casually structured paragraph a definite pattern and design.

As you study the stylistic paragraphs on the following pages, concentrate upon the specific characteristic that lifts each out of the ordinary and gives it its noticeable quality. If, for instance, the following paragraph were your model, you would note the many different stylistic characteristics. You would, however, concentrate on the major characteristic, the prevalence of questions. And you would compose a paragraph similarly based upon such questions.

Who has flown and not felt the paradox of man's power: the perfect, self-righting balance of this delicate machine, the pitiful mark left by human hands on the vast panorama stretching below? Who has flown and not gloried in the illusions of power created by gunning the ship on the runway, clearing a section of steel fence for the first time by ten feet, slipping wingwise with ailerons and rudders opposed into the uprushing earth? Who has flown and not felt closer to nature for learning to look for the wind's least messengers? for understanding the reasons for diminishing thrust as one climbs into the atmosphere's rarity? for seeing the wonder of the sun go down as the tight blanket of darkness draws in from the compass' quarters, making the very air small and the hangars' cylindrical black mouths fade away as the roads become rivers of light?—Seldon Rodman, The Poetry of Flight

When shall the nations of the earth find a lasting and enduring peace? When shall human beings truly lay down their arms and work together, rather than fight together? When shall men find it more profitable to cooperate? more advantageous to unite against the common enemies of poverty and disease? more realistic to build highways than weapons, to venture lunar probes rather than territorial invasions? When will men make a serious effort to solve the problems that lead to war rather than wage war itself?

Or you might even write such a paragraph as:

Is there any other place in the Western world comparable to the Acropolis in Athens? Where else can one encounter, so dramatically, the grandeur of the human experience and the human dilemma? Where else does one find in fallen marble, in fluted columns, in the well-worn marble steps the very essence of the human achievement? Where else can one see in the grand pediments and the shattered roof both the aspiration and the failure of the mortal spirit? Where else do unwearying caryatids lift up the marble beams? Where else does one walk among the fallen slabs of ancient glory? Where else does ruin mingle with such majesty? Where else is there such a marriage of grandeur and pathos?

19 THE SERIES PARAGRAPH

There were two stores in the village. My uncle, John A. Quarels, was proprietor of one of them. It was a very small establishment, with a few rolls of "bit" calicoes on half a dozen shelves; a few barrels of salt mackerel, coffee, and New Orleans sugar behind the counter; stacks of brooms, shovels, axes, hoes, rakes, and such things here and there; a lot of cheap hats, bonnets, and tinware strung on strings and suspended from the walls; and at the other end of the room was another counter with bags of shot on it, a cheese or two and a keg of powder; in front of it a row of nail kegs and a few pigs of lead, and behind it a barrel or two of New Orleans molasses and native corn whisky on tap. If a boy bought five or ten cents' worth of anything, he was entitled to half a handful of sugar from the barrel; if a woman bought a few yards of calico she was entitled to a spool of thread in addition to the usual gratis "trimmin's"; if a man bought a trifle, he was at liberty to draw and swallow as big a drink of whisky as he wanted.—Mark Twain, Autobiography

In writing either descriptive or narrative paragraphs, you may well make use of a number of series sentences to create a series paragraph. In such a paragraph nearly every sentence contains one kind of series or another, and the series are presented in some kind of order—from a long series to a short series, or vice versa. The overall effect of such a paragraph is quantity and abundance; and if the series order is from long to short, the effect may be one of increasing order and meaningfulness; if from short to long, the effect may be an increasing disorder and chaos. You can profitably use the series paragraph when presenting descriptive details, narrative events, or catalogues of people, things, or places.

Mark Twain's series paragraph is a good example. After the introductory sentences, he begins his various series in the third sentence.

The first series is, "a few rolls of 'bit' calicoes on half a dozen shelves; a few barrels of salt mackerel, coffee, and New Orleans sugar behind the counter; stacks of brooms, shovels, axes, hoes, rakes, and such things here and there; a lot of cheap hats, bonnets, and tinware strung on strings and suspended from the walls." Within this first four-part series there are interior series: "a few barrels of salt mackerel, coffee, and New Orleans sugar" (three-part); "stacks of brooms, shovels, axes, hoes, rakes, and such things" (six-part); "a lot of cheap hats, bonnets, and tinware" (three-part); and "strung . . . and suspended" (two-part).

A second major series reads, "and at the other end of the room was another counter with bags of shot on it, a cheese or two, and a keg of powder" (three-part). A third series follows, "in front of it a row of nail kegs and a few pigs of lead" (two-part), and "and behind it a barrel or two of New Orleans molasses and native corn whiskey on tap" (two-part). The concluding three-part series reads, "If a boy . . .; if a woman . . .; if a man. . . ."

You will notice that the series generally grow shorter as the paragraph continues. The general meaning is that, among the great abundance of items in the uncle's store, there was a definite scheme to things: The store may have looked crowded and confined, but there was system and order to it.

Copy Mark Twain's series paragraph; then *compose* a similar paragraph, keeping in mind that there is a difference between ordering content and ordering the presentation of content: Mark Twain could have used the same general spatial order that prevails in his paragraph without ordering the items into definite series that decreased in length. Good writers always organize and order their content in some way, but they may not always resort to such stylistic ordering unless they wish to produce the effect of variation or emphasis.

You may find it convenient to write a descriptive paragraph in which you present the details of your description in a set of series following a spatial order. Then, you should rewrite the paragraph, manipulating the length of the series—shortening the first series and lengthening the concluding series, or lengthening the first and shortening the final. If you decide to make the geographically ordered paragraph move from short series to long, you will be suggesting that what you are describing seems simple on first glance but as one continues to look at it it appears more complicated. If you move from long series to short, you suggest that what you are describing, though rich in details at first glance, actually has a certain simplicity to it as one's familiarity with it increases.

20 | THE ANTITHESIS PARAGRAPH

Winter and summer, then, were two hostile lives, and bred two separate natures. Winter was always the effort to live; summer was tropical license. Whether the children rolled in the grass, or waded in the brook, or swam in the salt ocean, or sailed in the bay, or fished for smelts in the creeks, or netted minnows in the salt-marshes, or took to the pine-woods and the granite quarries, or chased muskrats and hunted snapping-turtles in the swamps, or mushrooms or nuts on the autumn hills, summer and country were always sensual living, while winter was always compulsory learning. Summer was the multiplicity of nature; winter was school.—Henry Adams, The Education of Henry Adams

Basic paragraphs dealing with contrasting ideas, events, persons, or objects may be transformed into stylistic paragraphs by presenting the contrast in its most balanced antithetical form. Moving from a rather uncontrolled, loose presentation of contrasting matters to a sharply pointed presentation lifts a paragraph to a new level of stylistic intensity.

Henry Adams has written a striking example of the antithetical paragraph. The topic sentence declares the contrast and presents it in a sharp antithesis: "Winter and summer" followed by a balanced predicate, "were two hostile lives, and bred two separate natures." The second sentence continues the antithesis: "Winter was always the effort to live; summer was tropical license." The third sentence departs from the carefully constructed antithesis to present a long introductory series (an example of stylistic variation) followed, however, by the antithesis once again: "summer and country were always sensual living, while winter was always compulsory learning." The final sentence is a clear antithesis: "Summer was the multiplicity of nature; winter was school."

With every sentence containing an antithesis, Adams's paragraph becomes part of a grander-than-average style, revealing a concern not only with the idea in the paragraph, but also with the idea's verbal presentation. Consider, for instance, that the paragraph *might* have been written in this fashion: "Seasons have their own individual qualities; one season is sometimes actually hostile to another. I discovered this when I was a boy. In winter, for instance, the spirit of work, school, and study filled my life, and I hated it. To me, winter seemed to be the overt enemy of summer—summer with its tropical license, sensual living, and multiplicity of nature, all of which I loved. I began to have definite emotional feelings about these different seasons. . . ." Such a paragraph would have contained the *idea* of contrast, but it would not have had the antithetical form that Adams's paragraph actually took.

Copy Henry Adam's antithesis paragraph; then *compose* one of your own in which you contrast two elements, people, or events and in which you present clear, discernible antitheses.

21 THE QUESTION PARAGRAPH

But what use, pray, is man? Would anybody, besides his dog, miss him if he were gone? Would the sun cease to shed its light because there were no human beings here to sing the praises of sunlight? Would there be sorrow among the little hiding creatures of the underwood, or loneliness in the hearts of the proud and noble beasts? Would the other simians feel that their king was gone? Would God, Jehovah, Zeus, Allah, miss the sound of hymns and psalms, the odor of frankincense and flattery?—Donald Culross Peattie, An Almanac for Moderns

A paragraph that, in its basic form, might consist primarily of statements may, in its stylistic form, be presented as a set of questions. Such a striking paragraph always stands in sharp contrast with its neighbors and invites special attention from a reader.

All-question paragraphs are perhaps the most prevalent kind of monochromatic paragraphs—paragraphs that consist of sentences all alike in some noticeable way: all short simple sentences, all questions, all long conditional sentences, or all elliptical sentences. Monochromatic paragraphs, all of one "color" as it were, always stand out in a composition and are valuable for achieving instant variety and instant attention.

In the exemplary paragraph of questions above, Donald Culross Peattie has phrased his topic sentence as a question and then has "answered" this initial question with a series of rhetorical questions, each a challenge to man's sense of self-importance and to his anthropormorphic ideas about the universe. To appreciate the effectiveness of the all-question paragraph, you need simply rewrite Peattie's paragraph as one of assertions: "Man is of little use. Nobody would miss him, if he were gone, except his dog. . . ." What were barbed ironies in the all-question paragraph become ordinary comments.

A paragraph of questions engages your readers in your composition by making them more a part of your argument, by forcing them to look about for answers of their own, and by necessitating their answering your questions with their own "yes," or "no," with their own facts and judgments.

Copy the Peattie paragraph; then *compose* a similar paragraph of questions. Perhaps it will be helpful to write a basic paragraph of assertions and then to convert it to a paragraph of questions.

22 THE CIRCULAR PARAGRAPH

There in the mist, enormous, majestic, silent, and terrible, stood the Great Wall of China. Solitarily, with the indifference of nature herself, it crept up the mountain side and slipped down to the depth of the valley. Menacingly, the grim watch towers, stark and foursquare, at due intervals stood at their posts. Ruthlessly, for it was built at the cost of a million lives and each one of those great grey stones has been stained with the bloody tears of the captive and the outcast, it forged its dark way through a sea of rugged mountains. Fearlessly, it went on its endless journey, league upon league to the furthermost regions of Asia, in utter solitude, mysterious like the great empire it guarded. There in the mist, enormous, majestic, silent, and terrible, stood the Great Wall of China.— W. *Somerset Maugham,* On a Chinese Screen

Stylistic paragraphs usually assume a quality of pattern and design. One of the most obvious—but effective—ways to achieve stylistic design is to begin and end a paragraph with the same sentence. You may do this when presenting information that can tolerate the same summary sentence both before and after intervening details and illustrations. The result is a verbal circle, and it is an especially valuable way to present descriptions—for the beginning and ending sentences become something of a picture frame, enclosing a still life or portrait composed of descriptive sentences.

Somerset Maugham has used the circular paragraph in his description of the Great Wall of China. The concluding sentence is identical with the opening sentence; the circle is closed. Between these sentences are four descriptive sentences, all patterned alike: "Solitarily . . .," "Menacingly . . .," "Ruthlessly . . .," and "Fearlessly . . .," they begin. Each sentence is itself a "snapshot," the whole paragraph becoming a "picture album," bound and contained.

Copy Somerset Maugham's circular paragraph; then *compose* a circular paragraph describing a scene, an object, or a person. Make sure that your paragraph makes sense and make sure that it is the right length for its circular nature to be effective—long enough so that the opening and closing sentences do not seem to be needless repetition and short enough so that the reader has not forgotten the opening sentence by the time he comes to the paragraph's conclusion.

23 | THE PATTERNED PARAGRAPH (INCREASING SENTENCE LENGTH)

But not the same. There lies the hope of life. The old ways are exploited and remain, but new things come, new senses try the unfamiliar air. There are small scuttlings and splashings in the dark, and out of it come the first croaking, illiterate voices of things to be, just as man once croaked and dreamed darkly in that tiny vesicular forebrain.—Loren Eiseley, The Snout

One of the most interesting ways to establish design in a paragraph is to control the length of sentences—or, more accurately, to control the number of phrases that give each sentence rhythm and to control the strong, definite pauses created by periods at the end of sentences. All sorts of designs can be established in this way and a fine one with which to start is that achieved by using sentences of increasing length. As sentence length increases the paragraph itself becomes more substantial, more weighty, and a definite progression can be seen.

Though patterned paragraphs may be used simply in stylistic contrast with unpatterned paragraphs, they are most effectively used when they are in some way analogous with the paragraph's topic and development. Consider Loren Eiseley's paragraph. Moving from a short opening sentence of only four words to a long sentence of thirty-six words, Eiseley's paragraph pattern is appropriate for the subject of evolution. From a sentence of a single phrase to a sentence of multiple phrases, Eiseley supports the subject he is discussing with style—the evolving from simple to complex in nature, from simple, singular states of being to multiple, sophisticated states of being.

Copy Loren Eiseley's patterned paragraph; then *compose* a similar one in which the sentences become increasingly long. Discuss the evolution, progress, growth, or development of an object, idea, or person in your paragraph.

24 | THE PATTERNED PARAGRAPH (DECREASING LENGTH)

I do not hesitate to say, that those who call themselves Abolitionists should at once effectually withdraw their support, both in person and property, from the government of Massachusetts, and not wait till they constitute a majority of one, before they suffer the right to prevail through them. I think that it is enough if they have God on their side, without waiting for that other one. Moreover, any man more right than his neighbors constitutes a majority of one already.—Henry David Thoreau, On the Duty of Civil Disobedience

On April 3rd, with America still three days away from war, I speculated on the possibility of another canoe trip, for August—a journey on which I proposed to carry "a modified form of miner's tent." Apparently I was spending more time reading sporting goods catalogues and dreaming of the woods than studying news accounts of hostilities in Europe. I was also considering the chances of a summer job. Next fall I was to enter college.—E. B. White, First World War

You may also control the length of sentences in a paragraph by moving from long sentences to short ones, thus creating a pattern that looks something like an inverted pyramid. With sentences of decreasing length your paragraph surrenders substance and weight and moves toward singularity, restriction, isolation, and even deprivation. In such a paragraph there is the subtle sense of loss.

Thoreau's paragraph, for instance, urges a withdrawal of Abolitionist support from the Massachusetts state government. His paragraph is patterned with sentences of decreasing length: moving from the plurality of "themselves" in the first sentence to the singular idea in the last sentence that a single man can constitute "a majority of one." The first sentence contains forty-eight words, the second contains nineteen words, and the third contains fourteen words.

E. B. White's paragraph deals with the ominous threat of war hanging over a young man's life. Even as White speculates on the regular order of his life, the peacetime expectations of vacation, job, and college, the shadow of war falls darker and darker over the world. One can sense this shadow as the very sentences in the paragraph grow shorter and shorter; the full expectations of the first sentence are reduced to the abbreviated expectation of the last. The first sentence contains thirty-six words, the second sentence contains twenty-three words, the third sentence contains ten words, and the fourth sentence contains seven.

Copy both the Thoreau paragraph and the White paragraph; then *compose* a paragraph of your own discussing an idea or situation that you think would be enhanced by this particular paragraph pattern. Preferably, write on a topic dealing with individuality, isolation, independence, loss, or separation.

25 THE PATTERNED PARAGRAPH (SHORT SENTENCE TO LONG SENTENCE TO SHORT SENTENCE)

A man's wife, true enough, may envy her husband certain of his more soothing prerogatives and sentimentalities. She may envy him his masculine liberty of movement and occupation, his impenetrable complacency, his peasant-like delight

*in petty vices, his capacity for hiding the harsh face of reality behind the cloak
of romanticism, his general innocence and childishness. But she never envies him
his shoddy and preposterous soul.—H. L. Mencken,* The Feminine Mind

Another pattern you can achieve in a paragraph is the short
sentence–long sentence–short sentence pattern, a swelling forth in
the middle of the paragraph with a compact beginning and conclusion. The value of such a paragraph is primarily to achieve contrast
with unpatterned, surrounding paragraphs. On some occasions, however, it may be judiciously used to give "shape" to the topic you
wish to present: If you were discussing a nation's beginning, development, and decline, or the stock market's fluctuation from low to
high to low, or a young man's movement from alienation to involvement and back to alienation again, you might well use the short-
long-short pattern as a kind of subtle illustration.

In his paragraph Mencken has taken some care with pattern
and design. He opens with a short sentence and the sentence contains a balance, "prerogatives and sentimentalities." He closes with
a short sentence that also contains a balance, "shoddy and preposterous." Between these sentences he writes his long sentence containing a long series. He takes care that the first item in that series—
"his masculine liberty of movement and occupation"—contains a
balance, "movement and occupation," and that the last item in the
series—"his general innocence and childishness"—contains another
balance, "innocence and childishness." This particular paragraph
takes on a strong two-part nature then: balance here, balance there
and the whole paragraph a balance of two short sentences on either
side of the long central sentence. All in all, the design of the paragraph seems appropriate to a discussion of the battle of the sexes.

Copy the Mencken paragraph; then *compose* a paragraph that
similarly moves from a short sentence to a long middle sentence and
then to a short concluding sentence.

26 THE PATTERNED PARAGRAPH (LONG SENTENCE TO SHORT SENTENCE TO LONG SENTENCE)

*So many Christs there seem to be: one in rebellion against his cross, to which he
was nailed; one bitter with the agony of knowing he must die, his heart-
beatings all futile; one who felt sentimental; one who gave in to his misery; one
who was sensationalist; one who dreamed and fretted with thought. Perhaps the
peasant carvers of crucifixes are right, and all these are found on the same cross.
And perhaps there were others too: one who waited for the end, his soul still
with a sense of right and hope; one ashamed to see the crowd make beasts of
themselves, ashamed that he should provide for their sport; one who looked at*

them and thought: "And I am of you. I might be among you, yelling at myself in that way. But I am not, I am here. And so—"—D. H. Lawrence, Christs in Tirol

The patterned paragraph may also move from long sentence to short sentence to long. Again, the value of such a paragraph with its rather exact structure is to provide contrast with other paragraphs in which sentence lengths are of no consideration.

Lawrence has made effective use of this particular design, faced as he was with the problem of presenting his long list of diverse Christ-figures without surfeiting the reader. By breaking his list into two long series sentences and separating them with a short sentence, he has used this patterned paragraph in analogy with a two-act drama having an intermission between the acts. The play would have been too long without some interruption; the short sentence becomes the necessary relief.

Copy Lawrence's paragraph; then *compose* a paragraph using the same long-short-long design.

27 | THE PATTERNED PARAGRAPH (STATEMENTS AND QUESTIONS)

Ibsen once made one of his characters say that he did not read much because he found reading "irrelevant," and the adjective was brilliantly chosen because it held implications even beyond those of which Ibsen was consciously aware. What is it that made the classics irrelevant to him and to us? Is it not just exactly those to him impossible premises which make tragedy what it is, those assumptions that the soul of man is great, that the universe (together with whatever gods may be) concerns itself with him and that he is, in a word, noble? Ibsen turned to village politics for exactly the same reason that his contemporaries and his successors have, each in his own way, sought out some aspect of the common man and his common life—because, that is to say, here was at least something small enough for him to be able to believe.—Joseph Wood Krutch, The Modern Temper

What has been learned? What have we learned from one of the most instructive weeks in human history? If we have learned well, it is possible that the human race stands a fair chance of securing to itself the blessings of reason and fulfillment on earth to a greater degree than has been possible so far. If we have learned poorly, then it may be only a short time before the onset of new eruptions from which there can be neither recovery nor appeal.—Norman Cousins, What Have We Learned?

Patterned paragraphs can be achieved not only by manipulating sentence length but also by using various sentence forms. Questions and statements, being clearly distinguishable forms, are those most frequently used to create designs. Joseph Wood Krutch, in his paragraph above, has created a pattern with a statement, a question, a question, and a statement. Nor is the pattern an accident; the third sentence could easily have been a statement rather than a rhetorical question. And what is the rationale of the pattern? The rationale of interest if nothing else; certainly, when dealing with abstract ideas such as belief, relevancy, tragedy, or nobility, an author may well feel the need to support the abstract observations with a definite architectural paragraph and to hold reader attention by providing delightful and well-considered style during a generally abstract discussion.

Another version of the question/statement pattern is the one by Norman Cousins. Cousins presents two questions and then two conditional statements. The paragraph is carefully patterned since both conditional statements open with the same words. It becomes antithetical when "well" and "poorly" are contrasted.

This strongly patterned paragraph was used by Cousins to begin an an editorial in the *Saturday Review*. Patterned paragraphs of one kind or another are frequently used in opening positions, since they are exceptional and attract reader attention.

Copy the two paragraphs above; then *compose* two paragraphs that make use of questions and statements to create a pattern. In one paragraph use the exact pattern that Joseph Wood Krutch uses. Then compose a paragraph similar to that of Norman Cousins— with two questions followed by two statements. If you wish, write a third paragraph in which you make up a pattern of your own.

28 THE EXPERIMENTAL PARAGRAPH

Paris Exhibition: the Spanish Pavilion, the Italian Pavilion. The other pavilions. The Palaces of Glass and of Peace. The Eiffel Tower. The last named occasionally sings. Moved by an emission of Roman Candles from its flanks, it will break of an evening into a dulcet and commanding melody. When this happens the pavilions fold their hands to listen, and are steeped for a little in shadow, so that the aniline fountains may play more brightly in the Seine. The melody swells, inciting the fireworks as they the melody, and both of them swell the crowd. O synchronisation! O splendour unequalled! Splendour never to be surpassed? Probably never to be surpassed. The German and Russian Pavilions, the Chinese and Japanese Pavilions, the British and Italian Pavilions, any and all of the pavilions, will see to that. The Eiffel Tower sings louder, a scientific swan. Rosy chemicals stimulate her spine, she can scarcely bear the voltage, the joy, the pain. . . . The emotion goes to her tiny head, it turns crimson and vomits fiery serpents. All Paris sees them. They astonish the Pantheon and Montmarte. Even the Institute de France notices, heavy browed, dreaming of cardinals, laurels, and réclame in the past. O inspired giraffe! Whatever will the old thing turn into next? Listen and see. The crisis is coming. The melody rises by slight and sure gradations, à la César Franck, spiralling easily upward upon the celestial roundabout. Bell pop popple crack, is the crisis, bell pop popple crack, the senses reel, music and light, lusic and might, the Eiffel Tower becomes a plesioauros, flings out her arms in flame, and brings them back smartly to her vibrating sides, as one who should say, "la!" Bell pop crack pop popple bell. The carillon dies away, the rockets fall, the senses disentangle. There is silence, there are various types of silences, and during one of them the Angel of the Laboratory speaks, "Au revoir, mes enfants," she says. "I hope you have enjoyed yourselves. We shall meet again shortly, and in different conditions." The children applaud these well-chosen words. The German Pavilion, the Russian Pavilion, confront one another again, and a small star shines out on the top of the Column of Peace.—E. M. Forster, Two Cheers for Democracy

On some extremely rare occasion, you may wish to create a paragraph that adheres to no given formula and for which there is no existing model: you may simply want to experiment with words and sentences to create a paragraph of your own invention. However, when you do write an experimental paragraph, you will have to be judicious in your use of it. It might be too exceptional to fit into the prose compositions that you normally write. Yet, it is good to be prepared to do something different. You may someday have need to shock your readers into great awareness, and you may decide that the only way to do it is to give them a piece of writing that they normally would not encounter.

To give a formula for an experimental paragraph would be to negate its originality and uniqueness; but by studying experimental paragraphs of master writers you may get some ideas on how experimentation comes about. In E. M. Forster's paragraph you will find an effective accumulation of such devices as elliptical sentences, series sentences, figurative sentences, and rhetorical questions combined with alliteration, onomatopoeia, and the like—creating a readable, understandable paragraph that is, nevertheless, a unique experience in itself.

Forster's main device in creating his unusual paragraph is the metaphor, especially personification. He presents his personification of the Eiffel Tower in a variety of highly structured sentences, sentences with key-word repetitions, metrical sentences, and rhythmical sentences. Look especially at such sentences as follow: "O synchronisation! O splendour unequalled! Splendour never to be surpassed? Probably never to be surpassed. . . . Listen and see. The crisis is coming. . . . Bell pop crack pop popple bell. The carillon dies away, the rockets fall, the senses disentangle." Actually, Forster has drawn upon the full range of sentences to create his paragraph. Using a full spectrum of colors, he has created a vivid and dynamic description of a place, a vivid and dynamic account of an evening's event.

Copy the Forster paragraph; then *compose* an experimental paragraph of your own. Use as many types of stylistic sentences as you can to create a colorful picture of a place or an exciting account of some experience. Write as vigorously as you can. To get started, follow Forster's lead: Simply state the object you intend to describe or name the experience you are going to report—"The University: the green oval, the marble library. To the left: the temples of science. To the right: the temples of art. Science. Art. Staring across the green abyss. . . ." Use your imagination—and let yourself go, verbally.

THE WHOLE COMPOSITION

The following essay employs a variety of basic and stylistic paragraph patterns even in what is, for Norman Mailer, reasonably conventional prose.

Cities Higher Than Mountains

Norman Mailer

In Lyndon Johnson's book, *My Hope for America*, the fifth chapter is titled "Toward the Great Society." It contains this paragraph:

> *. . . fifty years from now, . . . there will be four hundred million Americans, four-fifths of them in urban areas. In the remainder of this century, . . . we will have to build homes, highways, and facilities equal to all those built since this country was first settled. In the next forty years we must rebuild the entire urban United States.*

It is a staggering sentence. The city we inhabit at this moment is already close to a total reconstruction of the world our parents knew in their childhood. If there is no nuclear war, if we shift from cold war to some kind of peace, and there is a worldwide rise in the standard of living, then indeed we will build a huge new country. It is possible that not one in a thousand of the buildings put up by 1899 will still be standing in the year 2000.

But what will America look like? How will its architecture appear? Will it be the architecture of a Great Society, or continue to be the architecture of an empty promiscuous panorama where no one can distinguish between hospitals and housing projects, factories and colleges, concert halls, civic centers, and airport terminals? The mind recoils from the thought of an America rebuilt completely in the shape of those blank skyscrapers forty stories high, their walls dead as an empty television screen, their form as interesting as a box of cleansing tissue propped on end. They are buildings which reveal nothing so much as the deterioration in real value of the dollar bill. They are denuded of ornament (which costs money), their windows are not subtly recessed into the wall but are laid flush with the surface like a patch of collodion on the skin, there is no instant where a roof with a tower, a gable, a spire, a mansard, a ridge or even a mooring mast for a dirigible intrudes itself into the sky, reminding us that every previous culture of man attempted to engage the heavens.

No, our modern buildings go flat, flat at the top, flat as eternal monotony, flat as the last penny in a dollar. There is so much corruption in the building codes, overinflation in the value of land, featherbedding built into union rules, so much graft, so much waste, so much public relations, and so much emptiness inflated upon so much emptiness that no one tries to do more with the roof than leave it flat.

As one travels through the arbitrary new neighborhoods of the present, those high squat dormitories which imprison the rich as well as the poor, one is not surprised that the violence is greater than it used to be in the old slum, up are the statistics for juvenile delinquency and for dope addiction. To live in the old slum jungle left many half crippled, and others part savage, but it was at least an environment which asked for wit. In the prison vistas of urban renewal, the violence travels from without to within, there is no wit—one travels down a long empty corridor to reach one's door, long as the corridors in the public schools, long as the corridors in the hospitals at the end of the road; the landscape of modern man takes on a sense of endless empty communications.

Sterile as an operating table is the future vista of suburban spread, invigorating as a whiff of deodorant is the sight of new office buildings. Small elation sits upon us as we contemplate the future, for the picturesque will be uprooted with the ugly, our populations will double, and in a city like New York, the brownstone will be replaced by a cube sixteen stories high with a huge park for parking cars and a little grass. The city will go up a little and it will go out, it will spread. We will live with glass walls in a cold climate. The entire world will come to look like Queens Boulevard. We will have been uprooted so many times that future man will come to bear the same relation to the past that a hydroponic plant bears to soil.

Yet some part of us is aware that to uproot the past too completely is a danger without measure. It must at the least produce a profound psychic discomfort. For we do not know how much our perception of the present and our estimate of the future depend upon our sense of what has gone before. To return to an old neighborhood and discover it has disappeared is a minor woe for some; it is close to a psychological catastrophe for others, an amputation where the lost nerves still feel pain. This century must appear at times like a great beast which has lost its tail, but who could argue that the amputation was not self-inflicted?

There seems at loose an impulse to uproot every vestige of the past, an urge so powerful one wonders if it is not with purpose, if it is not in the nature of twentieth-century man to uproot himself not only from his past, but from his planet. Perhaps we live on the edge of a great divide in history and so are divided ourselves between the desire for a gracious, intimate, detailed and highly particular landscape and an urge less articulate to voyage out on explorations not yet made. Perhaps the blank faceless abstract quality of our modern architecture is a reflection of the anxiety we feel before the void, a kind of visual static which emanates from the psyche of us all, as if we do not know which way to go.

If we are to spare the countryside, if we are to protect the style of the small town and of the exclusive suburb, keep the organic center of the metropolis and the old neighborhoods, maintain those few remaining streets where the tradition of the nineteenth century and the muse of the eighteenth century still linger on the mood in the summer cool of an evening, if we are to avoid a megalopolis five hundred miles long, a city without shape or exit, a nightmare of ranch houses, highways, suburbs and industrial sludge, if we are to save the dramatic edge of a city—the precise moment when we leave the outskirts and race into the country, the open country—if we are to have a keen acute sense of concentration and a breath of release, then there is only one solution: the cities must climb, they must not spread, they must build up, not by increments, but by leaps, up and up, up to the heavens.

We must be able to live in houses one hundred stories high, two hundred stories high, far above the height of buildings as we know them now. New cities with great towers must rise in the plain, cities higher than mountains, cities with room for 400,000,000 to live, or that part of 400,000,000 who wish to live high in a landscape of peaks and spires, cliffs and precipices. For the others, for those who wish to live on the ground and with the ground, there will then be new room to live—the traditional small town will be able to survive, as will the old neighborhoods in the cities. But first a way must be found to build upward, to triple and triple again the height of all buildings as we know them now.

Picture, if you please, an open space where twenty acrobats

stand, each locking hands with two different partners. Conceive then of ten acrobats standing on the shoulders of these twenty, and five upon the ten acrobats, and three more in turn above them, then two, then one. We have a pyramid of figures: six thousand to eight thousand pounds is supported upon a base of twenty pairs of shoes.

It enables one to think of structures more complex, of pyramids of steel which rise to become towers. Imagine a tower half a mile high and stressed to bear a vast load. Think of six or eight such towers and of bridges built between them, even as huge vines tie the branches of one high tree to another; think of groups of apartments built above these bridges (like the shops on the Ponte Vecchio in Florence) and apartments suspended beneath each bridge, and smaller bridges running from one complex of apartments to another, and of apartments suspended from cables, apartments kept in harmonious stress to another by cables between them.

One can now begin to conceive of a city, or a separate part of a city, which is as high as it is wide, a city which bends ever so subtly in a high wind with the most delicate flexing of its near-to-numberless parts even as the smallest strut in a great bridge reflects the passing of an automobile with some fine-tuned quiver. In the subtlety of its swayings the vertical city might seem to be ready to live itself. It might be agreeable to live there.

The real question, however, has not yet been posed. It is whether a large fraction of the population would find it reasonable to live one hundred to two hundred stories in the air. There is the dread of heights. Would that tiny pit of suicide, planted like the small seed of murder in civilized man, flower prematurely into breakdown, terror and dread? Would it demand too much of a tenant to stare down each morning on a flight of 2,000 feet? Or would it prove a deliverance for some? Would the juvenile delinquent festering in the violence of his monotonous corridors diminish in his desire for brutality if he lived high in the air and found the intensity of his inexpressible vision matched by the intensity of the space through a fall?

That question returns us to the perspective of twentieth-century man. Caught between our desire to cling to the earth and to explore the stars, it is not impossible that a new life lived half a mile in the air, with streets in the clouds and chasms beyond each railing could prove nonetheless more intimate and more personal to us than the present congestions of the housing-project city. For that future man would be returned some individuality from his habitation. His apartment in the sky would be not so very different in its internal details from the apartments of his neighbors, no more than one apartment is varied from another in Washington Square Village. But his situation would now be different from any other. His windows would look out on a view of massive constructions and airy bridges, of huge vaults and fine intricacies. The complexity of our culture could be captured again by the imagination of the architect: our buildings could begin to look a little less like armored tanks and more like clipper ships. Would we also then feel the dignity of sailors on a four-master at sea? Living so high, thrust into space, might we be returned to that mixture of awe and elation, of dignity and self-respect and a hint of dread, that sense of zest which a man must have known working his way out along a yardarm in a stiff breeze at sea? Would the fatal monotony of mass culture dissolve a hint before the quiet swaying of a great and vertical city?

Exercises

1. Identify the basic and stylistic paragraph patterns Norman Mailer employs in "Cities Higher Than Mountains."

2. Select one of the paragraphs from the essay to use as the model for a paragraph of your own composition on quite a different subject.

3. Transform a paragraph of Mailer's essay from one pattern to another somewhat different one making whatever revisions are necessary.

11. SENTENCES

Like the paragraph, the sentence is a basic unit of composition. It is—by traditional definition—a group of words, consisting of at least a subject and verb, which expresses a complete thought. To write well, we learn to write a basic kind of sentence—and then learn to develop the basic sentence into other sentence forms. With a little practice, we discover that virtually all sentences can be shortened or extended, compounded or complicated to serve our rhetorical needs. As we write our sentences, we try to keep three rules in mind: First, we must never let our reader lose sight of the central thought upon which the sentence turns. Second, we should keep in mind that complicated thoughts need to be expressed as simply as possible. And third, we should always be prepared to use, in order to achieve various rhetorical profiles, a full range of sentence forms.

To write effective sentences you must first realize that you have a wide range of sentence forms to choose from. Some of the most crucial decisions you make will be whether to use a virtual, simple, compound, complex, or combination compound-complex sentence. Though you may think that you write the kind of sentence that subject matter and content dictate, actually the choice is far from being that simple or automatic. If anything, the content itself has less to do with your decision than such considerations as variety, emphasis, and rhetorical profile.

The basic sentence pattern can be modified, combined, and elaborated in different ways to accommodate any thought of sentence proportions. This basic pattern is, in short, the axle upon which all your sentences turn, from the most elliptical virtual sentence to the most elaborate compound-complex sentence. *The basic sentence consists of a subject, an action verb or linking verb, and, almost always, an object or complement:*

Time flies.
I love you.

This sentence pattern can be infinitely adapted by varying one of its four attributes.

It is typically declarative; but by *altering the order of elements*, you can subtly shift its emphasis or change its function:

He was brave. (declarative)
Was he brave? (interrogative)
How brave he was! (exclamatory)
Be brave. (imperative)
Brave he was. (moves the complement ahead of the subject)

It can be *abbreviated, elaborated, compounded, or complicated.* By abbreviating the basic sentence, you can sometimes express a complete thought in a grammatically incomplete way:

Brave? Him!
The impenetrable mystery in those reptilian eyes.

By slightly elaborating certain elements you can make the basic sentence more flexible without sacrificing terseness:

The great god Pan is dead.

The Polynesians explored and colonized the Pacific.

He was brave from then on.

By more extensively compounding or modifying elements, the basic sentence becomes even more affluent. Ultimately you begin coordinating basic sentences to make compound sentences and subordinating added thoughts to make complex sentences:

He was brave, but his foolish lack of caution cost him his life.

Since there was no alternative, he was brave.

And by combining in various ways these compound and complex patterns, you can expand the basic sentence even further:

He was brave because there was no alternative to bravery but cowardice, and he feared being a coward more than dying.

So possibilities here range from the shortest simple sentence of two or three words (or even the virtual sentence of perhaps a single word) to the labyrinthine compound-complex sentence of ten or twenty times that length.

The sentence, whatever size or shape, *is most commonly loose, but can often be written as periodic.* Often in conversation and sometimes in writing you begin a sentence without really knowing how it will end, completing the sentence as you can by tacking on additional thoughts as they occur. Only the loose sentence, which expresses the main idea first and then adds details, permits such an easygoing approach to communication. While the loose sentence is so casual and instinctive that you use it most of the time, it is apt to be diffuse, anticlimactic, and overworked.

The following examples illustrate how the loose sentence grows:

Red-tailed hawks hunt my meadow.

Red-tailed hawks hunt my meadow for rabbits and field mice.

Red-tailed hawks hunt my meadow for rabbits and field mice on those sheet-metal days in February.

The first expresses only the main idea; the second expresses the main idea, then adds a couple of immediately related details; but the third expresses the main idea, then adds so many details that the sentence begins to falter at the end. The loose sentence pattern is not inherently interesting, and a succession of loose sentences can be terribly monotonous. The last sentence is better rewritten as partially periodic:

On those sheet-metal days in February, red-tailed hawks hunt my meadow for rabbits and field mice.

Or somewhat more periodic:

On those sheet-metal days in February when the rabbits and field mice creep out to feed, red-tailed hawks hunt my meadow.

Or almost wholly periodic—there being, of course, degrees of periodicity:

Hunting my meadow for rabbits and field mice on those sheet-metal days in February was a pair of red-tailed hawks.

Had the loose original been a complex sentence, the periodic revision would have been an even more striking improvement:

Red-tailed hawks hunt my meadow for rabbits and field mice on those sheet-metal days in February when the grey ice bows down the bluestem leaving rusty patches where the sedge grass grows. (basically loose)
On those sheet-metal days in February when the grey ice bows down the bluestem leaving rusty patches where the sedge grass grows, red-tailed hawks hunt my meadow for rabbits and field mice. (basically periodic)

While a compound sentence as a whole cannot be periodic, its parts can:

The red-tailed hawk hunts my meadow in soaring cricles by day; the barn owl scans my meadow in silent swoops by night. (basically loose)
By day the red-tailed hawk hunts my meadow in soaring circles; by night the barn owl scans my meadow in silent swoops. (slightly periodic)

The periodic sentence, which delays completing the main thought until the end, or near the end, is an interesting pattern because it holds the reader in suspense and forces him to keep all the details in mind. Most loose sentences can easily be translated into periodic:

by adding or moving forward a modifier (to the beginning of the sentence or between the subject and verb),

Red-tailed hawks, searching for rabbits and field mice, hunt my meadow.

by inverting the sentence,

Hunting my meadow for rabbits and field mice was a red-tailed hawk.

and by beginning the sentence with "It was."

It was February before the red-tailed hawks began to hunt my meadow.

Don't be too quick to change, for a succession of periodic sentences, even more than a succession of loose sentences, can be precociously self-conscious and thoroughly wearisome. But consider using a higher proportion of periodic sentences than you have in the past:

(1) *for varying your predominantly loose style and emphasizing your more important ideas,*

All the luck was on my side in the first encounter with the mysterious trade of teaching. I had found a personality not antagonistic to mine. His 'teenish gallantry rose to the challenge of my desperate determination to interest him. He offered me the gifts of believing that maybe I had "had something" in this Aeneid. At any rate I was a decent sort and he would listen long enough to give me the benefit of the doubt. Somehow or other, probably because there is nowhere else in life such unadulterated idealism and decency as the pure strain, if it can be tapped, than flows in the veins of sixteen—perhaps, too, because the impact of long weeks lounging about Europe had subconsciously released and stimulated his sense of the beautiful permanent things of civilization—he did get interested in the story itself and how Virgil had contrived to tell it.—Esther Cloudman Dunn, Pursuit of Understanding: Autobiography of an Education

(The last and most important sentence is strongly periodic.)

(2) *for putting the important ideas at the end of the sentence,*

Out of the wild, crumbling confusion born of the dissolution of the force and the last great shape, foamy fountains spurt, and ringlets of spray.—Henry Beston, The Outermost House

(3) *and for sustaining interest in a long sentence.*

Here, amid the throngs, the buses, the dodging taxicabs, the clanging streetcars; here, among the gaudy billboards and the glaring colors of the nighttime spectaculars; here, in this public and populous spot—fenced in by glass and brick, stone and asphalt, cement and steel—is a world so divorced from that of the open fields and woods that it seems impossible that the two should ever meet.— Edwin Way Teale, The Lost Woods

And, although it can be written in the passive voice, the basic sentence is most forceful in the active. In fact, if you used only the active voice, you would be right most of the time. The active voice, which preserves the natural order of sentence elements, is direct and forceful; the passive voice, which inverts the sentence, is frequently wordy and noncommittal. It is usually more effective to say "Darwin collected and popularized ideas that had been talked about for centuries," than "Ideas that had been talked about for centuries were collected and popularized by Darwin." And it is clearly better to write, "I climbed the Matterhorn," than, "The Matterhorn was climbed by me," for this implies something you don't mean.

Use the active voice regularly; use the passive voice only where it would be more effective:

to emphasize the receiver of the action rather than, as the active voice does, the doer of the action. If navigation were your subject you would write,

A form of stellar navigation was used by the ancient Phoenecians.

And if the Phoenicians were your subject,

The ancient Phoenicians used a form of stellar navigation.

to shift the real subject to the end position where it can sometimes be more easily modified,

The Ossianic poems were actually written by James Macpherson, a talented literary forger who apparently made use of genuine Celtic tradition but composed most of the epic *Fingal* himself.

to give the effect of detachment

The bride's worst fears were confirmed. (What they were is unknown.)
She was left waiting at the door of the church. (By whom is unimportant.)
But her tears were changed to smiles. (Modesty prevented, "I changed her tears to smiles.")

and sometimes to make the thought easier to phrase. It is simpler to write, "A horse can be taught to stand when the reins are dropped," than any equivalent in the active voice.

THE VIRTUAL SENTENCE

The basic sentence pattern can, on occasion, be foreshortened. Any thought or feeling put into words is a sentence. And sometimes not many words are required. "Mayday!" in certain circumstances means, "I am bailing out; get a fix on my signal and send help," and "Oh, yeah?" with the right intonation says "I don't believe that what you have just told me is true." Ordinary speech contains a good many of these abbreviations and fragments. So when you talk about sentences you have to begin with a construction that isn't really a sentence at all in the strictest sense—the virtual sentence. It is a short cut taken by a writer who knows the route extremely well and knows the reader is right behind. And it demonstrates the importance of context in writing, for the virtual sentence is a complete thought not because of what it says, but because of what is said or suggested elsewhere.

Occasionally use the virtual sentence to capture some of the snap and immediacy of speech and to shorten and simplify what would otherwise be an ineffectively complicated statement:

in dialogue (especially questions, answers, exclamations),

"Have your people got a car?"
"Yes."
"What sort of car?"
"Daimler."
"How many horse-power?"
(Pause, and leap in the dark.) "Fifteen."
"What kind of lights?"
The little boy is bewildered.
"What kind of lights? Electric or acetylene?"
(A longer pause, and another leap in the dark.) "Acetylene."—George Orwell, Such, Such Were the Joys

in description,

A restless morning, with clouds lower down, moving also with a larger round-ward motion. Everything moving. But to go out in motion too, the slow round-ward motion like the hawks.—D. H. Lawrence, Mornings in Mexico

for transitions,

So much for Raffles. *Now for a header into the cesspool.—George Orwell,* Raffles and Miss Blandish

for introductions,

Kimono. It covers her from throat to ankles; with a gesture as feminine as the placing of a flower or as female as the cradling of a child, the hands themselves can be concealed into the sleeves until there remains one unbroken chalice-shape of modesty proclaiming her femininity where nudity would merely parade her mammalian femaleness.—William Faulkner, Faulkner at Nagano

for conclusions,

The Greeks and Romans were the first comers in the fields of thought and literature. When they arrived at fairly obvious reflections upon life and love, upon war, fate or manners, they coined them into the slogans or epigrams for which their language was so well adapted, and thus preserved the patent rights for all time. Hence their reputation.—Winston Churchill, A Roving Commission

for emphasis,

They say here that great waves reach this coast in threes. Three great waves, then an indeterminate run of lesser rhythms, then three great waves again.— Henry Beston, The Outermost House

But use virtual sentences rarely, and don't confuse them with incomplete sentences. A fully intended and clearly effective "incomplete sentence" is not the same as an accidental and uncalled for "incomplete sentence." It would be pointless to write,

Washington's veterans encamped at Valley Forge not only to lick their wounds but to learn soldiering. To prepare for the day they could meet the British in a decisive action.

Either complete the sentence,

Washington's veterans encamped at Valley Forge not only to lick their wounds but to learn soldiering. Here preparations were made for the day they would meet the British in a decisive action.

or join it with another,

Washington's veterans encamped at Valley Forge not only to lick their wounds but to learn soldiering and prepare for the day they would meet the British in a decisive action.

THE SIMPLE SENTENCE

The basic sentence pattern is most prominent in the simple sentence, a routinely and sometimes strikingly effective form. Many of your best sentences will possess the clarity of the simple sentence, the directness and force of the active voice, and the suspense of periodic construction.

Use the simple sentence:
in its most austere form for variety, but mainly for emphasis,

I got up. The Burmans were already racing past me across the mud. It was obvious that the elephant would never rise again, but he was not dead.—George Orwell, Shooting an Elephant

I have never walked down the south side of Piccadilly without being all in a dither about what was happening on the north. This is folly.—W. Somerset Maugham, A Summing Up

or with parts compounded or modified to make it more variable, comprehensive, and periodic. In the familiar subject-verb-complement sentence, for example, you can elaborate the subject,

To come all the way to Europe, to arrive full of expectation, and then to find the monuments covered with scaffolding and the streets full of American tourists is maddening. (subject compounded)

That red Morocco volume, with the cracked spine and illegible gilt lettering, is a rare first edition. (subject modified)

or the verb,

Most quarter milers sprint for a good position going into the first curve, float much of the backstretch, and sprint again coming out of the last curve. (verb compounded)

The tidal wave advanced, slowly at first, then faster, then with awesome speed toward the beach. (verb modified)

or the object,

I relish spring mornings, summer evenings, fall afternoons—and winter not at all. (object compounded)

I read his reasonably artistic, but somewhat tiresome memoirs. (object modified)

or some combination of subject, verb, and complement. But don't overelaborate the simple sentence like this,

The tiger and the lamb live in peace and serenity in Edward Hicks's Peaceable Kingdom and in St. Francis' Paradise. (subject, object of preposition, and prepositional phrases compounded)

The courageous Gloucesterman sails across stormy seas to the lonely fishing grounds. (subject, verb, and objects of prepositions modified)

When you have this many details to communicate, you'd better think about coordinating them in some more effective way, perhaps even subordinating some of them. A succession of simple sentences is, especially in expository writing, likely to appear simple-minded and sure to be monotonous:

I was once seized by the desire to read Homer in the original. I bought an interlinear edition of *The Odyssey*. I also got a lexicon. Later I added a grammar. And I spent many long summer evenings with those books.

Writing more simple sentences is not the way to elaborate a simple sentence. You can even write the above five sentences as one and stay within the general framework of the simple sentence:

I was once seized by the desire to read Homer in the original and spent many long summer evenings with a grammar, a lexicon, and an interlinear edition of *The Odyssey*.

Contrary to what you might expect, the uncomplicated and insignificant thought often belongs in a compound or complex sentence, rather than in a simple sentence where it might appear ridiculously patent or overemphasized.

THE COMPOUND SENTENCE

The compound sentence, which is made up of what are essentially simple sentences joined by conjunctions or punctuation, coordinates thoughts of more or less equal importance. In the hands of an alert stylist, the compound sentence is swift and rhythmical, considering in the same breath thoughts that belong together because they are in either close agreement or close contrast. Thus you may write,

To many, democracy is phlegmatic, equivocal, and mean; but no one has found a better way to manage the housekeeping affairs of a nation. Only a few have tried—and their opinions are read only to be ridiculed.

rather than in the primer style,

To many, democracy is phlegmatic, equivocal, and mean. But no one has found a better way to manage the housekeeping affairs of a nation. Only a few have tried. Their opinions are read only to be ridiculed.

> Make a compound sentence more effective:
> *by coordinating only those ideas that are logically related and equal, and when necessary, by expanding the relation,*

St. Mark's and its Campanile stood out against the evening sky. Twittering swallows wheeled through the air. (Avoid simply tacking on an independent clause as in, "St. Mark's and its Campanile stood out against the evening sky, and twittering swallows wheeled through the air.")

As the birds and cumulus clouds became more numerous, we felt increasingly sure land was near. (Avoid coordinating what you should subordinate as in, "The birds and cumulus clouds became more numerous and we felt increasingly sure land was near.")

Indian Johnny was an old cowboy, and he could reminisce for hours about cattle ranching in the southwest. (Avoid leaving too much of the relationship up to your reader's imagination as in, "Indian Johnny was an old cowboy, and he could talk for hours.")

> *by coordinating with other than the all-too-inevitable "and" or by dropping the conjunction altogether and letting the punctuation support the connection.* There is nothing wrong with *and* in the right place, as when it subtly pivots a cause and effect:

Critics denounced the novel as pornographic, and most who read it agreed.

But too often *and* is used in place of a more exact coordinator—but, for, or, nor, so, consequently, therefore, thus, however, still, yet, otherwise, then.

The nations were still at war and the founding fathers were doubtful about whether a world organization could be made to work at all, so they inserted a clause or two to cover themselves in case it didn't.—E. B. White, The Shape of the U.N. (*And* would have obscured the causal relation.)

We intended to clean it out and live in it, but there were holes in the roof and the birds had come in and were roosting in the rafters.—Loren C. Eiseley, The Immense Journey (*And* would have obscured the sense of qualification and exception.)

The compound sentence with a coordinator is perhaps smoother and more natural; but the compound sentence with punctuation only is likely to appear more adroit and impressive. When the relationship of parts is so clear that no coordinator is necessary, rely on your punctuation to link the clauses.

Goodness is easier to recognize than to define; only the great novelists can portray good people.—W. H. Auden, I Believe

I bored my parents, they bored me.—Robert Lowell, Life Studies

by coordinating for special effect. The compound sentence, even more than the simple sentence, is the pattern of ordinary speech.

I was in the woman left on the shore; the canoe held my companions of the past summer; the island was to be my home until another summer should bring them back again.—Laura Lee Davidson, A Winter of Content

They rise out of the earth, they sweat and starve for a few years, and then they sink back into the nameless mounds of the graveyard and nobody notices that they are gone.—George Orwell, Marrakech

The sheep ran forward in little pattering rushes; they began to bleat, and ghostly flocks and herds answered them from under the sea. "Baa! Baaa!"—Katherine Mansfied, At the Bay

But in the hands of a wide-awake writer the compound sentence can have snap, as when one of the clauses is a brief anticipation or afterthought to a longer one:

The storm is gone, and here in the country a mild sun has bit by bit argued the cold and snow away.—Donald Culrose Peattie, Green Laurels

The act of dying is not of importance, it lasts so short a time.—James Boswell, The Life of Johnson

And is capable of long rhythms that are sometimes right for the context:

The rain began to patter down in broad and scattered drops; the wind freshened, and curled up the waves; at length it seemed as if the bellying clouds were torn open by the mountain-tops, and complete torrents of rain came rattling down.— Washington Irving, Bracebridge Hall

and by balancing the sentence. Since it is rather distinctive, the balanced sentence should be used mainly for emphasis and only occasionally for variety. Ordinarily balance is achieved when parts of the same sentence are similar in length and structure. But it may involve separate sentences of similar design. In either case, when the thoughts are in agreement, the effect is one of mutual reinforcement; and when thoughts are in contrast, the effect is one of tension. (This last sentence is essentially a balanced one. The slight variation from perfect symmetry, provided here by the short introductory phrase, is usually an improvement when the statement is rather routine.)

Love not pleasure; love God.—*Thomas Carlyle,* Sartor Resartus

I have loved individuals; I have never much cared for men in the mass.—*W. Somerset Maugham,* A Summing Up

The power of French literature is in its prose writers, the power of English literature is in its poets.—*Matthew Arnold,* Essays in Criticism

Outside, the flurry rain made muddy scallops in the street; but inside, dust particles floated serenely in the filtered evening half-light.

This kind of balance can involve the complex sentence or some combination of compound and complex as well:
The true American knew something of the facts, but nothing of the feelings; he read the letter, but he never felt the law.—*Henry Adams,* The Education of Henry Adams

The thunder burst in tremendous explosions; the peals were echoed from mountain to mountain; they crashed upon Dunderberg, and rolled up the long defile of the highlands, each headland making a new echo, until old Bull Hill seemed to bellow back the storm.—*Washington Irving,* Bracebridge Hall

Not a victory is gained, not a deed of faithfulness or courage is done, except upon a maybe; not a service, not a sally of generosity, nor a scientific explanation or experiment or text book, that may not be a mistake.—*William James,* Is Life Worth Living?

THE COMPLEX SENTENCE

The complex sentence, which consists of one independent clause and one or more dependent clauses, subordinates thoughts of lesser importance. It is vastly more sophisticated than either the simple or compound sentence because it not only contains more than one idea, but distinguishes the central idea from its details.

As separate simple sentences,

The sea boomed and hissed. I slept but fitfully.

and as a single compound sentence,

The sea boomed and hissed, and I slept but fitfully.

these two ideas are of undifferentiated importance. But rewritten as a complex sentence, either the sound of the sea,

The sea boomed and hissed, while I slept but fitfully.

or the fitful sleep,

When the sea boomed and hissed, I slept but fitfully.

can be emphasized. Whenever you possibly can, put the important thoughts into independent clauses and reduce the others to modifying clauses, phrases, and words.

You can make a complex sentence more effective by keeping sight of the central idea. The central idea belongs in the main clause, never in the subordinate clause or phrase.

When he happened to glance in the display case, he noticed a scarab of unusual design. (Not, "He happened to glance in the display case, noticing a scarab of unusual design.")

As the survivors watched from lifeboats, the doomed ship heeled over and slowly disappeared. (Not, "As the doomed ship heeled over and slowly disappeared, the survivors watched from lifeboats.")

The central idea should stand out clearly and never be obscured by unnecessary subordinate details or by a sequence of subordinate clauses, each dependent upon the one before.

Though I have coins from Greece, Palestine, and Egypt, my prize exhibit is a silver coin from Rome. (Not, "My collection includes a silver coin minted in Rome seventeen hundred years ago that bears a portrait of the Emperor Probus, and an assortment of bronze coins from Greece, Palestine, and Egypt that I ordered from a place in New York.")

At the opera I sat next to a friend of the leading soprano. They had been classmates at a musical conservatory that has produced several famous operatic sopranos. (Not, "At the opera I sat next to a woman who told me she knew the leading soprano, who had been her classmate when both attended a musical conservatory that has produced several operatic sopranos who have become famous.")

You can make a complex sentence more effective by using a subordinator that points up the most exact relationship. Some subordinators are often so smooth we are not aware of there being separate thoughts (who, whom, where, which, that, what).

The sprinter who leaves the blocks first usually wins.
Which she chose made no difference.
He didn't know what he wanted.

Some generally connect a clause modifying a word in the main clause (when, whenever, where, wherever, how, why, while, as, before, after, until, since).

When the wind is easterly we usually have rain.
She couldn't remember why she had come.
He got out while there was time.

And some distinguish between the central thought and its details more emphatically than other subordinators (although, as, as if, so, so that, because, before, if, since, that, until, till, unless, when, where).

She likes terra-cotta because it is a color associated with Sufism.
Since it is too late for tea, let's have dinner.
Until you learn to relax in the water you cannot expect to be a good swimmer.

Some subordinators have rather precise meanings. For example, *if* at the beginning of a dependent clause indicates that it is the cause of the effect described in the independent clause; and *although* suggests some kind of concession.

But some have more than one meaning; when you use *as, so,* and *while,* you especially run a risk of being ambiguous. In the sentence, "As the desert heat grew more intense, the travelers began to suffer," you would be much clearer if you replaced *as* with *when* (referring to time) or *because* (referring to cause). And in the sentence, "While Melville was at work on *Moby Dick*, he often rode over to visit Hawthorne," you would be better off replacing *while* with *when* (referring to time) or *although* (referring to concession). Even more serious is the tendency to say something like, "Fruit trees, which bloom early, are a poor risk on the central plains." (But this is partly a problem of punctuation; turn to page 251.)

Finally, *you can make a complex sentence more effective by suppressing the subordinator whenever possible.* Too many *that*'s and *which*'s and *whose*'s will ruin otherwise good prose by making it tedious and overformal. When the clauses are side by side and the relation clear, consider dropping the subordinator. Of course, this takes a good ear and an alert mind, for there is possibility of ambiguity, confusion, and unintended humor. But the fluency you gain justifies the effort.

There stood the oak, blasted by lightning. (Not, "There stood the oak that was blasted by lightning.")

Finally reaching the ledge, realizing how exhausted he was, he made camp for the night. (Not, "He finally reached the ledge. He realized how exhausted he was. He made camp for the night.")

The happy man with the trophy is a driver for the Ferrari team. (Not, "The man who is carrying the trophy and who looks so happy is a driver for the team that races Ferraris.")

The last two examples were streamlined further by simplifying the grammar of the sentence. A good way to keep the complex sentence from getting out of hand is to substitute a phrase for a clause, a word for a phrase.

THE COMBINATION SENTENCE

The English sentence is capable of great sophistication. Some of your most ingenious and intricate sentences will be neither compound nor complex but one of the numerous combinations of the two. The range of possibilities is limited only by the skill of the writer—and, sometimes, by the patience of the reader.

The combination sentence must have at least two independent clauses and at least one dependent clause:

When Columbus failed to find quantities of gold, he was disappointed; but he was not disillusioned.

But beyond that, the number of both independent and dependent clauses is variable:

Louis XIV, not the self-indulgent wastrel his grandfather had been, was a serious and compassionate man; and he was, particularly in view of the disastrous finances that prevailed in the French government, a fairly able administrator.

All sorts of combinations are possible:

Late one September night, as I sat reading, the very father of all waves must have flung himself down before the house, for the quiet of the night was suddenly overturned by a gigantic, tumbling crash and an earthquake rumbling; the beach trembled beneath the avalanche, the dune shook, and my house so shook in its dune that the flame of a lamp quivered and pictures jarred on the wall.— Henry Beston, The Outermost House

Over the whole earth—this infinitely small globe that possesses all we know of sunshine and bird song—an unfamiliar blight is creeping: man—man, who has become at last a planetary disease and who would, if his technology yet permitted, pass this infection to another star.—Loren Eiseley, The Time of Man

The front door is especially handsome: the door itself is dark green and equipped with a brass knocker, and the woodwork which frames it is white; it is crowned with a wide fanlight and flanked by two narrow panes of glass, in which a white filigree of ironwork makes a webbing like ice over winter ponds.—Edmund Wilson, The American Earthquake

Occasionally use a form of the combination sentence to achieve variety or emphasis, or to indicate more precisely the relationship among a number of details. Keep in mind, however, that important thoughts have a way of getting lost in the intricacies of the combination sentence; always put them at the beginning, or better, at the end.

The principal thing to remember about both short, simple sentences and long, combination sentences is that together they give you more control over style than would ever be possible if you used sentences from the middle range of the spectrum only. Certainly most of your sentences will be elaborated simple sentences, compound sentences, and complex sentences; and you can achieve variety and pattern using these alone. But real stylistic virtuosity requires the full range of sentence forms.

SUMMARY CHECKLIST
Ask yourself these questions:

1. Are the sentence forms in my compositions everywhere appropriate to the thought?
2. Are sentences drawn—for variety— from the whole range of forms?
3. Do I use as high a proportion of periodic sentences as is compatible with the desired rhetorical profile?
4. Do I use the active voice except in cases where the passive would be a clear gain?

THE WHOLE COMPOSITION
You will find John Baker's essay a catalogue of sentence forms. It opens with an austere simple sentence ("Stand up.") and closes with a more elaborate combination sentence ("Remember, the first travelers of all went on foot; before wheels were, walking was."). And the essay ranges in its complexity from a three-word virtual sentence

("A last word.") to a seventy-five-word combination sentence ("His legs stride along beneath him with what becomes amazingly soon an automatic motion. . . .").

You will find the phrasing declarative ("But the walker must steel himself. . . ."), interrogative ("But what, you may ask . . .?"), exclamatory ("How they walked and talked, and exalted in what they saw!"), and imperative ("Don a stout pair of shoes. . . ."). And you will find the sentence patterns are now loose ("Usually I am not much given to lamenting the vanished glories of the past."); now more periodic ("But there is something in the picture of these old writers, striding over the countryside along with their visions, or discoursing to a companion, as did Coleridge, 'in the most delightful explanatory way over hill and dale a summer's day,' that is remarkably touching."). Give special attention to the diversity and naturalness of Baker's sentences, and to their absolute appropriateness to his thoughts.

An Honest Day's Walk

John F. Baker

Stand up. Move one leg out in front of you, placing the foot firmly on the ground. Bring the other leg from behind it, placing that foot firmly in turn. Carry on with this motion and look around you. Objects are moving past, receding behind you, advancing to meet you. You are walking.

So much for the actual technique; basic pedestrianism, as it were. It's something you pick up quite early in life. The first step, in fact, is always regarded as something of a landmark. I know people who feel their whole life has been one long anticlimax, starting at the ecstatic moment when they tottered from one pair of out-stretched arms to another. But the chances are that, once having acquired the knack of walking, you never make much further conscious use of it, and your foot power is allowed to atrophy while you wallow in the back seats of limousines. This just isn't good enough. Think for a moment of what happened to the ability to waggle the ears. There was a time when we could all do that. Now it is a party trick of only a selected few, preserved from among multitudes by the stern principles of Darwinism.

Do you want that to happen to walking, too? Before you have a chance to say how little you care, I must stress that I mean walking as an art, not the automatic shuffling process that carries you out of the house in the morning and into the garage, or across the lobby and into the elevator. The sort of progress I have in mind takes you across the river and into the trees.

Time was when the sort of walking I mean was much in

fashion, when the activities of a man like Associate Justice William Douglas of the United States Supreme Court—who has been known to walk several miles at a stretch in country so remote as to be beyond the reach of news photographers—would have caused not the slightest inclination of an eyebrow. Time was, in fact, when a literary exercise was more than a mere English composition, and many of the great writers—Hazlitt, Wordsworth, Coleridge, Carlyle, Thoreau, Robert Louis Stevenson, to name a few—were dedicated trampers.

They marched about all over the nineteenth-century landscape, talking up a storm as they went, then settling down in the candle-lit evening to a bottle, and a blank sheet of paper on which to immortalize it all—and their eloquence survives them strongly. Usually I am not much given to lamenting the vanished glories of the past. But there is something in the picture of these old writers, striding over the countryside alone with their visions, or discoursing to a companion, as did Coleridge, "in the most delightful explanatory way over hill and dale a summer's day," that is remarkably touching. How they walked and talked, and exulted in what they saw! And how sweetly they set it all down—the changing landscape, the people met along the way, the evening peace of the inn.

But what, you may ask, can walking offer to those who have no wish to write about it afterward, and whose cars are in working order? It's no use pretending the physical effects are remarkable. You could develop better muscles by a good gym workout, get to live longer by a healthier diet, keep your weight down by running or playing handball. The benefits are philosophical and mental, rather. The British historian G. M. Trevelyan, a passionate advocate of walking as spiritual exercise, put it this way: "I never knew a man go for an honest day's walk . . . and not have his reward in the repossession of his own soul."

Fighting words; but consider a little. Man is becoming increasingly out of touch with the natural world, moving as he does through a universe of glass, plastic, rubber, metal. He is dwindling out of scale with the material world he has built around himself—a world scaled to the automobile rather than to the walking human, to wastage and satiety rather than a reasonable sufficiency. More than a hundred years ago the unnaturalness of human life was enough to drive a thinker like Thoreau into the wilderness; yet we now look on the period that he found intolerable as a golden age of lost innocence and quiet satisfactions. The pace is ever quickening, the pressures ever growing. But if you want to stop the world for a while and get off, you can.

Don a stout pair of shoes and drive out, alone or with only the very choicest of companions, to the nearest open country—and start walking. You should try to include on the route some forest and a few hills; but if there aren't any, just enjoy the sky and the sense of space. Don't try to set any speed records; the coming of evening will wait for you, as a train never would. Don't try to cover too much ground; the idea is not to stumble back at night exhausted, but to amble in with the sort of afterglow that comes from body and mind well extended.

I have found, and men more eloquent than I agree, that however miserable, anxious or tense the walker when he starts out, it is impossible for him to be long on the way without a degree of calm descending upon him. His legs stride along beneath him with what becomes amazingly soon an automatic motion; his eyes turn on leaves, grass, water, sky and distant views; preoccupations recede like the sounds of civilization behind him; his feet planted on the earth give him a certainty of himself he had come near to losing among the city's concrete ambiguities; in a natural setting his sense of human scale returns with a delightful shock. If he wants to talk to himself, he will not meet the blank stare of the city dweller warily recognizing yet another nut. (We have progressed a long way in unhappy self-consciousness since Hazlitt confessed that on his solitary walks, "I laugh, I run, I leap, I sing for joy.")

He may find, of course, that the brain stubbornly refuses to participate in his ramble, and that he becomes simply a walking vegetable, sensing a general dim enjoyment of his surroundings. This is a matter of taste; but I should have thought that, considering what the brain inflicts upon us when it is actively participating in our lives, a little rest would be all to the good. (Max Beerbohm used to experience this mental blankness while on a walk, and resented walking as a result—but then our brains are not such lively companions as his.)

I've made the whole process sound so simple: as if a bit more wear on the shoes will keep the shine off the psychiatrist's couch. But there are a few difficulties I haven't mentioned, which never had to be faced by the sages who set out for their constitutionals a century ago. They merely had to leave their inn in the morning, walk a little way along a quiet street, and they were in the country—a shining landscape full of trafficless roads, public rights of way across private property, and—well, inns.

Today's walker cannot hope to start walking where he lives (unless where he lives is so far away from it all that he has no need of a walk to soothe his soul). He must get in his car and drive along a few congested highways, then find somewhere to park, before he can step out into the wilds—and at that, the wilds are more likely to come in the form of a national or state park, with pictures of

Smokey the Bear gazing at him from the trees, and a litter of beer cans around picnic sites, than the idyllic landscape of the heart's longing.

And once he's on his way he must take care with his route, for nothing is more jarring to newly won peace of mind than to come, suddenly and unawares, on a highway replete with service stations, hamburger stands, used car lots and prefabricated discount stores. Yet no matter how far from the madding crowd today's tramper may succeed in fleeing, he must return at nightfall to the ignoble strife of that very same highway. For where, today, is the country inn that regaled his forebears? It has been hauled into the automotive age and now describes itself as a motel; and there he will probably have to stay, carless though he may be. Looking, and probably feeling, rather like a hotel guest without luggage, he must march from one motel office to another in search of a night's lodging. (Have you ever tried *walking* along a highway shoulder between "No Vacancy" signs? It's that business of inhuman scale I was talking about, all over again.)

The inn parlor will no longer form a background to his contented evening reverie. Highway diners will be his restaurants, the constant swish of tires past their windows drowning the day's last sleepy birdsong. And instead of enjoying a snug taproom, winking with pewter and old oak, he must down his evening dram—without which, naturally, no therapeutic walk would be complete—in road-side cocktail lounges where the only illumination comes from the jukebox, and where the drinks are cold and deadly in their power.

But the walker must steel himself to survive these assaults on the tender shoots of his new self. And if he is carefully following my formula for a life-enhancing walk, the time he spends in daily freedom from urban fetters will more than make up for his nightly thralldom.

A last word. Americans are gregarious creatures, and it may occur to the would-be walker that my experiment in asocial living would be best conducted in a friendly group. It wouldn't. The perils of even a single companion are considerable: Perhaps he wants to talk when you wish for silence, or is lost in rapt meditation just when you are particularly anxious to call his attention to something. And it's amazing how few poeple can share a notion of the ideal distance and speed for a worthy ramble.

As for organized hiking parties, our old essayists, determined individualists all, shunned them: too many people, too much concentration on sheer brute progress and miles per hour. You will find this stress on efficiency, output and performance whenever a quiet, self-indulgent occupation becomes a hobby of mass popularity. Compare today's cyclist, with his hunched back and his sinews etched in effort, to the stately, perpendicular pedaler round the lanes of fifty years ago, and you'll see what I mean about hikers as against the solitary walker.

They are, of course, admirably keen, these hikers; and there is some comfort in knowing that there are so many people who share your pleasure in perambulating through the countryside in preference to surveying it from the windows of a passing car. With that, however, their advantage ends. Let them march out of sight, with their rucksacks, their reckless pace and their jostling for position at the head of the line in which they go. They represent too perfectly the life we want to leave behind when we walk.

Off, then, into the trees, moving along beneath the leaves' dapple, hearing again the oldest sounds man has heard—chirp and rustle, and trickle of water. Soon you're back before the Fall. Remember, the first travelers of all went on foot; before wheels were, walking was.

Exercises

1. Abbreviate, elaborate, and complicate the same basic sentence until it exemplifies the whole spectrum of sentence forms from the virtual to the combination compound-complex. Write at least a dozen versions.
2. Using fairly difficult materials, write a paragraph dominated by simple and compound sentences. Then revise the paragraph to contain more complex and combination sentences. Notice how much more discerning the second paragraph is.
3. Write different versions of the same paragraph, one in which loose sentences predominate, a second in which periodic sentences predominate. Compare the interest generated by the two paragraphs.
4. Now write different versions of another paragraph, one in the passive voice, a second in the active. Compare the length and forcefulness of the two paragraphs.
5. In the following paragraph which sentences are loose, which are mildly periodic, which are strongly periodic—and why?

Washington Irving published his famous collection of short stories, *The Sketch Book*, in England in 1819. He published in that same collection a little essay called "A Rebuke to English Writers." In this nonfiction piece, Irving argues that English authors have failed in their writings to describe America accurately. He accuses the English authors of actually fomenting an unneces-sary international hostility. So vigorous is Irving's attack on the British, that the essay has been called "The American Declara-tion of Literary Independence."

6. Identify the virtual sentences in the following examples and explain their use.

I wish you could see La Spezia. The terraces of square, red-roofed houses. The palms and the umbrella-pines and rhodo-dendrons. But especially the soft blue Spezian bay.

So much for the Anglo-Saxons. Now a word about the Celts, those original inhabitants of Britain who were pushed into Wales and Scotland and Ireland by the invaders.

Alexander the Great quelled a revolt among the Illyrians and Greeks, conquered a Persian empire which included all of west-ern Asia and Egypt, and marched deep into India, creating a Macedonian empire larger than anything Rome would possess for several centuries. And died in his thirty-second year!

7. Rewrite the following overcoordinated paragraph, subordi-nating mere details to the more important ideas.

This happened when I was ten. I built a "man-carrying" glider. For my efforts I earned a neighborhood reputation as an aeronautical genius. But I was frightened of high places and persuaded a chum to test my muslin and lathe creation by jumping with it from a garage roof. He broke both the glider and his leg. He sent my reputation into a nosedive.

8. In the following sentences, substitute a more exact coordi-nator for the overused *and*.

It was a good lecture, and it was rather long.

Hemingway deserves his fame as a stylist, and he taught Ameri-can writers how to use the simple declarative sentence.

The captain ordered the anchor let go, and he scanned the beach for some sign of life.

9. Consider the preliminary work you did earlier (Chapter 9, exercise 6); are the beginnings and endings, the topic sen-tences as appropriate, forceful, and varied as they might be? Do you habitually favor one sentence form—the com-pound, for example—to such a degree that you overlook opportunities for effectively employing other forms?

12. SENTENCE MODELS

When we examine a sentence that someone else has written, we should be especially concerned with its structure: the sequence of words, the sequence of clauses, the way in which clauses are connected. We should ask ourselves: *what has the writer done? why did he do it? in what sort of composition would this sentence work best?* And as we examine the sentences of another writer, we should keep in mind Ben Jonson's famous bit of "Advice to the Writer": "For the mind and memory are more sharply exercised in comprehending another man's things than our own; and such as accustom themselves and are familiar with the best authors shall ever and anon find somewhat of them in themselves: and in the expression of their minds, even when they feel it not, be able to utter something like theirs, which hath an authority above their own."

Just as with paragraphs, a repertoire of sentence forms can be quickly acquired if you go about the process methodically. By imitating master writers, you can discover some of the traditional—and exciting—ways of developing sentences, and you can add to your writing craftsmanship a variety of sentence forms especially valuable to have on hand as you write your compositions—each composition with its own rhetorical profile.

On the pages that follow are a number of sentence models—both basic and stylistic sentences, ranging from the succinct elliptical to the metrically elaborate. Each sentence form is labeled, exemplified, and described, and you are urged in your study of these models to read, copy, and compose a version of your own.

BASIC SENTENCE FORMS
1 THE LOOSE SENTENCE

I remember one splendid morning, all blue and silver, in the summer holidays when I reluctantly tore myself away from the task of doing nothing in particular, and put on a hat of some sort and picked up a walking-stick, and put six very bright-coloured chalks in my pocket.—G. K. Chesterton, A Piece of Chalk

Most of the sentences you write will probably be loose. Loose sentences are those in which you express the main thought at the outset and afterward add whatever details you wish. In the Chesterton sentence the subject and predicate, "I remember," express the main thought. The object, to some degree, "one splendid morning," and certainly all other phrases in the sentence are an expansion of that initial, grammatically complete statement. In the above example the loose structure of the sentence is appropriately reflective and casual. And the modifying and compounding of elements is a source of rhythm. This sentence, which is more extended than most, shows for how long a loose sentence may be sustained. Chesterton's loose opening sentence is made effective by the clarity and excitement inherent in the specific, concrete language, by the alliteration, and by the overall simplicity of both the statement and the grammatical structure.

Although you may wish to use a higher proportion of periodic to loose sentences as you become a more conscious stylist, remember that the loose pattern is more expected and natural. Partly because of this the loose sentence is apt to be diffuse, anticlimactic, and overworked. A succession of loose sentences is almost inevitably monotonous.

Copy Chesterton's sentence; then *compose* a similar loose sentence, enlarging upon the initial, main thought by the addition of other details. Extend the sentence as long as you dare, sustaining interest as long as possible.

2 THE PERIODIC SENTENCE

Crossing a bare common, in snow puddles, at twilight, under a clouded sky, without having in my thoughts any occurrence of special good fortune, I have enjoyed a perfect exhilaration.—Ralph Waldo Emerson, Nature

As you gain skill in writing, an increased proportion of your sentences will be periodic, that is, sentences in which you delay completing the main thought until the end, or near the end. Delaying phrases and clauses postpone statement of the main thought, "I have enjoyed a perfect exhilaration," until the end of Emerson's sentence. Notice how the parallelism of the prepositional phrase "in snow puddles, at twilight, under a clouded sky" keeps the structure of the sentence simple and contributes to its suspense. There is a sense of development in the movement from the series of phrases to the final independent clause.

There are, of course, degrees of how effective a periodic sentence can be, depending on how late in the sentence the main thought is completed. Complex sentences are easily written as periodic; compound sentences cannot be periodic but their separate clauses can be. Most loose sentences can be changed to periodic ones by adding or moving forward a modifier, by inverting the sentence, or by beginning the sentence with "It was." You will shift from loose to periodic to give variety and add emphasis, to make the most important idea stand out more, and in a long sentence to sustain interest and suspense. You must, however, avoid using too many periodic sentences, especially in an informal context, for they will tend to reduce the ease and fluency of your style.

Copy Emerson's sentence; then *compose* a similar periodic sentence. Force the reader to keep all the details in mind by using preliminary phrases to delay the main thought as Emerson has done. For additional practice, you may wish to take several loose sentences and experiment with various ways of changing them into periodic sentences.

3 THE INVERTED SENTENCE

Immoral Ovid was, but he had high standards in art.—Gilbert Highet, Poets in a Landscape

The great majority of your sentences will follow the expected subject-verb-complement order, regardless of what modification or other elaboration complicates the sentence pattern. This is almost always the case with declarative sentences; in interrogative sentences the subject is often preceded by the verb; while in imperative sentences the subject may be implied rather than stated. Sometimes, however, to shift the emphasis in a sentence, you will alter the normal order of the basic sentence elements. The result will be an inverted sentence. Since the reader is surprised to encounter a complement or predicate before the subject, the entire sentence in which an inversion occurs is always emphatic; the upstart element is especially emphatic. Any type of sentence, from simple to compound-complex, can be inverted to serve the writer's purpose.

The first clause of Highet's two-part compound sentence, "Immoral Ovid was," is clearly inverted with the complement placed before the subject and verb. Had this been a simple sentence of only the three words, the inversion would have been justified as a means of achieving emphasis and variety. As one of two clauses in a compound sentence, the inversion is even more effective: The contrast of the clauses, which pivots on the punctuation and coordinator, is accentuated by the inversion of the first clause and the normal order of the second. The reader is momentarily slowed down by the opening words but flies through the remaining; the opening criticism of Ovid is quickly alleviated. The sentence is so constructed that the important matters, Ovid's "immoral" nature and his "art," are positioned at either end where they are certain to be noticed and associated. (Ordinarily the end position of a sentence is the most emphatic; the first position is only slightly less so. In an inverted sentence the first position is probably the stronger. Certainly the middle position in such a sentence is comparatively unemphatic.)

When the complement or verb is clearly the important element or when you simply wish to be emphatic, consider inverting your sentence. Remember, however, that it takes a good ear to distinguish between an inversion that is exactly right, perhaps even stunning, and one that is plainly awkward. Highet, for example, would not have inverted the final part of his sentence so that it read, "In art high standards he had."

Copy Highet's sentence; then *compose* a similar inverted sentence. Cast about for a subject that will give you such opportunity as the remark about Ovid's immorality and his art. Emphasize the comparison or contrast of thoughts in a compound sentence with a skillful inversion in one of the clauses. Then try your hand at the art of inversion with a variety of other sentence patterns.

4 THE VIRTUAL SENTENCE

Six o'clock. A cold summer's evening.—William Sansom, Eventide

Ordinarily all of your sentences will contain these three elements: a subject, verb, and complement. Occasionally you will prefer a grammatically abbreviated, fragmentary statement that is virtually complete, not because of what it contains, but because of what is said or suggested elsewhere. Sansom might have written "It was six o'clock *on* a cold summer's evening." Instead he chose to condense the longer, conventional sentence into two elliptical sentences—partly to economize on the use of accessory words and thereby to shorten and simplify what, in its context, would threaten to become an ineffectively complicated statement, but mainly to capture some of the snap and immediacy of speech patterns and thought processes.

You will, from time to time, find virtual sentences convenient for dialogue, for descriptions, for introductions, for conclusions, for transitions, and even for emphasis. Still, the virtual sentence is a rather special form, to be used *infrequently* and then for some clear purpose.

Copy the Sansom sentences, which together form the introductory paragraph to a short story; then *compose* similar virtual sentences that quickly introduce and describe a setting, while presenting only the essence.

5 THE SIMPLE SENTENCE

Centuries passed.—Gilbert Highet, Poets in a Landscape

London frightened him.—H. M. Tomlinson, A Lost Wood

The simple sentence in its most austere and succinct form is surprisingly rare and almost always striking. This despite the fact that the subject and verb or, more often, the subject, verb, and complement constitute the basic pattern in English. Still, because the minimal sentence is so striking, it is rarely written. When you wish to be forcefully clear and direct, however, you may choose to express yourself as Highet has done in "Centuries passed" (subject-verb) or

Tomlinson in "London frightened him" (subject-verb-complement). Standing alone, the briefest simple sentence is emphatic; used together with longer sentences it is the basis for sharp contrasts.

Do not be misled by the artless appearance of the flat statement, for there is great power in it. Many writers are strangely diffident about using the simple sentence of two or three words and, through a habitual exuberance with words or through fear of making unqualified assertions, they seldom write such sentences—even when they should.

Copy the Highet and Tomlinson sentences; then *compose* similar simple sentences. Cast about for thoughts that lend themselves to the intense, almost overwhelming clarity of such two- or three-word sentences.

6 | THE SIMPLE SENTENCE: ANTICIPATION

After skirting the river for three or four miles, I found a rickety footbridge.—Vladimir Nabokov, Conclusive Evidence

Even after dark the touch of the wind has the warmth of flesh.—Lafcadio Hearn, A Midsummer Trip to the Tropics

Compared with that of the Taoists and Far Eastern Buddhists, the Christian attitude towards Nature has been curiously insensitive and often downright domineering and violent.—Aldous Huxley, The Perennial Philosophy

Phrases that serve as the subject or complement are clearly part of the basic sentence, but phrases that modify the subject, verb, or complement are an elaboration upon the basic simple sentence. The part of speech a phrase modifies determines its location to some extent, and the length and complexity of the phrase has some bearing on how it is related to the rest of the sentence. Phrases coming at the beginning of a sentence often operate as mild anticipations, those in the middle of a sentence as interruptions, and those at the end as afterthoughts. The connection of a phrase to the basic sentence can be managed in various ways. Whether to use both a connecting word and punctuation, or whether to use punctuation alone, and if both, specifically which conjunction or punctuation mark is one of those very basic writer's decisions.

The sentence by Vladimir Nabokov, consisting of a phrase introduced by the connecting word, "after," and separated from the clause by a comma, illustrates one form of the simple sentence. Since the phrase, "After skirting the river for three or four miles," precedes the clause, "I found a rickety footbridge," it serves as an anticipation and dramatically delays the main thought. Had the phrase followed the clause, the sentence would have been just as clear, but the suspense would have been lost, along with the natural emphasis on the clause in its terminal position.

It would not have been incorrect for Lafcadio Hearn to have written "Even after dark, the touch of the wind has the warmth of flesh," with the comma after "dark," but it would not have been so effective. The brevity of the anticipation, the simplicity, and the informality of the entire sentence, and, most importantly, the close relation of the phrase and the clause, which together are part of the same impression, all justify his omission of the comma. (Did you also notice the metaphorical comparison in the sentence, "the *touch* of the wind has the *warmth* of flesh"? There is certainly more verbal excitement in such a line than in, say, "the wind felt warm," which is not only pedestrian but is also stated in the passive voice.)

It is clear from the first word of the Aldous Huxley sentence that a comparison, actually a contrast, is in the offing. The reader is, thus, fully prepared for the matter-of-fact comparison of Taoist and Buddhist attitudes toward nature with those of the Christian. A connecting word is simply not needed here. Indeed, if you were to rewrite the sentence employing a conjunction, you would quickly realize that such an alternative would be wordy and repetitious: "Although the Taoists and Far Eastern Buddhists have been responsive and cooperative with Nature, the Christian attitude towards Nature has been curiously insensitive and often downright domineering and violent." Such an imitation is inferior to the original. Incidentally, as you study the model sentence, notice the capitalization of "Nature," the surprisingly colloquial expression, "downright," and the compounding of modifiers toward the end of the sentence.

Copy the sentences by Nabokov, Hearn, and Huxley; then *compose* three similar sentences involving anticipation. Write at least one sentence in which the phrase is separated from the clause by a comma.

7 THE SIMPLE SENTENCE: INTERRUPTION

A barn, in day, is a small night.—*John Updike,* The Dogwood Tree: A Boyhood

The thought of her was like champagne itself!—*John Galsworthy,* The Man of Property

You, the listener, sit opposite me.—*Ford Madox Ford,* The Good Soldier

In each of these model sentences a phrase interrupts, either casually or dramatically, the flow of the main statement. The connection of these interruptive phrases to the basic sentence can be made in a variety of ways.

The John Updike sentence, with its brief phrase introduced by the connecting word, "in," and enclosed in commas (partly for emphasis and partly because the phrase does interrupt the syntactic flow of the sentence), is one form of the interrupted simple sentence. The phrase, "in day," by briefly stopping the movement of the sentence transforms a perfectly ordinary statement into something more impressive and significant.

In John Galsworthy's sentence the phrase, "of her," is so mildly interruptive, so much a part of the basic sentence, so essential to explaining what sort of thought, that it would have been a mistake to isolate the phrase by surrounding punctuation. The connecting word, "of," suffices to identify the phrase.

The short appositive phrase in the sentence of Ford Madox Ford is separated by commas as it should be, for "the listener" in this imperative sentence makes forcefully clear who "you" is. Ford could have introduced the phrase with a connecting word and written "who are the listener," but the connection is clear enough with punctuation alone.

Copy the sentences by Updike, Galsworthy, and Ford; then *compose* three similar sentences that contain interruptions—the first surrounding the phrase with punctuation and introducing it with a connecting word, the second relying on the connecting word alone, and the third on punctuation.

8 THE SIMPLE SENTENCE: AFTERTHOUGHT

How beautiful to die of a broken heart, on paper!—Thomas Carlyle, Sartor Resartus

There are our young barbarians all at play.—Matthew Arnold, Essays in Criticism

The steadiest winds are the trades, blowing diagonally toward the equator from the northeast and southwest.—Rachel Carson, The Sea around Us

In each of the above simple sentences one or more phrases follow the central statement as an afterthought. Here, the term *afterthought* is used in its most literal sense. It describes any syntactically subordinate thought that comes after the main thought. The afterthought may be a dramatic and significant turn or a casual and superfluous elaboration. There are three basic ways to mark the connection between the clause and afterthought: with a comma and connecting word, with a connecting word alone, with punctuation alone.

The Thomas Carlyle sentence is not the simplest possible illustration of a phrasal afterthought since it contains a pair of final phrases, "of a broken heart" and "on paper." If Carlyle had simply written, "How beautiful to die, on paper!", the phrase still would have been introduced by both a connecting word and punctuation to emphasize the surprising turn the phrase effects in the sentence. Also, since "on paper," which makes this an epigrammatic sentence, follows a much milder elaborating phrase that is not part of the afterthought, the comma is most essential.

In the Matthew Arnold sentence, "all at play" is such a natural extension and completion of the clause, "There are our young barbarians," that it should not be separated from it by punctuation, "all" casually indicating the connection.

Finally, the longer phrasal afterthought in Rachel Carson's sentence actually consists of two phrases, "blowing diagonally toward the equator" and "from the northeast and southwest." Clearly such an afterthought requires a comma, partly because of its length and complexity, but mainly because the writer desired to express what is essentially a single afterthought by using several phrases. Of course, this is not the simplest illustration of an afterthought with punctuation alone; for example, it is not so simple as "The steadiest winds are the trades, blowing diagonally toward the equator."

Copy the sentences by Carlyle, Arnold, and Carson; then *compose* three similar sentences containing afterthoughts—the first introducing the phrase by punctuation and a connecting word, the second doing so with the connecting word alone, and the third with punctuation. Elaborate on the basic sentence pattern as Carlyle, Carson, and Arnold have done.

9 THE ELABORATED SIMPLE SENTENCE

The gulls went in slanting flight up the wind toward the grey desolate east.—Stephen Crane, The Open Boat

Once you begin modifying various parts of the simple sentence by adding phrases at the beginning, in the middle, or at the end of the sentence, you find that the basic pattern can be extensively elaborated without sacrificing its inherent lucidity. One of the most important achievements in modern literature has been the rediscovery of the simple declarative sentence. Hemingway and others of his generation demonstrated that the simple declarative sentence could be the basis of a distinctive style. Yet, when students first begin trying very hard to write well, they often forget this and abandon the simple sentence for tangled and overblown syntax. Remember, a primer style is less to be feared than a pretentious one, for clarity is the writer's first objective. If you do not overuse or overelaborate the simple sentence, it can be the most useful and trustworthy pattern in your repertoire of basic sentences.

The basic statement in Crane's sentence is contained in the subject and verb—the minimal parts of an English sentence. The verb, however, is neither explicit nor exciting. So Crane, by adding three modifying phrases ("in slanting flight," "up the wind," and "toward the grey desolate east") went on to write a rather memorable elaborated simple sentence. Of course, Crane had another alternative: He could have used "slanted" as a verb and written, "The gulls slanted into the wind. . . ." Since the subject, verb, and complement of any basic sentence can be modified or compounded in not only different combinations but to different extents, the elaborated simple sentence is capable of almost infinite variation.

Copy the Crane sentence; then *compose* a similar elaborated sentence. Modify the verb as in the exemplary sentence. You might compose a second version of the same sentence in which you modify the subject or use a compound subject also or in which you modify the subject instead of the verb.

10 | THE COMPOUND SENTENCE

The great tragic artists of the world are four, and three of them are Greek.— *Edith Hamilton,* The Greek Way

Made up of what are essentially simple sentences joined by conjunctions and punctuation or by only punctuation, the compound sentence coordinates grammatically independent but logically related thoughts. Poor writers often coordinate where they should subordinate, and they show a marked inclination for a prose style that abounds in simple-minded compound sentences—the idiom of excited children and gossipy women. Because of this many writers regard the compound sentence as a comparatively unsophisticated pattern. It is, on the contrary, the basis of such stylistic effects as balance, the series, and repetition. In the hands of an alert stylist, even a standard compound sentence can be most sophisticated, as when it sharply accentuates a comparison or contrast, when the clauses are of strikingly dissimilar length, when narrative events or descriptive details are presented in quick succession, or simply when the longer rhythms it creates are appropriate in the context.

Develop a large vocabulary of coordinators and use them with precision: In addition to *and, or, but*, and *however*, you also have *for, nor, so, consequently, therefore, then, still, yet, otherwise*. Do not write *also* when you mean *yet*, or *thus* when you mean *furthermore*. Also develop a vocabulary of coordinating punctuation: Not only will semicolons and commas serve this purpose, but dashes and colons will also. (Remember, however, that some coordinating conjunctions—*also, however, nevertheless, therefore, consequently, hence, furthermore, indeed, still, then*—require a semicolon before and a comma after.) But most of all, be sure that the clauses joined by conjunctions are, indeed, of equal importance and clearly do belong in the same sentence.

The Edith Hamilton sentence coordinates independent clauses, pivoting them on the comma and the conjunction. In this case, however, coordination implies only that the thoughts are closely related, for they are most certainly not of equal importance. Since "three of them are Greek" is the main point, you may wonder why the author did not begin with a subordinator like *although*, and phrase the statement as a complex sentence. She chose, for two reasons, to write a compound sentence: First, consisting of succinct and strongly worded simple declarative sentences, the statement is extremely forceful as a compound sentence. Second, the more important final clause is, because of its position and brevity, and because the longer clause has been de-emphasized by the modifier, unmistakably emphasized.

Copy Edith Hamilton's sentence; then *compose* a similar compound sentence, one in which the final clause is the more important.

11 THE COMPOUND SENTENCE (WITH COORDINATOR ONLY)

We would walk out with a bottle of pop apiece and sometimes the pop would backfire up our noses and hurt.—E. B. White, Once More to the Lake

The compound sentence written with coordinators but without punctuation is so rare and risky that you should be wary of expressing yourself in such a sentence. Still, until you can at least appreciate the possibilities in such a form, you do not really know the compound sentence. Theoretically, none of the clauses in a compound sentence is emphasized, unless, of course, you have singled out one in some way. In practice, the final clause is emphasized slightly because of its position. To de-emphasize this and the separateness of the clauses, you may decide to drop the coordinating punctuation. Suppressing the comma before *and* is often justified, since *and* is a neutral coordinator; doing so before *but* and certainly before *yet* might be misleading, since these coordinators point up a meaningful distinction between the clauses.

Briefly, then, you may consider dropping the punctuation when you want to fuse the clauses of a compound sentence into a single, undifferentiated statement. E. B. White, by using the coordinator only in his compound sentence, has underlined the youth and informality of simple and hardly separate actions—"We would walk out with a bottle of pop . . . the pop would backfire up our noses. . . ." (Notice that White used *and* rather than a more precise connecting word, which would specify a time or cause-effect sequence.) Although you might have reservations about using a sentence of this kind in a more formal context, you will sometimes find a place for it; Edith Hamilton did in *The Greek Way*: "The Greeks were the first scientists and all science goes back to them."

Copy the E. B. White sentence; then *compose* a similar sentence with a coordinator only.

12 THE COMPOUND SENTENCE (WITH PUNCTUATION ONLY)

In the morning it was sunny, the lake was blue.—D. H. Lawrence, Twilight in Italy

The clauses of a compound sentence are almost always separated by some form of punctuation, ordinarily a comma or semicolon. Other punctuation marks may be used, however, and each varies in strength. The comma separates and emphasizes slightly the final clause; a comma may be used when the clauses are short and similar in form. The dash points up a hesitation or delay between the clauses—a moment of suspense before a surprising turn in the final clause. The semicolon is the standard coordinating mark, and it tends to emphasize the entire sentence, especially any epigrammatic qualities it may possess. Semicolons, however, are both too heavy and too formal to be used very often. The colon, an even more formal and special mark, suggests that what follows is a distinct addition to or explanation of what came before. A colon emphasizes the promise-fulfillment relation of the clauses.

When the relationship of clauses is so clear that no coordinator is necessary, rely on punctuation alone to make the link. By doing this you will, of course, accentuate somewhat the separateness of the clauses; but often this is precisely the effect you want, especially if the final clause represents a sharp contrast or dramatic turn. The second clause of D. H. Lawrence's compound sentence is an inevitable consequence of the first; hence, it was not necessary to show the relation of the clauses with a coordinating conjunction. To be sure, the model sentence is exceptional; many would say it had a comma splice. But it does illustrate a case in which the writer was evidently aware of the alternatives, for he chose something out of the ordinary.

Copy the Lawrence sentence; then *compose* a similar compound sentence using punctuation but no coordinator. Consider the alternatives and use the most effective mark, which may not be the semicolon. To observe the different effect of each mark, you might try writing a compound sentence that could be more or less correctly punctuated in a variety of ways.

13 | THE ELABORATED COMPOUND SENTENCE

We were somewhere near Sorrento; behind us lay the long curve of faint-glimmering lights on the Naples shore; ahead was Capri.—George Gissing, By the Ionian Sea

Without affecting its basic pattern, the compound sentence can be elaborated in various ways. The number of clauses can be increased from the usual two to three and even more. The elements within the clauses can be inverted or compounded and modified in different ways. The alternatives of correct punctuation and effective coordinators are many.

The Gissing sentence coordinates three clauses of quite different design: The first is simple; the long second clause is not only inverted but also contains several modifiers; and the third is as brief as possible and inverted as well. The compound sentence is capable of variation limited only by the writer's skill and imagination, the sentence pattern being fully as adaptable and sophisticated as any.

Copy the Gissing sentence; then *compose* a similarly elaborated compound sentence of three distinctly different clauses. Consider carefully what you are doing and why, for the effectively written elaborated compound sentence requires creative judgment.

14 | THE COMPLEX SENTENCE: ANTICIPATION (WITH SUBORDINATOR AND PUNCTUATION)

If there is magic on this planet, it is contained in water.—Loren Eiseley, The Immense Journey

Thoughts of lesser importance are subordinated in the complex sentence, which consists of one independent and one or more dependent clauses. The most mature and educated styles naturally make use of many complex sentences, because the writer has made decisions that would otherwise fall to the reader—decisions that clearly distinguish the major idea from its minor details and that specifically describe their relationship. Clarity and effectiveness, the basic attributes of every stylistic statement, are largely a product of the writer's successful control over emphasis and subordination.

Whenever you write a complex sentence, keep these two fundamental rules in mind: First, always phrase the main thought as an independent clause and subordinate details as dependent clauses. It is possible to write sentences in which the main idea is contained in the dependent clause rather than in the independent clause; for example, "He said that she was the most beautiful woman he had ever seen." In such exceptional cases, however, the dependent clause comes at the end of the sentence where it is naturally somewhat emphasized. Also because of the length and content of the clause, it clearly expresses the important matter. Second, never obscure the main thought with unnecessary subordinate details or by a sequence of subordinate clauses, each one dependent upon the one before.

You should develop a large vocabulary of subordinators, and always use them with precision. Some subordinators (*who, whom, where, which, that, what*) are so smooth you are hardly aware of the dependent clauses they introduce. Some more surely distinguish the dependent from the main clause. *Although, as, as if, so, so that, because, before, after, if, since, that, until, till, unless, when, where* are among these. Clearly, many, like *if* and *although*, have rather specific meanings; while others, like *as, so*, and *while*, have more than a single meaning, and if used carelessly may lead you to write an ambiguous sentence. Your choice of subordinator, therefore, should be neither automatic nor perfunctory.

The Eiseley sentence, consisting of a dependent clause introduced by the subordinator, "If," and separated from the independent clause by a comma, illustrates one form of the complex sentence. Since the dependent clause, "If there is magic on this planet," precedes the independent clause, it is an anticipation. The term "anticipation" accurately describes what the dependent clause does in all sentences of this kind; it dramatically delays the main thought. Had the dependent clause followed the independent clause, the sentence would have been just as clear, but the suspense that comes with periodic sentences and the natural emphasis of the terminal position would have been lost.

Copy the Eiseley sentence; then *compose* a complex sentence that contains an anticipation. You may wish to review what was said earlier about the periodic sentence. Use a subordinator other than *if*, and be sure it points up the relationship between the clauses exactly.

15 THE COMPLEX SENTENCE: ANTICIPATION (WITH SUBORDINATOR ONLY)

Whenever people are short on ideas they tend to use long words.—Clifton Fadiman, Plan Thoughts on Fancy Language

If the anticipation (dependent clause) is short and its relation to the independent clause is obvious, then consider omitting the usual comma. The momentum of your sentences will be improved if you exploit the principle of open punctuation whenever ease of reading and understanding is not likely to be affected.

It would not have been incorrect for Clifton Fadiman to have retained the comma and written "Whenever people are short on ideas, they tend to use long words," but it would not have been so effective. The brevity of the anticipation, the simplicity and informality of the entire sentence, and, most important, the close relation of the clauses, which are both part of the same impression, all justify his omission. Indeed, it would have been a stylistic lapse on Fadiman's part to have retained the comma. Some student writers, trying very hard to be formal and correct, place a comma after the anticipation in every complex sentence—but, you see, this may not always be intelligent.

Copy the Fadiman sentence; then *compose* a similar complex sentence, omitting the punctuation following the anticipation.

16 THE COMPLEX SENTENCE: INTERRUPTION (WITH SUBORDINATOR AND PUNCTUATION)

Richard's crown, which he wore to the last, was picked out of a bush and placed upon the victor's head.—Winston Churchill, The Birth of Britain

There is some advantage in placing a dependent clause within the sentence if it would weaken the initial effect as an anticipation or assume too much importance as an afterthought. By writing a complex sentence with an interruption, you can easily place one important element from the independent clause (for example, the subject) at the beginning and another (for example, the object) at the end, the most emphatic positions. If the dependent clause is clearly incidental, you should consider writing it as an interruption; but even if it is fairly important, you can point this up by proper punctuation. Of all the complex sentence patterns, this is perhaps the most subtle—the suspended thought and the periodicity conferred by interruption. The interruption is so adaptable, so varied in its possible contributions to a sentence that it is difficult to generalize about the construction. The writer has considerable freedom in the matter of his subordinator and punctuation and can bend the sentence to make it do his will.

The interruption in Churchill's sentence, introduced by the subordinator *which* and enclosed by commas, is incidental; but the effect of the remainder of the statement is so much stronger because of that interposed remark. The important details in this sentence are "Richard's crown" and "the victor's head"; one comes at the very beginning and the other at the end where they will be most noticed and best remembered by the reader. Notice, too, the balance of the verb-complement, verb-complement after the interruption, and how it is reinforced by the alliteration of the words "picked" and "placed."

Copy the Churchill sentence; then *compose* a similar complex sentence with an interruption. Elaborate the final parts of the sentence as Churchill has done, and place the important details at the beginning and end.

17 THE COMPLEX SENTENCE: INTERRUPTION (WITH PUNCTUATION ONLY)

This tree, I learned quite early, was exactly my age, was, in a sense, me.—
John Updike, The Dogwood Tree: A Boyhood

If the relation of the dependent clause to the independent clause is unmistakably clear, you may drop the subordinator and use only punctuation. Before surrounding an internal clause in a complex sentence with punctuation, however, you must be certain that it is, in fact, an interruption. A restrictive clause is essential to the sense of the sentence and cannot be separated from what it modifies without changing the meaning; it is not really an interruption and should not be isolated by punctuation. A nonrestrictive clause, although it may add a great deal to the sentence, is nevertheless incidental; it is an interruption and should be punctuated as one. In the Updike sentence both of the interruptive elements are nonrestrictive and require punctuation. Although it is technically an independent clause, "I learned quite early," is clearly subordinate to the main thought, "This tree was me," and to the sentence in which it appears complex rather than compound. The other interruptive element, "in a sense," is a prepositional phrase. What appears to be a third interruption is, because of the surrounding punctuation, a secondary verbal phrase. Together the interruptions delay the movement of the sentence considerably, and thereby emphasize the complement, "me." Since heavy stress also falls on the subject, "this tree," and the verb "was," the reader must keep in mind the periodicity of the sentence. Because of the short words and the rhythm, the brevity and simplicity of the statement, the sentence is complicated but not awkward. Even the most basic complex sentence with an interruption is a somewhat special pattern, not one to be written regularly.

The commas are, of course, right for the Updike sentence, but other marks can be used to punctuate an interruption. A true interruption must be surrounded by marks of some kind—commas, parentheses, dashes, semicolons, or colons—in a pair, except where the first comma or other mark of punctuation is replaced by a conjunction. As a rule, the longer and more interjectional the interruption, the stronger the punctuation. Commas mildly distinguish the interruption from the main clause; parentheses more decisively separate an interruption that is an aside or note; dashes strongly emphasize the interruption; semicolons and colons, rarely used to enclose interruptions, are most special and emphatic. At any rate, in punctuating an interruption you must decide, first, if the clause or other element is an interruption and if it should be punctuated, and, second, what punctuation should be used.

Copy the Updike sentence; then *compose* a similar complex sentence with interruptions. Indicate their relation to the main clause with punctuation rather than with a subordinator. Delay the movement of the sentence, as Updike does, with a variety of interruptive elements.

18 THE COMPLEX SENTENCE: RESTRICTIVE INTERRUPTION (WITH SUBORDINATOR ONLY)

All works of art which deserve their name have a happy end.—Joseph Wood Krutch, The Modern Temper

The dependent clause in Krutch's sentence is, in the strictest sense, not an interruption. Read the sentence without the restrictive clause, "which deserve their name," and the meaning is utterly changed. Krutch would never have written "All works of art have a happy end," for this is obvious nonsense. Still, even restrictive elements are interruptions in that they are something interposed between the subject, verb, and complement, and they separate these parts and delay completion of the sentence. Usually, such an interruption is identified by a subordinator, like the "which" in Krutch's sentence. Of course, too many *that*'s, *which*'s, and *who*'s can ruin otherwise fluent prose by making it tedious and overformal. When the relationship is clear you might consider suppressing the subordinator, but this takes a good ear and acute judgment. Ordinarily, you are better off casting about for a subordinator that accurately points up the relationship between clauses.

Copy the Krutch sentence; then *compose* a similar complex sentence with an interruption. Delay the movement of the sentence with a restrictive clause introduced by a subordinator but, of course, not separated from the dependent clause by punctuation.

19 | THE COMPLEX SENTENCE: AFTERTHOUGHT (WITH SUBORDINATOR AND PUNCTUATION)

Amory had decided definitely on Princeton, even though he would be the only boy entering that year from St. Regis'.—F. Scott Fitzgerald, This Side of Paradise

Because of its position in the sentence, the dependent clause is often more emphatic when written as an afterthought, especially when punctuated by something stronger than a comma. The Fitzgerald sentence, however, is an unexceptionally loose sentence. The main thought, "Amory had decided definitely on Princeton," is expressed in the independent clause; the longer dependent clause, "even though he would be the only boy entering that year from St. Regis'," marked by the comma and subordinator, is an afterthought that simply adds details and extends the sentence.

Copy the Fitzgerald sentence; then *compose* a similar complex sentence with an afterthought. Add subordinate details to the final parts of the sentence as he has done. But first, review the discussion of the loose sentence.

20 | THE COMPLEX SENTENCE: AFTERTHOUGHT (WITH SUBORDINATOR ONLY)

The trees stood massively in all their summer foliage spotted and grouped upon a meadow which sloped gently down from the big white house.—Virginia Woolf, Miss Ormerod

If the afterthought is fairly short and not decidedly subordinate to the independent clause, then punctuation alone might effectively mark the dependent clause. Of course, if it were clearly restrictive, as in this sentence of G. K. Chesterton's, "The artistic temperament is a disease that afflicts amateurs," then you would not consider placing a comma before the afterthought; this would change the meaning. And in the model sentence, the afterthought, "which sloped gently down from the big white house," is likewise unpunctuated and has only the subordinator. Virginia Woolf played down the separateness of the clauses as well as the subordinate relation of the afterthought, fusing them into a single unemphatic statement.

The independent clause in Virginia Woolf's sentence is complicated by the presence of an adverb, "massively," a minor interruptive modifier, "in all their summer foliage," and past participles used as adjectives, "spotted" and "grouped." The afterthought is made more specific and varied by adverbial and adjectival modification, "gently," and "big white." The sentence is, indeed, an example of a diffuse and extended style of writing, which in some contexts creates exactly the right effect; certainly, the easy sweep of the model is nevertheless unmarked by any punctuation.

Copy Virginia Woolf's sentence; then *compose* a similar complex sentence with an afterthought, unmarked by any punctuation.

21 THE ELABORATED COMPLEX SENTENCE

Early in May, the oaks, hickories, maples, and other trees, just putting out amidst the pine woods around the pond, imparted a brightness like sunshine to the landscape, especially in cloudy days, as if the sun were breaking through mists and shining faintly on the hillsides here and there.—Henry David Thoreau, Walden

Without changing its basic subordinate pattern, the complex sentence can be variously elaborated: The number of dependent clauses can be increased from one to two or more; these can be of many forms and take different positions in the sentence; punctuation marks and subordinators can relate the dependent clauses to the independent clause in several ways.

The Thoreau sentence is a fine example of the elaborated complex pattern, and it illustrates a surprising number of possibilities. "Early in May" is an anticipation; "the oaks, hickories, maples, and other trees" make the compound subject; "just putting out amidst the pine woods around the pond" is an interruption; "imparted . . . to the landscape" states the verb and its modifier; "a brightness like sunshine" is the object and its modifier; "especially in cloudy days" and "as if the sun were breaking through mists and shining faintly on the hillsides here and there" are afterthoughts. In spite of its syntactical complexity, the sentence is perfectly clear, partly because there is nothing abstract in the matter-of-fact observation and simple comparison nor in the vocabulary, and also because Thoreau in other ways (for example, by repetition—"sunshine," "sun," "shining") sped the sentence on its way.

Copy the Thoreau sentence; then see if you can *compose* a similar elaborated complex sentence, with anticipation, interruption, and afterthoughts. The elaborated complex sentence and, indeed, the next several sentence forms are apt to be diffuse and obscure. Since they are an essential, if infrequently used, part of your basic sentence repertoire, you must learn to write syntactically complicated sentences that are at the same time clear and effective.

22 THE COMBINATION SENTENCE

Years ago the British used to run a flying-boat service down through Africa, and although it was a slow and sometimes rather bumpy journey I can remember no flight that was quite so pleasant.—Alan Moorehead, No Room in the Ark

As the name implies, a combination sentence is a combination of the two patterns; it coordinates and subordinates several thoughts in some intricate way. At the very least the combination sentence consists of two independent clauses and a single dependent clause. Despite what you might suppose, the combination sentence is often no longer than any of the simpler basic patterns. Logan Pearsall Smith writes, for instance, in *All Trivia,* "People say that life is the thing, but I prefer reading." Generally, however, it is somewhat longer and provides a convenient source of variety.

Alan Moorehead's combination sentence is a classic example written in response to familiar circumstances. The closely related main thoughts, "Years ago the British used to run a flying-boat service down through Africa" and "I can remember no flight that was quite so pleasant," are where they should be, at the beginning and end of the sentence. The dependent clause, "and although it was a slow and sometimes rather bumpy journey," is all the more subordinate because it is sandwiched between the main thoughts. It is introduced but not concluded by a comma because it belongs with what follows, and it delays and reinforces the final and most important clause. Although this or, for that matter, any similar sentence could be written as two simpler sentences, by using the combination pattern the writer can indicate more precisely the relationship among a number of details.

Copy the Moorehead sentence; then *compose* a similar combination sentence.

23 | THE ELABORATED COMBINATION SENTENCE

Late one September night, as I sat reading, the very father of all waves must have flung himself down before the house, for the quiet of the night was suddenly overturned by a gigantic, tumbling crash and an earthquake rumbling; the beach trembled beneath the avalanche, the dune shook, and my house so shook in its dune that the flame of a lamp quivered and pictures jarred on the wall.—Henry Beston, The Outermost House

Consisting of multiple independent and dependent clauses, the elaborated combination sentence represents the upper limit of the sentence spectrum. The Beston sentence is composed of a dependent clause, five independent clauses, and a final dependent clause, almost all in some way modified and all concentrated into one sentence to emphasize the suddenness of the great wave's breaking and the instantaneous sequence of sound and shaking. Study also the alliteration and repetition, onomatopoeia and stunning diction—for example, "overturned" in that context—in Beston's sentence. You will encounter such a sentence now and then in a narrative or descriptive passage where the substance is relatively concrete, but rarely in expository writing, where its length and intricacy is apt to hopelessly fog a more abstract statement.

The variety of basic patterns, from the simple sentence of two or three words to the elaborated combination sentence of fifty or more, affirms the flexibility and sophistication of the English sentence. By making use of the full range of basic sentence patterns you have more control over variety, emphasis, and design than you would have if you drew only from the middle of the spectrum. While most of the time you will rely on elaborated simple sentences, compound sentences, and complex sentences, to express yourself always with clarity and effectiveness you must have all the basic sentence patterns in your repertoire.

Now, *copy* the Beston sentence; then *compose* an elaborated combination sentence, approximating the length and involvement of the model but not necessarily duplicating the pattern clause by clause. Be sure that the intricacies of coordination and subordination in your sentence are a natural consequence of what you wish to express.

24 | THE REPRESENTATIVE-SERIES SENTENCE: TWO-PART

How are we to find the knowledge of reality in the world without, or in the shifting, flowing fluid world within?—Archibald MacLeish, Why Do We Teach Poetry?

On many occasions in your writing, you must decide on the number of items to include in a series of examples, a series of modifications, a series of qualifications, or the like. Although at times the number of items is determined for you simply by the demands of truth and accuracy, more often the series you give to your reader is a representative one: Out of many, many possible items, you select a certain number that are representative of what you desire to say or present in the way of content.

In creating a representative list when you wish to suggest totality, certainty, and absoluteness, choose *two* instances, details, or examples and present them coordinately. By giving two items, and no more, as a representation of the whole, you create an alpha-omega structure, saying in effect, "Here are two examples and two only; that is all that you need to know; it is a settled matter." When you use the two-part series your writing "voice" becomes highly confident.

Archibald MacLeish, for instance, has summed up the dimensions of his concern by reducing his content to an either/or statement in two distinct parts: The two-part series, comprising two prepositional phrases, "in the world without," " in the shifting, flowing fluid world within." Although his two-part series may seem to be inevitable, it is actually the result of choice and decision. Instead, could he not have said something like, "How are we to find the knowledge of reality within ourselves, within our society, within our universe?"

Copy the MacLeish sentence; then *compose* a sentence that includes a definite two-part series.

25 THE REPRESENTATIVE-SERIES SENTENCE: THREE PART

All history teaches us that these questions that we think the pressing ones will be transmuted before they are answered, that they will be replaced by others, and that the very process of discovery will shatter the concepts that we today use to describe our puzzlement.—J. Robert Oppenheimer, Prospects in the Arts and Sciences

A representative series may be presented in three parts as well as in two. Less dogmatic and absolute than the two-part series, the three-part says in effect that you are willing to give one more example for the sake of fairness. Or, as Gilbert Highet says in his essay on The Gettysburg Address, in *A Clerk at Oxenford*, the three-part series "emphasizes basic harmony and unity." You will choose the three-part series when you wish to indicate a reasonable, judicious, and normal attitude toward your subject. Echoing the structure of the classical syllogism, this type of series is the most frequently used of the representative series simply because most writers, most of the time, wish to appear within the mainstream of order and reason. It is understandable that Professor Oppenheimer, speaking about history in an essay dealing with the arts and sciences (all matters within the province of academic concern and discipline) should use the three-part series to reflect the judicious, rational mode of the academic mind.

Like all representative series, the three-part series may be constructed from various elements—words, phrases, or even clauses—as in Professor Oppenheimer's sentence, for example: "that these questions that we think the pressing ones will be transmuted," "that they will be replaced," and "that the very process of discovery will shatter. . . ."

Copy the three-part series sentence given above, and then *compose* two similar sentences of your own. Use a different unit (word, phrase, or clause) in the series in each sentence.

26 THE REPRESENTATIVE-SERIES SENTENCE: FOUR-PART

London was hideous, vicious, cruel, and above all overwhelming.—Henry James, Italian Hours

You can also use a four-part series on those occasions when you wish to indicate a more emotional, human-oriented, or subjective attitude in your writing. The four-part series is the series of involvement. It indicates that you, the writer, are concerned or even emotional about the subject at hand, and that you are willing to add yet another example beyond the three that is "average" for the sake of making sure that your reader grasps and comprehends the situation.

In the sentence above, Henry James presents a description of London in emotional terms, and it is fitting that he used the four-part series rather than the two- or three-part series. James is presenting London not as an abstraction nor as an object of study but as the dwelling-place of human beings, and he is responding to the subject evaluatively, not judiciously or definitively.

In the four-part series, as in the other types of series, the units may be words (as in James's sentence) or phrases. They may also be clauses as in this sentence by Robert Louis Stevenson:

They have no curiosity; they cannot give themselves over to random provocations; they do not take pleasure in the exercise of their faculties for its own sake; and unless Necessity lays about them with a stick, they will even stand still.—Robert Louis Stevenson, An Apology for Idlers

Stevenson, making several quick and related observations about human beings, about idlers, has appropriately used the four-part series.

Copy James's four-part series sentence and also Stevenson's; then *compose* two sentences of your own—one with adjectives, one with complete clauses—dealing with human beings or some emotional situation, or taking an emotional view of some place or idea.

27 THE REPRESENTATIVE-SERIES SENTENCE: FIVE-OR-MORE PART

There is not a more mean, stupid, dastardly, pitiful, selfish, spiteful, envious, ungrateful animal than the Public.—William Hazlitt, On Living to One's Self

Although the four-part series is indicative of a human, emotional, subjective, involved attitude, each additional lengthening of the series increases and magnifies this attitude, and begins to add an element of humor, even absurdity. Hazlitt, writing about human beings, the Public, his own "kind," uses the long series to indicate great involvement, great feeling, and a certain sense of humor about it all. The Public is mean, but so ornery that we almost have to laugh.

You might consider the different effects that would have been produced if Hazlitt had written any one of these sentences:

1. There is no more stupid or ungrateful animal than the Public.
2. There is no more stupid, pitiful, or ungrateful animal than the Public.
3. There is no more stupid and selfish, envious and ungrateful animal than the Public.

Can you hear in these various sentences different tones of voice, different attitudes and approaches to the subject as a result of using different kinds of representative series?

Copy Hazlitt's long-series sentence, and then *compose* a sentence of your own in which you use a series of at least five units. Write on some subject that you think deserves just a touch of laughter.

SPECIAL STYLISTIC SENTENCE FORMS

A stylistic sentence is a basic sentence modified or transformed to produce some special effect.

Stylistic sentences can do a number of things for you: They can help establish emphasis; they can indicate climaxes; they can provide variation within a plain and common style; and they can help establish and maintain an elaborate and eventful literary style. In general, they can assist you in your manipulation of stylistic texture.

If you were to write using only basic sentences, you would not be writing poorly, but you would probably not be writing as effectively as possible. If you were to paint only with primary colors, perhaps you would not paint so colorfully and flexibly as you might if you mixed these primary colors to get secondary ones. Stylistic sentences are like secondary colors: They are the more subtle, at times even more exotic, hues that the skilled artist employs.

Clifton Fadiman once wrote, "Purely purposive prose can become so dull as to fail of its purpose, which first of all presupposes the engagement of the attention." Stylistic sentences are especially geared to engage the reader's attention. Indeed the stylistic sentence might be called the noticeable sentence, for it not only communicates with, but also begins to intrigue, the reader by the very way it is put together.

By mastering the various forms of stylistic sentences, you will be able to intrigue your readers, to engage their attention to the extent that seems best at any given time. On certain occasions you may wish your writing to be low-keyed, rather plain, but on other occasions you may wish to make it highly eventful, elaborate—even unusual. In between these two possibilities there are, of course, numerous shadings and gradations of stylistic intensity that you can establish. With the proper use of stylistic sentences along with basic sentences, you can usually produce the tone and manner that you have in mind. As you increase the number of stylistic sentences in your writing, you will increase the elaborateness and eventfulness of your prose. And, as you will soon discover, stylistic sentences themselves differ in their degrees of intensity: Some are more elaborate and eventful than others.

A stylistic sentence may be engendered from a basic sentence in various ways: by altering the basic sequence of words and their syntax; by introducing elements of design and pattern; by interrupting the normal flow of the sentence; and by adding repetitions, metaphors, alliterations, and various rhythms. Indeed, you will find many, many ways to construct stylistic sentences, many of these ways so well established in the art of composition that they have definite (and ancient!) technical names, names you may wish to learn when they are presented.

As you practice the various stylistic sentences given on the following pages, keep in mind that they are to be used in conjunction with basic sentences. Remember, that if you are to write well, you must always draw from the full spectrum of sentence types—both basic *and* stylistic. No one sentence form, no one group of sentence types, is better than another.

1 | THE REPETITION SENTENCE (WITH KEY WORD REPEATED)

A friend in power is a friend lost.—Henry Adams, The Education of Henry Adams

If your readers dislike you, they will dislike what you say.—F. L. Lucas, Style

Perpetual devotion to what a man calls his business is only to be sustained by perpetual neglect of many other things.—Robert Louis Stevenson, An Apology for Idlers

One of the things you can do to transform a basic sentence into a stylistic sentence is to repeat a key word. In Henry Adams's sentence, the repeition of the noun "friend" not only gives emphasis to "friend" itself, but also distinguishes the entire sentence from a more ordinary expression of the same thought. Adams might have written, "A friend in power is lost," or "Once a friend has power, he is lost" or "We lose our friends when they gain power." Adams chose, however, for stylistic reasons, a more structured form.

Such key-word repetition—it may be the repetition of a noun, or a verb as in F. L. Lucas's sentence, or a adjective as in Robert Louis Stevenson's sentence—often occurs in a separate phrase or clause that is clearly removed from the initial appearance of the key word. A part of this type of sentence's effectiveness results from the reader's encountering the key word after intervening words have occurred.

Sentences with a single key-word repetition in them frequently have an aphoristic quality, and therefore are valuable to use when you are expressing something you consider an indisputable, important, or memorable truth.

Copy each of the three sentences given above; then *compose* three sentences of your own, one in which you repeat the major noun in the sentence, one in which you repeat a verb, and one in which you repeat an adjective.

2 THE REPEATED-WORD SENTENCE (EPIZEUXIS)

For to mean anything high enough and hard enough is to fail, fail joyously.—John Ciardi, "Manner of Speaking," June 24, 1967

Surrounded by her listeners, she talked in a slow circle in her fine deep voice, the word 'perception' occurring again and again and yet again like the brass ring the children snatch for as their hobby horses whirl by.—Katherine Anne Porter, Gertrude Stein: A Self-Portrait

They hire English nannies, if possible, always nice middling women with sensible hairdos, sensible clothes, and sensible shoes.—Tom Wolfe, The Nanny Mafia

Another form of key-word repetition that is used to achieve the stylistic sentence is the repetition of the same word in close proximity. John Ciardi, in his sentence, has repeated the word "enough" with only two words between, and he has repeated "fail" with no words intervening. Such close repetitions are technically known as epizeuxis and are an important way to emphasize particular words. They also tend to give a sentence a certain focus and climax, and they frequently give the sentence a special type of rhythmical quality.

Epizeuxis can occur with any part of speech: In Ciardi's sentence it is achieved with an adverb and also with a verb; in Katherine Ann Porter's sentence, with an adverb; and in Tom Wolfe's sentence, with an adjective.

Copy each of the above three sentences; then *compose* three sentences of your own in which you repeat words in close sequence. Vary the part of speech of the repeated words from one sentence to the next.

3 THE REPEATED-WORD SENTENCE (WITH EXTENDED REPETITION)

All the more strange, then, is it that we should wish to know Greek, try to know Greek, feel forever drawn back to Greek, and be forever making up for some notion of the meaning of Greek, though from what incongruous odds and ends, with what slight resemblance to the real meaning of Greek, who shall say?—Virginia Woolf, On Not Knowing Greek

Word repetition can be extended to some length in the stylistic sentence, becoming something like a refrain or chorus. Virginia

Woolf has presented the word "Greek" five times to achieve extreme emphasis and to create a sentence seemingly "nailed together" with the repeated word. We can almost hear the hammer blows as Virginia Woolf pounds in the word "Greek," fastening the sentence together. Extended repetition is a valuable device to use when you wish to suggest a certain amount of compulsiveness, weary vexation, anger, or even irritation; it is a valuable kind of sentence to use in criticism, argument, and disputation.

Copy the above sentence; then *compose* a sentence of your own in which word repetition is carried on at some length. Write a sentence dealing with an issue or subject that especially concerns you or disturbs you.

4 REPOSITIONED-ADJECTIVE SENTENCE

Salisbury Plain is barren of criticism, but Stonehenge will bear a discussion antiquarian, picturesque, and philosophical.—William Hazlitt, On Going a Journey

Consider what dreams must have dominated the builders of the Pyramids—dreams geometrical, dreams funereal, dreams of resurrection, dreams of outdoing the pyramid of some other Pharaoh!—George Santayana, Soliloquies in England

Another easy way to transform a basic sentence into a stylistic one is to move words from their normal syntactical position into a more unusual position, and the easiest kind of word to manipulate in such a way is the adjective. Hazlitt achieved an interesting sentence simply by moving his three adjectives from in front of the noun "discussion" and presenting them after the noun. Instead of writing "Salisbury Plain is barren of criticism, but Stonehenge will bear an antiquarian, picturesque, and philosophical discussion," Hazlitt moved his adjectives to emphasize the adjectives themselves and to give the entire sentence a new and unusual structure and sound. In doing do, he lifted the sentence from a pedestrian level to a more noticeable level. The repositioned-adjective sentence can be used for variation in a passage of writing that relies heavily upon adjective modification.

In Santayana's sentence we find another dramatic version of the repositioned adjective. This sentence is certainly more dramatic than a more basic version: "Consider what geometrical and funereal dreams of resurrection must have dominated the builders of the Pyramids who yearned to outdo the pyramid of some other Pharaoh!"

Notice, too, that Santayana's sentence is doubly dramatic since it makes use not only of adjectives moved from their normal position but it also makes use of key-word repetition. This sentence is a good example of how a writer can begin to compound stylistic intensity and elaborateness in a sentence by doing more than one noticeable thing at the same time.

Copy the above two sentences; then *compose* two sentences of your own—one in which you present one or more adjectives after the noun rather than in front, and another in which you use not only unusual adjective placement but also some form of word repetition. You may wish to prepare for this exercise by first writing a descriptive sentence in which you employ a number of adjectives, all in the normal front-of-the-noun position, and then rewriting your sentence with one or two of your adjectives moved to an unusual position for the sake of emphasis or simple variation.

5 THE RHETORICAL QUESTION

Are they not criminals, books that have wasted our time and sympathy; are they not the most insidious enemies of society, corruptors, defilers, the writers of false books, faked books, books that fill the air with decay and disease?—*Virginia Woolf,* How Should One Read a Book?

A standard, and in many ways easy, method of giving stylistic aura to a sentence is to convert it into a rhetorical question. Virginia Woolf could easily have left her sentence in its basic form: "Books that have wasted our time and sympathy are criminals; writers of false books, faked books, books that fill the air with decay and disease are the most insidious enemies, corruptors, and defilers of society." By converting the statement into a question, she gave it a new stylistic dimension. You will note, however, that she could have presented the rhetorical question in the positive, rather than in the negative: "Are they criminals . . .; are they the most insidious . . .?", but by including the "not" she forces the reader into agreement and affirmation.

If you were to start with a basic statement, "The sky is dark blue," you might achieve a stylistic conversion by asking, "Is the sky dark blue?" in a context that suggests a "yes" answer or by asking the question "Is not the sky dark blue?" so as to *demand* a "yes" answer. The difference in the two forms of rhetorical questions is that the negative form is less subtle in its request for agreement.

Note that, stylistically, Virginia Woolf does several other things in her sentence: She shuns the ordinary syntax, "Are books not criminals," and uses instead "Are they not criminals, books . . ." and she repeats the key word "books."

Copy the rhetorical question given above; then *compose* a similar question of your own, that is based upon some prior declaration or statement. Write both your basic statement and your "question form" of it.

6 THE INTERRUPTED SENTENCE (THE EXPLANATION)

They have observed—that is to say, they have really seen—nothing.—Arnold Bennett, The Author's Craft

How then does a man—be he good or bad—big or little—a philosopher or a fribble—St. Paul or Horace Walpole—make his memoirs interesting?—Augustine Birrell, Obiter Dicta

Stylistic sentences may be achieved by the judicious use of interruptions. You have already copied and composed the interrupted sentence in your study of basic sentences, but now you will want to note the particular stylistic uses to which the interrupted sentence can be put.

The interrupted sentence is used in two ways. One, the interruption can draw attention to that element in the sentence that follows the the interruption. In Arnold Bennett's sentence the word "nothing" receives a special emphasis because of the suspenseful nature of the words preceding it. Two, the interruption frequently acts as a kind of brake on the rhythm of the sentence and consequently can indicate termination: The concluding sentence in a paragraph or whole composition is frequently of an interrupted nature—interrupted so as to "put on the brake" verbally, as the writer brings a particular unit of composition to its conclusion.

Interruptions may be of any length, of course, and may be of a complex nature, made up of various separate items. In Birrell's sentence, there is a deliberate use of the interruption to create stylistic suspense and to give greater emphasis to the concluding words. In this sentence you will note that the device of interruption has been joined with the device of the rhetorical question for a more complex stylistic effect.

Copy the two interrupted sentences; then *compose* two of your own—one with a rather simple interruption focusing attention upon the word that follows the interruption, and one with a complex interruption of several items.

7 THE INTERRUPTED SENTENCE (THE ASIDE)

Even mathematical solutions (though here I speak with trembling) can have aesthetic beauty.—F. L. Lucas, Style

Some interruptions are more digressive than others. While the usual interruption may be an appositive or a modification or a direct explanation, the interruption can become something like an "aside" and truly parenthetical, whether presented within parentheses or not. Such digressive interruptions may be more startling than other kinds of interruptions and are frequently placed within parentheses to indicate that they are to be "spoken with a whisper." Digressive interruptions, the whispered asides, can be used stylistically to soften content, to give increased importance to what follows the aside, to establish the very nature of the persona in a composition, or simply to relieve the bluntness of a direct style.

Consider Lucas's sentence. A basic statement, "Even mathematical solutions can have aesthetic beauty" has been modified by the interruption so that the reader is put in brief suspense following the word "solutions"; he is forced to wait a few words before finding out what Lucas has to say about his subject. Also, the aside, "though here I speak with trembling," gives a new quality to the sentence by adding—to a statement that sounds like the premise of a syllogism—a certain personal, human, and subjective quality. To keep the sentence from being strictly declarative and expository, Lucas uses the digressive interruption to introduce a softening tone. The sentence becomes less didactic and slightly more dramatic. In addition, the concluding words "aesthetic beauty" take on new emphasis as a result of their delay.

Copy the sentence above; then *compose* a similar sentence containing a digressive interruption by using parentheses.

8 THE STRUCTURED SERIES (BALANCE)

An event may seem to us amusing or pathetic.—Joseph Wood Krutch, Experience and Art

He who enters the sphere of faith enters the sanctuary of life.—Paul Tillich, The Dynamics of Faith

If we wish life to be a system, this may be a nuisance; but if we wish it to be a drama, it is an essential.—G. K. Chesterton, Heretics

You have written a number of basic sentences that contained

representative series. Such series can be part of a stylistic sentence if you attend to the length of the units within the series. Without thinking about it, you may create units of various lengths; but, on certain occasions, you can, if you wish, take care to see that the units are the same length, are equalized into a definite architecture. Such a structure, having units that are the same length, is called an isocolon. With equal-length units, a series becomes more noticeable, more controlled, and more emphatic.

When only two units are involved, the resulting equal-length structure is called a balance. The balance may consist of two words, as "amusing" and "pathetic" in Joseph Wood Krutch's sentence; or of longer units, as the phrases in Tillich's sentence—"the sphere of faith" and "the sanctuary of life"; or even of clauses, as in Chesterton's sentence. In the Chesterton example the entire sentence is involved in the balance and represents the most controlled structural form a writer can achieve with a two-part series.

Whenever you write a sentence, if you can add a dimension of perfect structure and architecture by using units of equal size, you will make your writing more noticeable and eventful—an effect you will desire when your rhetorical profile calls for some degree of heightening.

Copy the three sentences above; then *compose* three sentences of your own in which you balance first two individuals words, then two independent clauses, and then two prepositional phrases used as adjectives.

9 COMPOUND-BALANCE SENTENCE

The room was solid and rich; it was established and quiet.—Robert Allen Durr, The Last Days of H. L. Mencken

Two balanced structures can be joined in a single sentence to create an even more elaborate balance. You should master this sentence type that compounds the balancing effect. In Durr's sentence you find an overall balance—"The room was solid and rich" balanced with "it was established and quiet." Yet each item in that overall balance contains its own balance: "Solid" is balanced with "rich," and "established" is balanced with "quiet." By compounding a structural effect, the dramatic quality of a sentence is doubly increased.

Copy the above compound-balance sentence; then *compose* a similar sentence of your own.

10 THE STRUCTURED SERIES (TRICOLON)

He was, indeed, in every sense of the word, a wise, a good, and a great man.— Thomas Jefferson, A Letter on the Character of George Washington

Creation, property, enjoyment form a sinister trinity in the human mind.— *E. M. Forster,* My Wood

One of the most frequently used forms of the structured series is the tricolon—a three-part series with units of equal length. The tricolon is always dramatic, and it has been used for such grandiose announcements as Caesar's "I came, I saw, I conquered" and Lincoln's "of the people, by the people, for the people." The tricolon effects a dramatic presentation of the reasonable and judicious position; and perhaps for that reason, it is one of the most popular stylistic constructions. Jefferson has an exact tricolon in "a wise," "a good," and " a great." Forster has an exact tricolon with his three trisyllabic words, "creation," "property," and "enjoyment."

Because the tricolon is so effective a device of rhetoric and style, it can be overused; therefore, a writer should keep in mind the distinctions between two-part, three-part, and four-part series in general, and if he decides to use the three-part series, he should make sure he wants the series given the extra emphasis and attention that the tricolon will confer.

Copy the two sentences above; then *compose* two sentences of your own in which you use the tricolon.

11 THE STRUCTURED SERIES (FOUR-PART)

Logic, eloquence, wit, taste, all those things which are generally considered as *making a book valuable, were utterly wanting to him.—Thomas Babington* *Macaulay,* Review of Croker's Edition of *Boswell's Life of Johnson*

The four-part series can also have units of approximately the same length; indeed, any series can be so structured. In the sentence above, Macaulay presents four one-word units in his series; and, while the first two words are polysyllabic and the last two words are monosyllabic, the sense of exact structure prevails. Not only does Macaulay's series connote, because of its four items, "the human being," but because of its carefully structured one-two-three-four sequence, the series is given special importance, particular emphasis. Macaulay, indeed, would seem to be saying that not only are these the characteristics that sophisticated human beings put into their writing but also that these characteristics should not be ignored.

Copy the sentence above; then *compose* a sentence of your own in which the units in a four-part or even a five-part series are of approximately the same length.

12 | THE SYMMETRICAL SENTENCE

Effeminacy is fatal.—Dixon Wecter, The Hero in America

Imagination means individuation.—Stephen Spender, The Imagination in the Modern World

In addition to balancing the units of a two-part series, you may also write a sentence in which one part is balanced against the other. This sort of symmetrical sentence is achieved by presenting units of equal length on either side of a central verb. The symmetrical sentence is usually quite short, every word in it is involved in the balance. Wecter's sentence of just three words presents a noun on one side of the pivotal verb and an adjective on the other. Stephen Spender has done even more: He has not only a noun balanced with another noun, but he has also taken care that both words begin with *i* and end with *tion*. By placing on either side of the verb words of similar sound and spelling, Spender has given an additional intensification to the symmetrical sentence.

Structured as though on a fulcrum, the symmetrical sentence is emphatic and frequently aphoristic. It is often used—because of its startling and abbreviated structure—in opening positions at the beginnings of paragraphs or whole compositions, usually followed by explanations and details. It is a splendid kind of sentence for startling declarations and premises, even though some sort of proof or illustration must of necessity come after.

Copy these symmetrical sentences; then *compose* two, three words in length, of your own. Use *is* as the pivotal verb in one sentence; then try to find another equalizing verb for your second sentence.

13 | THE NEGATIVE-POSITIVE SEQUENCE

A tragic writer does not have to believe in God, but he must believe in man.— Joseph Wood Krutch, The Modern Temper

He suddenly saw the fields, not as solid flat objects covered with grass or useful crops and dotted with trees, but as colour in astonishing variety and subtlety of gradation.—Joyce Carey, Art and Reality

Many times you may present a two-part series in a negative-positive form: "not this, but that." Presenting the certainty of a two-part series and presenting it in so definite a no/yes or black/white version, you can create a particular and exceptional tension.

Such negative-positive two-part series are effectively used when you wish to communicate certainty—and at the same time wish to give the second part of the series special importance. By presenting the negative, you suggest that you are not only "certain" but also that you are taking into consideration any contrary argument, in order that your "certainty" will become imperative.

Consider how different Krutch's sentence would have been if he had written, "A tragic writer may be an atheist, but he must believe in man." The absoluteness of the two-part series would have remained, but a certain forcefulness would be lost. An additional degree of intensity was added to the sentence by Krutch's repetition of the key word "believe."

Consider, too, how different the effect of Joyce Carey's sentence would have been if he had written, "He suddenly saw the fields— normally viewed as solid flat objects covered with grass or useful crops and dotted with trees—now as colour in astonishing variety and subtlety of gradation." Carey added the negative in order to highlight his concern with the color.

Note that Carey has compounded his two-part series: the first item in the series, "not as solid flat objects covered with grass or useful crops and dotted with trees," contains its own two-part series, "covered with grass or useful crops" and "dotted with trees." And the first item of that interior series contains a two-part series, "grass" and "useful crops." In addition the second item of the overall series, "but as colour in astonishing variety and subtlety of gradation," contains an interior two-part series, "variety" and "subtlety." Whereas Krutch combined negative-positive presentation with key-word repetition to increase the intensity of his sentence, Carey has combined negative-positive presentation with interior two-part series to increase both tension and intensity.

Copy these negative-positive sentences; then *compose* two of your own. Compose one containing a negative-positive sequence without any additional device of intensity. Then compose another sentence containing the negative-positive sequence along with some additional device, such as key-word repetition or interior series.

14 POSITIVE-NEGATIVE SEQUENCE

I was told about missionaries, but never about pirates; I was familiar with humming-birds, but I never heard of fairies.—Edmund Gosse, Father and Son

Reason can dissect, but cannot originate; she can adopt, but cannot create; she can modify, but cannot find.—Horatio Greenough, Form and Function

High-tension sentences can also be created by presenting two items in positive-negative order. When the positive is presented first, however, the sentence takes on a particular negative note; there is more complaint in such a sentence, more criticism. When you write in "this, not that" form, you are giving a certain stress to the negative, the absent, the weak, the unfortunate within your content.

Edmund Gosse's sentence is essentially a complaint. It would have had a much more positive tone if he had written "I was never told about pirates, but I was told about missionaries; I had never heard of fairies, but I was familiar with humming-birds." At least the complaint and criticism would have been greatly softened. Likewise, Greenough's sentence would have been quite different if he had written, "Reason cannot originate, but can dissect; she cannot create, but can adopt; she cannot find, but can modify." Greenough's sentence, as actually written—in a positive-negative sequence—is a sharper, more militant criticism of reason and the rational mind.

Copy these two positive-negative sentences; then *compose* two of your own about something worthy of your complaint and criticism.

15 ANTITHESIS

The loftiest edifices need the deepest foundations.—George Santayana, Reason in Society

Sink or swim, live or die, survive or perish, I give my hand and my heart to this vote.—Daniel Webster, Eulogy on Adams and Jefferson

Extreme tension can be achieved in sentences by presenting balanced elements in direct opposition to each other. A balance of opposites is called an antithesis, and it is one of the most popular of the intensifying devices in style. Antithesis may be especially useful to you when you wish to emphasize discrepancies and contrasts, or wish to magnify unlikely relationships.

Santayana, in his sentence, has used antithesis to emphasize the relationship between the seen and the unseen parts of a structure; he has achieved intensification by balancing both his adjectives and nouns. Daniel Webster, in turn, has used a series of antitheses, not only to suggest the totality of his conviction, but also to suggest that this totality takes into consideration all polarities and that his conviction is so firm that it will survive whatever the circumstances.

Copy the two antithetical sentences; then *compose* two of your own. In your second sentence use a series of antitheses as Daniel Webster did.

16 ANTIMETABOLE

But if thought corrupts language, language can also corrupt thought.—George Orwell, Politics and the English Language

An even more elaborate form of intensification occurs in a two-part series when two elements constitute one part of a balance and are then reversed to compose the second part of a balance. In Orwell's sentence we see that "thought . . . language" becomes "language . . . thought." This reversal of parts in a balance, involving exact words, is called antimetabole. It is, of course, a powerfully intense construction and, as such, is used only on rare occasions.

Copy Orwell's sentence containing antimetabole; then *compose* a similar sentence.

17 ASYNDETON

He has had his intuition, he has made his discovery, he is eager to explore it, to reveal it, to fix it down.—Joyce Carey, Art and Reality

We hear the hum of life in the fields; a horse champs his bit; a butterfly circles and settles.—Virginia Woolf, The Novels of Turgenev

You can stylistically modify any series, whatever its length, by manipulating the conjunctions within the series. You usually write a series with one conjunction, which comes between the last and next-to-the-last items. If you omit that conjunction, you have employed the device of asyndeton, and your series is pushed together into a more definite, single event or action or condition: The sense of time is speeded up and you have given your reader the impression that what you are talking about is one event occurring all-at-once.

In the sentence by Joyce Carey and the sentence by Virginia Woolf, you can anticipate the difference in effect if a conjunction had been used: "He has had his intuition, he has made his discovery, and he is eager to explore it, to reveal it, and to fix it down," and "We hear the hum of life in the fields; a horse champs his bit; and a butterfly circles and settles." With the conjunction the sentences are more ordinary; without it they are more compressed, more instantaneous, and more dramatic.

Copy these two sentences; then *compose* two sentences of your own containing asyndeton.

18 POLYSYNDETON

It was a hot day and the sky was very bright and blue and the road was white and dusty.—Ernest Hemingway, A Farewell to Arms

It is his privilege to help man endure by lifting his heart, by reminding him of the courage and honor and hope and pride and compassion and pity and sacrifice which have been the glory of his past.—William Faulkner, Nobel Prize speech, 1950

The opposite of asyndeton is polysyndeton: an abundant use of conjunctions in a series. Polysyndeton enables you to stretch what you are saying out over a longer piece of time and enables you to distinguish each item of a series from its companions: Polysyndeton separates each item of a series into a distinct or discrete experience.

Hemingway is famous for his use of polysyndeton; and Faulkner, in his sentence from his well-known Nobel Prize speech, makes tremendously effective use of polysyndeton in conjunction with a long series. Faulkner is calling attention to the human and the emotional, but the virtues he lists are not simply those of a single moment (if they were, asyndeton would have been used), but these virtues persist through the "glory of the past" into the present moment.

Copy the above two sentences; then *compose* two similar sentences in which you use many conjunctions to indicate an extension of experience over a long period of time and to indicate the distinct identity of each item in the series.

19 ANAPHORA

The reason why I object to Dr. Johnson's style is, that there is no discrimination, no selection, no variety in it.—William Hazlitt, On Familiar Style

Art, for most Americans, is a very queer fish—it can't be reasoned with, it can't be bribed, it can't be doped out or duplicated; above all, it can't be cashed in on.—Louis Kronenberger, America and Art

Another intensifying device you can use in constructing a series of any length is anaphora: beginning each item in the series with the same word or words. In Hazlitt's tricolon, you will note that he has begun each item with the word "no": "no discrimination, no selection, no variety." In Louis Kronenberger's long series, each item begins with the words "it can't be."

You will use anaphora to give a pounding emphasis to each item in a series, and thereby elevate the entire series onto a more intense and dramatic level of writing. To create anaphora, you can employ more than one word; whereas Hazlitt uses only "no" in the anaphora, Kronenberger uses three words, "it can't be." As anaphora deepens, as more and more words are repeated at the beginning of each item, the more intense the device becomes.

Copy the above two sentences; then *compose* two of your own in which you employ anaphora.

20 EPISTROPHE

To the good American many subjects are sacred: sex is sacred, women are sacred, children are sacred, business is sacred, America is sacred, Masonic lodges and college clubs are sacred.—George Santayana, Character and Opinion in the United States

Raphael paints wisdom; Handel sings it, Phidias carves it, Shakespeare writes it, Wren builds it, Columbus sails it, Luther preaches it, Washington arms it, Watt mechanizes it.—Ralph Waldo Emerson, Civilization

Of equal intensity with anaphora is epistrophe: ending each item in a series with the same word or words. Epistrophe is a dramatic way of showing the common denominator that unites a diverse series of subjects, and epistrophe forces a reader to an inescapable awareness of each item by placing it before a recurring terminal word or words.

Santayana, for instance, makes us hear with startling clarity the words "sex," "women," "children," "business," "America," and "Masonic lodges and college clubs" because they are all placed against a common background: the word "sacred." How different would Santayana's sentence have been if it read in a simpler form: "To the good American many subjects are sacred: sex, women, children, business, America, Masonic lodges and college clubs." In such an ordinary series, neither the word "sacred" nor any individual item in the series would have challenged our attention.

Likewise, in Emerson's sentence we hear much more loudly and clearly the words "Raphael paints," "Handel sings," "Phidias carves," "Shakespeare writes," "Wren builds," and so on because they are noticeable variations in contrast with the constant "it."

With epistrophe, a sentence is given a rich, driving power. You will find this device valuable to use when you have to present a number of items that have some common characteristic or feature.

Copy the above two sentences; then *compose* two sentences in which you use epistrophe. Use a three-part series in one sentence and a five-part series in the other.

21 SYMPLOCE

I was born an American; I will live an American; I shall die an American.—Daniel Webster, Speech, *July 17, 1850*

Finally, you can combine anaphora and epistrophe to create the inescapable effect of symploce. By beginning each item with the same word and by closing each item with the same word, you achieve a double-barreled stylistic effect that is especially dramatic and emphatic.

Copy the above sentence; then *compose* one in which you use the device of symploce. Begin each item in the series, whatever its length, with the same word or words, and close each item in the series with the same word or words.

22 ANADIPLOSIS

And there they have it, the color called Landlord's Brown, immune to time, flood, tropic heat, arctic chill, punk rumbles, slops, blood, leprotic bugs, cockroaches the size of mice, mice the size of rats, rats the size of Airedales and lumpenprole tenants.—Tom Wolfe, Putting Daddy On

We have lost our concern with the ends because we have lost our touch with reality and we have lost our touch with reality because we are estranged from the means to reality which is the poem—the work of art.—Archibald MacLeish, Why Do We Teach Poetry?

This is great poetry, and it is dramatic; but besides being poetic and dramatic, it is something more.—T. S. Eliot, Poetry and Drama

Passing bells are ringing all the world over. All the world over and every hour, someone is parting company with all his aches and ecstasies.—Robert Louis Stevenson, Aes Triplex

In a long-series sentence where the series have been extended to the point of absurdity, Tom Wolfe has used yet another stylistic transformation: ending one item in the series with the word that begins the next item—"the size of mice, mice the size of rats, rats the size of Airedales. . . ." This device is called anadiplosis. You will use anadiplosis to give a sentence—or at least that part of the sentence in which it occurs—a greater continuity and a slower tempo (anadiplosis puts a sentence into something like slow motion). You will also use this device to give additional emphasis to the words involved.

You are not limited to the series in the use of anadiplosis, however. It can be used in any sentence that has two or more phrases or clauses. In Archibald MacLeish's sentence the words "we have lost our touch with reality" are repeated at the beginning of the next clause, "and we have lost our touch with reality."

Anadiplosis is sometimes muted—that is, more suggested than actually achieved in the technical sense. In T. S. Eliot's sentence the words "poetry" and "dramatic" are taken from the first part of the sentence and "poetic" and "dramatic" are used to begin the second part. The effect is that of anadiplosis, and the same continuity, emphasis, overlapping, and slow-motion is achieved.

Anadiplosis may occur at the end of the one sentence and the beginning of the next sentence, as in the sentences from Stevenson's *Aes Triplex.*

Copy the four sentences; then *compose* two sentences of your own containing anadiplosis.

23 THE CIRCULAR SENTENCE (EPANALEPSIS)

Across the United States of America, from New York to California and back, glazed, again, for many months of the year there streams and sings for its heady supper a dazed and prejudiced procession of European lecturers, scholars, sociologists, economists, writers, authorities on this and that and even, in theory, on the United States of America.—Dylan Thomas, A Visit to America

Beginning and ending a clause or a sentence with the same word or words is called epanalepsis. Epanalepsis creates something like a circular sentence in that it ends where it began. Using epanalepsis, Dylan Thomas has written a razzle-dazzle sentence—one that boasts a complex series and high diction as well—typical of the intense, elaborate style for which he is famous.

This fairly long sentence makes a complete circle: "United States of America . . . United States of America." Thomas has used it at the beginning of an essay to get the essay off to a rollicking start. Many writers do such a thing: Start a composition with an attention-getting sentence, employing some elaborate stylistic device, such as the circular sentence.

Copy Dylan Thomas's sentence; then *compose* a similar sentence that begins and ends with the same words.

24 THE CIRCULAR SENTENCE (MODIFIED EPANALEPSIS)

His illness was beyond all hope of healing before anyone realized that he was ill.—James Baldwin, Notes of a Native Son

America had to be made before it could be lived in, and that making took centuries, took extraordinary energies and bred an attitude of life that is peculiarly American.—D. W. Brogan, The American Character

Different ages have answered the question differently.—Virginia Woolf, The Patron and the Crocus

Sometimes circular sentences make use of modified epanalepsis, employing not the same word at the beginning and end but some form of the same word. (Whenever you use a variant form of a word, you are using the device of polyptoton.) In Baldwin's sentence "illness" and "ill" create a modified epanalepsis and effect a circular sentence. The circular sentence is especially effective if there is one central theme a writer wishes to emphasize, as James Baldwin wishes to emphasize illness. By beginning and ending with the same idea, Baldwin seems to say that illness was the sum of his father's final days; it was an all-encompassing and total event and experience.

Likewise, in Brogan's sentence no one can mistake the main concern: The subject, "America," is absolutely reinforced by being placed at the beginning and, as "American," at the end of the sentence. In Virginia Woolf's sentence the modified epanalepsis creates an aphoristic quality—closing the sentence off, rounding it into completeness, as though to say there is nothing beyond this sentence.

Copy these three sentences; then *compose* three of your own in which modified epanalepsis is used. Write one expressing the total domination of a subject that you name at the beginning and end of the sentence. Write another that expresses what you consider a truth about life, again naming the subject at the beginning and end of the sentence.

25 THE FIGURATIVE SENTENCE (SIMILE)

Like a piece of ice on a hot stove the poem must ride on its own melting.—Robert Frost, The Figure a Poem Makes

Ah, what a mistress, this Etna! with her strange winds prowling round her like Circe's panthers, some black, some white.—D. H. Lawrence, Sea and Sardinia

An idea is frequently presented in a most intense manner when it is compared—startlingly, dramatically, and unexpectedly—with some highly picturable object, person, or event. Comparisons that are literal are not especially exciting, but comparisons made between different worlds of experience, differing planes of reality become dramatic figures that are an essential part of a writer's stylistic material. Adding a figure to a literal basic sentence is a sure way to transform the basic into the stylistic.

Figures traditionally have a tenor—the idea or subject you are actually talking about—and a vehicle—the object, person, or event that you introduce for the sake of the startling comparison. In Robert Frost's figure, the "poem" is the tenor and "a piece of ice" is the vehicle. By comparing a poem to a piece of ice, Frost has concretized and made picturable something he wants to say about the nature of the poetic art. And by making the comparison very explicit, by using the word *like* so the reader will be certain to notice the comparison, Frost has used what is technically known as a simile.

Similes can be combined with other stylistic devices, of course. D. H. Lawrence, in his sentence, has combined the simile with another form of figurative language, personification, and has, in addition, used a two-part series, "some black, some white," intensified by balance, antithesis, and anaphora. Whereas Frost has compared an abstraction "poem" with the concrete "ice," Lawrence has compared the unseeable "winds" with living animals; the difference between the two similes suggests how diverse and creative a writer can be in composing figurative sentences.

Copy these two figurative sentences; then *compose* two of your own. Remember a good simile—or, any good figure—is novel and fresh and truly adds new insight to the subject you are discussing.

26 | THE FIGURATIVE SENTENCE (METAPHOR)

Nay, to conclude upon a note of grandeur, it is by ignorance alone that we advance through the rough seas of this our mortal life.—Hilaire Belloc, In Praise of Ignorance

Less explicit than the simile is the metaphor, wherein the words *like* or *as* are omitted. As figures become less explicit, they become stylistically more effective and intense. A metaphor may be presented in this fashion: "Our mortal life is a rough sea." Or it may be presented, as Belloc has done, in an even more subtle way: "the rough seas of this our mortal life." This form of metaphor is sometimes called a condensed metaphor, and it is one of the most effective devices you can use in your writing.

Copy Belloc's sentence; then *compose* a sentence containing a condensed metaphor.

27 | THE FIGURATIVE SENTENCE (REIFICATION)

The winds that scattered the Spanish Armada blew English Literature, which had been merely smouldering for generations, into a blaze of genius.—J. B. Priestley, Literature and Western Man

By comparing such an intangible subject as "English Literature" with so tangible a phenomenon as a fire "smouldering . . . into a blaze," Priestley has constructed a figurative sentence by means of reification: Reification simply means making whatever you are talking about into a *thing*. The tenor is abstract, the vehicle is concrete. Reification is one of the standard ways of establishing a figure, whether that figure is presented as a simile or a metaphor.

Copy Priestley's sentence; then *compose* a figurative sentence containing an example of reification.

28 | THE FIGURATIVE SENTENCE (PERSONIFICATION)

Far off, a little yellow plane scuttles down a runway, steps awkwardly into the air, then climbs busily, learning grace.—Robert Penn Warren, Segregation

Death stands at attention, obedient, expectant, ready to serve, ready to shear away the peoples en masse; *ready, if called on, to pulverize, without hope of repair, what is left of civilisation.—Winston Churchill,* World Crisis

Another way of establishing a figure is to compare a nonliving or inanimate subject with something alive. A figure whose vehicle is living and animate is called a personification. Robert Penn Warren has compared a plane (tenor) with a human being (vehicle) or at least with some sort of animal that can "step" and "climb" and "learn."

Winston Churchill has also used personification. He has compared death, an abstraction, with a soldier who can "stand at attention."

By knowing how to create personification and reification you can achieve different kinds of figurative sentences and thereby maintain variety in your composition even when writing at a highly intense figurative level.

Copy the two sentences above; then *compose* two similar sentences using personification as the means of achieving your figures.

29 THE COMPLEX FIGURATIVE SENTENCE

When the struggle with somnolence has been fought out and won, when the world is all-covering darkness and close-pressing silence, when the tobacco suddenly takes on fresh vigour and fragrance and the books lie strewn about the table, then it seems as though all the rubbish and floating matter of the day's thoughts have poured away and only the bright, clear, and swift current of the mind itself remains, flowing happily and without impediment.—Christopher Morley, On Going to Bed

A sentence may contain several separate figures, and some of these figures may be extended to considerable length. In Morley's sentence, you will notice various metaphors such as: "somnolence" (tenor), "something to fight with" (vehicle); "silence" (tenor), "something that can physically press in on a person" (vehicle); "tobacco" (tenor), "something that can be vigorous" (vehicle); "thoughts" (tenor), "something that can produce rubbish and floating matter" (vehicle); and "mind" (tenor), "a swift current" (vehicle). The metaphors concerning the day's thoughts and the mind are actually akin to each other and are an extension of the basic metaphor that the mind is a stream that can become contaminated, but that also can be purified.

Copy Morley's sentence; then *compose* one, just as long, in which you use at least two different and separate figures of any kind—similes, metaphors, reifications, or personifications. Extend one of the figures through several clauses.

30 THE ALLITERATIVE SENTENCE

All beauty comes from beautiful blood and a beautiful brain.—Walt Whitman, Preface to Leaves of Grass

A moist young moon hung above the mist of a neighboring meadow.—Vladimir Nabokov, Conclusive Evidence

Even if the facts are false, they are still very strange.—G. K. Chesterton, On Certain Modern Writers and the Institution of the Family

On occasion, you will transform a basic sentence by making use of noticeable alliteration. Alliteration can make a statement unified and more memorable. A sentence in which many words are alliterated becomes a sentence with a common phonetic theme running throughout it, a thread of sound that ties the meaning together. As a consequence alliterative sentences are more easily remembered.

Alliteration is achieved by repeating a consonant sound at the beginning of several words. Whitman, for instance, has alliterated the words "beauty," "beautiful," "blood," "beautiful," and "brain." There is a limit, of course, to the number of words that can be alliterated in any given sentence, and Whitman's use of the consonant *b* five times represents a maximum sort of use.

Nabokov uses the letter *m* four times in "moist," "moon," "mist," and "meadow"; but he has spread out the alliteration a bit with more intervening words. Perhaps the secret of good alliteration is to limit the number of accented words involved and to avoid too heavy a concentration of the consonant sound.

Many times more then one alliterative consonant is used in a sentence. Chesterton, for instance, alliterates *f* twice, then shifts to the letter *s*. This can create an especially delightful effect, as one sound is contrasted with another, and as a result each is heightened, without becoming monotonous.

Copy the three alliterative sentences; then *compose* three of your own. Write two sentences, each with a different letter used in alliteration. Write a third sentence that uses two different letters for alliterative effect.

31 THE RHYTHMICAL SENTENCE

He is capable of being shown of what consciousness consists.—Stephen Spender, The Imagination in the Modern World

Curiosity is a form of desire.—Marchette Chute, Getting at the Truth

Though perhaps all good sentences should be rhythmical, certain sentences have a much more obvious cadence and flow to them and are therefore more useful stylistically. The sentence that attracts us by its patterned flow is a sentence that can be used for all stylistic effects from simple emphasis to calculated grandeur.

In Stephen Spender's sentence we find a two-part rhythm, echoing old biblical rhythms, old Anglo-Saxon rhythms, and the free-verse rhythms that Walt Whitman popularized in *Leaves of Grass*. "He is capable of being shown" is the first phrase in the rhythm, "of what consciousness consists" is the balancing phrase. This pendulumlike rhythm, swinging back and forth, could become monotonous and stupefying if it were the prevailing rhythm in a piece of writing; but as a special effect on special occasions, it is a delightful and enjoyable device.

In Marchette Chute's sentence you will notice a three-part rhythm: "Curiosity" phrase one, "is a form" phrase two, "of desire" phrase three. Three-part rhythms can be used in contrast with two-part rhythms in passages of writing that need to "sing forth," yet cannot be maintained with one single rhythmic form.

Copy the two rhythmical sentences above; then *compose* two of your own. One should have a two-part rhythm, the other a three-part rhythm.

32 THE METRICAL SENTENCE (FOUR BEATS)

The sentence is a single cry.—Herbert Read, English Prose Style

Hitch your wagon to a star.—Ralph Waldo Emerson, Civilization

The world is very different now.—John F. Kennedy, Inaugural Address

On rare occasions you may wish to make a sentence actually metrical; that is, make its accents fall in a regular and patterned way. In Herbert Read's sentence, you can hear the beat: "The SEN tence IS a SIN gle CRY." The beat is a 1-2-3-4 beat or march step, the most common form of the metrical sentence. Metrical sentences are highly memorable because they are almost singable.

Emerson took advantage of the metrical sentence to make his transcendental philosophy understandable and popular; at least he took advantage of it in his famous sentence: HITCH your WAG on TO a STAR.

The modern writer sometimes uses the metrical sentence to make his points: John F. Kennedy included the metrical sentence in his Inaugural Address—a composition that is a rich display of most of the stylistic sentences you are encountering in this text.

Copy the three four-beat sentences above; then *compose* three of your own.

33 THE METRICAL SENTENCE (VARIOUS BEATS)

May in Venice is better than April, but June is best of all.—Henry James, Portraits of Places

He was the man that cannot steer, that cannot splice, that dodges the work on dark nights; that, aloft, holds on frantically with both arms and legs, and swears at the wind, the sleet, the darkness; the man who curses the sea while others work.—Joseph Conrad, The Nigger and the Narcissus

Henry James also makes use of word accents to create a strongly metrical sentence: MAY in VEN ice is BET ter than ÀP ril, but JUNE is BEST of ALL. In the first clause the metrical feet are a mixture of trochaic and dactylic measures, but in the second clause James shifts to straight iambic feet. The total effect of the sentence is something like a dance, a measured lilt around the room, an appropriate meter for the "vacation" atmosphere of the sentence.

In Conrad's metrical sentence, you will find an element of rhyme ("splice," "nights") added to meter, and the effect is almost sing-song. After the opening clause, "He was the man," the sentence becomes very metrical; it becomes almost a quatrain of iambic dimeter lines:

> that cannot steer,
>> that cannot splice,
> that dodges the work
>> on dark nights

Then each succeeding clause establishes a definite meter of its own, especially the last clause, which is basically iambic pentameter. This exaggerated form of the metrical sentence is rarely used. You may, however, have need for it on some special occasion; perhaps to be funny, if nothing else.

Copy the two metrical sentences above; then *compose* two metrical sentences of your own, experimenting as you wish with different kinds of metrical measures and feet.

34 | THE MASTER SENTENCE

The worst part of war is not death and destruction but just soldiering; the worst part of soldiering is not danger but nostalgia; and the worst part of a soldier's nostalgia is the lack of intimacy, the lack of privacy, and the deprivation of the rights of self-determination and ownership.—Robert Henriques, The Voice of the Trumpet

Master sentences are achieved by using a rich number of stylistic devices and by combining, weaving together, and juxtaposing various stylistic modifications and transformations. Robert Henriques has written such a master sentence. In it you will recognize alliteration—"worst," "war," "death," "destruction"; balanced two-part series—"death and destruction," "self-determination and ownership"; negative-positive sequence—"not death and destruction but just soldiering," "not danger but nostalgia"; modified anadiplosis—"soldiering; the worst part of soldiering is not danger but nostalgia; and the worst part of a soldier's nostalgia"; key-word repetition—"lack," "lack"; three-part series with anaphora—"the worst part of war . . .; the worst part of soldiering . . . ; and the worst part of a soldier's nostalgia . . ."; and three-part series without anaphora—"lack of intimacy, the lack of privacy, and the deprivation of the rights. . . ." Such a rich mixture of stylistic modifications does not make for confusion, but for a tremendously effective sentence, remarkably clear and sturdy.

Copy Robert Henriques's sentence; then *compose* a sentence that employs at least three of the stylistic devices that Henriques used.

35 | THE MASTER SENTENCE

Vengeance then is forbidden; sacrifice is forbidden; justice is impossible: what remains? the fourth choice? forgiveness? and how then forgiveness?—Charles Williams, The Forgiveness of Sins

In this sentence Charles Williams opens with a three-part series—a tricolon: "Vengeance then is forbidden; sacrifice is forbidden; justice is impossible." Then he dramatically concludes the sentence with a series of rhetorical questions: "what remains? the fourth choice? forgiveness? and how then forgiveness?" In the course of the three-part series and the four rhetorical questions, Williams uses key-word repetition: "forbidden," "forbidden" (not quite an epistrophe because the third item in the series differs) and "forgiveness," "forgiveness."

Also in the sentence are some splendid subtleties: Do you notice that the second word in the sentence is "then" and the next to the last word in the sentence is "then"? Do you also notice that the sentence opens with "vengeance" and closes with "forgiveness," two opposed or antithetical words?

Copy Charles Williams's sentence; then *compose* a sentence that • opens with a tricolon and closes with a set of rhetorical questions. Add as many subtle stylistic devices as you can.

36 | THE MASTER SENTENCE

Now the trumpet summons us again—not as a call to bear arms, though arms we need; not as a call to battle, though embattled we are; but a call to bear the burden of a long twilight struggle, year in and year out, "rejoicing in hope, patient in tribulation," a struggle against the common enemies of man: tyranny, poverty, disease and war itself.—John F. Kennedy, Inaugural Address

Opening with a metaphor, this splendid sentence proceeds through the negative-positive sequences—"not as a call to bear arms, though arms we need; not as a call to battle, though embattled we are; but a call to bear. . . ." It continues with such modifications as a balanced two-part series of which the negative-positive sequences are part; repositioned adjectives—"embattled we are"; balance with anaphora—"year in and year out"; and a concluding four-part series.

John F. Kennedy's Inaugural Address has become famous because of the use of such stylistic sentences. It serves to show that in all forms of writing, public and private, objective and subjective, logical and impassioned, stylistic sentences play a vital and important role.

Copy John F. Kennedy's sentence; then *compose* a similar sentence. Open with a metaphor, continue through a negative-positive sequence and through a separate and distinct balance, and conclude with a four-part series.

37 THE MASTER SENTENCE

I was born in a large Welsh town at the beginning of the Great War—an ugly, lovely town (or so it was and is to me), crawling, sprawling by a long and splendid curving shore where truant boys and sandfield boys and old men from nowhere, beachcombed, idled and paddled, watched the dock-bound ships or the ships steaming away into wonder and India, magic and China, countries bright with oranges and loud with lions; threw stones into the sea for the barking outcast dogs; made castles and forts and harbours and race tracks in the sand; and on Saturday afternoons listened to the brass band, watched the Punch and Judy, or hung about on the fringes of the crowd to hear the fierce religious speakers who shouted at the sea, as though it were wicked and wrong to roll in and out like that, white-horsed and full of fishes.—Dylan Thomas, Quite Early One Morning

In this magnificent sentence, loose and long, constituting an entire paragraph, great use is made of details placed in various forms of the series. After the initial statement the sentence proceeds descriptively, using double adjectives in front of nouns—"ugly, lovely town"—and double participles after the noun—"crawling, sprawling"—along with many instances of balance—"so it was and is to me," "long and splendid," "idled and paddled," and "bright with oranges and loud with lions." Note also the four-part series used: "castles and forts and harbours and race tracks." In the sentence abundant use is also made of sound devices: alliteration—"wicked and wrong"—and rhyme—"crawling, sprawling." And you will note the terminal rhythm of the sentence, after the long sweep of clauses and phrases: "as though it were wicked and wrong to roll in and out like that, white-horsed and full of fishes," with "white-horsed," a repositioned adjective, acting as a brake on the rhythmical flow.

You would rarely write so splendiferous a sentence, of course, But you may want to try it, just to say that you have done it. Someday you might even want to use such a sentence if you find yourself wanting to recreate some vital, exuberant experience.

Copy the sentence by Dylan Thomas; then *compose* a similar sentence: long, detailed, descriptive; with great attention paid to balanced constructions, various forms of the series, and repositioned adjectives; and with special attention paid to bringing your sentence to a rhythmical and cadenced conclusion.

THE WHOLE COMPOSITION

The following essay employs a range of basic and stylistic sentence patterns. The result is a vivid and vigorous prose with many sentences clearly designed to achieve particular effects.

The Search for Something Else

Jane Howard

Something oddly important began to happen a decade or so ago to the simple word "into." It changed. Once a modest preposition, it started to stretch way out of shape and erupt into the loose, all-purpose word it now has become. I was in California, birthplace of many a modern innovation, when I first noticed this new usage. The leader of an encounter workshop at the Esalen Institute told a roomful of us she hoped that in the week ahead we would take risks, share a lot of gut feelings, and not be, as she put it, "into secrets."

Now everyone is "into" everything. Only pedants describe their enthusiasms otherwise. A sporting-goods store advertises that it is "INTO RACQUETS." A cousin of mine, fully clad in chinos and a turtleneck, says he has never really been "into clothes." A man chopping onions is "into souffles"; his girl friend, reading in the next room, is "into death"; they're both "into androgyny." An outsized fellow claiming to be an ecologist, who one night last summer pushed a bunch of us off a pier and into a cold lake, had the gall to say he was "into awareness."

What we all are "into," it would seem, is an implosion of almost more awareness than we know what to do with—to a degree remarkable even for so self-conscious, introspective and stubbornly individual a Nation as everybody since De Tocqueville has found this one to be. Maybe the Bicentennial has something to do with it; the craze for wholesale stocktaking is not just individual, but collective and even patriotic. Wherever we look, we find more evidence of what some call the Consciousness Movement—a funny name for a phenomenon that doesn't look to be in motion at all, since its action is interior.

Much has changed since the candor and clangor of the '60s, when we first flocked to places like Esalen and paid large sums to master such "new" skills as confession, encounter and the methodical shedding of secrets. We would try anything, in those sometimes-naked days, to rid ourselves of the phony, girdled politeness that we felt had frozen us in the '50s. In our zeal to unfreeze, we didn't just thaw (restraint never having been conspicuous among our national virtues); we oozed, dripped and exploded all over the place, letting it—as the phrase went—all hang out.

"Out" was our chosen direction, all right. "Outasight!" we would exclaim, and "Far-out!" Outwardness suited us; it was showy and tricky, and we were a Nation of technological showoffs whose like the world had never seen. With a grandiose flourish we propelled ourselves all the way to the cratered surface of the moon, but even that feat didn't bring us enduring comfort or triumph. Even less were we warmed or cheered by our more protracted journey to Vietnam. No wonder our wanderlust diminished.

We came home. We came home not just to our houses but to the inside of our skulls, a place whose merits were being sung by a growing chorus of psychedelic adventurers. Maybe, we mused, isolationism might not be such a wrongheaded policy, for men and for nations, after all. Maybe we ought to forget about other planets and other countries and even other persons, for a while at least, and tend to our neglected selves. The pendulum was swinging for us as it had in Greece after the Peloponnesian War when, to quote Gilbert Murray, "Man's sense of failure and loss of hope threw him back upon his own soul, upon the pursuit of personal holiness, upon mysteries and revelations."

Mystery: now there was a word we hadn't heard for a while. All the commotion of encountering had distracted us from the sacredness of mystery, the elegant eloquence of certain silences. What balm, to think that maybe some questions weren't even meant to have answers. If mystery had been lost, if our old myths no longer fit us, then we would have to look for some new ones, and the only place to look was startlingly close at hand. The kingdom of heaven, as a wise man said many centuries and swings of the pendulum ago, is within.

It might be near, this new territory we sought to explore, but what little we could see of it looked frightening. Where were the maps? We had lost them, but that was OK, because cartographers bearing new ones began to swarm from everywhere. Gurus and swamis crossed oceans to guide us inside us. The flirtation we had been carrying on with Eastern wisdom since the days of the New England transcendentalists flared into a romance. Hare Krishna chanters' bells jingled as we twisted into the Full Lotus, uncoiled to try the Cobra and the Plough, and practiced 47 different ways of exhaling that were advertised on bulletin boards around town along with Tai Chi Chuan studies and lessons in Shiatsu, the needle-free acupuncture. We shook coins to get our messages from the *I Ching*, and nearly always the message was "Perseverance furthers." We persevered, or was it the inwardness that did?

A skeptical friend of mine came home to Chicago after 10 years in Asia, where he had vowed "never to become one of those starry-eyed Yankees spuriously hooked on the Wisdom of the Mysterious East." You know what he does now? He goes every morning to a *Zendo* in a Buddhist temple, there in Chicago, to sit *zazen*. Other people I know have taken to a system called Arica, imported from Chile, and others, by the thousands, choose their paths to enlightenment from confusing supermarkets of homegrown acronyms; est (Erhard Seminars Training) may have outstripped TA (Transactional Analysis), but not TM (Transcendental Meditation), whose salespersons, dressed as for Kiwanis luncheons, ask: may we show you something in mantras? For just $125, scarcely more than it costs to reclaim your towed car from the New York police, you can buy a Sanskrit sound which, regularly repeated, will edge you toward the peace that approaches, if it doesn't pass, understanding.

Not all paths to inwardness are imported or ethereal. Followers of a new technique called biofeedback attach themselves with electrodes and cords to machines that can monitor such internal processes as blood pressure, brain waves, and subtle changes in muscles and temperatures. If we are calm enough to pay proper heed to such messages from inside ourselves, we may learn to replace diseases with serenity, throwing open wider still what Aldous Huxley called the doors of perception. "These machines," one of their champions says, "don't pour anything new into you; they just tell you what's been there all along."

All this is heady stuff, literally; and so is the light that has been shed of late on the nearly atrophied right hemispheres of our brains. Right hemispheres, as Jack Fincher writes in his recently published book "Human Intelligence," are the source of symbols and feelings and artistic impulses. Rediscovering them might edge us even closer to the new renaissance, the new stage of human evolution, near whose brink some think we stand.

Not, of course, that anything is ever really new under the sun. Thoreau observed some time ago that wisdom is far less likely to turn up in our mailboxes, however stuffed they may be with messages, than inside our heads. Martin Buber remarked how deluded we were to claim more self-knowledge than any people before us, when we always had such trouble trying to "venture self-illumination with awake and unafraid spirit." He was right; we've had a good deal of trouble along those lines, and our efforts have been as absurd as they've been touching and idealistic. But with luck, and perseverance, and some grace, maybe we really can wake up and shake off the fearful, innocent arrogance that has kept us all along from the pathways that connect out with in.

Exercises

1. Identify some of the various basic and stylistic sentence patterns Jane Howard employs in "The Search for Something Else."

2. Select a number of interesting sentences (perhaps six to ten) to use as models for sentences of your own composition on quite different subjects.

3. Revise a passage from Jane Howard's essay altering the sentence patterns of the selection while holding to the original content. Comment upon any changes this produces in the character of the prose.

13. WORDS

■ We write with words—and to write with flexibility we need to have as many words on hand as possible. The more words we have the more accurately and effectively we can write—and the more choices we have when it comes time to consider the "best word" for a particular context and particular rhetorical profile. To build up the large supply of words that will help us put "the proper word in the proper place," we need to discover new words in our reading; review the words we already know to avoid vocabulary attrition; create new words of our own; revitalize old words by using them in new ways; go "shopping" in the dictionary every now and then; write down words we hear other people use in conversation; ponder the various connotations that any given word may have. Simply being interested in words—in the origin, history, spelling, pronunciation, current meaning, and use of every word that comes our way—contributes greatly to our writing capacity. ■

Basic to all good composition is a rich vocabulary and a perceptive understanding of words. Yet you can't learn diction in the same way that you can learn to write sentences and paragraphs. In spite of what you have been told, few words can be absolutely defined, once and for all, and few words have exact synonyms. Wild and sometimes exotic, they must be stalked in their natural habitat—in books and talk—not in dictionary preserves only. So if you aren't fascinated by the prospect of a hunt for accurate, evocative words, your reader is doomed to boredom.

A WIDE VOCABULARY

In writing effectively, you need to have as large and as varied a vocabulary as possible. Don't make the mistake of acquiring for yourself a limited vocabulary of simple, everyday words on the one hand or of florid, grandiose words on the other.

Make sure your vocabulary includes a large artillery of short, simple words for the sake of increased clarity in your writing, remembering that "short, simple" does not necessarily mean monosyllabic. With short, simple words you will be able to achieve increased clarity many times simply because *part* may reach more readers than *component* does. Likewise, in certain rhetorical profiles, *end* has advantages over *terminate, use* over *utilize, make up* over *constitute, belonging to* over *intrinsic.* Finding a short, simple word is fairly easy in English, since most longer words have shorter equivalents: *arrive, come; complete, finish; remain, stay.*

Short, simple words are valuable artillery also because they can be effectively used in contrast with long, sophisticated words in your composition. If you use a long word, you may wish to accompany it with several shorter ones: the effect of the long word will be more pronounced.

And obviously when you are trying for a generally simple style, a colloquial or informal level of diction, you will employ the short, simple word a great deal of the time. Since an informal composition of common texture could not tolerate this sentence—"Working with ferrous and nonferrous metals, the sculptor creates a fluid form of equilibrium, possessing a definite order depictive of both the microcosm and the macrocosm"—you can use short, simple words to say practically the same thing: "Working with iron and other metals, the sculptor creates forms suggestive of the universal drive toward balance and movement."

You will also want to have a full share of what some people like to call "big words." The long, somewhat uncommon word is valuable to you primarily because it is economical: *eclectic* is more direct and economical than *of elements from various sources,* and *onomatopoetic* than *of words whose sound suggests the sense.* But the long, uncommon word is also valuable because many times it offers dictional variation and emphasis; it can be used in effective contrast to the short, simple word. And many times it simply provides more interest and excitement than the short word or familiar word: *Arabesque* sounds more exotic than *Arabian,* and *vacuous,* because of its relation to *vacuum,* suggests a more intense hollowness than *empty.* The long, uncommon word may also serve you well because of sound or rhythm: in *sententious, didactic,* and *malevolent,* the repetition of sounds and the rise and fall of accents make the words interesting.

Foreign words and phrases can be extremely useful to you in creating a rich rhetorical texture and in extending the cultural dimension of your composition. You will avoid most foreign expressions on the colloquial level, of course, but on the high informal or formal level, they are welcome—if you use them judiciously. The foreign word you use should fit the subject and mood of the composition (even in a formal discussion of the American West, the foreign word might have a rough time of it); the foreign word you use should have no simple English equivalent; and the foreign word you use should be at least distantly familiar to your reader or be capable of interpretation from the context or translatable through its similarity to English. *Dolce far niente* (an Italian phrase meaning literally *sweet doing nothing*), *Weltanschauung* (a German word, sometimes used in criticism, meaning roughly *a comprehensive view of the world*), and *terrae filii* (a Latin expression, something of an allusion since it is associated with more than one nineteenth-century English essayist, meaning *sons of the soil*) would be effective in the right kind of formal or serious composition, or even in the highly literary informal essay.

General rule: Keep in mind that the modern reader is not only unimpressed by foreign expressions, but quick to consider them affectations, so don't be too free with your *bona fide* and *esprit de corps.* You should overuse foreign expressions only if you wish to create the effect of humor, parody, or satirical pomposity.

You will find that literary expressions—quick, subtle allusions or quotations—can be a way of putting a great deal of meaning into few words. You will use literary expressions most frequently on the formal level of writing (less frequently in informal writing, scarcely at all in colloquial writing), and you will use them only when you are sure your reader will respond knowingly to them. When you are sure your reader will understand your allusions and quotations, you can then use literary matter as a quick and effective way to expand the dimension of your writing and to relate your own composition to the great tradition of literature.

If you were to write, "This Earth is our Blessed Isle, our Elysian Field, our Garden of Eden," your references to the primitive, classical, and Hebraic utopias would carry with them numerous connotations. And if you were to write, "The wind-blown spray splashed into the street where it formed a rivulet and ran in serpentine curls, recalling for her the sleepy world of dreams," your last few words would remind the reader of Swinburne's "Garden of Proserpine" and its associations.

You will find that among the greatest sources for literary allusions are the Bible, Homer, Virgil, Shakespeare. And you will find, also, that when you draw a quick phrase from well-known literature of the nineteenth century or earlier you will present the phrase more effectively without citing the author or bracketing with quotes.

You will also do well to maintain a reasonable share of hard-hitting, tough, less-than-polished words in your dictional artillery. You may find it extremely advantageous to use a tough Anglo-Saxon word from time to time; such words can certainly sharpen colloquial writing, and even in the higher levels of diction, the tough word can sometimes be used for shock and surprise. The tough word can complete your dictional range, give you a chance for variety and emphasis, and can even at times increase the intensity of your rhetorical texture.

Just as there is a place in good writing for the expression "acquire a dictionary," there is a place for "get a dictionary." And surely you will want to be able to write such sentences as these: "In angry moments he spits out his words with surprising force"; "he's all verbosity and no guts." Even as there is a difference in writing between effective simplicity and just plain stupidity, there is a difference between a valuable toughness in diction and just plain crudity. You can use some tough words without being crude or offensive.

And you will also want to be able to create some words of your own, simply by using a noun as a verb, a verb as an adjective, or what have you. If you proceed judiciously, you can enliven your writing from time to time simply by transferring parts of speech. If *apple* is a noun, it can also be an adjective ("this apple weather," "the apple aroma") or a verb ("Why don't you apple that ice cream with a big Jonathan slice?" "We coffee in the morning, sherbet in the afternoon, and apple in the evening"). Though you may shock your grammarian aunt, you will have added a sparkle of interest to your writing.

(*Warning:* One such created word in a composition will be plenty unless you are deliberately striving for an exceptional, highly elaborate rhetorical texture.)

Here are some paragraphs, of differing rhetorical profiles, showing how these various areas of vocabulary can be employed in your writing:

The *sine qua non* of a good marriage is a sense of humor. Without a

fair share of laughter, all the serious love in the world won't hold
two people together. The old romantic notion that beauty and passion are the foundation of the successful marriage has long since disappeared into the wilds of fanciful legend. Modern lovers realize
that "Laugh and your mate laughs with you, weep and you weep
alone." (Short simple words—*good, humor, fair, share,* etc.; long, somewhat uncommon words—*foundation, fanciful;* foreign words—*sine qua
non;* hard-hitting words—perhaps *wilds.*)

Professor Hieronymous Blanck claims that the *sine qua non* of the
good marriage is a sense of humor. Without a capacity for laughter,
husband and wife cannot withstand the ravaging forces of the modern social order: their alliance will crumble. Even the grandest sort
of love will not, by itself, hold two people together. The old (and
false to begin with) Tristan and Isolde notion—that beauty and passion are the foundation of marriage—has long since been relegated
to the wasteland of cultural debris. Modern, enlightened lovers
know that an enduring marriage must begin in tolerance and that a
sense of humor is the handmaiden of tolerance. (Short simple
words—*claims, good, forces, sort, love,* etc.; long, somewhat uncommon
words—*capacity, withstand, ravaging, alliance,* etc.; foreign words—*sine
qua non;* literary expression—*Tristan and Isolde.*)

A good marriage needs a sense of humor. Unless it's spiced with
laughs, all the serious love in the world won't hold two people together. The old notion that good looks and sex are all you need to
make a go of things in marriage—that notion's long since gone with
the wind. Young people today one-hundred-percent their marriages
by being willing to laugh a little at themselves and their foibles.
(Short simple words—*good, needs, laugh,* etc.; long, somewhat uncommon words—*foibles;* literary expressions—*gone with the wind;* hard
word—perhaps *sex;* created words—*one-hundred-percent.*)

WORDS TO USE AND WORDS TO AVOID
In writing effectively on every dictional level, you will also want to
keep in mind some general dos and don'ts about the use of words,
some general directives that you can keep in mind regardless of the
level of your writing.

Use the Idiomatic Word
Keep on hand a large supply of idioms in your dictional artillery,
for with idioms you stand a better chance of writing with fluency
and of achieving an unstilted and believable style. (Learning idioms
is largely a matter of experience. You can't tell someone exactly
how idioms work—since idioms are never especially logical and cer-

tainly can't be defined word by word.) Idioms are used at all levels of diction—though recently established idioms are more likely to indicate colloquial diction. You will use idioms in order to place your writing in the mainstream of correct usage; your failure to use idioms may be effective on certain occasions, but only in the sense that your style will seem more foreign, more isolated—an effect you may decide you rarely want.

The idiomatic use of prepositions calls for your closest attention, for the nonidiomatic use of prepositions creates the aura not only of unorthodoxy in your style but, many times, of utter confusion. Your reader is prepared to hear "different from," "capable of," "there is no need for," "preferable to." And if you violate the idiom you will pay a heavy price in readership for the privilege of your eccentricity.

The eccentric way is:

I do not plan on acting in a manner any different than my usual manner. I will try and be as much the gentleman as possible. But if you have any worries as for my behavior, ring me down on the telephone and give me your last-minute instructions—as you always do.

The acceptable way is:

I do not plan on acting in a manner any different from my usual manner. I will try to be as much a gentleman as possible. But if you have any worries about my behavior, ring me up on the telephone and give me your last-minute instructions—as you always do.

Use the Exact Word

Communication is at best arbitrary and approximate. Try not to compound the problem through your own coyness or laziness. You know what you mean, but do your readers? They are, after all, readers, and not mind readers. Although most of the words in a sentence are not really subject to choice, the important ones are. Develop the habit of looking intently at those words. Don't be satisfied with a word that falls near; and don't be unnecessarily indirect.

In addition to an up-to-date dictionary, you should own Roget's *Thesaurus* or a similar treasury of synonyms. Also extremely useful are Fowler's *Modern English Usage* (Oxford) and, if your writing vocabulary is held back by your uncertain spelling, Leslie's *20,000 Words* (McGraw-Hill). These books will help you avoid making foolish mistakes or using words capriciously or vaguely. To develop a diction striking for its exactness you will need to begin thinking more about words. This means, among other things, that you should become sensitive to what are sometimes shadowy distinctions. Consider the connotative as well as the denotative value of words. Many have, in addition to their explicit meanings, certain emotional and associative meanings. Words like *doctrine* and *device* are relatively neutral, but not so *propaganda* and *gadget*. *Lost* (as in battle) and *stout* suggest meanings slightly different from *killed* and *fat*, as do *complete* and *inquire* from *finish* and *ask*.

Avoid Vague Words

Any word can be used in a vague way, but some have been carelessly used for so long that they have in most instances no definite meaning. Avoid words like *analysis, aspect, basically, case, element, factor, field, function, line, material,* and *thing*. Either cut them out by writing "She entered teaching" instead of "She entered the field of teaching"; or replace the offender by writing "He likes concerts, operas, and ballets" instead of "He likes concerts and other things along that line."

Distinguish between Near Synonyms

Perfect synonyms are rare, and the shade of difference is often enough to distort your meaning. To be *detached* is not the same as to be *disinterested, indifferent,* or *unconcerned*. Even though the definitions are similar, the words are not interchangeable. Neither are homonyms (words that sound alike but aren't), like *red* and *read, complement* and *compliment;* or even various forms of the same words, *beside* and *besides, informed* and *informative*.

Do Not Use the Tired Word

Some words are tired because they are overworked and some because they have nothing to do. Whatever the reason, give exhausted nouns and verbs, fagged adjectives and adverbs, and all their pooped companions a rest.

Avoid the Two Forms of Wordiness—Redundancy and Verbosity

Some writers seem dedicated to the proposition that two words are always better than one. Unless the two words are more exact and vivid than the one, they aren't. Redundancy creeps into your writing in various guises:

Refer back to page one. ("Refer to page one"; the list of such paired redundancies as "repeat again," "each and every," "forefront" is long indeed.)

The dowager was proud, haughty, and vain. ("The dowager was proud." *Haughty* and *vain* are so nearly synonymous they add little.)

Whatever Sophocles undertook he did it well. ("Whatever Sophocles undertook he did well" is an improvement.)

The blowing snow hid the climbers from sight, and nothing could be seen of them. (Preferably write, "Blowing snow hid the climbers from sight.")

The library is the center of every university. A library is more important than professors and classrooms. And if a student learns to use the library effectively he has learned the most important lesson the university can teach. (The simple repetition of *university* is not objectionable, but the three-time repetition of *library*—except for emphasis—may be. But the repetition of *important* is pointless and even confusing, and the repetition of *learns* and *learned* in the same sentence is awkward. It would be better to write: "The library, even more than professors and classrooms, is the center of every university. And learning to find in it what information you need is the first object of a university education.")

However, repetition for the sake of clarity and emphasis is desirable. Even repetition that borders on redundancy is preferable to an inelegant variation (like *treasury of tomes* for *library*) or to a synonym (like *bibliotheca* for *library*) if the reader momentarily thinks you are referring to something else, or to a pronoun if the reference is unclear. But redundancies, where no special emphasis is intended, should be eliminated by using pronouns or synonyms, or by rephrasing.

Verbosity also has its various guises; here are some:

There are many women who are driven more by the ambitions they have for their children than anything else. (19 words; "There are many women who are driven by the ambitions they have for their children," 15 words; "Many women are driven by the ambitions they have for their children," 12 words; "Many women are driven by ambitions for their children," 9 words; "Many women are ambitious for their children," 7 words)

We flew into a squall, and it was turbulent. ("We flew into a turbulent squall" is probably an improvement.)

It was on July 14, 1789, that the Bastille was stormed. ("On July 14, 1789, the Bastille was stormed" is preferable.)

I have always enjoyed walking. It's good exercise and it's fun. I most enjoy a walk in the country on spring mornings or fall afternoons. But my most rewarding walks have been taken on cold rainy days when my first impulse was to stay indoors. Let me begin at the beginning and tell you about why I enjoy walking. ("Let me tell you about the joys of walking" says as much.)

In general, you should use the fewest words you can and still (1) say what you want to say and (2) achieve the rhetorical profile you are seeking to establish. Whenever you discover you've used too many words in a piece of writing—as may frequently happen in a first draft of a composition—you can condense: by dropping spare words, by reducing clauses and phrases to single words, and by pruning inconsequential details.

Avoid Clichés

With some expressions and quotations, the price of distinction is apparently extinction. Clichés are fossils of once fresh and vivid expressions that have been calcified by overuse. There are so many scattered through the language that even the most original writer can't avoid unearthing one now and then. When you do, drop it. Dead expressions are infinitely less effective than living ones. Here are a few random specimens from the bone yard:

acid test	hit the ceiling
at a loss for words	in conclusion
ax to grind	it stands to reason
bitter end	know the ropes
blazing inferno	last but not least
bright and early	like a rat in a trap
brilliant performance	nipped in the bud
bring order out of chaos	play into the hands of
busy as a bee	quick as a flash
clear as mud	sad but true
depths of despair	sadder but wiser
dire necessity	shake like a leaf
dodge the issue	spur of the moment
drastic action	think out loud
equal to the occasion	tired but happy
force of circumstance	wended my way

Use them long enough and you yourself will become a cliché whose perception as well as expression of the world is contained in several dozen pat phrases: You will "wake with a start" in the "breathless silence" of the "wee small hours" to "view with alarm" the "vanished glory" of your own style.

Of course, this is an overstatement. Clichés sometimes say exactly what you want to say. And the doctrine of the *mot juste*—the idea that there exists for a given spot an inevitable expression—may force you to use one. If it's a trifling thought in a piece of routine prose and you don't have time to devise something better, a cliché may be excusable. There are, after all, degrees of triteness—"psychological moments" are not as bad as "bolts from the blue." (Metaphorical clichés are particularly risky.) In writing dialogue you will naturally use the clichés your characters would be expected to use. And you may use clichés because they are clichés. If you don't call attention to your cleverness with quotation marks, clichés can be humorous—although even here the effect is often flat, as you would expect from a stock gag. Sometimes you can get effects more subtle than broad humor, like whimsy ("The carillon echoed clear as a bell across the valley") or irony ("The nineteenth-century fascination with the utilitarian has been replaced by an obsession with the bigger and the better"). Parodies on clichés can be witty: "hazel-eyed monster" (from "green-eyed monster"), "bony knees of poverty" (from "lap of luxury").

Avoid Pseudotechnical and Pseudoliterary Expressions

When writers try too hard they are apt to use words in the wrong way for the wrong reader. Authentic technical words have their place—knowledge is, as you know, largely a matter of possessing a vocabulary. Even a somewhat elegant and poetic diction can be successful if supported by the subject. But the spectacle of a half-baked writer using words mainly to impress readers with his intellectual acumen and artistic sensibilities is nauseating.

Stripped of their original exactness, some technical words—*existential, subliminal, IQ, socioeconomic, viable*—pop up with the regularity of clichés, often in a style characterized by other similarly inefficient expressions—*appreciable degree, motivating factor, substantial segments, marked discrepancy.* Intelligent professional people don't write this way even for their colleagues; and historians, psychologists, oceanographers have written memorable essays for the lay person in a supremely lucid style. Remember, the more complex the thought, the more simply you must express it. As much as you can, avoid the technical word.

Here are two paragraphs, the first of which is especially burdened with inexact and weary language:

It is my considerable opinion that the thing wrong with this aspect of your article is its tried-and-true—but very unexciting—method of exposition. To an appreciable degree, there are lots of interesting examples here, but nevertheless substantial segments of your argument on these three pages remain hopelessly dull. Think seriously about giving some serious thought to the things you have to say and see if you can't face the issue head on to achieve a greater orientation to your reader's psychological need for entertainment as well as information.

My considered opinion is that the third section of your article fails simply because of dullness. Though you have used a number of case histories and anecdotes, you have failed to achieve a truly provocative style. Rethink what you have to say. Then write this section once again, kindling as much fire as possible—not only for light, but also for warmth.

SUMMARY CHECKLIST

In the concluding drafts of your composition, you will want to examine your diction once again and ask yourself these questions:

1. Have I at any place violated educated English idiom?
2. Have I avoided vague words and weary words? Have I avoided redundancy and verbosity, clichés, pseudotechnical and pseudoliterary jargon?
3. Have I made imaginative use of my vocabulary? Have I been willing to coin a word—if need be?
4. Have I given special attention to my verbs and adjectives?
5. Have I maintained an appropriate but interesting diction in my composition? Have I employed the dictionaries and thesauruses as an aid to finding the precise and provocative words that I need?

THE WHOLE COMPOSITION

You will enjoy the rich display of vocabulary in this essay. Phyllis McGinley relies on an essentially simple idiom, but one that sometimes takes the reader by surprise. Her playful use of language is apparent in the first sentence (in the juxtaposition of *flies* and *sits*). While not intimidated by "big words"—*dispense, pent, epitome, heterogeneous, gamboling, progeny, scintillate*—she derives the greatest effect from words unexpectedly encountered or combined. The extravagance with which she speaks of Main Street as a *thundering thoroughfare* and a vacation trip as a *seasonal hegira* is characteristic. But even more traditional are those lines in which she sets the reader up for the comic turn, as in "the houses reveal themselves as comfortable, well-kept, *architecturally insignificant"* and "not many families rich enough to be *awesome."* Typical of Phyllis McGinley's verbal wit is the familiar phrase or word turned slightly from its expected course, as in a line like "let the décor fall where it may."

But quite apart from the comic uses to which she puts language, Phyllis McGinley uses words in an uncommonly expressive way. In her hand they are always clear and direct, vivid and energetic. In short, you will find in this essay that broad range of vocabulary you will want to use in most of your informal writing, whether comic or serious.

Suburbia: Of Thee I Sing

Phyllis McGinley

Twenty miles east of New York City as the New Haven Railroad flies sits a village I shall call Spruce Manor. The Boston Post Road, there, for the length of two blocks, becomes Main Street, and on one side of that thundering thoroughfare are the grocery stores and the drug stores and the Village Spa where teen-agers gather of an afternoon to drink their cokes and speak their curious confidences. There one finds the shoe repairers and the dry cleaners and the second-hand stores which sell "antiques" and the stationery stores which dispense comic books to ten-year-olds and greeting cards and lending library masterpieces to their mothers. On the opposite side stand the bank, the fire house, the public library. The rest of this town of perhaps four or five thousand people lies to the south and is bounded largely by Long Island Sound, curving protectively on three borders. The movie theater (dedicated to the showing of second-run, single-feature pictures) and the grade schools lie north, beyond the Post Road, and that is a source of worry to Spruce Manorites. They are always a little uneasy about the children, crossing, perhaps, before the lights are safely green. However, two excellent policemen—Mr. Crowley and Mr. Lang—station themselves at the intersections four times a day, and so far there have been no accidents.

Spruce Manor in the spring and summer and fall is a pretty town, full of gardens and old elms. (There are few spruces, but the village Council is considering planting a few on the station plaza, out of sheer patriotism.) In the winter, the houses reveal themselves as comfortable, well-kept, architecturally insignificant. Then one can see the town for what it is and has been since it left off being farm and woodland some sixty years ago—the epitome of Suburbia, not the country and certainly not the city. It is a commuter's town, the living center of a web which unrolls each morning as the men swing aboard the locals, and contracts again in the evening when they return. By day, with even the children pent in schools, it is a village of women. They trundle mobile baskets at the A&P, they sit under driers at the hairdressers, they sweep their porches and set out bulbs and stitch up slip covers. Only on weekends does it become heterogeneous and lively, the parking places difficult to find.

Spruce Manor has no country club of its own, though devoted golfers have their choice of two or three not far away. It does have a small yacht club and a beach which can be used by anyone who rents or owns a house here. The village supports a little park with playground equipment and a counselor, where children, unattended by parents, can spend summer days if they have no more pressing engagements.

It is a town not wholly without traditions. Residents will point out the two-hundred-year-old manor house, now a minor museum; and in the autumn they line the streets on a scheduled evening to watch the Volunteer Firemen parade. That is a fine occasion, with so many heads of households marching in their red blouses and white gloves, some with flaming helmets, some swinging lanterns, most of them genially out of step. There is a bigger parade on Memorial Day with more marchers than watchers and with the Catholic priest, the rabbi, and the Protestant ministers each delivering a short prayer when the paraders gather near the War Memorial. On the whole, however, outside of contributing generously to the Community Chest, Manorites are not addicted to municipal get-togethers.

No one is very poor here and not many families rich enough to be awesome. In fact, there is not much to distinguish Spruce Manor from any other of a thousand suburbs outside of New York City or San Francisco or Detroit or Chicago or even Stockholm, for that matter. Except for one thing. For some reason, Spruce Manor has become a sort of symbol to writers and reporters familiar only with its name or trivial aspects. It has become a symbol of all that is middle-class in the worst sense, of settled-downness or rootlessness, according to what the writer is trying to prove; of smug and prosperous mediocrity—or even, in more lurid novels, of lechery at the country club and Sunday morning hangovers.

To condemn Suburbia has long been a literary cliché, anyhow. I have yet to read a book in which the suburban life was pictured as the good life or the commuter as a sympathetic figure. He is nearly as much a stock character as the old stage Irishman: the man who "spends his life riding to and from his wife," the eternal Babbitt who knows all about Buicks and nothing about Picasso, whose sanctuary is the club locker room, whose ideas spring ready-made from the illiberal newspapers. His wife plays politics at the P.T.A.

and keeps up with the Joneses. Or—if the scene is more gilded and less respectable—the commuter is the high-powered advertising executive with a station wagon and an eye for the ladies, his wife a restless baggage given to too many cocktails in the afternoon.

These clichés I challenge. I have lived in the country, I have lived in the city. I have lived in an average Middle Western small town. But for the best eleven years of my life I have lived in Suburbia and I like it.

"Compromise!" cried our friends when we came here from an expensive, inconvenient, moderately fashionable tenement in Manhattan. It was the period in our lives when everyone was moving somewhere. Farther uptown, farther downtown, across town to Sutton Place, to a half-dozen rural acres in Connecticut or New Jersey or even Vermont. But no one in our rather rarefied little group was thinking of moving to the suburbs except us. They were aghast that we could find anything appealing in the thought of a middle-class house on a middle-class street in a middle-class village full of middle-class people. That we were tired of town and hoped for children, that we couldn't afford both a city apartment and a farm, they put down as feeble excuses. To this day they cannot understand us. You see, they read the books. They even write them.

Compromise? Of course we compromise. But compromise, if not the spice of life, is its solidity. It is what makes nations great and marriages happy and Spruce Manor the pleasant place it is. As for its being middle-class, what is wrong with acknowledging one's roots? And how free we are! Free of the city's noise, of its ubiquitous doormen, of the soot on the windowsill and the radio in the next apartment. We have released ourselves from the seasonal hegira to the mountains or the seashore. We have only one address, one house to keep supplied with paring knives and blankets. We are free from the snows that block the countryman's roads in winter and his electricity which always goes off in a thunderstorm. I do not insist that we are typical. There is nothing really typical about any of our friends and neighbors here, and therein lies my point. The true suburbanite needs to conform less than anyone else; much less than the gentleman farmer with his remodeled salt-box or than the determined cliff dweller with his necessity for living at the right address. In Spruce Manor all addresses are right. And since we are fairly numerous here, we need not fall back on the people nearest us for total companionship. There is not here, as in a small city away from truly urban centers, some particular family whose codes must be ours. And we could not keep up with the Joneses even if we wanted to, for we know many Joneses and they are all quite different people leading the most various lives.

The Albert Joneses spend their weekends sailing, the Bertram

Joneses cultivate their delphinium, the Clarence Joneses—Clarence being a handy man with a cello—are enthusiastic about amateur chamber music. The David Joneses dote on bridge, but neither of the Ernest Joneses understands it, and they prefer staying home of an evening so that Ernest Jones can carve his witty caricatures out of pieces of old fruit wood. We admire each other's gardens, applaud each other's sailing records; we are too busy to compete. So long as our clapboards are painted and our hedges decently trimmed, we have fulfilled our community obligations. We can live as anonymously as in a city or we can call half the village by their first names.

On our half-acre or three-quarters, we can raise enough tomatoes for our salads and assassinate enough beetles to satisfy the gardening urge. Or we can buy our vegetables at the store and put the whole place to lawn without feeling that we are neglecting our property. We can have privacy and shade and the changing of the seasons and also the Joneses next door from whom to borrow a cup of sugar or a stepladder. Despite the novelists, the shadow of the country club rests lightly on us. Half of us wouldn't be found dead with a golf stick in our hands, and loathe Saturday dances. Few of us expect to be deliriously wealthy or world-famous or divorced. What we do expect is to pay off the mortgage and send our healthy children to good colleges.

For when I refer to life here, I think, of course, of living with children. Spruce Manor without children would be a paradox. The summer waters are full of them, gamboling like dolphins. The lanes are alive with them, the yards overflow with them, they possess the tennis courts and the skating pond and the vacant lots. Their roller skates wear down the asphalt, and their bicycles make necessary the twenty-five-mile speed limit. They converse interminably on the telephones and make rich the dentist and the pediatrician. Who claims that a child and a half is the American middle-class average? A nice medium Spruce Manor family runs to four or five, and we count proudly, but not with amazement, the many solid households running to six, seven, eight, nine, even up to twelve. Our houses here are big and not new, most of them, and there is a temptation to fill them up, let the décor fall where it may.

Besides, Spruce Manor seems designed by providence and town planning for the happiness of children. Better designed than the city; better, I say defiantly, than the country. Country mothers must be constantly arranging and contriving for their children's leisure time. There is no neighbor child next door for playmate, no school within walking distance. The ponds are dangerous to young swimmers, the woods full of poison ivy, the romantic dirt roads unsuitable for bicycles. An extra acre or two gives a fine sense of possession to an adult; it does not compensate children for the give-and-take of our village, where there is always a contemporary to help swing the skipping rope or put on the catcher's mitt. Where in the country is the Friday evening dancing class or the Saturday morning movie (approved by the P.T.A.)? It is the greatest fallacy of all time that children love the country as a year-around plan. Children would take a dusty corner of Washington Square or a city sidewalk, even, in preference to the lonely sermons in stones and books in running brooks which their contemporaries cannot share.

As for the horrors of bringing up progeny in the city, for all its museums and other cultural advantages (so perfectly within reach of suburban families if they feel strongly about it), they were summed up for me one day last winter. The harried mother of one, speaking to me on the telephone just after Christmas, sighed and said, "It's been a really wonderful time for me, as vacations go. Barbara has had an engagement with a child in our apartment house every afternoon this week. I have had to take her almost nowhere." Barbara is eleven. For six of those eleven years, I realized, her mother must have dreaded Christmas vacation, not to mention spring, as a time when Barbara had to be entertained. I thought thankfully of my own daughters whom I had scarcely seen since school closed, out with their skis and their sleds and their friends, sliding down the roped-off hill half a block away, coming in hungrily for lunch and disappearing again, hearty, amused, and safe—at least as safe as any sled-borne child can be.

Spruce Manor is not Eden, of course. Our taxes are higher than we like, and there is always that eight-eleven in the morning to be caught, and we sometimes resent the necessity of rushing from a theater to a train on a weekday evening. But the taxes pay for our really excellent schools and for our garbage collections (so that the pails of orange peels need not stand in the halls overnight as ours did in the city) and for our water supply which does not give out every dry summer as it frequently does in the country. As for the theaters—they are twenty miles away and we don't get to them more than twice a month. But neither, I think, do many of our friends in town. The eight-eleven is rather a pleasant train, too, say the husbands; it gets them to work in thirty-four minutes and they read the papers restfully on the way.

"But the suburban mind!" cry our die-hard friends in Manhattan and Connecticut. "The suburban conversation! The monotony!" They imply that they and I must scintillate or we perish. Let me anatomize Spruce Manor, for them and for the others who envision Suburbia as a congregation of mindless housewives and amoral go-getters.

From my window, now, on a June morning, I have a view. It

contains neither solitary hills nor dramatic skyscrapers. But I can see my roses in bloom, and my foxglove, and an arch of trees over the lane. I think comfortably of my friends whose houses line this and other streets rather like it. Not one of them is, so far as I know, doing any of the things that suburban ladies are popularly supposed to be doing. One of them, I happen to know, has gone bowling for her health and figure, but she has already tidied up her house and arranged to be home before the boys return from school. Some, undoubtedly, are ferociously busy in the garden. One lady is on her way to Ellis Island, bearing comfort and gifts to a Polish boy—a seventeen-year-old stowaway who did slave labor in Germany and was liberated by a cousin of hers during the war—who is being held for attempting to attain the land of which her cousin told him. The boy has been on the island for three months. Twice a week she takes this tedious journey, meanwhile besieging courts and immigration authorities on his behalf. This lady has a large house, a part-time maid, and five children.

My friend around the corner is finishing her third novel. She writes daily from nine-thirty until two. After that her son comes back from school and she plunges into maternity; at six, she combs her pretty hair, refreshes her lipstick, and is charming to her doctor husband. The village dancing school is run by another neighbor, as it has been for twenty years. She has sent a number of ballerinas on to the theatrical world as well as having shepherded for many a successful season the white-gloved little boys and full-skirted little girls through their first social tasks.

Some of the ladies are no doubt painting their kitchens or a nursery; one of them is painting the portrait, on assignment, of a very distinguished personage. Some of them are nurses' aides and Red Cross workers and supporters of good causes. But all find time to be friends with their families and to meet the 5:32 five nights a week. They read something besides the newest historical novel, Braque is not unidentifiable to most of them, and their conversation is for the most part as agreeable as the tables they set. The tireless bridge players, the gossips, the women bored by their husbands live perhaps in our suburb, too. Let them. Our orbits need not cross.

And what of the husbands, industriously selling bonds or practicing law or editing magazines or looking through microscopes or managing offices in the city? Do they spend their evenings and their weekends in the gaudy bars of Fifty-second Street? Or are they the perennial householders, their lives a dreary round of taking down screens and mending drains? Well, screens they have always with them, and a man who is good around the house can spend happy hours with the plumbing even on a South Sea island. Some of them cut their own lawns and some of them try to break par and some of them sail their little boats all summer with their families for crew. Some of them are village trustees for nothing a year and some listen to symphonies and some think Milton Berle ought to be President. There is a scientist who plays wonderful bebop, and an insurance salesman who has bought a big old house nearby and with his own hands is gradually tearing it apart and reshaping it nearer to his heart's desire. Some of them are passionate hedge-clippers and some read Plutarch for fun. But I do not know many—though there may be such—who either kiss their neighbor's wives behind doors or whose idea of sprightly talk is to tell you the plot of an old movie.

It is June, now, as I have said. This afternoon my daughters will come home from school with a crowd of their peers at their heels. They will eat up the cookies and drink up the ginger ale and go down for a swim at the beach if the water is warm enough, that beach which is only three blocks away and open to all Spruce Manor. They will go unattended by me, since they have been swimming since they were four, and besides there are lifeguards and no big waves. (Even our piece of ocean is a compromise.) Presently it will be time for us to climb into our very old Studebaker—we are not car-proud in Spruce Manor—and meet the 5:32. That evening expedition is not vitally necessary, for a bus runs straight down our principal avenue from the station to the shore, and it meets all trains. But it is an event we enjoy. There is something delightfully ritualistic about the moment when the train pulls in and the men swing off, with the less sophisticated children running squealing to meet them. The women move over from the driver's seat, surrender the keys, and receive an absentminded kiss. It is the sort of picture that wakes John Marquand screaming from his sleep. But, deluded people that we are, we do not realize how mediocre it all seems. We will eat our undistinguished meal, probably without even a cocktail to enliven it. We will drink our coffee at the table, not carry it into the living room; if a husband changes for dinner here it is into old and spotty trousers and more comfortable shoes. The children will then go through the regular childhood routine—complain about their homework, grumble about going to bed, and finally accomplish both ordeals. Perhaps later the Gerard Joneses will drop in. We will talk a great deal of unimportant chatter and compare notes on food prices; we will also discuss the headlines and disagree. (Some of us in the Manor are Republicans, some are Democrats, a few lean plainly leftward. There are probably anti-Semites and anti-Catholics and even anti-Americans. Most of us are merely anti-antis.) We will all have one highball, and the Joneses will leave early. Tomorrow and tomorrow and tomorrow the pattern will be repeated. This is Suburbia.

But I think that some day people will look back on our little interval here, on our Spruce Manor way of life, as we now look back on the Currier and Ives kind of living, with nostalgia and respect. In a world of terrible extremes, it will stand out as the safe, important medium.

Suburbia, of thee I sing!

EXERCISES

1. Try writing a paragraph (or whole composition) just as it comes to mind, just as you would say it, complete with "I mean" and "you know." Inarticulate as the result probably is, the language may have a swiftness and ease your style sorely needs. Now rewrite the paragraph, heightening it with an occasional unexpected and distinctive word, making it more vivid and exact, eliminating tired words. But retain as much dictional spontaneity as possible.

2. Write a dozen sentences, each heightened by a single word drawn either from the area of slang, neologisms, created words, or from the area of the long, uncommon words of classical etymology.

3. For three common, rather unspecific verbs list all the specific alternatives you can. Then search your dictionary and thesaurus for more.

4. Make a list of ten interesting nouns. Then write ten sentences, using the nouns as verbs and as adjectives.

5. Edit the following overwritten and weary-worded paragraph by cutting out unnecessary words and phrases and by substituting exact words for all vague, indefinite expressions.

When we initiated the new enrollment procedure for the first time, we realized that many would have difficulty getting used to the new plan. It takes people quite a bit of time to get used to new procedures. But after the necessary adjustments were made, the new method worked out pretty well. More people were taken care of than ever before and it took less time to do it. Everybody now agrees that the new enrollment procedure should have been in operation a long time ago.

6. In simple lists of words there is sometimes poetry (anise, basil, borage, caraway, chives, dill, fennel, lavender, marjoram, parsley, rosemary, summer savory, thyme . . .) and sometimes a certain sense of fact (cylinder, piston, crankshaft, connecting rod . . .). Copy down a list of words just as you find it—from a catalog or index or instruction man-

ual or cookbook. Using your dictionary, define and learn the accepted pronunciation for each word on the list.

7. Do the three compositions of the earlier exercise (Chapter 11, exercise 9) employ a rich diction? Rewrite where necessary to make the language more swift, vivacious, easy—precise, deliberate, and memorable. Heighten the diction especially at those points in the composition that need increased emphasis.

14.METAPHORS

We use metaphors in our writing not for simple ornamentation—but to make certain ideas more picturable and to add to the elaborateness of rhetorical texture. First we learn to write the various types of metaphors—from very explicit similes to subtle condensed forms. Then we learn to use these various types—increasing the quantity and intricacy of metaphors in a composition whenever we need to enrich our style. To make and use good metaphors, we need to develop our capacity to compare things in an imaginative way and to present our comparisons to readers in an appropriate manner. As with any enriching element in our writing, we strive to use a sufficient number and range of metaphors to achieve a stylistic goal—but never to use too many.

Metaphors can contribute to the effectiveness of your writing in two ways. In the first place, you can clarify your ideas by giving your readers a method of picturing what you have to say in terms they already comprehend. In the second place, you can add interest and richness to your writing, simply by suggesting a larger world of images and ideas beyond the ordinary level of your expression. Metaphors can help clarify what you are saying and can add valuable color and dimension to your style.

Primarily, metaphors are a form of comparison. You create a metaphor when you compare item A—that which you are actually discussing on a literal level—with item B, drawn from another plane of experience beyond your literal concern. Items A and B need to be similar in only one small way, a way that you have discovered and pointed out to your reader. The more disparate the items are otherwise, the better; the more removed they are from each other, save for their little facets of similarity, the more startled your reader will be. And metaphors are intended to startle. When they no longer open your reader's eyes, they are no longer usable. They are simply worn-out comparisons.

THE STRUCTURE OF METAPHORS

Since metaphors compare one thing with another, they obviously have two parts. The literal part of the metaphor is called the *tenor.* That part which comes from the different and removed level of experience is called the *vehicle.* In other words, the tenor (or basic sense) of what you have to say takes a temporary ride in the vehicle of another idea, object, image, or emotion. If you say, "The moon is like a ship cruising on a dark, gentian sea," you have created a metaphor in which the tenor is the *moon* and the vehicle is the *ship.* If you say, "My love is a red, red rose," you have compared *love* (the tenor) with a *rose* (the vehicle). If you say, "His mind is like a revolver, spitting out ideas like ammunition," the metaphor's tenor is *mind* and the vehicle is *revolver.*

In the following list of metaphors you can easily observe the two structural parts:

The two young men *were* statues *smoking, touch-capped and collarless watchers and witnesses* carved out of the stone *of the blowing room where they stood at my side with nowhere to go. . . .—Dylan Thomas,* Portrait of the Artist as a Young Dog

The instability, injustice, *and* confusion *introduced into the public councils, have, in truth, been the* mortal diseases *under which popular governments everywhere perished.—James Madison,* The Federalist

A few linger in memory, horrible even there: a crazy little church *just west of*

Jeannette, set like a dormer-window *on the side of a bare, leprous hill; the headquarters of the Veterans of Foreign Wars at another forlorn town, a steel* stadium *like a* huge rat-trap *somewhere further down the line.—H. L. Mencken,* The Libido for the Ugly

The tenor and vehicle are absolutely necessary in the composition of a metaphor. Yet they are not always overtly expressed. Many times the full form of a metaphor—tenor plus vehicle—is implied rather than spelled out. Many times, in a single word, you can suggest the nature of the full comparison and do not have to take time to write out the metaphor completely. You can condense your metaphors into small, compact packages that do the work of the full metaphor, but do it rapidly and intensely.

Before concerning yourself with condensed metaphors, however, you should deal with the more obvious and explicit forms. The ordinary metaphor usually contains both tenor and vehicle—overtly expressed. When you say, "The moon is a ship, cruising on a dark, gentian sea," you assume your reader will recognize the metaphor because of the literal impossibility of the equation. But you can make this regular metaphor even more obvious and explicit by converting it to a *simile;* that is, by making use of the words *like* or *as if* to label clearly the comparison for what it is. If you say, "The moon is like a ship cruising on a dark, gentian sea," your use of the word *like* will leave no doubt in the reader's mind about what you are doing.

You can clearly see the comparisons being made in the following metaphors and similes:

The burning candles were pale-stemmed flowers.
The candles glowed *like* pale-stemmed flowers.

The mirror was a cruel enemy who threatened her happiness.
The mirror was *like* a cruel enemy who threatened her happiness.

The right cornea is covered by a milky film, like clouded glass.—Robert Craft, Table Talk

The right cornea is a clouded glass.

Mainly because of their explicitness, fully expressed metaphors, including similes, are valuable whenever you are using figurative language to increase understanding and clarity. Though a precise formulization of use would be wrong, you may hazard the guess that when your main purpose in creating a metaphor is to clarify your meaning, you may well give preference to explicit forms. You will give preference to more condensed forms only when your concern

with stylistic effectiveness is equal to your concern with understanding and meaning.

Condensed metaphors are less obvious but perhaps more exciting
because the reader is not led so immediately to an identification of
tenors and vehicles. Certainly the tenors and vehicles are there, but
they are not so clearly labeled as they are in explicit comparisons.
You create a condensed metaphor when you remove any labels of
comparison, relocate the vehicle or tenor from its normal location in
the equation A is B, or so closely associate the vehicle and tenor
that they seem inseparable.

Three basic kinds of condensed metaphors are possible: those
based upon *renaming* the tenor with a vehicle; those based upon condensing the vehicle into a *verb;* those based upon condensing the vehicle into an *adjective.*

If you say, "Here comes Mr. Elephant," you have created a
condensed noun metaphor. The word *Mr.* is the tenor (you are talking
about some man) and the word *Elephant* is the vehicle (you are comparing the man with the elephant). You could have presented a regular metaphor—"Here comes a man who is an elephant." It's all
the same comparison. But in the statement "Here comes Mr. Elephant," you have condensed the whole comparison into a noun expression.

Consider the use of the noun metaphor in the following:

*Etna, that wicked witch, resting her thick white snow under heaven.—D. H.
Lawrence,* Sea and Sardinia

*It is by ignorance alone that we advance through the rough seas of this our mor-
tal life.—Hilaire Belloc,* In Praise of Ignorance

The one-eyed monster dominates the present-day cave in a manner
that many sociologists consider dangerous and ominous. The blaring
beast of television seduces pater and mater and all the little filiae
into a never-never land of shoot-'em-up and laugh-'em-down that is
psychologically destructive. But what can we do about the walnut-
stained, Danish-modern animal in the living-room corner? Do we
dare shoot it? Do we dare put it in the zoo? Do we dare return it to
the jungle whence it came?

If you say, "The moon sails across the sky," you have created a
condensed verb metaphor. The word *moon* is the tenor, and the word *sails*
is the vehicle. You could have said, "The moon is like a ship that
sails," or "The moon is a ship that sails," but here you have condensed the comparison into a single verb. Likewise, if you say, "His

mind shot out ideas, . . ." you are condensing the figure "His mind is a gun" into a single verb idea.

Consider the use of the verb metaphor in the following:

We had not known that he was being eaten up by paranoia.—James Baldwin, Notes of a Native Son

Joey cried, "He broke my feelings."—Bruno Bettelheim, Joey: A "Mechanical Boy"

Television sets growl and snicker at, claw at and caress the American audience day after day. And in wake of such vivid goings-on, apathy curls up on the love seat, lethargy stretches out in front of the fireplace, and all sorts of unfortunate psychological conditions settle down for a prolonged visit with the American family. Sociologists and psychologists are alarmed that television can so dominate human behavior.

If you say, "The full-sailed moon moves across the sky," you have condensed the whole comparison into an *adjective.* Again, you have condensed the metaphor "The moon is like a ship" into a single adjective expression. Consider these comparisons, "his rifle-bullet ideas," "the woven lawn," "his tarnished emotions," "the nervous trees," and "the scornful mirrors."

In the following sentences the adjective metaphor is used:

These generous traits are overcast by much that is dark, cold, and sinister, by sleepless distrust, and rankling jealousy.—Francis Parkman, The Conspiracy of Pontiac

. . . at night there would come the huge boiled-flannel splendor of the dinner.— Thomas Wolfe, Of Time and the River

And consider how the adjective metaphor is employed in this paragraph:

The beastly television set occupies a place of importance in the wasteland living rooms of America. Crouching in some sacred corner, the television set offers automaton papa, automaton mama, and the automaton kiddies a new shiny, unreal reality. The television set, cavorting, gesticulating, arguing, laughing in the living-room corner entertains hour after hour a wooden, enamel-eyed, wire-and-string puppet audience of good, solid Americans.

You will find that, in general, condensed metaphors lead to a more intense, poetic, and exciting style. Yet keep in mind that all forms of the metaphor, explicit and condensed, are a part of stylistic excitement, and do not hesitate to shift from explicit to condensed comparison and back again within a generally elaborate texture. You can use the regular metaphor, the simile, and all three kinds of condensed metaphors in order to achieve some variety.

But not only do you have a selection among forms of metaphor—condensed and explicit—you also have a selection among kinds. You will identify certain metaphors according to the relationship that exists between the world of the tenor and the world of the vehicle. Though there is no real limit upon the relationships that can exist, certain relationships are so popular they have achieved names.

The normal metaphor "The moon is a ship" is simply a comparison of one object with another, objects from different areas of experience, of course. Other ordinary metaphors are these:

The evening clouds wigwamed against the sky.

White radishes of ice hung from the eaves of the house.

The trickle of rain made a highway across the grass.

But if you say, "The moon is a beautiful woman," you have compared an object with a human being, and the resulting metaphor is called *personification*. Personification occurs whenever the tenor is inanimate and the vehicle is animate. If you say, "The wind growls like a lion," you have personification in that you are giving a living, though not human, characteristic to an inanimate or nonliving phenomenon. Examples of personification are:

A fat yellow moon appeared in the branches of the fig tree as if it were going to roost there with the chickens.—Flannery O'Connor, The Life You Save May Be Your Own

Comedy laughs the minor mishaps of its characters away.—Joseph Wood Krutch, The Modern Temper

My heart was knocking in its cage, and I felt that life contained an infinite number of possibilities.—Graham Greene, The Revolver in the Corner Cupboard

One note of warning, however, about the use of personification. Giving human life to flora and fauna can lead to an unfortunate sentimentality, called the pathetic fallacy. Weeping willows, shy violets, and dying sunsets are all taboo. Use personification only if the subject of your comparison has not already been extensively personified, and avoid comparing things of nature with the gentle, domesticated qualities of human beings. "Regiments of cannas marching across the lawn" is not nearly so disastrous as "the motherly sycamore stretching her leafy arms into the baby blue sky," simply because the vehicle "marching regiments" is not a part of the stereotyped mother-baby-family-sunshine-sweetness figure too often used in discussing flowers, trees, and ferns.

Reification is almost the opposite of personification. Reification occurs whenever you say something like "My love is a wine too rich to drink." It is the comparing of an abstract with a concrete, tangible, or material item. "His tarnished emotions" is reification, for the tenor is obviously an abstraction, *emotions,* and the vehicle, by implication, is an object, *silver,* or at least some *tarnishable metal.* Other reifications are:

. . . *the quality of the imagination is to flow, and not to freeze.*—*Ralph Waldo Emerson,* The Poet

A consistent native tradition has been formed, spreading over the country, surviving cleavages and dispersals, often growing underground, but rising to the surface like some rough vine.—*Constance Rourke,* American Humor: A Study of the National Character

This same truth is a naked and open daylight that doth not show the masks and mummeries and triumphs of the world half so stately and daintily as candlelights.—*Francis Bacon,* Of Truth

Obviously, both personification and reification can be presented in any of the metaphor structures—explicit or condensed. A personification can occur, for instance, as a simile or a condensed adjective metaphor. A reification can occur as an explicit metaphor or as a condensed verb metaphor. Personification and reification are ways of achieving metaphorical comparisons that can be expressed in any of the metaphor forms.

Creation and use of metaphors can be a pleasurable and intriguing aspect of your writing. Though the basic structure of metaphors is simple enough, there are some pitfalls in metaphor construction. Some of the things you should keep in mind as you build your metaphors are these:

Metaphorical comparisons on the same level of experience are not really metaphors. "John walks like Bill" is a simple comparison. "His old jalopy drives like a Cadillac" is not a metaphor; it's a comparison of two items from the same plane of experience.

Trite metaphors don't achieve much intensity or do much for your style. Such metaphors as "The moon is like a ship sailing . . ." is a good old, shop-worn metaphor that won't give you much mileage. Some comparisons to be avoided are these: lips/cherries; eyes/stars; love/rose; sky/sea; ship/state; sons/chips; fathers/old blocks.

Likewise, dead metaphors produce no metaphorical result. Dead metaphors are those so established in the language that they have acquired a literal meaning and effect. The arms and legs of a chair are no longer metaphors. They are now dead and consequently literal: you can saw off the leg of a chair and not cause anyone serious pain. Some other common dead metaphors are: eyes of potatoes, branch of government, head of state, seat of government, apple skin, a head of steam.

Mixed metaphors can be hazardous to use. A metaphor whose vehicle is really a compound—or mix—of two different vehicles can very easily produce humor—and though you may decide to use such a metaphor as "He was a foxy old goat," you should anticipate your reader's smile. If you're writing seriously on serious subjects, you may wish to avoid mixed metaphors completely. You can easily see in the following metaphors the sort of absurdity that is produced, an absurdity that you may—or may not—wish to incorporate into a particular piece of writing:

His storm of protest was nipped in the bud when he backed into an open manhole.

She loaded the cannon of her hate and viciously stabbed her enemy.

And some metaphors—though not trite, dead, or mixed—may nevertheless create unintended ludicrous images. If you say, "Snow-covered Mt. Whitney looks like an ice-cream cone," you've created an upside-down image that doesn't make sense. It may be good for a laugh—but is a laugh what you're after?

THE USE OF METAPHORS

With many different kinds of metaphor at your command, you have the opportunity within a metaphorical style to achieve ample diversity and variety. You also have the opportunity, in working with metaphors, to manipulate the metaphorical texture of your style. Starting from rock bottom, with no metaphors present at all, you can gradually increase your metaphorical texture in these ways:

You can, obviously, simply begin to add metaphors. One metaphor added to a nonmetaphorical passage increases the metaphorical intensity at that point.

If you are already using a given percentage of metaphors in your style, you can simply increase the number of metaphors per page, even though you keep those metaphors generally varied and diversified in their form of presentation.

Consider these paragraphs:

We had a good week at the camp. The bass were biting well and the sun shone endlessly, day after day. We would be tired at night and lie down in the accumulated heat of the little bedrooms after the long hot day and the breeze would stir almost imperceptibly outside and the smell of the swamp drift in through the rusty screens. Sleep would come easily and in the morning the red squirrel would be on the roof, tapping out his gay routine. I kept remembering everything, lying in bed in the mornings—the small steamboat that had a long rounded stern like the lip of a Ubangi, *and how quietly she ran on the moonlight sails, when the older boys played their mandolins and the girls sang and we ate doughnuts dipped in sugar, and how sweet the music was on the water in the shining night, and what it had felt like to think about girls then. After breakfast we would go up to the store and the things were in the same place—the minnows in a bottle, the plugs and spinners disarranged and pawed over by the youngsters from the boys' camp, the fig newtons and the Beeman's gum. Outside, the road was tarred and cars stood in front of the store. Inside, all was just as it had always been, except there was more Coca-Cola and not so much Moxie and root beer and birch beer and sarsaparilla. We would walk out with a bottle of pop apiece and sometimes the pop would backfire up our noses and hurt. We explored the streams, quietly, where the turtles slid off the sunny logs and dug their way into the soft bottom; and we lay on the town wharf and fed worms to the tame bass. Everywhere we went I had trouble making out which was I, the one walking at my side, the one walking in my pants.*

One afternoon while we were there at that lake a thunderstorm came up. It was like the revival of an old melodrama *that I had seen long ago* with childish awe. The second-act climax of the drama *of the electrical disturbance over a lake in America had not changed in any important respect.* This was the big scene, still the big scene. *The whole thing was so familiar, the first feeling of oppression and heat and a general air around camp of not wanting to go very far away. In midafternoon (it was all the same) a curious darkening of the sky, and a lull in everything that had made* life tick; *and then the way the boats suddenly swung the other way at their moorings with the coming of a breeze out of the new quarter, and the premonitory rumble.* Then the kettle drum, then the snare, then the bass drum and cymbals, *the crackling light against the dark, and* the gods grinning and licking their chops in the hills. *Afterward the calm, the rain steadily rustling in the calm lake, the return of light and hope and spirits, and the campers running out in joy and relief to go swimming in the rain, their* bright cries *perpetuating the deathless joke about how they were getting simply drenched, and the children screaming with delight at the new sensation of bathing in the rain, and the joke about getting drenched* linking the generations in a strong indestructible chain. *And the comedian who waded in carrying an umbrella.—E. B. White,* Once More to the Lake

You will note the first paragraph is almost nonmetaphorical, while the second paragraph has a fair number of metaphors.

If you are already using a given percentage of metaphors in your style, you can increase texture by (1) increasing the number (as above), (2) using more condensed metaphors than explicit metaphors, and (3) developing more continued metaphors and metaphorical sequences.

Continued metaphors are those that, in a series, maintain the same basic tenor and the same basic vehicle. Through a series of sentences, the tenor and vehicle do not change. A continued metaphor appears in these sentences:

At dusk, the moon lifts anchor in the eastern port and steers, with full sails, west across the darkening waters. (The basic metaphor is continued in *anchor, port, steers, sails, waters.*)

The life of Man is a long march through the night, surrounded by invisible foes, tortured by weariness and pain, towards a goal that few can hope to reach, and where none may tarry long. One by one, as they march, our comrades vanish from our sight, seized by the silent orders of omnipotent Death.—Bertrand Russell, Mysticism and Logic

And in this sentence the same metaphor is continued, with sufficient repetition of tenor and vehicle to keep the reader aware of what the basic metaphor is:

When a man becomes a member of a public body, he is like a racoon, or other beast that climbs up the trunk of a tree; the boys pushing at him with pitchforks, or throwing stones, or shooting at him with an arrow, the dogs barking in the meantime.—Hugh Henry Brackenridge, The Will of the People

The same metaphor could be continued through any number of sentences.

Metaphorical sequences, on the other hand, are a series of metaphors in which the tenor remains the same, but various vehicles are used. Consider the following:

The national economy is an elevator, jerking up and down from basement to penthouse to basement; a roller coaster, struggling slowly to its peak, then plunging to its valley. The national economy is a manic-depressive, high one day and low the next; a hypochondriac addicted to depressants and antidepressants, downers and uppers alike.

Continued metaphors and metaphorical sequences give an added elaborateness to metaphorical style that, coupled with a sheer increase in numbers, can lift the metaphorical texture to a great height.

Here are two paragraphs demonstrating the increase in metaphorical texture by using more varied forms of metaphors.

A garden is the mirror of a mind. It is a place of life, a mystery of green moving to the pulse of the year, and pressing on and pausing the while to its own inherent rhythms. In making a garden there is something to be sought, and something to be found. To be sought is a sense of the lovely and assured, of garden permanence and order, of human association and human meaning; to be found is beauty and that unfolding content and occupation which is one of the lamps of peace.

Gardens today seem often enough neither to seek nor to find. They make their effect, they attain a perfection, and they are curiously empty of human feeling or emotional appeal. In character they are pictures, painted with flowers as with oils, a colour being touched in here and a blossom there till the canvas is ready to be seen. So purely an objective appeal, however, touches but one small and sometimes rather childish side of us, and the methods used to forward it tend to disrupt and destroy the garden sense of order and abiding loveliness. What human meaning have for us these tableaux in the crinoline grand manner, these huge scenes made from everything under the sun, or this use of boorish weeds in a new and unholy splendour, rarities as outlandish as a savage with a skewer through his nose, and old favorites turned hideous by a destruction of proportion? Surely a garden angel with a flaming sword is needed at the entrance of the catalogues! The gardening ancients were more wise. Flowers for them were but an aspect, an incidental loveliness of something near to man, living, and green. Plants were identities, presences to be lived with, known, and watched growing; they were shapes and habits of leaves, powers, fragrances, and life-familiars. A sense of form gave the garden its tranquility, and one might hear there, in the full of one's own peace, the serene footsteps of the year.—Henry Beston, Herbs and the Earth

The number of metaphors in the second paragraph is not greatly increased, but the effect of the metaphors is more dynamic because of more varied metaphorical forms—the continued metaphor for instance.

You have the possibility of manipulating metaphors just as you do of manipulating other rhetorical devices, diction, sentence patterns, or what have you. You will want to manipulate metaphors for the same reason you wish to manipulate the other language devices, in order to establish a basic profile, in order to achieve monotony-relieving variation, and in order to achieve emphasis for some particular idea.

SUMMARY CHECKLIST

As you master the techniques of metaphor, you will want to examine each composition you write and ask yourself these questions:

1. Have I adequately employed metaphors to enliven my writing—to achieve variation and emphasis?
2. Have I adequately employed metaphors to achieve more elaborate rhetorical texture if such a texture is appropriate?
3. If I am using a great many metaphors in a single piece of writing, have I adequately varied them?
4. Are my metaphors original?
5. Are the tenors and vehicles of my metaphors from diverse areas of experience? At the same time, do the tenors and vehicles have the necessary point of similarity?

THE WHOLE COMPOSITION

Christopher Morley's use of metaphors in this essay is judicious and effective. His varied and provocative metaphors help to establish a vigorous and interesting rhetorical texture. So skillfully are the metaphors used that even those that are dead ("the hands of the clock") or stereotyped ("the departing skirts of the day") contribute to the overall effect of richness and amusement.

You will note Morley's use of nearly every possible metaphorical form. A number of condensed metaphors appear—"devil of drowsiness," "the will on its tottering throne," "the friable resolutions of the day are brought out again and recemented and chiselled anew,"—along with such an explicit metaphor as "the end . . . is a steady nasal buzz." Extended metaphors are found in the fourth paragraph—("the tide of sleep . . . borne . . . out to great waters . . . from the wharf . . .") and in the sixth ("rubbish and floating matter . . . bright, clear, and swift current. . . ."). And you will find a delightful metaphorical jumble in "this drastic weeding out which Night imposes upon her wooers. . . ."

Read this essay carefully to find as many metaphors as possible, and observe that without the metaphors both the effectiveness and clarity of the essay would have suffered.

On Going to Bed

Christopher Morley

One of the characters in *The Moon and Sixpence* remarked that he had faithfully lived up to the old precept about doing every day two things you heartily dislike; for, said he, every day he had got up and he had gone to bed.

It is a sad thing that as soon as the hands of the clock have turned ten the shadow of going to bed begins to creep over the evening. We have never heard bedtime spoken of with any enthusiasm. One after another we have seen a gathering disperse, each person saying (with an air of solemn resignation): "Well, I guess I'll go to bed." But there was no hilarity about it. It is really rather touching how they cling to the departing skirts of the day that is vanishing under the spinning shadow of night.

This is odd, we repeat, for sleep is highly popular among human beings. The reluctance to go to one's couch is not at all a reluctance to slumber, for almost all of us will doze happily in an armchair or on a sofa, or even festooned on the floor with a couple of cushions. But the actual and formal yielding to sheets and blankets is to be postponed to the last possible moment.

The devil of drowsiness is at his most potent, we find, about 10:30 P.M. At this period the human carcass seems to consider that it has finished its cycle, which began with so much courage nearly sixteen hours before. It begins to slack and the mind halts on a dead centre every now and then, refusing to complete the revolution. Now there are those who hold that this is certainly the seemly and appointed time to go to bed and they do so as a matter of routine. These are, commonly, the happier creatures, for they take the tide of sleep at the flood and are borne calmly and with gracious gentleness out to great waters of nothingness. They push off from the wharf on a tranquil current and nothing more is to be seen or heard of these voyagers until they reappear at the breakfast table digging lustily into their grapefruit.

These people are happy, aye, in a brutish and sedentary fashion, but they miss the admirable adventures of those more embittered wrestlers who will not give in without a struggle. These latter suffer severe pangs between 10:30 and about 11:15 while they grapple with their fading faculties and seek to reestablish the will on its tottering throne. This requires courage stout, valour unbending. Once you yield, be it ever so little, to the tempter, you are lost. And here our poor barren clay plays us false, undermining the intellect with many a trick and wile. "I will sit down for a season in that comfortable chair," the creature says to himself, "and read this sprightly novel. That will ease my mind and put me in humour for a continuance of lively thinking." And the end of that man is a steady nasal buzz from the bottom of the chair where he has collapsed, an unsightly object and a disgrace to humanity. This also means a big bill from the electric light company at the end of the month. In many such ways will his corpus betray him, leading him by plausible self-deceptions into a pitfall of sleep, whence he is aroused about 3 A.M. when the planet turns over on the other side. Only by stiff perseverance and rigid avoidance of easy chairs may the critical hour between 10:30 and 11:30 be safely passed. Tobacco, a self-brewed pot of tea, and a browsing along bookshelves (remain standing and do not sit down with your book) are helps in this time of struggle. Even so, there are some happily drowsy souls who can never cross these shadows alone without grounding on the Lotus Reefs. Our friend J-D-K-, magnificent creature, was (when we lived with him) so potently hypnophil that, even erect and determined at his bookcase and urgently bent upon Brann's *Iconoclast* or some other literary irritant, sleep would seep through his pores and he would fall with a crash, lying there in unconscious bliss until someone came in and prodded him up, reeling and ashamed.

But, as we started to say, those who survive this drastic weeding out which Night imposes upon her wooers—so as to cull and choose only the truly meritorious lovers—experience supreme delights which are unknown to their snoring fellows. When the struggle with somnolence has been fought out and won, when the world is all-covering darkness and close-pressing silence, when the tobacco suddenly takes on fresh vigour and fragrance and the books lie strewn about the table, then it seems as though all the rubbish and floating matter of the day's thoughts have poured away and only the bright, clear, and swift current of the mind itself remains, flowing happily and without impediment. This perfection of existence is not to be reached very often; but when properly approached it may be won. It is a different mind that one uncovers then, a spirit which is lucid and hopeful, to which (for a few serene hours) time exists not. The friable resolutions of the day are brought out again and recemented and chiselled anew. Surprising schemes are started and carried through to happy conclusion, lifetimes of amazement are lived in a few passing ticks. There is one who at such moments resolves, with complete sincerity, to start at one end of the top shelf and read again all the books in his library, intending this time really to extract their true marrow. He takes a clean sheet of paper and sets down memoranda of all the people he intends to write to, and all the plumbers and what not that he will call up the next day. And the next time this happy seizure attacks him he will go through the same gestures again without surprise and without the slightest mortification. And then, having lived a generation of good works since midnight struck, he summons all his resolution and goes to bed.

EXERCISES

1. Select a published essay or article and determine, by carefully examining two or three pages of the text, the metaphorical texture of the writing. How many metaphors per hundred words are there?

2. Identify the tenor and vehicle in the following metaphors.

The twisted tree forked its branches into the air like a grand antique candelabrum.

My brother is a veritable rock of Gibraltar.

Like some distant, luminous bird, the satellite moved across the sky.

Bulldozing time crushed our perfect afternoon.

No man is an island unto himself.

3. What kinds of metaphors are these?

The old hound paused a moment to say his prayers, then plunged into the thicket.

She could not break his diamond-hard sense of obligation.

The clock clasped its hands together, groaned once, then proudly announced the hour of twelve.

Her anger spilled out upon us.

The Lord is my shepherd, I shall not want.

4. Identify the metaphors in the following passage and consider the rhetorical texture the metaphors help create.

. . . . an air of solid comfort, of inordinate sobriety and permanence, of unadventurous middle-class domesticity—respectability is the word, at last—settled around the shoulders of the guest like a Paisley shawl, a borrowed shawl of course, something to be worn and admired for a moment and handed back to the owner. Miss Stein herself sat there in full possession of herself, the scene, the spectators, wearing thick no-colored shapeless woolen clothes and honest woolen stockings knitted for her by Miss Toklas, looking extremely like a handsome old Jewish patriarch who had backslid and shaved off his beard.

Surrounded by her listeners, she talked in a slow circle in her fine deep voice, the word "perception" occurring again and again and yet again like the brass ring the children snatch for as their hobby horses whirl by.—Katherine Anne Porter, The Wooden Umbrella

5. Create a basically interesting metaphor, writing out all the possible forms in which it can be presented.
6. Write a paragraph in which you use a continued metaphor.
7. Write three paragraphs, each of a differing metaphorical elaborateness.
8. Do the three compositions of the earlier exercise (Chapter 13, exercise 7) employ metaphors effectively? In those areas of your compositions where you need greater emphasis or greater intensification, convert some of your literal statements into metaphorical statements.

15. PUNCTUA-
TION

We punctuate our writing in order to help our readers find their way through our sentences and paragraphs. We give "signs" along the route—so our readers can more clearly follow our thinking; more clearly see what words and phrases and clauses go together; more clearly grasp the connections we are trying to make. Exactly *how* we punctuate a particular sentence or paragraph depends greatly upon the context in which the sentence or paragraph occurs, upon the particular nuances of meaning that we wish to communicate, and upon the rhetorical profile we are attempting to achieve. We have a range of punctuation marks to use—from commas to semicolons, from periods to parentheses, from dashes to exclamation points—and we learn the different effects these marks can produce on different occasions. In general, we try to maintain a consistent principle of punctuation in any given composition—letting our punctuation help create the style that seems most appropriate.

Accurate, creative punctuation can give final polish to a well-written composition; careless punctuation can spoil an otherwise good piece of prose. Writers sometimes forget that punctuation not only prevents misreading, but consists of symbols communicative in their own right; that it not only reflects spoken English through identifying pauses, but indicates variations in pronunciation necessary to understanding the character of the sentence. In short, to be an effective writer, you must be a more than competent punctuator.

Absolute guides, however, are surprisingly few. Even where convention stipulates some form of punctuation, choice of the specific mark is often a matter of personal judgment. The following advice is not intended as a complete discussion of punctuation. Rather, it suggests a few alternatives you might consider in writing situations where judgment and invention are especially involved.

PUNCTUATING COMPOUNDS

Convention and instinctive logic insist that you separate the main clauses of a compound sentence with some form of punctuation, ordinarily the comma. But don't ignore the other alternatives. Indeed, think of the comma-dash-semicolon-colon-period as a spectrum of increasingly emphatic separators. The choice of which to use is not a matter of eenie, meenie, minie, moe. They separate increasingly complete thoughts and represent increasingly apparent vocal breaks. Moreover, they are so specialized in their functions that it would be wrong to use arbitrarily one in place of another. The intended meaning, the length and structure of the clauses, the nature of the conjunction, and the rhythm of the passage determine which mark—if any.

Consider the alternatives in this sentence:

He pitched his rope over the steer's head, then he snubbed the end of the rope about his own hips.

He pitched his rope over the steer's head—then he snubbed the end of the rope about his own hips.

He pitched his rope over the steer's head; then he snubbed the end of the rope about his own hips.

He pitched his rope over the steer's head: then he snubbed the end of the rope about his own hips.

He pitched his rope over the steer's head. Then he snubbed the end of the rope about his own hips.

The effect of each is different. Briefly, the comma emphasizes the second action; the dash emphasizes the element of suspense between the two actions; the semicolon emphasizes the close and immediate relation of the actions; the colon emphasizes the intention-fulfillment relation of the actions; and the period emphasizes only the equality of the actions.

Generally Use the Comma between Independent Clauses Joined by a Conjunction (and, but, for, or, nor, still, yet, so)

The comma, like its companion at the other end of the spectrum, the period, is more useful grammatically than rhetorically. A mark relied upon so frequently (often indiscriminately) could hardly be otherwise. In a somewhat perfunctory way, the comma suggests the clauses are separate but related and mildly emphasizes the second clause or the contrast between the two. Often what you really want is something weaker or something stronger—but in the sentences below a comma is right.

He planted an orchard of apple trees, and neighbors were quick to remind him this wasn't the fruit belt.

The quarterback called a running play in the huddle, but he changed signals at the line of scrimmage.

This meeting may be a long one, for the chairperson has several resolutions to present.

Omit the comma to avoid emphasizing the second clause or the contrast between clauses. Admittedly risky, this sort of construction can be effective only if the clauses are brief, structurally similar, and close in meaning. To drop the comma before *and* is often justified since this somewhat imprecise conjunction was probably used for the same reasons the comma was omitted. To drop the comma before *but* is dangerous and before *yet* is certainly so. Failure to use the comma here would imply the clauses are parallel when the conjunction, by introducing a whole new idea, suggests the contrary. There are occasions, however, when running the clauses together achieves exactly the right effect. Consider the reasoning behind the punctuation of these sentences:

But the night comes and these flowers fade.—*Virginia Woolf,* The Patron and the Crocus

Men like white meat and women like dark meat.

Men like white meat but women like dark meat.

He didn't like white meat, yet he knew she preferred dark meat.

The Greeks were the first scientists and all science goes back to them.—Edith Hamilton, The Greek Way

I am a vegetarian and I prefer the company of vegetarians.

I am a vegetarian, and I loathe meat eaters.

If you choose not to join independent clauses with a conjunction, then a comma or something stronger is a must. The comma can be used with good effect, but be certain that the clauses are short and similar in form—or you will wind up with a comma splice. Use the comma only if the semicolon would clearly be too strong or too formal.

In the morning it was sunny, the lake was blue.—D. H. Lawrence, Twilight in Italy

She never could seem to get used to them, her opportunities went for nothing.— Mark Twain, Autobiography

His health is ever good, his lungs are sound, his spirits never flag.—Henry David Thoreau, Walden

Always use a comma between the independent clauses of a compound sentence if you expect to keep the separateness of the clauses distinct. Whenever a hierarchy or contrast exists among clauses, emphasize it with a comma or some stronger mark.

Use the Dash to Emphasize an Element of Suspense between Clauses

The dash calls attention to the meaningful hesitation or delay between the clauses and strongly emphasizes the second clause. Its functions somewhat overlap those of the comma, semicolon, and colon. And its weight on the punctuation spectrum varies considerably. The pause a dash symbolizes may be long and heavy with tension, or sharp and light, depending on the circumstances. In spite of its versatility, the dash is not an all-purpose mark—it has a more distinct personality than the comma, semicolon, or colon. In the compound sentence, the dash is a dramatic mark indicating a surprising shift or an abrupt break in thought. The effect of a forceful statement or marked change in attitude can be immeasurably heightened by the well-timed delay.

Pride goeth before a fall—but first it lifts men to real heights.—Herbert J. Muller, The Uses of the Past

Everything worked perfectly except for one detail—I didn't know what kind of birds were there.—Loren Eiseley, The Immense Journey

Strangely the Burckhard's sober continental bourgeois house was without golden mean—everything was either hilariously old Swiss or madly modern.—Robert Lowell, Life Studies

A primary fight, at any level, is America's most original contribution to the art of democracy—and, at any level, it is that form of the art most profanely reviled and intensely hated by every professional who practices politics as a trade.— Theodore H. White, The Making of the President 1960

Use the Semicolon to Emphasize the Close Relation between the Clauses

The semicolon, functionally more like the period than any other mark, occupies a position midway between that of the more essential comma and period in the punctuation spectrum. It separates clauses more decisively than the comma, yet not so decisively as the period; and it can lean one way or the other as the situation demands. In the sentence you just read the semicolon is being used as if to say: Look, here are two thoughts that should be considered together. The semicolon is especially justified when the clauses are parallel in structure or when a clear contrast exists between the two.

The semicolon will help you avoid the self-conscious, monotonous rhythm of too many short sentences. With it you can retain the snap of short sentences but overcome the choppiness. And independent clauses joined by semicolons have an epigrammatic quality missing in short sentences. More important, the semicolon will enable you to consolidate short related sentences that might otherwise drift freely in the paragraph.

Be sure that the nature of the relation is so apparent you don't need to specify it with a conjunction. One good reason for using the semicolon is that it enables you to eliminate a conjunctive word—almost always an advantage since these words tend to dissipate the force of the statement. The semicolon can be retained even when a conjunction seems advisable; moreover, in the case of some transitional conjunctions (also, however, nevertheless, moreover, therefore, consequently, hence, furthermore, indeed, still, then) a semicolon is required before and a comma after.

The child lives in the book; but just as much the book lives in the child.—Ivor Brown, Out of a Book

We had a grand afternoon; we got no fish.—Stephen Leacock, My Fishing Pond

The metaphor is not original; I do not claim it so; I copy it from others.—Hilaire Belloc, In Praise of Ignorance

We were somewhere near Sorrento; behind us lay the long curve of faint-glimmering lights on the Naples shore; ahead was Capri.—George Gissing, By the Ionian Sea

Until recently Thomas Hardy's reputation as novelist overshadowed that of poet; however, that seems to be changing now.

Beware of overusing the semicolon, however; a large part of its effectiveness is dependent on its uncommonness. And in writing narrative and dialogue the semicolon may introduce a tinge more formality than is desired.

Use the Colon to Emphasize the Promise-Fulfillment Relation of Clauses

The colon is functionally more like the dash than any other mark. Often you'll have to choose between the two. If you want to give emotional emphasis to what follows in a reasonably informal context, the dash would be the better choice since in such a climate the colon would seem pedantically precise or ostentatiously formal. If you want to emphasize the second clause in a compound sentence quietly but strongly, even impressively, the colon is your mark.

In general, the colon tells the reader that what will be said is a distinct addition to what has been said. The functions of the colon are so many that the exact nature of the promise-fulfillment relation it points up is not clearly defined. The second clause may be: explanation, example, definition, restatement, summary, conclusion, or some other type of elaboration, often some form of quoted speech— in first or third person, in full or abridged. As long as it is used with restraint and with this "as follows" purpose in mind the colon can be used with relative freedom.

I was right about the tar: it led to within half a mile of the shore.—E. B. White, Once More to the Lake

It was built at the end of the eighteenth century: the first event recorded in connection with it is a memorial service for General Washington.—Edmund Wilson, The American Earthquake

Men are ruled by imagination: imagination makes them into men, capable of madness and of immense labors.—George Santayana, Soliloquies in England

Use the Period between What Would Otherwise Be Independent Clauses in a Compound Sentence if the Clauses Are Not Conceived as Two Steps or Two Parts of the Same Thought

The period is the expected terminal punctuation for complete declarative or imperative thoughts. Sometimes a foggy compound or compound-complex sentence can be clarified simply by replacing the comma with a period. (Beware, however, of the drum-beat effect of too many periods.) No specific rule can be established for deciding when sentences should be written separately or combined to form a compound sentence. Length of the statements and relation of the ideas are factors, but often not determining ones. What you do depends on the statements themselves and the stylistic climate.

PUNCTUATING ANTICIPATIONS AND AFTERTHOUGHTS

Some of your most effective sentences contain words, phrases, clauses that are incidental to the basic meaning, such as a dependent clause coming at the beginning or end of a complex sentence. If not set off by punctuation, these interruptions will complicate the flow of the sentence; effectively signaled they not only clarify the idea but heighten its effect. Meaning is the determining factor in deciding whether a remark is an interruption or an essential part of the sentence. If the sentence makes grammatical and logical sense without the passage, the passage is probably an interruption. But frequently you will have to decide how you want the passage to be interpreted before it can be punctuated. Location is also a factor. Interruptions can be placed at the beginning, in the interior, or at the end of the sentence. Subordinate remarks occurring within the sentence are more interruptive than anticipations or afterthoughts, and present quite different problems for the punctuator.

Subordinate remarks coming before or after the main clause ordinarily require separating punctuation. Sense, emphasis, and ease of reading are at stake. But don't make mincemeat of your sentences by indiscriminately punctuating every anticipation and afterthought. Some are more effective without punctuation; some are better served by other marks than the usual comma; and some are more useful to the sentence as parenthetic interruptions. You have a spectrum of punctuation at your disposal for managing anticipations and afterthoughts—the comma, dash, colon—providing you keep in mind the special functions of each. (And much that has been said elsewhere about the individual marks is pertinent here.) Consider the effect of comma—dash—colon in this sentence.

Within us there are warring factions, the puritan and the libertine.
Within us there are warring factions—the puritan and the libertine.
Within us there are warring factions: the puritan and the libertine.

Clearly the comma distinguishes and mildly emphasizes the main thought; the dash delays and thereby heightens the effect of the main thought; the colon emphasizes both thoughts, and suggests that the second is an immediate consequence of the first.

Generally Use the Comma between Long Anticipatory Remarks or Afterthoughts and the Rest of the Sentence

The comma is in this situation a rather light mark, serving only to clarify and possibly emphasize the main matter of the sentence by separating it from the less important. When the phrase or clause is simply subordinate, the comma can sometimes be omitted; when its relationship is more distant, never.

English weather is delightful, occasionally.

Like the Romans and the Germans, we are not an artistic people.—Louis Kronenberger, Company Manners

After skirting the river for three or four miles, I found a rickety footbridge.— Vladimir Nabokov, Speak, Memory

How beautiful to die of a broken heart, on paper!—Thomas Carlyle, Sartor Resartus

Omit the comma after anticipations unless they are long, verbal modifiers, transitional expressions, or references to persons addressed. In order to exploit the principle of open punctuation and maintain the momentum of your sentences, use the comma only as an accessory to meaning and ease of reading.

Embarrassed, the high school tragedian looked wildly around for the prompter.

Indeed this prehistoric stage of education ended rather abruptly with his tenth year.—Henry Adams, The Education of Henry Adams

On the rough wet grass of the back yard my father and mother have spread quilts.—James Agee, A Death in the Family

In the opinion of their most ardent admirers they are less like a machine and more like a human brain than anything man has ever succeeded in making before.—Joseph Wood Krutch, The Measure of Man

By the end of the eighteenth century Adam Smith boasted that it took eighteen men to make a pin, each man doing a little bit of the job and passing the pin on to the next, and none of them being able to make a whole pin or to buy the materials or to sell it when it was made.—George Bernard Shaw, The Intelligent Woman's Guide to Socialism and Capitalism

However, he was game.

Geoffrey, would you like to come along with us to Canterbury?

•

Omit the comma before afterthoughts unless they are long explanations that should be subordinated, or contrasts that should be emphasized. Closely related afterthoughts—especially if they are part of a cause-and-effect sequence—seldom require punctuation.

I wore a black velvet cap with a peak and that was all wrong.—H. G. Wells, Experiment in Autobiography

I would wish that all of it were deserved or at least appreciated as I have tried to do.—William Faulkner, Faulkner at Nagano

Of course the family is a good institution because it is uncongenial.—G. K. Chesterton, Heretics

It is common rule with distance runners not to break stride, for this upsets a rhythm that is sometimes difficult to reestablish.

Lay off, if you don't want to get into trouble.

A neighbor objects to my keeping bees, although he keeps a pack of vicious wolf hounds.

Use the Dash to Emphasize the Anticipation or Afterthought

Clearly the dash is not an alternative to the comma since it may stress the very thing the comma subordinates—the anticipation or afterthought. The dash, which vigorously heightens the effect of following remarks, is particularly effective near the end of a sentence. Here, where it is reinforced by position, the dash may emphasize a humorous aside or epigrammatic turn or dramatic final word; or it may mark a change of pace in the sentence, often a moment of reflection; or it may indicate that the writer has abandoned a sentence that threatened to get out of hand in favor of a quick abridgement or summary.

Just a touch—be careful!—Stephen Leacock, My Fishing Pond

In a strange transmutation dancing is a form of asceticism—almost a form of celibacy.—Agnes de Mille, And Promenade Home

I believe in aristocracy, though—if that is the right word, and if a democrat may use it.—E. M. Forster, What I Believe

Use the Colon to Emphasize the Promise-Fulfillment Relation of the Main Clause and the Anticipation or Afterthought

Like the dash, the colon emphasizes the remark that follows, whether it is a main clause or an afterthought. Use the colon reservedly; it is a prominent fulcrum that emphasizes both parts of the sentence.

Not only is it a famous statement of purpose: it is also an admirable statement of purpose.—Archibald MacLeish, The National Purpose

Here Melville puts, as it were, his ear to reality itself: to the rock rather than to the hero trying to get his sword out of the rock.—Alfred Kazin, Introduction to Moby Dick

That's it: illusion.—Stephen Leacock, My Fishing Pond

Thus the genuine biological benefits of the suburb were undermined by its psychological and social defects: above all, the irreality of its retreat.—Lewis Mumford, The City in History

PUNCTUATING INTERRUPTIONS

Subordinate remarks occurring within the sentence always require surrounding punctuation if they are interruptive. Restrictive phrases and clauses are not interruptions because they are essential to the sense of the sentence. To separate a restrictive remark from the sentence is appreciably to change the meaning. Consider this sentence: "Writers who aren't on intimate terms with the whole spectrum of punctuation can't manage a sophisticated prose style." Commas before *who* and after *punctuation* would have suggested no writer was capable of a sophisticated style—obviously not what was intended. Restrictive remarks do just what you would expect: they restrict the meaning of the word they modify and, hence, are really a part of it. Nonrestrictive phrases and clauses are interruptions because they are extras, remarks added which may contribute but don't radically alter the meaning of the main clause. Whether a remark is most effective as restrictive or nonrestrictive is sometimes a problem only the writer can decide. But as a rule, if the remark cannot be omitted without changing the meaning of the sentence, it is restrictive and not interruptive; if the remark can be omitted without changing the meaning of the sentence, it is nonrestrictive and must be punctuated as an interruption. Of course, there are other interruptive elements—transitions, parenthetical explanations, names of persons addressed—that require punctuation as well.

Interruptions within the sentence are often superior to anticipations or afterthoughts because here they neither weaken the initial effect of the sentence nor assume too much importance by taking the emphatic end position. You need to know how to use a variety of marks—commas, parentheses, and dashes, even semicolons and colons—in order to control meaning and avoid monotony in punctuating interruptions. Remember this rule of thumb: *the longer and more abrupt the interruption, the stronger the punctuation.* Consider the effect of interruptive signals in this sentence:

Barbados, the most easterly of the Caribbean islands, is 95 miles from its nearest neighbor.

Barbados (the most easterly of the Caribbean islands) is 95 miles from its nearest neighbor.

Barbados—the most easterly of the Caribbean islands—is 95 miles from its nearest neighbor.

Briefly, commas simply distinguish the main clause; parentheses separate the interruption more decisively, possibly emphasizing it; dashes clearly emphasize the interruption.

Generally Use Commas to Surround Interruptions That Are Closely Related to the Rest of the Sentence and But Slightly Impede Its Flow

The effect of commas is sometimes ambiguous. While they are the lightest and smoothest marks, the interruption remains more in the sentence and may, in some instances, be more interruptive than if stronger marks were used.

Native bluestem, unlike most grasses, is difficult to reestablish once it has been killed out.

Cumulus clouds, which are most common in spring and summer, are sometimes the prelude to thundershowers.

There are, of course, more ways than one to skin a cat.

Ordinarily, in punctuating interruptions, use paired marks or none—except in cases where the first comma is replaced by an opening conjunction.

But to make a long story short, he moved on.

And to a culture which questions the freedom of the will, Aristotle's hero seems to be a little beside the point.—*Lionel Trilling,* The Morality of Inertia

Use Parentheses to Surround Interruptions That Are Clearly Incidental to the Basic Meaning of the Sentence

The relative weight of parentheses is indeterminate. They tend to interrupt the sentence less than commas while at the same time emphasizing the enclosed remarks more. You must decide in light of the specific context whether parentheses would be lighter or heavier than commas. Interruptions are often directed at a particular reader: definitions or explanations for the less informed, supporting details for the critical.

Combining words to create a single metaphorical term ("kenning") is a characteristic of Old English poetry.

While semantics (the study of the meaning of words) has not solved all man's earthly problems, it certainly has been a useful tool in mediation.

She says that you once flirted with her (did you?) and that she still blushes at the mention of your name.

If you win the Chancellor's medal (and I hope it's announced soon), you must let me be the first to know.

Tennyson's 1832 volume failed miserably. (Only 300 out of 800 copies were sold by 1835; critics damned the book with rare unanimity. And the poet wrote little during the next ten years.)

He violently jerked at the life preserver (tearing its cover and dooming himself to certain death) and jumped into the sea.

(Parentheses are not to be confused with brackets, marks used to surround a special kind of interruption—editorial explanation or comment within a passage of quoted material.)

Remember: Interruptions that are complete thoughts need not begin with a capital or end with a period. (For exclamations and questions, however, the terminal signal should be retained.) If the interruption is a separate sentence, it is written conventionally with the terminal punctuation inside the enclosing punctuation. Also, punctuation belonging to the part of the sentence coming before the interruption should be placed after the closing parentheses.

Use Dashes to Surround Important Interruptions

Lackadaisical writers use parentheses when they should use dashes. Dashes are the most emphatic of the standard marks and are typically used to surround rather abrupt, even violent interruptions.

Fiction—if it at all aspires to be art—appeals to temperament.—Joseph Conrad, The Nigger of the Narcissus

The chief charm of New England was harshness of contrasts and extremes of sensibility—a cold that froze the blood, and a heat that boiled it—so that the pleasures of hating—one's self if no better victim offered—was not its rarest amusement.—Henry Adams, The Education of Henry Adams

We know as much—and as little—about our own ancestors as we do about some other missing creatures from the zoological record.—Loren Eiseley, The Time of Man

Ellipses, sometimes used as dashes in punctuating interruptions, are better reserved for marking an omission in quoted material.

Use Semicolons and Colons Rarely to Surround Interruptions

Except in the case of semicolons to set off interruptions which contain commas or other punctuation, their use here is very special, very literary. But since they sometimes enable a fine distinction or necessary variation, experienced writers occasionally punctuate an interruption with semicolons or colons.

And he might have been equally irritated by lack of style; for he boasted of "my barbaric yawp"—he would not be literary; his readers should touch not a book but a man.—F. L. Lucas, On the Fascination of Style

To enjoy these advantages I was ready to carry it on; like Atlas, to take the world on my shoulders,—I overheard what compensation he received for that,— and do all those things which had no other motive or excuse but that I might pay for it and be unmolested in my possession of it; for I knew all the while that it would yield the most abundant crop of the kind I wanted if I could only afford to let it alone.—Henry David Thoreau, Walden

The faces: Van Gogh and Manet would have loved them: that of the pilgrim with staff and pack and dusty with walking, mounting the stairs toward the Temple in early sunlight.—William Faulkner, Faulkner at Nagano

PUNCTUATING A SERIES

Punctuating a series of items is sometimes considered such a simple affair that writers habitually fall back on the obvious and commonplace, failing to make the fine distinctions commensurate with stylistic prose.

As you would expect, the stronger the punctuation, the more distinct the series. Notice the effect on the following sentence of the most common serial marks:

Irony is one thing, sarcasm is another, invective is something else.

Irony is one thing; sarcasm is another; invective is something else.

Irony is one thing: sarcasm is another: invective is something else.

Commas are sufficiently clear; semicolons are more emphatic; colons are not only emphatic but suggest inevitability in the order of elements. This doesn't begin to suggest the subtleties involved, nor does it consider the other marks—dashes, question marks, exclamation points, and periods—that may also be used in punctuating serials.

Generally Use the Comma between All Words, Phrases, or Clauses in a Series When a Clear Distinction but No Particular Emphasis Is Desired

A conjunction before the last item does not substitute for the comma. Suppressing the comma here will lead your reader to suppose the last two items are really a single unit.

Guadeloupe, Saint Barthélemy, Martinique, and several smaller islands make up the French West Indies.

Children can't be expected to know the difference between a deliberate lie, an imaginative interpretation, or an innocent misconception.

He is articulate, he is self-possessed, he is capable.

Omit the commas when the adjectives in a series modify each other as well as the noun; retain the commas when the adjectives modify the noun independently. If the order of adjectives can be shuffled without playing havoc with the sense of the sentence, or if the conjunction *and* could be placed between each of the adjectives without seriously distorting the meaning, retain the commas. Otherwise drop the commas since writers usually err in the direction of too much scrupulosity. Blending the adjectives creates a more unified picture; often this is what you want.

One of the natives ran and got his camera to photograph a tourist wearing an iridescent flowered Hawaiian sport shirt.

A recent storm exposed the aged, rotten, worm-eaten timbers of a Spanish galleon.

The bookseller handed him a dirty, yellow, battered volume.

The bookseller gingerly handed him a dirty yellow battered volume.

Use Dashes between Items in a Series When You Want to Be Strongly Emphatic and Distinct

The relative strength of the series dash is indeterminate. It is useful in a wide range of situations and derives much of its force from the context. Dashes can be used to drive home a series of ideas with hammerlike emphasis. Or they can be used to represent vocal hesitations associated with a lazy, inarticulate, or thoughtful speaker. The dash is at its best when operating as the most emphatic of common serial marks.

I had no intention of shooting the elephant—I had merely sent for the rifle to defend myself if necessary—and it is always unnerving to have a crowd following you.—George Orwell, Shooting an Elephant

Where Hawthorne is known, he seems to be deemed a pleasant writer, with a pleasant style,—a sequestered, harmless man, from whom any deep and weighty thing would hardly be anticipated—a man who means no meanings.—Herman Melville, Hawthorne and His Mosses

But, in a larger sense, we cannot dedicate—we cannot consecrate—we cannot hallow—this ground.—Abraham Lincoln, The Gettysburg Address

If that inevitability breaks down—if the characters are compelled by the author to do what we instinctively know they would not do—then I think we feel that there is a flaw in the reality of the novel.—Elizabeth Bowen, The Novelist's Craft

We have no writers to match the giants of English literature: Chaucer—Shakespeare—Milton.

Five thousand—four thousand—three thousand, the plane lost precious altitude.

Use the Semicolon When Items in the Series Are Long or Contain Commas and Especially When You Want to Emphasize the Progression or Interrelation of the Items

Semicolons are more emphatic than commas and shouldn't be substituted for them without clear reason. Semicolons replace conjunctions with more authority than commas. The semicolon is most eloquent when alerting readers to the cumulative effect of a series of thoughts (often independent clauses) coming in quick succession or to the contrast or antithesis of thoughts.

Amos, for example, is like Milton in his sonorous, ringing lines; Hosea sounds the sad and minor notes of A. E. Housman; Second Isaiah is like Shelley in his ecstasy; certain of the Psalmists are like William Blake, or Thomas Traherne, or John Donne.—Mary Ellen Chase, The Bible and the Common Reader

He had caught his English at its living source, among the poets and prose-

writers of its best days; his literature was extensive and recondite; his quotations are always nuggets of the purest ore; there are sentences of his as perfect as anything in the language, and thoughts as clearly crystallized; his metaphors and images are always fresh from the soil; he had watched Nature like a detective who is to go upon the stand; as we read him, it seems as if all out-of-doors had kept a diary and become its own Montaigne; we look at the landscape in a Claude Lorraine glass; compared with his, all other books of similar aim, even White's Selborne, *seem dry as a country clergyman's meteorological journal in an old almanac.—James Russell Lowell,* Thoreau

The cracks between the logs were not filled; there was no carpet; consequently, if you dropped anything smaller than a peach, it was likely to go through.—Mark Twain, Autobiography

Use the Colon between Items in a Series When You Want to Emphasize That the Items Are Stages in a Development, Steps in an Argument, or an Accumulation of Items

The colon is oddly provocative, more so than the semicolon, which has something of the same effect. Whatever the explanation of its attraction, the series colon alerts readers to something special. Don't disappoint them.

He didn't dare: and I knew it: and he knew it.—D. H. Lawrence, Phoenix

Nothing happens: nothing can happen: nothing ever tries to happen.—Warren Weaver, Peace of Mind

A final word. When a series invites or, as when it is an interruption, requires some form of introductory punctuation, you are better off preferring a mark stronger than that used within the series—a dash or semicolon with internal commas, colons with stronger marks, parentheses or paired dashes with an interruption containing commas. Also, the stronger the introductory or surrounding punctuation, the more emphatic the series.

QUESTION MARKS AND EXCLAMATION POINTS

Even a word about the question mark and exclamation point, marks that occur in only 2 or 3 percent of sentences, seems extravagant— but is it? Both are often used with little restraint. Too many question marks suggest moronic puzzlement; too many exclamation points, hysteria. And both are used indiscriminately instead of a period. The difference between a direct and indirect question, a quiet and an assertive exclamation is a distinction worth preserving. These suggestions will help you to use the question mark and exclamation point more effectively:

A remark intended as mild or musing should not be distorted by a question

mark or exclamation point. The question mark can even be dropped after a direct question if it doesn't require an answer or isn't an emphatic statement. When in doubt always choose the period; understatement is invariably superior to overstatement.

Isn't this a beautiful evening.
Well, it's about time.

A shoemaker gives shoes for his bread. Well. A singer sings for his supper. Well. A capitalist leads a large enterprise. Well.—Herman Wouk, Aurora Dawn

A declarative statement can be transformed into a question or exclamation by punctuation only if this reading is supported by context.

Do you know of any essayist more knotty than Carlyle?
What! That can't be true! Why, it's perfectly absurd!

What is sweet to any of you in this world? Love? Nature? Art? Language? Youth?—Herman Wouk, Aurora Dawn

Generally, if your statement deserves a question mark or exclamation point the phrasing should reflect it. Don't get in the habit of depending too exclusively on punctuation.

Two words to the wise: There is no surer, quicker way to murder wit than to boast of your cleverness, your ironic perception with a question mark or exclamation point. Double, triple question marks? Exclamation points? Never!

In short, there exists a spectrum of increasingly emphatic interrogative or exclamatory signals: the period (following an indirect or mild question or exclamation), internal question marks or exclamation points, terminal question marks or exclamation points, the question mark or exclamation point followed by a dash, and a series of questions or exclamations so punctuated.

PUNCTUATING DIALOGUE

Modern prose—with its relatively simple diction, short sentences, and conversational rhythms—is remarkably like ordinary speech. And punctuation aids in recalling the pauses and inflections of speech and makes possible the casual syntactical arrangements used in conversation. Dialogue, either as literal or third-person speech, is becoming more common and with it certain punctuation techniques.

Cast more of your prose into the form of quoted speech when you want to

achieve a sense of immediacy. Quotation marks alert the reader to something emphatic or dramatic.

The student asks you, as a child his mother, "Where did I come from?" "Son," you say floundering, "below the Cambrian there was a worm." Or you say, "There was an odd fish in a swamp and you have his lungs." Or you say, "Once there was a reptile whose jaw bones are in your ear." Or you try again. "There was an ape and his teeth are in your mouth. Your jaw has shrunk and your skull has risen. You are fish and reptile and a warm-blooded, affectionate thing that dies if it has nothing to cling to when it is young. You are all of these things. You are also a rag doll made of patches out of many ages and skins. You began nowhere in particular. You are really an illusion, one of innumerable shadows in the dying fires of a mysterious universe. Yesterday you were a low-browed skull in the river gravel; tomorrow you may be a fleck of carbon amid the shattered glass of Moscow or New York. Ninety per cent of the world's life has already gone. Perhaps brains will accomplish the work of extinction faster. The pace is stepping up."—Loren Eiseley, The Time of Man

(Remember: Commas and periods go inside the quotation marks; semicolons and colons, outside. Dashes, question marks, and exclamation points go inside the quotation marks when they apply only to the quotation, outside when they apply to the entire sentence, inside when they apply to both.)

"There is no use going farther," he admitted, "when we've lost the trail."

According to Evelyn Underhill, the mystic seeks "union with Reality"; by this she means an intense awareness of the nonmaterial side of experience.

She said, "When are you leaving?"

Did she just say, "Let's go"?

Use a comma after most introductory statements preceding a quotation; omit punctuation after short, informal introductions; use a colon after long, formal, or emphatic introductions.

She cried "Ouch!" and shook her pricked finger.

Holding the flower gingerly she said, "Did Burns mean love was like a rose because it too had thorns?"

And, as you may have guessed, her next lecture to the Garden Club began: "Horticulturists have long sought to produce a thornless rose."

Use a comma after the first portion of a quotation broken by an interrup-

tion and either a comma, semicolon, dash, or period after the interruption, depending on the grammatical completeness of the parts.

"Soaring is possible," he said, "only when there are rising air currents."

"The writer assumes God-like prerogatives," he declared; "he creates characters that seem more alive than the living.

"I have always loved sailing," the lecturer said. "I built and sailed my first catboat when I was fourteen."

> *Use the comma between an opening quotation and concluding statement unless the quotation is punctuated with a question mark or exclamation point.*

"The plane is overdue," he said, rejoining the group on the field.

"You mean it's down somewhere?" he asked.

"Oh, surely not!" she gasped unbelievingly.

> *Use the name of the speaker followed by a colon when you want to emphasize strongly the speaker and the passage of dialogue; otherwise identify the speaker more casually.* In either case the speeches can be paragraphed conventionally or separated by dashes. As an interlude, the playlet can serve a variety of rhetorical purposes.

Reporter: And what advice do you have for someone like yourself, someone with money?

Millionaire: Remember, the only thing really worth having that money can buy is time.

He said, "I would give anything to be a bird."

"But," she reminded him, "a bird doesn't have a soul."

"I would trade my soul for a pair of wings," was his reply.

> *Use the run-together hyphen to suggest hurried or slurred speech; use the dash to suggest deliberate or labored speech.*

Let's-get-out-of-here!

"Weeawaugh, we-ee-eeelawaugh, weelawaugh," shrilled Mother's high voice. "But-and, but-and, but and!" Father's low mumble would drone in answer.— Robert Lowell, 91 Revere Street

Oh-o-o-o-o that I never had been born-r-r-r-n! *sighs one on this side of the pond, and circles with the restlessness of despair to some new perch on the gray oaks.—Henry David Thoreau,* Walden

I'd like to do it, but—er—you know—er, uh—well confound—I mean a person in my position can't make a habit of throwing his weight around.

Use the terminal dash to suggest that a statement suddenly breaks off; use the terminal ellipsis to suggest that it trails away.

As your C.O. I'll have to say no, but as your friend, well—.

The Victorians are secure, but the modern novelists. . . .

SPACING AS PUNCTUATION

Punctuation is in some ways but a substitute for spacing and typography. The naturalness of suggesting pause and rate by the space between letters and words, pitch and inflection by their position on a hypothetical scale, stress by relative boldness of the type is too obvious to miss—so is the impracticality. Spacing is not that important in conventional prose, but you should at least be aware that words on paper possess graphic qualities that affect meaning. Much of what could be said about spacing is too special to state as principle. This much can be said:

You may indicate major divisions by leaving spaces. The simple presence of such divisions implies order and design—sometimes more than is present. If the divisions are several, and if you want to identify them in some more particular way, use Roman numerals, Arabic numbers, or headings. In narrative writing, spacing or other punctuation can be used to suggest the passage of time; in expository writing, a change of tone or point of view. See, for instance, the essay at the end of Chapter 9.

You may emphasize the importance of items in a series by ordering them in vertical columns. Usually the items are indented and identified by numbers, letters, or preliminary dashes (useful but seldom seen marks).

You may, if the situation invites something truly exotic and esoteric, consider a typographical experiment. Since you are here assuming one of the prerogatives of the poet, this sort of thing is more appropriate in poetic or at least highly imaginative prose. Running words together without punctuation to suggest rush, deviating from the horizontal line to accentuate a rhythm, setting up a passage as poetry to emphasize its lyric qualities, italicizing to produce some rhetorical effect other than emphasis can be extremely effective in rare moments if you have the confidence and instinct for such stylistic acrobatics. Inspiration for experiment with space and typography must come from the context.

"There's cold chicken inside it," replied the Rat briefly; "coldtonguecoldhamcold-beefpickledgherkinssaladfrenchrollscressandwidgespottedmeatgingerbeerlemonadeso-dawater—"—Kenneth Grahame, The Wind in the Willows

Ford owned every detail of the process from the ore in the hills until the car rolled off the end of the assemblyline under its own power, the plants were rationalized to the last tenthousandth of an inch as measured by the Johansen scale;
In 1926 the production cycle was reduced to eightyone hours from the ore in the mine to the finished salable car proceeding under its own power,
but the model T was obsolete.

New Era prosperity and the American Plan
(there were strings to it, always there were strings to it)
had killed Tin Lizzie.
Ford's was just one of many automobile plants.—Dos Passos, The Big Money

The key-bugle remarked with singular distinctness to the dawn:

dy
I know a la   fair   kind
                    and
Was never face
            so   mind
            pleased my
                    y

—Ford Maddox Ford, George Herbert in the Trenches

SUMMARY CHECKLIST

As you give your compositions their final polish—as you use punctuation creatively, and as effectively as possible—ask yourself these questions:

1. Have I underpunctuated any sentences? If you're habitually somewhat hesitant or an overzealous champion of open punctuation, you'll want to be especially careful here. The simple addition of a mark can clear up an otherwise hopelessly ambiguous or misleading sentence.
2. Have I overpunctuated any sentences? Methodically acknowledging every joint in the sentence is not the best cure for haphazardry. If neither sound nor sense nor propriety absolutely require the mark, then drop it.
3. Have I considered the full spectrum of punctuation? In particular, have I overworked the comma and period and neglected the other marks?

THE WHOLE COMPOSITION

The following essay employs a great variety of marks in particularly effective ways. Richard Ketchum's use of the indispensable comma is abetted by his practice of open punctuation (for example, "When he went abroad in 1901 [no comma] the King of England asked that Morgan be seated at his right at a banquet. . . ."); his use of the inevitable period, by his readiness to use an alternative (in a sentence like, "In the depression of 1895 he had rescued the United States government (at a price) when it ran short of gold; in 1901 he had put together U.S. Steel, the world's first 'billion-dollar' corporation; six years later only his enormous courage, audacity, and prestige saved the country from financial disaster."). And when the intricacies of a thought demand something other than the comma or period, he is a capable stylist (as in, "Afterward Steichen described the impact of that formidable personality: meeting the man's eyes was something like confronting the headlights of an onrushing express train—if you could get out of the way it was only an awe-inspiring experience; otherwise it was calamitous."). Wherever there is a choice of marks, the author evidently considers the various possibilities; more than this, he clearly thinks of punctuation as one of the important constituents of style.

J. P. Morgan

Richard M. Ketchum

The great man could spare exactly two minutes. Like a huge, baleful dragon he sat, not posing but confronting the camera, defying it to do its worst, gripping the polished arm of the chair so that it looked like a gleaming pigsticker aimed at the vitals. The photographer, Edward Steichen, had time for two exposures; then his visitor rose, clapped a square-topped derby on his head, reached for the big black cigar he had laid aside, and departed.

Afterward Steichen described the impact of that formidable personality: meeting the man's eyes was something like confronting the headlights of an onrushing express train—if you could get out of the way it was only an awe-inspiring experience; otherwise it was calamitous. That was the effect John Pierpont Morgan nearly always had on people. What they saw first was the bulbous, flaming nose that was his affliction and his shame; to avoid staring at it they looked him in the eye and were struck dumb. Lincoln Steffens, who as a young financial reporter had interviewed him, recalled how "his eyes glared, his great red nose seemed to me to flash and darken, flash and darken." That was back in the nineties, a decade before Steichen's great photograph was made, when Morgan was at his office at 23 Wall Street every day. He sat alone, Steffens wrote, in a back room with glass sides; the door was open, as if anyone might walk in and ask a question. But no one dared; not even his partners went near him unless they were summoned, "and then they looked alarmed and darted in like office-boys."

Everything about Morgan bespoke solidity and permanence—his inevitable wing collar, Ascot tie, severe dark suit; the enormous bloodstone that hung from a heavy gold watch chain, the very stone and chain he had worn when he entered the business world in 1857. Everything he did was on a magnificent scale—his yacht, the *Corsair,* was the biggest, the collies he bred won the best blue ribbons, the works of art he brought back from Europe staggered the imagination. Truly, he was a man above men. As Mr. Dooley put it in an impersonation of Morgan, "call up the Czar an' th' Pope an' th' Sultan an' th' Impror Willum, an' tell thim we won't need their sarvices afther nex' week."

J. P. Morgan was easily the most powerful personal force in American life. In the depression of 1895 he had rescued the United States government (at a price) when it ran short of gold; in 1901 he had put together U.S. Steel, the world's first "billion-dollar" corporation; six years later only his enormous courage, audacity, and prestige saved the country from financial disaster. When he went abroad in 1901 the King of England asked that Morgan be seated at his right at a banquet; in Germany he dined alone with the Kaiser (when Wilhelm II mentioned the subject of socialism, Morgan glared at him momentarily and then announced: "I pay no attention to such theories"). The public image of him was evident in a song of the period, which told of a weary pilgrim seeking a place to rest, only to be turned away again and again with the words: "It's Morgan's, it's Morgan's . . ." Then, at last,

> *"I went to the only place left for me,*
> *So I boarded a boat for the brimstone sea;*
> *Maybe I'll be allowed to sit*
> *On the griddled floor of the bottomless pit;*
> *But a jeering imp with horns on his face*
> *Cried out as he forked me out of the place:*
> > Chorus:
> *It's Morgan's, it's Morgan's; the great financial gorgon's;*
> *Get off that spot, we're keeping it hot;*
> *That seat is reserved for Morgan."*

THE NEW STRATEGY OF STYLE

Inevitably the zealous young President, Theodore Roosevelt, and the crusty old financier ran afoul of one another. In 1902, only five months after Roosevelt took office, Wall Street shuddered with the news that the government planned to demand dissolution of the Northern Securities Company, the giant holding company created by Morgan and James J. Hill to control the Northern Pacific, the Great Northern, and the Chicago, Burlington & Quincy railroads. At 23 Wall the air was sulphurous; Morgan left immediately for Washington. In a dramatic meeting he criticized the brash young man in the White House for what was clearly a violation of vested rights, took him to task for not warning him of his plans, and concluded with the famous words: "If we have done anything wrong, send your man [meaning the Attorney General of the United States] to my man [a Morgan attorney] and they can fix it up." As the President was quick to see, Morgan regarded him as "a big rival operator"; privately, the banker considered him wildly irresponsible. "The man's a lunatic," he said. "He is worse than a Socialist." Nor was Morgan one to let bygones be bygones. When Roosevelt left the White House and announced his plans to go hunting in Africa, the financier growled, "I hope the first lion he meets does his duty."

Ironically, Morgan's last public appearance was in the nature of an accounting for the power he had wielded. In 1912, a year before he died, he was called to Washington to testify before the so-called Pujo Committee—a House subcommittee determined to prove that Morgan and a small group of New York bankers held the nation's economy in an iron grip. During the course of his testimony, J. P. Morgan revealed the credo which had governed his long career. The attorney conducting the examination asked whether commercial credit was not based primarily upon money or property. "No," Morgan replied firmly, "the first thing is character."

"Before money or property?"

"Before money or anything else. Money cannot buy it. . . . Because a man I do not trust could not get money from me on all the bonds in Christendom."

EXERCISES

1. In which of the following is the punctuation perfunctory? passively competent? truly creative?

    The metaphysical conceit is vastly superior to the Elizabethan. It is more elaborate, startling, and intellectual; at the same time too it is much less apt to become a cliché.

The metaphysical conceit is vastly superior to the Elizabethan: it is more elaborate, startling, and intellectual; at the same time too, it is much less apt to become a cliché.

The metaphysical conceit is vastly superior to the Elizabethan, it is more elaborate, startling and intellectual. At the same time too it is much less apt to become a cliché.

2. Punctuate the following sentences in the most effective way possible.

I listened to the music she watched the people

The sergeant showed us his collection of good luck charms then he was killed by a stray bullet

He hit an easy pop fly but the shortstop and third baseman collided under the ball and he made it to second

The rear cinch is a piece of useless paraphernalia on a riding saddle it is essential equipment on a roping saddle

Your punctuation is inclined to be rather tentative you must be both more precise and more confident

When you fire a shotgun keep the stock firmly seated against your shoulder

After his second novel he decided to become a professional writer

He will succeed in graduate school because of his dogged persistence

He was an eccentric fellow very eccentric as I recall

Read for this is the best way to experience vicariously what you could not dare not experience directly

Wilfred Owen who wrote much of his poetry under fire was the most experimental and meticulous of World War I poets

3. Write a paragraph in which you contrive to do without any punctuation beyond the period. Describe the problems you encountered.
4. Supplying illustrations from your own prose, classify yourself as a punctuator.
5. Write several sentences that can be "correctly" punctuated various ways with both subtle and not so subtle consequences.
6. Can you think of useful punctuation which does not exist? Compose a sentence employing such a mark. Explain why you think this new punctuation you have devised ought to be adopted. Did you have difficulty conceiving a truly

unique suggestion? Is there something to be said for a fairly restricted set of punctuation marks?

7. In the three essays written for an earlier exercise (Chapter 14, exercise 8)—or in a passage of your own or another's prose—see if you can't attain greater variety and exactness by replacing some commas and periods with other punctuation.

.

16. THE POPULAR ARTICLE

■ A professional attitude about writing presumes not only good *taste* and a degree of *skill* but some *knowledge of the published forms.* The most prominent contemporary prose form is the *popular article.* To shape our writing toward this preconsidered design in the confidence that the finished piece will be as we imagined requires an understanding of its purposes and characteristics. Such a *sense of form* provides us with not only a clear idea of the objective but a series of steps for achieving it, vastly simplifying the writing process. Even more important, we learn to express our ideas in the familiar, current, widely read context of the popular article. ■

You may not have literary ambitions at all, or you may never get beyond the stage of idly contemplating the prospect. But even if you have no immediate desire to publish, you will undoubtedly read more articles and essays than other published prose; and the best way to learn the intricacies of these familiar forms is to try your hand at them. As soon as you decide on a form, you make a commitment. You will follow pretty much the same steps in the writing process as other writers; you will work within a rather definite and sometimes elaborate framework; and you will produce something that is in many ways like others of its kind.

The article and essay have proved particularly convenient and expressive in the context for which each was designed, or they would be quickly discarded for something better. Though both are relatively modern, each is the product of a long evolution at the hands of publishing writers, many of them great stylists; and each continues to be modified to suit a changing society. For these are pragmatic forms, each providing a special kind of comment on the human condition in a technological age.

The article, a factual discussion of from several hundred to several thousand words on a fairly definite subject, is written to satisfy a practical reader in a utilitarian age. Informative rather than speculative, the article offers explanations and proofs rather than reflections and conjectures. It is written communication of the most direct and literal kind, avoiding the subtle, the suggestive, and the exquisite. The writer is an authority rather than a personality. In view of its impersonal preoccupation with subject and matter-of-fact idiom, the article can hardly be considered "literary." But this does not detract from the specific kind of skill required to write the article or, certainly, from the favor it has found with the reading public. Still, the term "article" is so commonly misused that we must remind ourselves it is a distinct form—more objective than the essay, less expressive of opinion than the editorial, and written in greater depth than the news story.

We cannot generalize about the article for very long without making a distinction between the *popular* and the *professional* article. The popular articles in magazines and newspapers are more likely to deal with subjects their numerous readers will find timely if not sensational and in a way that is rather more spritely than thorough. The scholarly or serious articles found in learned and professional journals are almost always the specialized, detailed, and closely reasoned treatments their somewhat more knowledgeable readers expect.

THE POPULAR ARTICLE AS A FORM

A more detailed description of the popular article must take up these topics: the accommodation of a subject to a class of readers, the selection and arrangement of details on the basis of interest, and the employment of a highly readable, journalistic style.

The accommodation of a subject to a class of readers is clearly the principal object of the popular article. You begin with a subject—but quickly look ahead to the reader. Not only is the choice of subjects influenced by the reader's preoccupations and psychology, but so is the way in which any subject is developed. For the subject, if not immediately attractive, must be quickly made so; you first find a relevant subject and then make it more relevant. The popular article is instructive, even persuasive, exploring those subjects which have something to do with "living the good life." But at the same time it brings pleasure to readers who enjoy indulging their curiosity. So you go looking for subjects, equipped with a fair knowledge of your reading audience and your subject. And most of your writing effort will be devoted to bringing this subject and these readers together.

Your subjects will invariably be the significant, the striking, the anecdotal, the inherently interesting (anything, in short, that appeals to those human hopes and fears which are the common lot and by so doing excites humor, pathos, fear, romance, and above all curiosity). And your reader will just as surely be one who through the article would become a part of the scheme of things (for not knowing is not belonging) and more affluent (for knowledge of the world remains the principal way of knowing and attaining our heart's desires). The article's greatest appeal is to that vast middle class of which we are virtually all members. Earnest, hard-working, eager to learn and succeed, we are fascinated by the odd and unusual, but especially attracted by the familiar and useful—people, places, new ideas, how-to-do-it pieces, exposés, personal experiences. A run-down of some published titles reveals a great deal about both the subjects and readers of popular articles: "G. H. Hardy: The Pure Mathematician" (C. P. Snow, *Atlantic*), "Cast Iron Furniture" (John Mebane, *Better Homes and Gardens*), "The Dawn, the Totem, the Drums: African Literature in the Grip of Harsh Realities" (Wilfred Cartey, *Commonweal*), "Dr. von Braun's All-Purpose Space Machine" (Gene Bylinsky, *Fortune*), "Gibraltar" (Anthony Burgess, *Holiday*), "Coming to Terms with the New Art" (Emily Genauer, *House Beautiful*), "Should This Sex Research Be Allowed to Go On?" (Lois Chevaliar, *Ladies' Home Journal*), "When an American Negro Returns to Africa" (Ernest Dunham, *Look*), "Young Marriage: What Happens When Parents Pay the Bills" (Samuel Grafton, *McCall's*), "College President: Salesman, Philosopher, Riot Preventer" (Andrew Hacker, *The New York Times Magazine*), "Big Fly: Big Trout" (V. C. Marinaro, *Outdoor Life*), "Change in Mixed Marriages" (J. C. Wynn, *Presbyterian Life*), "Better Coed Than Dead" (*Time*), "Medicare: Headache or Cure-all?" (Steven M. Spencer, *The Saturday Evening Post*).

In a form which would make the most of an arresting subject and a fascinated reader, *the selection and arrangement of details on the basis of reader interest* follows naturally. The popular article tells the readers all they want to know and need to know for their immediate purposes about the subject, but does not bore them with too many or with unessential details. And the popular article relies upon the most lively sort of details: anecdotes, quotations, examples, analogies, metaphors, similes, active descriptions, animated narratives. Extensive use of such means of amplifying and illustrating a subject would be out of place in scholarly writing, but here a departure from the more formal expository patterns is necessary if the popular article is to hold much appeal for readers who are motivated less by the desire to be edified, more by the desire to be entertained. And these details are arranged in such a way as to maintain interest at the highest pitch without distorting the subject or misinforming the readers: as unified, swift moving, forcefully stated, climactically ordered explanations and interpretations. The best popular articles are not sophistic, nor are they sensational. The authors have simply selected the most provocative details and arranged these in the most tantalizing way consistent with their instructive purpose. For the readers of popular articles are rapid readers, unwilling to pursue a lengthy and closely reasoned line of thought; they much prefer an article projected largely in terms of a few dramatic illustrations. The following paragraph, like the article on Tahiti from which it is taken, is composed almost entirely of such dramatic illustrations.

Papeete looks now much as it did in past years, which is to say like a weather-beaten Mexican border town. There are parks with magnificent trees, two-story wooden buildings, a cathedral, and plenty of debris and garbage in the streets. Here and there a new building amid the jumble of Chinese shops calls attention to itself by the gleam of white plaster; the colors of the older buildings are more muted, washed out. It used to be that when you got to Tahiti you went to the Cafe Vaima on the waterfront, and within an hour you would be included in all the local gossip and everyone you wanted to see would stroll by. Now the pace has picked up beyond a stroll: French military types in short-short pants and loose shirts buzz by on motorcycles, and the girls who would be gossip topics if they were walking careen by so quickly on their Vespas that they do not become a part of what is talked about. The girls are still in bright print pareus, golden shoulders bared, the calloused feet either bare or sandaled. When they smile there are not as many gaps as there used to be; more money, more dental work. Gold teeth flash. Exhaust fumes mix with the salt air. There are ocean-going yachts, with their connotations of timelessness and leisure, moored ten yards from the main street. Clothes hang out to dry on the Iota, *Sydney. Someone is having a cup of instant coffee on the afterdeck of the* Nina, *Honolulu, and someone else is just coming back onto the* Porpoise, *Los Angeles, with some mail. Farther on, at the jetty, the French are creating a naval base; gray LSTs are lined up, disgorging matériel, and beyond them, American tankers deliver the aviation fuel that keeps the fat Bregeut military cargo planes droning overhead on their way out to the Tuamotus.—George J. W. Goodman,* Tahiti

This selection and arrangement of interesting details is complemented in the popular article by *a highly readable, journalistic style.* If you think of style as an indirect expression of the author's personality, or personal idiom, you will find scant evidence of it in the popular article. While you may deduce something of the intellectual turn of mind from the way in which writers express themselves, you can know practically nothing of their private experiences, thoughts, tastes, values. That is to say, the popular article is communication rather than self-expression.

However, the author, in adapting his diction and syntax to the subject and reader, does make stylistic decisions: an article on karate will not use the same language as one written on early eighteenth-century formal gardens; nor will an article on how to roast a wild duck be written in the same way for a woman's magazine as for a man's. But knowing even a great deal about the subject and reader does not provide all the stylistic answers. Authors must finally choose their own manner of speaking: an article on poverty may be tough, hard-hitting, angry, or it may be tender, pathetic, sad.

The popular article is of uncertain origin. A form of journalistic prose, its fortunes have been linked with those of the newspaper and magazine. While the article was no doubt a feature of the eighteenth-century periodical, in no century has it been so dominant as in the present. Many regret the tendency for the popular article to replace the essay, sketch, short story, and other more literary forms; but others obviously appreciate the factual and topical article. For better or worse, it has become the dominant prose form of the twentieth century and is largely a product of the twentieth century. The popular article is, indeed, much too widely read and influential a form to be taken lightly. And many competent writers are for one reason or another attracted to the form, even though it carries with it a certain anonymity: the popular article, because it is current, is apt to become dated or irrelevant with the passing of time; the perishable nature of a newspaper or magazine works against the authors' lasting reputations; and even though most articles are signed, authors reveal so little of themselves that we are, indeed, apt to forget that each one was written by a skillful and discriminating personality. But the enthusiasm of the reading audience for popular articles on science, history, biography, travel, national and international affairs, domestic and office problems will continue to attract competent writers—especially those who wish to improve society by educating and informing the public.

HOW TO WRITE THE POPULAR ARTICLE

Because it is written with journalistic fidelity to fact and would communicate detailed truth to a reader in the most compelling way, considerable planning is involved in writing the popular article. Indeed, method is more important than sheer writing ability.

1. Even though you may already have a subject in mind, you must at the outset *form the clearest possible picture of your reader.* Your article will never find its audience unless you find it first—before the article is written. There are two ways of getting to know your reader: First, take whatever opportunities come along to learn the interests, tastes, values, motives, prejudices, hopes, fears of the class of people to which you expect to address yourself—sound people out on these subjects, try putting yourself in their place to look at life through their eyes, cultivate the arts of listening and observing. And second, study the ways in which well-edited magazines appeal to what they consider their particular audience. You must become a kind of arm-chair psychologist and social scientist, a student of at least a part of the human race.

2. *Look about for subjects that would likely interest such a class of readers.* Biography, history, travel and places, scientific progress, useful information, how-to-do-it, exposés or other controversial matters are all areas to consider. The best subjects are suggested by personal experience (college classes, hobbies, work) and by reading (many times another popular article which left you with a desire to know more). And the best subjects are often near at hand. The impression that articles are most often written on odd and unusual subjects is a false one. The great majority are on surprisingly familiar and commonplace subjects—revealed, to be sure, in a new light. Readers of popular articles are persons of mundane interests. Their preoccupations are with this world and this life of theirs. You must, of course, make a point of telling them something they do not already know, or they will not consider reading on. But the subject itself must be something they immediately recognize as timely and relevant to their experience.

3. *Appraise your reader's interest in this particular subject.* There are three important reasons for making such a check: to see if the subject is worth pursuing, to decide what aspect to take up, and to decide how to approach it. For each article assignment, at least until you are somewhat experienced, make a brief written analysis of your prospective reader. Include age, sex, cultural level, previous knowl-

edge, appeals the subject holds for the reader, and any other pertinent information. (If the popular article is to be turned in as an assignment, be sure it is accompanied by this description of the reader—especially if the article is not written for the class of readers represented by the students and the instructor.) Most of your planning will be based on what this reveals about your reader's relation to the subject.

4. Now you are ready to *decide what the specific subject and thesis will be.* Every article has a definite subject, a topic you can explore for this reader in this many pages in a satisfying way. Remember, the popular article relies on facts and illustrations; be sure that your subject is restricted enough that you can concentrate on specific details rather than generalizations. And every article has, for the sake of unity and purpose, a definite thesis, a statement which sums up the central idea of your article in a single sentence. If, for example, you wished to write a popular article on the early days of aviation, you might choose as your subject, "Wiley Post," and as your tentative thesis, "In proving the usefulness of the automatic pilot, radio direction finder, variable pitch propeller, and other systems, Wiley Post became the first of the world's true scientific test pilots." The thesis of a popular article is usually fresh and provocative. It would be pointless for it to be self-evident, though a general truth is sometimes worth expressing if the specific illustrations are sufficiently interesting. There is rarely any reason to be indirect in stating the thesis, unless the article is on an extremely controversial subject, and defends or proposes the unpopular view, or unless good taste forbids too explicit phrasing of the thesis—but exceptions to a matter-of-fact statement of the thesis are extremely rare. In any case, write out the thesis now, clearly and specifically. See if you can come up with a simple declarative sentence that not only names and limits the subject, but summarizes and concludes the entire article as well.

5. Since the popular article is factual and informative, you will undoubtedly have to *do a certain amount of information gathering.* The subject itself may have been suggested by some personal observation or experience, but unless you are an expert writing about your speciality, you will have to gather more material before going any further in your planning. Begin by taking inventory of what you already know about the subject. From there contrive how to get the information you need. Perhaps the library can supply all you need to know, but the writer of popular articles must often ask questions, interview, simply go and see for himself. Remember this about the popular article: while facts and figures are essential, details which stimulate human interest are equally important. So in gathering information about the subject, look for anecdotes, analogies, illustrations, examples that will lead the reader to appreciate the implica-

tions of the facts in familiar human situations and thereby vivify and enliven the article.

6. You may find it useful to *make a quick preliminary or inventory outline*. While this will not be quite the shape the article finally takes, such a brief outline will indicate where you need to fill out your popular article by gathering information. And even at this stage you should begin thinking of the five, six, or seven topics upon which the article will be based. A popular article on shell collecting, for example, could easily be written around these topics:

> Beginning: The simple beauty of seashells—shape and texture, color and pattern. Thesis: The seashell has, because of its simple and evocative beauty and the ease with which it is preserved and displayed, long been valued by collectors of natural objects.
>
> Common but beautiful shells
>
> Rare and valuable shells
>
> The earliest "collectors" (shells as utensils, currency, decoration, and objects of worship)
>
> The beginning of serious shell collecting in the seventeenth century
>
> Ending: the modern collector

7. After the brief outline comes *the full outline*. An outline holds you to a plan, presents the results of your research and other preliminary thinking in the most accessible way, discloses any major weakness in your conception of the article at a stage where it can be most easily corrected. The more extensive the outline the better—a noun-phrase or sentence outline will serve you best.

This outline is, of course, predicated on some knowledge of the popular article as a form. While you will not actually use these terms, it is useful to outline your article in terms of its beginning, middle, and end, with the proportions of something between 1:3:1 and 1:9:1.

8. The *beginning* of a popular article is almost invariably direct, it identifies the subject and in almost every case states the thesis without any delay. Professional writers speak of the beginning of a popular article as having two parts: the "lead" and the "transition." The *lead* is an arresting allusion to the subject and perhaps the thesis, one which at the same time demonstrates their relevance to the reader's experience. It may be a forceful statement, a pointed question, a quick summary, a provocative description or narrative—any-

thing that is reasonably striking and to the point. Some leads, like the following paragraph, are fairly dramatic.

It strikes without warning, usually before dawn, jolting its victim awake. Throbbing pulses of pain grip his big toe. Instinctively, he flexes his joint, only to feel the stabbing, searing pains shoot up his leg. Now the slightest movements, even the vibrations of a passing car, provoke new surges of anguish. And he knows, if he has suffered through similar attacks, that he is in for days— perhaps weeks—of continuous torture.—Albert Q. Maisel, An End, at Last, to Gout?

Obvious tricks to shock the reader into attention will not win you an audience—but neither will a flat, pedestrian lead. The *transition* does just what the term implies: it leads the reader into the discussion, the body of the article. Often you will need to explain the connection between the lead—which looks ahead to the article's conclusion—and the point at which you begin the article proper. At any rate, in the beginning you want to focus the reader's attention on the subject of your article and suggest what direction it will take.

In the following beginning of a popular article, the narrative account of a Mount Everest climb, the first paragraph constitutes the lead and the second the transition. "From my delicate perch I surveyed the rock above . . ." suggests the subject, mountain climbing. And "In a few days I would be leaving for Everest . . . to plumb that grey area near one's limits . . ." indicates for the reader the direction the article will take.

From my delicate perch I surveyed the rock above me. It swept up narrowing to a ridge as it steepened. Beautiful! I gauged the dropoffs to my left and right. Both lethal. Far below I could just hear the clock tower bells ringing on the University of Colorado campus at Boulder. I was running late. In 10 minutes my lunch hour would be over and I should be back at my desk. Never mind all that now; this rock was more important.

In a few days I would be leaving for Everest. It had been a lifelong dream of mine to plumb that gray area near one's limits, and succeed. So when a chance to go to Everest came, I accepted with enthusiasm. In addition to all the work of assembling our food and equipment, I had spent a great deal of time preparing myself both mentally and physically. Since January I had climbed 94 peaks, run 600 miles, mostly on rough mountain trails, chinned myself more than 4,000 times on that hated bar behind the house, done 10,000 sit-ups and 34,000 squeezes with those silly hand grips. I felt ready.—Gerard Roach, Robert Cormac, Dee B. Crouch, Everybody's Everest

9. The *middle* of the popular article is, of course, that comparatively lengthy section in which the main work of the article is done.

The materials are selected and arranged according to your purpose and your appraisal of the reader. Although you will not go about it with quite the directness of the newspaper reporter, the who-what-when-where-why-how of your subject now becomes imperative. The popular article is, after all, informative prose. The subject itself may suggest an approach; most by their very nature imply one of the traditional forms of order: spatial, chronological, cause-and-effect, emphatic. But often you have an alternative, and to say anything new on any subject you may need to consider something other than the inevitable. And certainly you will try to arrange your materials in terms of increasing relevance and importance, the earlier topics being for the most part preliminary to the later ones.

But the greatest problem for most writers is striking the right balance between generalizations and particulars. For example, while statistics are more significant than individual cases, most readers find the latter more appealing. The proportion depends on the subject and the reader, but certainly whatever you wish to say in a popular article must be projected largely as illustrations, examples, anecdotes, details which involve the reader in a way abstract generalizations could not. Throughout the middle you will alternate between the two ways of presenting information to keep the article varied and interesting, a statistic or other generalization followed by one or more specific illustrations. Too much generalization will lose your readers; too much specific detail will lose the overall conception of your subject. The more informed and motivated your readers, the better equipped they will be to absorb statistics and other generalizations. But every effective article must be richly provided with specific detail.

Notice in the following two paragraphs from the middle of a popular article how each generalization is clearly illustrated:

The test to be applied, when a new word is suggested or it is sought to give an old word a new meaning, is this: Does the change enrich the language? The easiest and silliest way in which to impoverish the language is to misuse a good existing word that conveys a clear and precise meaning and thereby to destroy that meaning and render the word useless. This is what Americans have done by using "alibi" when they mean "excuse." An alibi can never be an excuse, and an excuse can never be an alibi. A man pleads an alibi when he denies that he did an act and says that he could not have done it, since he was elsewhere (alibi) at the time. By an excuse, on the other hand, he admits the act, but says there was a good reason for it. The distinction should really not be too difficult for the ordinary intelligence to grasp. The misuse is a barbarism which has made the language poorer by depriving it of a once-useful word. It is like spoiling a chisel by using it as a screwdriver. It is linguistic murder.

Let me pass from American murder to American pretentious illiteracy;

from the destruction of an old word to the invention of a new word which clear-ly cannot bear the meaning assigned to it. "Underprivileged" is the leading ex-ample. This word appears to be used as a synonym for "poor," a word which strikes many Americans as mildly improper, though I do not know whether they propose to rewrite the Beatitudes. I have found in many conversations that, while they understand the criticism that the word "underprivileged" is preten-tious, they do not see immediately that it is illiterate, but it demonstrably is. A privilege is a special advantage which one person has over another or one class over another class. It is an inequality before the law. An underprivileged person must mean a person who has not enough privilege—a person, that is to say, who has not enough advantage over his neighbor. To pretend that you are in fa-vor of equality before the law and then to use a word which complains that there is not enough inequality seems to me to exceed the stupidity limit.—Lord Conesford, You Americans Are Murdering the Language

And notice the richly detailed development in this paragraph of the generalization "we cook everything thoroughly."

Although Southern dishes can vary significantly from state to state, there are certain principles that all Southerners have in common. For example, we cook everything thoroughly, from meat to vegetables to fish and hot desserts. But there is a reason, and a logical one. We must have rich flavor in everything we eat, rejecting any dish that is bland and that has not been enriched through a long cooking process by the addition of fats, oils, sugars and pungent spices. Also, ex-cept in rare instances, we demand that food be tender and easily digestible, as with a well-cooked rump roast, a "mess" of collard greens, dry rice, or an al-most liquid cobbler. When in the South, I cannot imagine eating string beans (preferably the superior Kentucky Wonder), turnip greens or black-eyed peas that have not simmered for hours with a piece of ham hock or a streak of lean (cured) hog's meat. What South Carolina housewife would take a highly sea-soned peach pie (made, of course, with Elbertas) out of the oven until the juices flowed over the sides and the crust was almost falling apart? What New Orle-ans black chef would not allow enough time for his fresh shrimp, crawfish, to-matoes, onions, herbs and pork sausage to blend into the rich stew that, when mixed with Louisiana rice, becomes the celebrated jambalaya? And who in Georgia would even so much as taste an okra soup in which the vegetable did not live up to its local appellation of "limping Susan"? Southerners may destroy much of the natural flavor of food by overcooking and overcuring, but in the pro-cess they create a cuisine that is both delicious and unique.—James Villas, The Truth about Southern Cooking

10. The *ending* either summarizes or concludes the article. If it is a summary ending, it should not be a tedious repetition, but a quick and revealing epitome, fresh because the reader sees for the first time the summation of the whole. If it is a conclusion ending, it

will of necessity be something new. Whichever ending you use, summary or conclusion, the nucleus of the ending is the restatement of the thesis. Having said it at least once before, at the beginning, this final statement of the thesis should certainly be more emphatic and sweeping. You may choose to end the article here, or you may go on to show that the thesis illustrates some greater truth about life, or you may vividly remind your reader of the relevance of the thesis by concluding with some illustrative material or an anecdote. Here are two endings—the first is a short summary ending:

It is certainly true that young people, speaking in a language of their own out of their special isolated world, have concepts different from ours with respect to love, marriage, work, war, racial relations, education, time, money, and whatever it is we mean when we speak of the American Way of Life. But the fact that their concepts are different does not always mean that they are correct, or even that the youngsters who espouse them actually believe in them. Like as not, the young people are trying to test them, and in any case our response cannot simply be to be scandalized and go "arrgh," but rather to try to figure out who these new people are, and how they got that way, and what they are saying that might be valuable; to give them the listening ear they most often badly need, and tell them what we think as plainly and as honestly as we can, whether they will like it or not.

It is not always easy to do this when a language barrier exists and when the concepts seem so different, but the fact that it is difficult to do something does not always mean that it is unnecessary to do it. And that, by the way, is a concept a good many young people seem never to have considered.—John Keats, Talking across the Generation Barrier

The second is a short conclusion ending:

Our studies thus far indicate that the moose and wolf populations on Isle Royale have struck a reasonably good balance. It seems likely that, for decades to come, the voice of primitive America will still be heard on winter nights on a remote wilderness island in Lake Superior.—Durward L. Allen and L. David Mech, Wolves versus Moose on Isle Royale

11. Now *look over your beginning, middle, and ending as you have outlined them.* Every idea and example should be accounted for. The transformation of an outline into an article is purely verbal. You will add some minor details, to be sure, but most of the expansion will be a result of your having added the words necessary to making an effective and pleasing prose statement. In short, it should be patently clear from the outline exactly what you will be writing at every point. To do this your outline will probably have to be from one-third to one-half as long as the final article.

As you assess the usefulness of your outline ask yourself these pertinent questions: First, is it all there? Outlines are naturally sketchy, but many times they are so far short of suggesting how an adequately developed article is to be written that they need to be expanded. You may need to expand your treatment of the subject *horizontally,* by adding on other related ideas, as in the following paragraph:

However, in Arizona today, and to a lesser extent in Alaska and elsewhere, everybody wants dams, or thinks he wants dams, like a panacea, or religion—to guarantee a better life, thus inducing increased bank deposits, freeway construction, congestion and sprawl. Where there should be fundamental research into problems of water storage and comprehensive long-range planning, political hysterics prevail. Harnessing natural features and improving upon rivers represent man's splendid ingenuity, beyond a doubt. But the greater ingenuity is to show that man can survive while leaving some few features of the earth to their own devices. This is the true test of our mechanical, intellectual and moral skills.— Michael Frome, The Politics of Conservation

Or you may need to expand *vertically,* by going into the idea (analysis, detail, illustration), as in this paragraph:

The social scientists have helped to make the U.S. the most self-analytic civilization ever known. Rome was not conscious of the "fall of the Roman Empire"; the Crusaders scarcely analyzed the infectious new ideas they brought back from the East; the romantics wrote new kinds of poetry, but did not turn out essays on the alarming death wishes in those poems. Americans cannot make a move without having it declared a trend, viewed critically in innumerable books deploring The Lonely Crowd, The Status Seekers, The Organization Man. *The exhortations offered to the U.S. public are always contradictory. No sooner had Americans learned that they must not be rugged individualists but must practice "adjustment," than they were told that they were all turning into conformists. No sooner had they learned that children must be raised progressively and permissively than they were told that children desperately want discipline. No sooner had they accepted the fact that women deserved and needed equal rights than they were informed that women had become too much like men.—* The Anatomy of *Angst,* Time

Also you may have started or stopped too soon and dealt with too few events or ideas; or you may have skipped over certain events or ideas essential to the sequence. Second, is it in the right order? Whatever scheme of order you choose, be sure that it is reasonable in view of the subject and your purposes, and that you stick to it. The reader should feel a sense of inevitability in the way these thoughts occur in this order. And third, is the relation of topics or parts clear? Later on you will have to worry about the smoothness of your transitions, but transitions can't do everything. At this point make sure that the ideas are such the reader can move easily from one to the next.

12. Since you are working from a rather extensive outline, you will need only *flesh out the discussion and add transitions to have a rough draft.* Follow the outline closely. If it proves inadequate, you had better revise the outline before going any further with your writing. But don't be bound by the tentative and abbreviated style of the outline. Even if you are working from a sentence outline, you should find yourself translating even those sentences into something more elaborate and felicitous.

See to it that every sentence is connected to the sentence that follows and the sentence that precedes, and that every paragraph is connected to the paragraphs that precede and follow, and that every major unit of the design and order of the article is connected with the preceding unit and with the following unit. A connection, or transition, must be of size enough to serve the units being connected. A single word may connect one sentence with another, even one short paragraph with another. But a unit of several paragraphs may need an entire sentence to connect to another unit of several para- graphs. In longer essays, paragraphs themselves may become transi- tional and connective.

13. Undoubtedly you have given some thought to a *title* before now, but this is a good time to do so seriously. The best titles for popular articles are short (ideally two or three words), descriptive, and provocative. But since the most descriptive titles are rarely short, you will probably find yourself compromising. Try one and then another, listening to the sound of it each time, until you come up with something that would be consistent with the article's pur- pose and at the same time would stimulate a browsing reader to pick it up.

14. Although you have kept the reader in mind all along, *take a critical look at the article you have written and the audience that will read it—* asking yourself, is it everywhere absolutely clear and compelling reading? Vagueness and dullness are death to the popular article. And these are not conditions you can recognize in your own work unless you can put yourself in the reader's place. Of all readers, yours are the most critical because they relate the article to their own experience and to the world's realities, expecting to discover something that is useful and true.

THE WHOLE COMPOSITION

The following popular article on John Benson, America's "finest sto- necutter and calligrapher," whose shop "may also be the oldest continuous business on the continent that still operates at its original site," combines several topics characteristic of the form. Readers of popular articles are especially attracted to personalities, to skills, to success, to arts and crafts, to history and tradition, and the like. And its objectives, not only to inform but to stimulate an appreciation, are familiar as well. "Life In Stone: A Young Master's Antique Art" exemplifies the best aspects of the popular article.

Life in Stone: A Young Master's Antique Art

Philip Kopper

John Benson lives in a drab house on a narrow street beside the Common Burying Ground in Newport, Rhode Island. His bedroom offers two views of the chic little city's hoariest graveyard, which he considers "beautiful, a friendly place." Just as operating rooms hold no terror for surgeons, boneyards don't spook Benson, whose work is often meant for cemeteries. He is, by all accounts, America's finest stonecutter and calligrapher.

Benson carved the Kennedy graves at Arlington, John D. Jr.'s gilt *credo* at Rockefeller Center, and the name over the new doors of the Boston Public Library. While hand-carved tombstones are his long suit, he also deals in memorial tablets for churches and schools, campus signs, mottoes for courthouse lobbies and corporate headquarters, and alphabet stones for esoteric collectors. He designed the National Geographic Society's lintel, West Point's MacArthur Memorial, and the back of a National Gallery of Art medal. Monumental or minute, his work is found across the nation.

Why does a modern young man practice the exacting, antique art of carving rocks? (Why did Hillary climb them?) At 36, Benson does it for love, money, and "the old pleasure center—the sexual rush" that comes with creating or contemplating something of rare beauty. He is quite serious about the Pleasure Center Principle, citing neurologists who say that both aesthetic excitement and sensual feeling occur in the same part of the human brain. He also quotes Veronese: "Given a large canvas, I enriched it as I saw fit."

A few months ago the brick-floored workroom in his shop contained a typical pair of major works in progress: polished slabs that fit together to name the New York State officials responsible for Albany Mall; and a big, black, gold-lettered pedestal to support Secretariat's statue at Belmont Park Race Track. At the same time, wooden tablets for a new Harvard library were being delicately cut upstairs under the 18th-century eaves.

Meanwhile, working between a wall of books on art, history, heraldry, lettering, etc., and an empty wall of rough white boards bearing a few antique stone shards, Benson designed his backlog of gravestones. "They're simple, well-established objects," he said. "All you can do is try to make the lettering as beautiful as you can. And that's a darlin' way to spend a day or two."

The work has nothing to do with death or afterlife. Asked for a theological opinion, Benson answered, "You die and you rot. . . . I believe in a great reservoir of human endeavor found in handmade relics of the past. You go back into that." A museum is such a reservoir, he said. "And that's what a graveyard is. Finest kind."

He treasures long-lasting objects in which "the concept and the material are one." Examples: handmade books; a machinist's vise some journeyman wrought a century ago; a stone fragment inscribed "In Memory of FREELOVE, Wife of MR. DANIEL VAUGHAN," who died in 1772. These objects say to him that their makers valued two things: utility, which is necessary, and beauty, which needn't be at all. His chosen profession is to combine the two.

Although John Benson is undoubtedly the best in his artful business today, he's the first to admit "there isn't much competition." Inheritor of the John Stevens Shop, he runs the only place in the nation where letters are still designed, laid out, and carved by hand. Thanks to two dynasties of Johns, the shop may also be the oldest continuous business on the continent that still operates at its original site.

The first John Stevens was born in Oxfordshire in 1646 and sailed for America in 1700. He began cutting stone in Newport four or five years later and built the shed that grew into the present building. His death's-head decorations seem gruesome now. Both his lettering and his spelling were irregular, cacographic. John Stevens died at 90, to be succeeded by a namesake son and grandson who carved cherubs and portraits instead of skulls on the native stone markers that John Benson's bedroom overlooks today.

"John II," as the founder's son now is called around the shop, was a fine artist. He developed a lovely alphabet of classic capitals and graceful lower-case letters whose curves were formed naturally by the way a hand-held chisel touches stone. "John III," the founder's grandson, copied ornate Baskerville letters from the latest books that reached the colonies. Priding himself on work "performed in the neatest and most elegant manner," John III hacked out hearths and printers' stones as well as gravestones. He accepted payment in "country produce or West Indies and dry goods," according to a newspaper notice of 1781.

"John III" was succeeded by his son Philip and two grandsons until the fifth generation of stonecutting Stevenses died out in 1900. Then the family business was taken over by a brother-in-law who hammered on until 1929, when he hired a remarkable apprentice and soon after died in his sleep. The apprentice, a native Newporter who'd studied at the Art Students League, bought the shop for $1,200 and established the second dynasty of Johns.

John Howard Benson became a legendary designer, calligrapher, carver, and teacher at the Rhode Island School of Design. A Catholic convert, self-taught scholar, and eccentric, he translated Italian Renaissance books and rediscovered ancient techniques for inscribing both paper and stone. Robert Flaherty filmed him for a documentary. The Academy of Arts and Sciences elected him to membership. Yale gave him an honorary degree. His likeness hangs in the National Portrait Gallery because Director Marvin Sadik believes "John Howard Benson was the greatest American ever to design and carve letters in stone—unless Fud is now."

"Fud," a.k.a. John Everett Benson, is John Howard Benson's son. He worked in the shop for one summer before his father died in 1955. After prep school at Portsmouth Priory, he studied sculpture at RISD and in Italy. When he graduated (with honors) he was already married and a father himself; he needed a job. His mother had kept the shop afloat, but it was doomed without a master craftsman and artistic designer. John, the second of three sons, had the manual skills, the grounding in art and art history, his father's inspired example, and the curiosity to learn lettering, which once bored him.

A perfectionist, he succeeded after some "horrendous" tangents, including "my blunderbuss Roman period." Leonard Baskin, the artist and designer, is one of the many experts who believe unconditionally that Benson *fils* has surpassed his once peerless *père*. "There's a fantastic strength and grace in his letters. That's what it's all about," says Baskin.

(The differences between good lettering and great calligraphy are as hard to nail down as the relative merits of vintage wines from neighboring Grand Cru vineyards. Calligraphic criteria are almost indescribably subtle, in part because they've been refined for so many centuries. The tradition dates back notably to Trajan's Column of A.D. 113, a Roman inscription that is to our letters what Moses' caveats are to modern law.)

Marvin Sadik says of Benson's work that "its ornamentation and legibility are one and inseparable." Benson says the challenge is "to do more and more with less and less," an idea not to be confused with the nonsense that "less is more." Were that the case, Crayola scribbles would suffice. Benson is an artist whose creative work involves a deep understanding of graphics and the deft skills of a disciplined artisan.

The actual chiseling of stone is only part of it. First he roughs out a design and refines it several times. Then a full-scale rendering is painted on paper, because a brush makes more plastic lines than pen or pencil to lend a grace that survives in the chiseled stone. The entire design is transferred to the stone with carbon paper and painted free-hand again before the carving begins.

Each step in the process includes small refinements. Even during the carving a space may be widened, the curve of a serif tightened in a "John Stevens Lower Case" letter, or the sweep of a curlicue extended to enhance cursive words. "You should get reinforcement at every stage of the game," Benson says. "The most fun is in the finishing."

He strikes two or three times a second—gentle taps—his left hand guiding the chisel at a constant angle along a painted letter's edge. The other side of the line is cut at the reverse angle to make a mitered groove, a V-cut of less than 90°. The chisel leaves light marks along the faces of the groove and there is a clear center line where the two faces meet. Since the cutting angles are constant, thick letters are deeper than hairline ligatures. All cuts would be the same depth if cutting angles varied, but different angles cause irregular shadows and spoil the visual unity.

By way of comparison, the typical epitaph on a Rock of Ages is sandblasted through cookie-cutter holes punched in a rubber sheet that protects the rest of the glossy stone. At close range such letters look like hard-edged pockmarks. Elsewhere, electric chisels— miniature jackhammers—speedily chip out shapes drawn with stencils. Still elsewhere, tablets are cast in bronze or iron with movable foundry type spaced as rigidly as street signs. These run-of-the-mill methods are economical and efficient. Relatively speaking, Benson's art is slow and expensive. For a simple headstone with name, dates, and a few words, he charges upwards of $800, about three times what some cemeteries charge just to dig a hole and fill it up again. Most of a stone's cost is in carving time at $16/hour. He pays himself barely twice as well as a union gravedigger.

Cost analysts would carp at the redundant steps in Benson's process, and some clients complain about the slow pace. Yet it is the best way to approach the perfection he seeks. As for mistakes, "We don't break out the center of an 'O' very often." But spelling can cause trouble. Though several mighty scholars approved layouts and renderings of one large tablet, a word lacked a letter when it was ceremoniously unveiled. Benson had to grind down the entire line by hand to correct the reminder of a famous library's "aquisition."

Time has a different rhythm in the shop on Thames Street in Newport's historical district. The antique clock on the office wall stopped at 4:42 years ago. There is no radio nattering out popular tunes, ads, and hourly news. This is a particularly quiet place.

Sometimes there is the feathery sound—inaudible two feet away—of wood chisels slicing birch. More often there is the bright tapping of carbide-steel stone chisels being struck lightly with a mallet, mell, or dummy. "The names aren't important," Benson confides. "We think of them as things to hit chisels with." ("We" includes Brooke Roberts, a summer helper who turned full-timer after graduating from college three years ago, and yet another John. Benson's contemporary and colleague for a dozen years, John Hegnauer is "the fastest chisel in the shop." An exceptionally skilled carver, he is a designer too.)

Once I watched Benson spend a day carving a seven-inch cross to match an existing marker. Then he passed several hours chipping away millimeters of stone around the cross until it emerged in relief. Then he spent most of an afternoon hand-polishing the surface with slivers of whetstone (because machine buffers leave scars). Tedious work? "When a job's finished, it no longer matters how much time it took." Unredeemable, time passes whether wasted or well spent.

A stone in Washington reflects Benson's view of stone letters and time. A memorial to diplomats who died in service, its original text read "their sacrifice *shall not be* forgotten." Benson declined the job until the words were changed, arguing that the purpose of a stone inscription is to be read for generations. He carved "their sacrifice *is* not forgotten." Slate holds the present tense nicely for centuries on end.

This stone shows "the infinite grace of the individual letter forms," wrote the art director of the Agency of International Development, Daniel F. Shea. The alphabet is a variant of Roman capitals with the slightest serifs. Examined closely, straight lines vanish; the top of each "T," for example, curves slightly and tapers. Vertical strokes broaden at both ends. The periods are perfect geometric diamonds, each composed of four triangular cuts that meet at a single apex like an intaglio pyramid. It is perfect writing flawlessly carved.

In contrast, Benson's carving for John F. Kennedy's grave is notable for its distortions. Though Arlington National Cemetery guides swear the letters are all regular, rubbings show them to be awkwardly tall. Neither parallel nor aligned, some of them are half again as large as others. All this is because they were cut in a sort of crescent tilted up on chopped-off ends, a stone surface that curves and slants. Seen straight on, the letters are misshapen; but nobody was supposed to see them dead ahead—you can't without a ladder.

Benson canceled the visually distorting effect of the surface's slant with elongated letters. Then he coped with the problem of putting something flat on a curved surface. (Mapmakers solve the opposite problem by using various projections to describe the earth's round surface on a flat page.) Words in straight lines would look clumsy, so the writing had to curve too. Because the surface's top edge curves less sharply than the bottom edge, each successive line of writing had to bend more sharply than the one above it. Finally, separate quotations (and the letters within them) had to grow imperceptibly larger toward the deep center of the crescent surface to make each letter fill the same fraction of the space.

Using invented tools, scale models, and mock-ups, Benson developed a unified design, which the architect and the President's widow came to Newport to approve. Hegnauer recalls that the visit prompted one of Benson's few bows to convention. "He went home and put on clean bellbottoms," a gesture Benson doesn't brag about.

If he is no longer perfectly pleased with his design solution, Benson doesn't regret the words he carved here—which is not always the case. Sometimes a commissioned text is enough to make stone curl, as when certain tastemakers wanted to remember one of their own as the "unstoppable visionary." Then there was a memorial to a "great pastor of Christian people whose vision penetrates the disturbances created by a new age engulfing the world in a divided Christendom." Verbiage like that can give lapidary calligraphy a bad reputation. Hegnauer's response is a tablet design that says "Writers in stone learn brevity."

The John Stevens Shop is not famous for composing texts. The crew fretted about one epitaph for so long that somebody finally suggested just carving "He stepped in front of a bus." When Benson was commissioned to design an alphabet for Washington's National Cathedral signs, he offered a fine dividend as well, a borrowed alphabetic sentence: "SPHINX OF BLACK QUARTZ JUDGE MY VOW." It is only three characters away from perfection, since it uses just three letters more than once. (By comparison, "The quick brown fox" takes 15 surplus letters to finish its business of using the entire alphabet in a cogent sentence.)

Benson tries to do everything perfectly. Last summer, for instance, he launched a lobstering venture with a friend and his major contribution to the effort was to weave rope "heads" for the lobster pots. Not content with the conventional, asymmetrically woven trap ends, he spent a week's coffee breaks and many evenings trying to invent a simpler, purer design—even though it wouldn't make a fishhead's difference to the lobsters.

By the same token, he's thinking of having "the finest tattoo in the Western world" drawn on his shoulder—a Viking beast struggling Laocoön-like with two mythical serpents. The design is borrowed from an ancient Scandinavian carving, and he'll make a stencil for his exterior decorator to follow exactly. Furthermore, the tattooist will work with a single needle, not the normal three-needle tool that makes lines too thick for this tattooee's practiced eye.

Sometimes Benson designs medals in precious metals for learned organizations, i.e., the National Gallery and the International Society on Thrombosis and Haemostasis. When the Franklin Mint held competitions for Bicentennial medals in every state, he entered and beat out 130 other Rhode Islanders for the $5,000 prize. He says the mint tampered with his design, but it still stands out from the other 49.

When the world's "tall ships" gathered in Newport, Benson contributed a compelling logo to the project, an abstract square-rigger seen bow-on. Plastered on posters all over town, it was later reproduced several million times on neckties, cigarette lighters, and the like. Visually addictive, it earned five-digit royalties for the event.

Benson has a mania for authenticity. A confessed "saloon singer," he appeared with friends at the Smithsonian Institution's Folklife Festival two years running. The group sang work songs, and to make the music make sense they hoisted a thousand-pound hunk of concrete with block and tackle in time to their sea chanteys.

Knee-jerk "progress" appalls him as much as gratuitous ugliness. Doris Duke bankrolled much fine restoration around Newport, then topped her mansion walls with barbed wire and floodlights. Goat Island, offshore from the 18th-century captain's house where Benson's mother still lives, is sprouting condominiums in the shadow of a massive modern hotel that looks like a derelict coal mine. An oddly comfortable century-old part of town was razed for tourist traffic and Benson fumes, "They destroyed the scale of the waterfront. It's not even honest whoring, not even hot dog stands, but boutiques."

He detests massive trash and minute artsy crafts, regarding both as mindless, undisciplined, and ugly. They insult a creative work ethic that had various flowerings—in 14th-century English architecture and American Revolution furniture. "The thing I'm talking about stopped on a national scale with the death of feudalism and the Renaissance. The Industrial Revolution is the real culprit." It made pride in individual work largely superfluous. Too many people are in current crafts movements for the wrong reasons, he says, for money, escapism, or the romance of it all.

The only right reason, so far as he's concerned, is a dedication to understanding the traditions of a medium, learning a craft's demanding techniques, and practicing the discipline of a creative art. "A beehive is beautiful because it's made by critters who ask nothing more than to be allowed to make beehives." The boutique merchants he hates are "trafficking in the arts," slapping gewgaws together out of whim, plastic, and Elmer's Glue-All.

In a manmade object he looks for natural relationships between materials, the way it is made, and its purpose. "When you make a quill pen you pick a primary feather from the right wing of a goose, because its curve fits the right hand." It works beautifully because what it is used for—writing—evolved with and from the object itself.

He has learned many skills from books and aging artisans, including how to rebuild violins. Still, he finds himself reinventing the wheel too often, to his own puzzlement, because "it doesn't occur to me there's something I don't know or can't figure out."

Bullheaded, he also has a mystical streak. Many people appreciate the idea that well-made things are to be valued because the maker's skill is palpable in them. Benson carries the notion a step further: creativity exudes something that can be physically absorbed. He quietly asserts that the John Stevens Shop resonates with the energy of the artists and artisans who have worked there for more than two and a half centuries. I agree, but can't explain it: the place has a rare ambience coming from the hand-hewn beams and random-width boards. There is a quiet presence, an echoing sense of purpose.

Looking ahead, Benson imagines he'll keep on doing what he's done for 15 years to make a modest living. He might limit his clientele to people of taste and vision, but the small market doesn't allow him to be too choosy. Beyond that, he wants to get in on the ground floor of more architectural work. He'd like to design all the graphics for a large building, from the parking lot signs to the "Push" on the lavatory doors, from the label outside the executive suite to the name inscribed on the lintel, if only he could find a client with "the courage of my convictions."

He has thought about his own gravestone, which John Hegnauer will carve for him. The writing will be in oghams, fifth-century Irish characters formed of straight lines along the corner of a stone. It seems the simplest form of writing in the world—words can't be written with any less. Few people can read it (without a source book in hand like Webster's Third International). But that might be just as well, since John Edward Benson's epitaph will say something about ⊢ and ⊣

Tracking the Common Burying Ground under a low gray sky, he gestured to the quarry of weathered stones—among them John I's death's-heads, John II's out-of-plumb cherubs, John III's fat letters, and John Howard Benson's simple slate marker. "Infinite stones set artificially for so long," John V said. "It has become an environment, a natural place with time and the lichens. It's beautiful, all this rock.'

EXERCISES

1. Go to the periodical department of your library, and look at several issues of the same magazine published during the last twenty years, e.g. the January, odd-year issues of *The Atlantic Monthly*. What percentage of the fare is made up of popular articles and what percentage is fiction? Has the proportion changed during that time?

2. From a study of the advertising in a particular magazine, to what kind of reading audience do you think the magazine is intended to appeal?

3. Write the same basic article for two distinctly different reading audiences.

4. Study a popular article you especially admire. Make a list of how and where you think the writer got each piece of information, "personal experience," "interview," "library research," etc.

5. See if you can turn an encyclopedia article or textbook discussion into an interesting popular article. What examples or illustrations would you probably have to bring from elsewhere in order to make the article compelling reading?

6. Make a structural analysis of a short published popular article, identifying the lead, the transition, the middle, the ending with marginal brackets; circling each clear statement of the thesis; marking statements of general fact with double underlinings and specific details (examples, illustrations, anecdotes, etc.) with a single underlining.

7. List some articles you were led to read principally because of their titles. What about those titles attracted you? Find articles with titles that you think are misleading in one way or another. (The common fault is overstatement, implying that the article and subject are more earth-shaking than they could possibly be.)

8. Read only the first paragraphs of several popular articles. Which of the articles do you really want to finish? What about those leads attracted you? (Of course, most often you choose to read or not read an article because of its

subject; but in a surprising number of instances the real deciding factor is not the subject but how it is introduced.)

9. Find two popular articles on the same subject, one decidedly inferior to the other. List all the reasons why you find the second article inferior. Or if you prefer, list all the reasons why you find the first article superior.

10. Now, in view of what you have learned about the popular article, write such a prose form following as nearly as possible the described procedure.

17. THE PROFESSIONAL ARTICLE

We have all written variants of the *professional article* in the form of term papers, research papers, and the like. And many of us are planning for careers in which some version of the professional article will be a most familiar writing task. No other prose possesses such a definite pattern, so established a set of conventions and procedures—this to emphasize the data, reasoning, and conclusions. Yet the form lends itself to a range of intellectual activities in which *sound research* and *clear reporting* are the uppermost considerations in your writing.

The professional article is difficult to generalize about since it comprises a number of specialized prose forms—scholarly papers, theses, textbooks, business and technical reports—each involving a special procedure. For the sake of simplicity, we shall limit the discussion to the kind of writing students and teachers are most familiar with in an academic framework, the scholarly article—but much of the discussion will apply to any writing of this kind you may do in your scholastic or professional careers.

THE PROFESSIONAL ARTICLE AS A FORM

Any reasonably complete description of the professional article must acknowledge that it involves: the critical investigation of a problem or proposition, a closely reasoned and methodically developed structure, and an accurate and learned style.

Since the *critical investigation of a problem or proposition* is the main object of the professional article, it is not surprising that writing one requires rather more preparation than do many prose forms. Indeed, far more effort is spent by writers in educating themselves generally about the subject and researching a particular aspect of it than writing up the results.

The professional article deals with a subject about which the author has some special knowledge or insight, a subject that is often difficult or obscure. And the subject appeals to a reader of somewhat specialized tastes who, for personal and professional reasons, wants to be better educated. Thus, the author does not have to show that the subject is relevant, but can get quickly to the heart of the matter and concentrate on making a complete and detailed comment on some specific subject about which the reader already has an interest. Moreover, the author's attitude is one of philosophical inquiry. In an utterly disinterested way he or she wants to get to the bottom of something—answer a puzzling question, explore the implications of some suggestive detail, scrutinize what other people pass over lightly not pausing to question. With luck and effort such an objective and penetrating look at a single, limited topic will lead to the expression of a thought which, if not wholly new, is revealed in a new light. The professional article is informative, but sometimes cautiously persuasive; the writer, having proved something to his or her own satisfaction, would now prove it to the reader as well. All speculative and theoretical scholarship depends on the professional article. For the professional article not only communicates knowledge and reports research, but preserves it as well, not only makes a reasonably independent comment, but along with a great many articles on other facets of the same subject makes a comprehensive statement.

In a prose form intended to enable a writer to make some original comment on a specialized subject for a knowledgeable reader, *a closely reasoned and methodically developed structure is essential.* Readers of professional articles do not have to be courted with quite the same enthusiasm as readers of most other prose forms in order to be won. Accustomed to much sophisticated reading, they are receptive to the article as soon as they recognize its bearing on a subject of professional interest. Even for this reader the writer must explain and support every statement that is not self-evident, but need not always feel compelled to be lively and colorful. To exploit the full repertoire of appeals available to the writer takes words and, for these readers, detracts from the main business. Indeed, readers of professional articles, more concerned with truth than appearances, are likely to become suspicious of what they will regard as condescension or sophistry or lack of objectivity. Consequently, writers of professional articles are more concerned with presenting convincing evidence rather than simply the most dramatic illustrations. Their first responsibility is to their subject, the selection and arrangement of details is made on the basis of pertinence rather than interest—though, happily, for readers of professional articles the two generally coincide. Hence, such serious and concentrated studies of what has heretofore been overlooked or misunderstood are developed as a studious reader expects them to be: deliberate and explicit from the first statement of the subject, problem, and thesis; through the step-by-step presentation of the argument; to the final commentary on the results.

There are, of course, the conventions of scholarship—those accepted forms for presenting notes and bibliography, and for preparing the manuscript generally—which have to do with the surface structure of the professional article. A convenience for both writer and reader, and pretty well established over the years, these conventions are a necessary part of scholarly, technical, and professional writing.

It follows that such a formal structure should be matched by an *accurate and learned style.* The style of the professional article is still "plain," though it does employ a professional vocabulary and educated idiom. There is nothing particularly formidable or difficult about it; certainly everything is done to avoid vagueness and obscurity. The authors subordinate themselves and their stylistic individualities in order to shun subjectivity and emotional connotation. Although scholarly and professional writing is more casual than it once was, and the first person is occasionally used, the third person is still the prevailing viewpoint. The rare instances of pedantry are more a matter of style than of conception; subjects are not in themselves inconsequential or soporific—yet some inept writers are like alchemists in reverse with their knack for turning gold into lead. Professional articles are, indeed, serious and studied, but almost never dull and artificial. The style of the professional article is nothing more than the natural manner of expression for an educated person writing for an educated reader of like interests. In terms of profile, the style is usually informal to formal in level and low to medium in texture.

In the academic, scientific, and technological world the professional article is the standard form of serious communication. And what many do not realize, the professional article is also a means of preserving knowledge. Research published in the form of a professional article will be accessible indefinitely for interested readers; it achieves a permanence few other short prose forms possess. The journals, reviews, quarterlies, proceedings, monographs, papers published by universities and professional societies are absolutely essential to human intellectual affairs—and the basic form of expression in all these publications is the professional article.

Because professional articles are written not only for today but also for tomorrow, and because they need not adapt to the capricious tastes of the popular reading audience, every effort has been made to find the best possible form for presenting truth as conceived by an original thinker and then to make it by mutual consent the standard of scholarly and scientific communication. The conventions of scholarship are one of the results. Thus, the history of the professional article is unique in that there has been little evolution of the form in the last fifty years and it is not likely to change appreciably in the future.

HOW TO WRITE THE PROFESSIONAL ARTICLE

The professional article is a more definite form than many, partly because it is so objective and partly because there are conventions regarding its contents and appearance. If you are not challenged by the prospect of doing any original thinking, and if you are not willing to work up to professional standards, you will find writing the professional article an altogether wearisome experience. You may, indeed, think you have already found it so despite your best intentions. But what you have written were, in fact, trumped-up research papers—cut and paste jobs made up of paraphrases and quotations from the usual obvious sources. The professional article is something else again—and most writers seem to follow this sort of plan.

1. *Begin by reading widely and in depth in some area.* Make it your own; become an authority. This really isn't so impossible as it may seem. (You may know comparatively little about, say, John Donne's poetry; but you could make it a point to know far more than most about the herbs alluded to in his verses, in this way providing another insight into the man's poetic vision.) It would be pointless to write a professional article unless you possessed a thought which

seemed to you true and revealing and original. And obviously such thoughts do not come to one who has only superficial knowledge of one's subject. The more pressed for time you are, the more directed your reading will have to be. This means you must specialize from the beginning, limit your reading to that which pertains most specifically to your particular interest. Surely your own instincts will lead you to consider the most worthwhile aspects of a subject. Naturally, the obvious and the trivial, the conjectural and the synoptic are not. And if the subject is current, you will have to depend largely on your own resources for facts and the opinions of others will be scarce. So first learn the basic facts about your subject, and then concentrate on some part about which you might reasonably become a qualified expert.

2. As you read, *cast about for a specific topic,* a facet of the larger subject you find especially provocative and promising. Life is so rich and mysterious and every subject so filled with possibilities that we perpetually try too much, spread ourselves too thin. But to write intelligently for a reader who is already well-informed on the subject, you will have to specialize. In fact, the less you know about the subject to begin with, the more you will have to limit yourself. Providing you know the basic facts about your subject, an intensive knowledge can make up for the lack of an extensive knowledge. Later, after you have come to know your subject better, you will be able to make more comprehensive assertions about it—this may come as a surprise to some students, who, accustomed to thinking the other way round, try to generalize about what they know very little. At any rate, the first object is to concentrate on a topic sufficiently specific that you can become acquainted with a significant part of what has been written about it.

3. And the next object, once you have got the boundaries of what is to be your province clearly marked, is to *begin looking for some hitherto unapparent or unappreciated truth about your subject.* You will probably not discover any such revelation right off, but ultimately you will come across something that will make you pause—a curious fact, an inner contradiction, a suggestive detail, a possible connection. If you are truly interested in the subject (and it would be inconceivable to make such a close study of something that didn't interest you) a great many questions will occur to you in connection with your study. Follow them up. And give yourself time, time for all the reading and thinking that will have to be done before all the pieces begin to fall into place.

4. *Jot down a tentative thesis and a preliminary outline* as soon as you can. At this stage the thesis is little more than a guess, or hunch beginning "I wonder if . . .?"; and the outline is more a plan for further reading than the design for a scholarly article. But even here, a

thesis should begin to take on the characteristics of one—that is, it should not be a purely personal notion ("John Donne is too obscure for modern readers."), or an impossibly broad thesis ("John Donne's poetic imagery is drawn from virtually every province of English seventeenth-century intellectual life."), or an obvious and indisputable fact ("John Donne was a metaphysical poet."), but rather some significant truth that could in the several thousand words you have allowed yourself be explored and defended to the complete satisfaction of your reader.

And even the preliminary outline suggests what direction you presume your argument will take and what evidence you expect to present in defense of your proposition. Be prepared for surprises. You may not find what you expect at all. In which case you will either make whatever changes necessary in your thesis, abandon it for a more promising one you discover along the way, or give it up altogether as a false or unsupportable conclusion. Armed with a thesis and outline—though both will be considerably revised later on—you can begin doing concentrated work.

5. *Now read further and compile a bibliography.* Some would begin taking notes at this point, and they would be premature on two counts. For one thing, there is much to be said for reading and thinking about your subject, in light now of your tentative thesis, a while longer before committing yourself. Try as we might to stay flexible, our thoughts on any subject tend to stiffen once we decide what our line is going to be. Even eminent scholars are guilty of hastiness here. So mull over your subject for a spell.

You will do a more discriminating job of research and come up with sounder evidence to support your thesis if you consider the problem of bibliography at the outset. Books, articles, and other items which comprise your bibliography are not by any means your only source of evidence, but they are relied upon so extensively by writers of professional articles that the term "source" has come to imply written works. There is an important distinction to be made between "primary" and "secondary" sources. A *primary source* is the most immediate written revelation of the subject. For the biographer this would include letters and diaries, for the historian eye-witness accounts and contemporary records, for the literary critic the work itself—in short, the subject itself or the most direct expression of the subject. A *secondary source* is the subject as reviewed and commented upon in writing by others. And for the biographer this would include impressions by those who knew the person and other biographies, for the historian contemporary views and subsequent histories, for the literary critic reviews and criticism—all interpretations which incorporate a good deal of opinion if not bias. (Of course, if your subject were the changing image of George Washington as reflected in major biographies of several decades, then the various biographies would be primary sources. What is secondary in one instance can be primary in another. And the same is true of the parts of any written work. A direct quotation in a biography would be considered primary even though the biography in general would be secondary.)

You will have the greatest opportunity for original thinking and the least chance of perpetuating the errors of others if you make it your practice to rely as much as possible on primary sources. And when you do depend on secondary sources, be certain that you cite opinions which are either prevailing or authoritative. (The best secondary sources are generally the recently published and highly specialized.)

What you want at this stage is a list of books and articles on your subject drawn from the card catalogue, the periodical indexes, the published bibliographies, the source footnotes and bibliographies in the written works you consult. Look these over, deciding what is most pertinent and significant. (The more discriminating you are here, the less time you will waste when you begin taking notes. And for each source you expect to use, jot down the author, title, and facts of publication on a separate 3- by 5-inch card.)

For a book: the library call number, the author's name, the title of the book, the place of publication, the publisher, and the date of publication:

70–114929
Slonimsky, Nicolas.
Music Since 1900
New York: Charles Scribner's Sons, 1971.

For an article (essay, story, poem): the author's name, the title of the article, the title of the publication in which the article appears, the volume number, the date of publication, and finally the pages on which the article appears:

Simmons, Jean.
"Sex Discrimination in Botany and the Biological Sciences," Plant Science Bulletin, 22
(December 1976),
38–39.

(There are, needless to say, many published sources that will require a slightly different description. To handle these variations, you may need to consult one of the many guides to scholarly writing.) On the lower half of the card you may wish to jot down a brief description of what you find most useful in this particular source. At any rate, having compiled a tentative bibliography, you will find it much easier to read, take notes, prepare the source footnotes and final bibliography.

6. *Now revise your tentative thesis and preliminary outline in light of what you now know about the subject.* Does your basic proposition still appear true and worth expressing? Has your reading exposed it as platitudinous or unsupportable? Is your basic line of thought clear and complete? Has your reading disclosed any omissions or any confusion in the present order of your argument? After making whatever revisions are necessary, you are ready to begin work in earnest on the professional article.

7. *Take notes:* there is no alternative. Those who don't wind up starting from scratch, as if they were the first ever to give the subject any thought, the first to write a word about it; or else condemn themselves to endless thumbing through a canyon of books looking for the first one and then another vaguely remembered but absolutely essential fact. And there is no more convenient way to record the facts and ideas that will later be incorporated into your article than by jotting each down on a 3- by 5-inch (or 4- by 6-inch) card. The utility of such a system is that later you can select and arrange the cards to jibe with your final working outline and write the article with all your materials at hand. To be useful, each card must contain three items: a brief bibliographical tag in the upper left hand corner (since you have a separate bibliographical file the briefest identification is all that is necessary—the author's last name and a page number are usually sufficient), a tentative heading in the upper right hand corner (tentative because it is either a heading from the preliminary outline or simply suggested by the contents of the note), and the note itself consisting, and this is important to remember, of a single fact or idea.

Empson, p. 12

The pastoral as a form of epic

When the traditional shepherd figure of the pastoral is associated with other rulers of flocks, like kings and bishops, then the pastoral begins to take on the qualities of an heroic epic.

You will typically find yourself making three kinds of notes: (a) If who expressed the thought or how it was expressed is important, you will probably quote the passage directly. Be unmistakably legible and accurate, identifying the whole with quotation marks and any omissions with ellipses, recording the exact page number(s) on which the passage appears. (b) If the thought is a prevailing opinion or reasonably apparent observation, you will probably paraphrase the passage. Be sure to express the thought in your own words, which means you must do more than change a word here and there. (c) If some more or less original thought occurs to you in the process of researching the article—and this is one of the main reasons for reading what others have had to say—jot it down on a note card. Indeed, while many of your ideas will have been incorporated into the outline, and many will later on, the note card is as convenient a way of keeping track of original ideas as it is for recording ideas from your study of primary and secondary sources.

8. *Prepare a working outline of the article and arrange your note cards accordingly.* As a result of your research you will make some changes in the content and order of your outline. Certainly you will add considerably to its length, for the working outline of a professional article is typically more detailed than that for any other prose form. Incorporate the more important notes into the outline and arrange the others according to the outline so they will be readily accessible as you write. You will, of course, be selective—putting aside many notes because they are irrelevant, or superfluous, or duplications, or unconvincing. And you will revise the headings of those note cards you plan to use—making them more specifically descriptive.

9. As you revise the working outline, *keep the traditional parts of the article in mind.* The *Beginning* may contain the following: (a) general remarks about the subject, (b) the question, or problem and its background—including, perhaps, some reference to other published discussions of the same question and a brief explanation of why still another article on the same subject is necessary, (c) the purpose and method, and (d) the answer, or solution—which is, of course, a quick statement of the thesis. But the Beginning is always short, and especially in a short article, the parts are frequently abbreviated and combined in various ways, presented in different order, or implicit enough that they need not be expressed at all.

The following is a reasonably standard beginning paragraph.

"Oh! To hear him!. . . . To hear the names he's giving me! That Or-lick! Oh! Oh!" With these words, Mrs. Joe Gargery reaches the climax of her hysterical fit and Dickens begins a series of violent incidents that seem to bear but an obscure relevance to the plot of Great Expectations. *A unified reading of the subsequent episodes that develop Mrs. Joe's character might treat her as an extended metaphor or allegory among the many others expressing the theme of the novel. Mrs. Joe's passion for respectability is central to the main theme of* Great Expectations, *because more than any other person she has had the shaping of Pip's conscience, his infantile and perdurable sense of right and*

wrong. The novel as a whole treats of social injustice and that theme too may also explicate Mrs. Joe's private struggle with her own conscience, for Dickens is apparently very concerned with the conflict between respectable prosperity and shameful poverty in the public scene and with the individual attempt to adapt private values to the status quo.—John Lindberg, Individual Conscience and Social Injustic in *Great Expectations*

The *Middle* consists of the steps in your argument, a series of subordinate assumptions in defense of your thesis with evidence presented in support of each. And the *Ending,* though it may include a summary, is basically a conclusion ending—a restatement of the thesis and discussion of its implications.

The following is a typical ending paragraph:

Such methods, together with techniques of biological control of insects already in use and under development, could greatly reduce the present reliance on hazardous insecticides. The insects have shown that they cannot be conquered permanently by the brand of chemical warfare we have been using up to now. After all, they had become battle-hardened from fighting the insecticide warfare of the plants for more than 100 million years. By learning from the plants and sharpening their natural weapons we should be able to find effective ways of poisoning our insect competitors without poisoning ourselves.—Paul R. Ehrlich and Peter H. Raven, Butterflies and Plants

Once you review your notes, and revise the outline, you are probably ready to write a first draft.

10. *Concentrate on expanding the outline and notes keyed to it into prose with as little deviation from plan as possible.* Elaborate each point in the outline as fully as you can within reason. And follow the outline explicitly. If other ideas or other ways of developing the article occur, by all means consider incorporating them—but make the changes in the outline before writing one, or you will risk losing your sense of direction. Since you will write a better first draft if carried along by the momentum of your enthusiasm, do what you can to keep from becoming bogged down with problems that can be put off until later. Specifically, don't worry over the manner of your expression. It is enough for now that the thought is clearly stated; in later revisions you can see that it is also effectively said. In the case of direct quotations, clip the note card containing the passage to the page. (This also reduces the chance of error through repeated copying.) Footnotes and other documentation can be abbreviated for the time being. (The author's last name and a page number usually suffices.) In order to get the heart of the article written with dispatch, some students prefer not to write the beginning until later, knowing it will be thoroughly revised. Still others prefer to write it first, feeling it

gets them off to a good start to have the way clearly pointed out. Experiment to find out which works best for you.

11. You may have hit upon the right *title* before now. But if not, this is a good point at which to begin considering possibilities. Since the title of a scholarly article must, above all, be descriptive, it is most difficult to invent one that is also short and provocative. If you can't come up with an effective conventional title, you might consider one which, in addition to a short, provocative, and reasonably descriptive main title, also incorporates a necessarily longer, less exciting, but more specifically descriptive subtitle.

Here are some suggestions how effective titles might be written: "Two Fossil Floras of the Negev Desert," "*Perkin Warbeck* as 17th Century Psychological Play," "*Blackberry Winter* and the Use of Archetypes," "Fallen from Time: The Mythic Rip Van Winkle," "Madagascar Lemurs: Isolated Primates," "October War: Doctrine and Tactics in the Yom Kippur Conflict, 6 to 24 October 1973."

12. *See to it that the article reads smoothly.* In addition to the usual measures taken to refine your expression, you will condense here and expand there (sometimes with the aid of scissors and paste or Scotch tape) in order to achieve the desired clarity and emphasis. And you will pay special attention to the salient parts of the article—the beginning and ending, the transitions at every level, the way the thesis is introduced and developed.

13. You will also *review* (and probably considerably revise) *the manner in which quotations are integrated with the text.* Some badly conceived professional articles appear little more than anthologies of pertinent quotations. To avoid making such an impression—and at the same time use a fair number of quotations, generally your most effective form of evidence—you must not allow them to impede the flow of your prose. It is, for example, much smoother to say,

Neither the vestiges of puritan pride nor the new-found sense of power over nature can permit man to accept life as "something in one cell that doesn't need to think" or as "merely strange dark interludes in the electrical display of God the Father!"

than it would be to write,

Neither the vestiges of puritan pride nor the new-found sense of power over nature can permit man to accept life as described by the two major characters in the play. Edmund Darrell decides that "Thinking doesn't matter a damn! Life is something in one cell that doesn't need to think." And later, Nina concludes "Yes, our lives are merely strange dark interludes in the electrical display of God the Father!"

Do not quote at all unless who expressed the thought or how it was expressed is important. Quote from a passage only what is necessary to illustrate your point. Use the ellipsis (to mark omissions) and square brackets (to enclose editorial comment) as a means of abbreviating the passage. There are basically three ways of weaving quotations into the text: (a) By holding the quotation down to a phrase or a sentence or two, you will be able to incorporate it into one of your own sentences. (b) If because of the length or nature of the quotation this is impossible, you must introduce the quotation in some more obvious way. (c) And if it runs to more than three lines, indent and single space the quotation as well.

14. *Documenting* your scholarly article is really not so difficult if you have kept track of where your evidence came from, and if you have reported or quoted it accurately. *The MLA Style Sheet* (a publication of the Modern Language Association), *A Manual for the Writers of Term Papers, Theses, and Dissertations* by Kate L. Turabian (University of Chicago Press), or similar guide will be useful, not only to answer the questions which are bound to occur in documenting your work, but to find out what professional practice is with regard to manuscript form. Basic rules are few and simple: You need not document a prevailing opinion or reasonably apparent observation even if it was suggested to you by another writer. You must document any term or idea that is clearly the product of one person's original thought. And you must document every quotation. In short, you must always acknowledge the source of your information when it is required by courtesy (and by law) and when authoritative opinion or textual evidence is essential in supporting your thesis.

Here is a summary of how notes are usually handled:

—Notes are indicated in the text by a raised (or "superior") number following the reference or quotation; the note itself is identified by a corresponding raised number.

—Whether notes are placed at the bottom of the page—becoming footnotes—and separated from the text by a line (or "rule"), or placed on a separate sheet at the end of the article, as they are most frequently done, they are numbered consecutively throughout the article.

—Ordinarily each quotation is noted, but if several excerpts from the same passage are quoted in the same paragraph of the article, a common note will suffice.

—The most common reference to a book is: the author's name, the title of the book, the place of publication, publisher, date of publication, and finally the page number(s).

[1]E. G. R. Taylor, *The Haven-Finding Art: A History of Navigation from Odysseus to Captain Cook* (London: Hollis & Carter, 1958), p. 61.

But many book references are, of necessity, exceptional.

[2]Winston S. Churchill, *The Birth of Britain* (Vol. I of *A History of English Speaking Peoples*, 4 vols.: New York: Dodd, Mead & Company, 1956), p. 332.

[3]Herodotus, *The Persian Wars*, trans. George Rawlinson (New York: Random House, 1942), p. 595.

[4]William Shakespeare, *The Tragedy of King Lear*, I. v. 56.

—The most common reference to an article is: the author's name, the title of the article, the name of the periodical, the volume number, the month and the year, and finally the page number(s).

[1]Sir John Glubb, "The Fate of Empires," *Blackwood's*, vol. 320 (December, 1976), p. 484.

But there are exceptions to the usual article references as well.

[2]"Medicine's Next Decade," *The New York Times*, 3 January 1967, p. 36.

[3]William Sansom, "A Country Walk," in *The Stories of William Sansom* (Boston: Little, Brown and Company, 1963), p. 355.

[4]Newton Chester Whittier, "Squall and Squall Line," *Encyclopedia Britannica* (1965), XXI, p. 267.

—For subsequent references, the author's last name followed by the page number(s) will normally suffice. (Both *op. cit.* and *loc. cit.* are unnecessary terms and are going out of fashion.) And, of course, if the author's name appears in the text, the page number(s) alone will suffice.

—If in a reasonably short and informal scholarly article you can incorporate some or all of your documentation in the text without impeding its flow, so much the better. If you quote repeatedly from a particular work, subsequent citation after the first note (in which you say in addition to the usual note something to the effect that, "Hereafter all page references to this edition will appear in the body of the text.") need be only a page number in parentheses following the reference.

Marsden says of himself, "I've never married the word to life!" (p. 624).

Should your article contain only a few references and should you wish to avoid notes altogether, you may present the complete bibliographical information in the text.

Gwen Benwell and Arthur Waugh, in *Sea Enchantress* (New York: The Citadel Press, 1965, p. 130), explain the representation of a lion suckling a mermaid as "a link with the cult of Artemis."

Or an incomplete source note in the text may refer implicitly to the complete facts of publication in the bibliography.

On page 3 of his informal study of the tropics, *Where Winter Never Comes,* Marston Bates dismisses Huntington's theories about the relationship between civilization and climate as the case of a man who "did not like warm climates" and who "documented his dislike with impressive learning."

And there are other variations of the form for in-text documentation.

There are, in addition to source notes, *explanatory notes* which are more a part of the text than its documentation. Occasionally you will wish to define a term or offer some incidental but pertinent information, to refer your readers to more detailed published discussion of a point, or to call their attention to another part of your article—but to do so in the text would be an intrusion, a violation of proportion. If it is not used to compensate for something having been omitted or presented out of order, the explanatory note is a useful device.

[1]See Moorhead, *The Fatal Impact*, for a more dramatic account of Cook's death.

[2]Oscar Cargill, in *Intellectual America* (New York: Macmillan, 1941), p. 72, comments that *Strange Interlude* is "a dramatized textbook of all the neuroses discoverable by psychoanalysis."

[3]A thousand years later these mooring holes would furnish the best indication of which shores and waterways the Vikings knew.

If your revisions have been thorough and discriminate, you are probably ready to write the final draft of your scholarly article.

15. One of the last things you will do is *prepare a bibliography.* When in a short article the notes are collected at the end, a bibliography is probably not required. But a longer or more formal article is expected to include a bibliography. The bibliography is both a testimony to your own thoroughness and a contribution to scholarship, providing the reader with a list of materials for further study.

Be selective, don't include every written source you know about on the subject or even all those you looked at. Limit your bibliography to those books and articles that were directly useful in your research, ordinarily items which have appeared in source notes. Arrange the bibliography cards alphabetically by the author's last name or, if the work is unsigned, by the first letter in the title (excepting "a," "an," and "the"). And type them pretty much as they appear on the card, neither numbering the entries nor dividing them according to kind.

Ardrey, Robert. *The Territorial Imperative.* New York: Atheneum, 1966.

Churchill, Winston S. *The Birth of Britain.* Vol. I of *A History of English Speaking Peoples.* 4 vols. New York: Dodd, Mead & Company, 1956.

Herodotus. *The Persian Wars.* Trans. George Rawlinson. New York: Random House, 1942.

Koenig, Marie. "Celtic Coins: A New Interpretation," *Archaeology,* vol. 19 (January, 1966), 24–30.

"Medicine's Next Decade." *The New York Times,* 3 January 1967, p. 36.

Sansom, William. "A Country Walk," in *The Stories of William Sansom.* Boston: Little, Brown and Company, 1963, pp. 355–69.

Shakespeare, William. *The Tragedy of King Lear.* "Arden Edition." Cambridge: Harvard University Press, 1952.

Whittier, Newton Chester. "Squall and Squall Line." *Encyclopedia Britannica* (1965), XXI, pp. 267–268.

16. Ordinarily a title page or cover is not required; instructors sometimes appreciate having one or both, editors much prefer neither. In the case of a longer, more formal work you may find it advisable to prepare not only a cover and title page, but a preface, table of contents, list of tables, list of illustrations, notes page, appendix, and bibliography as well. Then is the time to go to an authoritative guide.

To be sure, correctness and accuracy come at the price of tedious attention to detail. But with it goes all the fascination of unraveling a puzzle. And in a world that somewhat limits our personal access to mystery, here is an opportunity for scholarly adventure.

THE WHOLE COMPOSITION

The following professional article, a study of Melville's fiction, is written for the person who regularly reads such scholarly journals as *Dalhousie Review* or who has been attracted to the article by its descriptive title. Fred E. H. Schroeder does not claim that the thesis of "Enter Ahab, Then All: Theatrical Elements in Melville's Fiction" is an utterly new and original insight. "Aficionados are aware that certain chapters of *Moby Dick* are composed like a play script," he begins—before alluding to other theatrical elements readers may have overlooked. While such a close reading may strike some as superfluous or irrelevant, few will admit their understanding of Melville's fiction has not been deepened. Actually this article is much more accessible to general readers than the "pure scholarship" encountered in many reviews, quarterlies, journals, and the like. But all such publications provide writers and readers with a prose form which serves not only as the framework for research but as a means for reporting the results to others with a professional interest.

Enter Ahab, Then All: Theatrical Elements in Melville's Fiction
Fred E. H. Schroeder

Aficionados are aware that certain chapters of *Moby Dick* are composed like a play script, complete to stage directions, but few seem to have noticed how frequently Herman Melville employs many other theatrical devices (visual and aural effects) at crucial points in his works. Most often the theatrical effects are blended in clusters around dramatic plot-situations, but they can be reasonably classified into three general techniques: the use of the nineteenth-century "picture-frame" stage; the use of semi-operatic choruses and bombastic speeches; and the use of theatrical sudden disclosures which are intensified by means of carefully contrived visual focal points. Before analyzing examples of these theatrical elements, however, it is of importance to consider the question of whether theatrical effects—practical stage devices—are consistent with Melville's thematic or, if you will, his dramatic purposes.

The very first chapter of *Moby Dick* provides a clue which suggests that for Melville the stage is a metaphor rather than a mere place for acting. Ishmael, having discussed his reasons for going to sea, begins to inquire into his reasons for writing about the last voyage of the *Pequod*: ". . . I cannot tell why it was exactly that those stage managers, the Fates, put me down for this shabby part of a whaling voyage, when others were set down for magnificent parts in high tragedies, and short and easy parts in genteel comedies, and jolly parts in farces. . . ."[1], and he surmises that he was predestined to the voyage. It is evident that what follows is to be a drama, in which the actors are cast and directed by the Fates. But how large is the stage? Melville is hardly attempting to portray all the world. Rather he presents a small complement of men in the narrow confines of a ship, roaming the most deserted areas of the world, cut off from the rest of humanity except for occasional encounters with like men, on like ships, equally confined and limited in their movements. In this novel, Melville does not say any more about the stage on which he will perform his drama.

Forty years later, however, in *Billy Budd,* Melville falls into the same language of the theatre, although he does not compose any portions of this last novel in the manner of a stage script. Here he becomes most intent on explaining how and why a ship is a suitable microcosm for staging his ideas. In the first paragraph of Chapter 14, he says:

> *Passion, and passion in its profoundest, is not a thing demanding a palatial stage whereon to play its part. Down among the groundlings, among the beggars and rakers of the garbage, profound passion is enacted. And the circumstances that provoke it, however trivial and mean, are no measure of its power. In the present instance the stage is a scrubbed gun-deck, and one of the external provocations a man-of-war's spilled soup.[2]*

Earlier, in Chapter 11, he had stated why human contacts are intensified on shipboard:

> *Now there can exist no irritating juxtaposition of dissimilar personalities comparable to that which is possible aboard a great warship fully manned and at sea. There, every day among all ranks almost every man comes into more or less of a contact with almost every other man (p. 35).[3]*

By choosing a ship for his stage, Melville solves a problem that confronts every playwright: selecting a setting which will be limited in size, but which will still provide a natural arena for the interplay of the characters. A ship, when once properly provisioned, can exist independently of the rest of the world for months at a time, allowing the drama to be played out without outside human influence. Melville deliberately describes the independence of the *Pequod,* pointing out that it carries enough fresh water to maintain the crew on the Pacific for the greater part of a year. I believe that one reason for this isolation is thematic, reflecting Ahab's deliberate self-exile from humanity and, ultimately, from sophisticated manifestations of God's law. But the ship also provides a dramatically manageable environment for the exhibition of universal problems of good and evil. A desire to narrow the boundaries of action and focus the reader's attention at crucial moments seems to be characteristic of Melville as well as of the theatre. Focusing is one of the most basic stage devices of modern directorial practice, and Melville's methods are remarkably similar to those of the director. Melville had remarkable stage sense and an eye for vivid visual composition, and the way in which he used these abilities enhanced both the actions and themes of *Moby Dick, Billy Budd,* and *Benito Cereno.*

A most conscious passage which deliberately sets the stage is found in Chapter 19 of *Billy Budd.* The captain, having received Claggart's false report, has decided to confront the accuser with the accused: "The measure he determined upon involved a shifting of the scene, a transfer to a place less exposed to observation than the broad quarter-deck" (p. 48). Melville has used terminology which is peculiar to the language of the theatre, "Shifting of the scene." And later, in Chapter 22, when the cabin is described, the description reads like the setting of a scene in a play script:

> *The court was held in the same cabin where the unfortunate affair had taken place. This cabin, the Commander's, embraced the entire area under the poopdeck. Aft, and on either side, was a small stateroom; the one room temporarily a jail and the other a dead-house, and a yet smaller compartment leaving a space between, expanding forward into a goodly oblong of length coinciding with the ship's beam. A skylight of moderate dimension was overhead, and at each end of the oblong space were two sashed porthole windows . . .(p. 52).*

The description is complete to details of the light source and the doors leading offstage; and incidentally, as on stage, we never see the interiors of the offstage rooms. When Billy is closeted in the jail, he is out of sight, and when Captain Vere communicates the decision of the drum-head court to him, "what took place at this interview was never known." In other words, Captain Vere has left by the door "up-right," so to speak, and the audience cannot follow him. This is a convention of the theatre, not of the novel, but Melville has employed it as a means of keeping the focus on the courtroom where the strifeful action is played.

In *Benito Cereno,* Melville also uses the ship as a stage on which a drama is to be played, and he makes use of a more fanciful stage setting than is found in *Billy Budd.* Near the beginning of the narrative as Captain Delano first describes Cereno's ship the *San Dominick,* he speaks of the air of enchantment which a ship met at sea takes on, an enchantment which is a result of its sudden appearance and subsequent disappearance. He says, "The ship seems unreal; these strange costumes, gestures, and faces, but a shadowy tableau just emerged from the deep, which directly must receive back what it gave." An encounter with a ship on the ocean, then, is like a stage play—or a tableau—because the encounter is a limited period within the continuum of time. The ship, like the stage, provides in a neat package a distinct physical and social environment which, so far as an outside observer is concerned, has a beginning and an ending. When the ship pulls away or the curtain falls, the environment of the drama just observed is cut off and the onlooker sees only the neutral sea or the impartial drapery before him.

The *San Dominick,* however, is no mere tableau because Melville prepares the scene in a semi-operatic manner with a droning chorus and percussion orchestra sustaining a weird accompaniment which sets a particular kind of "stage" with its peculiarly appropriate stage effects: the ornate scrollwork and gilding of the old warship effectively intensify Spanish decadence and place Benito Cereno's apparent weakness of character in ironic contrast to the symbols of past glory. That comparing the fading grandeur of Spain to Cereno's degradation was one of Melville's methods is made clear when Delano watches Don Benito being shaved and notices that the royal banner of Spain is being used as a barber's sheet. The effects are contrived, but as will be seen in *Moby Dick,* Melville would go to great lengths to achieve a single visual dramatic effect.

Chapter 99, "The Doubloon," one of the most contrived scenes of theatrical staging in *Moby Dick,* for example, is significantly enough one of the most important portions of the book, summarizing the attitudes and prejudices of seven major characters. The doubloon has been nailed to the mast for most of the voyage and it had been a focal point for the crew when nailed up. Now it is a focal point again, but this time it is not the centre of histrionic action, but is rather the object of successive soliloquies. As each man goes to the coin, he is observed by the others, hidden about the ship like so many characters in a Shakespeare comedy or a Mozart opera. Each comes forward, speaks his peculiar thoughts in his own peculiar idiom, and retires to observe the next man. If we discount Ishmael's opening description—although it is written in his own bookish mode of speech—we notice another excellent piece of stage writing: Ahab, in his soliloquy, describes the imprint of the coin in detail, thereby communicating the details of its appearance to the audience, who naturally were not able to see its design. By the time we come to the last observer, poor mad Pip, we are told that the doubloon, this focal point, is "the ship's navel," the focus of sinful greed.

The presentation of this chapter is essentially theatrical—no novelist need crowd a scene unnaturally with seven people to provide seven different attitudes toward one symbol. Hawthorne, for example, used the same device of commenting on a visual image in *The Scarlet Letter,* when at dawn, a cloud shaped like an "A" catches the ruddy morning light. His approach, however, was to take the novelist's license to enter different homes, different rooms, different minds, to evoke a variety of interpretations of the vision. It should be noticed particularly that Hawthorne relates the unspoken thoughts of the viewers. But Melville, in his theatrical style, has each character speak aloud. The soliloquy, in fact, is one of the most characteristic methods in *Moby Dick*, and although—as is so strongly manifested in Chapter 99—Melville can make amazing distinctions between the speech idioms of his characters, none of them speaks a true vernacular. Rather, they all speak the language of the stage and the pulpit. Even Flask, the very essence of cold practicality, speaks metaphorically. He begins, "I see nothing here, but a round thing made of gold . . ." (p. 463); but in two lines, this round thing emobodies his values. It is for him "nine hundred and sixty cigars."

Another remarkable thing about the language is that it reads well aloud. It soon becomes apparent that one of the reasons for this is that the characters frequently break into regular metre. The following two passages from the Starbuck-Ahab dialogues in Chapter 132, "The Symphony," illustrate the rhythms of their theatrically unrealistic speech:

> *"Oh, Starbuck! it is a mild, mild wind, and a mild looking sky. On such a day—very much such sweetness as this—I struck my first whale. . . .*
>
> *Oh, my Captain, my Captain! grand old heart, after all! . . . Wife and child, too, are Starbuck's—wife and child of his brotherly, sisterly, play-fellow youth. . . ." (pp. 580–581).*

There are few actors who could resist reproducing the thick essence of a balmy wind in "very much such sweetness as this," or the metrical heaping of images of home and family bonds in Starbuck's "brotherly, sisterly, play-fellow youth." It is not only that the poetic language suggests the stage—most novelists indulge in some rhapsody, although ordinarily as narrators—but that the diction is often on the verge of bombast. It is the language of the theatre.

Melville has a way of saving reference to some of the symbols until they can be produced suddenly in a brilliant dramatic flourish, and the symbols are invariably large enough to be easily seen— sometimes seeming obvious to the point of crudity. An outstanding example of this is found in Chapter 100 of *Moby Dick*, "Leg and Arm." Ahab calls to the *Samuel Enderby:*

> *"Hast seen the White Whale!"*
>
> *"See you this?" and withdrawing it from the fold that had hidden it, he*

*held up a white arm of Sperm whale bone, terminating in a wooden head
like a mallet (p. 466).*

Then follows the meeting of the two maimed captains, in an almost
embarrassingly dramatic act. Ahab is hoisted to the *Samuel Enderby.*
We are told that this is done because Ahab could not manipulate
the ladder. This is undoubtedly true. But it is also done to set up
the stage for a symbolic action which would be ridiculous if Ahab
were not slung aloft:

> *With his ivory arm frankly thrust forth in welcome, the other captain
> advanced, and Ahab, putting out his ivory leg, crossing the ivory arm (like
> two swordfish blades) cried out in his walrus way "Aye, aye, hearty! let
> us shake bones together!—an arm and a leg!—an arm that can never
> shrink, d'ye see; and a leg that can never run" (p. 467).*

I think that most novelists would assume that a thrilling and darkly
significant effect was produced by the other captain's sudden
revelation of his arm; but a dramatist is compelled to illustrate
visually important relationships which may be apparent only in the
mind of one character, and Melville, whether consciously or
unconsciously writing in the theatrical mode, has therefore prepared
elaborate machinery to cross the ivory limbs.

The same type of theatrical sudden disclosure occurs frequently
in *Moby Dick.* Queequeg's "ramadan" in Chapter 17 is revealed by
having Ishmael shoulder the door down from a running start; at the
close of Chapter 47, Ahab's devilish yellow boat-crew spills forth
from below decks as the remainder of the crew stands transfixed;
and in Chapter 131, after the *Pequod* has encountered the *Delight* just
as it is burying another of Moby Dick's victims, it turns suddenly
away:

> *As Ahab now glided from the dejected* Delight, *the strange life-buoy
> hanging at the* Pequod's *stern came into conspicuous relief.*
> *"Ha! Yonder! look yonder, men!" cried a foreboding voice in her
> wake. "In vain, oh, ye strangers, ye fly our sad burial; yet but turn us
> your taffrail to show us your coffin!" (p. 578).*

In a similar situation, in *Benito Cereno,* just after it is suddenly
revealed to Captain Delano that Cereno is not the persecutor but
the persecuted, another stage-like sudden revelation places Delano's
reversal of attitude in brilliant relief as the sub-stage curtain is
suddenly lifted to reveal the figurehead:

> *But by this time, the cable of the* San Dominick *has been cut; and the*

THE NEW STRATEGY OF STYLE

> *fag-end, in lashing out, whipped away the canvas shroud about the beak,*
> *suddenly revealing, the bleached hull swung round toward the open ocean,*
> *death for the figurehead, in a human skeleton; chalky comment on the*
> *chalked words below, "Follow your leader." (pp. 79–80).*

And, in *Billy Budd,* there is another such example, as Billy is
hanged:

> *At the same moment it chanced that the vapory fleece hanging low in the*
> *East, was shot through with a soft glory as of the fleece of the Lamb of*
> *God seen in mystical vision and simultaneously therewith, watched by the*
> *wedged mass of upturned faces, Billy ascended; and ascending, took the*
> *full rose of the dawn (p. 62).*

This scene is one of perfect stage composition: the faces are all
directed toward a single figure who is above all the others, and he is
singled out to receive weird lighting effect.

There are in *Moby Dick* twelve chapters which employ stage
directions. Two blocks of such chapters occur: the first block,
Chapters 36 to 40, including the scenes in which Ahab swears his
men to his mission; the second, Chapters 119–122, being the scenes
of the great storm which demagnetizes the compass. Three isolated
chapters have stage directions as well: Chapter 108 with Ahab and
the carpenter, and Chapters 127 and 129 with Ahab and Pip. The
mere listing of these chapters reveals two important points: Melville
seems to use the playwright's method at exceedingly crucial
moments, and he uses this method at moments when dialogue and a
few elemental motions are needed to develop the basic action.
(Obviously the pursuit of the White Whale, while crucial, is all
action, and the narrative method is better suited to it.)

The first block of scenes is the finest, starting with words which
are as memorable as "Call me Ishmael": "enter Ahab: Then, all";
and building up to a frenzied scene representative of all mankind
dancing and singing to the steady beat of the tambourine. The
rhythmic background commences in the second paragraph—"Soon
his steady, ivory stride was heard . . ."—and leads into the
catechism of the sailors:

> *"What do ye do when you see a whale, men?"*
> *"Sing out for him!" . . .*
> *"And what do ye do next, men?"*
> *"Lower away, and after him!"*
> *"And what tune is it ye pull to, Men?"*
> *"A dead whale or a stove boat!" (p. 171).*

And the excitement builds up, interrupted only by Starbuck, until Ahab has his harpooners drink a pact with him from the hollows of their harpoon heads. This chapter is followed by three short chapters, each a soliloquy of a major figure. Here are the stage directions which open each of the chapters:

> Sunset: *The cabin; by the stern windows; Ahab sitting alone, and gazing out.*
> Dusk: *By the Mainmast; Starbuck leaning against it.*
> First Night Watch: *Stubb solus, and mending a brace.*

The very positions of the three men are carefully selected to reflect their characters, before each speaks. Stern Ahab, alone, at the stern windows; Starbuck in a position of anguish, but not standing alone—rather leaning against the mainmast. His first words show that he has relinquished his power to stand independently: "My soul is more than matched; she's over-manned; and by a madman!" And Stubb is disclosed, at work, totally business-like, but understanding in a shallow way, Starbuck's problem:

> "... who calls? Mr. Starbuck? Aye, aye, sir—(Aside) he's my superior, he has his too, if I'm not mistaken ..." (p. 182).

The first block culminates in Chapter 40, which is a play script opening with the stage direction to "raise the foresail" and carrying the men from song to dance, to contemplation of the sea as a sensuous woman, to a quarrel—until all breaks up as nature provides a squall to top the petty squalling of the men. In these scenes, then, we see the welding of the crew into a weapon of vengeance, and the stage-dialogue method has effectively portrayed the wildness and enthusiasm of the moment, while the musical accompaniment provides a steadiness in the background that, contrasting with the headlong drunkenness of the men's speech, creates a tension which probably reflects the tension that is felt on an intellectual plane by Starbuck and Ishmael. This method of producing tension is extremely powerful in the operatic tradition (consider virtually any Verdi opera) and, as we have seen, was used again by Melville in *Benito Cereno* where the inexorable droning of the oakum-pickers is punctuated by the clashing of the hatchet-cymbals, which provides a rigid regularity in tense contrast with Captain Delano's vacillating thoughts about Don Benito and his crew.

This fortieth chapter of *Moby Dick* is the most theatrical: never again does Melville bring the whole crew into the action as a chorus, and he uses only a few crew members other than the harpooners as single characters. But when he does, he returns to the stage technique. When lightning strikes the ship and all the crew gather around aghast, Ahab steals the show, posing before the "trinity of Flames." Finally, when Ahab does speak to crew members—the carpenter and the cabin boy—Melville also reverts to dramatic dialogue.

One is tempted to suggest that Melville meant *Moby Dick* to be a drama, but that the narrative of Ishmael, the digressions on cetology, and the violent action of the actual whale-hunts are too essential and could be dealt with only in the novel form. Melville did, however, make conscious use of theatrical conventions, probably to reinforce his view of a ship as a stage; as much of a microcosm as a stage, and yet as limited as a stage. He undoubtedly anticipated modern playwrights in accepting the limitations of a small physical environment, and in fact turned the limitations to his advantage by intensifying human contacts and intellectual problems through the use of highly selective and vivid symbols, placed in visual prominence. His dialogue is artificial, yet each actor has his characteristic mode of speech, usually established by means of distinctive metaphors. In short, the peculiar stage passages in *Moby Dick* enhance the narration, and support the ship-stage attitude which Melville expressed most fully in *Billy Budd.*

Notes

1. *Moby Dick; or, The Whale* (New York: Heritage Press, 1943), p. 7.
2. *Billy Budd,* in *American Short Novels,* ed. R. P. Blackmur (New York: Crowell, 1960), p. 38.
3. *Benito Cereno,* in *Shorter Novels of Herman Melville* (New York: Horace Liveright, 1928), p. 8.
4. An illustrated translation of Froissart appeared in New York in 1854, two years before the publication of *Benito Cereno.* Eighteenth-century architectural drawings in Chapman's *Architectura Navalis Mercatoria* 1768, Neu Herausgageben von Robert Loef (Berlin, 1930) indicate that the ship decks in 1768 were flat, and that even frigates were not built with a rear deck elevated more than five feet. Judging from illustrations in *Navires et Marins* (Paris, 1946), Volume II, in the section "Les Trois-Mats du Commerce", pp. 138–144, the *San Dominick* may have been built before 1679.

EXERCISES

1. Make a study of a work of fiction, poetry, or drama; decide what aspect you wish to treat; and formulate a thesis. Write a short professional article (500–1,000 words, which many journals would refer to as a "note") in support of your thesis, drawing exclusively upon the primary source for evidence.
2. Using a mixture of primary and secondary sources, write a short professional article (1,000–1,500 words) on a person or event of historical significance. You may wish to

choose a subject of local significance, for which you will have to do a certain amount of especially imaginative research.

3. Using secondary sources almost exclusively, i.e. newspaper and magazine stories, radio and television reports, make a study of some current and controversial event. Compare and weigh the evidence. Write a short but fully documented account which represents for you the truth. How did you evaluate the secondary sources?

4. Make a schematic analysis of a short published professional article, identifying the beginning, the middle and the ending with marginal brackets; circling each clear statement of the thesis; underlining each subordinate assumption; and, if it is appropriate, placing a "p" or "s" by each piece of evidence according to whether it is primary or secondary.

5. In three divergent scholarly or technical articles, estimate the proportion of primary and secondary source evidence. What influence does the nature of the subject seem to have upon the resulting ratios or percentages? Might the authors have used a higher proportion of primary sources to good advantage? What efforts did they make to choose the most pertinent and persuasive secondary sources?

6. Compile a bibliography for a specific topic. Be exhaustive but selective. Compare your list with those prepared by your colleagues for the same topic. How closely do they compare? How does yours compare with the best?

7. Retrace the steps followed by a writer in researching and supplying evidence for a professional article by running down every source footnote and every bibliographical entry. Have the sources been exploited well? Can you find other readily available sources apparently not consulted that would have been even more useful? Using the same sources as the writer, could you write an article on another aspect of the same subject?

8. Find two professional articles (on the same general subject if possible), one marred by a somewhat self-consciously pretentious style and the other written more naturally. From your study of these two articles, do you think it possible to be learned and precise without using technical jargon and pedantic expressions? Or do you think the dangers of overstatement and impressionistic writing are greater?

9. Rewrite a popular article as a professional article. Among

other changes, you will have to limit the subject further, supply more and different kinds of evidence, document your sources, employ a more cautious and explicit style. Compare the results.

10. Now, in view of what you have learned about the professional article, write such a prose form following as nearly as possible the described procedure.

18. THE PERSONAL ESSAY

The *essay* is not so pointedly factual or instructive as the article, but more ranging and speculative. Written for a reader of philosophical temperament and urbane tastes, it demands of us a thoughtful, impressionable, and original turn of mind. Of all prose forms the *personal essay* is the most literary and self-revealing, calling upon all those *strategies of style* we have acquired through practice.

Perhaps, as we are told, the mood of the age is not right for the essay, but a great many readers find it the best of all possible forms: the *personal essay* possessing the intimacy of a private conversation, the *formal essay* recalling the wise and prophetic dignity of a classical oration. The customary and quite real distinction between the two general types of essays is only a suggestion of its diversity and adaptability. Indeed, the essayical spirit is not likely to diminish.

THE PERSONAL ESSAY AS A FORM

Any description of the personal essay must include these qualities: the personal element, the suggestive treatment of the subject, the informal structure, the graceful and effortless style, and the literary effect.

The *personal element* is naturally a major attribute of the form. The personal essay is a fragment of autobiography, for it is inevitably self-revealing. The tastes and impressions and experiences of a unique individual dominate the essay to such an extent that it simply could not have been written by anyone else. Yet it is not autobiographical in the most limited sense. It is personal but not private. What the writer does is express an individual view of a universal subject—that is, objectifies subjective experience.

The reader's impression is of having broken in on a personal reverie. The essay has also been compared to a lyric poem. But it is more like a dialogue or, better, a quiet conversation with a friend; for it is in every way one writer speaking with one reader, as perfect equals. The persona, or speaker, may be any kind of personality. But generally essayists are sincere, modest, frank, curious, observant, calm, affable, fanciful. Even though the writing may have been provoked by something about which they are mildly discontent, essayists rarely lose their sense of humor. And their manner is always intimate and confidential, never pompous or distant, never platitudinous or cliché ridden.

In a form so dominated by the spirit and whims of the writer, a *suggestive treatment of the subject is inevitable.* The subject itself is often of no great consequence and may appear trifling. This is because the essayist's vision is miniature, focused on the little things and commonplaces (but not the silly, the ephemeral), fit subjects for reflection or reminiscence. Even if the subject is of apparent significance, the treatment will in no way be a complete and comprehensive statement. This isn't to say the personal essay is uninformed or frivolous; actually it reveals in a casual way an intimate knowledge of the subject. And it may well be that the really significant subjects in life are quite beyond formal explanation. Certainly the writer of personal essays will not describe, analyze, and evaluate a subject in a very methodical way. Moreover, since the essayist's view is comic—that is, detached, skeptical, amused by the human scene—the treatment of any subject is apt to be light, whimsical, humorous. Even when the essayist is deadly in earnest, anxiety and anger take the form of cynicism and satire.

The subject receives this treatment partly because of the *informal structure* of the personal essay. It is simply too brief and tentative a form to permit elaborate schemes of order and organization. Actually both are present, but the basis is more psychological than logical. The essayist depends more on the subtle devices of momentum and on simple association than on more obvious and closely reasoned schemes. The personal essay is more digressive and allusive than deliberate and explicit, more descriptive and narrative than expository or argumentative. Indeed, the most definite thing you can say about the structure of the personal essay is that it brings considerable knowledge to bear on a specific subject, that it has a definite point (or thesis) and a climax, and that it does have a beginning and middle and end. Despite the apparent lack of any itinerary, the personal essay always seems to get where it's going with surprising zip—suggesting that here at least, the shortest distance between two points is not a straight line.

The informal structure is matched by a *graceful and effortless style.* The personal essay could not, of course, be what it is without employing a style that is informal, sometimes colloquial, easy and relaxed, conversational, natural, spontaneous, even impetuous. But style is finally a personal affair, the distinctive idiom of this writer on this occasion. The personal essay is written with style, with a manner of expression that is never perfunctory, never simply correct, always preeminently expressive.

But whatever else it is or is not, the personal essay is *literary.* Its knowledge reflects a well-read and speculative mind; its allusions, wit, irony, satire evince a nimble intellect; its images, metaphors, symbols suggest a keen observer and lively imagination; its sounds and rhythms, appropriate always if not euphonic, are proof of a lyric sense. In the personal essay the fusion of form and content is particularly right; the means becomes the end. In short, this spectacle of a civilized human being describing the good life (perhaps lamenting its passing or yearning for its attainment) is intensely literary.

HOW TO WRITE THE PERSONAL ESSAY

Since you are assuming many of the literary prerogatives of the poet and short story writer, you may use their methods in writing the personal essay—and their methods are not the deliberate ways of the scholar and journalist. The creative process is, of course, largely a unique and private affair, especially that of essayists; for theirs is

in many ways the most subjective of literary forms. But most writers
for most of their essays seem to follow this plan or something like it:

1. *Begin with some abstract thought associated with concrete things or
specific events* to such an extent that the things and events stand (or
can be made to stand) as metaphors for the thought. Sometimes the
thought will come first, sometimes the sensory experience. But in
either case, the thought should be a personal sentiment, one which
has its origin perhaps in mild discontent, and one that speaks to the
reader's condition; and the things and events should involve a considerable quantity of the solid, perceptible stuff of life.

There is certainly no scarcity of ideas for essays. If you are
lucky, you may come upon the germ of an essay quite by accident;
you may even be surprised to discover that it has already begun to
develop. But most of the time you will have to go looking. And the
place to look is rarely among facts, for the personal essay is not a
scientific or inductive effort, but a speculative and far-ranging one.
Indeed, much of the time you will find yourself looking inward at
how a thing strikes you, or at what connection it has with something
else you once encountered. Remember, an essayist is first a curious
and observant and meditative person—hence, always on the look-
out for the subject matter, whether the essays get written or not.
(You can always stimulate this idea-getting process by asking yourself two questions: What have I just experienced? observed? How do
I feel about it now that I've had time to reflect?)

For example, on a walk across campus you might be struck by
the "straight" lines of buildings, of the street, of the angular books
in your arms, of the wings on that 727 flying overhead . . . and by
the "curved" lines of trees, of the creek, of the cumulus clouds in the
sky, of the curl in that girl's hair. The notion that human culture is
linked to the straight line, that people came into the world and began drawing straight lines where there were formerly only curved
ones, that it is "their mark" (possible title?) is an obvious enough
connection. While this thought is not yet a fully developed idea—
you may wind up writing about the aesthetics of efficiency or the
architectural tyranny of the post and lintel or the posters of Peter
Max or the art nouveau revival or something else—the association
you have made between the concrete and abstract is one of the most
likely places to begin that line of thought which will culminate in a
personal essay.

2. Next *summon up and inventory all the relevancies from your experience
and observation, reflection and reading.* Begin to build a reservoir of images, metaphors, symbols, allusions, quotations, anecdotes, etc., from
which to draw for this essay. Jot them down as they come to you by
association—this may be more or less the order of your mentioning
them in the essay itself. Suppose, for example, that in the course of

reading some rather bad verse by a minor poet you came upon
these surprisingly memorable lines,

> *Red o'er the forest peers the setting sun.*
> *The line of yellow light dies fast away*
> *That crowned the eastern copse: and chill and dun*
> *Falls on the moor the brief November day . . .—John Keble,* Christian
> Year

You might well be struck by the realization that our ideas about not
only art but life are based overmuch upon total effect, that we have
too little appreciation of the part. The thought that fragments and
ruins possess a beauty often surpassing that of the whole and perfect
(and sometimes even imperfect) original is exactly the sort of thing
about which essays are written. As you pursue this line of thinking—recalling the classical torsos you viewed in the British Museum,
Schubert's *Unfinished Symphony,* an intriguing scrap of overheard conversation, Rose Macaulay's *Pleasure of Ruins,* the oak ribs of a
wrecked schooner protruding from the sand of Cape Cod, etc.—concentrate on range and variety, even if the mix of details has about it
a suggestion of incongruity.

Although we speak of it as an expository form, the personal essay often begins by relating a story or painting a word picture, or
contains details which to all purposes do one or the other. And it
may be based almost exclusively on a narrative or descriptive framework. But usually the personal essay is a free-wheeling mix of anecdotal and descriptive detail linked by passages of expository comment.

3. *Add to that reservoir of materials, if necessary, by doing some research.*
You will probably have to check on the accuracy and relevancy of
quotations, allusions, details. Run down, for example, the exact
phrasing of Fromme's remark to the effect that great societies worship people and use things while we in America worship things and
use people; look to be certain that Gilbert White is, indeed, considered the first field naturalist; find out if those handsome gold-
hackled and russet-barred chickens, the kind old masters scattered
around the feet of milkmaids, were in fact golden Campines; and
simply reread the *Blackwood's* essay in which Sir John Glubb establishes the life-span of great national powers as never more than 250
years.

4. *Decide what your response will be toward the matter of the essay.* A
certain consistency of response, especially in those essays where subject and thesis are neither very definite, is basic to the unity of the
essay. You will probably need to establish in your own mind the

persona, the "speaker" in this personal essay. You may even choose to jot down a brief character sketch of this persona, whether or not it is you speaking—and, of course, you may well decide to assume for this essay a role other than the one in which you normally confront life. You might, for example, choose for the moment to be someone else—a cultured, bookish, fashionable, middle-aged woman of the world who has just thrown over her New York job with an advertising agency to go live in the country—in order to make a kind of observation about life you cannot as Pete, age 19, student at Midwestern U., left tackle, even though Pete is quite capable of making valid and even profound statements while being himself. (However, if Pete is going to attempt to "put on" such a persona, he had better be an avid reader of such authors as Marya Mannes and Dorothy Parker, have a girl friend who subscribes to *Vogue* and a mother who gave up bridge clubs to raise bantams in her suburban backyard—or settle for something a little closer to himself in the first place. But the value of sometimes making a distinction between yourself as the writer of the essay and the persona who is the speaker in the essay is obvious.) At the very least you will have to decide whether you will be whimsical and playful, or methodical and dignified, or something else. As author or persona, the role you play must be clear and consistent.

5. Only now are you ready to *put aside random speculations and begin thinking in terms of a specific subject and thesis.* Your essay will, no doubt, touch on many things, but in the end it will be clear that even the apparent digressions and irrelevancies all have some bearing on a single subject. And in almost every essay you write, the purpose, or central thought of the essay is summed up at least once. Some personal essays are more pointed than others. Most give the impression of being more unpremeditated and rambling than they actually are. But even in the freest, you are on safer ground if you provide your reader with a clear sense of what the essay is about and to what object it is written. And not only is a clear subject-and-thesis desirable, but the subject-and-thesis must be something you can handle in the brief and casual personal essay. You will, in fact, do better with a limited subject than with a broad subject. Your major problem will always lie, not in a lack of knowledge about your subject, but in your failure to present what knowledge you have in an effective way. So while the personal essay is in some respects far-ranging, it is largely addressed to a specific subject-and-thesis—even though both subject and thesis may be suggestively developed. For example, George Orwell's "Some Thoughts on the Common Toad," has as its apparent subject the phenomena of spring, especially mating toads; the essay is in truth a form of social criticism developing the thesis that

*by retaining one's childhood love of such things as trees, fishes, butterflies and
. . . toads, one makes a peaceful and decent future a little more probable, and
that by preaching the doctrine that nothing is to be admired except steel and concrete, one merely makes it a little surer that human beings will have no outlet
for their surplus energy except in hatred and leader-worship.—George Orwell,*
Some Thoughts on the Common Toad

6. *Jot down a list of topics for the essay in about the order you plan to
use them.* Don't be concerned about phrasing and don't be too detailed. Keep thinking of these notes as tentative. And try out one
scheme and then another until you find the most promising. From
this point form will be a major consideration. Look first at what design the material seems to call for. Then, within the confines of this
design, try to order your materials most effectively. In brief, what
you want here are from three to seven topics; providing for a beginning, middle, and end; with topics of the middle part, regardless
what other schemes may be used, ordered in terms of increasing relevance and importance; planning for something strong to occur toward the end of the essay. A personal essay on "old maps," for example, might be written around these topics:

—Beginning: Thesis—the disappearance of vast white spaces,
of *terra incognita* from maps of the world has cramped the fancy—for
the imagination is most stirred by the vaguely dreamed of and the
wholly unknown.
—Modern maps, in their detail and exactness and, above all,
in their practical uses, are dull affairs.
—Old maps with their showy hues and designs are the most
romantic expression of the imaginative spirit.
—The only unknown seas and lands remain in literature.
—But even modern writers only thinly disguise familiar places.
—Ending: In the blank spaces of old maps and in the make-
believe lands of childhood there was space for dreaming that has
quite gone out with the accurate charting of the world.

7. *Incorporate the minor details.* Don't work out a complete and explicit formal outline, the object is only to have the materials for
writing conveniently at hand. You may want to revise and certainly
you will have to enlarge the brief "outline" you jotted down earlier,
deciding what you can and can't use in this essay. This will be determined largely by the conception of form that has begun to
emerge.
8. *Consider what attitude will prevail in the essay.* This may have
been apparent from the beginning, possibly a consequence of your
choice of persona—but begin to indicate, in this draft, the particular

attitude you have chosen to maintain in presenting your material. If you have decided to be humorous or ironic, you can—even in this draft—begin to create the phrases and locutions that will reveal to your reader that "this is for fun" or "this means something other than what it actually says." If you choose to be humorous, you will use such well-established devices of humor as *exaggeration, surprise,* and *dehumanization.* If you choose to be ironic, you will use the standard devices of *inversion with exaggeration* ("The novel was brilliant" for "The novel was quite bad"), *negation* ("The novel was not bad" for "The novel was bad"), and *understatement* ("The novel was not very good" for "The novel was terrible"). Even at this stage what is said cannot be separated from how it is said.

9. Next, *attend to form.* Your essay should have the basic design of "beginning, middle, end," and that properly proportioned. You may need to elaborate and expand here, eliminate or condense there, in order to control proportion and emphasis. Though your personal essay can't do without a *beginning,* you may introduce your subject matter—the main task of any beginning—in a more casual and indirect way than would be possible in other forms of writing. You can construct a delayed beginning, not stating your subject in the first sentence of the first paragraph as you would normally do, but presenting the subject at the end of the first paragraph or even somewhere in the second paragraph. The delayed beginning is appropriate to the personal essay because it helps create the light and casual tone, and suggests the author is willing to spend a little time in setting the stage for the subject. But even in the more typical direct beginning a certain amount of edging toward the subject is characteristic of the personal essay—as in Jane O'Reilly's "On Daring to Be Romantic."

My notions of what is romantic were fairly well fixed when I was 10 years old and first heard the song about a stranger seen across a crowded room on some enchanted evening. I am still quite attached to those notions. Champagne is, of course, romantic. So are white lilacs out of season, long-distance telephone calls at midnight, Fred Astaire movies, fur rugs before bedroom fireplaces.

In time, some of my notions of the romantic had to be given up. Maribou bed jackets made me sneeze, red leather address books were too often lost. Lace-trimmed nightgowns hand-hemmed in Belgium were too often thrown into the laundry with the sweat socks.

As the proportion of sweat socks rose in relation to the tattered remnants of lace nightgowns, I reflected sorrowfully, and with considerable lack of originality, that life is not, as a rule, very romantic.

I was wrong. Life is romantic; infinitely unpredictable, endlessly possible. What was not romantic was my own stubborn attachments to a few ideas of what romance should be. Limousines and candlelight and meaningful glances are all right as far as they go, but they don't go very far. As concepts, they serve best in advertisements. In real life, they are somewhat banal, and the constant effort to avoid banality is the essence of romanticism.—Jane O'Reilly, On Daring to Be Romantic

10. In the *middle section be sure that your essay has an apparent and appropriate design, and enough continuity and momentum* that the reader will move from one thought to the next smoothly and swiftly. Notice the apparent design and the transitional devices in these first lines from the major paragraphs in J. B. Priestley's "On Education":

When I was sixteen I left school and found myself a job in a wool office. . . .
Looking back, I can see quite clearly now that the great formative period for me was neither school nor the Cambridge years. It was 1911–14, when nobody was trying to educate me nor paying for me to be instructed, when, in fact, I was working (though as little as possible) in the wool office. . . .
The truth is, I was fortunate during those years in my environment. . . .
Let us take a look at what seem at first to be more formal processes of education. . . .
Now we have to spend so much on the school that we cannot afford to educate the street. . . .
But no, I must not growl and grumble. I will simply state the case, as I see it. I owe most to a time when I was not being formally educated but when I enjoyed an environment favourable to a youth of my sort. . . .—J. B. Priestley, On Education

11. Whether the *ending* is a quick summary or a conclusion, it should come full circle by renaming the subject and referring once again to the matter of the beginning. The only exception to this rule is the occasional epilogue ending which follows a traditional ending and brings the essay to rest with a final anecdote or some other afterthought. The ending of E. M. Forster's "My Wood" is a conventional summary ending:

Enormously stout, endlessly avaricious, pseudo-creative, insensely selfish, I shall weave upon my forehead the quadruple crown of possession until those nasty Bolshies come and take it off again and thrust me aside into the outer darkness.—E. M. Forster, My Wood

And G. K. Chesterton's "A Piece of Chalk" employs an even more traditional conclusion ending, one which clinches the point of the essay:

And I stood there in a trance of pleasure, realizing that this Southern England is not only a grand peninsula, and a tradition and a civilisation; it is something even more admirable. It is a piece of chalk.—G. K. Chesterton, A Piece of Chalk

But Wolcott Gibbs's "The Country of the Blind," an essay on the resistance of the cinema to rational criticism, terminates with the more exceptional epilogue ending:

I once knew an educated and almost excessively cultivated man who really enjoyed reviewing the movies. He was, however, a special case, in that he was unfailingly amused in his wintry way by sex in what he was pleased to call its "contactual aspects," and the idea of an art form fundamentally based on the slow, relentless approach and final passionate collision of two enormous faces struck him as convulsing. He wrote about it all with a wonderful, maidenly distaste, and to the total bewilderment of the motion-picture industry, but he really had the time of his life. He was also a very valuable critic since, free from the terrible spell of Love, he saw a good deal that escaped his earnest colleagues.— Wolcott Gibbs, The Country of the Blind

12. And *consider again the location of the thesis.* In the personal essay, you need not spell out your thesis at the essay's beginning, of course—but there probably should be a concise statement of your thesis at the climax or in the conclusion of your essay. Occasionally, you may even use an implied thesis—refraining from stating your thesis altogether but revealing it to your reader by indirection and suggestion. Virginia Woolf, in "The Death of the Moth," muses about the dying struggles of a diminutive moth on a window ledge with the world's great landscape beyond, concluding with what is, because of its understatement, an implied thesis—"O yes, he seemed to say, death is stronger than I am."

13. *Finally, concentrate on style and on the literary touches.* Both, of course, have been a part of your conception from the beginning. But now that the larger problems of form are solved, you can turn more of your rewriting time over to these. See if there is any point where an image, metaphor, symbol, quotation, allusion, play on words could be sharper or richer. Do all you can to make the wording smooth and clear, possibly even lyrical or grand. Certainly at the essay's climax you will consider using the most impressive language that it will bear. At the same time, you will be consistent. Unless you are being inconsistent for effect, try to maintain the same general level of diction and the same general sentence and paragraph style throughout the essay. In the beginning of your essay, you commit yourself to a certain rhetorical profile and a certain approach throughout your essay. Do not violate this commitment without

good reason. At any rate, the personal essay is a literary form—and this implies a heightened vision and language not to be achieved in any quick and easy way. Even the poetry of G. K. Chesterton's "A Piece of Chalk" is possible in the personal essay:

With my stick and my knife, my chalks and my brown paper, I went out on to the great downs. I crawled across those colossal contours that express the best quality of England, because they are at the same time soft and strong. The smoothness of them has the same meaning as the smoothness of great cart-horses, or the smoothness of the beech-tree; it declares in the teeth of our timid and cruel theories that the mighty are merciful. As my eye swept the landscape, the landscape was as kindly as any of its cottages, but for power it was like an earthquake. The villages in the immense valley were safe, one could see, for centuries; yet the lifting of the whole land was like the lifting of one enormous wave to wash them all away.

I crossed one swell of living turf after another, looking for a place to sit down and draw. Do not, for heaven's sake, imagine I was going to sketch from Nature. I was going to draw devils and seraphim, and blind old gods that men worshipped before the dawn of right, and saints in robes of angry crimson, and seas of strange green, and all the sacred or monstrous symbols that look so well in bright colours on brown paper. They are much better worth drawing than Nature; also they are much easier to draw. When a cow came slouching by in the field next to me, a mere artist might have drawn it; but I always get wrong in the hind legs of quadrupeds. So I drew the soul of the cow; which I saw there plainly walking before me in the sunlight; and the soul was all purple and silver, and had seven horns and the mystery that belongs to all the beasts. But though I could not with a crayon get the best out of the landscape, it does not follow that the landscape was not getting the best out of me. And this, I think, is the mistake that people make about the old poets who lived before Wordsworth, and were supposed not to care very much about Nature because they did not describe it much.

They preferred writing about great men to writing about great hills; but they sat on the great hills to write it. They gave out much less about Nature, but they drank in, perhaps, much more. They painted the white robes of their holy virgins with the blinding snow, at which they had stared all day. They blazoned the shields of their paladins with the purple and gold of many heraldic sunsets. The greenness of a thousand green leaves clustered into the live green figure of Robin Hood. The blueness of a score of forgotten skies became the blue robes of the Virgin. The inspiration went in like sunbeams and came out like Apollo.—G. K. Chesterton, A Piece of Chalk

14. *Now look again at the essay*—especially at the first sentence of your essay and the last, and at the title. The first sentence—whether it leads the reader directly into a consideration of your subject or is part of a prelude—should arouse the reader's curiosity. The last sen-

tence should have about it a ring of finality, of farewell. And the title should be brief, descriptive or at least pertinent, and provocative. Above all, the essay should possess the kind of literary sophistication readers expect to find in the form.

If you get stuck along the way, as all writers do from time to time, here are some suggestions: (1) Go back to the beginning of the creative process and retrace your steps, checking at each point to see that you have made the best decision. Perhaps you made a wrong turn somewhere. (2) Forget about the immediate problem for the time being, loosen up and just write on—perhaps the problem will iron itself out, or perhaps you will be able to deal with it better later. (3) Come back to it later. Writing is hard work, perhaps you need to take a short rest from it. When you turn again to your essay, you may be able to deal more successfully with problems as they come up. (4) If you are really stuck, stop writing and start reading. See how other essayists have dealt with their materials. It may help if you use another essay as a model. (5) As last resort, put this essay aside and start afresh on a new idea.

THE WHOLE COMPOSITION

"Flirtation," that "small impermanent spark between one human being and another," hardly the topic for a more matter-of-fact study, is an ideal subject for the personal essay. But however light and amusing the essay, Marya Mannes is quite serious in the observations she makes about "social life today" and in her conclusion that "the function of flirtation is to bring the illusion of intimacy to a public encounter."

A Plea for Flirtation

Marya Mannes

In an age where the lowered eyelid is merely a sign of fatigue, the delicate game of love is pining away. This observation may, of course, be traced to the age of the writer and countered by an army of women under forty who find, in this country of youth, no such decline in the practice of flirtation.

But I doubt it. While so much of our life is confined to halfway measures (the middle-of-the-road is the security zone), love is the exception. A man and a woman are either in love or just friends. And this, I think, is a very great pity. For I remember from earlier years, as I know from present experience abroad, a highly stimulating area between these extremes in which the presence of sex in conversation can be a pleasure in itself, making a man feel more of a man and a woman more of a woman without requiring either mating or marriage. It can, in fact, be enjoyed by those happily married to others, by those maintaining, for whatever reason, a single state, and by those with dishonorable intentions. Flirtation is merely an expression of considered desire coupled with an admission of its impracticability. "I think you are very attractive," say the eyes of man to the eyes of woman, "and it would be nice if we could. But you know and I know we can't."

"If we were on a desert island together," say the eyes of woman to the eyes of man, "we could have a very pleasant time." In a good flirtation these semaphores are never translated into words. In fact, they may be waved back and forth during a conversation on theatre, pink-foot geese, or skindiving, though talk of the stock market might prove too competitive. (Money is not an aphrodisiac: the desire it may kindle in the female eye is more for the cash than the carrier.)

But if it is indeed true that these passages of arms and eyes are increasingly rare in our social life today, what are the reasons? We can eliminate those groups in which flirtation never flourished, and one of them is what we are now allowed to call "the lower economic bracket." They want what they want when they want it, and that's about it. And if we are to believe the dialogue of Paddy Chayefsky and other tape-recorder writers, words are out of the picture. Or rather, they come singly and painfully between man and woman as they shuffle toward a disordered bed. Not for them the time or the taste for sweet nothings; or the vocabulary.

And what of the middle bracket of our people, the happy suburbans? Well, it's hard to flirt with the kiddies underfoot, and if one is to believe what one reads about life in Oakwood, adults are never alone until after their third Martini, when lunges towards the neighbor's wife come under the heading of euphoria rather than flirtation. Alcohol, no matter where, precipitates the behavior which a controlled flirtation would evade. You can't be tight and tentative.

And what of the leisured people, the upper bracket, the intellectuals? Well, I would cancel out the contemporary intellectuals in our society: a great many seem to think that a free spirit and social graces are incompatible, and they find the frivolity of a compliment beneath them. I think also that Freud and flirtation are poor companions, for a search for meanings can spoil a lot of fun.

So now we come to the last rampart, the arbiters, the traveled, the sophisticated. We are not talking here of the young in search of marriage: their flirtations have deadly purpose. We are talking of those ostensibly stabilized, if not trapped.

Well, I have been to a legion of dinners with people like these, and I find the pattern between men and women something like this: if the man you sit next to is an old friend, familiarity precludes flirtation; you talk of friends or weekend traffic. You can't be both cosy and curious, and curiosity is a major ingredient in flirtation. If the man you sit next to is an old beau who still finds you attractive, he will usually be too fond of your husband and too afraid of his wife to say so. Affection for the mates of others is the Great Neutralizer.

If the man you sit next to is a stranger—presumably the ideal beginning—you have three problems as a woman. If you try to entertain him, he is inclined to think you are either garrulous or aggressive. If you wait for him to entertain you, the woman on his other side will grab him. And if you betray any interest in him as a man, panic will seize him (watch out for this woman). Your neighbor may be masterful on the golf course, but the fairways of flirtation are for him a terrain of hazards for which he is not equipped. More profoundly, what generic love of women and interest in women he may once have had has been long since overlaid by paper work: he has forgotten how to talk to women unless they are secretaries.

Unlike Europeans, then, our American man is more relieved than dismayed when the host bears him off to the company of men after dinner, and the women are segregated, spending together what seems to be the balance of the night. Whatever mood was established during cocktails and dinner is never recaptured after the sexes, at long last, are rejoined. The male eyes are on the wrist watch, the female eyes on their husbands, and the only semaphores waved spell "Let's go home."

Cocktail parties—particularly large ones—are better for flirting, although hostesses have a compulsive genius for discouraging its development. No sooner have you established some contact with your partner's eye and mind, than she pulls you away to meet a couple who are welded to each other by timidity as well as marriage. There is nothing more annoying, in fact, to the average hostess, than an unmated couple enjoying each other's company.

Now, travel used to be a magnificent field for flirtation and, in other parts of the world, still is. It is possible, if not inevitable, to play this game of attraction on a train or plane crossing the boundaries of Europe and carrying men of curiosity and courage; but something strange has happened to that former cradle of flirtation: the ocean liner.

Pick-ups, yes. You have only to stand at the rail of a ship alone for a while to have some man inch up alongside and break the silence. But always the wrong man with the wrong voice. Why? Because the attractive man, the desirable man, the right man, is in mortal terror of speaking to, or being spoken to by, the wrong woman. So, plunged in a book in remote deck chair behind a stanchion, or holed in his cabin till the last day, he keeps himself inviolate. Now this, of course, is not always the case. He may quite possibly engage in flirtation with a woman who is the wrong one merely because she is not yourself. (You call her The Obvious Type: Lays it on with a Trowel.)

But I think that women on the prowl have spoiled the gentle sport, and every ship is full of them looking for the single men who aren't there, or who have better prospects in port. And how is a poor man to know these days whether flirtation is a game without a goal or a strategy for life? The acquisitive intensity of American women who interpret a gallant compliment as a proposal of marriage is not only the dismay of European men but possibly the greatest single inhibitor of the instinct towards flirtation in all the men she meets.

So much for boats. As for rolling stock, since the American train has given up providing even the minimal comforts, it can hardly be expected to service flirtation. Men use parlor cars to catch up on work and bar cars to catch up on drink, and as for the dining car, eyes that are riveted on lurching coffee are hardly free to drown in the gaze of others. Besides, who rides in trains these days except commuters or those grounded by weather—hardly amorous conditions?

And what of the airplane? Having sat in a window seat for thousands of miles over this glorious land, I can only testify that the neighboring seat is occupied by a woman or not at all. Nothing seems to strike terror in the American male like a seat next to a female: he will avoid it at all costs. Why? Because he thinks he will be talked at, and because he finds the talk of most women deadly. This I understand, with a certain sympathy. For in a plane he is stuck for the duration; he can not move away. And the tragedy is that the faster we go, the more we are trapped. In the older and slower planes of the past—the Flying Boat of the forties, the Stratocruiser of the early fifties—there were places for meeting and ways to change seats, and I remember, wistfully, several trips across the sea when the company of strange men provided exhilaration without risk.

But now there is nothing but the sterile seat plan of the jetborne capsule and the cowardice of men who will not trade the *Reader's Digest* or *Business Week* for the brief knowledge of a strange woman. Who knows, she might be even more fun?

At this point, I am forced to admit that the average American male air traveler rarely compels curiosity. He is rather grey, inside and out, and he wears his clothes and his hat without any masculine dash. They are coverings, not statements. If he is old, his face is either hard-bitten or baby-soft; and if he is younger, he has no definite face at all: rather, an arrangement of features blurred to anonymity by adjustment. What's more, such men never look at a woman directly, although they study measurements. Such is our culture, in fact, that woman is not the sum of her dimensions, but her dimensions are the sum of woman. The nature of woman, the mind of woman, the spirit of woman—these, to most of our men, are irrelevancies. And when only the attributes of physical youth are able to arouse interest in a man, the value of a woman at any age lies undiscovered. Mature men know this. Grown-up adolescents don't. And it is they who form the enormous market for sex magazines, art stills, and girls for whom no preliminaries are required.

Now let me quickly, before an army of men protest, distribute blame equally for the decline of flirtation. Men and women make each other what they are; and if I have been concentrating on the conspicuous lack of masculine skill at this sport, or even engagement in it, it is because I am, so to speak, on the other side.

But I have observed enough to understand our share of the guilt and attempt to define it. The faces of most women on the street (literally speaking) hardly invite the gentler male approach. They are set, self-preoccupied, and cold-eyed. In fact, they seldom bother to look a man in the eye with that pleased appraisal that makes the passage of a man in the streets of Europe an adventure. And I am not speaking of professional appraisal.

Too many women either have no time to acknowledge the courtesies too few men pay them—opening doors, offering seats, picking things up—or assume that they are passes to be repulsed. It is the rare man who continues to suffer such bruises.

At parties, too few women accord the men they meet their whole attention. Either their gaze wanders, or their conversation is a monologue directed largely at themselves. Junior's school triumphs or the importance of World Federalism do not kindle the opposite eye. Nor does that narcissism, widely prevalent, that makes a woman more concerned with how she looks than with the man who is looking at her.

For the function of flirtation is to bring the illusion of intimacy to a public encounter; to warm, to amuse, to titillate, even to excite. It is a graceful salute to sex, a small impermanent spark between one human being and another, between a man and a woman not in need of fire. And it would make this impermanent life a lot more fun if more of us learned the art of keeping the spark alive, and glowing.

Exercises

1. Write a three-paragraph essay on a traditional topic, one which would have appealed to a Bacon or an Addison as much as to a Marya Mannes (e.g., Of Travel, Of Friendship, A Plea for Flirtation).

2. The shorter forms are always difficult—but try your hand at a one-paragraph essay. Notice how similar it is to the essay of more familiar length in terms of subject and thesis, beginning-middle-end, and structure generally.

3. Write an essay in the style of some well-known essayist, either using a particular essay as a model or simply appropriating the essayist's characteristic style.

4. Make a structural analysis of a published essay: underline every statement of the subject with single lines, each statement of the thesis with double lines, the topic sentence of each paragraph with dotted lines; circle each transition (connect by lines those working in combination); identify each paragraph form and some of the more prominent sentences in the margin; identify some of the more apparent literary touches (quotations, allusions, figures of speech, etc.); and comment upon the general development of the essay. You may wish to use the Marya Mannes essay. In any case read the essay again noting the way in which form and content supplement one another.

5. Make a list of several different essays on the same subject, noting the influence of form on content.

6. Write an openly humorous or ironic essay.

7. Write as stunning a personal essay as you can manage, adapting the form to your own interests and tastes.

19. THE FORMAL ESSAY

Even if we have not read many examples of the *formal essay,* we have undoubtedly listened to them in the form of addresses and sermons, scholarly lectures and ceremonial speeches. Reflective and critical, associated with special occasions and grand issues, formal essays are not one of the prose forms we are frequently called upon to write. Yet appropriate opportunities will arise—and meanwhile we will draw upon the rhetoric of the formal essay whenever we wish our words to carry particular weight and dignity.

Even in so informal a society as that of twentieth-century America, the formal essay is an important literary genre. Only the imperceptive and unduly practical writer would decide that "to be formal is to be phony" and would therefore ignore the art of the formal essay. Civilized and mature writers unhesitatingly include the genre in their repertoire of prose forms; they trust that even in a shirtsleeve society, submissive as it frequently is to riotous harangues, the formal essay still has its place, that there is need for the essay in which a thoughtful writer may consider public and social issues in a logical and reasonable way.

THE FORMAL ESSAY AS A FORM

The formal essay is characterized primarily by its serious purpose, its public orientation, its orderliness, and its dispassionate style.

The *serious purpose* of the essayist is actually what brings the formal essay into being. The form emerges from the desire of the writer to speak lastingly and meaningfully to a serious-minded audience on a subject of some importance. An essential aspect of this serious purpose is the essayist's desire to educate, rather than to entertain; to stimulate intellectually rather than simply to delight.

Yet the serious didactic intentions of the formal essay must be distinguished from the informative intentions of the professional article. The formal essayist educates more by "pondering" than by "proving," and is less likely to supply the reader with detailed information and scientific conclusions (as in the professional article), than to supply the reader with judgments and ideas designed to influence or change the reader's intellectual perspective. If the professional article presents data leading to a judgment, the formal essay presents judgments that lead to admonition. In the formal essay, fact is less important than the meaning of fact, and if analysis occurs it is not of a laboratory nature; the discussion is always less concerned with establishing the validity of evidence and more concerned with revealing the implications of conclusions and theses.

Serious in purpose, the formal essay is also *the most public of all prose forms:* it deals with matters in an overt way, in the social, political, and cultural forum; though it may be specialized or narrow in its range, it is never intimate or private. The formal essay is the form appropriate to the social, political, or cultural issue, and represents the discussion of a person, not involved in private reverie or confession, but involved in public debate or address.

To a certain extent, all prose forms are public—simply because they are written for an audience. But the words used by the formal essayist are especially geared "for all the World to hear," and the formal essayist meets the reader, not so much as personal friend or confidant or next-door neighbor but as fellow citizen or as fellow member of a well-defined social group speaking on matters, not of *tête-à-tête* interest, but of large value: life and death, the nature of institutions and movements, problems of government, economics, history, philosophy, art.

A good example of the public and serious subject common to the formal essay is seen in the opening paragraph of Joseph Wood Krutch's essay on "Creative America":

The story of man's adventures and achievements on this planet can be told in many different ways. Today it is most often told in terms of his technological advances—which is to say in terms of his assumption of power over his physical environment. Sometimes it is assumed, even, that any other achievements are mere consequences of his success in this grand enterprise, and extremists have gone so far as to suggest that the measure of a civilization is simply the horsepower available per unit of population. Nevertheless, the story can also be told in various other ways such as, for instance, in terms of his beliefs, ideals, convictions, and standards of value. Sometimes, though less often, it has been told in terms of his creative imagination as revealed in his art.—Joseph Wood Krutch, Creative America

Indeed, formal essayists speak for the record, not to reveal themselves privately and individually but to speak representatively for the society or public of which they are a part.

Speaking seriously and publicly, the formal essayist writes with a *great sense of order.* All writing, of course, demands organization and ordering of its contents, but the formal essay, more than all others, brooks few exceptions or variations from clear-cut and logical arrangement. Unlike the personal essay, that permits a certain amount of circuitous journeying from beginning to end, the formal essay marches straight through its ideas to its conclusion. The reason for this logical deliberateness is easy to understand. The very meaning of formality is the rational ordering of events or ideas or things. And formality would be drastically weakened and diluted if it gave way to entertaining digression or intriguing but obscure architecture. If one has something serious and important to say, can one endanger the clarity of one's statements by trying to be clever, subtle, or mysterious in their presentation?

And it is for this reason that the formal essayist adopts in his writing a *dispassionate style.* Though the essay may have its emotional moments, the essay itself is not emotionally oriented and does not seek to make emotional appeals. And though it may urge and promulgate definite plans of action, it maintains a certain matter-of-factness in its discussion.

This does not mean that formal essays are necessarily dull or that the formal essayist always writes "with a long face in a brown mood." Ideally the formal essay tries to be neither "sleepy" nor "noisy." Like all good pieces of writing, it strives for as much vitality of manner and grace of style as possible—without confusing any of its clear-cut ideas or without delaying the deliberate revelation of its thinking. A glow and luster may emerge from the words, but readers rarely comment upon the writing by saying "how beautiful"; readers are far more likely to respond by saying "how true."

Picture if you will a man speaking to a large crowd (the public occasion) on the matter of rebuilding the town devastatingly destroyed by a recent flood (the serious subject): he is sincere and serious, yet his task is not to stampede the crowd into an inefficient mob; he must speak calmly yet meaningfully; he must stir emotions to the grand task; yet he knows his address is not an occasion for propaganda or advertising; he must speak to his audience's better self, rouse them to duty. The manner he takes, dispassionate but not dull, is the manner and style of the formal essay.

Consider Abraham Lincoln's "Gettysburg Address," a formal essay in miniature. It is stirring and grandiose—without being intimate or emotional. It is serious, public, orderly, dispassionate—and extremely effective.

HOW TO WRITE THE FORMAL ESSAY

In writing the formal essay you will proceed as with all compositions in your gathering of ideas, reading for information and data, organizing and outlining your thoughts, preparing first, second, even third drafts, and then giving a final stylistic polish to your work. Certain writing procedures are the same, whether one is writing a popular article, a personal essay, a critical review, or what have you. However, in writing the formal essay you will need to keep in mind some special compositional tasks—tasks that will direct your writing into this particular genre with its own characteristics and identity.

1. First of all, *write down your subject and thesis*—and confirm their seriousness and social significance. Theoretically any subject can be handled in a formal way, yet "my trip to Hawaii" seems a less suitable subject than "the growing schism between Soviet Russia and Communist China." And even the generally appropriate subject—something from the province of religion, history, politics, art, and the like—will usually be treated in its more theoretical, abstract aspect as opposed to its practical, utilitarian aspect. (Subjects and theses of an immediate, utilitarian nature are perhaps best handled in articles rather than in essays.)

2. Next, *establish clearly the projected audience and occasion for your essay*. And the best way to do so is by writing it down on paper. Ask

yourself: for whom am I writing? And why? These are questions one should always ask when one writes—but especially so when writing the formal essay, for many times you will come to the formal essay more in consideration of occasion and audience than even in consideration of subject. Many times you will write the formal essay, not simply because you have a certain subject and thesis on hand, but because you need to deal with a certain audience in a certain way.

In determining audience and occasion keep these principles in mind: the formal essay is more appropriate to a well-educated audience than a poorly educated audience: the audience should have a serious interest in your subject and thesis; your audience should have a certain homogeneity, certain distinguishable values, beliefs, and behaviors in common. Also, your essay should speak to a general need; when we speak of occasion we mean, really, the *occasion of need*—the need to remind, to celebrate, to analyze, to redefine; in fact, occasions come into existence out of general need, and it is recognizing the general need that makes us write appropriately and effectively for an occasion.

Try very hard to state in words *why* you are writing your formal essay: "because I am disturbed by the recent monetary policies of the government" or "because I think that existential theology calls for a redefinition of God" or "because our conquest of space climaxes our technological revolution and raises the whole question of our real goals in the universe." Your "because" statement is your occasion—now all you need to ask is whether or not the occasion is public and general.

Would you plan to write a formal essay if the occasion turned out to be "my delight with Christmas" or "my fondness for my eccentric old Uncle Ben" or "my animosity toward glass-and-steel architecture"? No. For such subjects—and occasions—try the popular article or personal essay instead.

3. After establishing your subject, your audience, and your occasion, you will need to *establish your role in the composition.* In writing the formal essay, one of the most important things you must establish is the "voice" or "persona"—for even though every composition has voice and persona, in the formal essay they are of a special kind.

As a formal essayist, you will suppress your unique personality, your extreme individuality, and assume the role of the representative social person and write in a manner that is essentially detached and impersonal. You may write as a twentieth-century American citizen, but not especially as a citizen of Chicago, Illinois, in the grocery business, who attends the Methodist church. You will write as someone vitally concerned with your subject, but not as a propagandist, promoter, or special pleader. You may express personal judgments in the formal essay, but you will play down their personal quality and present them as self-evident truths.

4. To establish your impersonal, public voice in the formal essay, *you will most frequently write in the third-person singular.* The pronouns "one," "he," and "she," are most consistently used in formal expression—"One may not agree with the present administration, but one does not riot on the streets in protest" or "A man may have no personal knowledge of God, but he may hesitate to attack the tradition of revelation."

In some essays, however, you may compromise the utter objectivity of the third person with the personality of the first, and use the social or editorial first-person plural: "Those of us who have lived through two world wars feel that we have seen enough of modern horror" or "We do not believe that the new eschatology will replace the old," or "As victims of mass media, we no longer distinguish very clearly between truth and falsehood."

Only rarely will you ever use the first-person singular in the formal essay. You will do so only if it is vitally necessary to present your subject and thesis *from your special perspective:* Let us say you are a prominent authority in a certain science or art and you are writing from the perspective of that special, even unique knowledge; you may indeed be forced to say "I have never found evidence that these issues are simple" or "I have come at last to the conclusion that his ideas are pernicious." But in every instance, you would be using the pronoun "I" only to the extent that you hold some public or social role appropriate to the formal essay. "I, the mayor of the city . . .," "I, the president of the student body, . . ." or "I, the minister to this congregation, . . ." If you refer to yourself in the formal essay, be sure that you hold some sort of status as far as your subject, audience, and occasion are concerned.

Robert Maynard Hutchins, speaking as a former chancellor of the University of Chicago and as President of the Fund for the Republic, U.S.A., legitimately used the first person in his essay on "Freedom and the Responsibility of the Press," originally delivered as an address:

In 1930, some twenty-five years ago, I last had the honor of confronting the American Society of Newspaper Editors. The quarter of a century between has been the longest in history. That was a different world, before the Depression, before the New Deal, before the Newspaper Guild, before the suburbs, before they charged for newsprint, before the atom, before television. It was a world in which the press was powerful and numerous. Though the press is powerful still, some eight hundred papers that were alive then are gone. Twenty-five years hence, when I am eighty-one, where will the press be?—Robert Maynard Hutchins, Freedom and the Responsibility of the Press

5. Once you have determined your subject, audience, occasion, and voice, you will *begin the actual composition of the essay*—assuming that you have your ideas well organized and ordered. Ideally, you will have written down on cards the individual ideas, data, facts, judgments that you have developed in your prewriting preparations, and you will have arranged these cards—literally and physically—into well-ordered groups that now you can simply transcribe, with the necessary elaborations and transitions, onto the manuscript page.

6. As you move from notes to the actual text of your composition, you will work within the structure of the formal essay. This structure will be essentially conservative.

First, you will write what may be termed a slow or *unhurried beginning*, taking time frequently for a certain amount of intellectual preparation before you officially announce your thesis. Your delayed beginning will not, however, be in any way oblique—for from the very first word of the formal essay you are committed toward a straight and direct path of exposition and discussion. In your opening words, you will declare the area of the essay's concern—the general subject matter—but you may feel that you need to make a few preliminary statements, not to entertain but to inform, to establish a context of significance, before you begin the step-by-step presentation of your thinking. While the professional article makes much greater use of direct beginnings—*here it is, this is what I'm talking about*—the formal essay, by its very meditative nature, may (without, of course, completely ruling out the direct beginning) take a slightly longer time to get completely underway.

In the following example, for instance, you will note the setting of an intellectual and philosophical stage, broad in scope, before the essay narrows to its specific discussion:

We live in an unusual world, marked by very great and irreversible changes that occur within the span of a man's life. We live in a time where our knowledge and understanding of the world of nature grows wider and deeper at an unparalleled rate; and where the problems of applying this knowledge to man's needs and hopes are new, and only a little illuminated by our past history.

Indeed it has always, in traditional societies, been the great function of culture to keep things rather stable, quiet, and unchanging. It has been the function of tradition to assimilate one epoch to another, one episode to another, even one year to another. It has been the function of culture to bring out meaning, by pointing to the constant or recurrent traits of human life, which in easier days one talked about as the eternal verities.

In the most primitive societies, if one believes the anthropologists, the principal function of ritual, religion, of culture is, in fact, almost to stop change. It is to provide for the social organism which life provides in such a magic way for living organisms, a kind of homeostasis, an ability to remain intact, to re-

spond only very little to the obvious convulsions and alternations in the world around.

Today, culture and tradition have assumed a very different intellectual and social purpose. The principal function of the most vital and living traditions today is precisely to provide the instruments of rapid change. . . .—J. Robert Oppenheimer, On Science and Culture

And in this beginning, though it is much shorter, there is still a certain amount of "leading into" the essay proper:

H. G. Wells is quoted as having said, "There is no more evil thing than race prejudice. It holds more baseness and cruelty than any other error in the world." Race prejudice is bad, in the first place, because all *prejudice is bad. Prejudice, by definition, is pre-judgment—the forming of opinion in advance of the evidence, and without knowledge of the facts: an unintelligent and unjustifiable procedure. It is bad, in the second place, because it is a manifestation of one of the worst confusions and abuses that have plagued men for generations—the misunderstanding and vicious application of the notion of race itself.*

So noisesome has this jungle become that some writers seek to escape it by discarding the concept of race entirely. But this is sheer evasion; the only constructive solution lies in discovering the truth about race and facing it squarely and courageously.

In the first place. . . .—Henry Pratt Fairchild, The Truth about Race

7. Likewise, your *conclusion* will not be abrupt, but will neatly tie the essay together, either summarizing or evaluating or coming to logical conclusion. Sometimes the ending is slightly longer than the ending of a personal essay or popular article—simply because in the formal essay all structural parts (beginning, middle, conclusion) are more definitely and clearly marked and maintained. You may, in the formal essay, take your time to conclude.

Here is a standard conclusion to a formal essay—an essay that discusses the subject of "Morals, religion, and higher education," for some 7,000 words and then comes to these final paragraphs:

How, then, can higher education escape dogmatism, narrowness, the invasion of academic freedom, and failure in its proper intellectual task and still do its duty by morals and religion? A possible answer lies in the Great Conversation. The Great Conversation began with the Greeks, the Hebrews, the Hindus, and the Chinese and has continued to the present day. It is a conversation that deals, perhaps more extensively than it deals with anything else, with morals and religion. The questions of the nature and existence of God, the nature and destiny of man, and the organization and purpose of human society are the recurring themes of the Great Conversation.

There may be many ways in which a college or university can continue the Great Conversation, but it would seem offhand that one of the best ways is through the reading and discussion by all the students of the books in which the Great Conversation has been carried on by the greatest men who have taken part in it. I emphasize discussion because of the contributions that this method makes to the moral and intellectual habits we desire; and I emphasize reading and discussion by all the students and faculty because in this way the formation of a community can be advanced. To continue and enrich the Great Conversation is the object of higher education.

The Civilization of the Dialogue is the only civilization worth having and the only civilization in which the whole world can unite. It is, therefore, the only civilization we can hope for, because the world must unite or be blown to bits. The Civilization of the Dialogue requires communication. It requires a common language and a common stock of ideas. It assumes that every man has reason and that every man can use it. It preserves to every man his independent judgment and, since it does so, it deprives any man or any group of men of the privilege of forcing their judgment upon any other man or group of men. The Civilization of the Dialogue is the negation of force. We have reached the point, in any event, when force cannot unite the world; it can merely destroy it. Through continuing and enriching the Great Conversation higher education not only does its duty by morals and religion; it not only performs its proper intellectual task: it also supports and symbolizes the highest hopes and the highest aspirations of mankind.—Robert Maynard Hutchins, Morals, Religion, and Higher Education

8. As for the *middle* or fundamental section of your essay, you will *match structure to content:* what you have to say will determine the design and organization of your materials.

If for instance you are writing on "The Consequences of American Involvement in Asian Affairs," the structure of your essay may rather inevitably proceed through an identification of the various consequences, and since the consequences are, in all likelihood, going to be of differing value and significance, you will probably proceed in some sort of climactic order. The structure of the middle section of your essay may well look something like this:

Discussion of first consequence (150 words)

Discussion of second consequence (275 words)

Discussion of third consequence (300 words)

Discussion of fourth consequence (325 words)

Discussion of fifth consequence (450 words)

Or if you are writing an address to be delivered on the occasion of a Beethoven birthday celebration the structure of your essay may follow directly from your thesis, say: "Beethoven remains a 'modern composer' because the diversity of his achievements permits him to speak to generation after generation in one way or another." Inevitably the structure of your essay will be built upon the "diversity of his achievements" and you may come up with the following outline for your writing:

Part I: Beethoven's achievement as a performer and creative artist
Beethoven's achievement as a conductor (150 words)
Beethoven's achievement as a pianist (250 words)
Beethoven's achievement as a composer (425 words)
Part II: Beethoven's achievement in musical forms
Beethoven's achievement in opera (100 words)
Beethoven's achievement in chamber music (250 words)
Beethoven's achievement in concerti (375 words)
Beethoven's achievement in the symphony (550 words)
Part III: Beethoven's achievement in instrumentation
Beethoven's achievement in writing for tympani and brass (175 words)
Beethoven's achievement in writing for the human voice (200 words)
Beethoven's achievement in writing for string instruments (300 words)
Beethoven's achievement in writing for piano (400 words)
Beethoven's achievement in writing for full orchestra (650 words)

The overall essay might finally look like this:

Beginning: The occasion for the address; statement of subject and thesis.
Middle: Part I: Beethoven as performer—825 words
Part II: Beethoven's musical forms—1,275 words
Part III: Beethoven's instruments—2,725 words
Conclusion: Summary of middle section, and restatement of thesis.

In addition to this topical arrangement, however, you may note that traditionally the formal essay, once past the beginning, establishes the basic situation or problem upon which the essay is based; that is, establishes the seriousness, the sense of occasion, that the audience needs to understand in order to understand your discussion.

Then follows a detailed demonstration or proving of the situation, problem, issue in question. And finally, before the conclusion, comes the evaluation, judgment, analysis, criticism of the matter. This traditional arrangement of the formal essay is, of course, the arrangement found in classical rhetoric—where the parts are called the exordium, narration, confirmation, refutation, and conclusion.

9. With your structure established (topical or traditional) you will—as in all writing—need to *expand your basic ideas* into the full body of your composition. But in the formal essay you will be less inclined to expand your ideas by horizontal movement; you will rely more heavily on vertical exploration. That is to say, you will be less inclined to "go on to the next possible idea" and will concentrate rather on in-depth exploration of any given thought. Whereas in the popular article there may be a kind of rushing from one idea to another, an exciting dash toward conclusion, in the formal essay there is a slower movement, a more deliberate examination of illustrative and explanatory material, a greater desire to make sure that no misunderstanding occurs about the ideas that you present. Whereas in other prose forms the quantity of facts and data may be extremely valuable, in the formal essay quantity gives way to quality.

10. After you have developed your essay into something like its final shape, *you will want to pay careful attention to your transitions.* Moving from paragraph to paragraph, from idea to idea, you will want to use transitions that are very clear—you should leave no doubt in your reader's mind how you are getting from one idea to another. Yet your transitions should not be hard and monotonous: though your essay will be so well-organized you may easily use such indications of transitions as "one," "two," "three" or "first," "second," and "third," such words have the connotation of the scholarly or technical article and are usually to be avoided, or at least supplemented or varied, in the more formal composition. Use "one," "two," "first," "second," if you wish, in certain areas of your essay, but also manage to use prepositional phrases and conjunctive adverbs and subordinate clauses and brief transitional paragraphs to achieve your momentum and continuity. Clarity and variety together are what you want.

11. And finally in your writing of the formal essay you will take care with your rhetorical profile—that is, with the entire complex of tone and style that comes out of your vocabulary and your sentence and paragraph structures.

Consider your words, for instance. Formal essays are generally written on the formal level of language, with a precise and thorough manner of expression. And you will use a rich, full-range of vocabulary—monosyllabic and polysyllabic words, words of Greek, Latin, and Anglo-Saxon origin, common and unusual words. But if your vocabulary leans in any direction, let it lean toward the learned and the allusive, and avoid (save for very special effects) contractions, colloquialisms, slang, or jargon. You would probably not use these words—"We don't think too many jet-set darlings are going to contribute to a true 'peace on earth' "—but rather these—"We believe that very few of today's affluent and uncommitted young men and women, devoted as they are to pleasure and play, will make any sort of serious contribution to a lasting 'peace on earth.' " Not that the first version is wrong, but it would be inappropriate in a formal essay; its words are too heavy with connotation, they are too emotive. Likewise avoid words too specialized, technical, or childish.

A typical example of formal vocabulary is found in this passage from the work of Carl Becker:

The natural rights philosophy made its way in America with far less opposition than it did in Europe. It was accepted as a convenient theory for justifying the political separation of the American colonies from Great Britain; but with that object attained no further revolution of serious import, such as occurred in France, was required to bring the social and political institutions of the United States into harmony with the philosophy that presided at its birth as an independent nation. The state and Federal constitutions were scarcely more than a codification of colonial institutions with the Parliament and king left out, and the natural rights philosophy of the Declaration of Independence was accepted without much opposition as the obvious and necessary foundation of the new political structure. If the colonies had ever been governed by a king, it was only by a king in absentia *exercising a merely nominal control. Monarchical absolutism and the theory of divine right, the vested interest of a ruling landed aristocracy based on birth, the moral and political influence of an organized state religion—none of these obstacles to political and social democracy, which had to be overcome in all European countries, was ever in any real sense a part of the American political practice or tradition.—Carl Becker,* The American Political Tradition

12. *Consider now the structure of your sentences.* You are free, even in formal style, to write any kind of sentence you wish—virtual, loose, simple, long, short. But note that your sentences should *not be predominantly* short, simple, elliptical: you should be sure that enough long, complex, and periodic sentences occur to handle the seriousness of your subject matter. Also, sentences in the formal essay are generally more studied and structured: you will find in formal style more of the definitely recognizable rhetorical devices of balance, parallelism, antithesis, anaphora, rhetorical question, and the like. Some examples of formally structured sentences are these:

In the Renaissance, art is so available and so evident that those productive years of the fifteenth, sixteenth, and seventeenth centuries in Italy, France, and England offer us advantageous examples in a discussion of what art is and what the creation of it involves.

Art is the making intellectually—even emotionally—bearable that which is otherwise not bearable, to wit—the black and the white, the agony and the joy, the birth and the death.

Some poetry is prose, some prose is poetry.

After the literature of the absurd, what shall we have? After the literature of sadism, what shall we be given? The future of American letters remains in question.

Critics themselves need critics. Never should the judgments of the few go unchallenged by the many.

13. Likewise your *paragraphs are going to be relatively longer* than paragraphs in the popular article or the informal essay, and your paragraphs will be more definitely structured, more decisively controlled in their expansion; you will more rigidly adhere to the traditional construction of the paragraph—topic sentence and examples, topic sentence and illustrations, topic sentence and relevant details.

A representative formal paragraph is the following from Thomas Babington Macaulay—representative both in its conventional structure and in its length.

The Puritans were men whose minds had derived a peculiar character from the daily contemplation of superior beings and eternal interests. Not content with acknowledging, in general terms, an overruling Providence, they habitually ascribed every event to the will of the Great Being, for whose power nothing was too vast, for whose inspection nothing was too minute. To know him, to serve him, to enjoy him, was with them the great end of existence. They rejected with contempt the ceremonious homage which other sects substituted for the pure worship of the soul. Instead of catching occasional glimpses of the Deity through an obscuring veil, they aspired to gaze full on his intolerable brightness, and to commune with him face to face. Hence originated their contempt for terrestrial distinctions. The difference between the greatest and the meanest of mankind seemed to vanish, when compared with the boundless interval which separated the whole race from him on whom their own eyes were constantly fixed. They recognized no title to superiority but his favour; and confident of that favour, they despised all the accomplishments and all the dignities of the world. If they were unacquainted with the works of philosophers and poets, they were deeply read in the oracles of God. If their names were not found in the registers of heralds, they were recorded in the Book of Life. If their steps were not accompanied by a splendid train of menials, legions of ministering angels had charge over them. Their palaces were houses not made with hands; their diadems crowns of glory which should never fade away. On the rich and the eloquent, on nobles and priests, they looked down with contempt: for they esteemed themselves rich in a more precious treasure, and eloquent in a more sublime language, nobles by the right of an earlier creation, and priests by the imposition of a mightier hand. The very meanest of them was a being to whose fate a mysterious and terrible importance belonged, on whose slightest action the spirits of light and darkness looked with anxious interest, who had been destined, before heaven and earth were created, to enjoy a felicity which should continue when heaven and earth should have passed away. Events which short-sighted politicians ascribed to earthly causes had been ordained on his account. For his sake empires had risen, and flourished, and decayed. For his sake the Almighty had proclaimed his will by the pen of the Evangelist, and the harp of the prophet. He had been wrested by no common deliverer from the grasp of no common foe. He had been ransomed by the sweat of no vulgar agony, by the blood of no earthly sacrifice. It was for him that the sun had been darkened, that the rocks had been rent, that the dead had risen, that all nature had shuddered at the sufferings of her expiring God.—Thomas Babington Macaulay, The History of England

14. And one concluding word about *length in general:* because formal essays have a tendency to be more full-bodied, more complete than other prose forms—and therefore longer; because formal essays, avoiding in their seriousness the superficial and slight, give full expression to ideas and concepts—and are therefore longer; because of this frequent length of the form, you do not want to make the mistake of padding out your material to make it look bulky and substantial and pseudo-formal. In your attempt to be formal and serious and orderly and public, you may overwrite, put on unnecessary airs, and effect pomposity rather than profundity.

Your final task then, in writing the formal essay, is to go over your last draft carefully—prune and trim your words, remove mere verbiage, and tighten up your style. One should always do this in writing, of course—but the temptation *not* to do it seems especially great with this genre. Make sure that your formal essay contains no idle words—but is as perfectly and meaningfully wrought as possible.

THE WHOLE COMPOSITION
In the following formal essay, an eminent historian confronts what he considers a crisis in the humanistic tradition—the divorce of history, classics, and literature from life. J. H. Plumb's subject has particularly to do with the contemporary view of history, a false view and one uncorrected by historians. Such sweeping cultural issues, especially when tinged with urgency and a keen sense of the high stakes, are the métier of the formal essay.

The Sorry State of History

J. H. Plumb

Quips from Cicero are uncommon in the engineers' lab; Ahab and Jael rarely provide a parable for biologists; and few civil servants seek a guide for policy in the examples of Jefferson or Pitt. Yet a hundred, or even fifty, years ago a tradition of culture, based on the classics, on Scripture, on history and literature, bound the educated classes together and projected the image of a gentleman.

It was a curious mixture of humanistic principles and national pride. The Renaissance made literary breeding fashionable; a gentleman was expected to be conversant with all knowledge, well-read in Plato and Cicero, from whom he obtained his sense of civic virtues, familiar with the Scriptures as a never-ending source of parable and aphorism, fortified in his patriotism by the story of his nation's heroes, his experience deepened and enriched by his extensive knowledge of his country's literature.

These subjects—History, Classics, Literature, and Divinity—were, with Mathematics, the core of the educational system and believed to have peculiar virtues in providing politicians, civil servants, administrators, and legislators. In them, in England certainly, the arcane wisdom of the Establishment was preserved and handed down from generation to generation.

Alas, the rising tide of scientific and industrial societies, combined with the battering of two world wars, has shattered the confidence of humanists in their capacity to lead or to instruct. Uncertain of their social function, their practitioners have taken refuge in two desperate courses—both suicidal. Either they blindly cling to their traditional attitudes and pretend that their function is what it was and that all will be well so long as change is repelled, or they retreat into their private professional world and deny any social function to their subject.

And so the humanities are at the crossroads, at a crisis in their existence; either they must change the image that they present, adapt themselves to the needs of a society dominated by science and technology, or retreat into social triviality. This is the crucial problem facing all the subjects—History, Classics, Literature—that are to be discussed here.

Adaptation is the great difficulty. Homer sells millions; Thucydides hundreds of thousands; even Tacitus tens of thousands. The hunger to know about the ancient world is almost insatiable. The professional classicists, however, rarely provide the diet (more often than not the providers live on the fringe of the profession).

The professionals prefer to cherish their ancient skills, to concentrate their abilities on turning a piece of Burke into Ciceronian prose or on similar masterpieces of obvious triviality.

As with classics, so with history: the demand to know about the past is greater than ever before in human history, but it is rarely the professionals who satisfy it. It is more often gifted amateurs such as Mrs. Woodham-Smith or Christopher Herold. In spite of the acerbities of Dr. F. R. Leavis, Sir Charles Snow's opponent, tens of thousands still enjoy Galsworthy, Wells, or Bennett; ordinary men and women still search for their imaginative satisfactions in the whole of the world's literature, untouched by the corrosive acid of literary criticism.

Yet perhaps the situation is worst of all in my own subject— History. For this reason: it has lost all faith in itself as a guide to the actions of men; no longer do historians investigate the past in the hope that it may enable their fellow men to control the future. Its educational value, they feel, lies in the exercises it provides for the mind and not in what it contains. History, well taught, they argue, is admirable discipline in clear and precise thinking. It extends the memory, sharpens the sense of logic, teaches the rules of evidence, and gives practice in lucid exposition and clarity of thought.

And these exercises, they maintain, can best be performed on subjects upon which historians have been active the longest or where the source material—as in medieval history—makes the greatest demands on these faculties. Therefore, it is the old, tried subjects— English history, European, medieval, and modern—that must provide the core of historical education.

Within this core, it seems, there are certain problems which, because scholarly talent has battened on them for decades, make the best exercises of all for historical training; hence the importance of certain topics that bewilder most outsiders and often reduce others to uncomprehending mirth, such as endless discussions of the importance of the coronation of Charlemagne on Christmas Day, 800, or whether or not the accession of George III brought about a break in constitutional practice.

So sixth-form English schoolboys will be familiar with the entire historiography of the controversies about George III from Horace Walpole to Sir Lewis Namier, yet remain totally ignorant of the scientific revolution of the seventeenth century, or even—and this, too, is quite possible—of the Industrial and American revolutions in George III's own reign. To the American counterparts of these sixth-formers, of course, George III will remain, apparently, perpetually the villain, and nothing more, in that last revolution.

Of course, the educative argument is spurious: memory, sense of logic, critical use of evidence, lucidity in exposition—all can be trained by large subjects as well as small, by problems relevant to modern society as well as by matters indifferent. But the whole sickening, deadening process of increasing specialization within history destroys half its value for education in its broadest and best sense: the major purpose of historical studies should not be to produce professional historians, but to explain the past for our time and generation and by so doing deepen human experience and breed confidence in the capacity of man to master his environment.

And if it is to do this, what it teaches must be central, not peripheral, to the human story and concerned with the whole history of mankind and not with patriotic enclaves. Then and then only will the study of history be meaningful to the scientists, social as well as natural, who are going to dominate our society.

Although a reorganization of what is taught in the schools and in the universities might diminish the present crisis in historical studies and help to bridge the chasm between professional history and public needs, it would not solve the problem. The root of the trouble lies deeper.

One of the greatest recent successes on Broadway is Edward Albee's *Who's Afraid of Virginia Woolf?*, an appealing title for a savage, grim, searing, three-hour dialogue between a historian and his wife. The personal situation, dominated by a screeching Earth Mother (the historian's wife), provides the focus of the play's power, but its magnetism, the disquiet it breeds, derives from its deeper implications.

The historian of the plan is sterile and impotent. He talks endlessly of an imagined child (the Future) and babbles bewilderingly about his past. Did he or did he not kill his parents? There is a conflict of evidence, and great uncertainty. No one, including himself, can ever know. His wife, who possesses all the force, the violence, the passion, of an instinctively living woman, hates his failure, his verbosity, his inadequacy. But her desire is also strong, and she cannot disentangle herself from his needs.

History and Life, therefore, are doomed to live it out in hate, in distrust, in mutual failure. They are lost in timeless falsehood, bound by dreams of the past that may not have existed, and enslaved by their own lies about the future. And this, as the audience streams out into the flashing neon lights of Broadway, seems to have the force of truth. History is without meaning, without power, without hope. The present exists: the past is our own cloud-cuckoo-land. Albee presents dramatically what most historians and philosophers of history believe. That is the cruel truth. He merely puts symbolically and more harshly what R. G. Collingwood and Benedetto Croce preached elsewhere.

Toward the end of the nineteenth century historians both in Europe and in America began to reject the idea that history possessed any meaning, any purpose, any dialectical pattern. Just as the novelists withdrew their interest from man in society to investigate the stream of consciousness, and painters rejected the traditions of European art for a more personal exploration of reality, so the historians came to accept that history, all history, was but a personal vision, that the past could not exist separate from themselves; what existed was a personal reconstruction of the past; all history, to quote Croce, the great Italian historian and philosopher, was present history, a contemporary construction, and so a world entire unto itself, true only for one time and one place.

As might be expected, there has been a minority of historians, largely those who concern themselves with economic history, who have resisted this attitude and maintained that the study of history could mean more than a personal world. But they have tended to argue that function and not dialectic was the true goal of history; i.e., that historians should be more concerned with the interrelations of society at a given epoch and not with those aspects which might, or might not, lead it to develop into something different.

Such an attitude is inimical to the concept of progress, or of history having much social value; so, too, is the other fashionable view which has shown great resilience in this century: the belief that history can only be explained as the working of Providence. But, as man cannot understand the mind of God or know His purpose, we must accept history as it is and regard historical analysis as little better than a guttering candle in a fathomless cave. Only at the Day of Judgment will light blaze forth. Therefore, to try to impose a pattern on history, to attempt to extract useful, broad generalizations for the guidance of man, is understandably human but intellectual folly. These, with a plethora of variations, are by and large the basic attitudes of the profession. And most of them are not very far from Albee's.

Even if the professionals hold up their hands in horror at the idea of drawing lessons from history, others, far less capable, do not. Toynbee has no hesitation in trampling where Namier feared to tread. And before Toynbee, Spengler displayed no less confidence and no less absurdity. Both regarded history as a whirligig in which decay was as frequent as growth.

Toynbee dismisses the last four hundred years of European history as an uninterrupted disaster; Spengler declared in 1928 that the West was in its "sunset epoch," that the world had gone straight downhill since the eighteenth century. Both of them encouraged despair about the present, neither considered material progress as relevant. They were Albee's progenitors, if anyone; and their vision of history persists, and distorts the truth.

Yet if there is one idea that makes sense of history, it is the idea of progress. The idea is simple: over the centuries, in spite of frequent setbacks, the material condition of man has improved. Men live longer, get more to eat, are freer from disease, possess more leisure. The speed of progress has accelerated phenomenally over the past one hundred fifty years and shows all prospect of continuing to do so. Place a hand loom by a computer; the case is unarguable.

With this material progress has gone an increase in civility. And this, many, for obvious reasons, find difficult to believe. To those not well grounded in history but conscious of Hitler's Jewish policy, two world wars, and Hiroshima—to say nothing of Guernica, Lidice, Stalin's camps, the Warsaw Ghetto, and the continuing bestialities of men—this claim may appear almost naïvely optimistic. Yet it is true. The world is less savage, less brutal, less tyrannical than it was a hundred years ago.

How progress has happened and is happening is complex, not entirely understood, but it is certainly the most intellectually fascinating aspect of history. It ought to be the core of historical study and education, particularly the latter. It relates directly to the scientific and technical world in which we live. And furthermore the interpretation of how this has happened and might be accelerated would give a renewed sense of social purpose to the teaching of history. The history of progress, well taught, would at least breed confidence in the present and the future, dispel Albee's nightmare, and fortify those qualities in man that have helped him to drag himself from the cave to the industrial suburb. But there lies the rub.

To many the idea that men should pursue material progress is an anathema: for them, as for Toynbee, it is vulgar; destructive of spiritual values; repellent in its social and artistic manifestations; totally destructive of what the good Dr. Leavis calls the "organic community."

Now the opposition to the idea of progress, conscious or unconscious, derives from three of its aspects. It is essentially secular; it is socially radical; it is, wrongly, assumed to be tainted with Marxism. (Its father, however, was not Marx but Francis Bacon, an almost respectable capitalist.)

Certainly progress has quickened when man has applied his deductive powers to the material world, whether it has been to the method of working flints or to making electricity. The more scientific his approach to the problems of his environment, the more speedily has he solved them. Neither prayer nor exorcism will stop smallpox, but vaccination will.

The idea of progress is essentially materialist and makes an uneasy bedfellow for religion: wisely, Pius IX anathematized the idea in 1864.

However, the social radicalism implied in the idea of progress has probably been a greater enemy than its rationalism. And this is particularly true of this century. Industrialization impels social change: old certainties of class, status, education, get washed away. Nor is it a gentle process: it has in its early stages been as brutal as any historical movement. Slums, industrial tyranny, a ravaged countryside, speak too vividly of its evils. Sensitive men, bred in middle-class traditions, frightened for their values and their status, have lost all sense of historical judgment. They have fled to a never-never land of rustic glory where every peasant is a craftsman and—no matter how illiterate—radiates with "inner life." Or, like the New England historians of the nineteenth century, they have escaped into a bogus medievalism that exalts Mont-Saint-Michel as the pinnacle of human achievement.

Yet such absurd attitudes, understandable as they are, and propagated endlessly by Dr. Leavis and his disciples, are eagerly believed. They are taught day in, day out, in our schools and universities, and swallowed wholesale. Do such men know nothing of the past or of the sheer horror of pre-industrial society: its filth, its disease, its hunger, the brutishness of its pleasures, its frustrations, its tyrannies, its gross superstitions? Do they never look at Bruegel or Hogarth or even Rowlandson? Do they never read?

Would it surprise them to learn that, in the societies they adulate, dying Negroes were thrown by the score into the Atlantic for the sake of the insurance; that small girls and boys were strung up on gibbets for petty theft; that men were castrated, disembowelled, and quartered in public; that these were not exceptional events but commonplace and repeated without protest?

Such happenings might be matched by incidents of evil and cruelty today, but these rarely pass unrecorded and rightly create a sense of public horror. They are not accepted as a part of life, like the seasons, unchanging and unchangeable, as they were in the pre-industrial societies of Europe and America. (Indeed, to think that a peasant's life was more enriching than a modern factory-worker's borders on lunacy.) Yet hardly a historian's voice has been raised at this constant denigration of the present or at the corruption of scholarship that passes as literary and social criticism.

This would not matter if it were a minor eccentricity of a few literary critics or reactionary historians, but it is only the most aggressive aspect of a general attitude. Most current teaching in the humanities undermines confidence not only in present society—that is of no great importance—but in those qualities by which man has bettered himself: technical cunning, applied intelligence, and a capacity to risk change.

Instruction of this kind makes scientists impatient of the humanities and leads them to dismiss them as absurd or trivial or both. There is a growing danger, as science grows, of their being pushed farther into the academic background. Yet if ever there was need for the humanities, it is now, before the educational system required by a scientific society sets in a rigid pattern.

To many influential sections of Western society, particularly Western European society, industrialism and its concomitants are distasteful, not merely in their manifestations—no one would pretend that industry does not bring plenty of horrors in its wake—but in their essence. They wish to reject them. They prefer to retain the social and cultural exclusiveness of an agrarian and commercial society, of the world of Jane Austen, of Anthony Trollope, of Thomas Arnold and Rudyard Kipling. Hence the cult of D. H. Lawrence, who was but a gifted beatnik version of Thoreau or W. H. Hudson, men who loved life and hated humanity, men of sensitive hearts and thick heads.

Although this crisis in the humanities primarily springs from the nature of our backward-looking, tradition-drugged society, it has been encouraged by the treason of historians to their subject. They have permitted, almost without protest, a false image of history to be projected. Except as mind-trainers they have almost contracted out of education, leaving to others, and to others far less worthy, the formulation of a social attitude to the world about us.

It is an odd situation. Technically, history has never been so superbly equipped. Its methods are more refined, its practitioners more skilled, its knowledge greater and more exact than ever before in the long record of man. Yet rarely has history been so socially impotent.

And some responsibility must lie on its own shoulders, on the reticence of historians, their ambiguities, their reluctance to accept the social responsibilities that their subject imposes on them, and their adamantine conservatism toward the teaching of history.

Yet as humanity crawls up the face of the Eiger, hesitates, slips, and then miraculously scrambles back, it seems a little hard that those who plot its course should give no encouragement.

Exercises

1. Make a list of twelve to fifteen subjects that would be suit-

able for discussion in a formal essay. Indicate for each subject the sense of need or occasion that lifts it to the formal level.

2. Looking through the last twelve issues of such magazines as *The American Scholar, Yale Review, Horizon,* or *The Centennial Review,* locate at least three formal essays and determine as precisely as possible what each essay is trying to do: criticize, celebrate, inspire, reform.

3. Choose a formal essay that especially appeals to you and make an analysis of its structure; that is, identify beginning, middle, and end—as well as subject and thesis. How well organized is the essay? How easy is it to outline?

4. Choose a formal essay that especially appeals to you and make an analysis of its language. Select three paragraphs, one from the beginning, one from the middle, and one from the end. By listing, counting, and comparing, describe as best you can the vocabulary, the sentences, and the paragraphs used in the essay.

5. Using the "Gettyburg Address" as a model, write a miniature formal essay for some contemporary occasion: the razing of a landmark in your city, the retirement of a favorite professor, the dedication of a new library or hospital.

6. Write a full-length formal essay on some issue of serious concern to you. Assuming you have an intelligent and educated reader waiting for you, probe in depth the pros and cons of the problem you wish to discuss.

20. THE CRITICAL REVIEW

As educated people, we're asked, often enough, to make critical evaluations of various items and events in our culture: to share with others our judgment of books, records, performances, exhibitions. If we're at all active in our society, we're asked—from time to time—to write critical reviews of plays, films, art shows, new books at the library. In writing our critical reviews, we want clearly to identify what it is we're reviewing; use valid and meaningful criteria in our judging; present both the good and bad "aspects" in an intelligent manner; come to as clear and useful an evaluation as possible. By mastering the form and procedures of the standard critical review, we can make a sensible, rewarding presentation of our opinions and responses.

A large complex society depends a great deal upon the critical review to direct cultural traffic, to weed out the unworthy and call attention to the laudable. And involved in today's culture explosion, in which we are pursuers of culture whether or no, all of us depend on the critical review to guide us through the pleasant plethora of books, movies, dramas, concerts, exhibitions, recitals, and performances (of whatever kind) that is so perpetually available.

To write the critical review is indeed to write one of the prevalent forms of prose—a form to be found in the daily newspaper, in the weekly review, in the special journals devoted to cultural diagnoses, as well as in campus tabloids and literary magazines. And to write the critical review is to take an important and responsible part in modern social life. For better or worse, the critical review has wide influence: many readers (too many perhaps) will take the review as gospel and will act accordingly.

Responsible reviewers must therefore pay especial attention to the form of their reviews, for in giving thought to the form they will be led to write more carefully, more convincingly, and it is to be hoped—more wisely.

THE CRITICAL REVIEW AS A FORM

Several things a critical review is *not*. First of all, a critical review *is not simply a summary or report:* it is not a book report, a movie report, a concert report. Reports and summaries simply present a factual, non-evaluative synopsis or contents-listing of a work of art or a performance, while a critical review has something to say about the success or failure, the good or bad of the subject under consideration.

And second, a critical review *is not a work of literary criticism.* A critical review may be based upon values discussed in a critical essay, but while literary criticism deals more with an explanation or interpretation of a work, the review concerns itself with the "good or bad."

Literary criticism—and critical essays dealing with other media—tell us what is and what is not present in a work, pointing out its form, its tradition, it technical achievements—and many times illuminating its very meaning. Literary criticism is primarily concerned with identification, in the broadest sense of the word. A critical review, however, assuming identification, tries to come to a sane and practical evaluation—and guide the reader to some particular action: read or not read the book, watch or not watch the show, listen or not listen to the record.

A good critical review (and one must realize that a lot of bad ones are published) is marked primarily by clear and definite criteria, and by a sense of moderation and reasonableness.

It is almost impossible to discuss the merits and weaknesses of anything unless one has *a definite set of values* by which to measure. Criticism is based upon values—and a good critical review presents value judgments in a convincing way. A review based on other than clear and discernible values will be ambiguous, evasive, and meaningless. Even if one is a wholehearted relativist as far as the universe is concerned, when it comes to writing a critical review relativism should be set aside. In a critical review, one must simply take one's stand—and take it on the basis of predetermined values, predetermined criteria of judgment. A good review doesn't stammer around, trying to make up its mind.

The criteria involved in the critical review may be either (1) impersonal, objective, even scientific, or (2) personal and subjective. Sometimes the critical criteria are those to which many educated people subscribe—they are the criteria established by tradition or established within some professional discipline. Based upon such standard or accepted criteria, a review is impersonal and objective. But sometimes the criteria are those in which the reviewers alone believe—and this is their privilege. Good criticism, after all, can help establish new criteria as well as demonstrate the old. One's only obligation, when using subjective and personal criteria, is to spell out one's values with a certain amount of clarity or imply them so strongly that they are easy for the reader to formulate. And having once identified them, overtly or by implication, to maintain them consistently within the review.

Some traditional criteria used in judging works of art—including literature—are these: A work of art is good if it is "true to life," if it "communicates," if it is "significant to the times," if it is "well made," and if it "encourages and supports the morals and ethics of the community." You may not agree with these criteria at all. Indeed you may want to reject them altogether and present more meaningful criteria of your own. To do so, you will do well to jot down your criteria in advance—to clarify them for yourself and to have them in verbal form to include in your review. To establish your own criteria, write down a series of statements in the following manner: "I will consider the work I am going to review good if it____," and then spell out the precise conditions of excellence that you have in mind. A series of three or four criteria statements will usually be adequate. Five would about be the limit. If you try to employ too many criteria in any one review, you may find yourself unable to handle any one criterion adequately and will be unable to prove or illustrate sufficiently to what extent the criteria are satisfied or ignored.

Here for instance would be a usable set of criteria:

I will consider the book of poetry I am reviewing a good one if the individual poems deal with significant and universally valuable subjects.

I will consider the book of poetry I am reviewing a good one if the individual poems are technically well done as far as rhythm and form are concerned.

I will consider the book of poetry I am reviewing a good one if the poems as a group are held together by some common theme.

I will consider the book of poetry I am reviewing a good one if the book itself is presented in a readable and attractive form.

Though you may not make an actual list of the criteria for inclusion in your review, you may give some indication of what values you have in mind in making your judgment:

Wholly heartfelt and wholly in hand, these poems are convincing and sympathetic portraits, dramatic and yet philosophically aware.—Charles Philbrick, Debuts and Encores

In that one sentence, the reviewer has pointed out some of the things he thinks a good book of poetry should be.

One method of evaluation, however, is anathema to most educated readers. The good review *avoids irrelevant criteria*—judging a particular work or performance, for instance, by the morality or politics of the creator or performer. To attack the architecture of the Upstate Insurance Building on the grounds that the architect is an alcoholic would be silly at best, irresponsible at worst. Such *ad hominem* arguing—and evaluation—is always to be avoided.

Another attribute of the good review, in addition to its clear criteria, is its *balanced or moderate vision*. Ideally a review contains a balance of praise and censure—though, admittedly, such balance is not always possible. Sometimes a terrible performance is simply a terrible performance and that's all there is to it. But ideally, the critical review does not let itself become entirely an encomium—if it does, it actually moves out of its genre into another. Nor does the critical review let itself become a 100 percent jeremiad—if it does, it ceases to be useful and effective.

In general, the balanced vision of a work is best, and the critical review, at *its* best, incorporates moderation into its form. By and large, within the critical review, to validate weaknesses—one must note strengths; to validate strengths—one must note weaknesses. One cannot create the strengths or weaknesses out of whole cloth, of course—but in most cases, as with all things in life, there is both something good and bad to be said. Noting both leads one to wiser conclusions.

As for literary style, *one cannot claim any particular style for the critical review*—the style depends a great deal on the place of publication, the subject being reviewed, the occasion of the criticism. In general, the critical review is more likely to be short and informal than formal and long—simply because of the exigencies of the periodicals in which reviews nowadays appear. But there are notable exceptions— reviews by George Steiner in *The New Yorker*, for instance.

The style may range from dead seriousness to flippancy, from solemnity to wit, from formality to brashness. The good review avoids, however, being so delightful or humorous or petulant or grandiose that the style overwhelms the review—good reviewers try not to steal their own show with a heavy stylistic performance.

And as a general practice, good reviewers do not inject themselves into their reviews, save when they have had some relevant experience or possess some first-hand information appropriate to the review. A reviewer who has served in the Peace Corps in Africa and is now reviewing a documentary film about Africa may indeed refer to personal knowledge. But otherwise, as a reviewer, one does not flaunt one's identity.

All in all, the critical review is the most utilitarian of the prevalent prose forms. It, more than other forms, has a definite goal in mind—other forms seek to entertain or instruct, but the critical review goes even further: it seeks to provide the reader with the basis for an immediate decision—to accept or reject, to spend or not to spend time or money. Every aspect of the critical review as a form is devoted to this utilitarian end.

Nearly any responsible member of any profession is likely to have opportunity—or need—to write the critical review on occasion—professors, physicians, and air force generals review books, plays, events, and objects close to their areas of interest and special knowledge.

With a continuing information explosion in modern life, the critical review becomes more and more important: the busy scholars and scientists, or even the busy pursuers of culture in general, more and more live in the world of reviews in order to be at least partially informed and aware of the world around them.

HOW TO WRITE THE CRITICAL REVIEW

Before you undertake the actual writing of the critical review, you must make a careful preparation: *examine, experience, and understand the work you are going to evaluate.* If you are not willing to pay close attention to the movie, the recording, the book—then you should not attempt to review it. It would be unethical to review the half-read novel, the slept-through performance. And even if you do observe a work carefully, but do not know what to make of it—you may wish to leave the reviewing to someone else.

Good reviewers know their own capacities and limitations, and nothing can be more disastrous than the review written by the wrong person. Not that one always has to be an authority; great and significant reviewing is done by educated lay persons. Yet one should not be so irresponsible as to attempt to review that for which one has no feeling, no concern, no comprehension. One does not have to be a Fonteyn or a Nureyev to review a ballet, yet one should at least enjoy ballet in general, know something about its techniques and traditions, and have attended a fair number of performances.

Once, however, you feel prepared to make a review then you may proceed in this way:

1. *Write down your first general impression of the work.* Though you finally want, as much as possible, to match specific evidence drawn from the work against specific criteria of judgment, you may start out with overall reaction and worry about "proving" it later on. Sometimes we know a work is good or bad, but are actually hard pressed to prove it the way a scientist would. You will want to give as detailed a demonstration as possible of how you came to your reaction, but we might as well all candidly admit that a critical review is not a laboratory report: it does involve educated taste and judgment.

2. Having written down your overall impression, *write down as many details of that overall judgment as possible.* If your first impression was, "I found the symphony a beautiful and moving piece of music," you will now want to go into detail about what you meant: "I found the symphony a beautiful and moving piece of music—the first movement seems especially novel and lyrical all at once; the third movement seems to be the symphony's greatest achievement." You will go on to note particular passages, or particular use of instruments, and the like.

3. And now, one step further. *Jot down the specific things in the work that led you to your judgments.* "I like the third movement of the symphony because of its intricate but understandable theme, because of its effective use of the string instruments, and because its resolution is adequate without being prolonged."

If you are dealing with literature, as in a book review, you will be able—at this stage—to copy out phrases, sentences, even paragraphs from the work itself in order to provide evidence supporting your conclusions. In the book review, you will want to use a judicious amount of quotation (and in other reviews, too, if the medium of the work in question makes quoting possible) in order to give a certain sense of reality to what you are saying. In quoting from a literary work for review purposes you do not have to worry about the problems of citation as you do in the professional article; you will have already identified the work, and you do not very often have to pin down your quotations to the exact page number. Take care, however, not to quote too much—never let your review become more quotation than commentary. And take care, also, that you do not quote too long a passage at any one time. A few select and choice quotations will serve you better than a whole army of them.

4. And this leads to the observation that in your gathering of judgments and evidence, *you should deal only with the salient characteristics of the work.* Decide what is important in the work, good or bad; what should be truly noted. Don't make the mistake of reviewing insignificant aspects of a work. You may find a ludicrous typographical error—but does it deserve your attention? Or you may find an error in a footnote (a flaw that some nitpicking reviewers from academe love to light upon)—but would it be worthwhile your straightening that particular matter out? Unfortunately, some reviewers amble off the beaten path into the byroads of minutiae simply to display their erudition.

5. Once you have gathered your ammunition, as it were, and have the cannon of your criticism loaded and carefully aimed, you will proceed, most of the time, according to this structural program:

Give a *general identification* of the work you are reviewing. Within the first paragraph of your review, give the name, genre, creator, and any other pertinent information about the subject: "In his new novel, *The Gemini Murder,* Leslie Buchanan has . . .," or "Ella Fitzgerald's great range of singing style is revealed in her new album, *Whisper Not,* in which she sings love ballads and jazz classics accompanied by seventeen-piece and ten-piece bands conducted by March Piach (Verve V6-4071, $4.79; stereo, $5.79)."

In some instances, the technical identification of the work in question will be given outside the review proper. Reviews in *The New York Times Book Review,* for instance, are always headed in this fashion:

Madame Sarah. *By Cornelia Otis Skinner. Illustrated. 356 pp. Boston: Houghton Mifflin Company. $6.95.*

In such cases, you may plunge in without telling your reader who, what, when, where, and why—but at all other times, you will have to provide the identification within the text proper—within the very first paragraph.

6. After this identification, you will in the first or second paragraph give *a quick evaluation* of the work. You will state in a sentence or two your overall opinion of it. In general, this work is good. In general, this work is bad. In general, this work will appeal only to children. In general, this work represents a great literary triumph. In the critical review, you should not play guessing games with your readers, and you should not insist that they wait until the end of the review to find out what your judgment is. Though you will go on to give the details of your judgment, you should give your opinion—your thesis as it were—early in your writing.

Immediate evaluations, elaborated upon as the reviews proceed, are given in these opening paragraphs from items published in *Saturday Review:*

The New Industrial State, *by John Kenneth Galbraith. (Houghton-Mifflin. 427 pp. $6.95).*

For some years John Kenneth Galbraith has been poking, prodding, and irritating America toward a measure of understanding of its economic life. His sardonic Affluent Society *devastated one section of sanctified generalizations. This time he has tackled the more serious task of laying out an economic theory corresponding to its major facts. The book is long overdue.* The New Industrial State *will make economic history.—Adolf A. Berle,* Analyzing the Corporate-Complex

Washington, D.C., *by Gore Vidal. (Little Brown, 377 pp. $6.95).*

Gore Vidal's new novel starts with a rainstorm that promises literary lightning. Instead, Mr. Vidal has produced a squall that spends itself on a sea of sex, self-destruction, and cynicism, and ends by dismissing the human race as "no more than bacteria upon a luminous slide." His characters all but drown themselves in cliches and predictable situations, which make his work neither heroic, tragic, nor humorous—just tired and threadbare. Although Washington, D.C. *is saved from total bankruptcy by occasional flashes of fine prose, the book leaves a lingering frustration because Mr. Vidal's diagnosis of our democratic dilemma is too pat and all surface, as the plot and characters clearly indicate.— Jeffrey St. John,* Brutus on Capitol Hill

7. On many occasions, you will give—early in the review—*necessary background information* in order to orient your reader to the terms and conditions of your criticism. Not every review takes time out to present a context, but when reviewers are not confined to a few hundred words they often will give historical background or ideological background or biographical background to make the work they are discussing more meaningful and more significant for their readers. If the review is of a new piece of sculpture, the reviewer may

say something about the state of sculpture today in America and about the particular category of sculpture in question. If the review is an author's seventh novel, some word about the author's previous novels may be appropriate. Or if the review is of a biography of Handel, something may be said about the eighteenth century, about English musical society in that time—or, in another direction, something may be said about the current writing of biography, or how this particular work compares with previous biographies of Handel.

The following example demonstrates a reviewer's need to "set the stage" for criticism of a particular work:

Self and Society: Social Change and Individual Development, *by Nevitt Sanford. (Atherton. $8.95).*

Nevitt Sandford is a distingished American psychologist whose career has been unusually rich and complicated . . . and now he has gathered . . . past writings and some new observations into a first-rate book whose title, Self and Society, *indicates its almost daring breadth of concern.*

Social scientists essentially sort themselves out into two camps, those who look at the individual's mind and attitudes (whether kept to himself or shared with others) and those whose chief interest is in the "world" people must every day confront, be it the concrete neighborhoods they frequent or the intangible but equally influential climate of values and traditions they call their own enough to pass down over the generations. Although an intellectual division of labor is necessary in any field, the nature of man's life on this planet does not lend itself very well to the process of abstraction, unless the abstractions are worded in a gracefully self-defeating way that ensures theoretical flexibility and protects the truth of our contrariness, our stubborn capacity as diverse human beings to resist the descriptions we so much want to make about ourselves. Concepts like "self" or "society" are thus at once, a necessity, a temptation and very real danger. Somehow we have to gather together our thoughts and our observations, yet in doing so we can confuse our ideas (often pridefully discrete) with the "facts" of existence, hard to convey with any words or generalizations. The bitter and childish fights between psychiatrists (and indeed social scientists) over the relative importance of "nature" and "nurture," of the unconscious and the street scene, in the individual's fate, show how much we simply don't know or have yet to clarify—and thus must turn into a cause for intellectual war.

This book will help make for peace . . .—Robert Coles, in The American Scholar

In all cases, giving background information or establishing a context for the work to be reviewed is an extension actually of identification. Reviewers must decide to what extent they must make so detailed and educative an identification for their reader.

8. Also, reviewers many times feel that they must give *a brief*

summary of a work's contents; a quick trip through the work; a recreation of the work in miniature. In doing so, they remain fairly objective—they give nonevaluative description, read from the program, or repeat the table of contents. This helps the reader comprehend the dimensions and form of the work being reviewed, and is, of course, presented early in the review—in the first few paragraphs.

Franklin Edgerton, ed. and trans. The Beginnings of Indian Philosophy. *Cambridge: Harvard University Press, 1965, 362 pp. $8.75.*

Those who know the writings of Professor Edgerton will undoubtedly welcome the new volume from his pen as an authoritative pronouncement on early Indian philosophy. . . .

The book consists of six parts. The first part of the book gives a lucid introduction, in about thirty pages, and supplies a necessary background for the materials translated in the later parts. The author has also prefixed an introductory note to each of the later sections regarding the nature and the context of the extracts translated. The translations are further accompanied by elaborate notes on the text and by interpretation of individual passages. A consistent attempt is made throughout to avoid the use of Sanskrit words. A very useful Glossorial Index, which furnishes brief definitions of those Sanskrit words used, is included at the end.

The author knows the difficulties of translation and interpretation . . .
—K. L. S. Rao, in Literature East and West

9. And now you are ready to go into details. Having identified the work and given a basic judgment, *you will now want to point out the specific weaknesses and the specific strengths.* In fact, the body of your critical review will be devoted to this citation of evidence and a guiding of your reader down the road to final opinion.

A good rule to follow is this: if your overall judgment of the work is favorable, then you will present the weaknesses first and get them out of the way. If, however, the review is generally unfavorable, you will present the good points first—and then go on to the things that led to the unfavorable conclusion. "This novel has many weaknesses. They are. . . . But, of course, they are almost unnoticed in the light of the novel's many virtues, which are. . . ." Or: "This movie has some exciting and wonderful moments. They are. . . . But, unfortunately, the greater part of the movie is a dud. Consider for instance such scenes as. . . ."

One can, of course, do just the opposite. In a favorable review, give all the good points first—and then, unobtrusively suggest the bad points. Or vice versa. But to end a favorable review with the bad points has a tendency to negate the previous praise; and to end a bad review with the few good points has a tendency to weaken the criticism in general—to leave a slight hint of apology and compromise.

The only workable alternative to the general rule—con/pro in pro reviews; pro/con in con reviews—is to intermix praise and censure throughout the review. This alternative is frequently used when reviewers are following the work in its own sequence—that is, they are discussing a book chapter by chapter, and comment on the good and bad of each chapter as they go along; or they are discussing a drama in some topical order—plot, acting, set, direction—and find good and bad in each of the parts. Also, by intermixing praise and censure throughout, the reviewers give less emphasis to either one: though running the risk of a meaningless neutrality, they can, if successful, give an impression of great judiciousness on their part.

10. You will, after giving the details of your criticism, *restate your general evaluation,* and then—if possible—*make some sort of recommendation to the reader or come to some sort of significant conclusion.* The recommendation or conclusion may take different forms: Because this movie is a good one, (1) you should see it. Or (2) it should inspire similar movies. Or (3) it will achieve a certain influence on the political climate of the nation. Or because the movie is bad, (4) we should see in it a dangerous influence in our society. Or (5) it will contribute to the vulgarization of certain subjects. Or (6) we certainly hope the playwright will shift to a more conventional type of drama next time.

The recommendation or conclusion should point out the significance of the work (good or bad) in our society, our culture, our lives. A good review does not just hang upon a work like a price tag—but suggests not only what the worth is, but what the worth implies.

Some typical review "endings" are these: From *The New York Review of Books*—"I hope that, he will carry on, and provide a similar measured, intelligent work on Richardson or Fielding," and "At a time when the behavioral scientists are hot for certainties and computers are unfed in the laboratories of personality research, Anna Freud's book makes it clear that psychoanalysis has little fare to offer the machines. Will it ever? To put it another way, one small child, infinitively complex, can still confound the fortune tellers." From *The New Yorker*—"The post-apocalyptic irresolution of 'Two Views' may well be where European man, after history's extravagant demands, is glad to settle." And from *Saturday Review:* "Projecting this mode of procedure further into the future, it is not impossible that some soloist may commission a work for violin and magnetic tape, say, which he will then proceed to perform without the intervention of an orchestra. Or, by logical extension, without a conductor. Perhaps, there is something to the whole idea after all."

11. One special note about the form of the review: Most reviews deal with single works, of course, but on certain occasions you may wish to attempt some judgment of a set of related works. In such cases you will most likely establish—as a means of unifying your review—some common theme, letting this common theme become your main subject as you proceed to discuss a series of novels, a series of recordings, or a group of paintings.

In a review dealing with several items, you will begin by identifying your theme—and only then will you proceed in the regular manner of the review (identification, evaluation, and the like) as you discuss one work after another. Your conclusion will, of course, deal with the unifying theme—and frequently your final judgment will be of the theme (its significance, its effect on society, and the like) as well as upon the individual works.

Here are excerpts from a review of three books. In writing the review, Douglas M. Davis identifies and discusses the common theme of "black humor":

"Black humor" keeps getting blacker. That is the only safe conclusion from the latest products served up by three of its major practitioners—John Hawkes and The Innocent Party, *a collection of plays; James Purdy and* Eustace Chisholm and the Works, *a novel; and William Burroughs and* The Ticket That Exploded, *another novel.* [First paragraph]
    Let me feed you just a few of the essential goings-on. . . .
    As I say, black humor is blacker than ever. I am not sure, however, that it's better than ever. . . .
    [Final paragraph] *The black humorists need to get off dead center esthetically. Rage and disgust alone will not carry a novelist—not through more than one or two books, anyway.—Douglas M. Davis, in* The National Observer

12. You will write out your review, of course, in a length determined primarily by the journal, magazine, or newspaper in which the review is likely to appear. If you are writing a review simply for teacher or friends, you may make the review as long as you wish, taking into consideration your audience's depth of interest. But if you are writing for any sort of publication—and that can be anything from a five-minute radio broadcast to a magazine article—you will shape your review to the physical limitations of your medium.

If you are writing a five-minute radio review, you will write some 500 words. If you are writing for *World Literature Today,* you may limit yourself to a quick review of some 100 to 150 words, or whatever limitations the editor prescribes. If you are writing for *Saturday Review,* you may range, it seems, from 500 words to 1,000 words. And in some publications, such as *Yale Review* or *The New Yorker,* reviews are sometimes as long as 3,000 to 5,000 words.

Whatever the length, you will normally use the same basic outline of presentation: identification, quick evaluation, background, weaknesses and strengths (or strengths and weaknesses), restatement of evaluation, and final recommendation or conclusion.

13. And you will, of course, write your review in a rhetorical profile appropriate to your audience and your subject matter. Admittedly, most reviews are written today in a journalistic style—simple, straightforward, deliberate. But there are exceptions. In a long review dealing with some major event, you may have need for a more formal manner; if for instance you were writing about the performances that closed the old Metropolitan House and opened the new, you might write a bit more grandly than otherwise. Or if you are speaking in depth to a highly educated audience, you may allow yourself more linguistic graciousness.

And if you are speaking to an audience especially well-informed in the art form or subject matter of your review, your review may be somewhat more technical. Or in a review for some special, sophisticated "inside" audience, you may inject into your review a certain amount of "entertainment" value—as Dorothy Parker did, delightfully, in her book reviews for *Esquire* magazine.

An example of a fairly popular style in writing a review is seen in this passage from a movie review by Wilfred Sheed:

A mighty clash of censors has been heard over the movie Ulysses, *a beating of tin pans and tooting of penny-whistles, but this must surely be one of their more foolish battles. . . .*

As it turns out, the picture is hardly worth the fuss anyway. The first half hour or so is fine, with Stephen Dedalus pacing the sands to the tune of Joyce's finest, and then the men in the coach jogging moodily to the funeral. But after that, things come tolerably unstuck. Milo O'Shea makes a pedestrian Leopold Bloom and his night-town fantasies are drawn to peep-show scale. Standing by while Joyce's diabolically gorgeous language is being boiled and watered down to B-movie images is nasty work and calls for a moral.—William Sheed, Films

The following review—by Russell Kirk in *The Sewanee Review*—comes from the other end of the style spectrum: it is written more conventionally and more learnedly.

Much the best stylist of our present company, Mr. Bredvold dissects the principal errors of the Enlightenment: the rejection of the theory of natural law; scientism; the sentimental view of human nature; a fashion of "following nature" which is inimical to civilization; a disastrous Utopianism. Contemptuously rejecting the transcendant understanding of man and society which arises from religious knowledge, the philosophes *exposed modern man to the inner disorder of the soul and the outer disorder of the total state: thus, fancying themselves liberators, they enslaved the world to appetite and unchecked power.—Russell Kirk,* Ideologues' Folly

All in all, your style can vary from the more formal manner of *The American Scholar* to the standard journalistic manner of *Saturday Review* to the cute and breezy way of *Time* magazine to the almost anonymous, scholarly oriented language found in the back of many professional journals.

When you have finished writing your review, put it aside for a day. If possible, reread the book, re-view the movie, listen once again to the music. You may have second thoughts. And you may want to check out your criticisms once again, to make sure that in trying to serve an audience by guiding them toward or diverting them from some particular experience, you have always written with honesty, sincerity, and good taste.

THE WHOLE COMPOSITION

In this review, Harold Taylor first attempts to identify the sort of book *The Leaning Ivory Tower* is and at the same time imply a quick evaluation of it: "very badly needed." He next gives some background material—primarily about Warren Bennis, the author. Then, after making note of some of the book's weaknesses—both in style and content—Taylor turns to a positive evaluation of the work, indicating what some of his critical criteria are: "courage and insight to analyze" and "useful conventional wisdom." Without providing a point-by-point summary of the book's content, Taylor nevertheless gives us a good idea of the material covered and the book's overall thesis. Taylor concludes his review with a discussion of the book's general significance and suggests the sort of "action" that readers should take: use the book as a model for "honest expression of the truth about what is actually happening" in various areas of modern institutional life.

Administration 101b

Harold Taylor

THE LEANING IVORY TOWER. By Warren Bennis, with the assistance of Patricia Ward Biederman. 154 pages. Jossey-Bass. $7.75.

In one sense, this is a book about institutional loyalties and the way they can corrupt both institutions and the people in them. In another sense, it is a book about a man with ambitions for institutional power who was lost in the jungle of higher education until found by a presidential search committee from the University of Cincinnati. In still another, it is a piece of confessional literature in a field where that kind of writing is phenomenally scarce and very badly needed.

Warren Bennis had been chairman of the Organizational Studies Group at the Sloan School of Management at MIT before President Martin Meyerson and his assistant, Saul Touster, persuaded him in 1967 to become provost for the social sciences at the State University of New York at Buffalo. In 1968 he became vice-president for academic affairs and, later, acting executive vice-president of the university.

Why a man who already had his hands full with two such posts should then begin to cultivate so great a passion for a university presidency that he would submit to review by 12 separate presidential search committees, or why a man would leave his post, as Bennis did in 1970, at the height of his university's most agonized policy struggle—the calling of the police to put down a student uprising—merely to be interviewed by Northwestern University, are questions that he failed either to raise or to answer at the time.

But these acts are recorded, among other things, and in the aftermath of his struggle to find his way to the post he now occupies, one is forced to a certain kind of admiration by the fact that he is willing to write about it all so openly. He is capable of some atrocious sentences; for example, about his organized campaign for the presidency of the University of Buffalo: "My own image for the job was not right for the times," and about his relation to Martin Meyerson: "His patina had rubbed off on me, for better or worse."

He is capable of some of the most banal pronouncements in the history of social science: *"Unchecked disruption leads to more external intervention at successively higher levels"* (italics in original); "As a student of organizational behavior, I have come to realize that images are central to all our political processes."

He is also capable of extraordinary lapses in judgment: "Over the next two months, my work in my continuing role as academic vice-president was largely sacrificed to presidential ambition." In protest against the acting president's decision to call the police to the campus in Buffalo, Bennis resigned one of his two positions but kept the other, and then was surprised that the resignation not only had no effect on policy but was interpreted as a clever move in his campaign for the presidency.

The behavior he reports shows in part the characteristics of an organization man on the make, with some of the naïveté of a sophomore running for president of the student council or John Lindsay trying to become President of the United States. The recital of the record arouses in the reader at various points a mixture of impatience and annoyance with the way things were done.

Yet the saving virtue of the book, and of the record, is that Bennis has the courage and the insight to analyze what he and the others did, draw conclusions from the analysis, and share the knowledge publicly. As he says in his introductory chapter, "Personal Knowledge as Social Science," "Too little has been written about the backstage life of *any* of the large bureaucratic institutions that dominate our 'organized society.' . . . Mute loyalty is the favored emotion; according to this code, members can complain nonstop among themselves but never express their grievances in public." In the preface he says of his book, "There are pages of confession, expiation, apology, justification, and self-congratulation."

There are also pages of useful conventional wisdom about the university as a social system and how to make it function, how to choose its leadership, how to create institutional change that not only lasts but improves the quality of the intellectual environment. After all that experience with presidential search committees, Bennis has become one kind of expert in how they work and how they can be improved. With the startling clarity of hindsight, Bennis sees that most of his acts had predictable consequences that he should have foreseen at the time. He now knows what he wished he had known then.

On the other hand, without him we would never know the bizarre story of Northwestern's complicated dance with a management firm in applying management techniques to the job of finding a president-manager, or that the mere mention of Kingman Brewster's name could actually cause a Northwestern board member to choke on his fruit salad. Nor would we know as much as we now do about why things went wrong at the university in Buffalo after such a brilliant beginning in 1966 with Martin Meyerson's ideas and intentions.

When Bennis first went to Buffalo as provost of the social sciences, he decided to keep a journal for a research project of his own on how administrative and organizational theory is related to the practical experience of running an institution. He soon gave it up. He found so slight a relationship between his own theories and what he was doing day by day that his journal became useless.

Now that he has gone through his years of trial by fire, Bennis has come out on the other side with a deep appreciation of the reality of institutional problems and the need, not for theories of organization, but for a new empirical science of education that draws its metaphors and methods from something equivalent to the new journalism. He is right. That is to say, if contemporary society has to be organized through bureaucracies simply to get things done, then the individual members of those bureaucracies must understand that their first loyalty is not to the institution they serve but to the human values it represents.

University presidents, faculty members, students, and everyone else must speak openly of what they know, and educational research must be concerned with the honest expression of the truth about what is actually happening. Otherwise, we have the Pentagon without the Pentagon Papers and Daniel Ellsberg, General Motors without Ralph Nader, the universities without leadership, and America without a conscience.

Exercises

1. Identify the criteria, stated or implied, in the front-page review in a recent issue of *The New York Times Book Review.* Are any of the criteria unacceptable? Are the judgments in the review consistent with the stated criteria?

2. After seeing a movie that you have especially liked, look up a review of it in *Time, Holiday, The New York Times, Saturday Review,* or your local newspaper. Do you agree with the review? If not, why not? Do you feel the review has erred in the use of criteria or in the use of evidence?

3. Compare two reviews of the same book—say a review from *The Atlantic* or *Harper's* with one from *The American Scholar* or *Western Humanities Review.* How do you account for the difference?

4. Write a review of a book you have recently read. Write first a 250-word review. Then write a longer review, say of about 1,000 words.

5. Write a 1,000-word review of a television comedy show. Prepare for the review by establishing in advance some of the specific things you will be looking for, by establishing your criteria, and by watching some other television comedy show for the sake of comparison.

6. Write a review of a building, a painting, or a piece of music. First, find one of these that you dislike; write a negative review—and yet at the same time a fair and just review. Second, find one of the subjects—building, painting, musical composition—that you like very much; write a favorable review—and yet at the same time avoid meaningless praise and panegyrics.

A NOTE ON MANUSCRIPTS AND PUBLISHING

■ What do we think as we thumb through our finished manuscripts? "Well, I've managed to nail down some passing thoughts . . . catch up with a few fleeting experiences." That alone would make it worth doing. To have transformed those vague and illusive ideas of ours into something reasonably clear and substantial would in itself justify our efforts. But the creative objective of our writing is a more tangible and public product—a manuscript which is not only readable but, in one way or another, publishable. ■

With the completion of the finished manuscript your work is done; the manuscript is quite literally out of your hands; and no explanations or apologies can have any effect on its reception. The handing over of your manuscript to a reader is a kind of symbolic gesture. You imply that the subject has been treated knowledgeably and fairly, that the art of the personal essay (or whatever the form) has been upheld, that the reader will find something significant and accessible, and that you have written your best—in short, that you have created something of publishable quality.

THE READABLE MANUSCRIPT

And attention to some final details will do much to insure your manuscript a considerate reading. Many of these final details have to do with what will be for your reader's first impressions, the physical appearance of the manuscript. Paradoxically, you don't want your reader to notice the typewritten page at all. You want him to look through the page to what thoughts and visions lie beyond. And the best way to avoid misdirecting his attention is to be utterly correct, neat, and conventional.

Paper

Always use white, standard size (8½ by 11 inch), medium weight (16 or 20 pound) bond (25% cotton fibre is ideal). Do not use any of the so-called erasable papers for their tendency to smear is such that you cannot have a neat page for very long. And do not use onion skin except for carbons for your own files.

Typing

A typewriter is the best investment a writer can make and is absolutely essential if you expect to write for publication. The portable electrics are good and cost little more than many portable standards. Except for the inconvenience, an office typewriter is often a good buy—it will always give you better copy than a standard portable. The conventional pica or elite is safest, but some of the less radical newer typefaces are acceptable. Script-style type, however, is definitely out. Use a nylon or possibly silk ribbon, not cotton. An all black ribbon is a better buy than a red and black one since you can turn it over to get twice the life. But don't use any ribbon so long that the type becomes illegible.

Margins, Spacing, Page Numbering, Identification

Margins on the first page should be two inches above the title, four spaces below, with the title centered. Margins on subsequent pages should be one and one-half inches at the top and on the left side, one inch at the right and bottom. Indent five to seven spaces for paragraphs. Double space, except for prose quotes running to two or more lines; these should be indented approximately one inch more and single spaced. (On earlier drafts you may want to triple space, leaving yourself more room for revisions.) All pages after the first should be numbered with Arabic numerals (2, 3, 4, etc.) in the upper right-hand corner. Your name plus address or other information requested by the instructor should appear in the upper left-hand corner of the first page.

Proofing and Correcting

Your final proofreading must be the most critical and careful of all because it is the last. Any manuscript submitted to an editor or instructor must be neat and error free. To get it this way you may need to retype certain pages or even the entire manuscript. Minor errors—spelling, punctuation, and typographical bloopers—can sometimes be corrected by a neat erasure followed by retyping. (The various liquids and films made for this purpose work pretty well, but once the page is out of the machine you really have to erase.) More serious errors require more drastic measures. To delete, draw a line horizontally through the words. To add, there or elsewhere, print (or type) the correction above and place a caret ($_\wedge$) below the line. Other proofreader's marks are often useful: ¶ (paragraph), no ¶ (no paragraph), ℵ (reverse these letters, words), > (vertical space), ∧ (horizontal space). Corrections on the final manuscript, even obvious ones, are not damning if they are few, neat, and clear. Errors, no matter how neat the copy, are still errors.

Some Additional Good Advice

Keep a copy, preferably a carbon or photocopy of everything you write. Don't even be too quick to throw away early drafts and working notes. Build a library of writer's reference books: at the very least you should own a really good dictionary and a thesaurus or dictionary of synonyms.

THE VARIETIES OF PUBLISHING

This manuscript of yours must now be published (just as a painting must be exhibited and a musical composition performed) for the creative act to be completed. You may be asked to *read your article or essay aloud to the class*. This is the earliest form of publishing, going back to a time before there even was a written language. The difficulties of such publication did not discourage the authors of *Genesis* or *Beowulf*. Some literary forms, like the ballad and drama, are written to be performed orally. There has been a revival in recent years of readers' theater where, along with the usual program of poetry and closet drama, you sometimes hear a kind of lyric essay. And although they may later appear in print, sermons and certain other examples of the formal essay are written for the platform.

Whether you read your manuscript aloud to the class yourself or listen while someone else reads your words, it is a forceful reminder of the communicative function of writing, that it is "one person speaking to another," even when the other person is an unknown and out-of-sight reader. You seem to hear the article or essay for the first time, becoming one of the audience yourself. And this objective hearing enables you to check on such matters as the adequacy of your information, the clarity of your line of thought, the rhythm of your sentences.

Circulating copies of your work among friends is the second oldest form of publishing. Great literary reputations have been achieved on the basis of such publication. The classical writers had little alternative; and Gerard Manley Hopkins and Emily Dickinson seemed content that only a few acquaintances read their work. Movable type didn't come into use until the fifteenth century; and only during the last 200 years has printing been really commonplace. Dissident writing in Russia and elsewhere takes the form of privately circulated copies. The pamphleteer and the broadside balladeer have always published with the handout. Now the existence of low-cost duplicators—like the mimeograph and photocopier—makes it easier to reproduce numerous copies of a manuscript for distribution. Even your personal letters are a form of publishing. So when you have written something appropriate, why not casually pass it along to your friends or to other readers who would be interested in what you have to say?

Certainly clean *copies of your best writing should go into a portfolio.* Increasingly the world is paying for skill rather than simply information. And if you can demonstrate your writing ability with samples of your prose, a potential employer is likely to be more confident about hiring you. Also, the basic executive functions are communicative, and many jobs specifically involve writing. Even though only a handful of readers glance through your "anthology," this could be one of your most rewarding publishing efforts!

Copies of virtually everything you write should be kept on file as a base from which to build at a later date. You will undoubtedly make progress as a writer, and some of your work will in retrospect seem naïve, but some of it will strike you as perceptive and articulate. In any case, the writing you've done—with its data and insight and experiment—can often be revised for later publication or used as a basis for other writing.

But there is no reason why you should not *make an effort to be published in the usual sense.* The realities of publishing are such that you may not feel committed enough to your writing to pursue the matter. (It takes a certain amount of persistence and audacity to get into print.) But even if the present state of your art is inauspicious, it may not always be so. With experience you will become a more confident and articulate writer. And the odds are not so great that any reasonably competent writer cannot sooner or later publish. But whether you are writing for publication or not, your object should always be to write as professionally as you can. Make every writing job—notes, letters, minutes, reports, research papers, essay exams, the articles and essays and reviews you write for English Composition—an occasion for practicing and perfecting your art. With that sort of attitude you will achieve a reputation with all who read your prose as being that most rare and envied person, "a good writer"; and you may, if you follow more or less the procedures outlined here, become a publishing writer as well.

Writing for publication is not the same as writing to please yourself. The criteria editors apply to your work are likely to be quite different. They are looking for special qualities—relevance and novelty, flash and sophistication, smoothness and succinctness. Since they read infinitely more manuscripts than they could ever use, editors will reject yours for the slightest of reasons. Certainly they will not very often be indulgent and encouraging critics. So you will want to take your writing seriously if you expect to publish. If you don't, who will?

Surveying the Field

Find out which journals and magazines publish the forms you write best. Notice which lengths, subjects, styles editors seem to favor. Find out for yourself what is being published these days. Don't aim too high at first; get published anywhere; begin building up a list of credits; then you will be assured of a more attentive reading by editors who see your work.

Writing for a Particular Audience

You have probably already noticed that magazines and journals have distinct preferences about what they print. Your chances of getting published by an editor are much greater if you have written something or can write something that appeals to the editor's tastes. "Slanting" what you write, as it is sometimes called, is not difficult. Writers have always adapted their material to a particular audience. And editors' preferences are generally based on what they believe to be those of their readers. The kind of material that would interest one editor would probably be of interest to others whose publications were in a similar class. Read the publication to see if there is any statement made about editorial policy or submitting manuscripts. Quite often they will request that you follow a particular style sheet, or ask for two copies of any material, or say that they do not read unsolicited manuscripts and must be queried first.

The Manuscript
Naturally all that has been said about the readable manuscript applies here. A manuscript of professional quality is correct, neat, and conventional. Anything less will not receive a very favorable reading and will likely be summarily returned. Right or wrong, it's that old matter of first appearances again.

The Cover Letter
A very brief letter should accompany your submission. It need say no more than, in effect, "here is my manuscript." It should not try to explain or justify what you have written, but may contain information about yourself and your publishing record which might induce the editor to give the material a more careful reading. Be brief, however—one page at the most—or you will do more harm than good.

Mailing the Manuscript
Address the editor by name if you know it (and you can usually find out by consulting the current *Writer's Market*) or simply "The Editor" if you do not. Send the manuscript first class if it is light or by the special rate if it is heavier. Shorter manuscripts can be folded once in a 5- by 7-inch envelope or folded as a letter in a standard business-size envelope; longer manuscripts should be mailed flat in a 9- by 12-inch envelope, with perhaps a piece of cardboard enclosed to stiffen and protect it. Be sure to enclose a self-addressed, stamped envelope. And always keep a copy of your work. Above all, keep your manuscripts in circulation; if one is rejected by an editor, send it immediately to the next most likely place.

Keep Writing
The true professional stays at the typewriter. If what you have written isn't accepted, what you write next will be better—and may be published.

ACKNOWLEDG-MENTS

John Updike, "Central Park" from *Assorted Prose,* reprinted by permission of Random House, Inc.

Kenneth Rexroth, "The Iliad" reprinted by permission from the *Saturday Review.*

E. M. Forster, "My Wood" from *Abinger Harvest,* copyright, 1936, 1964, reprinted by permission of Harcourt Brace Jovanovich, Inc., and Edward Arnold Publishers Ltd., London.

Yi-Fu-Tuan, "The Desert and The Sea," from the *New Mexico Quarterly,* Vol. XXXIII, no. 3, Autumn 1965; reprinted by permission of The University of New Mexico Press.

Mark Van Doren, "The Creative Heritage" reprinted by permission from *Creative America.* New York, The Ridge Press, 1962.

James Baldwin, "Encounter on the Seine: Black Meets Brown" from *Notes of a Native Son.* Copyright 1955 and reprinted by permission from Beacon Press.

Joan Didion, "On Self-Respect" from *Slouching toward Bethlehem,* copyright 1961, 1968; reprinted by permission from Farrar, Straus & Giroux, Inc.

Dylan Thomas, "A Visit to America" from *Quite Early One Morning,* copyright 1954 by New Directions. Reprinted by permission of the publishers, New Directions Publishing Corporation, and J. M. Dent & Sons, Ltd., and the literary executors of the Dylan Thomas Estate.

George Orwell, "Marrakech." From *Such, Such Were the Joys* by George Orwell. Copyright 1945, 1952, 1953 by Sonia Brownell Orwell. Reprinted by permission of Harcourt Brace Jovanovich, Inc., and Martin, Secker & Warburg, Ltd., London.

Norman Mailer, *Cities Higher than Mountains,* reprinted by permission of the author and the author's agents, Scott Meredith Literary Agency, Inc., 845 Third Avenue, New York, NY 10022.

John F. Baker, "An Honest Day's Walk," reprinted by permission from *Venture: The Traveler's World,* vol. 2, no. 2 (April, 1965). Copyright 1965 by Cowles Magazines and Broadcasting, Inc.

Jane Howard, *"The Search for Something Else,"* reprinted by permission of The Sterling Lord Agency, Inc.

Phyllis McGinley, "Suburbia: Of Thee I Sing". From *A Short Walk from the Station* by Phyllis McGinley. Copyright 1949 and 1951, reprinted by permission of The Viking Press, Inc., New York.

Christopher Morley, "On Going to Bed". From *Essays* by Christopher Morley. Copyright 1927, 1955 by Christopher Morley; reprinted by permission of Lippincott Co.

Richard M. Ketchum, "J. P. Morgan" From "Faces from the Past—IX" in *American Heritage.* Reprinted by permission of the author.

Phillip Kopper, "Life in Stone: A Young Master's Antique Art." From *QUEST/77,* March/April, 1977. Reprinted by permission of the Ambassador International Cultural Foundation.

Fred E. H. Schroeder, "Enter Ahab, Then All: Theatrical Elements in Melville's Fiction." From the *DALHOUSIE REVIEW.* Reprinted by permission of the *DALHOUSIE REVIEW* and the author.

Marya Mannes, "A Plea for Flirtation" from *But Will It Sell.* Copyright 1964 and reprinted by permission of the author.

J. H. Plumb, "The Sorry State of History", reprinted by permission of The Sunday Times of London.

INDEX

Abbreviated paragraph, 182–184
Active voice, 218–219, 221
Adams, Henry, 129, 158, 199, 225, 261, 333, 338
Adjective metaphor, 314
Adjectives, 136–137, 143, 254
Adverbs, 139–140, 254
Afterthoughts, 224, 243–244, 253–254, 332–335
Agee, James, 333
Allen, Durward L., 363
Alliteration, 141, 148, 188, 207, 237, 256, 280–281, 283, 285
Alliterative sentence, 280–281
Allusions, 120, 292–293
Alphabetical order, 32
Anadiplosis, 148–149, 275
  (*See also* Circular paragraph)
Analogy, 8, 190–191, 202
Analysis, 7
Anaphora, 273, 283
And, 223
Anecdote, 57, 120, 187
Anglo-Saxon words, 128–130
Anticipations, 224, 241–242, 248–250, 332–335
Anticlimactic order, 37–38
Antimetabole, 272
Antithesis, 199–200, 206, 271–272
Antonyms, 85–86
Aphorism, 49
Aphoristic writing, 269

Argumentation, 87, 283
Arnold, Matthew, 114, 225, 243
Article, definition of, 353
Asides, 266
Assonance, 141
Asyndeton, 272–273
Audience, 14–15, 17–19, 56, 144–145, 422–423
  (*See also* Readers)

Bacon, Francis, 90, 316
Baker, Carlos, 49
Baker, John F., 230–234
Balance, 119, 141–142, 204, 224–225, 245, 266–267, 271–272, 283, 285
Baldwin, James, 94–98, 277, 314
Basic paragraph forms, 175–195
Basic sentence forms, 237–260
Bates, Marston, 193
Becker, Carl L., 129, 430
Beginnings, 45–52, 57–60, 147, 206, 220, 240, 269, 359–360, 384–385, 409–410, 412, 425–426, 447–448
Belloc, Hillaire, 278, 313, 330
Bennett, Arnold, 106, 162, 265
Benton, Thomas Hart, 102
Berle, Adolf A., 448
Beston, Henry, 217, 220, 228–229, 256, 320
Bettelheim, Bruno, 314
Bibliography, 381–383, 389–390
Birrell, Augustine, 265

Books, 5
Boswell, James, 224
Bowen, Elizabeth, 340
Boyard, Anatole, 106
Brackenridge, Hugh Henry, 319
Brogan, D. W., 277
Brown, Ivor, 111, 113, 330
Burke, Edmund, 111
Business reports, 377
But, 88

Capitalization, 106–107, 242
Carey, Joyce, 269, 272
Carlyle, Thomas, 107, 225, 243, 333
Carmac, Robert, 360
Carson, Rachel L., 91, 157, 243
Cataloguing, 197
Cause-and-effect development, 36–37, 67, 71–72, 193
Causes and consequences, 193
Chase, Mary Ellen, 340
Chesterton, G. K., 85, 237, 266, 280, 334, 411–412
Chronological development, 34–36, 67, 186–187
Churchill, Winston, 220, 250, 279
Chute, Marchette, 281
Ciardi, John, 262
Circular paragraph, 201
Circular sentence, 276–277
Clarity, 245, 249
Clark, Walter Van Tilburg, 106
Classification, 29–31
Cliché, 298–299
Climactic order, 37–38
Climax, 20, 161, 260
Coles, Robert, 449
Colloquial diction, 242
Colloquial level, 128, 131–132, 142, 291
Colon, 120 246–247, 252, 327–329, 331–336, 339, 341, 343–344
Combination sentence, 107–109, 113, 214–215, 228–230, 255–256
Comma, 246–248, 250, 252–253, 255, 327–330, 332–334, 336, 339, 343
Common texture, 128, 142–143, 145–146
Comparisons, 73, 190–192, 242–245
Complex figurative sentence, 280
Complex sentence, 214–215, 225–228, 238, 248–255
Compound-balance sentence, 267

Compound-complex sentence (*see* Combination sentence)
Compound sentence, 214–216, 222–225, 238, 245–248, 327–332
Conclusion, 20, 53, 161
    (*See also* Ending)
Condensed metaphor, 277–279, 313–315
Conesford, Lord, 361–362
Confined metaphor, 319
Conjunction, 88–89, 222–223, 241–242, 244–246, 272–273, 328–330, 339–340
Connally, Cyril, 49
Conrad, Joseph, 113, 188, 282, 337
Consistency, 21–23
Content, 2, 6, 21–23, 30
    (*See also* Subject)
Context, 219
Continuity (*see* Momentum)
Contractions, 128–130, 132–133
Contrast, 73, 191–192, 199, 241–242, 245
Coordinating punctuation, 246
Coordination, 223
Cousins, Norman, 205
Craft, Robert, 312
Crane, Stephen, 161, 244
Creative writing, 21, 187, 207–208, 404–405
Criteria, 443–444
Critical review, 441–457
Criticism, 263
Crouch, Dee B., 360

Dash, 120, 191, 246–247, 252, 327, 329–340, 343–344
Davidson, Laura Lee, 224
Dead metaphor, 317
Declarative sentence, 214, 230, 239, 244, 246
Delayed beginning, 46–47, 57
de Mille, Agnes, 334
Denials and negations, 73, 194–195
Dependent clause, 249–256
Description, 72, 158, 160, 176–177, 182, 187–188, 197–198, 201, 219, 240, 245–256
Details, 34–36, 68–73, 182–183, 187–191, 193, 355–356, 361, 408
    (*See also* Expansion)
Dialogue, 50, 86, 148, 187, 219, 240, 331, 342–345
Dickens, Charles, 86
Diction, 127, 135–138, 140–143, 147–148, 291, 429–430
    (*See also* Words)
Didion, Joan, 48, 120–124

Direct beginning, 45–46
Direct ending, 53
Disputation, 263
Documentation, 386–390
Dos Passos, John, 346
Dunn, Esther Cloudman, 217
Durr, Robert Allen, 267
Durrell, Lawrence, 49

Edman, Irwin, 180
Ehrlich, Paul R., 385
Eiseley, Loren C., 202, 223, 229, 248, 329, 338, 343
Elaborate texture, 128, 141–142, 260, 315
Elaborated simple sentence, 244–245
Eliot, T. S., 275
Ellipses, 338
Elliptical sentence (*see* Virtual sentence)
Ellison, Ralph, 157
Emerson, Ralph Waldo, 56, 108, 158, 238, 274, 282, 316
Emphasis, 101–119, 183, 185, 191, 196, 214, 217, 220–221, 226, 239–241, 246, 249–253, 260, 274, 331, 340
Emphatic order, 32, 37–38
Ending, 44, 52–57, 161, 220, 240, 362–363, 385, 410–411, 426–427, 451
Enumeration, 89–90
Epanalepsis, 276–277
Epistrophe, 274–275
Epizeuxis, 262
Essay, definition of, 353
Essay length, 432
Examples, 72, 189–190
Exclamation points, 341–344
Exclamatory sentence, 214, 230
Expansion, 61–73, 361–362, 364, 429
Experience, personal, 3–5
Experimental paragraph, 206–208
Experimentation, 207–208
Explanation, 265
Expletives, 217, 238
Explicit metaphor, 277–279, 312–313
Exposition, 176–177, 180, 256
Expository paragraph, 160
Extended paragraph, 182, 184–185

Facts, 7
Fadiman, Clifton, 250
Fairchild, Henry Pratt, 426

Faulkner, William, 220, 273, 334, 338
Fiction, 176
(*See also* Creative writing)
Figurative sentence, 277–280
Fitzgerald, F. Scott, 253
Flashback, 35, 187
Ford, Ford Maddox, 242, 346
Foreign words, 292
Foreshadowing, 35, 187
Form, 44–57, 352
(*See also* Structure)
Formal diction, 128–129
Formal essay, 403, 419–440
Formal level, 128–130, 142, 144, 180, 185, 247, 292
Forster, E. M., 39–42, 49, 52, 102, 206–207, 268, 334, 410
Frazer, James George, 189
Frome, Michael, 364
Frost, Robert, 277

Galsworthy, John, 242
Generalization, 70, 361
Geng, Veronica, 49
Geographical order, 32
(*See also* Spatial order)
Gibbon, Edward, 104
Gibbs, Wolcott, 411
Gissing, George, 162, 175, 248, 331
Goldsmith, Oliver, 102
Gosse, Edmund, 270
Grahame, Kenneth, 346
Greco-Latin words, 128–130
Greene, Graham, 315
Greenewalt, Crawford H., 131
Greenough, Horatio, 271

Hamilton, Edith, 111, 159, 178, 245, 329
Hardwick, Elizabeth, 106
Hazlett, William, 104, 109, 259, 263, 273
Hearn, Lafcadio, 241
Hemingway, Ernest, 273
Henriques, Robert, 283
High pointing, 161
Highet, Gilbert, 111, 158, 239, 240
Horizontal expansion, 63–69, 71–73, 364
Howard, Jane, 286–289
Hoyle, Fred, 176
Hume, David, 49
Humor, 51, 153–154, 187, 259, 409

Hutchins, Robert Maynard, 424, 426–427
Huxley, Aldous, 241
Huxley, Julian, 194–195
Huxley, Thomas Henry, 83, 159, 164, 182
Hyphen, 344–345

Idioms, 128–131, 294–295
Illustration, 72–73, 189–190
Images, 82–83
Imagination, 7–9
Imitation, 174–208, 237–286
Imperative sentence, 214, 230, 239, 242–243
Impersonal *you*, 128–131, 133–134
Implied thesis, 21
Indefinite *you*, 133–134
Independent clause, 249–251, 253–256, 329
Induction, 7, 158, 177
Informal level, 128, 130–131, 142, 144–146,
     238, 247, 291–292
In medias res, 35, 187
Interrogative sentence, 214, 230, 239
Interrupted sentence, 265–266
Interruptions, 242–243, 250–253, 335–338
Introductory paragraphs, 176
Invention, 1–9, 30, 357–382, 405–407
Inversions, 217
Inverted sentence, 239
Irony, 409
Irving, Washington, 224, 225
Isocolon, 267
Italicizing, 106–109

James, Henry, 108, 225, 258, 282
Jarrell, Randall, 106
Jefferson, Thomas, 268
Journalistic style, 127, 356–357
Journalistic writing, 20

Kael, Pauline, 124
Kazin, Alfred, 143, 162, 335
Keats, John, 363
Kennedy, John F., 282, 284
Ketchum, Richard M., 347–349
Kirk, Russell, 453–454
Kopper, Philip, 366–374
Kronenberger, Louis, 273, 333
Krutch, Joseph Wood, 161, 183, 205, 252,
     266, 269, 315, 333, 421

Labyrinthine sentence, 215
Lamb, Charles, 52, 143
Langer, Susanne K., 160, 179
Lawrence, Barbara, 49
Lawrence, D. H., 86, 106, 142, 204–205, 219,
     247, 277, 313, 329, 341
Leacock, Stephen, 111, 330, 334, 335
Lead, 359–360
Lincoln, Abraham, 268, 340
Lindberg, John, 384–385
Lindbergh, Anne Morrow, 84
Lists, 9
Literary criticism, 442
Literary expressions, 292
Literary form, 14–16
Logic, 7–8
Loose sentence, 113, 130–131, 215–217, 230,
     237–238, 253, 285
Lowell, James Russell, 340–341
Lowell, Robert, 224, 330, 344
Lucas, F. L., 191–192, 261, 266, 338
Lyell, Charles, 161

Macaulay, Thomas Babington, 88, 268, 431–
     432
McGinley, Phyllis, 301–308
Machlis, Joseph, 159
MacLeish, Archibald, 256, 275, 335
Madison, James, 311
Mailer, Norman, 164, 208–212
Maisel, Albert Q., 360
Mannes, Marya, 413–417
Mansfield, Katherine, 224
Manuscript, 463
Manuscript preparation, 459–460
Master sentences, 283–286
Maugham, W. Somerset, 201, 221, 225
Mech, L. David, 363
Melville, Herman, 340
Mencken, H. L., 203–204, 311–312
Metaphor, 2, 82, 113, 115, 118–120, 127,
     141–143, 147–148, 191, 207, 242, 278–
     280, 284, 310–325
Metaphorical sequence, 319–320
Metrical sentence, 282–283
Middle, 360–362, 385, 410, 427–429
Mixed metaphors, 317
Momentum, 81–93, 182
Monochromatic paragraphs, 200
Monosyllabic words, 130
Moore, Crary, 142

Moorehead, Alan, 255
Morley, Christopher, 280, 322–324
Muller, Herbert Joseph, 107, 329
Multiple reviews, 452
Mumford, Lewis, 103, 162–163, 335

Nabokov, Vladimir, 280, 333
Narration, 158, 160, 176–177, 182, 186–187, 197, 245, 256, 331
Negations, 194–195
Negative-positive sequence, 269–270, 283–285
Newman, John Henry, 160
Nonrestrictive clause, 251, 335
Note-taking, 9
Notes, 382–384, 387, 425
Noun metaphor, 313
Nouns, 135, 137
Novak, Michael, 50

Observation, 2–3, 6, 9, 405
Occasion, 14–15, 19, 144
O'Connor, Flannery, 315
Onomatopoeia, 207, 256
Open punctuation, 250, 333
Opening sentences, 48–50, 412
Oppenheimer, J. Robert, 257, 425–426
Order, 29, 32–38, 361, 421, 427–429
O'Reilly, Jane, 409–410
Organization, 198, 408
Orwell, George, 56, 166–171, 190, 219–221, 224, 272, 340
Outline, 359, 365, 380–381, 383–385, 408, 453

Paper, 459
Paragraph, definition of, 155
Paragraph emphasis, 115–119
Paragraph length, 116–117, 127, 130–132, 155, 163–166, 183, 185, 431–432
Paragraph pattern, 193
Paragraph position, 115–116
Paragraph structure, 127, 147, 156–161, 175–208
Paragraphs, 21–22, 91–93, 115–119, 155–212
Parallelism, 81, 87–88, 113, 119, 141, 142, 183, 238
Parentheses, 252, 336–337
Parkman, Francis, 314

Parts of the whole, 72
Passive voice, 218–219
Pater, Walter, 130
Pathetic fallacy, 315–316
Patterned paragraph, 117–118, 202–206
Peattie, Donald Culross, 200, 224
Perception (*see* Observation)
Period, 327–328, 330–332, 343–344
Periodic sentence, 113–114, 120, 129–130, 215–217, 221, 230, 237–238, 249
Periodicity, 183, 250, 252
Perry, William G., Jr., 50
Persona, 144–145, 406–407, 423–424
Personal essay, 402–418
Personification, 207–208, 278, 279, 315
Persuasive writing, 158, 177
Petrunkevitch, Alexander, 52
Phrases, 241–242, 244, 251
Plumb, J. H., 433–439
Poetic devices, 127, 141
Polyptoton, 277
Polysyllabic words, 128–130
Polysyndeton, 273
Popular article, 352–375
Porter, Katherine Anne, 262, 324
Positive-negative sequence, 270–271
Prewriting, 9, 38
Priestly, J. B., 194, 279, 410
Pro-con sequences, 87
Professional article, 353, 376–401
Progressive order, 35, 187
Prolonged ending, 53
Promise-fulfillment clauses, 331
Pronoun reference, 81, 83
Proofreading, 460
Proportion, 30–31, 55
Proverb, 49
Publication, 460–463
Punctuation, 191, 222, 224, 241, 243–248, 251–254, 326–351

Question and answer, 86
Question marks, 341, 344
Question paragraph, 196–197, 200
Questions, 49, 113–114, 195–197, 200, 205–207, 264–265
Quotation marks, 106–107, 343–345
Quotations, 48–49, 181, 386–387

Rao, K. L. S., 450

Read, Herbert, 282
Readers, 354, 357–358, 361, 380, 422–423, 453
(*See also* Audience)
Reading, 5–6, 9, 379–380, 405–406
Redundancy, 296–297
Reference pronoun, 84
Regressive order, 35, 187
Regular paragraphs, 67
Reification, 279, 316
Repetition, 83–84, 102–103, 179–180, 183, 194, 245, 255–256, 273–275, 283–284
Repetition sentences, 261–263
Repositioned-adjective sentence, 263–264
Repositioned adjectives, 285
Representative-series sentence, 256–260
    five-part, 259–260
    four-part, 258–259
    three-part, 257–258
    two-part, 256–257
Research, 6, 358–359, 375, 377, 381–384, 406
Research papers, 379
(*See also* Professional article)
Restatement, 73
Restatement paragraphs, 194
Restrained texture, 128, 143–144
Restrictive clause, 251–253, 335
Review length, 452–453
Revision, 363–365
Rexroth, Kenneth, 23–26
Rhetorical consistency, 145–147
Rhetorical profile, 126–148, 214, 293–294, 326, 408–409, 421–422, 429–432, 445, 453–454
Rhetorical profile selection, 128, 144–145, 148, 423
Rhetorical question, 141, 148, 264–265, 284
Rhetorical texture, 161, 292–293, 317–321, 411–412
Rhyme, 283
Rhythm, 87, 141, 207–208, 224, 237, 245, 252, 281–282, 285–286, 381–382
Roach, Gerard, 360
Rodman, Sheldon, 196
Rogers, Will, 132
Rourke, Constance, 316
Ruskin, John, 164–165
Russell, Bertrand, 319

St. John, Jeffrey, 448
Samson, William, 240
Santayana, George, 263, 271, 274, 331

Scholarly papers, 377
Schroeder, Fred E. H., 290–301
Scientific writing, 189
Semicolon, 246–247, 252, 327–331, 336, 338–341, 344
Sentence, definition of, 213–214, 219, 240
Sentence emphasis, 107–115
Sentence length, 110–111, 120, 127, 129–130, 202–205
Sentence position, 111–113
Sentence structure, 127, 129–132, 141, 147, 214–230, 236–286
Sentences, 49–50, 107–115, 213–289, 430–431
Series, 197–198, 205, 207, 245, 256–260, 266–269, 271–275, 283, 285, 338–341, 345
Series paragraphs, 197–198
Shaw, George Bernard, 333
Sheed, William, 453
Simile, 277–278, 312
Simple sentence, 214, 221–222, 240–245
Single-sentence paragraph, 182–183
Skinner, Cornelia Otis, 186
Slang, 131
Smith, Logan Pearsall, 172–173, 181, 255
Sommer, Robert, 104
Southern, Terry, 48
Spacing, 345–346
Spatial order, 33–34, 188, 198
Speculation, 7–9
Spender, Stephen, 269, 281
Statement and question paragraph, 205–206
Statistics, 361
Stevenson, Robert Lewis, 131, 259, 261, 275
Storytelling, 187
Strand of an idea, 82
Structure, 31, 45–57
Structured series, 266–269
Stylistic commitment, 45, 57, 146–147
Stylistic determinants (*See* Rhetorical profile)
Stylistic intensity (*see* Stylistic texture)
Stylistic level, 128–134, 145
Stylistic paragraph forms, 195–208
Stylistic shift, 105–106, 113–115, 117–119
Stylistic texture, 128, 135–145, 147
Subject, 14–23, 30–31, 45–47, 57, 354, 357–358, 380, 383, 403–404, 407–408, 422
Subordination, 223, 225–228, 249, 255, 332, 335
Subordinating words, 226–227, 249, 251–253
Succinctness, 62
Summarizing paragraphs, 67, 176, 182–183
Summary ending, 53, 57

Sundberg, Johan, 114
Swift, Jonathan, 115
Syfers, Judy, 108
Symmetrical sentence, 269
Symploce, 275
Synonyms, 85, 296
Syntax, 214, 217, 239, 245, 254, 263
  (*See also* Sentence structure)

Talese, Gay, 48
Taylor, Harold, 454–457
Teale, Edwin Way, 218
Technical reports, 377
Technical words, 299
Technical writing, 20, 51
Tenor, 278–280, 311–312
Term papers (*see* Professional article)
Terminal dash, 345
Terminal sentence, 161–162, 175–176, 412–413
Tetracolon, 268–269
Textbooks, 377
Theses, 377
Thesis, 14–23, 30–33, 45–47, 53–54, 57, 65–67, 144–145, 358, 380–381, 384, 407–408, 411, 422
Thinking (*see* Speculation)
Third person, 134
Thomas, Dylan, 148–152, 276, 285, 311
Thoreau, Henry David, 184–185, 202, 254, 329, 338, 344
Thought process (*see* Speculation)
Tillich, Paul, 266
Title sentence, 176–177
Titles, 354–355, 365, 386, 413
Tomlinson, H. M., 87, 114, 160, 240
Topic sentence, 90–91, 156–161, 166, 175–182, 200
Transition, 359–260
Transitional paragraphs, 67, 91–93, 176, 182–183
Transitional sentences, 90
Transitional words, 89, 161, 191, 193
Transitions, 81, 88–93, 219–220, 240, 365, 429
Tricolon, 268, 284
Trilling, Lionel, 336
Tuan, Yi-Fu, 57–59
Tuchman, Barbara, 164
Twain, Mark, 51, 197, 329, 341
Typographical emphasis, 106–107
Typography, 345–346

Updike, John, 9–11, 242, 251

Vagueness, 3
Van der Post, Laurens, 82
Van Doren, Mark, 74–78
Variation, 53, 147, 196, 214, 217, 221, 260
Vehicle, 278–280, 311–312
Verb metaphor, 313–314
Verbosity, 296–298
Verbs, 138–139, 143
Vertical expansion, 64–69, 72–73, 364
Villar, James, 362
Virtual sentence, 49, 207, 214, 219–220, 229–230, 240
Vocabulary, 2, 5, 290–291, 429–430
Voice, 423–424

Warren, Robert Penn, 279
Warshow, Robert, 144
Weaver, Warren, 341
Webster, Daniel, 271, 275
Wecter, Dixon, 269
Welles, Orson, 48
Wells, H. G., 334
West, Rebecca, 91
White, E.B., 49, 50, 114–115, 203, 223, 246, 318, 331
White, Theodore H., 330
Whitman, Walt, 280
Williams, Charles, 283
Williams, George C., 106
Wilson, Edmund, 229, 331
Wolfe, Tom, 49, 262, 275
Woodward, Grace Steele, 113
Woolf, Leonard Sidney, 83
Woolf, Virginia, 48, 56–57, 108, 253, 262–264, 272, 277, 328, 411
Word emphasis, 102–107
Word position, 103–105
Word repetition, 102–103
Words, 128–129, 290–309
Wordsworth, William, 144
Wouk, Herman, 342
Writing habits, 1, 9, 81
Writing procedures, 51, 353, 357–365, 379–390, 403–413, 422–432, 445–454, 459–463
Writing situations, 14–15
  (*See also* Rhetorical consistency)
Wyre, Dorothy Otis, 132

Young, Edward, 142